Praise for *The Baja Adventure Book*

"[*The Baja Adventure Book*] is a...superior, authoritative work...with...smoothly written text, ...superb, magnificently detailed maps, ...lavish illustrations and entertainment value...an outstanding travel guide, one of the best of its kind. Highly recommended."   —*Coast Book Review Service*

"*The Baja Adventure Book* is like the bible to us in La Paz. The author's experience and dedication are clearly reflected in his writing."
                                                     —Jonathan Roldan, Cortez Club, La Paz

"...probably one of the best bargains in the world...This book goes way beyond the information in [other books on Baja]...you couldn't ask for a better guide."
                                                                                —*San Diego Log*

"...it's a wonderful, well written publication, the most complete Baja information and guidebook I have ever seen."
                                                     —Bill Johnson, Diving Charters, Inc., San Diego

"[*The Baja Adventure Book*] is by far the most informative and enjoyable book on Baja that I have ever seen."
                                                     —Barbara Littlemore, Baja California Tours, Inc

"For kayakers and smallboaters, this book is a gold mine of information on little-used beach access roads, launching sites, unspoiled camping and the best diving and fishing 'secret spots' in Baja...an indispensable companion on any Baja trip."   —Ed Gillet, Southwest Sea Kayaks

" ...a unique contribution to the literature on Baja...readable, well organized and offers a sensible view regarding the need for conservation of natural resources."
                        —Dr. José A. Mercadé, Professor, Glendale Community College

"As 'first-timers' setting out on a two month voyage of discovery in Baja, we felt like we had a friend and Baja expert along with us. *The Baja Adventure Book* became our single most-used reference...Mr. Peterson's humorous asides and personal encounters gave us many hearty laughs en route."
                                —Nancy Lattier Nash, video producer, *"On The Road in Baja"*

Peter Kuhn makes friends with a very relaxed, upside-down manta

The BAJA ADVENTURE BOOK

Walt Peterson

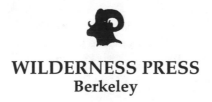

WILDERNESS PRESS
Berkeley

FIRST EDITION July 1987
Second printing July 1989
SECOND EDITION January 1992
Second printing March 1995
THIRD EDITION December 1998

Design by Thomas Winnett and Kathy Morey
Maps by Judith Peterson
Cover design by Larry B. Van Dyke
Photos by the author except as noted
Front cover photos: copyright © 1998 Rob Williams *(background)*; Insets: copyright © 1998 Walt Peterson *(left)*,
    copyright © 1998 Lou Perez *(center)*, copyright © 1998 Will Waterman *(right)*.
Back cover photos: copyright © 1998 Mark Wilford *(top)*, copyright © 1998 Will Waterman *(bottom)*.

Library of Congress Card Number 98-8746
International Standard Book Number 0-89997-231-4

Manufactured in the United States of America

Published by Wilderness Press
    2440 Bancroft Way
    Berkeley, CA 94704
    (800) 443-7227
    FAX (510) 548-1355
    mail@wildernesspress.com

    Contact us for a free catalog
    Visit our Web site at **www.wildernesspress.com**

Library of Congress Cataloging-in-Publication Data
    Peterson, Walt.
        The Baja adventure book / Walt Peterson. — 3rd ed.
                p.   cm.
        Includes bibliographical references (p.) and index.
        ISBN 0-89997-231-4 (alk. paper)
            1. Outdoor recreation—Mexico—Baja California—Guide-books.
    2. Natural history—Mexico—Baja California. 3. Automobile travel—
    Mexico—Baja California—Guidebooks. 4. Baja California (Mexico)—
    Guidebooks. 1. Title.
    GV191.48.M6P48   1998
    917.2'204836—dc21   98-8746
                                                              CIP

Contents

Using *The Baja Adventure Book* vi
Acknowledgments viii
Chapter 1. Natural Wonders 1
Chapter 2. The Bottom Line 15
Chapter 3. Fishing Fundamentals 24
Chapter 4. Wind, Water, and Waves 38
Chapter 5. Going Self-Propelled 46
Chapter 6. Wheelin' It 59
Chapter 7. Extra Added Attractions 71
Chapter 8. A Baja Survival Kit 78
Chapter 9. Tijuana to El Rosario 94
Chapter 10. El Rosario to Guerrero Negro 129
Chapter 11. Guerrero Negro to Loreto 161
Chapter 12. Loreto to Cabo San Lucas 199
Chapter 13. Tecate to San Felipe 247
Chapter 14. The Midriff Region 273
Appendix A. Map Key, Distances, Measurements, Peso/Dollar Calculator 283
Appendix B. Directory 285
Appendix C. A Baja Fishing Calendar 297
Appendix D. A Baja Bookshelf 300
Index 301

Using *The Baja Adventure Book*

Operating instructions

The Baja Adventure Book is not an "everywhere" book. Some geographic locations in Baja are of limited interest to most readers. In locations having numerous RV parks, such as San Felipe, which has perhaps 50, coverage is limited to those judged to be of the greatest interest to readers, based on their price, location, facilities, ambiance, and general level of cleanliness and repair. Some RV parks and restaurants in strategic locations are included because they are the only ones available. A number of RV parks are not included because they cater only to permanent residents. Since this is a book on outdoor adventure and natural history rather than conventional tourism, information on restaurants, bars, trinket stores, and the like is limited. Some hotels and resorts are listed because they have dive shops, sportfishing fleets, sailboard or kayak rentals, or other facilities or services relevant to the adventure travel/natural history themes of the book.

The addresses of most businesses and organizations mentioned by name in the text are contained in Appendix B, which also contains a number of useful e-mail addresses and almost 100 Internet sites. A number in parentheses following a name in the text indicates that its location is shown by that number on the accompanying city map. The sequence of such numbers commences at the north end of a given map and increases going south—number 1 will be the first encountered as you go from north to south, number 2 the next, etc. This system makes numbers easy to locate on the map. Many businesses and services not specifically mentioned in the text, such as grocery stores and bus stations, are shown on the city maps with a two-character alphabetical key, described in Appendix A.

All maps in the book are based on Mexican and US topographic maps and marine charts, updated and corrected with recent GPS fixes and tracks, and information from many sources. All are oriented with true north at the top, but compass roses showing magnetic bearings are provided on the regional and topographic maps. The variation on the peninsula ranges from 13° east at the north to 11° east at the south, with an average of 12°. Official place names assigned by the Mexican government have been used throughout the book, although a few have been converted to their English equivalents to promote euphony and brevity. Alternate names used locally are provided in the text in some cases. The State of Baja California is referred to as "Baja Norte" or "Baja California Norte" to avoid confusion with the popular name of the peninsula. The English translations of Spanish place names having a provocative or descriptive meaning (Isla Piojo is "Louse Island") are provided at the appropriate places in the text. Unofficial names assigned by surfers, climbers, cave explorers, and anglers, like "Zippers," "Gorin's Gully," "Cueva Tres Pisos" and "6$^1/2$ Spot," are placed in quotation marks when first used and should be obvious. Ranches and small settlements shown on the maps may be abandoned or in operation only seasonally, and their names change frequently. Only those mountains discussed in the text are shown on the maps.

Appendix A provides a key for symbols used on the town/city maps, a table of distances along the Transpeninsular Highway, conversions between metric and standard measurements, and a "calculator" for conversions between pesos and dollars. Most road travel descriptions in later chapters are keyed to the kilometer markers found on virtually all paved highways and on many unpaved roads. **Wait! There is no cause for panic! This system requires no knowledge of the metric system!** Just look at each KM marker as a little lighthouse, providing unmistakable identification as to geographic location. A "+" after a kilometer number means that the site occurs about half-way between that marker and the next **higher** marker. The numbers on the KM markers along some stretches of the Transpeninsular are ascending, along others descending, so take care not to become confused. Where markers are absent, the distances cited were measured with a calibrated odometer, but to take full advantage of them readers must know the error rates of their own odometers.

Distances over land are given in statute miles, except those pertaining to backpacking, climbing, and hiking trips, which are expressed in the amount of time normally required by persons in good physical condition carrying packs and equipment appropriate to the venture being described. Distances over water are given in nautical miles. Coastal routes are measured closely following the shoreline. All compass bearings in the text are magnetic, and all elevations are in feet. Temperatures are expressed in degrees Fahrenheit.

The term "off-road" is often encountered in advertisements for tires and shock absorbers, and in tales told around evening campfires. However, readers should keep in mind that what is meant is **off-pavement** driving. Other than driving on beaches, dry lakes, and similar special situations, there is no "off-road" driving in Baja, nor should there be. Driving across untracked desert creates environmental havoc, tearing up slow-growing desert vegetation and leaving scars that endure for generations. Such driving is almost always unnecessary, since unpaved roads will usually be found to take you anywhere you could want to go. In addition, it can often result in severe tire damage within a few miles, and even the fabled Baja 1000 racers wouldn't go a mile if the race were truly off-road.

Chapters 9 through 13 classify unpaved roads as sedan, pick-up, or four-wheel-drive. The ratings have little to do with comfort, but rather with the physical ability of the vehicle to get down the road. They are subjective, and your own experience with individual roads may differ. Equally important, time will bring change to the roads. Most unpaved roads in Baja are either poorly culverted or not culverted at all, and often have unstabilized slopes, and even a minor storm can change everything. On the other hand, road crews are busier than ever, and you may be pleasantly surprised. Use the ratings as rough guides and remember the Baja Adventurer's motto, "Remain rigidly flexible."

Chapter 13 is organized in a similar manner except that it involves Routes 2, 2D, 3, and 5, rather than the Transpeninsular. Since the Midriff region of the Sea of Cortez has no roads, towns, or cities, Chapter 14 contains only "trips by water" and short stories, the special topics being integrated into the text.

Chapters 9 through 13 classify unpaved roads as sedan, pick-up, or four-wheel-drive. The ratings have little to do with comfort, but rather with the physical ability of the vehicle to get down the road. They are subjective, and your own experience with individual roads may differ. Equally important, time will bring change to the roads. Most unpaved roads in Baja are either poorly culverted or not culverted at all, and often have unstabilized slopes, and even a minor storm can change everything. On the other hand, road crews are busier than ever, and you may be pleasantly surprised. Use the ratings as rough guides and remember the Baja Adventurer's motto, "Remain rigidly flexible."

The border cities

Tijuana, Tecate, and Mexicali are sizable modern cities having many of the services, facilities, and businesses found in cities of similar size in the US. However, their urban nature and close proximity to the border render them of limited interest in a book on adventure and natural history, at least the types of adventure and natural history discussed in *The Baja Adventure Book*. In addition, each city has a tourist bureau that can provide information by mail or telephone, the addresses and phone numbers of which are found in Appendix B. Thus, other than providing border crossing information and the location of consulates and places where local information can be obtained, *The Baja Adventure Book* does not describe these cities.

Caveats

Sincere efforts have been made to insure that *The Baja Adventure Book* is correct and current as of the date of publication. However, to err is human, and Baja California is a land of rapid change. Readers planning activities that are regulated, such as fishing and diving, or making trips that involve travel to mainland Mexico by ferry, and those planning to leave a boat, vehicle, or trailer in Mexico, should obtain current information from the many sources identified in the text and in Appendix B. None of the maps are intended to replace official government-issued charts for the purpose of air or marine navigation, and they should be used for planning purposes only. Although the author and the publisher cannot be responsible for the consequences of errors, they will gladly receive corrections, comments, and constructive suggestions; write in care of Wilderness Press.

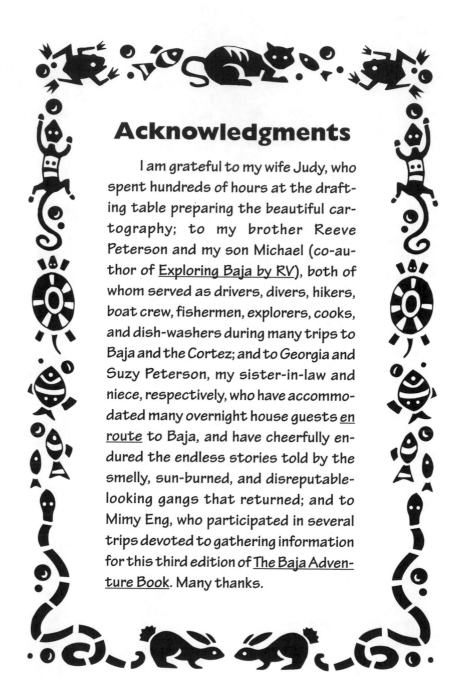

Acknowledgments

I am grateful to my wife Judy, who spent hundreds of hours at the drafting table preparing the beautiful cartography; to my brother Reeve Peterson and my son Michael (co-author of <u>Exploring Baja by RV</u>), both of whom served as drivers, divers, hikers, boat crew, fishermen, explorers, cooks, and dish-washers during many trips to Baja and the Cortez; and to Georgia and Suzy Peterson, my sister-in-law and niece, respectively, who have accommodated many overnight house guests <u>en route</u> to Baja, and have cheerfully endured the endless stories told by the smelly, sun-burned, and disreputable-looking gangs that returned; and to Mimy Eng, who participated in several trips devoted to gathering information for this third edition of <u>The Baja Adventure Book</u>. Many thanks.

Chapter 1

Natural Wonders

The adventures described in this book depend in many ways on what Mother Nature provided when she designed Baja, so a basic knowledge of the natural history of the peninsula and its nearby islands and surrounding waters will contribute to the enjoyment of everyone traveling there.

The lay of the land

Five million years ago the land mass of today's Baja California was firmly attached to what is now mainland Mexico. However, the Pacific Plate, on which Baja and all the land west of the San Andreas Fault lie, eventually separated from the North American Plate and began moving to the northwest. Today the peninsula and the deep gulf to the east that were formed are among the most striking geologic features on Earth. The Kamchatka, Malay, and Antarctic peninsulas are longer, but none is so narrow in relation to its length. Baja averages less than 70 miles in width along its 798-mile length, the narrowest part being 26 miles from the Pacific to the western shore of the bay near La Paz, and the greatest being 144 miles at the latitude of Punta Eugenia. Land area is 55,634 square miles, and the shoreline on both coasts totals 1,980 miles, excluding the interiors of large enclosed bays. The southernmost extent of the peninsula is an unnamed and otherwise undistinguished point several miles west of Los Frailes, the famed rocks at Cabo San Lucas that are incorrectly granted that honor by many T-shirt and postcard artists.

There are seven principal mountain ranges. The Sierra de Juárez and Sierra San Pedro Mártir, extending south about 160 miles from the border, form the backbone of the northern part of the peninsula. The western slopes of both ranges are fairly gentle and descend to coastal plains along the Pacific. The eastern slopes, however, are mostly steep escarpments plunging down to sweltering lowlands along the Río Colorado and the Sea of Cortez. Both escarpments have been eroded into a series of major canyons. The massive double peak named Picacho del Diablo, at 10,154 and 10,152 feet Baja's highest, rises just east of the San Pedro Mártir escarpment. A broken series of mountain ranges runs south from the Sierra San Pedro Mártir, including the Sierra San Borja, the Sierra de San Francisco, the Sierra de Guadalupe, and the Sierra de la Giganta, end-

ing north of La Paz. The central part of the Cape region south of La Paz is occupied by the Sierra de la Laguna, the highest mountain in the range being 6,855-foot Cerro las Casitas.

There are three great lowland areas: the area east of the Sierra de Juárez and Sierra San Pedro Mártir, the area

Rick Tinker and Will Ashford hike up the mouth of one of the great canyons in the escarpment of the Sierra San Pedro Mártir

south of Guerrero Negro along the Pacific coast past Laguna San Ignacio, and the area around Bahía Magdalena.

Pacific coastal waters

The southern sweep of the California Current carries cool water from more northerly regions, and surface water temperatures range between 50° and 75°. Northern coastal areas are characterized by cool water, ocean swells, heavy surge, and upwellings of nutrient-laden deep water, producing an underwater environment almost indistinguishable from that of Southern California. To the south, the California Current eventually becomes submerged under the Davidson

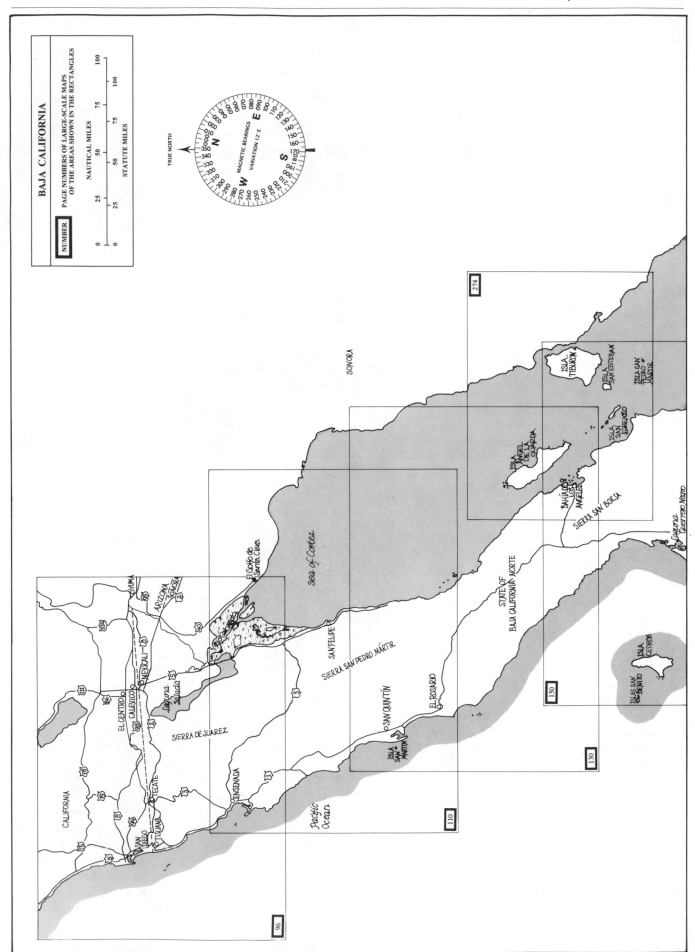

Current, a body of warm water moving north during part of the year. The infamous El Niño greatly alters these patterns. By early winter, 1997, the current El Niño had devastated the kelp fields around the Benitos, but if history is any guide they will return soon. For this reason, descriptions of kelp fields along Baja's Pacific coast from this point on reflect normal conditions, not those prevalent during an El Niño.

The Sea of Cortez

The Cortez is the scene of some of the world's greatest oceanographic extremes. Its long, narrow configuration produces one of the largest tidal ranges in the world, up to 31 feet at the northern end. Materials eroded out of today's Grand Canyon and surrounding lands over millions of years have been deposited at the north end of the Cortez by the Río Colorado, and low tides uncover mud flats up to 3 miles wide. Until it was tamed by dams, the tidal bore that ran up the Colorado was so powerful that it once sank a sizable ship. Tidal currents form huge whirlpools and rips in the Midriff region of the central Cortez, and velocities of over 6 knots have been recorded. Because there is no long fetch, large swells do not build up as they do in the ocean and there is thus little surge.

The Cortez has deep basins in its central and lower parts, one over 14,000 feet deep. Surface water temperatures range between 57° and 78° along Baja's Pacific coast. In keeping with its reputation for extremes, variations in the Cortez are also are extreme, surface waters reaching 91° in small, sheltered areas the south during summer and 57° in the north during winter. Since freshwater transport into the Cortez is less than evaporation, it is more saline than the Pacific.

Rivers and streams

Except for the Río Colorado, now reduced to a relative trickle because of increasing human demands, only about a half-dozen small streams flow into the sea on a more-or-less permanent basis along Baja's entire coastline. The famous "river" at Mulegé is actually an *estero* (a bight or arm of the sea), although springs above a dam near the highway bridge provide a small flow of fresh water. There are only two sizable lakes in Baja. Laguna Salada, in the lowlands south of Mexicali, receives widely differing amounts of water from the Río Colorado from year to year; in 1987 the lake was 60 miles long, but by 1991 the drought prevalent in the Southwest had reduced it to perhaps 20. Laguna Hanson in the Sierra de Juárez is less than a mile across and is shallow and muddy.

Climate

Baja's Pacific coastal areas have generally mild weather, and a number of fairly dependable seasonal patterns are recognizable. In winter, winds offshore tend to be steady from the northwest, averaging about 7 knots and occasionally reaching 25, with lesser velocities toward the southern end of the peninsula. Winds near the coastline are moderated by the influence of land, and nights and early mornings tend to be calm, with northwest winds beginning in late morning and blowing until sunset or even 2 or 3 hours into the night. Fog and overcast are common around Isla Cedros and Bahía Magdalena.

A large sea cave on the north coast of Isla Carmen

Rob Watson

North Pacific cold fronts disrupt this pattern, primarily between November and February. Fronts often bring winds from the southeast-to-southwest quadrants, which rise in velocity, sometimes carrying driving rain, later shifting to northwest, then moderating, and finally clearing. Strong north winds generally lasting 2 or 3 days are common in December and January. A high often forms over the interior of the southwestern US, creating a strong, persistent northeasterly wind. Known in Southern California as the Santa Ana, it can affect the coast from Tijuana to the Cape, with winds strongest near shore and lessening south of Cedros. Strong northwesterlies are common in the spring and early summer, but as summer wears on, wind strength tends to drop.

Between November and May prevailing winds in the Cortez are northerly, generally light and unpredictable, often following coastlines, and sailing yachts become festooned with cans of fuel. However, the winds are strong and dependable enough in the Punta Chivato and the East Cape that the areas have become Meccas to boardsailors. ("East Cape" is an unofficial name for the area between Punta Pescadero and somewhere short of San José del Cabo.) In the summer most winds are from the south or southeast, but in the spring and fall the winds become variable. Calms are frequent all year and fog is uncommon. However, wide changes in wind velocity and direction occur over short periods of time, and prevailing oily calms can turn into cauldrons of whitecaps in minutes. Most of these winds do not last long, but during winter ridges of high pressure often lie over the southwestern US, causing cool, dry winds to rip

down the Cortez, sometimes lasting more than a week and bringing joy to boardsailors looking for speed sailing, and gloom to anglers, divers, kayakers, and cruisers.

Tropical storms known as *chubascos* form far to the south and affect the southern part of the peninsula and surrounding waters from mid-May to mid-November, peaking in August and September, although abnormal water temperatures can cause exceptions. Most such storms affect only the southern part of the peninsula, but a few extend far to the north, occasionally moving up the Cortez to go ashore at San Felipe or into Sonora. Prodded by their insurance companies to be elsewhere during the *chubasco* season, many yachtsmen follow a migratory pattern as regular as any swallow, leaving San Diego after Thanksgiving with fair winds and following seas, and slogging back against the prevailing winds and the California Current before Memorial Day.

There are other, more local, weather patterns. The *cordonazo* is a short but severe storm encountered in the Cortez, generally developing in the summer months during periods of southerly winds and often accompanied by lightning. A breeze known as the *coromuel* blows from the south in the La Paz area almost every day from late spring to early fall, starting in the afternoon and continuing until morning. Thermal winds, created when air rushes in to fill the partial vacuum created by rising air currents over land heated by the sun, can occur anywhere. Mountains along Baja's eastern coast often cool rapidly at night, causing gravity to funnel strong winds through arroyos. Termed gravity—more properly katabatic—winds, they cause discomfort in villages

A **chubasco** *devastates the Cape Region (satellite photo)*

Courtesy NOAA

and anchorages along the shore. Bahía de los Angeles is famous for gale-force katabatic winds, sometimes lasting a week while surrounding areas remain relatively calm. Local topography can influence the strength and direction of winds in other ways, and prominent capes along the Pacific coast like Punta Eugenia often see heavy weather.

Much of the peninsula lies between two rainfall zones. Winter storms provide northwest Baja with up to 12 inches per year, while summer storms account for much of the 8 to 16 inches received annually by the Cape region, micro-climates in the Sierra de la Laguna receiving up to 30 inches. A few storms stray from their normal routes and provide rain in the central zone, but between El Rosario and La Paz rainfall is extremely low, averaging as little as 2 to 4 inches a year, sometimes only traces for years at a time. The pattern of rainfall is complicated by the ranges of mountains, which form an almost unbroken barrier up to 2,000 feet, half the length of the peninsula being blocked up to 3,000 feet. The cooling of damp westerly winds causes them to lose much of their moisture over western slopes, leaving the eastern slopes much drier. Higher areas of the Sierra de Juárez and Sierra San Pedro Mártir receive enough rain to support sizable forests, the latter accumulating up to 8 feet of snow in winter, while the coastal area in the "rain shadow" to the east is among the driest in North America.

Air temperatures along the Pacific coast are moderated by prevailing winds and the California Current, providing cool-to-moderate shirt-sleeve weather most of the year. In contrast, the Mexicali region, with an average summer maximum of 104 to 108° and extreme highs of 120°, is the hottest on the continent. The Cortez coast lacks the moderating influence of the ocean and can become very hot in summer. On a windless summer day Santa Rosalía can seem as hot as a blast from the town's copper smelters. The Cape region at the southern end of the peninsula tends to have moderate temperatures year-round. Mountain areas can be downright cold in winter; water jugs can freeze solid overnight at the 8,000-foot level west of Picacho del Diablo. As in desert areas elsewhere, day-to-night temperature variations are extreme, and it is not uncommon for drivers to run their heaters early in the morning and their air conditioners in the afternoon.

Living things

The peninsula is rich in native and introduced plants; almost 3,000 species, sub-species, and varieties of vascular plants (the "higher" plants, having vessels or ducts carrying sap) have been recorded. The number of endemic species (species found only in one area on Earth) is lower than what might be expected in a long, narrow peninsula, only 23% of the total. The reason for this appears to be that the peninsula split off from the mainland relatively recently, so isolation has been limited. In addition, its

mountains are not very high, snow and freezing temperatures are uncommon, and rainfall is low.

The plants of northern Baja are closely related to those of Southern California. Much of the land below 3,000 to 5,000 feet west of the Juárez and San Pedro Mártir escarpments is covered by chaparral consisting of chamise, manzanita, laurel sumac, sage, and other plants, giving way at lower elevations to a coastal scrub of *agave*, cliff spurge, buckeye, buckwheat, and bladderpod. Juniper-pinyon woodlands are found at higher elevations, and some mountain areas have forests of pine, cedar, fir, aspen, and oak. The highest areas of the Sierra San Pedro Mártir even have an impoverished version of a Canadian boreal forest, with lodgepole pine, white fir, and an endemic cypress. Plants in the Cape region and the Sierra de la Giganta are closely related to those of the nearest areas on the mainland, with oak-pinyon woodlands at high elevations and complex communities of cacti, yuccas, various shrubs, and trees like *palo blanco* and *palo verde* below. Between these two northern and southern areas many familiar desert plants are found, including *ocotillo*, ironwood, cholla, creosote bush, mesquite, *agave*, and various cacti, along with a number of striking plants adapted to extreme dryness such as "boojum," *cardón, copalquín,* and *torote*.

These distinctions are not sharp, and there are transi-

Rob Watson studies a Rubensesque "elephant tree" on Isla Cerralvo

A verdant palm oasis in Cañon San Pablo, Sierra de San Francisco

tion zones combining features of the communities on both sides. In addition, scattered accidents of geology and meteorology provide micro-environments containing interesting plant communities, including the verdant palm groves of the east-side canyons of the Sierra de Juárez and Sierra San Pedro Mártir; the park-like meadows of the higher reaches of the Sierra San Pedro Mártir; the complex plant communities of La Laguna, a meadow high in the Sierra de la Laguna; the fresh- and salt water marshes along the Colorado; the mangrove lagoons along the Pacific and Cortez coasts, and the pines of Cedros, surviving on the moisture provided by fog. Chapters 9 through 14 describe a number of the more interesting plants and plant communities.

Large land mammals include only mule deer, mountain lions, bighorn sheep, and a few antelope, but there are many smaller mammal species, including coyote, fox, rabbit, bobcat, skunk, badger, raccoon, ring-tailed cat, ground squirrel, chipmunk, gopher, mouse, and rat, plus feral (domestic species gone wild) goat, cat, and pig.

Well-adapted to Baja's climates, many reptile species inhabit the peninsula, including such familiar and expected animals as various species of rattlesnake and whiptail, king and gopher snakes, and numerous iguanids, geckos, and lizards. Tree frog, salamander, and pond turtle don't seem to be the sort of animal species you would encounter in Baja, but they are present, along with a number of species of toad.

Baja's diverse mix of deserts, bays, mangrove lagoons, forested peaks, and remote islands, together with its strategic location on many flyways, promotes an equally diverse mixture of bird life. Check lists differ, but some identify over 400 species that live in, breed in, or pass through Baja and over surrounding waters. Extended isolation has produced four endemics. The Xanthus hummingbird is a common resident of the Cape region north to San Ignacio. The gray thrasher is common along the Pacific coast south from Punta Cabras and throughout Baja California Sur in desert scrub at low elevations. San Lucas robin, a colorfully feathered sub-species of American robin, is common in the Sierra de la Laguna. Two sub-species of Belding's yellowthroat are found—the northern from San Ignacio to the Comondús, the southern from La Paz south, both normally seen in marshy locations. The yellow-legged gull breeds entirely within the Cortez, and its range is almost, but not quite, limited to those waters; some get as far north in summer as the Salton Sea in Alta California, and several have been recorded in the Bahía Magdalena area, so it perhaps could be termed a Cortez "almost-endemic." The mangrove yellow warbler is listed as a Baja endemic in some books, but it is also found widely in mainland Mexico. There are odd habitat-species relationships—places where birds appear though not expected—and unusual species compositions—birds keeping unusual avian company. Even after more than a century of professional studies, Baja's birds are not well known, and although the peninsula is not likely to appeal to the birding-from-the-bumper crowd, amateurs might be able to make real contributions.

An osprey feeds its young in a nest built in an unlikely place

A number of prominent bird areas are described in Chapters 9 through 14—see the index. Use great care when visiting these places, especially when in the vicinity of nesting seabirds. Most species react to humans as if they were large ground predators, and if disturbed adults may abandon their eggs and chicks, leaving them vulnerable to hypo- and hyperthermia, falling off ledges, and other accidents. Gulls are major predators of eggs and chicks, and since they are less afraid of humans than other species are, they can be seen escorting visitors through nesting colonies, darting in to take advantage of every opportunity. Stay at least 100 yards away and use binoculars. You will have an adequate view of the birds going about their natural business of raising their young, rather than of frightened parents poised to take flight. Never allow a pet near a nesting area.

Marine life

Along the northern part of the Pacific coast divers and anglers will be hard-pressed to differentiate the flora and fauna from those of Southern California. At Isla San Martín, however, cool-water plants and animals begin to disappear and more tropical forms are increasingly common, and south of Punta Abreojos the underwater environment becomes distinctly tropical, although some cool-water life like abalone can be found all the way to the Cape. The diversity of fish in the Cortez is also extreme due to its great variations in water temperature and depth, and great differences in bottom topography, which ranges from great shallows with flat, silty bottoms to vertical rock walls. In the north end there are isolated assemblages of cool-water fish that seem to have been taken from the Pacific: white seabass, ocean whitefish, several species of rockfish, and even sheephead and California halibut. At the southern end of the Cortez, Indo-Pacific species like Moorish idols and longnose butterfly fish can be seen, and there is even a sizable coral reef.

The Pacific coast and the Cortez are home to over 800 species of fish. Three species, Pacific manta, whale shark, and hammerhead shark, have become the object of attention by divers and are described in the following chapter, and Chapters 9 through 14 describe a number of underwater communities. A few of the more than one hundred species pursued by anglers are discussed in Chapter 3.

While a visitor to Baja is unlikely to see a large, wild land mammal—the four-legged kind anyway—the waters surrounding the peninsula contain an abundance of marine mammals. Over 20 species of cetaceans (whales, porpoises, and dolphins) have been identified. The most numerous large whales in Baja waters are the gray whales, discussed in the following section. A full-time resident population of finback whales lives in the Cortez, often concentrated in the Midriff, and others can be seen in the Pacific in winter. Finback whales are large; at up to 80 feet, they are second only to blue whales. They sometimes swim in groups of 2 to 10, their spouts shooting up like geysers, followed by the slow roll of dark backs, with a small tell-tale fin set well aft. On rare occasions they get together in larger groups; 27 have been seen feeding together in the Cortez. Similar in appearance but smaller and less gregarious than finback whales, Bryde's whales are also seen along the Pacific coast and throughout the Cortez. In 1980 boaters in a 24-foot cruiser were crossing Bahía de los Angeles when a large whale, possibly an adult fin or Bryde's whale, breached next to the boat. (During a breach a whale "jumps," so that all or most of its body is out of the water.) It landed across the bow, driving the boat down to the gunnels and leaving several pounds of hide aboard as it slid off. The boat was a shambles, with a smashed bow and a two-foot crack in its hull, but it did not sink and no one was hurt.

Humpbacks, with their long white flippers and musical talents, inhabit the Cortez and waters off the Cape in win-

A fin whale almost engulfs a brown pelican while feeding on krill

Bernie Tershy/Craig Strong

ter, especially the latter. Blue whales, at 100 feet and 150 tons the largest animals ever to live on Earth, cruise off the Pacific coast, some visiting the Cortez between late winter and late spring. A "school," or better yet a "university," of 12 blues was once seen feeding west of Cedros. Other whales that might be encountered include Sei, Minke, Cuvier's beaked, sperm, pygmy sperm, northern pilot, orca, and false killer. Orcas often stay near the Islas San Benito, where they are attracted by large numbers of sea lions, a favorite delicacy. In 1978 a pod of 40 orcas was seen attacking a blue whale off Cabo San Lucas, biting its lips and flukes (tail fins) for over an hour. Sperm whales are seen occasionally, sometimes traveling in large groups. Fifty-two of them stranded on a beach north of Mulegé in 1979 and died in the hot sun.

The smaller cetaceans in Baja waters include harbor porpoise, Dall's porpoise, common dolphin, Risso's dolphin, Pacific white-sided dolphin, Eastern Pacific spotted dolphin, spinner dolphin, Pacific bottlenose dolphin, and Gulf of California harbor porpoise. Bottlenose and common dolphins are abundant, often racing at the bows of passing boats. Several friends and I were rounding the south cape of a small island south of Tiburón when we came upon an unbelievable sight to the west: although the Cortez was flat calm, an area of several acres was being churned into whitecaps. Only when great numbers of black and white shapes leaped into the air did we realize that it was a group of several dozen common dolphins. At the other end of the spectrum, the Gulf of California harbor porpoise, found only in the northern

Cortez, has the smallest range of any cetacean and is one of the least-known marine mammals on Earth.

Pinnipeds (seals and sea lions) are common in Baja waters. California sea lions, elephant seals, and harbor seals breed and calve on the larger islands along the Pacific coast. California sea lions frequently seem quite friendly and accompany divers on the reefs at Isla San Jerónimo and the Benitos, to the great disgust of spearfishermen. There is a very large rookery of sea lions on the Benitos. Sea lions are the only pinnipeds common to the Midriff, and often haul out on beaches at San Lorenzo and San Pedro Mártir and southeast of Puerto Refugio at the north end of Guardian Angel Island. They entertain human divers at the islands north of La Paz with barrel-rolls and somersaults. The best place to meet an elephant seal is at the Benitos, although they haul out on the Islas los Coronados, San Jerónimo, and San Martín as well. Harbor seals often can be seen on San Martín, San Jerónimo, and the Coronados, and occasionally on the Islas de Todos Santos west of Ensenada. Steller sea lions and northern fur seals are seen from Cedros north, but only rarely.

Be extremely careful when in the vicinity of pinnipeds, for their sake and as well as yours. In the wild they can be extremely shy and if frightened may stampede for the safety of the sea, crushing pups and seriously injuring adults, some even throwing themselves off cliffs. If they feel cornered they may defend themselves, moving with unexpected swiftness on land. California sea lions occasionally nip at the fins of divers in a seemingly playful way. Elephant seals may appear largely indifferent about people, but during the breeding season males can be very aggressive. Although there seem to be no reports of attacks on humans, local commercial divers at the Benitos give elephant seals healthy respect and a wide berth. Still, elephant seals may not be entirely aloof—there have been reports of friendly encounters at Los Islotes, a small islet north of La Paz, one diver receiving a hug.

The gray whale

No aspect of Baja California's natural history has been the subject of more public attention than the life and times of the California gray whale. The first years of this attention nearly resulted in their extermination.

Gray whales make a variety of sounds, and many people believe they communicate with one another by verbal means. If so, today's mariners and yachtsmen are fortunate that the whales do not seem to have an oral history to be passed from generation to generation. In the mid-1800s large-scale whaling began in the eastern Pacific. Whales found in Bahía Magdalena were taken in such large numbers that the business soon became unprofitable. In 1857 Captain Charles Scammon rediscovered a lagoon visited by Juan Rodríguez Cabrillo in 1542, which became known as Scammon's Lagoon. Due

A troop of passing acrobats puts on an impromptu circus for author's wife Judy, and niece Suzy Peterson

A male sea elephant exercises his territorial rights to a few square yards of Isla Benito Este

to their large size, slow movements, and frequent surfacing habits, the whales inside the lagoon were highly vulnerable, and Scammon returned home with a full cargo of oil after a short voyage. It was not long until the secret was out, and large-scale slaughter began again. Whalers often harpooned the babies first, knowing that their mothers would return to defend them and offer a second target. Scammon later discovered a similar lagoon to the south, now known as Laguna San Ignacio. Between whales taken by ships in the lagoons and those taken along the coast by shore-based operations, the number of grays declined rapidly. Scammon estimated the gray population at between 30,000 and 40,000 in 1853; 28 years later it was between 5,000 and 9,000. These estimates were little more than guesses, and scientists now believe the population in 1846, before commercial whaling for grays began, to have been between 12,000 and 15,000. Regardless of which figures were used, many naturalists thought the species was headed for extinction. However, in 1937 the grays were given legal protection. In 1994 the US Fish and Wildlife Service took the grays off its endangered species list, and their numbers are now estimated at 21,000, possibly more than before whaling commenced.

Gray whales have become the subject of public interest of a more gentle nature in recent years, occasioned by two aspects of their behavior: their annual breeding migration and the fact that some are "friendly." Most grays inhabit the protein-rich waters of the Chukchi and Bering seas between April and October. Early in October they start the 5,000-mile journey south to Laguna Guerrero Negro, Scammon's

Lagoon, Laguna San Ignacio, and Bahía Magdalena, the longest migration of any mammal. A small number continue on to the western coast of mainland Mexico, and a few end up in the Cortez. Some females return consistently to the same lagoon year after year, others return to different lagoons, and still others circulate among the lagoons during the same season. Whales begin to arrive in the lagoons in late November, stragglers arriving as late as February. About half of the mature females conceived the prior year and are about to give birth. Most others are ready for breeding, many having given birth the previous year, while some are in season for the first time. They are hotly pursued by amorous adult males and precocious adolescents, who outnumber receptive females two to one. Although the females respond with feigned disinterest, they are promiscuous, copulating with a number of partners. At times the event turns into a free-for-all, with as many as 20 individuals involved.

Water temperature may have an influence on whale migration. The 1997-98 winter "whaling season" at Puerto Lopéz Mateos and San Carlos in Bahía Magdalena was poorly attended by the whales, while the lagoons farther north were crowded with them. Like so much else that has gone wrong in recent years, the warm water of the infamous El Niño got the blame, the theory being that the whales kept swimming south until the water was warm enough for their reproductive rites, and they simply stopped at this point, short of their normal route.

A few calves are born along the migration route, but most births occur in the lagoons, where warm, safe waters insure a high success rate. Approximately 1,500 grays are born each year, about half in Scammon's. A whale calf is about 15 feet long and weighs between 1,500 and 2,000 pounds. The mother nurses it from 2 nipples, providing up to 50 gallons of milk a day. Containing 53% fat, the milk enables a calf to grow rapidly, and within several months it may reach 20 feet and 4,000 pounds. The return migration to Arctic waters begins in late January, a few mothers and calves remaining as late as May or June. Those leaving early may encounter stragglers still heading south.

This annual migration has become the object of a great deal of attention. Large numbers of people watch from shore or go out on private boats, hundreds of commercial craft offer daily whale-watching trips out of coastal ports, and trips to the lagoons are offered on large sportfishing boats out of San Diego. It is estimated that over a million humans see these whales each year, making them the "most-seen" whales in the world.

A phenomenon that began in 1976 caused a new surge of interest, the "friendly" whales. A whale thought by some to be Gigi, a gray captured in 1971 and studied at Sea World in San Diego until she was released a year later, surfaced next to the vessel *Royal Polaris* while it was in Laguna San Ignacio. She was so curious about inflatable boats that she would lift them with bursts of exhaled bubbles and balance them on her head or back, always being careful to do this only when passengers were not aboard. Other whales have

A friendly whale pays a call in Laguna San Ignacio

apparently learned that humans can be trusted, some of them anyway, and the number of such incidents increases each year. Perhaps calves once petted by tourists have grown up and now allow their youngsters the same experience. Originally observed only in Laguna San Ignacio, these encounters have occurred recently in Bahía Magdalena, near Vancouver Island, and in the Bering Sea. Also, it is not limited to grays; recent incidents with southern right whales in the waters off Argentina indicate that they too are willing to forget the past and want to become friends, and an incident with a blue whale has been reported off Iceland.

Whale fans with their own boats can see grays at many coastal locations, and a yacht trip down the Baja coast in midwinter will result in dozens, perhaps hundreds, of sightings. Boaters anchoring just inside the entrance to Bahía Magdalena may be treated to an incredible sight: two, three, or even four whales breaching or spy-hopping at the same time. (A spy-hopping whale vigorously beats its flukes, or if in shallow water pushes its flukes against the bottom, so that its body is vertical and about a third out of the water.) Another good place is the inside waterway running north from Bahía Magdalena, where Jacques Cousteau filmed his television program "Desert Whales." Michael and I were fishing in our cartopper on a calm day north of Isla San Martín when a gray appeared on the horizon, showing his flukes every 3 or 4 minutes. We could hear his pulsing sounds when he was still 100 yards away and soon had the wonderful thrill of

seeing him pass directly under our boat. There are occasional surprise encounters: I was diving in a kelp bed south of Punta Eugenia when a gray plowed through only yards away. When he was 13 years old, Michael had the wonderful experience of snorkeling for a short time with a mother and baby.

To see a whale traveling offshore, first look for a "blow," and start timing the rhythmic breathing pattern to predict when it will surface. The powerful flukes disturb the water, leaving what appear to be oil slicks on the surface, showing its course. So that you won't harass the whale and expose yourself to danger, your boat should not be operated at speeds faster than the whale when paralleling it and within 100 yards. If more than one is present, go no faster than the slowest. Never try to overtake a whale from behind or to drive or herd it, and keep your speed and course as steady as possible. Take no action which causes it to use escape tactics such as frequent changes in direction or rapid swimming at the surface, prolonged diving or underwater course changes or which causes underwater exhalation. Never separate a calf from adults or cause a female to shield her calf by tail swishing or other maneuvers.

Whales can be encouraged to come right up to a boat in the lagoons and in Bahía Magdalena. The Mexican boatmen of Laguna San Ignacio say that grays are attracted by the sound of outboard engines and that they have a definite preference for the sound of certain engines, or possibly engine sounds of certain pitches. This seems to be true, per-

Ron Yarnell

Two kayakers venture close to a gray whale

haps because the sounds generated by outboards have about the same frequency as those emitted by the whales themselves, so to encourage a visit by a "friendly," the boatmen stop their boats, but leave their engines running in neutral. This also keeps the whales informed of where the boats are, an obvious safety precaution among breaching whales. If nothing happens, they alter the idling speed of their engines. They do not use their engines to get closer; when the whales want to pay a visit they will come to the boats, sometimes from quite a distance.

The lagoons are closed to private power boats without permits. Paddled and rowed boats, canoes, and kayaks have been permitted in the past, but are currently prohibited during the mating season. At present there are no restrictions on boats in Bahía Magdalena. Regulations concerning these areas may change in future years, so check with the nearest Captain of the Port (see the index for their locations) or civil authority. A visit with the friendly whales of Laguna San Ignacio is described beginning on page 170.

Great caution must be exercised while visiting the whales, for not all have such easy-going dispositions. During a whale-watching expedition to Laguna San Ignacio in 1982 a gray slapped a boat with its flukes. All 13 passengers were dumped into the water, and 2 hit their heads and were killed. Several years ago two divers in an inflatable were approached by an apparently friendly whale who seemed to want a backrub, when suddenly they found themselves, their equipment and their boat "flying like leaves in a storm." Yet, on another occasion, one of these divers spent a great deal of time in the water with a mother and her calf, all three swimming peacefully together. However, a diver later made the mistake of swimming directly at a whale and got a tremendous whack from a well-aimed fluke, causing broken bones. Other people have encountered "bumpers" and "thrashers," males who play a rough game with inflatables and skiffs, slamming into them repeatedly with consider-

able force, often for as long as an hour. This sport seems to be something other than simple light-hearted highjinks, and if these animals were human, we would call them bullies.

By far the best location to see whales from shore is at Laguna San Ignacio. Grays also can be seen from Parque Natural de la Ballena Gris on the northern shore of Scammon's, from the beaches along the waterway north of Bahía Magdalena, and from the old salt pier at Guerrero Negro. Although you will probably need binoculars to get a good look from these places, grays have occasionally cruised within 20 yards of the salt pier.

Given the popularity of the whales and the many dollars expended in seeing them, it seems only a matter of time until the economic value of live whales will exceed everything ever realized from killing them. There is still plenty of time; the Pacific Plate is being carried to the northwest, and in about 40 million years Baja California will be part of an island lying off British Columbia. One wonders whether the gray whales knew something about this when they selected the lagoons for the end of their annual migration; after all, the route is getting shorter every year.

Unfortunately, the travails of the whales at the hand of man may not be over. In 1995 the Mexican government and the Mitsubishi Corporation of Japan announced that they had entered into an agreement to establish a major salt extraction plant at Laguna San Ignacio. This would involve pumping 462 million metric tons of salt water from the lagoon into huge evaporation ponds each year. The expected annual yield of 6 million tons of salt would then be transported by a 15-mile conveyor belt to a mile-long pier at the mouth of the lagoon. Environmentalists say that the construction and operation of such a facility would have a disastrous effect on whale breeding. Two departments of the Mexican government are at odds over the project, and many environmental groups have submitted protests. Japan has earned an unenviable reputation in ecological matters, being one of the few nations still hunting whales, taking 300 Minkes each year with the transparent excuse that this slaughter is necessary for "scientific research." Whale meat from many species continues to be a popular menu item in Japan, and in 1994 American scientists were stunned when DNA analysis of whale meat routinely purchased in Japanese markets proved it to be from humpbacks, the taking of which had been banned world-wide for 27 years. In this case, let us hope that the "good guys" win, and that Mitsubishi leaves Laguna San Ignacio to the whales and returns to more acceptable pursuits.

The Mexican Galapagos

From a distance many of the 100 or so islands and islets in the Cortez seem almost barren, just some scattered desert scrub and a few cactus and *agave* being visible to the average person. However, a trained naturalist can find more diversity than most people would dream possible. Tiburón, for instance, has 298 species of vascular plants, while Isla las Ánimas Sur, little more than a rock sticking out of the sea northeast of Isla San José, has 11. Even Isla San Pedro Mártir, with its seemingly impenetrable covering of guano, has 27. The islands have the most spectacular concentrations of nesting southern seabirds on the west coast of North America, San Pedro Mártir, Partida Norte, Raza, and San Lorenzo being among the most important. Reptiles and amphibians thrive, ranging from Tiburón, with 25 species, to Islotes las Galeras, a group of small islets north of Isla Monserrate, which have a species of lizard. Many islands have land mammals: Tiburón has 13 species, and tiny Mejía, located at the north end of Guardian Angel, has 3. Larger mammals, such as ring-tailed cat, fox, coyote, brush rabbit, and jackrabbit, are found only on Espíritu Santo, Tiburón, and San José, and mule deer only on the last two.

Freed from many of the predators and competitors found on the mainland, the species that have become established on the islands have evolved under very different conditions from their mainland ancestors, some to the point that they are now considered separate species. Of about 581 plants found on the islands, 18 are endemic. The more curious animals include the "rattle-less" rattlesnake of Santa Catalina and the black jackrabbit of Espíritu Santo. As noted earlier, the yellow-legged gull seldom leaves the Cortez area except for forays to the Salton Sea. In addition, there are three other species of seabirds whose breeding ranges are almost totally confined to the islands of the Cortez: Heermann's gull, elegant tern, and Craveri's murrelet. The last is the southernmost member of a family of cold-water birds, an example of the curious mix of the temperate and tropical found in the Cortez area. Raza is the nesting site for over 90% of the world's Heermann's gulls and elegant terns.

The Cortez islands are a treasure of genetic diversity and scientific interest, and it has been suggested that had Charles Darwin visited them instead of the Galapagos he would have arrived at the same conclusions. Even today they are incompletely explored biologically, and the inventory of their terrestrial, avian, and marine life is far from complete. In the past the islands have been preserved by a blessing in disguise; they had little in the way of direct economic potential other than fish, seabird eggs, salt, guano, and gypsum, and except on several of the largest islands, no potable water was present. There has been some damage: seabird rookeries have been subject to heavy pressure by egg collectors; green turtle and *totuava* (a large bass-like fish) have been taken to near-extinction; there is a major gypsum mine on San Marcos; salt works have been in operation on Carmen and San José; and some guano collecting still goes on, especially on Patos. However, most communities of flora and fauna have remained largely intact, and many scientists consider the Cortez islands, especially those in the Midriff, to be among the world's last major refuges of relatively undisturbed island life.

In recent years the islands have become popular stops for yachtsmen, boaters, and tourists on natural-history tours, and increased numbers of outboard motors have made possible more frequent visits by the local people. While all or most of these visitors may be caring and well-meaning, their mere presence on the islands sometimes has hidden consequences that work against the preservation of the natural order. Some islands are more sensitive than others, and laws have been passed controlling many activities. Raza became a seabird sanctuary in 1964, and in 1978 all Cortez islands were granted wildlife-refuge status. Hunting and foraging are prohibited, and a permit is needed to collect or otherwise disturb the flora and fauna. Proposals have been made to include many of the islands in a national park.

Natural history trips and courses

Nature lovers have a virtual cornucopia of choices. Many organizations offer vessel-based trips, most with qualified naturalists aboard to present programs and answer ques-

One of the famous Espíritu Santo black jacks. Can you spot it?

tions. The more prominent organizations offering such trips include Baja Expeditions, Natural Habitat, Horizon Charters, Special Expeditions, the American Cetacean Society, Pacific Sea Fari Tours, Oceanic Society Expeditions, and Spirit of Adventure Charters.

A number of organizations combine nature-watching with other pursuits, so a rich diversity of interests can be accommodated. Baja California Tours offers a guided bus tour that visits many towns along the Transpeninsular, turns west at Ciudad Constitución to do some whale-watching at Puerto San Carlos and Puerto Lopéz Mateos, and visits La Paz, the participants then flying back. Baja Outdoor Activities in La Paz offers kayak/whale-watching. Baja Discovery has a tent camp at Laguna San Ignacio where visitors can meet the whales, expand their birding check lists, and do some local exploring. Some Wilderness: Alaska/Mexico kayak trips visit Bahía Magdalena. Baja Expeditions offers kayak trips to Bahía Magdalena to see the whales at close quarters. Part of the National Outdoor Leadership School (NOLS) "Spring Semester in Mexico" course involves a visit to Bahía Magdalena for some natural history, whale-watching, kayaking, and camping, as well as many other activities. Aqua Adventures offers Baja whale-watching ventures aboard kayaks.

Day-trips are offered in many locations. Sergio's Sport Fishing Center often takes whale-watchers on local trips from Ensenada. A number of organizations in Guerrero Negro offer trips to the nearby lagoons. Fishermen at Puerto Lopéz Mateos, Puerto San Carlos, Scammon's, and Laguna San Ignacio are often willing to take people out to see the whales. Cabo Acuadeportes and Amigos del Mar in Cabo San Lucas also offer whale-watching trips.

● ●

❝ *A glow-rious occasion*

Perry Studt, my brother Reeve, and I launched our Columbia 22 sailboat at San Felipe and headed south, encountering fierce winds almost immediately. Several days later our prayers were answered, too well in fact, and we had to resign ourselves to the noise of the outboard. At midnight I relieved Perry at the helm and soon lapsed into a reflective mood, wondering how such absolute peace could be possible in such a turbulent world. Our passage through the water was the only detectable motion, and even the sound of the engine did not seem to intrude into the silence. Gradually I became aware that something had been added to the velvety darkness of the water and the moonless sky: a dull glow of indefinite proportions could be seen to port. My eyes struggled to focus on the object, but due to its lack of form and substance I could not get a fix on it. Faint apprehensions began to stir; a gigantic glowing object was coming closer, and it was on a collision course. Thoughts raced through my mind, but evasion did not occur to me. No ripple or wake was evident, and it appeared to be below the surface. Sorting through all the possibilities I hit on the absurd: a giant squid! Captain Nemo! It shot toward the boat like an oversized torpedo, and as I braced for the crash, I realized I had not warned Perry and Reeve. Too late! At the last possible moment the object dove and then reappeared some distance to starboard. My mind still had not caught up with events as the glow faded in the distance, and it wasn't until my heartbeat returned to normal that the obvious became apparent: it was a whale. Perhaps with amorous designs on the shapely hull of our sailboat, he had homed in on the sound of the outboard engine. Finding the boat unresponsive, he dove under us and continued on his way, with billions of the famous Cortez bioluminescent plankton signaling their objections to his passage by switching on their tiny lanterns. Relieved, I laughed so loudly that Reeve and Perry started from their bunks and fell into a heap on the cabin sole. We spent the rest of the dark night in quiet speculation on the wonders of Baja, the only other sounds being the purr of the engine and the gurgle of the coffee pot. **❞**

● ●

I found wonderfully sculpted rock formations on Isla Espíritu Santo

Chapter 2

The Bottom Line

Baja California has the most diverse and interesting diving attractions of almost anywhere in the world. On a single trip a diver can hunt for lingcod in a cool-water kelp environment, visit a coral reef, make friends with a huge manta ray, hitch a ride on the fin of a gigantic whale shark, watch sand cascade down steep underwater canyons, and photograph such Indo-Pacific beauties as Moorish idols and longnose butterfly fish. A visit to a mysterious Pacific seamount, where life competes so vigorously for living space that not a square inch of bare rock can be seen, may be followed days later by a dive on a pristine sand bottom devoid of life; devoid, that is, unless you approach slowly and quietly, to find hundreds of slim garden eels swaying in the underwater breezes, ready to disappear instantly into the sand. Individually, these marvels are found elsewhere; collectively they make Baja unique.

Favorite dive locations

A dive trip to Baja, perhaps more than most places, requires careful planning, plenty of time, and a high degree of flexibility. Many of the best locations on the Pacific coast are around offshore islands and can be reached only by boat, or are in exposed locations, where wipeout conditions can prevail for weeks at a time. The greatest attractions in the Cortez lie far to the south, or are otherwise hard to reach. Although the peninsula's extreme length and narrow configuration create problems of distance and access, they also provide an advantage shared by few areas in the world: widely divergent weather and water conditions are only a short-to-moderate distance apart. If Sacramento Reef is a wipeout, entirely different conditions are only 189 road miles away at Bahía de los Angeles, and if the surf is up at Cabo San Lucas, Pulmo Reef could well be calm.

Until the recent diving boom at the southern end of the peninsula, the Islas de Todos Santos and the Punta Banda peninsula near Ensenada and the Islas los Coronados west of Tijuana traditionally attracted more divers than all other areas of Baja combined. They have much to recommend them: close proximity to the border, easy access, and a variety of underwater life. However, people able to make greater investments in time and effort will find far more beautiful and exotic locations farther south. Roca Ben and Johnston's Seamount, jutting up almost to the surface south of Isla San Martín, mark the first really unusual dive sites south of the border. Surrounded by marvelously clear deep-blue water, their soaring walls, and jagged pinnacles are celebrated for their beauty. If these are beyond the safe limits of your boat or your diving ability, you can get a fair idea of what they are like by visiting Rocas Soledad, 1.2 miles off Punta Santo Tomás.

At Sacramento Reef and the Benitos, divers will encounter marine life so dense that the areas have been called "biological miracles." The Cape region has good beach access, underwater sandfalls, a number of wrecks, and exotic fish. Pulmo Reef, around the turn of the Cape into the Cortez, is one of the few coral reefs on the west coast of North America. Most of the islands along the coast between La Paz and Mulegé and those in the Midriff are among the finest and least spoiled in the world, especially less accessible spots like Isla las Ánimas Sur. Chapters 9 through 14 contain detailed information on these and many other dive sites.

Diving with the mantas

In 1863 Baja explorer J. Ross Browne summarized the then-current understanding of the Pacific manta ray:

> The manta ray is an immense brute of great strength, cunning, and ferocity, and is more the terror of the pearl divers than any other creature of the sea. The habit of the animal is to hover at the surface over the pearl divers, obstructing the rays of the sun, and moving as the diver moves, and, when he is obliged to come up for breath, hugging him in his immense flaps until he is suffocated, when the brute, with his formidable teeth and jaws, devours him with gluttonous voracity. Many fishermen and pearl divers have been killed by them.

Events at Marisla Seamount (El Bajo Seamount), located northeast of the north end of Isla Espíritu Santo in the Cortez, have shown mantas to be something entirely different from what Browne would lead us to believe. In September 1980 a boat carrying a television crew was anchored on the seamount, filming an American Sportsman show about the schooling hammerhead sharks. Aboard were Stan Waterman, Howard Hall, Ted Rulison, Marty Snyderman, and novelist Peter Benchley, of *Jaws* fame. Soon a 16-foot manta came by, swimming slowly, something obviously wrong; ropes were fouled around its left wing and ala, a horn-like appendage used to sweep food into its mouth. Closer inspection showed it also had a number of fish hooks embedded in its wings, and a rope had cut deeply near an eye. Sensing the divers wanted to help, the manta let them come close, cut off the rope, and remove the hooks. It began swimming more vigorously and allowed one of the divers to climb on its back, taking him for a swooping, soaring ride. Returning the first diver, the fish gave the others a chance, and if a diver dropped off, it would circle back and pick him up. It hung around the entire time the crew was on the seamount, offering rides to whoever wanted them.

Marty Snyderman/Baja Expeditions

Tim and Nora Means hitch a fantastic ride at Marisla Seamount

No one knows whether the manta knew that humans like to go for rides and was rewarding them, or whether it considered the divers a species of cleaner fish, a sort of giant black wrasse useful for removing hooks and line. In any event, it was not an isolated incident, and other Cortez divers have had similar experiences. Trips were offered to Marisla Seamount for visits with the mantas until 1984, when the fish became scarce, possibly due to a change in water temperatures induced by an El Niño. They returned unexpectedly during the summer of 1989, and there have been recent encounters at Cabo San Lucas. Encounters with friendly mantas are too rare to allow accurate predictions, but the best months at Marisla Seamount have been August and September, and the encounters at Cabo San Lucas were in January and February.

A dive with the mantas is always an interesting experience, even if you can't get a ride. They are common along the coast from Loreto to La Paz, especially between July and October. There is no certain way to get close to a manta. They are aware of your presence long before you are of theirs, and may turn before you come into view. They often nose over in an outside loop, perhaps to see an approaching diver better. Occasionally they will move straight in, make a 90° turn at the last moment and glide away. Chasing them is futile, for they can swim far faster than any diver; when they want to play they will come to you. Some have gray backs, with lighter, **V**-shaped markings, and are generally less skittish than darker fish (this color difference may be sexual). They quiver all over when touched, and a few seem playful, or at least curious. Divers have hand-fed them with small fish and the mantas soon begin to hang around like hungry dogs.

Diving with the hammerheads

Schooling hammerhead sharks have been another major attraction at Marisla. Up to almost 100 have been seen swimming in synchronized fashion in large, endless circles. At intervals they conduct maneuvers described as "body tilting, head shaking, and corkscrewing." They look tough, but are very shy and will flee *en masse* at the pop of a strobe. Most seem disturbed by the noise a scuba regulator makes, and free-divers have a better chance of approaching them than tankers. The sharks appear to present little danger, but there have been minor incidents. During a study a number of years ago, 6 snorkelers were in the water with about 500 hammerheads for a week, and several bumping incidents occurred. No damage was done, but the sharks apparently wanted to get a message across. Some years ago, a diver, accompanied by his wife, was photographing the hammerheads when she nudged him to get his attention. Too intent on the sharks to be distracted, he ignored her, generating another nudge, and then another. Finally he turned around and found it wasn't his wife at all! The best time to visit the sharks is late summer and early fall, although evidence is accumulating that they may be present year-round.

Diving with the biggest fish in the sea

Because they do not breach or spy-hop like gray whales, making them difficult to spot, whale sharks have been considered rare in Baja. However, recent organized efforts to locate them have proved that they are more common than was once believed, and they have become the object of a good deal of interest. A small number of Baja divers have been able to approach them, sometimes spending considerable periods of time swimming alongside, and a lucky few have had the extraordinary experience of riding on their huge dorsal fins like jockeys.

Can a fish be friendly? Judge for yourself. During a June, 1997, boat trip to Isla Santa Cruz, north of La Paz, a group of divers from the San Diego area had a wonderful experience. Steven Salas was lowering a kayak to another diver, who was in the water, when something big appeared nearby, something "so big and so vivid it was like looking at a moving billboard." A fraction of a second after the cry "shark" went out, the diver in the water "levitated" himself and "walked on water" to the kayak and boosted himself aboard, "eyes like saucers." However, he quickly collected his wits and dove down into the path of the oncoming leviathan, which proved to be a huge whale shark. At first, everyone was convulsed with laughter, but there was a quick scramble for fins, masks, and snorkels, and soon eight divers were hanging onto the great fish. It seemed to love the attention, and kept circling the boat and giving rides to all comers for over an hour. If that's not friendly, what is it?

Adult whale sharks can approach 45 feet in length, and there have been reports of specimens 70 feet long. They are among the few sharks whose mouth is located at the end of the snout, rather than being underslung, making them look like wingless underwater 747s. With their 6-foot-wide mouths open, they swim at about 3 knots, collecting vast quantities of plankton, crustaceans, and small fish with sievelike gill rakers, straining almost a million gallons of water an hour. They prefer deep water, and surface only occasionally to bask and feed, often at rips where currents meet. Small schools have been seen, but they tend to be solitary animals.

One event has suggested that there may be more to their intellect than might be believed. Ted Rulison and Flip Nicklin were riding on the dorsal of a 40-footer when it stopped and rested its chin on their vessel's anchor chain. It then pressed down until finally the chain was curved in a **U**-shape. Then it slowly swam forward, dragging chain along its entire underside. It was scratching its tummy! Not so dumb!

There is no great difficulty in approaching a whale shark once one is located. When it wishes to break off the encounter it will make a steep dive, as if it knows the tiny creature clinging to it is an air-breathing mammal. In spite of its bulk, a whale shark can move fast when spooked; Sigurd Tesche bumped a 20-footer with a camera, and within seconds it was out of sight. The only danger encountered by divers has occurred when they have attempted to hang onto the tail and have been violently swished back and forth in a 15-foot arc,

Two divers record the passage of a gigantic whale shark

Jim Tobin/Baja Expeditions

tearing off fins, masks, and scubas.

Because of their habits and relatively small numbers, a dive with a whale shark is largely a target of opportunity. Anglers have reported them to be most numerous off the Cape region, especially around the Bancos Gorda, between May and October. As many as a dozen have been spotted in a single day in this area, although this is highly unusual. They also have been seen around Marisla Seamount, primarily in August and September. Baja Expeditions offers a whale shark trip utilizing a spotter aircraft.

Spearfishing locations

Baja California has many fine spearfishing areas. On the Pacific side the Benitos have the best white seabass and yellowtail hunting found anywhere, and Sacramento Reef has moderate numbers of black seabass. The Midriff, especially around the southwest coast of Isla Tiburón, probably has the best spearfishing in the Cortez. In 1972 Don Barthman bagged a 550-pound jewfish off Punta Willard on Tiburón, the largest ever taken free-diving. Punta Púlpito, south of Mulegé, has exciting spearfishing for grouper and yellowtail.

The above areas are relatively difficult to reach, but there are many other places where off-the-beach divers and those with only small cartop boats or inflatables can find good spearfishing. Los Candeleros, a group of rocky islets south of Loreto, have many fish and are only a few miles off a beach with close road access. The reef areas centered around Roca Lobos south of Isla San Marcos are within easy range of a boat launched at Caleta San Lucas. Several new roads and improvements to existing roads now provide easy access to a number of fine spearfishing areas, including that from KM 63+ on the Transpeninsular Highway south of Loreto to Bahía Agua Verde. The road from Bahía de los Angeles to Bahía San Francisquito allows cartoppers and small trailerboats access to Islas Salsipuedes and San Lorenzo in the Midriff. Isla Santa Cruz, north of La Paz, is not often visited by spearfishermen, but during the warm months, the surrounding waters offer heart-stopping action on large game fish, including marlin and roosterfish. On the Pacific coast, Isla Asunción and the reefs off Punta Abreojos are much easier to approach since road improvements were completed.

Although easy to reach and home to innumerable large game fish, the waters off the Cape do not attract many spearfishermen. However, in 1992 a diver at the Bancos Gorda managed to get a shaft into a marlin seen finning on the surface nearby. The fish almost instantly spooled the reel on his gun, the diver then setting up a large wake as he was dragged through the water, and with his friends on the boat cheering him on, the scene became reminiscent of a water-ski contest. The fish lost, but the diver had to steady his nerves with a few jolts of tequila when safely ashore.

Lloyd Whiteneck

Barthman's big fish. Left to right: Gary Falkner, Bill Bishopp, Bob Jackson, and Don Barthman (hand on spear)

Spearfishermen should stay away from a few places. Pulmo Reef, the harbor at Cabo San Lucas, and Scammon's Lagoon are underwater parks. Many biologists and sport divers believe certain other areas should also be given park status because of their profusion of underwater life (not necessarily big fish) and unspoiled nature, including the reef southeast of Isla la Ventana in Bahía de los Angeles, Isla las Ánimas Sur, and the wreck of the *Salvatierra* near La Paz. Foragers should not remove slow-growing shellfish and other sessile life from the tiny diveable areas of seamounts like Rocas Soledad, Roca Ben, Johnston's Seamount, Roca Pináculo (the one at the Benitos), and Marisla Seamount, for this quickly destroys their beauty and their value to others.

Licensing requirements, species, seasons, and so forth described in the following chapter generally apply to spearfishermen as well. Specific bag limits apply to spearfishing, and the taking of corals and gorgonians is prohibited. The Mexico Ministry of the Environment, Natural Resources, and Fisheries limits spearfishing to free-diving and rubber- or spring-powered guns only. These regulations change frequently, and it is essential that divers get a current copy and study it. Mexico enforces wastage laws, and due to the remoteness of many spearfishing locations it is often difficult or impossible to place fish under refrigeration, so limit what you shoot to fish that can be consumed right away.

A fine collection of wrecks

During Baja's 400-year maritime history, over 850 vessels, and possibly twice that number, have been lost along its Pacific coast and in the Cortez—a wonderful array of barks, barges, barkentines, brigs, tugs, ferryboats, full-rigged ships, junks, LCIs, Liberty ships, paddlewheel steamers, schooners, screw steamers, sloops, sportfishing vessels, submarines, tuna clippers, yachts, subchasers, and a destroyer. Their nationalities include the US, Mexico, Canada, Colombia, England, Denmark, Japan, Greece, Ecuador, and Peru. Many sank in deep water and are beyond reach, but some are in known locations shallow enough that they can be reached by sport divers. Many lie in remote areas and others require decompression diving, but some are easy to get to, and a few can even be explored with mask and snorkel.

The sea has strange habits, and a few wrecks in the most exposed locations on the west coast of North America still have major parts visible, like the tanker *Swift Eagle*, run ashore on Benito Oeste in 1934. Many others lying in protected locations are quickly reduced to rubble, such as the shrimper *San Gabriel*, sunk in placid Bahía Concepción in 1981. Novice divers often have unrealistic expectations about what they will encounter—an almost intact "Hollywood" wreck sitting sedate and upright on a flat bottom—and will almost certainly be disappointed, for these are rarities in Baja, and the term "wreckage" diving is often more appropriate. It often takes careful examination even to tell that anything is there at all, such as the remains of the paddlewheel steamer *Sacramento*, lost on Sacramento Reef in 1872.

Although most Baja wrecks are widely scattered, a few areas contain the bones of many ships. The outer shores of islands forming Bahías Magdalena and las Almejas contain more major shipwrecks than anywhere else in Baja, including the steamers *Indiana, Colombia*, and *Westbank Park*, and the US submarine *H-1*, as well as lesser wrecks like the fishing vessel *Shasta*. Although not diveable, the great paddlewheel steamers *Independence* and *Golden City* were also lost there, and there are a number of sizable wrecks on the beaches north of Cabo San Lázaro. Another interesting site is Sacramento Reef, where dozens of vessels have been lost, the schooner *Goodwill* and the *Sacramento* being of prime interest. The San Roque/Asunción area also has a number of wrecks, including the steamer *San José*, aground on Isla San Roque in 1921. The Midriff and Canal San Lorenzo near La Paz each has one major wreck, the great sailing ship *John Elliott Thayer* and the ferry *Salvatierra*.

The descriptions in this book have been limited to wrecks of interest to divers and a few of historical or human interest. Maritime histories usually include only vessels above a given size, say 50 tons, but no limit has been made here, because some very small wrecks, such as that at Isla el Racito, provide better diving than larger ones, like the steamer *San José*.

Mexico has strict laws concerning salvage diving, especially on wrecks of historical or archaeological interest. In addition, the US is a signatory to a United Nations multilateral convention on cultural property, and US law prohibits importation of certain objects of historical or archaeological value. There seems to be no law restricting casual hands-off visits to wrecks, but unless you are part of an authorized expedition having the required permits, you would be well advised to touch or remove nothing. You may be judged by the equipment you carry; possession of air lifts and sand blasters may be taken as *prima facie* evidence of intent.

Trips, sales, service, and air

As this edition of *The Baja Adventure Book* went to press, dive operations were located in Ensenada, Punta Banda, San Francisquito, Mulegé, Loreto, La Paz, East Cape, Cabo San Lucas, and San Felipe (see the index for a comprehen-

Joe Harold Brown investigates a "blip" near the wreck of the ship **John Elliot Thayer**

Ramon Carballo tells of wrecks that occurred near Bahia Magdalena when he was a young man

sive list). Even though they may lack an in-house dive shop, most beach-front hotels and resorts have snorkeling equipment available for guests and can arrange dive trips.

Further information on dive shops can be found in later chapters. A few of these businesses are not the full-service dive shops you may be used to. Sales and rentals are normally confined to basic equipment and then not in all sizes, styles and types, and few regulators are available. Repairs and spare parts are virtually nonexistent (some of the shops at La Paz and Cabo San Lucas may be able to help). Some hotel/resort operations limit sales, rentals, and services to guests only, and a few close during the off-season. Several independent shops operate at the whim of the owner, who may be off pursuing turtles when you need to have your tanks pumped. None of the shops will pump out-of-hydro tanks, and a few ask for VIP. All require certification from those requesting air, scuba equipment sales or rentals, and scuba trips. Some have only one compressor, and since parts are difficult to obtain, a breakdown can leave a shop without air for months. Air is not subject to periodic testing, and a visiting diver cannot assess its quality, so it is advisable to ask to see the compressor. While a clean and obviously well-maintained compressor does not guarantee good air, the reverse is frequently true. Many sporting goods stores, hardware shops, and supermarkets carry masks, snorkels, and fins.

Boats and diving equipment

Excellent off-the-beach diving with good road access is available, especially at Punta Banda, located just south of Ensenada, at San Sebastián, south of Mulegé, and in the Cape

region at Pulmo Reef and between San José del Cabo and Cabo San Lucas. In addition, a number of the dive shops offer day-trips on various kinds of boats. However, true to the Protestant work ethic, almost all of the most interesting and least picked-over dive sites are in remote and inaccessible areas, and a boat is almost a necessity for full enjoyment of Baja diving. Because distances from launch to dive site are generally too great, paddleboards have limited usefulness, although in a few compact locations with close road access, like Punta Banda, San Sebastián, and Pulmo, they can be great fun. See Chapter 4 for information on bringing your own boat to Baja.

Traditional 12-foot aluminum boats are too small for most Baja diving conditions, lacking the seaworthiness, speed, range, and load-carrying ability necessary to make them useful in any but the most limited circumstances. Years ago Reeve and I made a night dive off Punta Banda using a 12-footer. Afterward, we arrived alongside at the same time each with a huge bag of goodies. Not realizing the other person was there, each of us tried to hoist himself aboard, tipping the boat over. It was rough and we could not bail, and we had to free-dive to the ocean floor to recover our equipment. I had dropped my light, but fortunately it was turned on, and I could see the shaft of light on the bottom. It took almost an hour to collect our gear and swim the sodden mess to shore. The occupants of our goody bags were recovered and shortly thereafter were boiled and served with garlic butter and Chianti.

Reeve suits up for a night dive

Divers traveling by private vehicle have a great deal of mobility and may encounter a wide variety of conditions, requiring a full range of equipment. Most people need a full quarter-inch wet suit year-round along the Pacific coast south to Punta Abreojos, and from late fall to late spring in the Cortez south to the Midriff. Lighter suits may be in order elsewhere, depending on your metabolism and the thickness of your subcutaneous fat. In protected areas of the Cortez even shorty suits may not be necessary during summer. There is no ready access to a scuba compressor in vast areas of Baja, but a portable compressor or hooka will provide complete flexibility in the location and duration of dives. Take special precautions to protect such equipment from dust. Since you will probably end up doing a lot of free-diving, a low-volume mask and a shotgun snorkel are assets. A supply of batteries, bulbs, O-rings, rubbers, wishbones, and wet-suit cement is essential.

Underwater photography

The realities of Baja diving are such that you will probably be happier with the reliability, simplicity, and small size of a Nikonos rather than a big pressure cooker with your Nikon SLR inside. Because of the great tides in the northern Cortez, visibility can change radically in a short time, and a variety of lenses is needed, especially wide-angle. Dust is pervasive, so every piece of camera equipment should be sealed in a Ziplock bag, and accessible O-rings should be checked before each dive. Bring all the film you plan to use, for selection in Baja is limited, especially slide film. Common camera batteries and flashlight batteries for strobes can

usually be found with little trouble. If you use rechargeables, bring a charger; RV parks, hotels, resorts, and dive boats operate on 110-volt, 60-cycle. Processing for color-print film is available in most larger towns, but slide films can take a great deal of time.

Dive safety

Heavy kelp, ocean waves, surge, and currents occur along the Pacific coast. Although kelp is absent and heavy surge is uncommon in the Cortez, strong tidal currents are frequently encountered, especially in the northern end and in the Midriff. When diving out of a boat, always leave someone aboard who knows how to operate it, and use a long trailer linc. A diver's knife is essential, for there has been an explosive growth of fishing in most of Baja's waters, and there is a remote danger of becoming entangled in a length of monofilament or a gill net. Although shark incidents are remarkably few, there are large numbers of sharks present in some locations, and standard avoidance techniques found in any good dive manual should be followed. All in all, the greatest dangers to divers in Baja are self-inflicted: inadequate equipment, poor training, overexertion, and foolishness, such as running into cows while unwisely driving at night on the Transpeninsular.

Recompression facilities

Use your dive computer! The laws of physics and physiology have not been repealed, and divers can get the bends as easily in Baja as anywhere else; In 1987 a diver doubled over in pain soon after 2 or 3 dives to about 100 feet

Divers working Baja's Pacific coast for sea urchin and abalone

at Marisla Seamount and had to be flown to San Diego. There are three privately owned recompression chambers in Baja Sur, one at La Paz and two in Cabo San Lucas (see the index). A new chamber has been established by a sea urchin cooperative just south of Ensenada. Manned by a doctor, it is located on the road to Punta Banda. The nearest chamber in the US is at Hyperbaric Technology, Inc. in San Diego. Chambers also exist at El Rosario, Isla Cedros, Isla Natividad, San Carlos, and Bahía Tortugas. These are owned by the local fishing cooperatives, and except in the most dire of emergencies, you should not depend on these chambers. An ailing diver should be rushed to the facility in San Diego, or to the chambers in La Paz, Cabo San Lucas, or Punta Banda. However, since no one can foresee all possible circumstances, directions to these chambers will be found in later chapters.

Liveaboards, package trips, and local excursions

A liveaboard trip on a vessel operating out of San Diego, La Paz or Cabo San Lucas is a fine introduction to Baja diving. They visit the best areas and provide comfortable accommodations, lots of good diving, and minimum hassle. Baja Expeditions offers trips aboard the *Don José* and *Río Rita* that visit Los Islotes, Marisla Seamount, the wreck of the *Salvatierra*, Isla Cerralvo, Isla las Ánimas Sur, Isla San Diego, and other diving attractions in the Cortez. The *Solmar V*, a luxurious 112-foot, compressor-equipped liveaboard based in Cabo San Lucas, makes dive trips to Isla Socorro, Isla Clarion, Pulmo Reef, and the Sea of Cortez—contact Amigos del Mar for information. La Paz Diving Service of-

Waltraude Kuhn spots a playful octopus at Los Islotes

Helmut Horn

fers dive trips throughout the southern Cortez on the *Marisla II*. The Cortez Club offers liveaboard trips on 3 vessels based in La Paz, ranging from overnight to 10 days.

Horizon Charters offers 5- to 12-day dive trips from San Diego down Baja's Pacific coast and into the Cortez aboard the *Horizon*. Blue-water hunters are welcome, and the vessel has a refrigerated hold. Their other vessel, the *Ocean Odyssey*, makes one- to three-day trips as far south as Isla San Martín. At this time, she doesn't have a refrigerated hold, but will probably have one soon. Both vessels are specially equipped and licensed for such ventures, and have onboard compressors, swim platforms, plenty of storage space, and areas for maintenance and storage of camera gear. There are currently only two shore-based organizations actively catering to spearfishermen, San Francisquito Resort and Baja Spearfishing Adventures.

All boats operate seasonally, so get a schedule before your plans get too far along. If you are a spearfisherman or a shell collector ask first; some boats allow it, some don't. There is often an unwritten rule: no large groupers or jewfish. Most boats supply tanks, weights, and backpacks, but check before going. All limit scuba diving to certified divers.

The Cortez Club and Scu-Baja Dive Center in La Paz and Pepe's Dive Center in East Cape offer package trips in the Cape region. Fiesta Sportfishing & Diving provides a variety of diving excursions, including such attractions as Pulmo and the Bancos Gorda. Want a try for a marlin or sailfish? Blue-water hunters are welcome if arranged for prior to a guest's arrival. In addition, many Baja dive shops, both those associated with hotels, resorts, and independent shops, offer local excursions—see the index.

• •

" *Four hard lessons*

Some learn about diving at a NAUI or PADI course, others must attend the school of hard knocks. Many years ago I learned four hard lessons at this school during a dive trip with Dick Mandich and Reeve to Isla Turners in the Midriff. On the first day we were exploring a cave when we saw two groupers, one behind the other. Wow, we thought! What a chance—two fish with one shot! Urged on by my brother, I aimed and pulled the trigger, and the 6-foot shaft shot through both fish and hit the back of the cave. Unfortunately, the three heavy rubber slings had not ended their travel, and they drove the gun backwards, dealing a sharp blow to my chin. I saw stars for a few minutes, but when I recovered I found I still had both fish, and the only damage was a painful jaw. Had the gun hit my glass faceplate things would have been quite different. The fish were not as big as they seemed and we ate them for supper.

The next day we went for a night dive, and in the first cave our lights shone on an almost unbelievable object, a giant, fluorescent goldfish. About 3 or 4% of leopard groupers assume this coloration when they reach 10 inches, for reasons not understood. Suddenly, it spooked and came rushing out of the cave, its nose dealing a painful blow to the inside of my leg, avoiding major tragedy only by inches.

Although I could barely walk the next morning and my jaw was so sore I could hardly hold a snorkel in my mouth, we decided to do some foraging. We kicked north toward a large bird rock several hundred yards away. Visibility had decreased and we could not see the bottom, a clue that we carelessly ignored. Like three black submarines with their sonars out of operation, we blindly proceeded. Uneasy feelings finally descended on us, and when we looked up to get our bearings we knew we were in big trouble; a strong current was sweeping us away from the island. Kicking against the current proved futile, so we turned in hopes that we could reach the edge of the current. Although we knew we could outflank it sooner or later, we faced a long swim, and no one was around to help if we cramped up or became exhausted. We were about to abandon our goody bags when we began to make some progress, and we finally arrived back at camp cold, extremely tired, and considerably smarter.

It was time for more innocent pursuits, so I rigged up my Nikon F in its housing and attached a big strobe. Cruis-

ing along, I hyped up, kicked down, and started to take photographs of the beautiful nudibranchs. There were some great scenes through the viewfinder, and I began to fantasize I was no longer man-the-hunter but an artist, paying homage to beauty. However, on the tenth dive I learned something about human nature, mine at least. A lobster convention was in progress in a cave, which was chock-full of them. Did I back off, focus the lens, set the f-stop, compose the picture, and take a marvelous photograph of this amazing scene? No! I threw my $1,500 rig aside, shot to the surface and raced back to the boat to get Reeve and several gunny sacks. Within 20 minutes we were back in the boat with 2 bulging sacks (we didn't know at the time that the Mexican Fish and Game people frown on such conduct), celebrating our luck with cold cervezas (beers), when I suddenly remembered my camera. It took a dozen free-dives to find it, and as I lay panting in the bottom of the boat, sore jaw throbbing and leg aching, I realized I could have had it all: I could have taken some great photos and then bagged the bugs. **99**

● ●

John Anglin and the author's son, Mike, head out for a day's diving near La Bufadora

Chapter 3

Fishing Fundamentals

"Fish pileup!" "A...continuous school [of tuna]...a hundred miles long!" "Acres of roosterfish!" "Terms such as 'schools,' 'shoals,' or even 'armies' are inadequate to convey the enormity of a ten-mile-long horde of gamefish feeding on a still larger body of forage fish." Like thousands of others, I can still remember the first time I read Ray Cannon's marvelous tales of Baja fishing in his classic 1966 book, *The Sea of Cortez*. Today they provide a magical spice that flavors fond memories of long-ago trips to the Sea.

It is hard to comprehend the changes that have occurred since Ray's book was published. At that time paved roads heading south from the US border ended at San Felipe and north of San Quintín. Fishing in the western and southern Cortez was limited largely to fly-in anglers and those who came in off-road vehicles, although if you had the time you could drive to Mazatlán and take a ferry to La Paz. Fishing along the Pacific coast south of the roadhead was limited to off-road drivers and to those with the price of a trip on a long-range boat or access to a yacht. In those days you had to be either rich or rugged, and for the average man a Baja fishing trip was the stuff of dreams.

All this changed when the Transpeninsular Highway opened in 1973, making it possible to fish Baja waters without a huge outlay of time or money. Dozens of hotels and resorts, ranging from modest to magnificent, now cater to anglers, and rental and charter boats are available in many locations, from humble skiffs to fine diesel cruisers. Ramps for trailerboats have been constructed in a number of key locations, and cartoppers and inflatables can be launched across hundreds of beaches. Although paved roads still reach Pacific shores in only a small number of locations between El Rosario and the Cape, and facilities are extremely limited, drivers with ordinary pickups can now fish hundreds of miles of remote coast, and trailerboat sailors have access to huge Bahía Magdalena and its rich offshore banks, and to Bahía Tortugas and the islands to the northwest.

The big eight

Four of the eight most sought-after gamefish in Baja's waters are billfish: black, blue, and striped marlin, and sailfish. The other four gamefish are wahoo, roosterfish, dolphinfish (dorado, mahi-mahi), and yellowtail. The sources of their popularity are threefold: they are powerful, often spectacular fighters; they exist in fairly large numbers; and

they are found in waters close enough to shore that anglers with trailerboats, cartoppers, and inflatables can reach them safely.

Billfish

To many people, when you talk Baja fishing, you are talking about billfish in the Cape region, which offers a world-class fishery for these magnificent fighters. In fact, striped marlin fishing at the Cape is almost 4 times better than in Southern California, requiring an average of only 1.95 days of effort per fish as opposed to 7.29.

Billfish feed on almost anything in the sea, including squid, yellowfin tuna, albacore, mullet, mackerel, dorado, flying fish, paper nautilus, and their own kind. Although most are caught on surface baits, they feed at any depth, even taking bottom-dwellers such as octopus. When hungry they are fearless, and have been known to use their bills to stun and stab. They have poor memories, proved by the fact that there are many records of individual fish being hooked over and over again. Most large "bills" are females.

Black marlin are among the most prized gamefish in the world. Large, powerful, and determined, they have been called "the bulls of the sea." They can be differentiated from other marlin by the fact that their pectoral fins cannot be folded flat against the body, and by relatively small, rounded anal and first dorsal fins. Mackerel and squid are favorite foods. Blacks are encountered from May through December at East Cape, although their appearance is erratic and there are a number of year-round residents.

Found in the Cape region primarily from May through December, Pacific blue marlin are the strongest fighters of all billfish. They are more acrobatic than blacks, often jumping and sounding to great depths, and probably no more than 1 out of 10 hookups is boated. More numerous and slightly slimmer than blacks, their anal and first dorsal fins are more pointed and proportionately longer, and their pectoral fins can fold flat against the body. Their food is largely offshore fish, especially skipjack. Baja's memorable "Year of the Blues" was 1983, when daily catches of as many as four 300-pound blues per boat were recorded.

There are probably more stuffed striped marlin hanging on the barbershop walls of America than all other billfish combined. The most abundant and most frequently caught of all Baja billfish, they are fantastic jumpers, often

Gary Kramer

A magnificent striped marlin loses a fight

wearing themselves out more with their leaps, pirouettes, and greyhounding (swimming rapidly while breaking the surface with a series of long, low jumps) than in fighting the drag: a few jump more than a hundred times. They can be distinguished from other marlin by an obvious lateral line and vertical stripes, and their high, pointed first dorsal fin, which is usually equal to or slightly longer than the greatest body height. They are primarily surface feeders. Stripers are found in Cape waters all year, and May through July near La Paz. They migrate as far north as the Midriff and San Diego in the warm months, often coming close to shore.

Easily identified by a prominent lateral line and tremendous first dorsal fin, Pacific sailfish are a favorite with anglers because of their hard fight and acrobatic skills, although light tackle is preferred since they lack the staying power of their larger marlin cousins. They feed at all hours, but are most active at night. They tend to form schools, sometimes with as many as 40 members. Sailfish are common between June and the end of December from Bahía Magdalena to East Cape. Smaller numbers are present in the Cortez as far north as the Midriff in the hot months, and a few stay year-round in the Cape region.

Sailfish can drive men to a certain madness. A number of years ago Rich Brown was fishing off Loreto, when he hooked a big one. He finally got it alongside, but when the guide whacked it with a billy, the leader broke and the fish

started to sink. Fully clothed and wearing boots, Rich dove in and caught it about 30 feet down. On the way back to town, Rich and his partner toasted their good luck with a six-pack of Tecate. Their guide joined in, but his toasts were to luck of a different sort. Because the guide could not speak English, it was not until they returned to the hotel that they learned that three days earlier a customer in the same boat had also caught a sailfish, but only the bloody front half.

Since they are pursued by legions of skilled anglers, a great deal is known about baits and techniques for billfish. While there are differences among the four species, it all boils down to just two basic methods: drifting a live bait or trolling with a large whole bait like bonito, mackerel, or ballyhoo, or an artificial lure specially designed for bills. A marlin lure is generally about a foot long and has a clear plastic head with large eyes and prismatic strips of color embedded inside, and a brightly colored vinyl skirt. A heavy 15-foot monofilament (mono) leader runs through the head to a hook hidden in the skirt. Record marlin have been caught with everything from 2-pound "button thread" to 130-pound "telephone cable," so there is hope for anglers using almost any type of tackle, but those who are after blues and blacks will be better off with the heavy-duty trolling rig described later, and those after stripers and sailfish with the medium-duty trolling rig. Use a ball-bearing swivel, and set the drag to one-third of line test.

Since bills tend to be unevenly distributed, asking around for recent information before you go out often pays off. They don't move far during the night, so if you find them one day, they should not be far away the next. Different species have slightly different habitat preferences. Blacks are sometimes found near seamounts and pinnacles, stripers a half mile or so away, and blues in deeper water still farther away. Search for an area of clean, clear, warm water, determine its limits, and stay there by trolling in large circles or back and forth in straight lines. Troll an artificial just past the wake, at a speed high enough that it occasionally breaks the surface, probably about six knots. If a fish follows an artificial but won't take it, slow down, reel in and simultaneously let out a live bait on another line. They have good color vision, so experiment with different colors if you are using artificials.

Stripers, and to a lesser extent other billfish, will "fin" or "sleep" on the surface with the top of their dorsal and caudal (tail) fins exposed, especially in calm weather. Binoculars are thus a vital piece of equipment. In good years it is not unusual to see 20 or 30 finning stripers in a day of fishing at the Bancos Gorda off San José del Cabo, often keeping company in groups of 2 or 3. Careful helmsmanship can place a bait in an irresistible position. When you see a fish, put on a live bait, let it out 60 or 70 yards, and troll slowly in a large circle, with no changes in throttle. Try to place it within sight of the fish, then stop and let the bait swim freely. Stripers are sometimes not too concerned about boats and may let you troll within 20 or 30 yards without spooking. However, don't put a wake over a finning or sleeping fish. If this scheme doesn't work and you have heavy casting gear aboard, stop the engine, drift down on the fish from upwind, and drop a bait or lure right in front of it.

Sometimes "tailing" fish are seen swimming with the swell, at about the same speed. This usually occurs in the late afternoon when the winds have come up. The most effective way to handle such fish is to get well ahead, start trolling a lure or bait, and then slow down, letting the fish catch up.

You don't have to be an experienced angler to get a shot at a billfish, and you don't need a yacht equipped with outriggers, a fighting chair, and a spotting tower. A modest trailerboat, an inflatable, or even a cartopper will do. In addition to rod and reel and other tackle, bring a large cooler and a bucket. Get up early and launch in the inner harbor at Cabo San Lucas. Fill your cooler with sea water and buy live mackerel offered from boats in the harbor; four or five per person should last for an entire day. The bait should stay frisky if you drain half the water every half-hour and refill. Run between three and six miles south of Cabo Falso and shut off the engine. Rig a hook and leader, but do not use a weight. Hook a mackerel through the nose, damaging it as little as possible, and simply let it swim about 60 or 80 yards away from the boat before setting the drag, and wait.

It might take 5 minutes, 5 hours or 5 days, but your chances of getting a hookup using this method are excellent, the most likely fish being a striper of between 125 and 150 pounds. When it happens, your modest boat has a number of distinct advantages over larger craft: your engine can be tilted up, the shallow hull offers few opportunities for snags, and if the fish runs under the hull you can put the tip of your rod underwater if necessary to keep the line from touching the

John Anglin's striper was over half the length and three-quarters the weight of our cartop boat

hull. A fish may drag you for miles, but it will be a fight to remember. Release the fish unharmed if you can, but if it is too badly injured, don't believe the rumor that stripers are poor eating; They are excellent eating, especially if they are bled by cutting the gills and quickly cooled. In 1998 marlin was being sold in fish markets in the Seattle area for $8.99 a pound, more than double the price of salmon.

Wahoo!!

It has been claimed that the name is derived from the shouts of people who catch them, for wahoo are among the swiftest fish in the sea, capable of reaching 50 miles an hour, and they can spool you before you know what happened. Related to mackerel and tuna, they inhabit tropical and warmer temperate waters. Their bodies are slim and powerful, with a shape like barracuda, except that the first dorsal fin of a wahoo is much longer. They are pelagic and tend to swim alone or in small groups. Their migratory habits are hard to pin down. Wahoo are found in the warm months off Bahía Magdalena and the Cape region, and in the southern Cortez. However, during El Niño years, they travel farther north and have been caught at the Islas los Coronados. Most are taken in water of at least 76°. Although they grow to over 155 pounds in the Atlantic, Baja waters typically produce fish from 30 to 60 pounds.

Wahoo feed on almost anything they can catch, which is almost everything, but they prefer flying fish, mullet, ballyhoo, mackerel, and squid, and will take artificials, especially those that make surface noise. Trolling or casting vinyl-skirted and natural feather lures and jigs are the most popular methods, but on long-range trips down the Pacific coast between half and three-quarters of all wahoo are taken on live bait. They are not plentiful, but good numbers are taken at Banco Thetis and Rocas Alijos off Baja's Pacific coast, in the Cape region, especially at Bancos San Jaime and Gorda, at the south tip of Cerralvo, and off the east side of Isla Espíritu Santo. Wahoo are notorious morning-biters, and the best time of day is from first light until two hours after dawn. Since the hotel boats get going too late, plan to use your own. Because they have bony mouths and often shake their heads violently when they feel the hook, a relatively stiff rod and dacron line are best, and hooks must be needle-sharp. A wire leader is necessary, but don't use bright-finish snaps and swivels. Make sure swivels do not ride at the surface, for wahoo will strike at the trail of bubbles, cutting the line. Because they are attracted by turbulence, place your lure at the end of the wake and be ready for close-in strikes. Wear shoes and use a billy at the first opportunity, for a wahoo will bite you if given the chance.

Wahoo are great jumpers, sometimes causing surprises.

A wahoo comes over the rail

Many years ago an angler trolling for marlin in an outboard at Banco Gorda reeled in his lure to clear a foul. This done, he started to let out, when all hell broke loose; a wahoo grabbed the lure only 30 feet out, dove straight down, turned under the boat, and headed for the sky, flying right over the boat, the line making a full circle. The man instantly considered the alternatives and dove in with rod in-hand, coming up on the other side of the boat. The fish started to tow him away, but someone managed to snag him by the collar with a boat hook. His efforts were not in vain, and the fish ended up on the barbecue that night. A number of years ago another wahoo was similarly unlucky when it smashed through the galley window of the long-range boat *Red Rooster* during lunch and landed on a table in front of a group of startled anglers. It too ended up on the barbecue. They are fine eating, with firm, fine-grained white flesh. Wahoo don't always come out on the short end—several years ago an angler aboard the *Royal Star* was attacked by a wahoo while on a long-range trip and had to be flown back to San Diego, where surgeons reattached three ligaments in his left arm. To make it worse, the wahoo had not even been hooked! While chasing another angler's lure, it jumped 12 feet into the air, smashed into the unlucky man, landed on the deck and escaped over the side with a tale to tell its children!

Roosterfish

Roosterfish have gray and silver bodies, with spectacular dorsal rays, which they erect when excited. Voracious predators of small fishes, they generally are found on shallow reefs and sandy bottoms from the surf line out to very moderate depths, usually no more than 15 feet, especially where shallow rocky bottoms come up to meet sandy beaches. Fishable populations extend from Bahía Magdalena to the Cape and as far north as Loreto, the greatest concentrations being at East Cape.

Baja is the best place in the world to fish for large roosters. Fishing for these finicky, exciting fish is a real challenge. Often reputed to take only live bait, they will sometimes fall for artificials, especially in the surf or during a feeding frenzy. However, no single artificial produces consistently, and most fish are taken by slow trolling live bait, especially ladyfish, needlefish, halfbeaks, grunts, and mullet, the last being the bait of choice. Roosters have no sharp teeth, so metal leaders are unnecessary. Live baits tend to be too large for roosters to swallow immediately, so they drop them and hit again, especially if a feeding frenzy is not going on, making it difficult to know when to strike. Trollers often proceed at about one or two knots with the reel clutch out, the spool held with a thumb. When a strike is felt, the spool is released, allowing the fish to take the bait without resistance, and after 5 or 10 seconds the hook is set. Once a school is located, usually involving less than a dozen fish, it pays to stop and drift a live bait. Roosters hit hard and are powerful, long-range fighters, often greyhounding with their great dorsal fins raised, and some have been known to beach themselves in an effort to get away.

Favorite areas include the coast south from La Paz to Cabo Pulmo, especially near Punta Arena de la Ventana and

A roosterfish comes aboard off Punta Colorada

Gary Kramer

Punta Colorada, and the best months are May through December, primarily July and August, the very best usually being the last two weeks of July and the first two of August. The older fish disappear in the cold months, and no one knows where they go. Opinion is divided as to their culinary value, but some claim they are good eating if bled and cooled quickly.

Dorado

Dorado are the perfect gamefish; they take artificials readily, put on a fantastic aerial ballet of leaps, flips, twists, somersaults, and tailwalks when hooked, and if these efforts fail, they provide fine eating. Found throughout the world in tropical and warm temperate seas, they are migratory and tend to be found in schools. Extremely beautiful, they have iridescent blue backs and compressed flanks. Freshly caught

Gary Kramer displays a dorado taken off Buena Vista

Larry Rauen

dorado often turn the color and sheen of gold lamé, with waves of blue and green shimmering over their entire bodies.

Their favorite diet consists of squid, flying fish, and other small fish, and they can be taken in many ways, primarily by fast trolling dead or strip baits or artificials such as Rapalas or silver spoons 50 or 60 feet back of the boat, or by drifting live bait. Marlin anglers often catch dorado, but they are at their best on light tackle—a big meat stick takes the fun out of it. Individuals and small schools sometimes hang around floating objects like oil drums, forklift pallets, planks, logs, or seaweed, a habit of great usefulness to an angler. They are not afraid of boats; it is often possible to look down and see schools milling about, and double and triple hookups are common. They can be chummed, and chunk or strip bait works well once a school has been attracted. It often pays to let them have a free spool for a five-count before clutching in and setting the hook, but from that point on never give a dorado an inch of slack line. When a fish is caught, his fellows often will escort him to the boat, and they can be taken by casting vinyl skirt or feather lures, especially those with a red-and-white color scheme. You don't always need a hook and line; in 1986 Sue Dippold and Bernie Eskesen were hiking on a beach south of Bahía Agua Verde when they saw some fish feeding in the clear water of the shallow bay. To their surprise one large fish became so intent on chasing his lunch that he ran right up on the beach! Bernie threw off his pack and scrambled down the cliff in a matter of seconds. The prize? A beautiful three-foot dorado.

Dorado are found primarily from Bahía Magdalena to Mulegé in the hot months, although some stay off Cabo San Lucas and East Cape all year. Dorado pileups have been reported in the Midriff, especially around Isla San Pedro Mártir. In years with unusually warm water they are found as far north as Bahía de los Angeles, but occasionally things are so cool that few are taken in Baja waters. Superb eating (probably sold as mahi-mahi in your local fish market), dorado do not keep well and should be consumed immediately.

• •

❝ *A two-part tale*

Reeve, my friend John Anglin, and I were drifting live bait for stripers off the Cape one year when John hooked a dorado. After a lengthy battle he began to gain some line, his eyes all aglow and warwhoops resounding across the water—his first dorado! The fish spooked when it saw the boat, and spooked again and then a third time. Finally it was alongside, but just as I bent down to scoop it up with the net, the line broke. I was blamed, of course, and had to endure an hour of criticism and heated instruction. Finally satiated, Reeve and John dozed off, but I kept scanning the horizon for marlin fins. About 20 minutes later I saw something out of the corner of my eye—a large dorado trailing a line was jumping repeatedly a hundred yards away. Reeve and John leaped up and began to reel in, but they soon found their lines were in a terrible tangle. Efforts to straighten out the mess were futile, and the two of them finally agreed that Reeve's line should be the one to be cut away—it was the one with no tension on it. As the last cut was made John's line went limp—they had cut the wrong one! This two-part tale has been repeated endlessly around campfires ever since, but guess which half? 🙰

● ●

Yellowtail

The California yellowtail is one of the most abundant and popular gamefish in Baja's Pacific and Cortez waters. Related to amberjack, yellowtail are blue-gray to olive above and silver-white below, and have yellow-tinged fins and a yellow stripe down their sides. Large fish tend to be solitary and often stay in one area, but smaller ones usually join schools and migrate in season. "Psyching" out these migratory patterns is the key to productive fishing. March through December is often best on the Pacific coast south to Bahía Magdalena. In the Cortez their migratory pattern is regular but the dates are hard to predict. As the northern Cortez cools down in winter, yellows head south, leaving Bahía Gonzaga and showing up at Santa Rosalía, then Mulegé and so on, and in summer the migration is reversed. From Gonzaga to the Midriff the warmer months are thus often the best, but from Mulegé to La Paz winter and early spring are the most productive. In the Cape region large numbers are found from January through May. To complicate things, small groups of year-round fish provide good fishing in many locations any time of year. Because of these tendencies it does not pay to fish one area too long; if you are not getting bites, move on.

Yellows are structure-oriented, hanging around rocky points, headlands, and reefs, rather than flat, featureless underwater terrain, and are often found under kelp paddies. They feed in the morning and late afternoon on small fish, crabs, and other invertebrates, and will take live, strip, or chunk bait and cast, trolled, or yoyoed jigs, and trolled or cast chrome spoons or swimmer-style lures like Rapalas. Live bait or slabs fished on the bottom in deep water with plenty of lead often take the largest fish. Yellowtail can be strangely unpredictable; when crazed by the sight of squid, they will hit anything in the water, but

sometimes they carefully ignore anything with even a suggestion of a protruding hook as they gobble up chum. When schools are "breezing" (swimming at the surface and creating a slight disturbance that looks like a wind ruffle), they may go into a frenzy of competition to see who can get to the bait first, may follow it without biting, or may spook and disappear. A full moon often, but not always, shuts off the bite. They are masters at taking advantage of propellers, rudders, kelp, and rocks to break lines. If one tries this, give him a free spool, deceiving him into thinking he has escaped. Yellows hit hard, make long sizzling runs, and provide excellent eating.

Favorite spots along the Pacific coast include San Martín and the Benitos, the latter being the most consistent yellowtail fishery on the west coast of North America. In the Cortez, the chain of islands in the Midriff from Partida Norte to San Lorenzo is highly productive, as is the Loreto area. A washrock 200 yards west of the north tip of Isla Turners may be the most productive location in the Cortez.

Reeve and I took a fine pair of yellowtail off Isla San Esteban

Perry Studt

Season and location

When is the best time of year for the Baja angler? If you ask the question at a sportfishing office in Ensenada, you will get an inevitable answer, "Today! Today is best!" However, if the last boat has already left, the best time of year becomes "Tomorrow!" There is a certain logic to this, for any day is good to go fishing, but there are definite seasonal aspects to most locations and most species.

A great deal is known about when and where people have caught fish. The calendar in Appendix C was developed from a detailed review of over 250 books and magazine articles, some ranging as far back as the days of Zane Grey, a sportsman and popular writer of the early part of the century, as well as a review of the records maintained by the International Game Fish Association, and the scientific literature, all tempered with my own experience. It shows without question that the summer months are the most productive for most species, but that there is something biting almost everywhere throughout the year. So, using Appendix C, pick your location and species and the dates of your trip, and see how things are likely to pan out. Remember, however, that water temperatures vary widely in some years and have an effect on fishing, especially when El Niño is raising havoc, and be prepared for surprises.

Rods, reels, and equipment

Because Baja is home to several hundred species of gamefish, ranging from delicate ladyfish to great black marlin, a one-rod angler is likely to be disappointed. To take full advantage of what is available you will need four rigs: a heavy-duty trolling rod with roller guides and a 6/0 revolving-spool reel loaded with 50- to 80-pound mono; a medium-duty 6-foot trolling rod with aluminum oxide or hard alloy guides and a 4/0 reel loaded with 30-pound mono; a medium-duty 8- or 9-foot spinning outfit handling 20-pound mono; and a light spinning outfit with 8-pound mono. This array will handle almost any fish Baja has to offer and permit almost any technique except fly fishing and surf casting.

Be prepared to fish both natural and artificial baits. Your tackle box should include shrimp-fly rigs and small shiny lures for catching live bait, and you should have a bait tank or large cooler to keep it alive. A shovel is useful for taking clams and other tidal critters. The vast assortment of trinkets turned out by tackle manufacturers is proof that no artificial works all of the time everywhere, and specific advice as to make, model, and color has filled generations of fishing magazines. However, the basic guidelines are simple: you will need a variety of colors, types, and sizes of artificial baits, and those imitating natural foods, such as feathers, plastic shrimp, leadheads, and chrome spoons, continue to be sold year after year, while highly publicized gimmicks usually disappear in a year or two. Probably the most effective all-around lures are the jointed Rebel plug and its look-alikes; one in my tackle box has worked so well that all the

paint is gone and the underlying plastic is grooved by teeth marks, in some places so deeply that the eyes holding the hooks are in danger of pulling out. They come in a variety of sizes and three types, surface, medium depth, and deep-diving. Krocodile spoons also produce well.

Binoculars, preferably 7 x 50s, are a great asset, since they can be used to spot schools of baitfish, feeding fish, and birds, especially frigates, boobies, gulls, and pelicans. In addition, they can save you time by letting you determine whether a commotion on the surface is being caused by seals or sea lions instead of fish. If you wish to avoid problems, bring all the tackle you will need and a good supply of snaps, swivels, weights, leader, line, hooks, lures, and spare parts for reels. Many supermarkets, hardware stores, hotels, and fleet reservations offices have a limited assortment of tackle, but the best independent full-service tackle shop is Minerva's Baja Tackle in Cabo San Lucas. There are smaller shops elsewhere—see the index.

Obtaining natural baits

Natural bait, especially live or fresh-dead, often takes more fish than artificials, but since it is rarely for sale except in resort areas you will have to catch it yourself. According to the regulations of the Mexico Ministry of the Environment, Natural Resources, and Fisheries, "reasonable amounts" of bait fish can be taken. Almost any kind of small fish makes good live bait, including herring, Pacific mackerel, sierra, ballyhoo, and goatfish. Mackerel-like fish form dense schools and can be spotted with a fish-finder and taken with Lucky Joes, Handy-Dandys, mackerel snatchers, flies, or small chunks of bait. If they will not bite, cast a snag line with a half-dozen treble hook and a 3-ounce torpedo sinker through the school. Ladyfish, excellent gamefish in their own right, and other small species can be caught with feathers, chrome spoons, or flies.

There are useful baits besides fish, including sand flea, crab, mussel, clam, lobster, limpet, sea worm, and abalone. Shrimpers are often seen at anchor along the western shores of the Cortez, and it is possible to buy whole shrimp or heads. A few cans of inexpensive shrimp pieces or abalone bought locally are a useful backup. It would be well, of course, to bring a supply of natural baits from home. If your RV has a refrigerator, packages of frozen mackerel, anchovy, and squid will undoubtedly come in handy.

Fishing from small boats

Rather than chartering or hiring a local boat, many people prefer to bring a cartopper, an inflatable, or a trailerboat, and the following chapter discusses the ins and outs of bringing your own boat. If you don't have a boat or choose to leave it home, there are two basic types of boats available in Baja—*pangas* and fishing cruisers. A *panga* is an open skiff, usually made of fiberglass, often 22 feet in length, powered by an outboard engine of about 40 horsepower. Widely used for commercial fishing on both coasts, they are normally hired on a daily or hourly basis with a skipper-guide, and can comfortably fish three or four anglers. They are inexpensive, a quarter or a third the daily cost of a cruiser, and are fast and maneuverable, permitting access to rocky areas and shallow reefs. However, they often have no accommodations beyond bench seats, no head, and no protection from the sun, although a few are starting to sport Bimini tops and other amenities. Cruisers come in a wide variety of sizes and types and are more expensive than *pangas*, but usually offer live bait tanks, fighting chairs, a cabin, and a head, and they can travel farther and can keep fishing in heavier weather than *pangas*.

There are many cruiser and *panga* fleets scattered in strategic locations throughout Baja; see the index. Appendix B provides the mailing addresses, telephone numbers, e-mail addresses, and Internet sites of many. *Pangas* are also available in the beach area of almost any commercial fishing settlement, although they are sometimes hard at work and unavailable. Practices vary from place to place, so make sure you clearly understand what will and will not be provided in the way of tackle, bait, food, and drink, when to arrive in the morning, how long you will be out, and the price.

Beach-casting

The beaches and rocky points along Baja's 1,980 miles of coastline are its least-known and most under-utilized fishery. These offer outstanding fishing for everyone from surf anglers casting into crashing waves with highly specialized 12-foot poles, to children with light spinning outfits dropping chunks of clam into rocky holes. A large number of species are available, including corbina, corvina, croaker, surfperch, ladyfish, flatfish, opaleye, cabezon, and ocean whitefish. The great sweep of Pacific beaches between El Rosario and Guerrero Negro, and between Bahías Tortugas and Magdalena, especially the outer beaches of the islands forming the latter bay, are usually deserted and frequently offer outstanding surf fishing. Some beaches north of Guerrero Negro even yield such unlikely species as white seabass and halibut. A few other Pacific locations in Baja Norte have good roads and see fair numbers of anglers, including Eréndira and San Quintín.

The coast between San José del Cabo and La Paz offers some of the most unusual and exciting shore fishing in the world, especially for roosterfish at Punta Pescadero and Punta Arena Sur. Ray Cannon's famous "Tuna Canyon" is

Reeve makes a slight miscalculation as to the state of the waves while surf fishing

John Anglin wings out bait at Conejo

located 4 miles south of Punta Pescadero, where a submarine canyon runs in close to the beach, providing a year-round population of yellowfin tuna that can occasionally be caught from shore. An isolated population of white seabass lives in the upper Cortez, and they can be taken by casting from rocky points. Most yellowtail are caught from boats, and while they are not commonly thought of as an onshore species, they also feed in shallow water and even in the surf zone, although they don't stay there any longer than necessary. When they drive a school of bait into shallow water it can be a real melee and they will savagely attack anything offered. Don't expect to catch many yellowtail this way, for they fight hard, and by the time you beach the first fish the bite is usually over.

Getting "unskunked"

Mythology to the contrary, there are times and places where it is difficult to catch fish in Baja, and some anglers return home skunked. You rarely hear about them, but it happens; who can admit spending an entire vacation in fabled Baja without catching a single fish? There are two solid reasons why some people join this silent minority: a failure to experiment and an unwillingness to change location. Some people have a favorite method of fishing and either have strong fixed ideas about how to go about it, or no ideas at

all. They arrive, fish from dawn to dusk, and return home in total humiliation. If they are willing to talk about it at all, you will probably hear the excuse, "They were not biting. We tried everything, we flung everything in the tackle box at them, but nothing worked." Check closer and you will almost certainly find, far from trying "everything," that they limited their fishing technique to, say, slow surface trolling off two or three rocky points on one island off one village. At no time did they experiment with natural baits, change depth, try fast trolling, jigging, or beach-casting, or buy a few artificial baits not already in their tackle box, and they didn't even bother to check out an island a few miles away or consider moving to an entirely new location.

Real estate salesmen like to joke that the three most important factors in successfully selling a house are "location, location, location," but for Baja anglers, success comes from "variety, variety, variety." No place on Earth provides more species of fish, or more habitats and more conditions of temperature, depth, and current in so compact and accessible an area as Baja, and the key to getting "unskunked" is being willing and able to change and experiment. Bring all

We told Mike that it was unlikely he would catch a grouper in the shallow sandy-bottomed flats off our camp in Bahía Concepción—they just don't hang around such environments

four rigs recommended above and a wide variety of natural and artificial baits. Ask around to find out what fish are biting and what baits and lures have been successful. If artificials don't work, try natural baits, and *vice versa.* Experiment with different depths. Downriggers and paravanes are not widely used in Baja waters, but they greatly expand the depths, temperatures, and habitats that can be exploited. Try bottomfishing in 400 or even 600 feet of water, where the habitat and the species are entirely different. If trolling off rocky points doesn't work, troll off sandy points, or offshore. If trolling doesn't work, try jigging or beach-casting or drifting a live bait. Try night fishing—some species that are seemingly absent appear magically after dark and feed actively. Any skin diver can tell you that fish are unevenly distributed, and large areas have low populations, either seasonally or permanently, so if nothing else works, move on.

Long-range fishing

In addition to small-boat fishing and beach-casting, there is another major category of Baja fishing: long-range. Through the years a growing and evermore elaborate fleet of sportfishing vessels has been carrying anglers south from San Diego and Ensenada to enjoy some of the most exciting fishing the world has to offer. These trips usually take one of three basic forms: mini-, midi-, and maxi-long-range trips, differing in their length, places fished, and species of fish encountered. The definitions are not precise, but mini-trips usually last between 2 and 5 days and range between 75 and 350 miles south of the border, fishing Islas San Martín, San Jerónimo, Cedros, and Guadalupe, the Benitos, and a number of coastal locations. A wide variety of species is caught, including yellowtail, yellowfin tuna, ocean whitefish, lingcod, barracuda, bonito, calico bass, and black sea bass. Midi-trips vary between 6 and 10 days and range south to Bahía Magdalena, Rocas Alijos, and various seamounts and banks, as well as stopping at the locations visited on mini-trips. Since they encounter warmer water, midi-trips often produce species not usually seen on mini-trips, such as wahoo, dorado, and occasional marlin. Maxi-trips usually take 14 to 17 days and usually concentrate on the Islas de Revillagigedo, located 250 miles south of the Cape, and places *en route* like Rocas Alijos, the quarry often being wahoo, dorado, and yellowfin tuna.

There is a fairly well-established annual cycle in the schedule of these boats. May through July is often devoted to midi-trips, June through September to mini-trips for albacore, late August to mid-December to mini- and midi-trips, and mid-December through June to maxi- and midi-trips for the larger boats, mini- and midi-trips for the smaller ones. Four of the most prominent organizations offering long-range trips from San Diego are H & M Landing, Point Loma Sportfishing, Lee Palm Sportfishers, and Fisherman's Landing. Out of Ensenada, Gordo's Sport Fishing makes mini-trips to San Martín. Tony Reyes Fishing Tours offers trips from San Felipe to the Midriff, as well as trips out of La Paz, the last ranging south to the Bancos Gorda and north of Mulegé. Upon request, all fleet offices will send brochures describing schedules, rates, reservation procedures, and suggestions on tackle—see Appendix B.

Hotels, resorts, package trips, and charters

Many Baja hotels and resorts cater to anglers and hold tournaments and clinics, and some have their own cruiser fleets. A few, such as Rancho Buena Vista, have held an international reputation for world-class fishing for many years. Fishing International has a variety of package fishing trips to the Cape, East Cape, Loreto, and La Paz. A few organizations specialize in specific locations, such as Fisherman's Fleet, which offers package trips to the La Paz area, Ensenada los Muertos, and Isla Cerralvo. Cortez Yacht Charters specializes in fishing charters at Cabo San Lucas and Bahía Magdalena, and has vessels ranging from *pangas* to a 57-foot motor yacht. Fiesta Sportfishing & Diving Co. offers

Tom Selman prepares for the next day's action on the **Royal Polaris**

Our catch of 47 yellowtail, 169 wahoo, 48 yellowfin tuna, 138 grouper, 4 dolphinfish, and 1 marlin was hoisted out of the refrigerated hold of the **Royal Polaris** *just before we returned to San Diego*

fishing trips to the Cape region, and fly- and light-tackle fishing are available.

Staying legal

Licenses are available for periods of one week, one month, and one year. All persons aboard a boat, regardless of age, must have a fishing license if any fishing tackle is aboard—even if it's just fish hooks and line in life rafts. Licenses can be obtained by mail from the Mexico Ministry of the Environment, Natural Resources, and Fisheries office in San Diego (cashier's check or money order only, payable to "Oficina Recaudadora de Pesca"), from the Discover Baja Travel Club, and the Vagabundos del Mar Boat and Travel Club, and in person from some fishing tackle stores in San Diego and Baja, and all *Oficinas de Pesca* in Baja. The latter offices, referred to from this point on simply as "*Pesca* offices," are found in numerous locations in Baja, many of which are identified in Chapters 9 through 13. Allow at least two weeks when obtaining licenses by mail. Daily licenses

are available from some of the larger sport fishing operators in Baja, but the smaller ones usually don't have them, which can lead to problems at the border if you try to bring fish back (see the following page). Long-range boats usually provide these aboard at cost. Some fishing operations in Baja include the cost of an excursion license in their fee, but to make sure you don't run into problems at the border due to the lack of a license, get and keep a copy if you intend to bring fish back.

Only one rod per person is allowed to be in use at one time, and no "long-lines" with multiple hooks, nets, or explosives may be used. Specific bag and possession limits are established. The license is applicable only to fin fish—taking mollusks (including pismo clams and oysters), crustaceans (including crabs and lobsters), *totuava*, and turtles are forbidden. There is no limit on catch-and-release as long as the fish are returned to the sea in good survival condition. If you purchase seafood, make sure you get a receipt. Cleaning and filleting fish for storage and transportation are permitted if the species can still be identified, but you cannot leave remnants of cleaning ashore. Underwater ecological reserves have been established at Scammon's Lagoon, Pulmo Reef, and the harbor at Cabo San Lucas. Mexican sportfishing regulations are enforced, and game wardens are afield. In addition, military personnel sometimes check licenses and the contents of coolers. It is essential that anyone planning a fishing trip to Baja obtain a current copy of the regulations along with the license and read it carefully

There are US regulations concerning importation of fish taken in Mexico. The Lacey Act authorizes US border officers to enforce Mexican licensing and possession limits. A declaration must be filled out at the port of entry, and you must have a Mexican fishing license. The Mexican possession limit is the maximum that may be imported. An entry-dated tourist card, receipts or other satisfactory proof of the time spent in Mexico must be available to import fish in excess of the daily limit. (Information on tourist cards is found on page 79.)

Fishing for the future

Mexico has aggressively expanded commercial fishing in Baja waters in recent years, permitting major increases in local gill-netting and purse-seining for species like anchovy for reduction to fish meal, and even allowing Japanese long-liners to take massive numbers of billfish. (In 1991 Mexico announced that long-lining had been banned to protect the sportfishing industry.) While this was going on, the Transpeninsular Highway was completed, air transportation was improved and a number of hotels were built, bringing in new hordes of anglers. All this has placed stress on the fisheries, and there is no doubt that the fabulous fishing in Baja is declining and will continue to do so in coming years. Visiting anglers can do little about laws that permit this decline, but they can help in a number of very direct and important ways.

"Catch-and-release" has been promoted in recent years as a way to allow people to experience the fun of fishing without damaging the biota. Since released fish are never seen again, anglers assume that all is well. However, Bill Johnston, ex-owner-skipper of the dive boats *Bottom Scratcher* and *Sand Dollar*, says his divers find dead fish littering the bottom after sportfishing boats have been in an area at the Islas los Coronados. There is much that individual anglers—you—can do to reduce this waste.

If you intend to consume any of your catch, keep all fish of legal species caught, regardless of their small size; there are no current minimum size limits for any species in Baja waters. When you have enough for a meal or have reached the bag limit, either quit fishing or practice catch-and-release. However, you can't just jerk the fish off the hook, throw it back, and expect it to survive. Unless special precautions are taken, fish often succumb to shock, disorientation, suffocation, internal damage, or wounds. Anglers go to great lengths to learn how to catch fish, but few know

anything about how to let them go! Blued, unplated, long-shank iron hooks can be removed easily, and salt water and fish juices will eventually rust them away if the line breaks. Never use treble hooks, or hooks made from stainless steel. Consider using barbless hooks, or crimping down barbs with a pair of pliers. When a fish comes alongside keep it upright and try to get the hook out while it is in the water and can breathe. A fish hung vertically can sustain internal injuries, so don't hoist it out of the water. A fish's slimy coating protects it from bacteria, and fatal infections can occur if this is damaged, so try to get the fish off the hook without touching it. If you must bring a fish aboard use wet hands and grasp it by the lower lip or behind the gill plates, or ahead of the tail fin if it is toothy. Grasp a billfish in the obvious location. A net removes slime, and a gaff is almost always fatal. If the fish is deeply hooked, simply cut the line as close to the hook as possible. Bleeding fish are probably going to die, especially if their gills are involved, so keep such fish for food.

The largest individuals of most species are often females with high reproductive value, so let the big ones go. Large fish are probably going to be wasted anyway, since they cannot be consumed immediately, and it is difficult or impossible to keep one under refrigeration until you get home. Besides, big fish don't taste any better than little ones. There is a lot of ego involved in dragging home a huge trophy, and letting one go may be about as popular as *coitus interruptus*, but it helps greatly, for the opposite reason.

Anglers often crank up their catch from great depths, their eyes bulging and stomachs protruding from their mouths (the fish, that is). This is no place for catch-and-release, for the fish will almost certainly never make it back to the bottom, but if you decide to release such fish, there is a right way to do it. All of the above ideas about hooks and release techniques apply, and in addition anglers should be prepared with a number 14 hypodermic needle, available from farm and ranch supply stores. Lay a pectoral fin back against the fish's body, and with the point of the needle remove a scale from the body at the tip of the fin. Slowly insert the needle through the skin and abdominal wall. When the needle penetrates the gas bladder, air will rush out the end of the needle, telling you that it has penetrated far enough. Compress the sides of the fish until they appear normal or concave, pull out the needle and return the fish to the water. The fish will probably swim rapidly to the bottom, but if it doesn't a few prods from the blunt end of a gaff or net handle should send it on its way. This method works on almost any species of "bottomfish," regardless of size. No vital organs are harmed, and the chance of infection is slight if you keep the needle clean and store it in a vial of alcohol. Thus, for a dollar's worth of equipment and 30 seconds of effort you can greatly reduce this unnecessary waste, and who knows: perhaps the fish will eventually grow to monstrous proportions and fall for your bait a second time.

Anglers occasionally catch sea birds, most often pelicans and boobies. If this happens do not cut the line, for the part still attached to the bird may become fouled in vegetation, rocks, or driftwood, and the bird will die of starvation. Slowly reel the bird in and get it under control by grasping the bill and one wing, near its base. A cloth put over the bird's head will help calm it down. A landing net can be used to restrain the bird and bring it aboard a boat. Beware: a bird may defend itself by pecking, sometimes at eyes. Find the hook and push the barb through the skin, cut the barb off and back the hook out, just as you would with a person who has been hooked. Good judgment is required if the hook is in a joint or near an eye or other vulnerable area, and it may be better to leave the hook alone and simply cut the line as close to the eye of the hook as possible. If the bird has swallowed the hook and it is not visible, cut the line at its bill. Inspect the bird carefully and remove all fishing line from it before letting it go. Look closely; it is often hard to see mono among the feathers.

• •

66 *The world's worst fisherman*

Fishing tales are inevitably about the man who caught the biggest and the most, but I once had the opportunity to fish with The World's Worst Fisherman. This short biography is authorized, but by mutual agreement I will simply refer to him as Mr. Worst. Mrs. Worst told me that her husband "had always wanted to go fishing, but never had the time," which meant that he had been a busy fellow, for he was 45. After a month of planning we finally embarked on a trip to a secret location in the Cortez which was always teeming with big yellowtail. In the first 10 minutes of the first day, I hooked a beauty, then my brother got a bigger one, then I got one, then my brother, then I, then my brother, while Worst got nothing. This was also the pattern for the second day, broken only when I would get two or three in a row, followed by my brother.

Worst's morale was high at the campfire that night, for no reason other than he still had five days to connect. By the third night, however, his lower lip was protruding a bit, so we decided to figure out the reason for his bad luck. The next morning we identified the problem—although it wasn't simple bad luck. If yellowtail could be seen chasing forage at the surface, Worst's lure would come up covered with scratches from bouncing along the bottom. If they were near the bottom, his bait was skipping across the waves. Rather than trolling just in back of the wake, he would be back either 10 feet or 300 yards. If an examination of stomach contents showed the yellowtail were after squid, Worst would bend on a gaudy green Rapala. We discussed this with him, but got no signal that he understood. On the fifth day he continued, his technique unmodified and his stringer empty, and by the last day Worst seemed destined to break some sort of yellowtail non-record. Finally, with only one hour left, he let it all hang out. "You guys are doing something," he informed us, and threw down his rod and pouted. We finally persuaded him to try again, with our coaching. We selected a lure of the exact right size, type, and hue. I adjusted the throttle to the exact speed required, and told him to start letting out line. Finally, when the lure was in the right spot just beyond the wake I told him to flip the clutch lever on his reel. At that exact instant a bruiser of a yellowtail grabbed the lure and headed for parts unknown. His reel smoking, Worst finally turned the fish and gained some line, then he lost all of that and more. Back and forth the battle raged, until the fish was finally brought to gaff. Did this ease Worst's frustrations? No, for this certainly proved that we had been "doing something" all along—if we could turn on the fishing just like that, we could certainly turn it off. On the way home, though, he could finally joke about his "bad luck" and we started to plan a book about his fishing techniques, which we would sell worldwide through animal-rights organizations and vegetarian societies. 99

• •

Chapter 4

Wind, Water, and Waves

Unless your interests are strictly land-locked, you will probably want to bring a boat to Baja. Although there are many *pangas* for hire throughout Baja Norte and Baja Sur, and a number of cruiser fleets are available in Baja Sur, they are not always to be found when and where you need them. Besides, many anglers, divers, campers, and explorers find that piloting their own boat is part of the fun. In addition, the Cortez has some of the finest cruising waters in the world, and while yachts are available for charter, it is difficult or impossible to obtain a small sailboat or outboard in Baja for this purpose.

There have been many fine boating adventures in Baja waters. One of the earliest extensive trailerboat cruises occurred in 1960, when Spencer Murray and Ralph Poole brought their 22-foot lapstrake to San Felipe and cruised to Bahía Gonzaga, Bahía de los Angeles, Santa Rosalía, and Loreto, crossed the Cortez to Topolobampo, and recrossed to La Paz. After visiting the Cape, they left the boat in La Paz and flew back to the US. A number of months later the boat was returned to Ensenada aboard a Mexican freighter. Since then outboard cruisers as small as 17 feet have crossed from Guaymas to Mulegé repeatedly without incident, and even cartoppers have made lengthy trips in the Midriff. I have crossed the Cortez twice in a 15-foot aluminum boat, not a recommended activity unless a left-sided tilt to the adventure/safety scale is acceptable to you.

A few small-boat adventures have involved both the Pacific and the Cortez. In 1980 Joe Seidenthal piloted an open 22-foot Paceño outboard, the *panga* seen throughout Baja, from San Felipe to San Diego, and in 1983 David Steed carried things a step farther when he "circumnavigated" Baja. Aboard a 15-foot inflatable powered by a 50-horse engine, he voyaged from San Diego around the Cape to the mouth of the Río Colorado in 4 months. A friend with a trailer picked him up in San Felipe and drove to Ensenada, from where Steed launched and completed the run to San Diego.

The fun has not been limited to powerboats. Many small sailboats have cruised the Midriff and sailed the length of the Cortez, and a number of sailing dinghys have made the Loreto-to-La Paz run. The premiere small-boat sailing voyage in Baja waters is the Hobie Cat trip made by Jeff Hardgrave, Eric Guenther, and Dan Mangus. After 10 months of preparation, they sailed from San Diego on June 25, 1980, Jeff on a Hobie 18, the other two on 16s, their trampoline bags packed with a vast array of supplies and equipment. After many close-calls and adventures, disaster finally struck at El Conejo, when Jeff pitchpoled backward while leaving the beach. The boat was a mass of fractured fiberglass, broken aluminum, and torn sails, and the trip was over for him. Fortunately he did not sustain a scratch. Dan and Eric continued on the next day. Sailing through the night with a full moon, they rounded Cabo Falso and arrived at Cabo San Lucas at 3 in the morning of July 25, greeted by 2 barking dogs. Their magnificent voyage was over, 1,000 miles, 30 days, 5 capsizes, 2 dismastings, 1 wrecked boat, and 23 rudder pins later.

Favorite cruising grounds

Among the most interesting and adventurous small-boat cruises in the Cortez are: the Circumnavigating Guardian Angel Trip beginning and ending in Bahía de los Angeles and the Coasting to Santa Rosalía Trip from Bahía de los Angeles to Santa Rosalía (described in Chapter 10); the Coasting to Loreto Trip from Mulegé to Loreto, and the Island-Hopping Trip and the Coasting to La Paz Trip between Loreto and La Paz (Chapter 11); and the Stepping-Stones Trip through the Midriff to Bahía Kino, Sonora (Chapter 14).

Boaters wanting a pleasant, undemanding trip often gunkhole around Isla Espíritu Santo or Islas Carmen and Danzante for a week or two. Lengthy cruises along the Pacific coast like that taken by the Hobie sailors are rarely undertaken, due to logistics and weather problems, although it is great fun to explore vast Bahía Magdalena, and larger rigs can head for Banco Thetis for marlin and wahoo. Trailerboaters often launch at San Quintín and spend time at Isla San Martín, diving and fishing around Johnston's Seamount and Roca Ben and exploring the lava tubes on the island.

New roads and improvements to existing roads have opened up great adventures for small-boat sailors, especially the roads to Bahías Tortugas and Asunción. In the past, this stretch of coast was very difficult to get to with anything short of an oceangoing yacht, but it is now possible to haul in cartoppers and inflatables with only modest vehicles, and although there are no paved ramps and over-the-beach launches are necessary, adventurous trailerboat sailors can make the trip without undue difficulty. Best of all, the fine fishing and diving at the Benitos and Isla Cedros are now within the range of small-boaters. The San Evaristo road makes it possible to dive the wall at Isla las Ánimas Sur and the caves of Isla San Diego out of an inflatable or a cartopper, and the road south from Bahía de los Angeles to Bahía San Francisquito makes it easier to get to the Midriff.

Portable boats

The ultimate boat for fishing, diving, and short-range cruising and for exploring Baja's inshore waters may be the largest aluminum boat you can carry on the roof of your vehicle, probably a 15-footer if you have a full-size pickup or van. A 15-footer can be launched and beached almost anywhere, and can be taken far off-road to remote locations, near-impossibilities with even the smallest trailerboats. In an emergency, a person of average strength can launch and retrieve it alone once the engine and equipment are removed, by "walking" it—lifting one end and carrying it in an arc, then the other, etc. Best of all, you won't have to deal with the mechanical, insurance, and hassle problems associated with trailers. An engine as small as 15 horsepower, weighing less than 80 pounds, will keep it on a plane with several campers, divers, or anglers and their gear aboard and provide ad-

equate range and safety. A bit more horsepower is helpful, but engines over 20 horsepower are ordinarily too heavy for one person to carry across a rough cobble beach and install on a boat. As pointed out in Chapter 2, traditional 12-foot aluminum boats are too small for most Baja activities.

Recreation Industries Co. makes loaders that allow carrying a boat on the top of various types of vehicles, including large motor homes, cab-over campers, and pickups towing fifth-wheel trailers. A bow line and extra tie-downs are necessary to resist lateral and vertical loads caused by crosswinds and wind-blast from 18-wheelers on the narrow Transpeninsular. These are also necessary when traveling off-road to resist bouncing and swaying. Loader supports should be checked frequently, especially if they connect to rain gutters.

Another nice rig, on a larger scale, is a 17- or 18-foot aluminum boat. At 350 pounds or more, they are best carried upside down on the top of a low utility trailer. Several men can manhandle the boat on and off the trailer, which can also carry engines, fuel, tackle, ice chests, and other gear. Such a rig will require more manpower and fuel, and much off-road mobility is lost, but it will provide greater range,

Catamarans clutter the beach as the Hobie adventurers take a break from the rigors of the sea

Dan Mangus

safety, and load-carrying ability than a smaller boat.

The qualities of inflatables make them useful for Baja adventuring: they are light and portable, and their low free-board, stability, and load-carrying ability make them especially attractive to divers. In heavy weather, an inflatable is far safer than an open aluminum boat. While driving off-road, an inflatable in the back of a pickup will be a lot less hassle than a boat on top. On the negative side, they tend to be wet, take more engine horsepower, use more fuel, can carry relatively little load volume, and are vulnerable to hooks, knives, and fish spines, and attaching downriggers, rod holders, and transducers can be a problem. In addition, they take valuable cargo space; an aluminum boat on the roof takes less usable space than an inflatable in the bed of a pickup.

Some things to think about: In 1992 2 fishermen in a Zodiac at the Cape were repeatedly charged by a 9-foot sail-fish they had hooked, which seemed determined to use its bill for its intended purpose. Only by scooting out of the way with their engine were they able to avoid disinflation. The fish lost the battle. However, a hole in an inflatable is not necessarily a disaster. Peter Jensen was on a voyage out of Cabo San Lucas when a speargun caused a bad leak, but one of the crew simply stuck his finger in the hole, and the trip continued uneventfully.

Trailerboats

A wide variety of boats have been successfully trailered to Baja, ranging from miserable 1950s fiberglass runabouts with imitation Cadillac tailfins to the latest in Boston Whalers, but no one type or make is clearly best for all situations and interests. I find my Toland 18-foot, 8-inch "pocket cruiser," powered by 45-horse and 15-horse Honda 4-cycle engines, provides an excellent balance between range, speed, and accommodations, and it obediently follows my Toyota 4-cylinder, four-wheel-drive pickup, although it is admittedly a bit slow on the upgrades.

Among small sailboats, Westwight Potters, Hobies, Dovekies, Drascombe Luggers, and Ventures are frequently seen. Sail or power, the choice depends on how and where you plan to use it, seaworthiness, personal preference, and pocketbook. While the comfort, safety, and range of large "trailerable yachts" are desirable, they are hard to handle on the Transpeninsular and difficult to launch in most locations, and obtaining a supply of gasoline can be a problem in some areas. There is no sharp limit, but it is probably unwise to trail boats over 24 feet or any keel sailboat to Baja. Chapter 6 has information on preparing trailers and towing under Baja conditions.

Launch ramps

A few of the ramps in Baja, the ones at Puerto Escondido and Cabo San Lucas, for instance, are as good as anything north of the border, but most leave something to be desired. The most common problem is that waves have undermined

Reeve Peterson and Rob Watson found an inflatable to be the ideal dive boat while looking for the wreck of the tanker **Swift Eagle** *at the Islas San Benito*

the outer end, providing a big surprise as you back the trailer out. In addition, the northern Cortez is subject to enormous tides, often leaving the toe of the ramp a great distance from the water at low tide. All ramps in East Cape and San Felipe are in exposed locations, making it difficult to launch and retrieve when a sea is running, even with a trailer with guide-boards. The slope of the ramp can make things difficult: below about 12%, the boat may not float off the trailer until the back of the tow vehicle is in the salt water. If the ramp is too steep, above about 15%, getting enough traction to pull the boat out is difficult, especially when the bottom of the ramp is covered with slippery vegetation or sand.

For trailer-sailors with relatively small boats, these ramp problems are minor nuisances at most. Skippers of large boats, especially those with deep-**V** hulls, and those having sailboats with keels, have more significant problems, just as they do with ramps in the US. The ramp may not extend far enough to permit such boats to float off the trailer before the paving ends, especially at low tides, putting trailer wheels into the sand and mud. If the end of the ramp is undermined, getting the trailer wheels up on the concrete again can be a problem. The best advice is to inspect the ramp thoroughly, and plan to launch and retrieve at high tides.

Later chapters describe every paved ramp open to public use known to exist in Baja. Those in excess of 15% are termed "steep," while those of less than 12% are termed "shallow." There are, of course, many rock and sand areas where boats can be launched, too many to list individually. However, some are in important locations that have no other launch facilities, and are therefore identified and described.

Boat permits and marine insurance

In addition to the fishing licenses noted in the previous chapter, the Mexico Ministry of the Environment, Natural Resources, and Fisheries requires that all boats carrying fishing equipment have a boat permit. This includes inflatable, cartop, trailerable, and "non-trailerable" boats, as well as dinghys and additional boats aboard larger vessels. These can be obtained from most of the same sources providing the fishing licenses. As required for vehicles and trailers, you must carry your registration papers and a notarized letter from any lienholders giving you permission to bring the boat into Mexico. The details of these requirements and the prices of permits seem to be in a continuous state of flux, so telephone the Ministry office in San Diego to get current information well before you plan to depart. **Also, be sure to read the requirements noted beginning on page 90.**

Various forms of marine insurance are available from the Discover Baja Travel Club and the Vagabundos del Mar, as well as some commercial insurance companies.

Entering Mexico by boat

If you enter Mexico by sea, even in a kayak, you must comply with *Migración* (Immigration), *Aduana* (Customs), and *Capitán del Puerto* (Captain of the Port, COTP) proce-dures for yachts; consult with a yacht agent or refer to a yachting guide. The locations of many COTP offices are noted in Chapters 9 through 13. Once in Mexico and traveling by sea, there are procedures established for checking in and out of the various COTP jurisdictions. The COTPs seem to have little interest in boats brought in by road. However, because of increased anti-drug-smuggling activities by Mexican authorities, the chances of being asked for COTP paperwork by naval or law-enforcement personnel are higher than in the past. If you bring a boat into Mexico by road and plan a lengthy trip, say from San Felipe to La Paz, it would be wise to check into the COTP office nearest the launch point to get the latest information, especially if your boat is the kind that may attract interest, say a large cruiser with big engines, radar, and lots of antennas. Like everything in Mexico, these requirements concerning boats are in a continual state of change, so check before you go.

Marinas, fuel, oil, parts, and service

Yachtsmen will find the situation much better than a few years ago. After endless talk and a few false starts there are now modern marinas in Ensenada (Hotel Coral & Marina and Baja Naval), La Paz (Marina de La Paz, Marina Palmira and Marina Pichilingue), and Cabo San Lucas (Marina Cabo San Lucas). These facilities offer virtually everything you would find in a marina in the US, from floating docks with power and water to parts and repair services. Santa Rosalía also has a marina, although its facilities are more limited than the others. Descriptions will be found in later chapters, and their addresses and telephone numbers are listed in Appendix B. (A large complex that includes a marina has been planned for Puerto Escondido, but construction has been at a halt for a number of years.) Other than these locations, don't expect to cruise into a full-service marina and find a business catering to yachtsmen and maintaining normal business practices.

The marinas offer fuel, and there is a new fuel dock at Cabo San Lucas. Fueling facilities are also available at some commercial fishing docks, but your boat may be an intrusion and a disruption. In other areas, most of your fuel is thus going to come from ordinary PEMEX stations, and if you are on a cruise or are otherwise unable to take the boat to the fuel, you must be prepared to bring the fuel to the boat with numerous large cans. Fuel purchased from an individual, a cannery, or a boat yard is not price-controlled, and you will be charged what the traffic will bear. Two-cycle outboard oil can be hard to find, so carry enough to meet your needs.

Parts, service, and repairs for Johnson/Evinrude, Yamaha, Force, and Mercury/Mariner outboards are available in Baja—see the index for their locations. These dealers cater almost entirely to local fishermen and divers, and parts for very small and very large engines are often not in stock. In addition, some engines sold in Mexico may be "international" models, whose parts are not interchangeable with those of the same make and size sold in the US. There are a few independent repair shops shown on the city maps in Chapters 9 through 13. Mercury/Mariner dealers in Ensenada and La Paz handle MerCruiser sterndrives. Automotive parts may fit and seem to work well in sterndrives and inboards, but they can be dangerous in marine service. A shop service manual and parts list will greatly simplify handling engine problems.

Equipment and seamanship

Every powerboat should be equipped with a small outboard capable of being started manually and steered independently, and sailboats should have an auxiliary engine. The sun can be fierce and a Bimini top is a real asset. You should carry at least two anchors suitable for your boat, each with appropriate chain and rode. Since waves are often in one direction and wind in another, a flopper-stopper and a stern anchor are handy if you plan to sleep aboard. Local boats have rough sides and no rub-rail padding, so bring fenders if you intend to dicker for fish or shrimp. The best bailing equipment is a sturdy metal bucket. Tie it to the boat so it will not be lost should you swamp. Due to the lack of swell in the Cortez, the disturbances and foam that mark rocks and shoals are often absent, and a depth finder is essential for larger boats. In the Midriff and upper Cortez, tides

Johnny Neptune executes a daring sea rescue off Danzante, **pushing** *the author's boat back to port, while Will Ashford photographs the exploit*

and tidal currents will probably be greater than anything you have ever experienced outside of Alaska, so bring tide tables to help plan the voyage.

Make sure you know how far your boat will go on a gallon of fuel when the boat is fully laden, and insure that your tanks and fuel cans are adequate for the trip. Outboards get surprisingly poor mileage; the 15-foot, 15-horsepower rig recommended above will get only about 5 or 6 nautical miles per gallon when loaded to rated capacity. Remember that fuel use in choppy water or fighting winds and currents will be greater than in calm water, and that sediment may get stirred up and clog the fuel filter.

An aluminum folding chair weighs only about three pounds and contributes greatly to the comfort of a trip if you camp ashore. A propane outfit consisting of a cylinder, safety post, stove, and mantle lantern will allow cooking without the need to build fires and will provide light during the long evenings of winter. A double-mantle Coleman lantern burns $1/8$ of a pound of propane per hour when set at full brilliance, while one burner on a Coleman stove set at a moderate flame uses $1/3$ of a pound per hour. A winter trip typically requires about $3/4$ of a pound per day, so 5 disposable 16.4-ounce cylinders or one 5-pound refillable cylinder would be appropriate for a week-long trip. The hoses on most stoves are too short, so bring an extension. The next chapter has additional information on camping and camping equipment that may be useful to small-boaters.

One problem is common to cartoppers and inflatables—keeping things dry. The big bags used by river rafters are light and can take a lot of abuse, and the smaller ones used by sea kayakers may be handy. Things like cameras and radios that need protection from bumps as well as moisture can be packed in ammunition cans. A tarpaulin should cover the entire load.

Stay well within the weight and power ratings of your boat. Heavy objects like fuel and water cans should be put in the center, fore and aft as well as athwartships; by keeping the moment of inertia of the boat and its load low, the bow and stern can rise quickly to the waves. The load must be arranged so it can't shift—it may fall to the low side if you roll too far—but never tie heavy objects like weight belts to the boat, since they may overwhelm the floatation of the boat should you swamp. In addition, the center of gravity of the load and the passengers must be adjusted to allow the boat to plane efficiently. Don't compensate for a poorly balanced load by putting an extreme angle on the engine mounting bracket—work to get the balance right. Even a heavily laden boat can broach in a following sea (i.e., increase speed down the face of a wave and suddenly turn broadside to the waves and roll over), so hold your speed down and drag the bailing bucket if you have to.

To repeat an earlier caveat: the maps in *The Baja Adventure Book* should be used as a planning guide and are not a substitute for the appropriate nautical charts, so bring a full set. However, since they camp ashore at night and may need to put ashore in heavy weather, sailors of dinghys, Hobies, cartoppers, and other very small craft need highly detailed information on coastlines. Due to their small scale and absence of shoreline detail, most marine charts are of little value, and the 1:50,000 scale Mexican topographic maps or the charts and guides offered by Cruising Charts will be much more useful. See Chapter 8 for further information on maps and charts.

Most sailors recognize the inherent dangers of Baja's Pacific coast and keep their guard up, but the tranquil conditions prevalent in the Cortez can lull you into believing that things are always like that, and tragedies have occurred. In November 1980 a group of 29 young men and 11 staff members from an organization helping troubled teenagers left Guaymas bound for Baja in 4 converted life boats equipped with sails and oars. A storm hit, "the worst on record for that area." Three boats arrived safely at Mulegé, but the fourth, with eight people aboard, never made it.

Emergency assistance and communications

Boaters in Mexican waters will not find the extensive communications and rapid response they expect from the Coast Guard in US waters. Mexico has established a Rescue Coordination Center that has improved coordination between the two countries, but the Mexican Navy's search-and-rescue (SAR) capabilities are still limited. COTPs sometimes have boats or can arrange for local assistance. Under a bilateral agreement between the US and Mexico, the US Coast Guard can provide limited SAR coverage off the west coast of Mexico, directed by the Coast Guard Command Center in Alameda, CA. Surface units and HH-601 Jawhawk helicopters from San Diego normally can respond to SAR cases as far south as Cedros, and C-130s from Sacramento can operate as far south as Acapulco. Club Deportivo Bahía Kino at Bahía Kino, Sonora, at the east edge of the Midriff, finances and manages Rescue One with volunteers 365 days a year. Working under the auspices of the Bahía Kino COTP and the Mexican government, Rescue One sends out search-and-rescue boats and aircraft in the Cortez when needed, and maintains a coordination center for emergencies, illness, accidents, police assistance, etc.

The Coast Guard can be contacted on VHF channel 16, sometimes as far south as Ensenada, although at this distance it is unreliable. Many other organizations guard VHF channel 16, including Mexican government coastal radio stations at Ensenada, La Paz, Guaymas, and Mazatlán, COTP

The heavy tides encountered in the upper Cortez can be used to simplify engine and boat maintenance and to allow the loading of fuel and equipment with a minimum of hassle

A small problem at sea: **Andale's main backwinded and the boom broke at the preventer. Clockwise from the bottom: Paul Payne, Gerry Fulmer, and the author's brother Reeve clear the wreckage**

offices, vessels of the ferry system, commercial shipping, Mexican naval vessels and bases, and some marinas. Some operators speak English, although not necessarily fluently. Club Deportivo "Bahía Kino" guards CB channel 11 and VHF channel 16. Many other organizations and individuals guard CB channels; see page 89.

Clubs, charters, rentals, and commercial trips

The Vagabundos del Mar offers its members organized trips and flotillas to the Cortez and to Baja's Pacific coast; see page 80 for more on the club. Cortez Yacht Charters and The Moorings can provide a variety of yacht charters in Baja waters. The NOLS "Semester in Mexico" courses and their "Baja Coastal Sailing" course include travel in 22-foot Drascombe Longboats along Cortez coasts. A number of hotels, resorts, and other organizations rent Hobies or other small sailing craft. All are listed in the index, and the addresses, phone numbers, e-mail address, and Internet sites of many will be found in Appendix B.

❝ *For want of a pin the boat was (almost) lost*

We had heard that large groupers inhabit the waters around Isla Alcatraz in Bahía Kino, so Reeve and I decided to dive the area. We made camp on the shore northwest of town, launched our small cartopper, and loaded it with spearguns, underwater cameras, and dive gear. It was a long run to the island, about 7 miles, but the water was calm and we made excellent time. Anchored on the south side of the island, we suited up and hit the water. Grouper are very spooky fish, and hunting them proved to be difficult. The visibility was only 6 feet, which was about the range of our guns, so intense concentration and stealth were necessary. Their lateral lines told the fish of our presence far sooner than our eyes told us of theirs, and the first evidence we had that one was nearby was usually a loud "thump" and a swirl of silt as the fish spooked. Driven by curiosity, one would occasionally stay an extra second or two to see what was happening, and we got a few shots. It was nerve-wracking, each shot requiring instant reflexes and near-perfect aim, but we finally managed to bag several barbecue-size fish.

We were getting into the boat when we noticed white-caps rolling around the east and west points of the island; a heavy wind had sprung up from the northwest. We started the engine and pulled the anchor, but just after I engaged the shift lever and twisted the throttle the engine raced wildly—the shear pin had broken. We had three extra pins taped to the handle of the motor and I had tools in my underwater camera box, but replacing the pin was a bit tricky in the small and tippy boat. Reeve dropped the anchor, and I had to unclamp the engine from the transom, lift it into the boat, remove the propeller, put in a new pin, replace the propeller, and clamp the engine back on the transom. After the repair the engine behaved normally, but as we came out of the lee of the island things looked bad; a heavy sea was up and the bay was a mass of whitecaps. Our boat would be sorely challenged, but we would be safe if the engine kept working and we kept the bow into the waves. Several hundred yards from the island the engine again raced wildly; the new shear pin had broken. We quickly dropped the anchor before the boat had a chance to swing broadside to the waves. It was hairy removing the engine in the wildly pitching boat, but we finally got underway.

About four miles from camp the pin broke again. This time we were in big trouble, for the water was too deep to anchor. We swung broadside and began to roll heavily and take on green water, but a hastily improvised sea anchor consisting of a bucket on a length of rope finally swung us back perpendicular to the waves. Since our trip back to camp was parallel to the shore we were only a mile or two away from land. We rejected the idea of rowing for shore, since we would be broadside to the waves and might roll over or swamp, and the surf on the beach looked bad. Besides, it would be a long walk back to camp carrying our gear, if any of it survived the ride through the surf. We were in no great physical danger since we were in wet suits and had masks and fins close at hand—the real danger was the loss of our cameras, guns, boat, and motor.

In a great spray of wind-driven water I unclamped the engine and started to lift it, when a large wave hit, throwing me against the gunnel. I almost went over the side, motor and all, but Reeve grabbed me and I managed to get my footing. We installed the last pin, started the motor, shifted into gear—and the pin broke almost instantly. Several times the bow of the boat did not rise quickly enough into the ever-growing waves, and the bilges were soon awash in six inches of water. As Reeve frantically bailed I searched for something to serve as a shear pin, and finally found a set of five small jewelers screwdrivers in my underwater camera box.

Using a pair of sidecutting pliers, I nipped the hardened steel shaft of one of them and bent it back and forth until it broke. The diameter of the impromptu shear pin was too small, but it lasted about a mile. The second screwdriver broke almost immediately, but the third, fourth, and last one got us to within 500 yards of camp. What now? The wind was blowing us rapidly away from the shore, far faster than we could hope to row. It then dawned on us that when a shear pin breaks, it breaks into three pieces, one long and two short, and that the broken remains of some of the pins were still in the bilges. After a mad scramble on our knees, we removed the propeller and installed two of the long pieces in the propeller shaft, providing new shear surfaces. It worked! We started the engine, held our breaths and rode the crest of a breaker to land triumphantly on the beach in front of our camp. An examination of the engine revealed that a defect in the shifting mechanism was causing the engine to violently slam out and into gear, breaking the pins. **99**

● ●

Chapter 5

Going Self-Propelled

Since it carries virtually all road traffic south of Ensenada, the Transpeninsular Highway has greatly influenced the public image of Baja. To most people, the scenes passing outside the car window are the only Baja: mile after mile of asphalt road winding across scrubby desert and through desolate canyons, interrupted only by occasional villages, gas stations, and glimpses of the sea. The traveler's focus of attention is usually on reaching the next air-conditioned oasis, avoiding contact with everything in between as much as possible. Propose a bicycle or backpacking trip to someone and you are apt to be greeted with a snort and an incredulous, "Whataya, crazy or somethin?" Baja California is certainly the last place where anyone of sound mind would voluntarily forsake the advantages of the internal combustion engine for a trip propelled by human muscle. Right?

Wrong! Despite the common impression, Baja is a joy for adventurous bicyclists, backpackers, hikers, climbers, and kayakers. Bicyclists can watch whales mating, visit an Indian art site, challenge a roadrunner to a race, explore a cave, camp on a pristine beach, and catch a fish for supper, all during a single trip. Backpackers, climbers, and hikers can find another Baja, one not served by roads and thus rarely visited, of high mountains, plunging canyons, pines and oaks, flowing water, and emerald pools. Kayakers can revel among remote islands and beaches along the western shore of the

This cartoon from an 1868 article by J. Ross Browne portrays a typical impression of Baja backpacking

Cortez, an area that is becoming one of the more popular sea kayaking areas in North America.

Not everyone will appreciate Baja; it may be a paradise, but certainly not the Moslem version. Most self-propelled trips in Baja are made in winter, which is the "off" season for vigorous physical activity for many people, so they will have lots of sore muscles until the kinks get worked out. And once self-propelled in a remote area for the first time, some people experience an uncomfortable psychological shock, a reaction to the utter openness of the empty desert. Accustomed to conditions in the US, where towns are rarely more than 10 or 20 miles apart, some people find Baja's vast empty stretches threatening; they seem to doubt their ability to survive, self-contained and alone, no matter how well-prepared and well-tuned their bodies and their equipment. Some begin to refer to tiny *ranchos* as "towns" and small settlements as "cities," perhaps a manifestation of a subconscious wish. A few people begin to press for a return to a more crowded, familiar, and thus comfortable environment, constantly suggesting that the group get up early, ride late, or skip *siesta* time (a period of time traditionally set aside for an afternoon nap) so that they can "get somewhere." Most people adjust within a few days, and learn to slow down, accept, and enjoy. A few don't.

Clothing and camping equipment

True to its desert image, Baja is often warm or hot, but there are great variations in temperature, and it can occasionally get downright cold, even in summer. The existence of this variation, together with the need for ventilation and sun protection, should form the basis for planning clothing and bedding. Clothes should be loose fitting, light in weight, and made of cotton, with long sleeves and legs to prevent sunburn. Bathing suits, shorts, and G-strings lead to burns, dehydration, abrasion in case of falls, and unwelcome attention. A sweater and a jacket will be appreciated, and since the wind-chill law has not been repealed, the jacket ought to have a tightly-woven outer fabric. It is usually unnecessary to bring a lot of extra clothing along simply to stay clean, for even though water is scarce, there will be opportunities to wash clothes. Winter hikers and climbers should be prepared for frost in the Sierra de Juárez and Sierra de la Laguna, and snow and hard freezes in the upper reaches of the Sierra San Pedro Mártir.

Light-colored, broad-brimmed straw hats provide the

Ted Robinson and Wayne Campbell backpack through Parque Nacional Sierra San Pedro Mártir on a brisk spring morning

best sun protection and ventilation. Backpackers may want to pin up the back brim to prevent it from rubbing on their packs, and kayakers should glue styrofoam into the crown, since some straw hats sink. Don't forget your sun glasses, and a Swiss Army knife—the kind with tweezers—or a Leatherman multi-purpose tool, or one of their clones. Everything must be clean, presentable, and in good repair; look like a bum in Baja and you will be treated like a bum.

A 2-pound down bag or a 2^1/2- or 3-pound polyester bag should keep most people comfortable most of the year. Bags should have full-length zippers for heat control. A bag liner will facilitate cleanliness and can be used alone on hot nights. Your sleeping gear should be carried in a waterproof cover, since heavy dew is common on the Pacific side and rain is possible. Since ground temperatures also range from hot to cold, the thermal insulation provided by a foam pad makes it preferable to an air mattress. Bring lots of patches if you use an air mattress. Since they do not absorb sweat, plastic and rubber air mattresses become uncomfortable in hot weather, so a cotton sheet will be appreciated.

Most people bring a small, self-supporting tent. It must be designed to allow plenty of ventilation. A poncho is useful, serving as raingear, groundcloth, tent, table cloth, sun shade, kayak sail, and extra insulation on cold nights. Scorpions don't seem to like plastic, so people sleeping out in the open should use a plastic ground cloth.

Scouting up fire materials every time you want a cup of coffee can become a pain, especially during physically demanding trips, and some hard-working bicyclists don't bother to cook, since meals can be purchased from hotels and cafés along the Transpeninsular, and the weather is often so warm that frequent hot meals are not missed. In any event, if you camp near settled areas, it may not be possible to find adequate materials for a fire and you will need a stove anyway.

Gasoline is the only liquid fuel universally available in Baja, so multi-fuel stoves from MSR and Optimus are good choices. (See page 85 for more information on gasoline). Kerosene is difficult to find, and butane cartridges are very rare. Hardware and supply stores sometimes carry Coleman fuel, although you may not recognize it because it is often sold in a cylindrical container rather than the familiar rectangular can, and if you ask you may get a blank look—the locals pronounce it koh-lee-mahn, with the stress on the second syllable. Because of the extreme temperature differences, fuel is best carried in a metal container with a tight top.

Food and water

A self-propelled trip in Baja does not necessarily mean poor food and discomfort. In fact, with adequate planning it can be quite the opposite. Michael and I were to provide a sag wagon for a group of off-road bikers making a trip to Bahía Tortugas and Punta Abreojos a number of years ago, but we were delayed and did not catch up with them until they had been underway about a week. The contrast was priceless: Michael and I, in our new one-ton four-wheel-drive pickup, equipped with air conditioning, stereo, and deep-pile upholstery, had been underway three days and were tired, dirty, and cranky, having been living on Pringles and Coke. The bicyclists, underway for a week, were clean, fresh, and cheerful, and had been dining on fresh fish and scallops smothered in garlic and butter sauce. It all depends on how you go about it.

Supplies are apt to be less of a problem in Baja than in similarly remote parts of the US. Stores are found in many villages, and locally produced staple foods such as *tortillas*, fruit, eggs, and fish are often of good quality and quite inexpensive. A special treat is ranch eggs, produced by hens who have to scratch for a living, a world apart from US-style production-line eggs. When you pedal, paddle, or walk up to a tiny *rancho* or fishing camp in need of a meal you will probably be greeted courteously and offered beans, eggs, and *tortillas* at a low price. Fishermen sometimes have lobsters too small to be legally sold, and may offer you a mess of them, pan-fried and delicious. Foraging can produce clams and mussels—an army could not starve at the south end of Bahía Concepción—and a fishing kit with a handline, hooks, and a few sinkers weighs and costs almost nothing. Ranches and fish camps are not evenly spaced, and may be abandoned or in use only seasonally, and fish don't always bite, so this is apt to be a take-it-while-you-can-get-it proposition. For variety, flexibility, and insurance, bring a supply of lightweight foods not available in Baja, including freeze-dried meals, dried fruits, gorp, dried soups, and granola bars. Keep your food tightly bundled up—gulls, mice, rats, and coyotes like many of the same foods you do.

Active people may require up to a gallon of drinking water a day on warm days and up to 2 gallons in really hot conditions. In extremely difficult conditions, like the back-packing route from the La Milla campground to the mouth of Cañon Tajo, the requirements can even be higher (fortunately this particular route has water). Although kayakers may be able to bum safe water from passing yachts, and bicyclists from RVs, most will soon be dependent on un-treated local water. During their 1975 Cape-to-the-border backpacking trip, Alan Ehrgott and John Cox were forced at one point to drink dark-brown water so full of tiny beetles that they had to use their teeth as strainers. The nasty little critter named *Giardia lambia*, a protozoan that causes diar-rhea, abdominal pain, nausea, and other unhappy conditions, is alive, well, and waiting in Baja, as Michael proved during a recent backpacking trip to the high country in Parque Nacional Sierra San Pedro Mártir.

Don't depend on the opinion of locals as to water qual-ity, since they are used to it and will truthfully answer that the water is safe—for them. However, if they say the water is bad, believe them! If you must obtain water from a *rancho*, view it with suspicion, and if you don't see a well or wind-mill on the premises, crank up the anxiety level one notch. The basic rule is to treat all local water, no matter how clean and sparkling it looks. See Chapter 8 for information on water treatment.

Favorite bicycle trips

The ultimate Baja bicycling adventure is the 926-mile tour from Tecate to La Paz, or to Cabo San Lucas, 1,057 miles. Taking three weeks or so, most trips start in Tecate to miss the hassle and traffic in Tijuana. Many have made the trip, including a few coming from as far away as Switzerland and New Zealand. The first to make the trip were six people in the HEMISTOUR group, who started out from Alaska, bound for Patagonia. In February 1973 they crossed the border at Mexicali and took the unpaved road south of San Felipe, reaching the then-still-unpaved Transpeninsular north of Punta Prieta. They hit pavement at Guerrero Negro and continued on to La Paz. Two of them eventually made it to Patagonia. Age seems to be no barrier; in 1975 Claire Harvey made it to La Paz at 66, and in 1982 Phil Martín at 73.

There are shorter alternatives. The Mexican bus sys-tems or an airline can be used to get to jumping-off points in Baja or to bypass areas of limited interest. Some bikers find they enjoy Baja Sur the most and go by bus to San Ignacio or Santa Rosalía or fly to Loreto, the most northerly town in Baja Sur with an international airport, and bike south from there. Still another variation is to bike south to Santa Rosalía or La Paz, cross the Cortez by ferry and return home through Sonora, although the road north has headwinds and lots of traffic. If you like prime desert, the Transpeninsular between El Rosario and Bahía de los Angeles is the best in Baja.

Loop trips starting and ending in the same location are of special interest to Baja bicyclists. The only good paved loop trip is from La Paz to Cabo San Lucas on the Transpeninsular, and then north on Route 19 through Todos Santos back to La Paz, a moderate ride of 226 miles, taking

To reach an isolated beach, Lee and Elaine Waters had to ford a stretch of salty tidal water

6 or 7 days and visiting some of the nicest towns in Baja. A number of loop trips of interest to off-road bicyclists are described starting on page 51.

Bikes and equipment

The Transpeninsular has been conquered by a wide assortment of bikes, ranging from exotic racing machines to Channell Wasson's 1920s-era Westfield 3-speed, purchased from a thrift shop for 3 dollars, and even a unicycle. How-ever, the choice of a bike is of major importance, for a fine piece of machinery well-adapted to Baja conditions adds greatly to the fun. The roads tend to be rough, the distances long, and the weight to be carried heavy, so a sturdy, easy-riding touring or off-road bike is a better choice than a stiff and fragile racing bike. A compass and a cyclometer will help you locate any attractions noted in this book. A kickstand is a welcome addition, since your panniers may become a home for scorpions if you lay your bike on the ground; try to find the kind that holds the bike upright. Bike locks and chains are a judgment call; in areas south of the border cities crime is rare, a lock doesn't protect your gear, and other than tall cactuses and boojums there sometimes isn't much to lock your bike to. A set of front and rear panniers of at least 2,000-cubic-inch capacity and a seat bag should carry all your food, water, clothing, equipment, and camping gear, and a handlebar bag is handy for wallets, cameras, and maps. Most bicyclists find daypacks too warm for comfort. Racks are a source of problems, and steel is best, if only because Mexican welders can repair steel but rarely aluminum. The best way to carry water is in bladder bags in the front pan-niers.

Baja has a wealth of rocks, loose gravel, ruts, and cracks waiting to pitch you on your head, so a hard-shell helmet designed for biking is a necessity. Get the kind with a sun visor. The Transpeninsular is narrow and you must not drift left when turning your head to look back, so get a rear-view mirror that attaches to your helmet or glasses. Since bikers are not common and are thus unexpected, you should maintain high visibility with a bike flag and a safety vest. A bike flag is not a toy; nothing reveals the presence of a biker more quickly and surely than a shocking-pink bike flag darting back and forth on top of a flexible mast.

Preparation, spare parts, and repairs

Baja's long distances and rough roads require that a bike be specially prepared. Screws and nuts worked loose by vibration are a constant problem, so use lock washers everywhere and squirt on the Loctite liberally. Service all bearings, including bottom bracket and pedals, tighten the headset, replace worn brake blocks, brake cables, and shifter mechanisms, true the wheels, and tighten the spokes. If you are breaking spokes in the US you will break more in Baja. Tires must be new or near-new, with a thorn-resistant strip between each tire and its tube. The rolling resistance of heavy-duty tires and tubes is high, but most people find their much lower rate of flats and failures to be a good trade-off. Do your tires have Presta or Schrader valves? Will your air pump fit them? Remove any fenders—you won't need them. Individuals should carry a basic tool kit, chain repair links and tool, a few spare spokes, and tire repair equipment. A few small hose clamps, some boot material to repair gashes and sidewall cuts, a roll of wire, and some duct tape may be appreciated later. A group of worriers can split up the weight and carry a freewheel assembly, front and rear derailleurs, bottom bracket assembly, crankarms, and chain rings.

Chapters 9 through 13 identify a number of bike shops known to be in operation in areas south of the border cities shortly before publication. It is often easier to find a bike shop than an automobile repair shop, but don't expect too much; these shops carry parts for bikes owned by the local people, and you probably won't find, for instance, a Campagnolo bottom bracket tool. The most common wheels on local bikes are 26 x 1^3/8 and 27 x 1^1/4, and tires, tubes, and spokes for these sizes are fairly easy to find. Tires for off-road bikes are hard to find in the sizes used by adults, although 26 x 2.125s are encountered occasionally. The mechanics in these shops are not factory trained, but they have a good deal of experience in solving problems, and some can weld and braze. Some general stores and hardware stores carry common bike parts.

A cactus-garden picnic along the Transpeninsular Highway

Bonnie Wong

Underway

Early morning and late afternoon are best for riding because of the climate. Never ride at night, for bike lights are notoriously poor and Baja drivers are not expecting bikers. There are not many trees available and most cacti are too skinny to provide usable shade, so many bikers have taken a *siesta* in the shade of a dry culvert. Thirty-five to 45 miles a day is a good pace for beginners on the Transpeninsular. More experienced bikers may cover 50 or 60, and a few have made 130.

Drainage is usually poor at dips and at the bottom of grades, causing sand and gravel to collect and making coasting at high speed dangerous. The greatest moving hazards are not 18-wheelers, but the big motor homes driven by *gringos*, who often have little experience with their big toys and are accustomed to wide roads and shoulders. With mirrors projecting out like antlers, these giant rigs occupy the entire lane, and many drivers will try to pass in the same lane even though the other is unoccupied. Most Mexican truckers are distinctly more courteous and will usually pass in the opposite lane if they can.

Most flat tires are caused by cactus thorns. Big ones can be seen and pulled out, but the little ones escape detection and keep pushing through the casing, causing repeated

Cycling in cactus country can pose a few problems

Bonnie Wong

flats. Most thorns are picked up on unpaved areas, so experienced Baja bikers carry their bikes from the pavement to campsites. Ho-ho, you say! Is this like a Boy Scout snipe hunt, something to humiliate the new guys, getting them to carry their bikes around under the hot sun like a bunch of dummies? No, it's for real, and people who do this have far fewer flats than those who stand and smirk.

Chapters 9 through 13 describe all paved highways and all important unpaved roads in Baja, as well as many obscure by-ways. Information of interest to bikers is provided, such as important grades, bicycle shops, places to eat and obtain food and water, etc. In areas where they are easy to find, no specific information on campsites is necessary, but along roads with extensive fencing and agricultural areas, such as Route 3 southeast of Ensenada, places to stop are identified. In some cases these are modest indeed, often little more than a way to get off the road. With their slow speed, eagle eyes, and ability to get their bikes into areas inaccessible even to four-wheelers, bicyclists will discover many more places and should have less trouble finding a place to stop than any other type of traveler; no Baja biker has ever had to pedal all night for want of a campsite.

Hitchhiking and commercial transportation

Like bikers everywhere, those in Baja occasionally have a lazy day and hitchhike a lap or two. The locals are often friendly and curious about bicyclists. Most are willing to provide a free ride, and many a biker has made a lap in the back of a rickety stake truck jammed between a goat, a bale of hay, and Grandpa. Tinker and Brian Rovira were once offered a ride in the back of a water department truck and got more than they bargained for. A large section of corrugated metal culvert almost crowded them out, but when the driver stopped and pulled off the cover, it proved to be full of lobsters and scallops, packed in ice. Some were already cooked, so the group broke out fresh limes and had an impromptu feast.

Trips on the Transpeninsular are one-way for virtually everyone, most bikers pedaling south with the prevailing winds and returning home by plane, bus, or private vehicle. Bicyclists often have little trouble hitching rides home on pickups or RVs. There is another attractive alternative. Baja California Tours offers a series of bus tours throughout Baja, described on page 62. The company is willing to bring along bikers and bicycles on a space-available basis. Also, the company's "Follow-the-Whales" trip ends in La Paz, where the guests catch a plane back, and the company will provide bikers transportation back to the US on an otherwise empty bus. A bicyclist thus can take a fine guided bus tour one way and bike home, or do the biking first and return by bus. The company will also let bikers get on and off at intermediate stops.

Drivers for the Mexican bus companies are usually willing to take bicycles in the luggage compartment on a space-available basis, but may ask you to remove wheels and handlebars. To preserve your chrome and paint, it would be well to have several large plastic garbage bags and some duct tape available. If you are with a large group there may be problems, for drivers sometimes won't take more than two or three bikes. Current information on the bus companies can be obtained from the State Secretaries of Tourism. Airlines flying between airports in the US and Tijuana and airports farther south in Baja will carry bicycles, but their policies differ concerning extra cost, whether a box is required, and whether they will supply it. A given airline may have different requirements depending on whether you are flying to or from Baja. Their policies change from time to time, so get current information and make sure you understand the situation before you depart. Bicyclists can use the ferry system with no problems beyond those experienced by everyone else.

Off-road bicycling

Groups of off-road bicyclists have opened a new spectrum of adventure in Baja, topped by a 25-day trip from La Rumorosa to La Paz led by Bonnie Wong that included 600 off-road miles. On earlier trips her groups have conquered the road south of San Felipe past Bahía Gonzaga to the Transpeninsular; the road south from Bahía de los Angeles to Bahía San Francisquito and then southwest over La Cuesta de la Ley to El Arco and south to the highway; and the road from San Ignacio past Laguna San Ignacio to La Purísima, the Comondús, San Javier, and Loreto. Her groups have also visited Cueva Palmarito, a rock-art treasure located north of San Ignacio. These are remarkable accomplishments involving some of the most remote areas left in Baja.

Tinker and Brian Rovira had a surprise on one of these trips. They were pedaling down a slope when Tinker saw a huge rattlesnake crossing the road ahead. It was too late to brake or swerve, and with her feet almost at shoulder level and "yelling bloody thunder" (Brian's terminology), she ran over it. Shaken and fearful of finding an angry rattler intertwined among her spokes, she jumped off and waited while Brian inspected. The snake escaped to an uncertain fate.

Off-road bicyclists often feel the trip is over when they hit pavement, but a variety of excellent trips is possible if they can relax their standards a little. The following paragraphs list four loop trips combining on- and off-pavement riding. All starting points have bus service, two have air service, and if you drive to the point of beginning, you should have little trouble finding a place to leave your vehicle. All have water and some food available *en route*, although not necessarily at convenient intervals, and all have been successfully traveled by bicyclists. The direction (clockwise, counterclockwise) has been chosen to have shakedowns occur in settled areas, to take advantage of prevailing winds, and to miss long, steep upgrades where possible, although there are conflicts in some cases.

Laguna Hanson Loop Trip: El Cóndor, Laguna Hanson, El Coyote, north via Rosa de Castilla, KM 98, El Cóndor, covering 110 miles off-road, 9 miles on pavement. This easy-to-moderate, five- or six-day trip, passing through pine forests and meadows and encountering a number of *ranchos* along the way, involves few navigation, logistic, or road problems and is the best Baja route for novices.

Vizcaíno Loop Trip: Vizcaíno, Bahía Tortugas, Bahía Asunción, Punta Abreojos, KM 98 on the Transpeninsular, Vizcaíno, covering 276 miles off-road, 40 miles on pavement. This trip is easy but long, requiring 10 to 12 days. Most of the road is graded and fairly level, but there are stretches of washboard. The scenery is not always inspiring, but there are many fine deserted beaches.

Mountain Villages Loop Trip: Loreto, KM 118, San Javier, San José de Comondú, San Miguel de Comondú, La Purísima, KM 60, Loreto, covering 115 miles off-road, 38 miles on pavement (An alternate route returns to Loreto from the Comondús by way of Villa Insurgentes and the Transpeninsular back to Loreto, covering 113 miles off-road, 76 miles on pavement.) This trip is moderate to difficult and requires at least seven days. The road to San Javier is steep, and some later stretches are rough and remote and involve walking, but the towns and the terrain are unique.

Cape Coast Loop Trip: La Paz, Las Cuevas, Cabo Pulmo, San José del Cabo, Cabo San Lucas, Todos Santos, La Paz, covering 44.9 miles off-road, 210.3 miles on pavement. This trip is easy, requiring seven to eight days. The dirt section is graded, with no major hills. Although most of it is on pavement, this is

Tinker Rovira and Bill Gibson head up one of the "Terrible Three," the steepest and roughest grades in all of Baja

Bonnie Wong

the most interesting and varied of all the loop trips, including three of Baja's liveliest towns, magnificent deserted beaches on both the Cortez and Pacific sides, and excellent off-the-beach diving on Baja's only coral reef. A mask, snorkel, and fins weigh only 6 pounds, but if this is too heavy or bulky to bring along, you should have little trouble renting them when you get to the Pulmo. Several variations of this trip are possible; bikers could fly into Los Cabos International Airport instead of La Paz, and the Transpeninsular could be substituted for either the Pacific or Cortez segments.

In addition, there are loop trips recommended to four-wheelers in Chapter 6 that may be of interest to the more experienced, determined, and physically able off-road bicyclists. Chapters 9 through 13 contain detailed information on these loop trips and many other routes.

Many of the ideas on equipment, preparation, and so forth presented above for bicycle travel on the paved road system apply off-road as well. Often the most difficult and important aspect of Baja off-road biking is navigation, and a compass and accurate maps are essential. A cyclometer is also a necessity, since speed can be difficult to judge and there are often no kilometer posts to help you gauge distance. Compared to off-roading in the US, Baja roads are generally worse, and your daily mileage will be less.

Commercial trips, rentals, and other attractions

Backroads offers "Baja Hike, Bike, and Kayak" trips

in the Cape region, with options for primitive camping or luxurious hotel accommodations, and many other activities, such as snorkeling, tennis, horseback riding, boardsailing, and fishing. Baja Outdoor Activities in La Paz has trips that combine mountain biking and sea kayaking. Vela Windsurf Resorts and Baja Adventures, both at East Cape, have mountain bikes for rent, subject to first call by guests, and they are available at some RV parks, motels, and travel agencies—see the index. Bicycling West sponsors a number of bicycle fun rides, relays, triathlons, and similar events in Baja. The fun rides are especially popular and often involve more people as participants, crew, and spectators than the widely publicized Baja 1000 auto race.

Backpacking, hiking, and climbing

There is a simple way to tell if you are a true desert rat: simply make a list of your 10 favorite Baja locations, and then go back and see how many are associated with water. The chances are that you will fail the test miserably, and that most or all of them are "water places." You won't be alone, for in addition to obvious physiological needs, we all have strong psychological attachments to water. For either or both reasons, Baja's arid climate renders much of the peninsula of limited interest to most backpackers and hikers. Few will choose to follow Alan Ehrgott and John Cox, who worked for three months caching food and water at 75-mile intervals before their 110-day Cape-to-the-border backpacking

The start of the Rosarito-to-Ensenada Fun Ride

Ann Kendellen

Will Waterman

Celia Keisling, Jim Clark, and Bruce Barrus explore a pool in Cañon San Bernardo

trip, or Graham Mackintosh, who made a remarkable 3,000-mile trip along Baja's Pacific and Cortez coasts.

However, accidents of geology and meteorology have provided a number of places with permanent surface water, allowing lengthy and enjoyable visits. Later chapters describe backpacking adventures in Arroyo Grande, Parque Nacional Sierra San Pedro Mártir, Cañons Tajo and Guadalupe in the Sierra de Juárez escarpment, Cañon del Diablo in the Sierra San Pedro Mártir escarpment, Cañons Dionisio and San Bernardo in the Sierra de la Laguna, and to La Laguna, a mountain meadow, also in the Sierra de la Laguna.

Also described are a number of "day hikes," short ventures to interesting locations, beginning and ending in the same place, including the tip of the Punta Banda peninsula, the Islas de Todos Santos, Isla San Martín, Isla San Jerónimo, Isla Partida Sur, the Gran Cañon on Isla Cedros, the La Milla-Cañon Tajo overlook, the "Bell Dome" route into Cañon Tajo, Cueva Palmarito, the Puerto Balandra-to-Bahía Salinas hike on Isla Carmen, Playa Independence, Parque Nacional Constitución de 1857, Parque Nacional Sierra San Pedro Mártir, El Volcán, Tinaja de Yubay, and Mike's Sky Ranch, the last four of which have permanent surface water.

Baja has some excellent climbs, the most popular being the challenging class 3 climb on Picacho del Diablo, at 10,154 feet Baja's highest mountain. Cerro Salsipuedes, Picacho San Lázaro, and Cerro Zacatosa in the Sierra de la Laguna, and El Pilón de Parras near Loreto are less demanding class 3 climbs. Teta de la India, Pico Banda, and the volcano on Isla San Martín are easy class 1 or 2. (Class 1 is ordinary walking. Class 2 is scrambling, sometimes requiring that hands be used. Suitable boots or shoes are needed, but special knowledge and equipment are not essential. Class 3 is at the limit of climbing without specialized equipment, although boots are required and a rope may be useful for handling packs. Some specialized knowledge is helpful.)

The number of technical climbing areas (class 4, where ropes are used for safety purposes, and class 5, where they are used to support climbers, specialized knowledge and equipment being essential for both) in Baja is limited, but one area provides outstanding conditions. Located on the Juárez escarpment east of the road from Route 2 to Laguna Hanson, it is jealously guarded by San Diego climbers through a conspiracy of silence and hence is largely unknown to "outsiders." The centerpiece of the area is "El Trono

Wayne Campbell scouts Picacho del Diablo from a pinnacle on the escarpment of the San Pedro Mártir plateau

Blanco," a 1,600-foot big wall. The approach will put off the belay-from-the-bumper-crowd, but more energetic climbers should not miss this magnificent wall. There are literally hundreds of other climbs in the area, including at least 20 involving upper-class 5 moves. Technical climbs in other regions include the rock face at El Pilón de Parras and Cerro Blanco in the Sierra de la Laguna. Technical climbing in a very unusual setting is possible on Los Frailes at Cabo San Lucas.

The equipment and techniques required in Baja are no different from those for warm, arid, and remote regions elsewhere. You may get away with using running shoes for short forays, but for longer ventures boots are necessary. Stay away from extremes; neither lightweights with nylon uppers nor heavyweight clunkers are necessary or desirable. The best boot is a matter of preference, but many desert backpackers, hikers, and climbers prefer a medium-weight boot with Vibram lug soles, full-grain uppers, and a reinforced toe cap. They should not be of insulated or waterproof construction, and waterproofing compounds should not be applied, for the chances of getting them wet is low, and sweat must be free to dissipate.

No trails are maintained for recreational use anywhere in Baja, even in the national parks, and there are no signs or route markers, although the more popular ones may be marked by "ducks," small piles of stones or other physical means of showing the route. It is easy to get lost, so carry a compass and a topographic map, and leave your itinerary with family or friends. There are a few rangers, but the chance of encountering one in a time of need is remote. In fact, most areas are so little used that it is unusual to meet anyone once off the roads. Although permanent surface water is available in some places, it is not necessarily where you want it,

so you must carry a sizable amount and be prepared to alter your route and your plans if necessary. Chapter 8 describes the topographic maps produced by the Mexican Government.

Most backpackers, hikers, and climbers recognize the dangers inherent in a hot, arid climate, but cold and snow can be problems too. The Sierra San Pedro Mártir can accumulate up to 8 feet of snow, and the Ensenada rescue squad has been called out a number of times. In 1987 9 teen-agers on a late-April camping excursion at elevation 4,200 feet in the Sierra de Juárez were reported missing when 5 feet of snow fell. A comic-opera rescue attempt resulted when helicopters, ham radio operators, the State Judicial Police, forest rangers, rescue squad contingents from Ensenada, San Felipe, and Mexicali, the Mexican Army, several ranchers, a detachment of "commandos," and numerous cousins and uncles mostly got in each other's way. However, six days later a convoy of farm tractors, military vehicles, and four-wheel-drives, led by a bulldozer, broke through the snow to find the boys holed up in a cabin, out of food and firewood. Given hot showers and filled with *tortillas*, tuna casserole, and hot chocolate (they were too young for tequila), everyone survived, although three of the boys sustained frostbite.

The NOLS "Fall Semester in Mexico" course is designed to develop skills in backpacking, rock climbing, kay-

NOLS instructor Jim Clark introduces his students to the realities of the Sierra de la Victoria

aking, and sailing. It involves hiking in the remote high country of the Sierra San Pedro Mártir, rock climbing instruction, and travel by kayak and sailboat along the Cortez coast, all over a period of almost 3 months. The "Spring Semester" is similar, except that climbing is done in the Sierra de la Laguna in the Cape region, and students visit Bahía Magdalena for some natural history, whale-watching, kayaking, and camping. Wilderness: Alaska/Mexico offers an 8-day backpacking trip to La Laguna.

Sea kayaking

Sea kayaking has a long history in the Cortez. The Seri Indians once used their kayak-like reed boats to cross the Cortez in the Midriff region. In 1933 Dana and Ginger Lamb crossed the Cortez from the vicinity of Santa Rosalía as part of their epic San Diego-to-Panama trip. Today, as noted earlier, increasing numbers of kayakers have "discovered" the Cortez, and it is becoming one of the most popular sea kayaking locations on the continent.

You don't have to be a 40-miles-a-day, open-water kayaker to enjoy the Cortez. Two of the most popular kayak trips, the Coasting to Loreto Trip from Mulegé to Loreto, and the Coasting to La Paz Trip from Loreto to La Paz, are well within the ability of most kayakers and are described in Chapter 11. These are favored not only because of their fine scenery, abundant wildlife, and lack of civilization, but also because they are the right distance apart for 1- or 2-week trips, about 84 miles and 147 respectively. In addition, they begin and end at sizable towns on the Transpeninsular, making it possible for those on one-way trips to hitchhike or take the bus back to pick up vehicles.

Bahía de los Angeles is also an increasingly popular kayaking area. There are many islands to explore and numerous sandy campsites, and its relatively compact area makes it a fine place for a slow-bell kayak/camping trip. More ambitious kayakers can head to Puerto Don Juan and south along the coast to Bahía las Ánimas, a round trip taking a week or so, or head north to Isla Coronado. The more ambitious can try the Coasting to Santa Rosalía Trip, described in Chapter 10, and those with the requisite open-water experience can choose the Circumnavigating Guardian Angel Trip, Chapter 10, or the Stepping-Stones Trip, Chapter 14.

Bahía Concepción is calm and scenic, and is a great place to practice paddling, self-righting, and self-rescue procedures. Once you have these down pat, you can head for the open Cortez to try out your skills in waves. Kayakers like to launch at Loreto and head south along the coast past Isla Danzante for Bahía Agua Verde. The deeply indented western sides of Islas Espíritu Santo and Partida Sur north of La Paz have many fine sand beaches, making them popular destinations for novice kayakers and those interested in leisurely kayak/camping. Boats can be hired in La Paz to carry kayaks and gear to the islands if the 5-mile crossing of Canal de San Lorenzo is deemed unwise.

A trip down Baja's Pacific coast from the border to

Hazel Wolf was eighty-one when she made her second trip to Isla Espíritu Santo

the Cape can be recommended only to intrepid kayakers, for tales of being overpowered by currents and wind, getting lost in fog, and pitchpoling are the central themes of many of the accounts of such trips. While skill, practice, and planning can greatly reduce the risk, even experts have serious problems. In spite of this, there are some excellent locations for shorter trips. Bahía Magdalena is a popular destination, where kayakers can seek out gray whales and explore the mangrove-lined waterways, moving camp when the mood strikes. The coastline north of Santa Rosalillita has much to recommend it to kayakers, including secluded beaches, plenty of firewood, and excellent fishing and foraging. The coast along the southwest shore of the Punta Banda peninsula from La Bufadora is pleasant and undemanding, an ideal place for a first ocean trip, and a trip out to the Islas de Todos Santos can be made once the basics are mastered.

Equipment and preparation

Most Baja kayakers prefer a rigid boat, with high hull volume, a narrow curved bow, a straight stem, little rocker, and a foot-operated rudder. The same basic equipment and provisions normally used on any kayak voyage are required, except that more water and reserve food should be taken. Most routes pass settlements and ranches, and kayakers often encounter anchored yachts where water can be obtained. Down bags are a poor choice for a kayak trip, even in sunny Baja. A kayaker's tent should have fine mesh screening, for all Cortez routes pass through prime *jejéne* territory. (A *jejéne* is a blood-thirsty insect found in salt marshes, mangroves, and decaying seaweed; see the stories beginning on pages 146 and 198.)

Because of their small scale and absence of shoreline detail, most marine charts are of little value to Baja kayakers. Cruising Charts, with the assistance of kayaker Ed Gillet, has developed "Paddle Charts" of the best areas of the Cortez. These charts, printed on waterproof material, are specially designed to unfold to no more than 11 by 17 inches, making them easy to handle in the confines of a kayak cockpit. The 1:50,000-scale topographic maps produced by the Mexican government are useful, although a bit difficult to deal with in a kayak. The swift tidal currents of the upper- and mid-Cortez make tide tables essential. See Chapter 8 for more information on maps, topos, and tide tables. Kayakers will profit by re-reading the sections of the previous chapter regarding paperwork, safety, and emergency assistance. Remember, kayakers, all over-the-water distances in this book are expressed in nautical miles. Appendix A provides the conversion factors for nautical miles, statute miles, and kilometers.

Underway

The most favored months for Cortez kayaking are October through April, when the weather is cool. North-to-south trips with the prevailing winds recommended to bicyclists favor kayakers as well. Wind-driven waves in the Cortez can be sizable, but the short fetch allows little swell to build up, and waves usually die down quickly once the wind stops, so landings can usually be made without great difficulty. Tidal currents are not normally a major factor in open water, but if you are nearing prominent points, like Quemado, San Francisquito, or Púlpito, they can be fierce. Winds often spring up in mid-day, so an early start is necessary. Ten miles a day is a good average, 20 too much for most people. Beaches given a place name on the topos are often good places to stop for the night. (Mexican fishermen don't stop at a poor campsite often enough to have a name become widely accepted.)

Baja kayakers must be prepared to wait out weather. Winter winds in the Cortez can be stronger than those on the Pacific side. The number of days for the Mulegé-to-Loreto and Loreto-to-La Paz trips noted above, 7 and 14 respectively, are generally adequate for experienced kayakers in light weather, but extra food and water for 4 or 5 days should be maintained. Equipped with tide tables, a skilled and flexible Baja kayaker can turn the tide into a friend rather than an enemy; if you are headed north from Bahía de los Angeles to Puerto Refugio, pick a flood; if you are making the Mulegé-to-Loreto run, take advantage of the ebb.

Despite its normally placid appearance, the Cortez can change quickly and it deserves respect. In 1978 two groups of inexperienced kayakers were on a trip south along the Cortez coast headed for Loreto. The water was glassy as they started off one morning, but the wind soon came up and one group turned back. The other group of nine pressed on and were trying to round Punta Púlpito, when one kayak

Landlubbers learn the ways of the sea before getting their feet wet

Will Waterman

Kayakers take impromptu advantage of the wind

capsized. Others tried to raft up and help right it and bail it out, but they soon swamped as well. After spending more than 12 hours in the water, suffering from hypothermia and exhaustion, 6 of the 9 made it to shore.

The fun of Baja kayaking is not just in plying the waters. Fishing with a hand line or a short pole can produce fine meals and great sport. A mask, snorkel, and fins can provide marvelous sightseeing, as well as allow you to forage for supper. The silence and the unobtrusiveness of a kayak make it possible to get close to whales and sea lions without alarm. Only a kayaker, away from civilization's mechanical sounds, can appreciate the intensity of the sound of a huge whale spouting a few yards away. Some areas are so remote that animals there have little fear of humans. One paddler in Bahía Magdalena had a visit from a small seal, which slid up on the deck of his kayak and looked him over for 15 minutes. During a kayak trip to Magdalena, Lolly Flowers awoke to find a coyote tugging at her hair. It let go when she yelled, but far from being intimidated, it sniffed around for a while, grabbed a sweater and took off for the sand dunes. A few days later a stowaway was discovered in her kayak, a fat rodent of a species known to the locals by the all-purpose name "*rata*." He avoided capture by scurrying into the bow of her kayak while they were ashore, but during the paddle he would suddenly appear. Manuel, as he was named, became something of a pet, but after several days he disappeared. Someone later saw an osprey lifting

off the beach with a furry brown cargo, and it soon became apparent that Manuel had hitched his last ride.

Trips and courses

There is a rich offering of trips and courses. Southwest Sea Kayaks is one of the leaders, offering the most innovative and extensive array of trips available, ranging from short ventures to Estero Beach and the Islas de Todos Santos through Punta-Banda-to-Eréndira, San-Diego-to-Ensenada, Punta-Baja-to-Santa-Rosalillita, and Mulegé-to-Loreto trips, to a 10-day circumnavigation of Isla Tiburón. If you are a whale fan, they offer whale-watching trips to Bahía de los Angeles, Bahía Todos Santos, and Laguna Manuela. These areas are the best Baja has to offer, and the various trips meet the needs of paddlers ranging in experience from beginners to experts. Lectures, clinics, and instruction on kayaking are offered at Southwest's San Diego headquarters, along with frequent swap meets and sales, demonstration days, and special events. A large array of kayaks and equipment are available for rent or sale.

Baja Expeditions offers a trip to visit Isla Espíritu Santo, a coastal trip between Loreto and La Paz, and a Bahía Magdalena trip to see the whales and wildlife. Wilderness: Alaska/Mexico has a Bahía Magdalena kayaking/whale-watching venture, and a trip out to Isla Espíritu Santo. The NOLS "Fall Semester in Mexico" and "Spring Semester in Mexico" courses are designed to develop skills in kayaking,

Will Waterman

Lolly Flowers and Manuel

as well as backpacking, rock climbing, and sailing. NOLS also offers a "Baja Sea Kayaking" course. Venture Quest Kayaking offers package trips in the Bahía de los Angeles area, accompanied by a support boat.

Outland Adventures has a wilderness kayak trip from Puerto Escondido to points south, and offers kayak rentals and trips in the Bahía de los Angeles area. Sea Trek Ocean Kayaking Center trips explore the remote areas of the Cortez north of Loreto. Trips are accompanied by a motorized support boat, which not only provides additional safety, but carries coolers full of fresh produce, water, and *cervezas*. Baja Outdoor Activities in La Paz offers imaginative and eclectic kayak trips and activities, and rentals, day trips, and outfitting services and a beginner kayak certification course are available. Some Backroads trips to the Cape region include kayaking and hiking. Baja Discovery offers innovative van trips that combine visits to attractions along the Transpeninsular and desert walks to visit rock art sites, and whale-watching at Laguna San Ignacio with some kayaking in Bahía Concepción. Aqua Adventures offers a wide vari-

ety of trips, including package trips to Loreto, Bahía de los Angeles, and the Islas de Todos Santos off Ensenada, a "Baja Sea Cave & Rock Garden" trip along the south shore of Punta Banda, and unusual kayaking activities at Laguna Manuela—kayak wave-surfing and whale-watching.

Mulegé Kayaks/Baja Tropicales, located at EcoMundo, their headquarters at Bahía Concepción, offers a day-long kayaking activity that is of special interest, a "paddle, snorkel, dive, and dine" kayak trip, visiting beautiful coves, hot springs, a shipwreck, etc. They are also a full-service outfitter, offering kayak and camping equipment rentals. Villas de Loreto is home to several kayak companies. Although their primary business is package trips, all will accommodate walk-ins on a space-available basis. The La Concha Beach Resort and Club Hotel Cantamar in La Paz also offer trips. In addition, many hotels and resorts have kayak rentals—see the index.

• •

❝ *A desert encounter*

During a length-of-Baja bicycle trip, Bonnie Wong and several female companions were crossing Laguna Diablo, a desolate dry lake near San Felipe, when two male motorcycle racers roared up out of the mirages in a huge cloud of dust. Very macho, they were dressed from top to bottom in magnificent leathers, topped off with giant helmets, goggles, and heavy boots armored with shining studs, and plastic vests providing protection against rocks thrown up by the motorcycle ahead. Their machines gleamed of chromium, and most exterior surfaces not chromed were emblazoned with oil company slogans. Sweltering in the midday sun, they could only manage to stammer a shocked, "Are you ladies lost?" Bonnie explained that they had left from Tecate, had pedaled through the Sierra de Juárez and were headed for San Felipe, where they would take the "back road" through Puertecitos and Bahía Gonzaga, joining the Transpeninsular north of Punta Prieta. At San Ignacio they planned to head south past Laguna San Ignacio, hitting pavement again north of Villa Insurgentes, and then ride on to La Paz. At first there was no reaction, but as the magnitude of the adventure sank in, the two motorcyclists finally erupted in a torrent of warnings about the difficulties that lay ahead and heated questions as to how the ladies intended to survive the savage desert. Their concern was well meant, but the absurdity of the scene was priceless, and the "lost" bicyclists laughed for days. **❞**

• •

Chapter 6

Wheelin' It

At the height of the winter season over half the traffic on the Transpeninsular Highway carries US or Canadian plates, and 80% of these are motor homes, trailers, pickup campers, or vans. During a two-week vacation you might encounter people from 40 states and 5 Canadian provinces. They are a diverse lot: a British Columbia logger, a senior citizen from New Jersey, youthful surfers from Santa Cruz, a teacher from Illinois, a Saskatchewan wheat farmer, a Mennonite family towing their tent trailer through Ensenada, the bearded men in severe black coats and flat-brimmed hats, the women in frocks and bonnets. A few come from afar: a cook from Australia, a roofer from Tonga, a postman from Sweden. Their rigs are equally diverse, ranging from a ratty

VW camper showing every one of its quarter of a million miles to a gleaming new Blue Bird land yacht sporting a satellite dish and a gold Cadillac dinghy and showing every one of its quarter of a million dollars. Many are visiting Baja for the first time, but it is not unusual to meet people on their tenth or even twentieth trip. One crusty old codger told me he was "wheelin' it" in Baja for the 24th time.

An RV trip to Baja has many attractions, and there is something for almost everyone. To some people the RV is simply a means of transportation and a place to stay while pursuing other activities. A angler can park for weeks on a beautiful sand beach near Cabo San Lucas, the water off-shore being one of the world's great marlin fisheries, while

RV life in Baja is full of problems

a skin diver can drive a sizable rig to Pulmo Reef, one of the few coral reefs on the west coast of North America. A whale-watcher can spend time at Scammon's Lagoon or at Laguna San Ignacio, the winter home of the friendly whales. To others, who simply want to find a felicitous RV park and settle down for a relaxing vacation at San Felipe, Bahía de los Angeles, Mulegé, La Paz, or the Cape, the trip itself is the adventure. The weather is usually fine and living is inexpensive: local staple foods are cheap, some RV parks charge as little as three or four dollars a night, and there are innumerable beaches, coves, and clearings that cost nothing. The crowd at TRIPUI Resort RV Park will appeal to the most gregarious, and loners will appreciate hundreds of miles of remote beaches that rarely see a human being. You can learn something of the ways of a foreign culture in the exotic Comondú, or stick with your own kind at Posada Don Diego, as you choose.

Equipment and preparation

A Baja trip requires better preparation than one in the US or Canada, for there are only a few shops providing RV parts and service (see the index and directory). An ordinary magnet box may not be able to withstand the jolts of off-road driving, so use stainless wire to fasten a set of keys under the vehicle. Lost keys can be real problem, especially those for the ignition, and there is little opportunity to get to a near-by pay phone, consult the Yellow Pages and have a locksmith on hand in 20 minutes, as in the US.

Most wheel bearings for autos and trucks can be obtained fairly easily in Baja, but would be well to bring a bearing, race, and seal assembly for your trailer, grease, and a grease cap, which is often lost when a bearing fails. Many RV problems involve tires and springs, reflecting the excessive weight and speed to which they are often subjected, and the rough roads. Tires should start in excellent condition, and spares should be carried for both vehicle and trailer. A few careful trailer owners carry an extra spring assembly. Because of the warm climate, transmission coolers are even more important on large rigs than they are north of the border. Narrow, rough roads, and frequent crosswinds make a load-leveling hitch and a sway-control device necessary on all but the smallest trailers. Since shoulders are rare and the side of the road is often rough, skid wheels are needed on rigs with long overhangs.

Leveling jacks or a supply of wood blocks will be needed. Bring extra lengths of water and sewer hose and an electrical extension cord, since water, electric, and sewer connections in many parks are on the "wrong" side or are otherwise distant. Thirty-amp service is not too common, so a 30-20 amp conversion plug may be essential if you have a 30-amp plug. Bring holding-tank chemicals, for they are very hard to find in Baja. More than one person has found to his sorrow that the lug wrench from his tow vehicle would not fit the trailer, or that his scissors jack had inadequate capacity for a large trailer.

The circuit boards controlling refrigerators, air condi-

tioners, and other equipment found on all modern RVs and travel trailers, and those found in radios, CDs, televisions, satellite receivers, and computers are subject to damage by voltage spikes, which are unfortunately common in Baja. You can avoid all the hassle and expense of damaged circuit boards by obtaining a surge guard. This electronic gadget should not be confused with the small surge protectors used to protect individual pieces of electronic equipment, for it filters all the electricity coming into your rig. The cost may seem formidable, but if it saves even one piece of equipment it will pay for itself.

Some parks in remote areas do not have full hookups, and problems with water and electrical systems are common at almost all, so you should be equipped to operate self-contained for at least short periods of time. Unless you plan to stop only at RV parks with electrical hookups or have a generator, you may wish to leave 110-volt appliances at home. If you do intend to operate 110-volt appliances having 3 prongs directly from Mexican outlets (in a motel room, for instance) you should bring along a 3-2 prong converter plug, since ungrounded (2-prong) outlets are often encountered. Broadcast TV is very limited south of the border cities, although some RV parks now have satellite systems.

Underway

Speeds over 45 are too fast everywhere, and 25 is sometimes excessive. The Transpeninsular has been kept in better condition than in previous years, but potholes can quickly develop, and fate seems to have placed them at points where it is too late to slow down by the time you see them, especially if you are towing a less-than-nimble big trailer rig. If you are taking even a few heavy blows from potholes, you are driving too fast and are risking loss of control, blowouts, and broken springs. A checkoff list will help you make sure that drawers and cabinets are locked and equipment properly stowed. Before starting each day inspect the hitch and check all tires with an air gauge, or whack them with a hammer, trucker style. So you won't lose a wheel or enlarge lug holes, especially in aluminum wheels, check all nuts once a week.

Many RV parks are described in Chapters 9 through 13. Expect change and occasional problems; parks open and close, electricity and water can fail, the more popular parks may be full, and some are reserved largely for permanent occupants. Parking is available on thousands of beaches and flat spots along the road, but most of these are described in later chapters only if they are in strategic locations. If you belong to Good Sam, Discover Baja, the Vagabundos del Mar, or a similar club, if you are a senior citizen, or if you plan to stay for more than a week or so, ask if discounts are available at RV parks, as well as at restaurants and other businesses.

Extended self-contained operation

Most rigs can manage self-contained operation for three or four days, but comfortable living conditions can be maintained for longer periods if extra equipment and supplies are brought along. There are three primary problems to

A trailer rig unloads from a Cortez ferry

deal with: water, sewage, and electricity.

Unless there is a local source, potable water is likely to be the factor that limits the time you can operate self-contained. Consumption can be greatly reduced by using paper plates and visiting the wilds for calls of nature. If you have the proper soap it is possible to wash pots and pans and take baths in sea water (see Chapter 8). If local water comes from wells or other unpressurized sources, a large plastic jug with a spout or a funnel may be needed for filling tanks. If you introduce untreated water into your tanks, you should treat all of it that is used for drinking and cooking from that point on, and when you return home the system must be chlorinated.

You will need a shovel. From both the ecological and the social standpoints, the best place to dump sewage is at a dump station. However, if the circumstances are such that you must do it elsewhere, gopher holes should be dug for black water. This is ordinarily not a big chore, since soft and uninhabited ground is easily found. Before you depart, fill it in, tamp it down, and return the area to its prior condition. Gray water can be dumped in a gravel or sand area away from the road and settled areas without lasting harm.

Few things are more depressing than to be without electric lights and heat during the long, cold nights of winter. If you drive regularly, your alternator ought to keep the batteries charged, but if you stop for long periods you will need a generator. If your rig does not have one built in, a portable will provide all the AC and DC power needed. You can minimize the hours of operation of such a dual-voltage generator by running it at night, operating the RV on 110 volts while the DC system charges the batteries. If your rig does not have cooking or lighting facilities, the portable LPG outfit described in Chapter 4 may be useful. LPG is not likely to be a major problem if you start with full tanks and hold heater operation to a minimum. Shut off all pilot lights, and operate the water heater only when needed.

Clubs, organized trips, tours, and caravans

Some RVers choose to join an organized trip or caravan, and it is not uncommon to see a million dollars worth of Southwinds, Winnebagos, and Airstreams pull into a Baja RV park. Discover Baja and the Vagabundos del Mar sponsor trips for their members; see page 80 for more on these clubs. Airstream, El Monte RV Rentals & Sales, Good Sam Club, Point South RV Tours, and Tracks to Adventure also operate Baja RV caravans, often accompanied by a wagonmaster, a mechanic, and a tailgunner. Every RV rental company has its own policy concerning taking rigs into Mexico. El Monte RV Rentals & Sales and Cruise America rent RVs and will allow them to be taken into Baja Norte, while some of the others will not. The best way to find out is to get on the phone and start making telephone calls. If you are planning to make the trip with an organized caravan, you might ask the company or club for suggestions.

If you don't have your own RV or would like to leave the driving to others, Baja Discovery offers a number of van trips, including a visit to Laguna San Ignacio for some whale-watching, a visit to the Bahía de los Angeles area, and a trip devoted to photography. Baja California Tours offers guided bus tours that visit San Felipe for festivities during the *Cinco de Mayo* holiday, Ensenada for wining, dining, and art appreciation, and Puerto Nuevo for a Mozart concert, as well as visits to historic Rancho San José. Green Tortoise offers 9- and 14-day bus tours that visit many of Baja's prime destinations, with stops to shop, visit Indian art sites, fish, hike, kayak, loaf, and watch the whales.

Repairing a broken spring on our bike/boat trailer

Boat, motorcycle, and utility trailers

Problems with small trailers are fairly common in Baja—the rough roads will find the weakest link in your rig— but virtually all can be avoided. Tires 13 inches and smaller are not advisable, for they are easily damaged and replacements will not be found in Baja tire shops. I once blew out a 5x13 on my boat trailer, and after 2 days of searching finally found a cracked and worn-out tire of the same size on a wheelbarrow in Guerrero Negro. Its owner knew he had a corner on the market and quoted an astronomical price, but the next day I was surprised to find a large automotive wheel with the same bolt pattern in the Parador Punta Prieta junk yard. The tire was flat and unrepairable, but my boat was light and didn't squeeze the carcass completely down, so I bought it and limped the 750 miles back to San Francisco with a 30° list, the object of much levity from passing motorists.

The general rule in Baja is that small trailers should not be loaded beyond two-thirds of rated capacity. This may be impossible with boat and motorcycle trailers, which are inherently loaded close to their maximum. There is a lower limit too—trailers should not be loaded less than a third of their capacity as they may bounce, straining tires, suspension, and frame. Avoid putting heavy coolers and containers of fuel and water in boats carried on trailers; if you must do so, put them directly over the axle. Due to gravel and tar thrown up from the road, all trailers should have fenders. If you are towing a boat, tie a red flag to your propeller—Mexican police occasionally pull over rigs without such flags.

Off-road driving

Except perhaps for fishing, nothing has played more of a part in the lore of Baja California than off-road driving. In 1918 there were 24 cars in Santa Rosalía, and 3 in Mulegé. By the 1920s auto travel from San Diego to the onyx mine at El Mármol had become fairly routine. However, little or nothing was done by the Mexican government to upgrade the roads from the needs of mules and burros to those of the new gasoline-powered vehicles, and passage remained problematical.

A cactus collector once set out on a trip in a Model T Ford truck, his only companion a fox terrier. The roads were so terrible that he had the misfortune of tipping over sideways, twice. Blessed with foresight, he had included a railroad tie, a shovel, and a block and tackle among his equipment. After each upset, he climbed out, dusted off the dog and himself, dug a hole and buried the railroad tie standing upright, rigged the block and tackle between the truck and the tie, and started pulling!

Erle Stanley Gardner told of a man named Outdoor Franklin who drove from Tijuana to Santa Rosalía in the mid-1920s, supposedly the first ever to make the trip by car. In 1926–27, the government finally appropriated 3,500 pesos to extend the automobile trail south from El Mármol to San Ignacio. By 1928 automobiles could get to Mulegé, and soon a twice-monthly stage ran between Tijuana and Santa Rosalía. The Automobile Club of Southern California sent an expedition led by Phillip Townsend Hanna as far south as Mulegé that year, resulting in the first reasonably accurate road map of the peninsula. Completion of the "missing link" south of Mulegé in 1930 provided a road from Tijuana to Cabo San Lucas, one of the longest roads in Mexico.

By the late 1940s travel by sportsmen and adventurers down the peninsula in pickups and war surplus Jeeps was becoming common, although it never seemed so to the drivers—tales of broken axles, of hours spent digging out of sandy washes, and of days spent traveling a dozen miles filled their books and articles. Even as late as the 1960s things could still be tough. During a 1967 trip to La Paz, Willis Tilton had to deal with over 40 mechanical problems with his Jeep pickup, including a broken main drive shaft and bent front drive shaft; cracked exhaust manifold; broken transfer case, front drive-line support, front spring main leaf, and front differential; several starter failures; a number of gas tank punctures; and numerous flat tires. He made it.

Paving of the Transpeninsular was completed in 1973, but a vast system of unpaved roads still covers much of Baja. Although some have felt the bite of a bulldozer, most remain as the laws of physics intended. To offset this, there have been improvements in trucks, tires, and equipment, and the expansion of the paved-road system has greatly reduced the mileages involved in "rough-stuff" trips. In the days before the Transpeninsular everything was rough between distant north and south roadheads, but now you can cruise on pavement or an improved road until close to your destination, only then turning off. Today most "off-road" trips accumulate only a few hundred miles, often much less. Rugged four-wheel-drive trucks were once the kings of Baja roads, but ordinary pickups and vans are now encountered in even the most remote locations. Well prepared, properly equipped, and driven with care, a standard two-wheel-drive pickup or van will take you to almost every location discussed in *The Baja Adventure Book*.

Tools, spare parts, and preparation

The most common problems off-road are the same ones encountered in driving anywhere: flat tires, overheating, failure to start, getting locked out, and running out of gas, plus ones that can be attributed to extreme conditions, such as

Kenneth Brown, superintendent in the onyx quarry at El Mármol, figures out his next move during a 1920 flood

Courtesy John Mills

bent tie rods, punctured gas tanks, drive-line damage, and getting stuck. Every vehicle venturing into Baja should carry a good spare tire, lug wrench, jack, flashlight, double-bitted screwdriver, medium adjustable wrench, pliers, fan belts, air gauge, water, fuel filters, spare keys fastened to the vehicle with stainless wire, extra fuses, and emergency flares. Also, carry a small plastic drop cloth or a dish towel. This should be placed under the scene of all repairs—nothing can be more maddening than a search for a small part in the sand. Vehicles engaged in extensive driving on unimproved roads should also carry a large adjustable wrench, side-cutting pliers, a set of socket and open-end wrenches of conventional or metric sizes as appropriate for the vehicle, duct tape, a set of slotted and Phillips screwdrivers of various sizes, a ball-peen hammer, medium-size Channelock pliers, automotive and utility wire, jumper cables (especially if you have an automatic transmission), siphon hose, tow line, shovel, plywood jack pad, extra gasoline and engine oil, suitable amounts of food and water, a compass and appropriate maps, tire repair equipment, and a Loctite Instant Gas Tank Repair Patch, repair part 12020. Although they are not often viewed as off-road equipment, every person along should have a pair of shoes or boots suitable for long-distance walking; bathroom thongs are the wrong footwear for hiking out to get help.

Cheap jacks that come with new vehicles are unsatisfactory off-road; their lifting height is too limited, as is their capacity. John Anglin and I got stuck once near Bahía Asunción and used a scissors jack to get several pieces of plywood under the wheels, forgetting there was a great deal of weight in the van. Without warning the jack screw stripped through its threaded pivot. A fraction of a second before it collapsed, John decided that he really ought to get his arm out from beneath the van, and that tiny lead time averted disaster. A serious off-roader ought to have two jacks, a hydraulic jack of at least three tons capacity and a HiLift. The latter is a heavy-duty bumper jack of about 7,000 pounds capacity and a lift height of about 36 inches. A jack pad a foot square cut from three-quarter-inch plywood can be useful, since jacks usually just push down into soft ground, and flat stones can be hard to find.

Traditional five-gallon metal GI cans are the safest way to carry gasoline. Plastic jugs can puncture or chafe while being bounced around, they melt quickly if subjected to fire, and their caps often leak. A surprising amount of grit can be thrown up into the engine compartment, especially if the vehicle scrapes the crown of the road while you are moving, so every vehicle should have an air filter. I have found pebbles as big as robin's eggs in the air cleaner of my van. Batteries are a common source of problems on Baja trips, especially off-road, where the banging around causes sediments to drift down to the bottom of the case, resulting in internal shorts in older batteries. Replace the battery if you are experiencing symptoms, and make sure it is held firmly in its mount.

All loose equipment should be wedged or tied in place to stop chafing and banging. Think small; I once put a lead fishing weight and a tube of fishing-reel lubricant together in a tackle box, resulting in a thin gray covering of oil over everything in the box, and a quart of olive oil once got together with 10 pounds of flour, producing a mess of instant pasta. The large rear door found on some campers can be forced open by shifting cargo while climbing hills, so lash it closed. Finally, aluminum beverage cans should be stowed so that they cannot be damaged, for there are few things more vulnerable than that miracle of modern packaging. After a few hours of hot, sweaty driving, many a thirsty off-roader has opened his cooler anticipating a cold beer, only to find the entire six-pack punctured and bereft of its precious fluid.

Tires and tire repair

If you are a typical Baja driver, with a pickup or a van loaded with people, food, drink, and sporting goods, who plans to head for Baja, drive off-road to a favorite campsite, and do some local exploring, ordinary skins of good quality and adequate load rating with plenty of tread left are all you will need. Tires of extreme diameter and width provide greater ground clearance and may help on soft ground by increasing the size of the tire footprint, but they add to unsprung weight and inherently lower gear ratios, possibly taking the engine out of its optimum torque range. Aggressive tread designs are noisy on pavement and cause steering and braking difficulties.

Tire problems are normally limited to simple punctures, and today's tires have far fewer flats than the tires old-time Baja drivers used to complain about. The best flat preventer is lots of tread. It is not necessary to carry more than one spare unless unusual conditions will be encountered, assuming the ones in use are in good shape. The spare should not be a treadless wreck. Sub-size "tem-

Soft ground provides Victor Cook with healthy outdoor exercise during a mineral-collecting trip into Arroyo del Boleo

porary" spares are miserable, but you may not be able to bring a decent one due to space limitations in the cubby-holes where they are designed to fit. Liquid preparations like Super Fix-A-Flat sold to eliminate flat tires work well and are convenient, but you should have the leak "permanently" repaired fairly soon.

There are two basic types of flats, the "good" kind and the "bad" kind. No flat is enjoyable, and the "good" kind is good only in the sense that the other is much harder to deal with. The "good" kind is a puncture through the tread of a tubeless tire, which can usually can be dealt with without removing the tire from the rim, dismounting the wheel from the vehicle, or even jacking up the vehicle. Pump up the tire and spray the stem, tread, and sidewalls with water and a little detergent from a bottle brought for that purpose, moving the vehicle forward as necessary. Even a slow leak should be obvious, and with luck it will be in the tread, not the sidewall. When the leak is located, pull out the offending nail or cactus spine and plug the leak with a push-through patch, following the directions on the patch kit, pump up the tire, and away you go—ten minutes max!

Push-through patches come in various forms. Small kits with a simple insertion tool and a half-dozen patches are available in any parts store. These are inexpensive, but the patches tend to work loose, and sometimes will not seal at all. NAPA auto parts stores carry a specialized insertion tool, lubricant, and higher quality patches. A Safety Seal kit is probably what your local repair shop uses, and although it is more expensive, the repairs are permanent, and damage to the carcass of the tire is less likely. Always wear safety glasses when installing push-through patches.

The "bad" kind of flat involves a sidewall puncture. The sidewalls of modern radials are thin, and *agave* spines seem custom-designed by the Devil to puncture tires in this vulnerable location. A push-through patch can be used in an emergency, but it may not seal properly, and the flexing of the sidewall may open up a hole before you get very far. Even if it works, the tire should be limited to low speeds until a proper repair can be made. If you get a sidewall puncture, put on the spare and hope that you will make it to a tire repair shop before the next flat. It may not even be necessary to put on the spare, since most sidewall punctures are caused by *agave* spines, and these sometimes leak very slowly, often taking a day or more to get near "the bottom." If the leak is slow enough, just pump up the tire to rated pressure and continue on until you can get to a tire repair shop, stopping occasionally to add air. Once you get to a shop, the proprietor may advise an innertube, although some install a special 6″ tire patch (tire patches are not the same thing as innertube patches). Shops in Mexico often use "hot" (vulcanizing) innertube patches on tubeless tires, but these may peel away before long.

If you are among the unlucky few who have to repair a sidewall puncture out in the desert, expect a struggle. Pump up the tire, find the leak with a spray bottle, and mark its location with a piece of tape or a pencil. Breaking the beads loose is the first problem, for they are usually frozen on the rim. Deflate the tire completely, place it under the vehicle, put the jack on the sidewall, and break the beads loose by jacking against the weight of the vehicle. Pull the tire off the rim with a tire tool or jack handle, and install a tire patch, the special large size. This will require a NAPA 710-1062 6" by 6" tire patch, a can of NAPA 765-1197 cement, and a stitching tool, NAPA 710-1179. (This large patch is also useful in the rare event of a sidewall or tread cut.) The second major problem will then be encountered, seating the beads when the tire is remounted. If your air pump can't put out enough volume to seat them, wrap a length of rope around the circumference of the tread, tie a knot, insert a jack handle under the rope, and start twisting, compressing the tire (this is called a Spanish windlass).

A serious off-roader's tire repair kit ought to include a tire pump, an innertube for large leaks or cuts, a push-through patch kit, the items noted above, a spray bottle filled with water and detergent, a tire iron or other means of getting the tire off the rim, and a length of line. The most useful type of air pump is a hose that screws into a sparkplug hole, NAPA 90-366. This nifty gadget has a 16-foot hose and a built-in pressure gauge, produces up to 130 psi and can fill a tire in a minute and a half with no effort on your part. The air pumped has no gasoline or oil fumes and the pressure is easily controllable, making it good for tires, inflatable boats, air mattresses, and rubber ducks. Tiny electrically operated pumps cost twice as much, tend to be unreliable, and take almost forever to pump up a tire.

Despite all the advice in the previous paragraphs, you should not get overly concerned about flats—well prepared, yes, paranoid, no. Sidewall punctures are not common on pavement, so most flats will be 10-minute problems. In many years of off-road driving in Baja, I have averaged only 1 flat per 600 miles, have had only 4 occasions on which it was essential to demount a tire from a rim off-road, and have had only 3 sidewall punctures where installation of an innertube was eventually necessary. As an experiment, I once fixed a sidewall puncture with an innertube hot patch, and it was still holding air after 6,000 miles.

Off-road driving techniques

In rough conditions, slow is good; you will not be breaking axles, spindles, or springs, banging passengers around, or losing control. In fact, almost all off-road damage results from excessive speed. A careful driver will go up to 25 miles an hour on the best stretches of unimproved road, and down to a crawl on the worst, but over the long run will average about 12 miles an hour. Always wear seat belts, and keep them tight; hitting the ceiling can do serious damage to your head. In brushy areas mirrors should be folded back, and arms kept inside.

Grades over about 15% on unpaved roads begin to spell trouble for heavily loaded standard pickups and vans with small engines and three-speed transmissions. The classic boo-boo is to drive down into a steep arroyo and find that the opposite grade is too steep to ascend, then to try to go back and find the slope you went down is also too steep, especially if the arroyo bottom is soft or rough. Experienced drivers can eyeball such situations well, but if you have any doubts it pays to carry a small clinometer and measure steep grades before you attempt to drive them in a standard vehicle. If the problem is simply a poor power-to-weight ratio, you may have to unload and carry your goodies up the hill, a method Reeve and I used many years ago to conquer the "Terrible Three" south of Puertecitos in our overloaded VW van.

Washboard is encountered on unpaved roads in arid regions throughout the world, and Baja is no exception. The ride can be made more comfortable by letting air out of the tires to perhaps half normal pressure, but nothing lower, since beads may come loose or casings may move on the rims. Driving at a suitable speed also helps; it's a matter of harmonics, and if you drive very slowly or very fast you will avoid the maddening hammer. However, driving fast can be dangerous, for you can quickly lose steering control, and brakes lose their effectiveness, especially on curves.

● ●

❝ Valuable lessons

During one trip, our Toyota 4x4 was new, "right out of the box," and on the first day of off-roading Reeve and I were headed into "Mission Impossible" (Misión Santa María). We got as far as the truck could go, and I had to turn around in a space only a foot wider than the truck was long, and managed to squash an agave. You guessed it; the result was one of the infamous sidewall-punctures-in-a-radial-tire, on a tire with just over 2,000 miles on it. The lesson? Don't run over agaves. We then noticed that one of the hubcaps was missing, the expensive kind found on mag wheels, and we were unable to find it on the way out to the pavement. Lesson? Remove your hubcaps before doing any off-roading. The leak was slow, and by pumping up the tire occasionally we postponed the day of reckoning until we were camped on the beach at Playa Bufeo. Mellow from cold Dos Equis and freshly speared halibut cooked in tempura, we began to remove the wheel. The first lug nut came off only with great reluctance, making squealing sounds, and the second and third were so tight that the nuts got hot from friction. The next two were not even finger-tight, and the last one would not even budge. I put my full weight on the wrench and nothing happened, so we lengthened its lever arm with a piece of pipe, and still the nut would not move. What a predicament— how do you deal with a such a flat when you can't even get the wheel off? Finally, with both of us using our full weight— generating perhaps 800 foot-pounds of torque—the stud finally sheared off. Apparently a mechanic at the Toyota dealership had decided to play a joke with his air wrench. The lesson? Make sure your wheel nuts are torqued properly and will back off properly.

I drove a four-wheel-drive Dodge pickup more than 8,000 miles off-road on my last trip to Baja before the first edition of this book went to press and had a number of problems. Three tiny screws in my underwater light meter backed out, leaving part of the mechanism loose. Eight bolts holding the camper shell to the truck, all lock-washered, vibrated loose, almost depositing it on the side of the road before I discovered what was happening. The constant jiggling caused the steel striker plate on the rear door lock of the shell to saw almost through the brass bolt, twice. Finally, one day I heard an explosion and saw smoke pouring out of the back. Fortunately, just weeks before, I had decided to replace several 5-gallon plastic gas cans with metal GI cans. I had to reach through the flames to jerk them out, singeing my arms, but I managed to get them out and to put out the fire. The jostling had apparently caused a box of old-fashioned farmer's matches to ignite. The explosion was a can of overheated beans. The lesson? Watch for mischief done by vibration.

In another lesson, we had loaded a large chunk of ice into our cooler, and all was well for a few days, until it had melted to half its original size. During a particularly rough trip up a dry arroyo, the chunk was thrown back and forth and acted like a battering ram, mashing cups of yogurt, a package of weenies, a carton of milk, a stick of salami, and just about everything else into a unappetizing pulp. The lesson? Each day, brace the ice with cans or bottles so it can't gain any kinetic energy. Finally, the water we saw coming out of the bottom of the truck was not melt-water from the cooler; it was the last of our drinking water coming from a split seam in a plastic jug. The lesson? Keep your jugs from banging around, just like the ice. **❞**

● ●

Road problems come in two extremes: soft ground and rough, hard ground. Weight is one of the most important controllable variables in driving on soft ground, and the less you carry the better you will fare. It helps to reduce tire pressure, since this increases the area of the tire in contact with the ground. Knowing how much power to use and how long to use it is the key to driving on soft ground. Use too much power and you will be banging and slamming; too little and you simply can't keep moving. Drive at moderate speed, with a smooth, steady throttle. Avoid stopping if you can. If you must stop, get out and dig away the ridges that build up in front of the tires; even small ones may keep you from getting rolling again. If you get stuck on a beach, use a bucket to wet down the sand around the wheels and make a track ahead. Don't try to return to harder ground by running straight uphill, but drive at an upwards angle of 20 or 30°.

If you have four-wheel-drive, stay in compound low and drive in higher gears, rather than in high range and lower gears, allowing you to downshift almost instantly to "stump-pulling" gear if you start to bog down. Don't give in to the temptation to keep your foot on the accelerator when progress

In one of his foul tempers, Reeve does a little impromptu road work while the author supervises from the comfort of the air-conditioned cab

has come to a halt, especially with two-wheel-drive, for the powered wheels will dig in, making it harder to get out, and grit may be driven through universal joint seals if they touch ground, causing a mysterious failure months later. A little digging early on saves a lot later, and with a HiLift and a shovel, you should be able to work your way out of some pretty hairy situations. A HiLift can walk a vehicle sideways; jack up one end and push the vehicle sideways, toppling the jack, then jack up the other end, push it sideways, etc. This procedure can be dangerous and is not recommended by the jack manufacturer. Backing out of a hole is frequently best, but the passage of wheels sometimes breaks up the structure of packed sand and fine gravel, turning it into thousands of tiny ball bearings. When pulling out, make sure the front wheels are pointed straight ahead, or else they may simply skitter along half-sideways, wasting a great deal of power.

Surface hardness is not necessarily a good measure of "sinkability," especially on dry lake beds and sand. A crust can form which seems solid when you walk on it, and appears to support the vehicle at first. I once drove out on a beach that had a rock-hard surface. I got 50 yards into it when there was a crunching sound and down she went. Nothing I could do with a HiLift could get the van to stay on top of the crust, so I finally had to hire a local with a long rope to pull me out. One early traveler parked for the night on the hard surface of dry Laguna Chapala, only to find the next morning that his vehicle had broken through the crust and was slowly sinking into the bottomless muck below.

Few problems with sand turn out to be serious, since firm ground is rarely far away, but with mud and water things can be very different—see the stories on pages 70 and 128. No one wants to move every time there is a little sprinkle, but if it rains steadily or hard, consider moving to pavement or at least to an improved gravel road. If you must drive through a flooded stream or dip in the road, find out how deep the water is first. If it is deep but otherwise driveable, remove the belt driving the fan, which throws water over the engine, and put a Baggie over the distributor, which is vulnerable. Drive slowly, maintaining a constant speed. If you are pulling a trailer beware of water approaching spindle-deep; the inner hub seal on some rigs is not completely waterproof because a nasty little gadget called a "**Z**-ring" has been inserted between the spindle and the seal, apparently to avoid the cost of machining a smooth surface on the spindle. I once crossed a knee-deep stream a half-dozen times pulling a 16-footer and got about a half mile down the pavement when huge clouds of black smoke appeared in the rearview mirror. Water had gotten past the **Z**-ring and wiped out bearings, races, electric brakes, and the seal, requiring a trip back to San Diego while the rig stood on the side of the Transpeninsular for two days.

Problems encountered on rock may result in damage to tie rods, oil pans, differentials, and suspension, which is much more serious than just the hassle of digging out of a soft spot. Most problems can be avoided by holding speed down and mentally "driving ahead," planning your route farther in advance than you normally do. Sometimes you might have to get out and move loose rock or fill in a hole, but a few minutes of labor can save endless problems later. If you have any doubts, have someone walk ahead and look things over. Avoid getting high-centered on the crown of the road, don't let large rocks pass under the vehicle, and don't hit big holes with brakes locked, for the stress on the suspension and rolling gear becomes terrific.

Sand or pebbles on top of rock can mean trouble, since the material can act like ball bearings, reducing traction. If the road tilts to one side, this can be downright dangerous, and on numerous occasions I have found myself skittering sideways towards seeming disaster. Pebbles can also cause a loss of steering control, and several times my four-wheel-drive has decided to go where it wanted, regardless of the commands conveyed to it with the steering wheel. If you get stuck in an area with pebbles or cobble, beware: I once was pushing on the back of a van, when it started to get some traction. As it pulled away a rock the size of a baseball was ejected backwards by one wheel, striking me forcibly in the chest. If the wheels are turned to one side, stones can be ejected from the front wheels if the vehicle has front-wheel or four-wheel drive.

Favorite off-road runs

Chapter 5 describes 4 loop trips for off-road bicyclists, including the Laguna Hanson, Vizcaíno, Mountain Villages, and Cape Coast Loop Trips. All of these also make fine trips by off-road vehicle. The Two Parks Loop Trip, described below, is too long for all but the most intrepid bicyclists, but for off-road drivers it is in many respects the ultimate off-road trip in Baja, since it has everything: both national parks, long easy stretches where you can relax, a few short, difficult places to test yourself and your machine, empty beaches, the ocean, and the mountains.

Two Parks Loop Trip: El Cóndor, Laguna Hanson, KM 55+ on Route 3 to KM 138, Mike's Sky Ranch, Mile

29.7 on the Observatory Road, Parque Sierra San Pedro Mártir, KM 140+ on the Transpeninsular, Colonet, Johnson Ranch, Eréndira, Punta Cabras, KM 23 on the Santo Tomás-Punta San José Road, Santo Tomás, Uruapan, Ojos Negros, El Coyote, KM 98 on Route 2 and back to El Cóndor, covering 306 miles off-road, 76 miles on pavement.

The following route provides a long and challenging trip passing through some of the most interesting places Baja has to offer:

Hitting the High Spots Trip: El Cóndor, Laguna Hanson, KM 55+ on Route 3 to KM 164+, across Laguna Diablo to San Felipe, Puertecitos, KM 229+ on the Transpeninsular, Bahía de los Angeles, Bahía San Francisquito, El Arco, Vizcaíno, then follow the route of the Vizcaíno Loop Trip to KM 98, San Ignacio, Laguna San Ignacio, La Purísima, the Comondús, San Javier, and Loreto, covering 970 miles off-road, 110 on pavement.

There are many obscure wheel-tracks shown on the maps in Chapters 9 through 13 that can be used to reduce the amount of pavement travel, and it should be possible to devise many other trips, including a border-to-the-Cape trip.

Trailering and RVing off-road

RV trips on unimproved roads require careful thought. Excessive vehicle width, height, and length, long overhangs, low power-to-weight ratios, and limited maneuverability may make the probability of damage and excessive hassle unacceptably high. Some rigs simply are not up to heavy pounding: joints will begin to work loose, causing leaks, and vegetation along the road will scratch that new airbrush mural of the Last Supper of which you are so proud. In addition, getting stuck in a big RV is a much more serious proposition than in an ordinary vehicle. Even turning around may be impossible, a problem more serious than many imagine—try backing a trailer a half-dozen miles.

In spite of this, improvements to some unpaved roads make it possible for small- to moderate-sized rigs to get to locations previously unreachable, including the road from Vizcaíno to Bahía Tortugas and Bahía Asunción, La Ribera past Pulmo Reef to San José del Cabo, Bahía de los Angeles to Bahía San Francisquito, La Paz to north of San Juan de la Costa, and others. Bob and Bonnie Rauch have made a number of such off-road trips in their 20-foot Champion motor home. Powered by a 318 Dodge and equipped with oversized tires, duals in the rear, this rig has taken them to Bahía Tortugas, Malarrimo, Puerto Chale, San Juan de la Costa, the Comondús, and San Sebastián. Although a heavy jolt once lifted the front wheels 18 inches off the road, the only damage incurred was a shock-absorber bracket sheared off and some deep scrapes on the bottom. Chapters 9 through 13 identify a number of unpaved roads that may be suitable for such trips, but the final judgment lies with the driver.

Towing small utility, motorcycle, or boat trailers on unimproved roads can be risky, since the high crown of the road may damage low axles. I once bent the axle on a motorcycle trailer, but managed to shackle a chain to each end and bend it straight again with a HiLift. On another trip a spring broke and it looked like we were in trouble—how do you fix a spring or get a replacement in the geographic center of the Baja boondocks?—but we made a temporary repair by removing a **U**-bolt from a bracket holding the winch and using it to shackle the axle to the frame. Horizontal and vertical forces caused by bumps and potholes are considerable, and the resulting strain on tie-downs and their attachment points can be enough to break the tie-downs or bend boat, bike, or trailer parts. More than once I have looked in the rearview mirror to see a motorcycle fallen over, and once to see a friend's Trail 90 dragging behind us. Firm tension must be maintained on tie-downs, so use adequate line and trucker's hitches, or better yet use nylon strap and a lever device, or a small strap winch. There must be a large area of contact between boat and trailer or you will experience stress cracks and other damage. Fenders and guide-boards often flap like bird wings on washboard sections and finally break off due to metal fatigue. Fenders should not be removed, since gravel and sand will eventually erode that shiny gel-coat, and there seems to be no solution other than to insure that the brackets that hold them are sturdy and to inspect them frequently.

Motorcycling

Baja has been conquered by everything from humble Vespas to grand Gold Wings, and every rider has his own opinion on the ideal Baja bike. In general, however, a rider touring Baja on the paved road system but planning off-road forays will be happiest with a 4-stroke machine of moderate weight, with a 250-350 cc engine and a range of at least 200 miles. Two-stroke enduro machines also work well, but motocross bikes, due to their small tank sizes and difficult-to-use power curve, leave something to be desired.

The tool and parts kits on most bikes are inadequate, and plugs, condensers, chain lube, a spare tube (two if the tires are of different sizes), tire repair kit, air pump, and tow rope should be carried. All this will probably not fit in the bike's tool kit, so make a cylindrical container out of plastic drainage pipe and hold it on the rear rack with bungee cord. Tube liners help reduce the number of flats, and plastic hand guards will keep thorns and cactus spines away from vulnerable hands. All Mexican dogs hate all bikers, and a can of Halt carried on a handlebar clip may save tooth marks on

We crossed a meandering stream thirty-four times on the round trip to La Bocana

your boots or worse. Wire a spare ignition key in a hidden location. A small plastic painter's drop cloth spread under the bike will avoid the loss of small parts if repairs become necessary. Switch to conventional oil or bring what you need, since synthetic oil is not available in Baja. If you don't already have a washable air filter, get one.

Bikes should be serviced and brought up to top condition before heading south. A bike breakdown in the desert can be a far more serious proposition than one in a truck, so file a "flight plan," and carry adequate food and water. The uniform of the day should be a brain bucket, eye protection, gloves, and boots suitable for hiking. Use sunblock cream and lip glop generously. In dusty conditions check the oil level, wash the air cleaner, and lube and adjust the chain every day. Engine oil is a major factor affecting the life of a bike engine, and in dusty conditions a change every 200 miles would not be excessive.

There are a few motorcycle repair shops in Baja, but their parts selection is poor, and the brands they handle are often unfamiliar; see Chapters 9 through 13. Mike's Sky Ranch and Hacienda Santa Veronica are the only resorts in Baja catering specifically to off-road drivers and motorcyclists.

● ●

66 *Campfire tales*

No aspect of the legend and lore of Baja California generates more fun at campfire gatherings than tales of what goes wrong when driving off-road in the desert. Here is a sample of what you might hear over the crackling of a Baja campfire and the pop of freshly opened cervezas.

Backing-down is not a skill ordinarily associated with off-road driving, but it can be vital. Michael and I were driving north on the "low road" between Cadajé and Laguna San Ignacio. Consisting of just a single pair of wheel tracks, it crossed many miles of mud flats. It seemed firm enough to drive on, but when we stopped and tested the sides of the road we went in over our boot tops in gooey mud just 2 feet off the wheel tracks. Driving carefully, we seemed to be in the "middle of nowhere"—nothing was visible but mud and sky—when a truck appeared on the horizon. I slowed down and stopped, but the other driver aggressively kept coming until his bumper was only inches from ours. Three Mexicans, very large and rough-looking and not exactly exuding empathy and good humor, got out and in unison suggested in unmistakable terms that it was going to be us who pulled off to the side of the road. We could see tequila bottles on the floor of the cab and a shotgun in a rack in the rear window and quickly began to appreciate their logic; after all, it was their country. Our wheels got no more than 6 inches off the tracks when they started to sink into the mud, and we barely

managed to pull back. The three men were becoming impatient, perhaps anxious to see the tip of our aerial disappear into the muck, and we had to do something, fast. We couldn't go around, over, or under them, and that left only one direction. I shifted into reverse and started down the narrow wheel tracks, using the rearview mirror to steer. Steering with a mirror is confusing—every turn of the steering wheel must be the opposite of what the mirror suggests—and after a dozen close calls, I found I had to twist myself around to actually see where I was driving. Finally, after almost an hour, we came to a place where I could safely get out of the way, and the truck pulled away in a cloud of blue smoke and a shower of beer cans. When I tried to drive normally, I found I had a "crick" in my neck, which I couldn't straighten out for several days.

That wasn't the end of the mud problems. Reeve and I had parked our van near Puerto Chale while on a wreck dive near Punta Tosca, and when we returned a week later we found it perched on an island, surrounded by acres of mud caused by a series of high tides. Lacking traction and four-wheel drive, only kinetic energy would save us from an enforced month-long camp-out, so it was "pedal-to-the-metal" while we were still on firm ground. In a great spray we hit the liquid mud, our rear wheels throwing up roostertails, swerved back and forth, totally out of control and unable to see through the windshield but headed, we thought, in approximately the right direction, hit a rise, bounded 4 feet into the air and skidded to a stop in front of the astonished other half of our party, who had slowly crossed to dry land earlier in their fat-wheel 4x4, calm, clean, and unconcerned.

Small pickups are light and agile and do well off-road, but their low clearance sometimes produces startling results. Victor Cook and I were bouncing down a rocky road, checking out mineral collecting sites. I had just finished commenting on how well his Toyota was handling the terrain when there was a loud crunch and we saw something lying in the road behind us. It proved to be the left front torsion bar, torn off the truck by a rock. It was badly bent, but spare Toyota torsion bars are hard to come by 50 miles from the nearest pavement, so we decided to try to forge it back into shape. We turned up the regulator on our propane stove, heated the bar, and with a sledge used for cracking mineral samples and a rock for an anvil, I hammered the bent part back into shape. Miraculously, it fit perfectly on the first try. We smugly thought that our ingenuity had overcome a once-in-a-million fluke, but two days later there was another crunch. This time the right front torsion bar had been ripped off, giving us a second chance to perfect our newly acquired blacksmithing skills. 99

● ●

Chapter 7

Extra Added Attractions

Boardsailing

The number of boardsailors visiting Baja has increased by a factor of ten in recent years. Baja has finally been "discovered," and for good reason, for there is everything anyone could want, ranging from mill ponds to rolling ocean swells, from gentle zephyrs to boom-bending blasts, and vast rideable areas that never see more than a board or two at a time. The orientation of both coasts is roughly northwest-southeast, and since prevailing winds are northwest along the Pacific coast and north in the Cortez, fine, reliable, side-shore conditions are frequently encountered.

Bahías San Quintín, Magdalena, and Almejas provide long rides in good winds, with no ocean swells. Bahía Santa María (the "outer bay" at San Quintín) sometimes has a refracted swell and there are ocean swells at the point, but the winds are good and there are fine sand beaches. Bahía Santa Rosalillita, also a favorite with surfers, often has strong, reliable winds, giving it a reputation as something of a "jock" area. One boardsailor spent six weeks there, and was skunked only two days. Waves range from the calm of the bay to perfect sets of big waves off the point, providing a fine place for intermediate sailors making the transition to waves. Bahía Tortugas is not often visited by boardsailors, but is free of ocean swell and frequently has heavy winds, and you can't get carried too far if you are still having trouble with waterstarts and tacking. Punta Abreojos is very windy, and the heavy June thermals that are the bane of local fishermen are a joy to boardsailors. El Conejo, too, is a favorite with heavy-weather sailors. There are, of course, many small "secret" locations, small bays, and coves offering fine sailing, but by and large, most other Pacific coast locations are for experts only, due to large swells, tidal currents, and fog.

At the Cape, Playa el Médano at Cabo San Lucas and the small coves to the east attract novice and intermediate boardsailors. Cabo San Lucas is generally out of the area affected by the heavy north winds that funnel down the Cortez in winter, but southern fronts provide fine onshore and cross-onshore conditions in summer. With a body of warm water and a major land area to the east, an ocean to the south, and mountains and an ocean to the west, East Cape gets brisk, dependable winds between mid-November and mid-March, making it the most popular boardsailing location in Baja, the La Ventana, Cabo Pulmo and Bahía las Palmas areas being favorite places. There are also fine beaches and good boardsailing around Cabo Frailes, Punta Arena Sur, Punta Colorada, and Punta Arena de la Ventana. During the warm months a strong afternoon breeze of almost clock-like regularity blows at La Paz, providing fine conditions, especially at Balandra.

Loreto has good winds and general side-shore conditions. Placid Bahía Concepción is the ideal spot for beginners, for the wind that often funnels down the bay produces side-shore conditions in many locations. The shape and orientation of the spit at Playa Requesón allow novices to find good conditions with wind from almost any direction. Santispac is fun and compact, but the surrounding hills keep the winds down. At the north end of the bay, Punta Arena often has the heaviest winds, since the surrounding land is low. Low Punta Chivato north of Mulegé sticks out well into the Cortez, freeing it from the influence of the higher topography to the west and providing the best in speed sailing conditions during the north winds of winter.

Bahía de los Angeles is the eastern end of the famous "Baja Shuttle." In winter the bay has frequent katabic winds, but no swell builds up since they come from the north and the west. When the winds are up, boardsailors try speed sailing, and when it's calmer they play and explore the many islands. When a Pacific front approaches, they pack up and head west for Santa Rosalillita, only 74 miles away, to take advantage of the wind and the waves. When the front dies, everyone rushes back to Bahía de los Angeles. Since the two types of wind have separate causes, one or the other is often at work, providing almost continual boardsailing action in a variety of conditions.

Like their surfer cousins, Pacific-side wave sailors should watch the weather maps for fronts in winter and for tropical storms in summer and consult the Internet weather sites provided by some of the organizations in Appendix B. Speed sailors should look for a stagnant high over Southern California, hopefully with another high to the east, good indicators that strong north winds are blowing down the Cortez. Local thermals and katabic winds cannot be identified from weather maps, of course.

Due to the wide variety of conditions, it will pay to bring both a short and a long board and a full quiver of sails. A kayak paddle can turn your board into a vessel for exploring on no-wind days. Make sure your equipment is in top

Windsurfer Keir Becker takes a big one at K 38

shape and bring essential spare parts and plenty of sail tape. Baja's remote conditions require additional attention to safety matters. Rig a leash between mast and board in case the universal breaks or pulls out of the mast foot, and let someone know where you are. A wet suit is a necessity on both coasts because of wind-chill—if it isn't blowing you won't be out there. Watch for changes in wind direction, especially if you are riding a short board and/or aren't big on tacking, and for increases in velocity—if winds get up too much, head for camp. Unless you like being stranded miles from camp don't stray too far, certainly in areas with heavy currents, for Baja winds, especially in the Cortez, can drop to nothing in minutes. Boardsailors construct elaborate arguments for not wearing life jackets: they are not needed, sailboards can't sink, and they always stop when a rider falls off, there is no place to stow a jacket, you can't swim well in a jacket, and the best place to be in the surf is often 5 or 10 feet down. These arguments have a certain validity, but all are based on conditions "back home," where there is safety in numbers—if you get in trouble there is always someone around to help. However, few boardsailors have any experience out on the water alone, really alone, so think it out—what will you do

to stay afloat if you are injured and no one is around? The same thing holds for helmets—you may be the biggest thing around in hot-dogging and wave-sailing circles back home, but what will you do if your mast decides to bend itself double over your skull?

There are a number of fine companies offering package trips to Baja, including Ventana Windsurf, Vela Windsurf Resorts, and Baja Adventures, all at East Cape. These will accommodate walk-ins subject to first call by guests, and Vela has a limited supply of gear and replacement parts for sale. Rental boards are available in Ensenada, La Paz, La Ventana, East Cape, Cabo San Lucas, and San Felipe (see the index). Aereo Calafia offers airborne boardsailing trips to Punta Pequeña from the Cabo San Lucas airport. As noted earlier, Baja Outdoor Activities in La Paz offers a boardsailing/sea kayaking combo trip.

Surfing adventures

Baja is the last frontier of California surfing, the last place where you can escape the crowding and the confrontation that have marred the scene in Southern California for many years. There are two basic surfing regions. The first, between Tijuana and Ensenada, is essentially an extension of Southern California conditions. The weather, water, beach litter, and most of the people are the same, and San Miguel is as well-known to generations of Southern California surfers as Rincon. Tame and familiar stuff, but fun, friendly, and dependable.

The second region, the 1,032-mile coastline from Ensenada to the Cape, has almost every conceivable kind of surfing condition. Prevailing winter northwesterlies produce a succession of highly reliable point breaks on the many capes dangling south from the Pacific coast like icicles. Stretches of beach sweeping between them may work well only a few days or weeks a year, but so many miles are involved, with so many combinations of exposure, fetch, bottom terrain, beach curvature, and angle to the swell, that there is usually little difficulty in finding something that is working well. With the coming of summer, south winds and waves from tropical storms produce a far greater variety of conditions and enough lefts to keep an army of goofy-foots happy, and opening up locations that work best in south waves like Isla Natividad and the Cape. Individual surfers have favorite sea-

sons, but there is really no best time of year; the big southern boomers of summer may be more fun, but they tend to be less consistent than the waves of fall and winter.

Any list of the top surfing locations on the coast from Ensenada to the Cape would include Puntas San José, San Telmo ("Quatro Casas"), San Jacinto ("Freighters"), Baja, San Carlos, Santa Rosalillita, Punta Abreojos, Pequeña, and Juanico, plus El Conejo. Reliable breaks, with easy access and good camping, all can be reached with two-wheel-drive vehicles. In addition, there are two fine island sites, "El Martillo" ("The Hammer") and Natividad, both objects of a great deal of current interest, El Martillo being compared with such world-class locations as Waimea Bay in Hawaii and Maverick's in California. Surfers are a tight-lipped lot when it comes to recently "discovered" locations, and a magazine article raving about El Martillo's "good juicy all around high performance wave[s] with ... nice steep takeoff[s]" failed to inform readers where the place is located (the Islas de Todos Santos near Ensenada). El Martillo often has 10- or 12-foot faces when surfers at San Miguel, only 7 miles away, are sitting in their pickups wishing. The

Willy Morris rides a frothy face at "Open Doors," Isla Natividad

Photograph by Flame

islands can be reached easily by boats launched at Ensenada or Punta Banda. Surfers without their own can rent *pangas* or charter one of Gordo's Sport Fishing fleet boats. La Bufadora Dive offers surfing trips to El Martillo.

Natividad is more difficult to reach, but it's worth it; there are those who claim that "Open Doors," the break on its east end, is the best beach break on the west coast of North America. The island is only five miles off the village of Punta Eugenia, which has good road access and *pangas* available for hire. However, Natividad is primarily a summer site, dependent on big south waves that often wipe out the landings at Punta Eugenia and the island. These and many other surf sites are described in later chapters.

Surfers are among the great storytellers of our times, and their legends have given the region south of Ensenada a lurid reputation. These run the full gamut from the usual *bandido* roadblock, iguana-up-the-pant-leg, and flash-flood-washes-away-tent-with-people-in-it stories to imaginative creations about the killer whale that chased a surfer through the waves and floundered in the shallows as the wave receded, and the surfer who tried to outrun a pack of sea snakes. The weavers of most of these tales would probably refuse a polygraph test, but there is no doubt that a trip to these distant regions is a very different proposition than a day trip to San Miguel. There are no hotels or RV parks in the better locations, and a few may require an off-road vehicle. There are no Coast Guard stations your buddies can call when a rip carries you out to sea, and medical attention for bumps, bangs, and sea urchin stabs can be hours away. There is an extensive lobster fishery along Baja's Pacific coast, and pots are sometimes anchored in or drift into surfing areas, their buoy lines waiting to ensnare surfboard leashes. Despite these difficulties, the southern region offers fine surfing under a variety of adventurous conditions, and the lack of a crowd allows working on form and technique without the constant distraction of watching for collisions.

As with any trip to Baja, preparation is everything. Surfers planning to camp should study Chapter 5, and Chapter 6 will be of interest to those traveling in RVs and off-road. There are surf shops in Rosarito, Ensenada, Punta Banda, San José del Cabo, and Playa los Cerritos, on Route 19 north of Cabo San Lucas. (There are unfortunately two towns named Rosarito in Baja Norte, one just south of Tijuana, and one north of Guerrero Negro. To avoid mixing them up, the second one will be referred to as Rosarito Sur.). Rental boards and surf kayaks are available at the Aqua Adventures operation at Laguna Manuela. Aereo Calafia offers airborne surfing trips to Punta Pequeña from the Cabo San Lucas airport.

Extrapolating Southern California wave reports as far south as Ensenada is not too risky, but obtaining reliable information on surf conditions farther south is difficult, although you might get some valuable information by telephone or from one of the Internet weather-reporting sites. Surf Check's Internet site provides current video clips, reports, and forecasts for a number of locations along Baja's Pacific coast. If

There are breaks for surfers of almost every experience level: Mike catches a good one on his boogie Board at Cieto Lindo

you are in a Baja location that has an Internet café or computer services office, it's easy to get a current report and forecast. Surf Check is a membership site, and surfers currently pay about $10.00 per month for access. Reports on Baja surfing can be obtained from Surfline for $1.50 a minute.

Rock-art treasures

At more than a hundred sites scattered from the US border to the Cape, explorers, miners, ranchers, and archaeologists have discovered that early Indian tribes had graced the barren peninsula with art treasures ranging from simple petroglyphs pecked on rocks to enormous murals painted on cave walls. The most spectacular lie in the southern Sierra de San Francisco and the northern end of the Sierra de Guadalupe, an area bisected by the Transpeninsular Highway near San Ignacio. The murals depict figures of humans and animals painted life size or larger, and can extend hundreds of feet in length and to heights of 30 feet, a scale so grand that local legends insist the artists were giants.

The murals were executed in a flat wash technique in red, black, white, and, occasionally, yellow, using mineral pigments and brushes made from short pieces of *agave* or milkweed fiber. They generally depict humans, deer, bighorn sheep, and rabbits, but also may include mountain lions, birds, fish, sea mammals, raccoons, and rats, frequently rendered near life-size, in a realistic but static style. Many human and some animal figures are "bicolor"—a figure was divided in half and each half painted a different color, usually black and red. Another important characteristic is "overpainting," where the artist painted new images over those painted at an earlier time. The effect can be startling, a cacophony of animal and human figures with no apparent order or logic. In addition to representational paintings, there are many examples of abstract art, often taking the form of curvilinear figures or "checkerboards," intersecting lines forming squares filled with colors.

The few artifacts found at the sites around San Ignacio indicate that the murals were painted by Cochimí Indians between the mid-14th and early-16th centuries. Scattered descriptions occur in writings of the Jesuit missionaries, and in 1883 Herman Ten Kate, a Dutch physician, published an account of his archaeological activities in Baja that mentioned a few sites. Leon Diguet, a French chemist at the copper mines in Santa Rosalía, published a paper in 1895 describing many sites. However, it took mystery writer Erle Stanley Gardner to bring the art to public attention and generate the great interest that it now enjoys. Having heard rumors about a site north of San Ignacio, he assembled 2 expeditions in 1962 and found a number of art sites, including the crown jewel of Baja Indian art, known as Gardner Cave or Cueva Pintada. The local people, of course, knew about most of them all along.

Burro trips to see Gardner Cave and the other sites in the area can be arranged in the village of San Francisco,

Ron Smith and Robert Connick discuss the fine points of a mural at Gardner Cave

north of San Ignacio. Cueva Palmarito, also north of San Ignacio, can be approached within several miles by vehicle and hence can be visited in the course of a day. Guides can be obtained at nearby Rancho Santa Martha. Guided trips to Palmarito and other sites can be arranged in San Ignacio. Las Pintas, a minor site near El Rosario, can be visited by off-road vehicle.

Some art sites are accessible to casual travelers. The "Playhouse Cave" near Cataviña is an easy 15-minute hike from the Transpeninsular. Cueva Ratón, a site near San Francisco, can be visited by auto, requiring only a 2-minute hike. Gruta San Borjitas, north of Mulegé, is considered a major site and is only a 15-minute hike from a roadhead, and guided trips can be arranges at the hotels in town. The "Unhappy Coyote" in the Bahía Concepción area is just a 15-minute walk off the pavement. Green Tortoise bus trips stop at some minor sites. There are a number of museums in Baja which display rock art and Indian artifacts—see the index.

You are well advised not to attempt a "freelance" trip. Most sites are remote, and problems in learning their location, arranging for guides, burros, and equipment, compounded by language barriers, are formidable and costly. In addition, laws resulting from severe damage by unthinking tourists and pothunters restrict many activities. In 1977 an article appeared in a backpacking magazine about a trip to an art site. The people were described as intelligent and caring, but the article went on to describe how they despoiled the site by removing artifacts. Even professional anthropologists can be guilty. I once conducted an "FBI style" search of a nasty trash pile at one site and found the name and address of a prominent anthropologist on a number of magazine wrappers and letters. Mexican law now requires visitors to rock art sites to have a licensed guide.

Shelling

Baja's diverse underwater habitats, especially in the Cortez, produce an astounding variety of mollusks, and many beaches and flats are so remote that their conchological treasures lie undisturbed, providing fine collecting opportunities. Many of the more prominent sites are identified in Chapters 9 through 13. There are some opportunities to purchase shells in shops in Ensenada and La Paz. There are also less conventional ways to obtain them. An abalone fishery exists along the Pacific coast, and divers offer specimens of black, red, green, corrugated, and "blue" abalone (apparently a hybrid), as well as other creatures encountered during their travels along the bottom. Divers take vast quantities of sea urchins, whose sex organs are flown to Japan to be sold fresh at high prices, and a fine "basket" should be easy to obtain. In addition, local fishermen harvest pismos, scallops, *chocolates* (a common species of clam with a vitreous, light tan shell), and butter clams, several species of cockle, owl limpets, rock oysters, and mussels, and wavy turbans are taken for bait. Commercial divers land near the old salt pier in Guerrero Negro and may have shells for sale at low prices,

Suzy, Georgia, and Judy search for sea buttons on the beach at Isla San Francsco in the Cortez

most notably lion's paw. Scallop divers around Bahía Concepción usually have a variety of shells available. Shrimp trawlers working the Cortez bring up loads of live mollusks and often have specimens. The museum at Bahía de los Angeles has an extensive collection of local shells.

Mineral collecting

Jesuit Father Johann Jakob Baegert, who served in Baja in the mid-1700s, found the main ingredients of the peninsula to be largely "...petrified sea shells, mountains...of flint, ...wacke stones held together by a mortar-like substance, ...smooth polished stones...and...a mixture...which [defies] identification and can only be classified as 'pieces of California.'" Baegert's description didn't deter too many prospectors, and for over 400 years men have searched the arid peninsula for economic minerals, primarily gold and silver. However, remarkably little is known of Baja's potential for amateur mineral collecting. The geological knowledge of early prospectors was generally limited to locating gold or silver and getting it out of the ground, and papers in the recent professional geological literature are devoted to economic or descriptive geology, rarely touching on subjects of direct interest to collectors. Until completion of the Transpeninsular, large areas of Baja were accessible only at the cost of a great deal of time and money, which relatively few collectors were able to afford. Even today little has been published, and much of Baja remains unknown to collectors.

There are only about 250 known mines and mineral sites in Baja's 55,634 square miles, an amazingly small number for an area so large. When the sites are plotted on a map, three things become apparent: most sites are in Baja Norte, enormous "blank spots" exist without a single site, and the locations of non-economic mineral sites are strongly correlated with accessibility; few are far from roads. The cause of this uneven distribution could be that Mother Nature was stingy with Baja California and decided to locate most of her meager allocation in northern areas and near roads to insure that collectors could get to them easily, but the more likely reason is that many sites remain undetected or unreported.

Collectors thus have choices ranging between two extremes: confining their collecting activities to areas of proven mineralization or heading for unknown country. Six areas have extensive mineralization: (1) a broad band extending south from the border through La Rumorosa, El Alamo, and San Vicente, including areas west of Parque Nacional Sierra San Pedro Mártir; (2) areas on both sides of the Transpeninsular between El Rosario and Rosarito Sur; (3) the area around El Arco; (4) the Santa Rosalía area, where almost 60 minerals have been found; (5) the Concepción peninsula; and (6) around El Triunfo, where 35 have been identified. The major areas with few or no sites are located: (1) in the interior east of the Transpeninsular between the latitudes of Camalú and of El Rosario; (2) in Pacific coastal and interior areas from the latitude of Santa Rosalía to that of Loreto; and (3) the entire peninsula south of the latitude of Loreto, with some exceptions like El

A specific gravity of 58? Don Nelson and Jim Smallwood find something amusing about Jim's analysis of a mineral sample

Triunfo, magnesite deposits on Isla Santa Margarita, and phosphate deposits on the coast between Loreto and La Paz.

Chapters 9 through 13 identify many mineral sites, some prominent and even world-famous, others minor. Although of little direct interest, the latter have been included to help readers identify general areas of mineralization. The Mexican government produces topographic maps which show many mines, as well as a series of geologic maps—see Chapter 8.

People living in the old mining areas south of La Rumorosa occasionally have specimens for sale, primarily epidote. Small-scale miners, especially those working around El Alamo, sell raw gold at market prices. In 1983 an American was able to purchase an unusual and beautiful half-ounce gold nugget from an Alamo miner. Miners at El Arco sell copper-bearing minerals, and people living around El Aserradero south of Laguna Hanson often have specimens. The museums in Bahía de los Angeles and Santa Rosalía have mining and mineral displays. American Continental Travel offers a six-day package tour to the mineralogical and mining areas east of Ensenada, led by professional geologists.

Cave exploring

Sometimes those "pieces of California" have big holes between them. Other than a sentence here and there in the scientific literature, generally related to the life and times of the resident bats, my efforts in the library to learn of the existence of caves in Baja proved fruitless. However, after asking every bartender, butcher, cab driver, waiter, captain of the port, rancher, shepherd, goat driver, fisherman, and sea urchin diver within earshot, and passing out hundreds of handbills in Spanish, I came up with a fair number, which are described in later chapters. Solution, lava-tube, and sea caves are included. Several caves have been omitted to avoid disruption of their bat colonies. All are modest, but are of-

Don Nelson and Jim Smallwood examine strange, dust-covered speleothems in "Cueva Tres Pisos," the Three Story Cave

fered as proof that caves do exist in Baja. Some of the natural history cruises down the Pacific coast mentioned in Chapter 1 stop at Isla San Martín to see the lava tubes.

● ●

❝ *Trapped!*

I wanted photos of sally lightfoot crabs, so I decided to enter a small sea cave south of Bahía San Francisquito in my aluminum cartop boat. I cut the engine and rowed into the entrance, but soon the channel was barely wider than the boat and the ceiling became so low that I had to kneel. With my mind in neutral, I pressed on, propelling the boat by pushing an oar against the sides of the cave, my camera strobe illuminating the scene at intervals in brilliant white light. The channel turned several times and soon it was pitch-black. The water had been calm, but without warning there was a heavy surge, perhaps from the wake of a passing vessel, and the boat was rammed through the rapidly narrowing channel, screeching and slamming against the rough rock. When it finally came to a halt, the boat was firmly wedged in place and the flat ceiling had dipped so low that the tops of the outboard engines were almost touching rock. Pushing on the sides of the cave would not budge the boat an inch. Trapped, *but not for long! I thought. Kneeling in front of the engines was awkward, but I managed to pull the starter on one and it coughed into life. I shifted into reverse and raced the throttle, but nothing happened, except that I was enveloped in clouds of acrid smoke. Gagging and gasping for breath, I hit the stop button.*

I sat in the darkness for a few minutes, deciding what to do. If I could not break free I was going to have to abandon ship, but I could not quite squeeze over the transom because the engines and several rod holders were blocking the way. What would happen if the tide came in—would it fill the cave? I could see myself, nose pressed against the ceiling, sucking in the air from the last small bubble. It might be possible to get over the bow, but I would have to free-dive under the boat in the pitch-darkness, swim to the entrance, where there were only sheer bluffs for hundreds of yards on either side, and hike for many miles to find help. I cursed myself over and over: What a dummy! What a dummy! How could I have let this happen? *I had no water and no food except for a fish that had been baking in the bilges all day, and no shoes other than a pair of wet-suit booties, and I had told nobody where I was going. Later, I don't know how long, I was lying on my back, sick from the smoke, shivering, hungry, and cursing, when another idea popped into my head. I lay on my back, put my feet against the ceiling, and gave a heave with all the strength of my legs and back. Instantly the boat broke loose, and a few minutes later I was bobbing up and down off the entrance to the cave in the rose-colored twilight.* **❞**

● ●

Chapter 8

A Baja Survival Kit

Uninformed Americans are sometimes reluctant to travel in Baja, fearing the legendary "Mexican roadblock," hassles with police demanding *mordida* for inadvertent infractions of unfamiliar laws, and bouts of Montezuma's Revenge. However, in many trips to Baja, some almost five months long, I have paid *mordida* (a bribe, literally, the "bite") only twice—traffic cops nailed me in Tijuana and in La Paz and promised to "pay the fines for me," totaling less than $20. I was twice cheated by PEMEX attendants, for less than $10 each time. With these small exceptions, experienced over a period of many years of active travel and adventure in Baja, I have never had a problem with the locals, and have in fact been treated with almost uniform courtesy and honesty. I once had to leave a camper in Santa Rosalía for three months while I returned home. Although it was jammed with outboard motors, scuba gear, a diving compressor, cameras, camping equipment, and tools, I returned to find it intact, not so much as a dust mote disturbed. Could you do this in your home town?

Only once have I been aware of being deliberately misled—three young Mexicans in a pickup told me that I absolutely must not turn right at the next dirt road if I wanted to find Gruta San Borjitas. Fortunately they were such unpracticed liars that their intentions were obvious. By far the most dangerous and disagreeable part of my travels to Baja has been driving through Los Angeles on the way to the border, and the worst drinking water I ever had to endure in Baja was some I filled my tanks with while in San Diego.

Still, Mexico is a very foreign country; the language, money, customs, laws, and regulations are distinctly different, and traveling there is not like traveling in Canada. In fact, the cultural and economic factors that separate the US and Mexico may be among the greatest found between adjacent countries anywhere in the world. There is a great deal to know, and the following "survival kit" of facts, opinions, and ideas is intended to promote a pleasant Baja adventure.

Obtaining current information

What's the weather like? What's biting? How warm is the water? These questions are natural ones for anyone about to expend a considerable amount of time and money on a trip to Baja, but unfortunately there is little of value in the newspapers, and information in magazines and advice from returning friends is almost always too old to be meaningful.

However, readers will note that Appendix B lists many hotels, resorts, RV parks, and organizations that have Baja telephone numbers, as well as many Internet addresses where a wide variety of relatively fresh information can be found.

Current fishing information should not be too hard to obtain. Pisces Fleet and Minerva's Baja Tackle, both in Cabo San Lucas, can also be reached by telephone, and Point Loma Sportfishing, H & M Landing, and Fisherman's Landing maintain telephone hot lines describing the success on their long-range trips. Also, most of the cruiser and *panga* fleets either have Baja numbers or are associated with hotels that do.

Maps, guides, and tide tables

Mexico publishes useful topographic maps, though there are gaps in coverage and place names are often missing or applied to the wrong locations. They are generally accurate in their physical representations, although some "phantom" islands are shown, those northwest of the south tip of Guardian Angel Island, for instance. Although catalogs list topos for many Pacific and Cortez islands, the Mexican government has never gotten around to actually printing them, and even when smaller islands are within the geographic coverage of given maps, they are often not shown—San Nicolás G12A68, for instance, does not show Isla Ildefonso. Most topos were developed years ago and do not show recent road construction. Beware of roads that a map labels "*en construccíon*" (in construction)—they are often planned but rarely built. The US, Great Britain, and Mexico publish nautical charts of Baja's Pacific waters and the Sea of Cortez. Charts published by Mexico are usually copies of US charts, although a few are original and useful.

The Map Centre, Inc. sells a vast array of Baja nautical charts, topographic maps, books, and other products by phone, by mail, and in person. Map World sells charts, maps, and books on Baja, by phone, by mail, in person, or over the Internet. Crusing Charts sells a variety of useful products, including Cruising Guides of the southern and middle Cortez; Chart Packets covering Baja's Pacific coast, the La Paz area, Bahía Concepción, and Bahía de los Angeles; Mini-Guides for Cabo San Lucas, La Paz, Isla San José, Agua Verde, Puerto Escondido, Bahía Concepción, Santa Rosalía, Bahía de los Angeles, Puerto Refugio, and the Midriff; and Paddle Charts of the areas between Isla Carmen and La Paz, Bahía de los Angeles and Bahía San Francisquito, and Bahía Concepción and Isla Carmen. The Paddle Charts are of special interest to kayakers and small-boat sailors because they are printed on waterproof Tyvek, and can be folded to pocket size. Agencia Arjona in Ensenada and La Paz sells US and Mexican nautical charts. *Tide Tables for the West Coast of North and South America*, published by NOAA, has tidal stations for Ensenada, San Carlos, La Paz, and the entrance to the Río Colorado, plus stations on the east coast of the Cortez. The University of Arizona publishes tables for the northern Cortez. Also, tide and current information is available on the Internet.

Compasses

Many descriptions of the locations of shipwrecks, geological features, dive sites, fishing "holes," etc. in later chapters depend on compass bearings. To be able to take full advantage of this information, the reader should obtain a bearing compass, which has a sighting mechanism and a circular compass card with degrees marked on its periphery, allowing accurate readings. Coghlan's lensatic engineer compass, stock number 8164, available at many outdoor stores and large drug chains for about $10, is suitable, although they last only a year or two until their magnets go dead. If you want a dependable, long-lasting model get a military-specification engineer's lensatic compass, often found in military surplus stores.

Off-road drivers should obtain an auto compass. Make sure it is of the "compensating" type, allowing the compass to be adjusted for the deviation caused by the magnetic influence of the vehicle. Non-compensating compasses are subject to deviation in excess of 30°, often making them worse than useless. Airguide stock number 1699, found in many auto supply stores, is a compensating type, costs less than $10 and can be attached with double-faced tape to the windshield, where deviation is normally at a minimum.

Tourist cards

US citizens must have a tourist permit (everyone calls them tourist "cards," for reasons obscured by the mists of time) in order to stay more than 72 hours in border areas, or to travel south of Maneadero or San Felipe. There are two types of cards. A single-entry card is good for one visit of up to 180 days—the exact length will be determined by the Mexican *Migración* official who validates the card. If you get less than the full 180 days, you can ask for a longer period at the time the card is validated, or at any *Migración* (Immigration) office in Mexico at a later date. The second type, multiple-entry, allows any number of visits during its 180-day period. Both types can be obtained at the Mexican Consulate General, Mexican Consulates, or Mexican Government Tourism Offices, and single-entry cards can also be obtained from some airlines, insurance companies, and travel agencies, and from *Migración* offices. Obtaining a card before crossing the border will save time and hassle, especially

on holidays and weekends. There is no charge for either type, but you must show proof of US citizenship, such as a valid passport or certified birth certificate. Driver's licenses and Armed-forces IDs are often rejected as proof of citizenship. Naturalized citizens of the US can use a valid US passport, a Certificate of Naturalization, or a Certificate of Citizenship. The cards must be used within 90 days of issue, and the document used to prove citizenship must be carried while you are in Mexico.

Having a card in your possession is not enough—you must also have the card validated at a *Migración* office in Mexico. The offices at Tijuana, Otay Mesa, and Calexico West are often busy, and parking is hard to find. There is an office in Rosarito, but it is a bit out of the way for those heading south. The office in Ensenada is conveniently located, but it is often unexpectedly closed during business hours when the officials are dealing with cruise ship passengers, and it is sometimes closed on Sundays. Traffic at the new border crossing at Calexico East has not built up and there is plenty of parking, and there are normally few problems at Tecate. If you pass south of Maneadero or San Felipe without possessing a validated card you are breaking the law, and transgressors have recently received hefty fines. If you are headed for areas south of San Felipe you must have your card validated before you arrive there, for there is no *Migración* office. A few travelers have been able to get their cards validated at the agricultural inspection station just north of Guerrero Negro with no hassle, but this is obviously a hit-or-miss proposition—if the station is still there, if it is open, if the immigration official is there, and if he is feeling amiable, you might get by. There are a number of *Migración* offices in Baja, including the international airports and ferry offices—see the index.

Technically, you must return your single-entry card at the border when you depart Mexico, but few people actually do so, and border officials might be suspicious if you tried. This is the big problem with multiple-entry cards—there is no parking provided for this purpose at the border stations, and yet you must "check-out" properly if you intend to return without a hassle. Also, multiple-entry cards may be a source of complications if you attempt to validate them anywhere except at the border crossings.

In addition to a tourist card, a person under 18 traveling without both parents present must have a notarized letter granting permission to travel in Mexico. It must be signed by both parents if the minor is traveling alone, or by the parent not present if traveling with just one. If the child's parents are separated or divorced, the parent having custody must sign the letter, which must be accompanied by the separation or divorce papers. If one parent is dead, the living parent must sign the letter, which must be accompanied by the death certificate. If both parents are dead, the child's guardian must sign, and the letter must be accompanied by the guardianship papers. These requirements are rarely enforced in Baja.

Canadians

The rules described above for US tourists generally apply to Canadians as well. A valid passport or birth certificate is required to get a Mexican tourist card. A Canadian consulate is located in Tijuana—see the map on page 94, and Appendix B. Because of unfamiliarity with the currency and a lack of information as to the current exchange rate, Canadian dollars and travelers checks are not readily accepted in Mexico, and problems are sometimes encountered even in Southern California. Canadians should change their money into US dollars at the US-Canadian border and into pesos at the US-Mexican border. Because of the automatic conversion on billing or because the locals don't know the difference, Canadian credit cards seem to be as acceptable as US cards. The Canadian Department of Foreign Affairs and International Trade publishes a useful booklet, *Bon Voyage, But...*, describing visas, medical matters, import controls, consular matters, foreign laws, money, and many other subjects. The information in the booklet, together with other useful facts, is also available on the Department's Internet site—see Appendix B.

Pets

To take a dog or cat into Mexico you must obtain a rabies vaccination certificate and an Official Interstate and International Health Certificate for Dogs and Cats (Form 77-043), both signed by a licensed veterinarian, and have both

Dogs like to go to Baja, too; Soni the surfing Shorthair grabs a nice right at "Zippers"

approved by a Mexican consul. In practice, these requirements are often ignored in Baja.

To get back into the US, cats and dogs must be free of evidence of diseases communicable to man when examined at the port of entry. Dogs must have been vaccinated against rabies at least 30 days prior to entry into the US, except for puppies less than 3 months of age and for dogs located for 6 months or more in areas designated as being rabies-free. If a certificate is not available or the 30-day period has not elapsed, the animal can still be admitted with some hassle; information can be obtained at the border. US Customs has a booklet available, *Pets, Wildlife*, publication number 509, describing regulations on dogs, cats, birds, monkeys, and other pets and wildlife.

Canned dog food is available in many stores in Baja Norte. Cat food is hard to find south of the border cities, but inexpensive canned tuna and mackerel are readily available. In Baja Sur both canned and dried dog and cat foods are usually easy to find in the large towns. Cat litter is hard to find everywhere. Although most are involved in large-animal practice, there are many vets and a number of veterinary pharmacies.

Baja travel clubs

The Discover Baja Travel Club is one of the best of its kind. It offers monthly presentations at its San Diego office, covering topics ranging from plant identification to the history of the Spanish missions, as well as fishing seminars and Spanish classes. A resource center is available, providing more than 80 books on Baja and mainland Mexico, and displays Indian pottery and basketry. It publishes a lively, well-written bi-monthly newsletter, with feature articles of interest to Baja *aficionados*, news items, road reports, Customs regulations, peso exchange rates, and weather and fishing reports. Mexican insurance is offered at deep discounts for vehicles, motorcycles, boats, aircraft, and homes, together with discounts at hotels, RV parks, golf clubs, and restaurants, and at kayaking, diving, sportfishing, and other businesses throughout Baja. The club sponsors trips to Baja, and has books and maps, tourist cards, fishing licenses, and boat permits available. The $39 per year membership is a bargain, and you will more than recoup its cost in savings on your first trip.

The Vagabundos del Mar is another excellent club. The club sponsors fiestas, outings, and parties, long-range fishing trips out of San Diego at group rates, guided adventure tours to Baja and other locations, and fishing tournaments. The club offers: Mexican auto, RV, motor home, marine, aircraft, and homeowner's insurance; full roadside services; Mexican legal assistance for travelers; medical air service in the US and Mexico; books on Baja and elsewhere at special rates; discounts at many RV parks, restaurants, and other businesses in Baja, the western US and other locations; and discounts on marine accessories. In addition, the club can provide boat permits, tourist cards, and fishing licenses. *Chubasco*, the club's monthly newsletter, provides information of interest to Baja RVers and boaters.

The Vagabundos del Mar raft up during a July 1997 trip, and party time begins

Money and credit cards

Although US dollars are accepted almost anywhere, the Mexican national currency is pesos, and that is what the locals use and understand. If you use dollars, businessmen outside of the major tourist towns may not know the current exchange rate and will protect themselves by requiring an unfavorable exchange rate. If the person is dishonest, the transaction provides opportunities for flim-flam. Most money problems can be avoided by a simple expedient: convert some of your money to pesos. The decimal system is used and is easy to understand, and since almost all businesses make change in pesos anyway, you would soon be dealing with an impossible mix of pesos and dollars whether you like it or not. If this makes you uncomfortable, use a small calculator to figure the dollar equivalent of each purchase. If you don't have a calculator, Appendix A has a simple diagram that can enable you to convert back and forth between dollars and pesos.

The best way to convert dollars to pesos is by using an ATM (*cajero automatico*), available at most banks in Baja: the exchange rate is fair (eight ATM transactions during a recent foray into Baja were at almost exactly the "official" rate published in US newspapers for that period of time); there is no language barrier (instructions are available in both Spanish and English); there is no opportunity for dishonesty; it is far quicker than waiting in line in the bank; they often can be used when the bank is closed; and the ready availability of ATMs means you need not carry large amounts of cash on your trip. Cash withdrawals are normally limited to 1,500 pesos (about $150 at current exchange rates).

Money can also be changed at numerous *casas de cambio* (money-changing businesses), found at most tourist towns and all border crossings, and at many hotels and airports. While most money-changing businesses seem honest, it pays to ask for a calculator tape of the transaction and

study it closely before slipping your money through the window. Hoping you will not notice, a few businesses may try to figure a "commission" into the transaction, something not announced in the advertising of their buy and sell conversion rates. This is sometimes as much as an outrageous 10%, so ask first, and if any commission is charged, take your business elsewhere. You can convert pesos back to dollars when you return. There is competition, so shop around for the best rates. Hotels and airports offer the worst rates.

In 1875 a peso was worth almost exactly a dollar, but in recent years it has experienced an irregular but precipitous slide to about 3,500 to the dollar. Rather than dealing with the underlying reasons for the decline, the Mexican government issued "nuevo (new) pesos" in 1993, simply knocking three decimal places off the old, and then devaluated the nuevo peso by letting it "float" on world currency markets. (From this point on, nuevo pesos will be simply refereed to as pesos unless otherwise noted.) The peso, presently (1998) worth about 11 cents US (9.1 pesos per dollar), seems in danger of dropping even more, so don't convert large amounts into pesos or plan to hold them for long periods. Get your pesos in small denominations, for many businesses and gas stations can't make change for large peso notes.

It is very difficult to cash personal checks in Baja, so the remainder of what you expect to spend should be converted to small-denomination traveler's checks from large, well-recognized institutions such as Bank of America or American Express. Many tourist establishments will honor major credit cards, but don't plan to use them in smaller towns or at businesses catering to the local people.

Mail

Outside the larger towns, the post office is often in a small store, a tiny sign sometimes proclaiming "*Correo*," sometimes not. If you can't find it ask; everyone knows. Postage is very inexpensive. Hours of post office operation are erratic, and service ranges from mediocre to extremely bad. If you are lucky, delivery times to the US range from 5 days for Ensenada; 6 for La Paz, Bahía de los Angeles, and Loreto; 8 for El Rosario; 10 for Bahía Asunción, Cabo San Lucas, and Bahía Tortugas; to 13 for Mulegé, Isla Cedros, and Guerrero Negro. If you are not lucky, the sky is the limit—in preparing this book, about 50% of all letters written to Baja addresses took as long as 3 months to arrive, and the other 50% disappeared into thin air. I have had letters that took two years to get to their destination, and letters received from Baja often look like they had been trampled by wild horses.

Telephone

In the past, the telephone system in Baja provided poor service. However, automatic direct-dial equipment is being installed, and additional areas are getting service. Even Bahía de los Angeles and Cabo Pulmo now have phone systems. The system has been privatized, which should speed further improvements. In 1997 crews were digging trenches and installing fiber-optic telephone cable along the Transpeninsular, promising a new era in Baja communications.

Making a direct-dial call from the US or Canada to a location in Baja is simple. First, dial 011, telling the system that this is an international call, then the country code, which for Mexico is 52, and then the area code. All area codes in Baja have 3 digits, except for Ensenada, Mexicali, and Tijuana, which are 2-digit, 61, 65, and 66, respectively. Finally, dial the local number, which has five digits, except the three cities just named, which have six. Baja telephone numbers are listed in Appendix B in their full 13-digit form:

011 + 52 + area code (2 or 3 digits) + local number (6 or 5 digits)

The least expensive way to make a direct-dial call to the US or Canada while in Baja is to purchase a pre-paid TELNOR card, available in 25, 35, and 50-peso denominations from many stores in Baja. These are designed to work in pay phones labeled LADATEL or TELMEX. Simply insert the card, dial 95 and the area code and number. When 20 seconds is left on the card's balance of pesos, a countdown will appear in the readout window. Calls by this means to our home near Seattle cost 10 pesos ($1.13) per minute.

Many pay phones will accept Mexican coins. However, things usually seem to go awry, and there are often long and unexplained silences, ending when a computer bursts in with rapid-fire instructions in Spanish. The simplest way for those who do not speak Spanish but want to make a credit card call is to use AT&T, Sprint, or MCI. Each company has a toll-free 800 number that can be dialed directly from Mexico: AT&T is 95-800-462-4240; Sprint 95-800-877-8000; MCI 95-800-950-1022. These numbers directly access company facilities in the US, and from that point things are routine; you can then dial the area code and number you are trying to reach and your credit card number, or, if you must, you can place a collect call. Placing calls with the three companies in this manner can be done from private phones at hotels and RV parks, or from many pay phones.

Direct-dialed credit card calls from Mexico to the US and Canada cost about the same as the TELNOR pre-paid calls. A series of Sprint calls to the Seattle area, made at night from pay phones all over Baja during a recent trip averaged $1.14 a minute. A similar series of direct-dialed AT&T calls averaged $1.27 a minute, but since the calls over the two systems were from different locations in Baja, the difference is probably not meaningful. Operator-assisted and collect calls are much more expensive, and may involve a substantial surcharge: a number of AT&T operator-assisted calls from San Ignacio to the Seattle area cost us $1.75 a minute.

Large towns have telephone company offices, where international calls can be made. There are also private long-distance stations in smaller towns, usually staffed with an operator and often located in a pharmacy or other business; look for the sign LARGA DISTANCIA. Many hotel operators can also place international calls. If you use the services of these private companies or a hotel operator, they will add a surcharge.

You will see phones having signs proclaiming "Call USA, Canada or Worldwide, simply dial 0." Unless you are independently wealthy, these phone should be avoided. In early 1998 a call from Cabo San Lucas to my home east of Seattle would have cost $27.47 for the first 3 minutes, and $4.37 for each succeeding minute. That's no mis-print; $27.47 and $4.37!

Local and long-distance calls within Mexico are relatively inexpensive. All the Baja numbers listed in Appendix B are listed in their full 13-digit, international-call form. To make a call to one of these numbers from within the same area code, dial the last five digits (six in Ensenada, Mexicali, and Tijuana). To direct-dial a Baja number outside the local area code, dial 91, then the area code and local number.

Although public telephone service is absent in small villages along the Transpeninsular, many have at least one official telephone, often located in the *delegación municipal* building, which might be made available in an emergency.

Cellular phone service is available from a company named, appropriately enough, Baja Celular (there are others), with offices and coverage in Rosarito, Ensenada, Maneadero, San Quintín, Villa Insurgentes, Ciudad Constitución, La Paz, San José del Cabo, Cabo San Lucas, Tecate, San Felipe, and surrounding areas. Service can be established by visiting any of their offices (see the index), or by contacting your US cellular company, which may be able to establish roaming service in Baja. Take your phone to the Baja Celular office (analog only, no digitals), and they will activate the phone and provide it with a Mexican telephone number at which people in the US can call you. Ask for a list of emergency numbers and a coverage map.

You will be charged for activation (presently $38), which is good indefinitely. However, you must make at least one call every 60 days, or the service will be canceled. You will also be asked for a deposit for air time and long distance charges. Air time costs $0.47 per minute. They will accept most major credit cards or cash, and someone proficient in English is usually available at the offices. Your account balance can be determined at any time by calling a free number. If you exceed this balance during a call, you will not be cut off, but you will not be able to make any more calls until you visit an office and make a further deposit. Calls to emergency services (police, fire, etc.) can be made even if you have no balance. They offer several types of service and a number of payment plans, and service will be activated in all regions in Baja Norte served by Baja Celular. However, if you visit Baja Sur, you will have to activate there too if you wish to receive calls. When you return to the US, you can revert to your US phone number using a code provided by Baja Celular.

The altitude of the antennas at the Cape is high enough that the service extends well off-shore, and if you catch a marlin you can immediately call the gang at work to brag. In fact, why not dial them up when you make the hook-up and give them a blow-by-blow account?

Internet and e-mail

Need to check with your astrologer to see how the fishing will be tomorrow? Want to see what Motley Fool says about that stock you bought before you left? Oh, oh, bad news, and you need to tell Fidelity to sell it right away? Want to keep in touch with the sexy lady from the chat room? Worry not, for the Cyber Age has come to Baja! A small number of "Internet cafés" and computer service offices are now in business, variously providing computers (you will not find many Macs), modems, black-and-white and color printers, and scanners. The cafés also provide coffee, beer, wine, mixed drinks, snacks, and light meals. All cafés and offices offer a number of standard applications such as word processing, image processing, and spreadsheets (don't worry, they are in English), and walk-ins are welcome. Although the downloads from US addresses are rather slow, the cost of half-hour and one-hour blocks of time are quite reasonable. See the index for a list of cafés and service offices.

The problems with the mail and the telephone systems, terrible service and cost, respectively, were described earlier. The preferred communications system to and from Baja is now e-mail, the Cyber Age equivalent of the telegraph. Appendix B provides the e-mail addresses of many businesses and organizations on both sides of the border. All of the Baja Internet cafés and computer service offices provide e-mail service, and Eudora, Explorer, Navigator, TelNet, and similar programs are usually available. Make sure you know the password to your e-mail account, and remember to erase your mail once finished.

Public transportation and rental vehicles

International airports are located at Tijuana, Mexicali, Loreto, La Paz, and San José del Cabo. At present (early 1998) AeroCalifornia, Aerolitoral, AeroMexico, Alaska, America West, American, Continental, Mexicana, and North-

west offer flights between the US and Baja. Some have Internet sites where information and schedules can be obtained, and a few accept e-mail reservations.

A few airlines operate only within Mexico. Dubbed the "Cannery Airline," Aero Cedros flies Convair 440 cargo planes from Ensenada to Isla Cedros and Guerrero Negro. Flights leave the airport at El Ciprés south of Ensenada at 9:30 A.M. Tuesday through Friday. Delays and interruptions to service are frequent, but fares are low. Aerolineas California Pacifico offers flights between Guerrero Negro, Cedros, and Bahía Tortugas. Also, see Aereo Calafia, page 238.

The Mexican ferry system operates between Santa Rosalía and Guaymas, between La Paz and Topolobampo, and between La Paz and Mazatlán. The system is ill-managed and inefficient, information is difficult to obtain, and the reservation system is unreliable. The system is now run by a private company, and although increases in the quality of service have been promised, to date the most noticeable effect has been an increase in fares. However, fares are still not all that high, especially for foot passengers, the people are friendly, and the trip can be an interesting experience. The ferries can take RVs of any size, and bicycles and motorcycles are no problem. Accommodations range from inexpensive salon class, where you get a reclining chair, to private suites with bathroom and shower. There are frequent changes in schedules and in the regulations concerning boats and vehicles, and it would be wise to get current information before you depart the US. Also, you should make sure your Mexican insurance policy covers you in mainland Mexico—some apply only to Baja.

A number of Mexican bus companies operate in Baja California, several of which run between Tijuana and La Paz. A trip on one of these can be an unusual and inexpensive adventure, and bicyclists sometimes use them to great advantage. Information on schedules, routes, and terminal locations can be obtained from the tourism offices listed in Appendix B.

California Baja Rent-A-Car offers rental vehicles that can be taken anywhere is Baja, not just the border cities. The vehicles available include Jeep Wranglers and Cherokees, Hummers, and Ford Explorers, as well as Suburbans, passenger vans, and conventional autos. If you only want to go one way, a drop-off can be made in Cabo San Lucas for an extra charge.

Other US automobile rental companies vary in their regulations on bringing their cars into Mexico. Most prohibit it altogether, but a few—Dollar, for instance—will allow them to be taken into Baja as far south as Ensenada. Most of the tourist hotels have a rental agency in the lobby or can otherwise arrange rentals, and all the international airports have rental desks. Taxis are available in all large cities and in some of the smaller ones like Loreto.

Vehicle regulations

Your US or Canadian driver's license is valid for driving your own vehicle or a rental vehicle. You must have valid original registrations or notarized bills of sale for all vehicles, driven, towed, or carried, and for trailers and boats. Bring the original and two copies. If there is a lien on any of these, or if any are borrowed, you must have a notarized letter from the lienholder or owner authorizing you to take it into Mexico, who will probably require proof of insurance. You cannot lend, rent, or sell your vehicle to a Mexican.

Temporary import permits for vehicles are not required in Baja as they are on the mainland, but if you decide to take the ferry to the mainland they are available at the ferry office in La Paz **but not in Santa Rosalía**. With stunning logic, a Customs official in Santa Rosalía recently explained why: "We can't issue the permits because we don't have the forms." There are several important complications involved in obtaining these permits. For instance, only one permit will be issued per person. If you are alone and have your motorcycle aboard your pickup, you have a problem. The number of permits issued is also limited to the number of licensed drivers. Those anticipating taking the ferry from Baja to the mainland should obtain current information from a Mexican Consulate or Tourism Office concerning the requirements for temporary import permits. Ask them to mail you a copy of *Traveling to Mexico by Car*, published by the Secretary of Tourism. This booklet describes the procedures required to enter mainland Mexico, as well as those required when you leave—you must "check out" properly. Later chapters will provide the locations of ticket offices and the ferry terminals in Santa Rosalía and La Paz.

Vehicle insurance

Mexico does not require vehicle insurance, but it would be foolish to drive without it. Mexican law treats accidents seriously, and they may be considered as criminal as well as civil matters. If you have an accident, the police will determine whether you are responsible. You will usually be free to leave in a few hours if you are not at fault, or the next day if written statements are necessary. If you are at fault, your vehicle may be impounded, and you will be charged and brought before a judge. You may be held until judgments against you are satisfied, and a Mexican insurance policy is a swift way of proving financial responsibility and reducing red tape. Although some American and Canadian policies partially cover vehicles while in Mexico, the Mexican government does not recognize such insurance as proof of financial responsibility.

In general, Mexican policies can be written to provide the same five basic coverages available in the US: collision and upset; fire and total theft; property damage liability; bodily injury liability; and medical payments. Unfortunately, uninsured motorist coverage is not available. According to one company, about 92% of Mexican drivers do not carry auto insurance, so if you are in an accident and the other party is at fault, you almost certainly will never collect a dime. Theft coverage provides only for total theft, not pilferage of contents (your homeowner's policy may cover this).

You will invalidate coverage if you are drunk or under the influence of drugs, if you are unlicensed, or if you permit an unlicensed driver to drive. If you are towing a trailer, it has to be insured along with the tow vehicle. Under such coverage, a boat is insured only while being towed or attached to the insured tow vehicle, not while afloat.

These policies are designed for tourists, and there are additional restrictions: your citizenship and your street address must be anywhere except Mexico; you may not reside year-round in Mexico; your vehicle may neither have Mexican license plates nor be kept year-round in Mexico; and the purpose of your visit must be pleasure, not business, commercial, or organized charitable activity. Also, items carried on the top, front, or bed (except 5th wheelers) of any vehicle, and vehicle and boat accessories not bolted on, are not covered.

Policies for one day or more are available at many insurance offices in the US near all border crossings, some having drive-up services open seven days a week. Instant Mexico Auto Insurance Services, for instance, located at the last exit before the San Ysidro border crossing, is open 24 hours a day, and will write policies for a stated number of days while you wait. You must present your registration or notarized affidavit from lien holders and your driver's license. They offer discounts for long policies, ranging from 10% for 30 days to about 70% for 360 days, and accept VISA, MasterCard, and American Express cards. In addition, they offer tourist cards, fishing licenses, and boat permits. There are other companies offering such around-the-clock, drive-in services. The best insurance rates are offered by the Discover Baja Travel Club and the Vagabundos del Mar.

Where is the break-even point, where it pays to buy an annual policy, even though you plan to be in Baja less than a year? The conventional wisdom says 30 days, but an analysis of the daily and annual rates from a number of companies and organizations says something different. To some extent, it will be comparing apples and oranges, since the policies and benefits are not exactly the same, but, roughly, if you own a rig valued at $10,000, the break-even point is about 13 days, and it ranges down to about 10 days as the value of the rig increases. Despite the fact that some companies selling daily policies offer discounts ranging from 10% at 30 days up to about 70% at 360 days, the savings of an annual policy grow with the length of the trip. The bottom line: if you will be in Baja for more than several weeks, savings can be obtained by getting an annual policy, rather than a daily policy.

Some American insurance companies provide full coverage while in Mexico. United Services, for instance, extends all coverages, including uninsured motorist, to vehicles within 75 miles of the border. In addition, the company's umbrella policy will extend the liability limits of a Mexican policy, providing that it covers at least $100,000/person and $300,000/accident for bodily injury. If your Mexican policy has lower limits, you will be responsible for the "gap" between the Mexican policy and your umbrella policy. There are problems, however. For instance, the 75-mile limit will let you go as far south as Ensenada, but not to San Felipe, nor even to the junction at Crucero la Trinidad, and your American policy will not be accepted by Mexican authorities as proof of financial responsibility. Other American insurance companies have their own rules, so you should check with your company about coverage. Some American insurance companies can provide Mexican policies for their customers through Mexican affiliates.

Gasoline and diesel fuel

Petroleum products are sold by PEMEX, a government monopoly. In the US, different oil companies may have service stations on all four corners of an intersection, each competing vigorously by offering clean rest rooms, computer-assisted tune-ups, parts, and repair services, as well as gas and oil. Operating under monopoly conditions, PEMEX does not find it necessary to work so hard. Stations rarely offer more than gas and oil and a small selection of filters, additives, fan belts, and minor parts. Multi-grade oils and oils of 30 weight and less are hard to find. Encountering an operational rest room is a cause for surprise, and one both clean and operational a cause for a telegram to the Vatican. If you are lucky enough to find a suitable rest room, don't press things too far—bring your own toilet paper. PEMEX does not take plastic, so payment must be in cash. Dollars are usually accepted, but expect to get an unfavorable exchange rate. Stations are rarely open all night and they offer no mechanical services; they are gas stations, not service stations—if you need mechanical assistance you go to a *mechánico*. You will probably have to check your own oil and tire pressure, and many stations do not have an air compressor. If you run out of gas do not expect to find a container to borrow at the station.

Mexican gasoline now comes in two grades, Magnasin and Premium. Both are lead-free and cost roughly what similar grades would cost in the US. The actual octanes of Magnasin and Premium are considerably lower than advertised, leading to pinging problems in some engines. If your engine pings with Magnasin, start using Premium. If this doesn't solve the problem "octane boosting" additives are available on both sides of the border. Some people report success with JB Gas Treatment and Moroso. Diesel fuel comes from a red pump, and can be easier to find than in the US. It too goes for about the same as diesel would cost north of the border.

In fairness to PEMEX, it must be noted that real efforts are being made to upgrade existing stations with new paint and facilities, new stations are being constructed at a number of locations on the peninsula, and they have finally ceased production of Nova, a grade of gasoline heavily laced with lead, a health hazard to both humans and catalytic converters. Now, if they could only keep some fuel in the tanks at Parador Punta Prieta and Cataviña.

Chapters 9 through 13 identify all PEMEX stations known to be in operation in Baja south of the border cities, as well as a few places where local entrepreneurs sell gasoline out of drums or tanks. In the larger towns and cities their locations are shown on the maps. The text identifies the others and the types of fuel normally available as M (Magnasin), P (Premium), and D (diesel).

LPG (Liquefied Petroleum Gas)

The LPG sold in Baja is not 100% propane. To enable excess quantities of butane produced by the manufacture of gasoline to be disposed of, butane and other gases are often mixed with propane in Mexico. The amount of butane present varies widely from place to place and time to time. The characteristics of butane are quite different than those of propane, but the mixture seems to have no major adverse effects on refrigerators, stoves, water heaters, or other appliances designed for straight propane. Chapters 9 through 13 identify all LPG yards known to be in operation in Baja south of the border cities. Although village stores often lack an LPG pump, they can sometimes provide gravity fills from tanks, but it will not be possible to completely fill your tank. LPG is not available at PEMEX stations.

It is inadvisable to drive LPG vehicles into Baja. LPG is widely used for domestic purposes in Baja, and it is not uncommon to find two dozen cars and trucks lined up at the local yard early in the morning, some with a dozen or more 25-gallon cylinders to fill. The line does not always get shorter as the day wears on, and spot shortages are common. It's one thing to have to wait in line once a month to fill the cylinders for your trailer, another if it's every day to keep your engine humming along. Mechanics and parts for LPG vehicles are not available in Baja.

Parts, service, and repairs

Parts stores in Baja tend to be small, often with incomplete inventories, but they can obtain what you need, given enough time, and you might find parts for your RV such as gas regulators in general and hardware stores, and potable water pumps and other useful gadgets in marine supply stores. A few marine parts stores, several marinas, and the parts departments at some auto dealerships have limited parts for small boat and utility trailers, such as bearings, springs, tires, wheels, and bunker rollers, and their mechanics should be able to get you going again. Specialized parts for four-wheel-drive and all parts for off-brand vehicles may be hard to get, as may those for diesel vehicles. Chapters 9 through 13 list many parts stores and mechanics.

If needed parts are not available locally, there is a quick way to get them: telephone a dealer in the US, order what you want, have it shipped to you by way of DHL Worldwide Express, and pay for the parts, shipping, and customs fees with a credit card. You can save a great deal of time and hassle if you tell the dealer to ship the parts "DDP" (delivery duty paid). DHL has offices in Tijuana, Mexicali, and

La Paz (addresses and telephone numbers in Appendix B), and delivery time is normally only a day or two. DHL can also provide delivery to other locations; for instance, the La Paz office can deliver to San José del Cabo, Cabo San Lucas, Todos Santos, and Ciudad Constitución; the Tijuana office to Tecate, Ensenada, and Maneadero; and the Mexicali office to San Felipe. Local delivery to the towns surrounding La Paz, Tijuana, and Mexicali usually adds a day or two. If you have access to the Internet, you can track your shipment using the address provided in Appendix B. United Parcel Service offers similar services, and they claim they can deliver to any address in Mexico.

There are US-style automobile dealerships in Ensenada (Chevrolet, Dodge/Chrysler, Nissan, Volkswagen, and Ford), Ciudad Constitución (Chevrolet and Nissan), La Paz (Chevrolet, Dodge/Chrysler, Nissan, Volkswagen, and Ford), the San José del Cabo area (Nissan and Volkswagen), and Cabo San Lucas (Chevrolet). Souto Performance and Auto and Truck Repair in Ensenada offers virtually every service associated with the maintenance and repair of street-, off-road-, and recreational vehicles.

Wahoo RV Center in San José del Cabo specializes in RV service and repairs and can supply parts. Other than this, non-automotive RV parts and tires are almost unavailable in Baja. Marina de La Paz and Marina Palmira in La Paz, and Marina Cabo San Lucas in Cabo San Lucas carry an inventory of common parts oriented toward boat trailers but possibly useful on other types as well.

Most towns and some smaller settlements have a mechanic, but he may not be in business full-time and may not even have a sign posted. While these mechanics often show great ingenuity, parts may take a week or more to get, and they can do little with electronic ignition, smog-control, or fuel-injector problems. They do not have machine-shop equipment needed for turning down brake drums and discs, planing down warped heads, or facing off flywheels. Work on automatic transmissions must be scrupulously clean, an impossibility in most locations.

New tires are difficult to purchase outside of the larger towns, but many *llanterias* (tire shops) make repairs and sell used tires at very low prices, some in fairly good condition. Batteries are available in most parts stores and in some PEMEX stations, but you may have difficulty in locating a battery with side terminals or deep-cycle RV or marine batteries.

Local motoring traditions

Mexicans have driving habits that are distinctly different from those of Americans and Canadians. They often use the left-turn signal for highly ambiguous purposes, such as signaling a left turn to indicate that it is safe for you to pass. Intended as a courtesy, this signal can be dangerous. I have seen this signal from a vehicle moving at highway speed and have started to pass it, only to have the vehicle swerve into a left turn, its brake lights out of operation. In periods of reduced visibility, truckers often signal a left turn to oncoming traffic to mark the left margin of their rig, since their clearance lights are often burned out. I once had an oncoming trucker signal a left during a rainstorm, only to have him suddenly swerve left in front of me, leaving me shaken and angry in the ditch. Both the "safe-to-pass" and "left-side" signals should be greeted with great suspicion—don't leave the driving to others.

Some locals are poor drivers, with no training and little experience, and their vehicles are often in bad condition, with poor brakes, worse tires, and headlights missing or out of adjustment, although Baja's increasing prosperity is making these less common each year. Their low beams are frequently burned out, and in approach situations they will sometimes turn off their lights in an effort to avoid blinding you, a startling courtesy. What appeared to be an approaching motorcycle once blinded me with his high beam. When he switched to low beam, he suddenly seemed to swerve across the road. To avoid a head-on crash I swerved right and thumped across the desert for 50 yards. I was cursing all the world's motorcyclists as he sped away, until I saw a pair of tail lights and realized what had happened; it was a pickup with burned-out right low-beam and left high-beam lights.

Not rain, nor darkness, nor heavy traffic, nor fatigue, nor worn tires, not even monstrous potholes slow Mexican truckers in keeping their appointed rounds, and the resulting wreckage can be seen scattered along the Transpeninsular. Some big rigs sport muffler cutouts. Ostensibly installed to save fuel, their real purpose is to terrorize. Many trucks are graced by hand-lettered slogans, including the Spanish versions of such familiar American standards as "King of the Road," "Passing Side-Suicide" and, yes, even "Death Before Dishonor." Most convey mere bravado, but one should elicit deep respect, a skull and crossbones with "*Precaución: Benzedrinos*" lettered on each side. Believe it.

It is becoming increasingly common to encounter military checkpoints, perhaps a dozen or more on a trip the length of the Transpeninsular. No "probable cause" is required for a search of your vehicle, and the personnel are usually military, not police, with sub-machine guns close at hand. This is very threatening to people from countries like the US, where military personnel are normally prohibited from enforcing civil law. The purpose of these inspections is, of course, the control of drug and gun trafficking, so if it happens to you remember that we, the US, have put heavy pressure on Mexico to do just this. The soldiers are neatly dressed and very polite.

● ●

Under attack

During a recent trip, Michael and I stopped at a checkpoint manned by military personnel, the guns dangling carelessly over their shoulders making us a bit nervous. We were about to open the back of our pickup for inspection, when there was a loud BANG, and we both scurried for cover on the opposite side of the truck. After a few seconds of heavy anxiety, we found out what had made the noise—a tire on a soldier's bicycle had blown out. The adrenaline was still flowing as we drove off, and each of us was a bit keyed up. We were still talking about the incident 30 minutes later, when there was a much louder BANG, and we both flinched and ducked for cover below the level of the windows in the truck. It sounded like a mortar or a hand grenade, but an anxious look in the rear-view mirror revealed its source—a huge rear tire on a tractor had blown out as its driver was filling it with air in a PEMEX station. We were nervous wrecks for the rest of the afternoon.

• •

Driving the Transpeninsular

Paved road systems have existed in the northern part of Baja Norte and the southern part of Baja Sur for many years, but it was not until 1973 that the Transpeninsular Highway was finally completed. The only paved road extending the length of the peninsula, the Transpeninsular was built to modest engineering specifications. It is narrower than its US counterparts, shoulders are often nonexistent, striping and safety signs are normally absent, and culverting and drainage are poor. The sub-base is inadequate and the paving thin, often as little as a half-inch thick, and heavy traffic quickly produces a moonscape of potholes. However, in recent years the government has made an effort to upgrade the highway. Concrete bridges have been completed at a number of stream crossings that used to cause trouble after rains, parts of the

The road department has been busy, and chuckholes like this five-incher being measured by John Anglin are not as common as they used to be on the Transpeninsular

highway are even beginning to sport center lines and warning signs, and road crews are trying to keep ahead of the potholes. Things still go wrong; winter storms washed out 6 short stretches of the Transpeninsular near Loreto one year, and 6 months later not a shovel or a pick had been lifted to make repairs.

There are two basic safety rules on the Transpeninsular: never speed and never drive at night. In level country 45 miles an hour is the highest speed than can be sustained safely under the best of conditions, and in hilly terrain the safe speed may be less than 30. Much of Baja is open, unfenced rangeland, and cattle, burros, and goats wander onto the highway. At night a black cow may be draped over your hood before your foot can reach the brake pedal. The short days of winter require that additional driving time be scheduled; a border-to-the-Cape trip takes three full days in winter if driving is limited to daylight hours and safe speeds. A table of distances between points on the Transpeninsular will be found in Appendix A.

Do not depend on finding gasoline at every station along the Transpeninsular, especially on long holidays and during winter. The PEMEX stations at Cataviña and Villa Jesús María are remote from shipping terminals, and tank trucks are sometimes delayed by mechanical, weather, or road problems. The station at Parador Punta Prieta is the most notorious on the Transpeninsular Highway for unreliability. It will be pumping gas one month, and appear deserted the next, its pumps even being removed. Later, several months perhaps, it reappears and begins pumping, only to unaccountably disappear soon after. **Do not depend on obtaining gas at this station.** If you plan to drive to Bahía de los Angeles, be sure to read the comments on the PEMEX station there before you go—see page 139. Some stations depend on locally generated electricity, often produced by tiny gasoline-driven generators, and if these will not run there is no way to operate the pumps. A pump failure a few years ago put the station at Cataviña out of operation for two months. If one station can't pump gas, those on either side quickly run out and problems spread like falling dominoes. The basic rule for drivers in this notorious "gas gap" is to top off before your tank is half-empty.

Speaking Spanish

An inability to speak Spanish is apt to be far less of a problem than many people imagine. English and Spanish share a Latin root and have many words in common. Many locals have been to the US or have dealt with Americans for years and hence speak a bit of English. If you can't get through verbally, there still may be hope. Once, Michael and I needed answers to some rather complex questions about the services offered by Baja Celular. We stopped at their office in Villa Insurgentes, but our Spanish and their English were not up to the task. We were stymied for several minutes, when I remembered that my laptop computer in the truck had Spanish Assistant, a translation program, on its hard drive. In a few minutes there was a lively exchange of

Most of the time you are out of luck if the electricity fails, but sometimes local ingenuity can solve the problem

questions and answers, with huge grins on everyone's faces. There are other ways. If you don't know the word for a physical object, draw a picture; if you need a spare part, bring the broken one. In the El Rosario supermarket, my friend Rob Watson and I wanted to buy some honey, but could not find it. Neither of us could remember the word, and we did not have a dictionary, so Rob tried to act out what we wanted. Fluttering his hands at his shoulders and skipping down the aisles on tiptoes emitting loud buzzes, he stuck his face into a display of plastic flowers. At first there were dumfounded looks, but with a roar of laughter everyone got the idea at the same time, and there was a rush to show us where the *miel de abeja* was to be found. An American lady once tried to use this method to explain to a La Paz pharmacist that she needed a box of suppositories. There was a great deal of confusion at first over exactly what was required, but the correct message was finally understood.

Getting into and out of trouble

The things that are illegal in Baja are probably the same sorts of things that are illegal in your home town. The most common causes of jail sentences or deportation are possession of recreational drugs, problems resulting from alcohol consumption, and working without a permit. Public drunkenness is against the law in Mexico. Leave your stash and your nose candy at home—offenders found guilty of possessing more than a token amount of any narcotic substance, including marijuana and cocaine, are subject to a minimum

sentence of 10 years—read it again: a minimum sentence of 10 years—and it is not uncommon for persons charged with drug offenses to be detained for up to a year before a verdict is reached. Worldwide, Mexico has the highest number of arrests of Americans abroad—over 1,000 per year—and the highest prison population of Americans outside the US, about 450 at any one time. Jailbirds are not coddled in Mexico—the sign MUNICIPAL DUMP pointing to the Ensenada prison says it all.

Most legal rights enjoyed in the US are also found in Mexico, and foreigners (you) have virtually the same rights as citizens, but there are important procedural differences. If you need help, there is a US Consulate General in Tijuana, and a Consular Agency in Cabo San Lucas. (The Consular Agency in Mulegé has been closed.) The US State Department maintains a Citizen's Emergency Center in Washington, D.C., which can be reached by telephone. Both the State Secretary of Tourism of Baja California [Norte] and the State Secretary of Tourism of Baja California Sur have Tourist Assistance Departments to provide free legal assistance to

This boy could not speak a word of English, but he was able to make his intentions clear—he was going to carry Jim Smallwood's pack all the way up Cañon San Bernardo

tourists—see the index for locations. In the towns and villages, civil authority is exercised by the *delegado*, an elected official who can be found at the *Delegación Municipal* or *Subdelegación* building. In remote areas a local citizen may be appointed to perform similar duties.

If you need physical assistance, help can come from a number of sources. There are teams providing ambulance, paramedical, off-road, mountain search and rescue, and similar services, located in Tijuana, Mexicali, and Ensenada, with smaller organizations in a number of towns and villages. These can be contacted through local civil and military authorities. The famous Green Angel patrol operates over most paved highways in Baja. It consists of green pickups, each normally crewed by two men, one of whom hopefully is proficient in English. They can assist with minor repairs, provide small parts, sell gas and oil at cost, and arrange for towing and repairs. Although some routes are patrolled twice a day in mainland Mexico, in Baja it is more often once a day and sometimes not even that. Tow trucks are based in the border cities, Rosarito, Ensenada, San Quintín, San Felipe, Guerrero Negro, San Ignacio, Santa Rosalía, Loreto, Ciudad Constitución, La Paz, San José del Cabo, and Cabo San Lucas. Should medical problems become serious and the facilities in Baja prove to be inadequate, all is not lost—Aeromedical Group and Critical Air Medicine specialize in transporting critically ill and injured patients to the US by aircraft, and operate throughout Baja. Marine emergencies are discussed in Chapter 4.

Hmmmmmmm; let me think about that for a minute

Radio communications

CB radio is monitored by many boaters, RV drivers, and organizations such as the Green Angels, various rescue teams, and CB clubs in Ensenada and La Paz. Local citizens often use CB as a substitute for a telephone system. There is little agreement as to the proper channel for emergency communications. As in the US, channel 9 is the most frequently monitored, but some organizations monitor channel 1, 3, 4, 7, 10, or 16, so if you are listening for others needing help, use your scanner. You are allowed to broadcast only on channels 9, 10, and 11, and only for personal communications and emergency assistance. Some caravan operators strongly advise participants to get a CB.

Since January 1, 1991, permits for CB radios are no longer required for US and Canadian citizens. However, the regulations concerning permits frequently change, and if you plan to bring a CB, contact a consulate or tourism office beforehand and get the latest information. Marine communications are discussed in Chapter 4.

Staying clean

Laundromats can be found in towns along the Transpeninsular from the border to Guerrero Negro and from Santa Rosalía to the Cape (a laundromat can also found at Bahía Tortugas, far off the Transpeninsular). In areas off the Transpeninsular, you may be able to find a traditional Mexican washerwoman, and some hotels, motels, and RV establishments provide laundry service if you are a guest. Vel, a solid detergent bar widely available in Baja, washes human bodies satisfactorily in salt water, but to avoid a sticky film, don't air-dry yourself; use a towel. Joy dishwashing detergent has long been the standard among yachtsmen for washing dishes in salt water.

Staying well

Diarrhea is the most talked-about and feared malady in Mexico, but during many trips to Baja, I have experienced it only once, its source being the most expensive restaurant in Cabo San Lucas. Although there are other causes, the water usually gets the blame. However, all cities and most larger villages have installed modern systems. Some of the remote villages, including Punta Abreojos, La Bocana (the one north of Asunción), and Bahía Asunción, have desalinization plants that turn out better water than anything you have probably ever drunk. In addition, clean, inexpensive bottled water is available from many reverse-osmosis plants and virtually all food stores in Baja. It is thus possible to completely avoid water problems with little expense or trouble by simply using bottled water for drinking and food preparation, and reserving local water for washing and flushing. If you must use local water, treat it with bleach (8 to 16 drops per gallon), or with Microdyn or boil it for 30 minutes. Microdyn and bleach can also be used for disinfecting fruit and vegetables. Even so, bring some Imodium A-D along in your first aid kit—it is highly effective. Microdyn and Imodium A-D are available in many Baja supermarkets and pharmacies.

Don't forget about the purity of ice. If you have an LPG refrigerator with a freezer, make your own ice for drinks out of purified water. If you have only a cooler, be careful with block ice, for it is often not made from purified water. Keep food in contact with the ice in Ziplocks, and carefully wipe dry cans and bottles that get wet. Cube ice can be obtained in plastic bags in many stores, but look for the word *purificada* (purified) on the bag.

There are other causes of diarrhea, but you can easily make yourself virtually diarrhea-proof: take care with water, avoid greasy, highly seasoned, and unaccustomed foods; wash, peel, and/or cook all fresh food; and take care in selecting restaurants. Also, according to recent articles in the scientific literature, studies have shown that two of the most common diarrhea-causing bacteria, *Shigella* and *Salmonella*, are vulnerable to alcohol. So if you want to take a tot or two of tequila or several margaritas with your meals, you now have a scientific excuse.

If you do get diarrhea and there are no unusual symptoms, take your Imodium A-D according to the instructions on the box, get plenty of rest, and practice diet control. Drink plenty of fruit juices and treated water, and avoid milk and diuretics like coffee and tea.

Sunblock lotions of number 15 or higher are essential, at least for light-skinned people. Bull Frog SPF 36 Waterproof works well for people in and out of the water. If you start using a sunscreen, keep using it, for it offers no residual protection and your skin will not have had a chance to acclimate. I have a light complexion, and it used to seem that I could even get "moon-burned," but with modern sunblocks I can now make a two-week trip to Baja and return home only slightly pink. Lips are highly susceptible to burning and resultant lip cancer, but effective lip balms containing sunblocks are available. No matter how good your sunscreen is, nor how religiously you apply it, wear a hat, a long-sleeved shirt, and long pants. Also, be careful of exposed feet: sunburned feet can be very painful, especially when returned to the confines of shoes. Sunblock and lip balm are available in many Baja pharmacies and food stores. If you do get burned, get out of the sun and apply cold, wet dressings or a commercial burn preparation. To avoid infection do not break blisters, but instead let them dry up naturally.

One of the insect pests found in Baja are the *jejénes*, tiny biting insects. They are small enough that they can squeeze through the screening on your RV or boat, or through the netting of your tent. Sometimes they react to DEET, sometimes not, but they are found near areas with rotting marine vegetation and are very localized, so moving your rig a few hundred yards often removes you from the menu. Some Baja old-timers swear by Avon Skin-So-Soft bath oil. "Come on now," you are thinking, "you gotta be kidding," but there is a report in the scientific literature that the product has four ingredients insects avoid, coumarin being the most effective. Coumarin is a natural product used by many species of plants to repel insects, so it all figures out. So, if DEET doesn't do it, try some Avon.

Everyone likes an occasional evening campfire, and burnable materials like wood and cactus and *agave* debris are usually not hard to find. However, scorpions love to hide in such fuel materials, and most stings occur while people are making and maintaining fires, often when they have their minds on cooking. Use a pair of leather work gloves to handle firewood, and never stack it in your arms or allow it to touch the rest of your body. Also, since scorpions are nocturnal, never go barefoot at night. In the morning, shake out your bedding and shoes. I have always followed these simple precautions and have never been stung, but one evening a friend told me it seemed that I was over-reacting to the threat of scorpions—he didn't worry about them and had never been stung. Not five minutes later he was returning to the campfire with an armload of *agave* when a big one nailed him.

Other than applying cold compresses to the site of the bite and taking analgesics like aspirin or Tylenol, there is little that can be done in the way of first aid, and the symptoms generally last less than four hours. There is an immediate sharp pain, like a bee sting, followed by swelling and bruising, a "pins and needles" sensation, and/or numbness. A victim showing unusual symptoms should be taken to a doctor.

A prescription is not needed for many common drugs, and in rural areas the people often rely on the pharmacist for medical advice. There are numerous local physicians and dentists, many of whom speak some English, hospitals and clinics can be found in most settled areas, and some of the small villages have a Red Cross station, a few of them equipped with ambulances manned by enthusiastic drivers. Rob Watson once cracked up his trail bike while speeding down a beach near Colonet—witnesses said both he and the bike flew 10 feet into the air after he hit a hole, but the bike unfortunately came down second and landed on top of him. I drove him into town to get stitched up, the ambulance drivers quickly loaded him up, and with siren blaring and lights flashing they roared down the road to the clinic—200 yards away, the most exciting event in Colonet in 6 months.

Leaving your rig

Mexican law says a pleasure boat can remain in the country for the duration of its owner's tourist card, for up to six months. This law is still in effect, but in April, 1996, Mexico established new regulations concerning the importation of boats and trailers into the country. It was well-intended—it supposedly made things simpler—but as is so often the case in Mexico, it was poorly drafted, leaving it open to differing interpretations among *Aduana* personnel who must enforce it and travelers who must comply.

Basically, it requires the issuance of a 20-year temporary importation permit for boats and trailers that are to be in Mexico longer than six months, or that will remain in the country while the owner is absent. The permit is issued at no cost by the *Aduana* having jurisdiction where the boat or vehicle is to be left. A current, valid registration and a copy of the title is required, along with tourist card and a passport, a birth certificate or other means of proving citizenship and identity.

Two years have passed since this law went into effect, and there are many unanswered questions, and interpretations seem to change month-by-month. I recently interviewed officials from four *Aduana* offices in Baja, and there was no agreement even on the most basic questions: to whom and to what does it apply? Are kayaks and prams boats? What kind of trailers: boat, travel, motorcycle, and/or utility? Does it apply to yachts that enter Mexico by sea and/or boats brought into Mexico by trailer or car top? Is a permit required even for short visits, say a week at San Felipe? One official thought it applied to all boats and trailers brought into the country, no matter how short the visit; another said it applied only to boats and trailers that would be in the country for more than six months; and one claimed there was no such permit.

Travelers who are planning a trip to Baja with a boat or trailer should contact the Discover Baja Travel Club, the Vagabundos del Mar, a Mexican Consulate or Consular Agency, a Mexican Government Tourism Office, the State Secretary of Tourism of Baja California [Norte], or the State Secretary of Tourism of Baja California Sur to get the latest interpretations.

Bringing things back

Most people like to buy things in Baja that they need or that will remind them of the good time they had. However, you can't haul back just anything. The most common "tourist" items, like T-shirts and other clothing, leather work, ceramics, glass products, *serapes* (brightly colored, blanket-like shawls), *huaraches* (leather sandals), arts and crafts like ironwood carvings, figurines, silver jewelry, and so forth are no problem. Some other things are either prohibited or restricted, including certain kinds of fruits, vegetables, plants, plant products, soils, meats, meat products, hard corals, feathers, reptiles, and snails, as well as other live animals and animal products. Common items offered for sale in Baja that are illegal to import into the US include Cuban cigars, sea-turtle products such as jewelry and cosmetics containing turtle shell or oil, whale bones, teeth, and baleen, wildlife curios such as stuffed iguanas, some species of cacti, and virtually all live birds. All jewelry made from black coral is prohibited, and it is wise to avoid glazed cups, dishes, and other items intended to serve food—many contain unacceptable levels of lead. Remember, just because it may be legal to buy something in Mexico does not necessarily mean that it is legal to import it into the US, neither will the excuse "The man I bought it from said it was legal" carry any weight.

Upon returning to the US from Mexico, you are currently (1998) allowed a maximum of $400 in duty-free personal and household goods, including one liter of alcoholic beverage (if you are at least 21 years old), 100 cigars, and 200 cigarettes. Sales slips, invoices, or other evidence of purchase is helpful when you complete your customs decla-

ration. Gifts mailed from Mexico to people in the US are free of duty if the value of the entire package does not exceed $100. Non-gift purchases mailed to the US may pass without collection of duty if their value does not exceed $200. This exemption does not apply to perfume containing alcohol if it is valued at more than $5 retail, nor to alcoholic beverages, cigars, or cigarettes. The outer wrapping of packages must be marked with the contents, fair retail value, and whether the package is a gift ($100 exemption) or for personal use ($200).

Both the US and Mexico are signatories to a United Nations convention which makes it illegal to remove from Mexico or import into the US certain cultural property. In addition, US Customs enforces the Convention on Cultural Property Act. The provisions of these are complex, but basically what they boil down to is that if you intend to bring back something that is old or unusual, outside the realm of ordinary tourist items, it would be well to discuss it with US Customs first.

US Customs has a useful booklet, *Know Before You Go*, publication number 512, which contains detailed information on restricted and prohibited articles. Customs also maintains an Internet site containing a traveler's information page with information on restricted and prohibited merchandise; medications, and drugs; arriving by private boat, plane, or car; exiting the US; mailing goods to the US; pets and animals; and frequently asked questions, as well as the materials in the booklet *Know Before You Go*.

Canadians returning home should make themselves familiar with Canadian regulations, and those returning by way of the US should obtain *Customs Hints for Visitors (Nonresidents)*, publication 511-A, available from the US Customs Service.

Survive the savage desert?

The early sportsmen and adventurers who visited Baja were concerned with finding ways to survive the "savage" desert, but today the problem is the reverse. Slowly in most places, and not so slowly in others, Baja is showing increasing signs of the stresses of civilization.

One of the major problems involves the disposal of trash. Cans, bottles, and other trash disfigure arid landscapes for years and perhaps "forever." Plastic products are being recognized as particularly dangerous to wildlife. Surveys have shown that plastic items account for half of the man-made products on the ocean's surface, and sandwich bags, styrofoam cups and pellets, six-pack yokes, picnic utensils, and bottles are being found on even the most remote beaches of the world. Some scientists believe that these are an even greater source of mortality among marine animals than the highly publicized oil spills and heavy metals. Discarded fishing nets, monofilament line, and six-pack yokes are especially dangerous to fish, seabirds, and marine mammals, who often die when they become entangled in them. Some species of turtles are attracted by plastic bags, which look like

Rob Watson

This fellow almost strangled in a net until we rescued him

the jellyfish they eat. Birds have been found with pens, toy soldiers, poker chips, and fishing bobbers in their stomachs. A few years ago yachties headed for Cabo San Lucas spotted a sea bird with its head rammed through the side of a large plastic jug; apparently the bird thought the jug was prey of some sort and dove on it head first! With the aid of scissors the jug was cut off and the bird flew away.

The best policy for short visits is a conscientious effort to bring back home everything—every wrapper, every can, every bottle, every toothpaste tube, every inch of discarded fishing line. Many Baja kayakers and bicyclists, despite their extremely limited space and ability to carry weight, seem to be able to leave immaculate campsites, with nothing to mark their passage but foot prints and tire prints. Some other Baja travelers with far more ability to carry out their trash are real slobs—it sometimes seems that the bigger the RV the more trash that is dumped. While on a recent circumnavigation of Isla Guardian Angel in our cartopper, my son and I encountered two yachties anchored in Puerto Refugio. Invited to supper, we dined royally over four very large lobsters obtained from the local fishermen and a generous supply of tequila diluted with Tang. However, for the better part of an hour, the two men ranted and raved about how "the locals were raping the Cortez," all the while subjecting the waters of the beautiful bay around them to a constant stream of bean cans, well-worn copies of the *National Enquirer*, a number of empty Frito bags, and other debris, all in such an off-hand way as to suggest they were innocent of any comprehension of the damage they were doing—the

degradation of the Cortez was seen as someone else's fault. The observation that Mexicans are often the worst offenders may be correct, but it is certainly no excuse.

If the length of the visit is such that it is not possible to bring back everything, trash should be collected until it can be disposed of at a proper dump site. However, you should not get rid of everything indiscriminately. Baja dumps are informal affairs, and trash and garbage are never bulldozed under, so items that may blow around, like Frito bags and Twinkie wrappers, should be saved and burned at the evening campfire. If you need to wrap food for storage, use plastic wrap rather than aluminum foil, and burn it when done. Aluminum foil is also used in juice cartons and food containers, so if you burn them, pull the foil out of the ashes the next morning and discard it properly. Don't have your engine or transmission oil changed while in Baja, for used oil is inevitably dumped behind the shop. If it must be done, do it yourself, funnel the used oil into a suitable container, and bring it home where it can be recycled.

Instead of limiting yourself to maintaining the status quo, why not try to make things better and clean up a campsite when you arrive? Collect all plastic, paper, cardboard, rubber, cloth, rope, fishing line, nets, and man-made wooden objects and burn them. If you can haul out non-burnable objects to a proper disposal site, do so. Set a goal—how about a "125%" policy; 100% of your trash and 25% more of that left by the inconsiderate oafs ahead of you? If you can't, but are in a coastal area and have a boat or kayak, place steel cans in the fire to burn off paper labels and corrosion coatings. Collect these cans and other metallic items from the fire debris the next morning, gather all glass containers and other items, and sink them in very deep water. Since aluminum cans and foil might be carried back to the beaches by currents, haul them out with your own trash. The result of perhaps an hour's work will be an immaculate campsite you can enjoy for the remainder of your stay. If you are on a 10-day trip this will involve less than 0.5% of your time, a small price to pay for the sense of accomplishment it will bring. In addition, those who follow may be more likely to leave the campsite clean for your next visit.

There is another major problem: the human brain has a hard-wired set of criteria for campsites, and a small number of places end up getting the majority of use. As time passes, human wastes and toilet paper collect behind every rock and bush within walking distance, and because of the arid climate stay there for a long time. In coastal areas, there is a very simple and effective way to avoid contributing to the mess: use the ocean for your bathroom. This requires some psychological adjustment, but it can be done in complete privacy and cleanliness. Maintain personal hygiene in the European manner rather than by using toilet paper. If you are inland select a sandy area and follow the example of your cat.

Don't break in virgin territory. Avoid driving off the paved and unpaved road system, for vegetation crushed under wheels may show no new growth for years, and wheel tracks can remain visible for generations. Ruts provide a channel for erosion, and visitors returning after a number of years often find a small canyon where they expected to find a road to the beach. When camping, use existing campsites and fire locations. If you must build a fire in a virgin location, the best place is at the bottom of an arroyo or on a beach below the high tide line, where the ashes will be carried off and dissipated. Be careful about setting wildfires—several years ago a fire started just west of Parque Nacional Sierra San Pedro Mártir, jeopardizing the priceless, tinder-dry forest, a fire so large astronauts could see it from space. Fortunately, it was confined to lower elevations.

When hiking stay on established trails. If you go ashore on a small island, confine your visit to beaches and don't hike inland. For biogeographic reasons, the rarest flora and fauna are often found on the smallest islands, especially in upland areas, and many Baja islands, especially those in the Cortez, are home to some of the rarest living things on Earth.

Chapter 1 has suggestions for safely viewing birds, whales, and pinnipeds, and Chapter 3 describes practices that can increase the survival rate of fish and birds that have been hooked and released.

• •

66 *Mechanical marvels*

Groggy from the long drive home from Loreto, I did not realize at first that the pickup ahead of me was not moving. I came to my senses at the last moment and screeched to a stop in a shower of dust and gravel, inches from its bumper. Two anxious young Mexicans scrambled from underneath the truck and dusted themselves off. Embarrassed, I got out, apologized, and offered to help with the repairs they were making. With obvious pride, they refused, announcing that they were mechanics. Judging by the condition of their vehicle, that seemed to be a dubious claim. Although its original heritage was Ford, circa 1954, it was now the bastard son of a dozen parents. Parts of the body had been appropriated from a rusted wreck of unknown vintage and summarily bolted on. The steering wheel was so large that it almost touched the windshield, the only intact piece of glass aboard. All other windows, all the lights, even the face of the speedometer, were shattered. The engine was leaking oil and emit-

ting little gurgles of steam. The upholstery appeared to have been savaged by army ants, and the right front tire, considerably larger than the others, pointed to starboard, obviously far out of alignment. Both bumpers and the right front fender had either disintegrated or been appropriated for more important uses. If these fellows were mechanics, I thought, I was Fred C. Dobbs.

The truck would not shift into second gear—a clevis had fallen off the transmission and was nowhere to be found. Within 20 minutes they had fashioned a replacement from a piece of scrap metal, using a rock for a hammer. They got in and tried to start the engine, only to find that the battery was almost dead. Cursing and laughing, they quickly diagnosed the problem; the generator was not charging. With no test equipment more complicated than a piece of wire, they found that the source of the problem was the voltage regulator. They removed the cover and bent several electrical contacts with a pair of pliers. We rigged jumper cables from my battery, and the truck started immediately. Having little faith in their repair, I expected it to stop when I removed the cables. Grinning when I was proved wrong, they handed me a cold grape Fanta and pulled away in an eye-watering cloud of purple smoke.

I never expected to see them again, but as I approached El Rosario the battered truck was parked by the side of the road and my two friends flagged me down. They said their fuel pump was broken and asked if I had a piece of tubing 8 or 10 feet long. I didn't see the connection, but I dug through my junk box and found an old piece of outboard fuel line. They lashed a plastic jug full of gas to the roof of the truck, ran the fuel line from the jug down through a glass-less window and a hole in the firewall into the engine compartment. After sucking on the line to create a syphon, they connected the end of it to the carburetor. To my surprise the engine came to life immediately, and they started across the dry river bed. I expected to see them again at any moment, but as the miles passed I came to realize that I had finally met two of that legendary but dying breed: honest-to-goodness, real live do-anything-with-nothing Baja mechanics. Rather than a rolling comic opera, their hurdy-gurdy wreck of a truck was a monument to great mechanical skill and ingenuity. I never saw them again, but remain confident that they safely reached their destination: Sacramento, CA. 99

• •

Chapter 9

Tijuana to El Rosario

Should you visit 50% of the destinations described from this point on, you can begin to claim to have seen "the real Baja," at 75%, you can add the title "Baja" in front of your name, and if you achieve 90%, you will be privileged to use the honorific "Desert Rat" after your name.

On the US-Mexican border at the San Ysidro crossing

The border crossing at San Ysidro is open 24 hours a day, and is the busiest border crossing in the world. Those entering Mexico will normally encounter little delay; those returning to the US may wait in line for lengthy periods during business and rush hours, and at the end of holiday periods. Tourist cards can be obtained and vali-

dated at the *Migración* office (1), located in a building on the right immediately south of the border. Tijuana is a major city, and there are many hotels, restaurants, theaters, night clubs, and other facilities catering to tourists, and virtually any product or service you can think of is available, including a few your mother would not approve of. Information can be obtained at the tourism office (2) at the border crossing, and the Tijuana Tourism and Conventions Bureau offices downtown (3) and in San Diego. The Consulate General of the US is located in Colonia Hipódromo (6), and there is a Canadian Consulate (4).

If you are heading for Ensenada, you should take the Tijuana/Ensenada Toll Road. The traffic pattern immediately south of the border crossing requires quick wits, since you

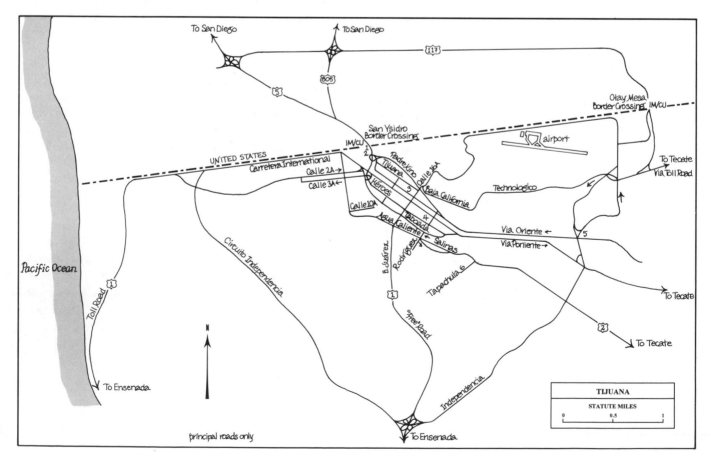

94

must get in the correct lane on very short notice. Look for signs saying ENSENADA-ROSARITO and then ENSENADA CUOTA. After a dizzying counterclockwise overpass, you should end up going west on Carretera Internacional, paralleling and adjacent to the border fence. After the road climbs a hill and swings south, go right (west) at the first major interchange, and you will soon be on the Toll Road.

If you plan to head east to Tecate or Mexicali via old Route 2 or Route 2D, the new Tijuana/Mexicali Toll Road, you should use the Otay Mesa border crossing; see page 297.

Bicyclists should cross the border at Tecate, although the Otay Mesa crossing is convenient for those heading for the Tijuana airport or the central bus station (5). The crossing at San Ysidro is difficult to approach without riding on freeways, and once across the border the bicyclist is plunged into the midst of the most reckless drivers and most sign-free streets on the continent. The Toll Road is closed to bicyclists and it will be necessary to pedal through the heart of Tijuana to the "Free Road" (old Highway 1). If you insist on crossing at Tijuana despite this advice, use the Otay Mesa crossing and head for Av. Independencia and its junction with the Free Road. Once south of the city, the Free Road is a fair-to-good, 4-lane road, crossing rolling hills until it reaches the coast near Rosarito, 16 miles from the border crossing. It then heads inland near La Misión, ending near El Sauzal in 40 more miles, with occasional places along the way to obtain food and drink and spend the night; see page 98 for a description of the Free Road from Rosarito south.

Bicyclists are prohibited on Route 2D, and should avoid Route 2, which has become dangerous and disagreeable due to heavy truck traffic. If you are in the San Diego area and wish to bike east to, say, San Felipe, the best way is to cross at Tecate and head south for Ensenada on Route 3 and then head east from Ensenada, again on Route 3, or else cross the border at Calexico East or Calexico West and then head south on Route 5.

■■■■■■■■■■■■■■■■■■
On the Tijuana/Ensenada Toll Road

KM	Location
9+	Toll booth, information, rest rooms, sodas, snacks. There are many solar-powered emergency telephones along the road from this point to Ensenada.

■ The Islas los Coronados

The islands 8 miles to the west at KM 14 are the Islas los Coronados. Often, so many dive boats,

sportfishing vessels, and yachts are often present that the place looks like an American lake. In spite of this, fishing and diving are excellent, perhaps because the islands are closed to commercial fishing. Many anglers pursue yellowtail between April and October, but many other species are taken in season, including bonito, barracuda, various species of rockfish, and a few white seabass. Productive fishing locations include the "Middle Grounds" north of Middle Rock, "85-Foot Reef" ("Jack-Ass Rock Ledge") 0.75 mile east of the lighthouse on the south tip of Coronado del Sur, and the "Rockpile," 7 miles, 131° from the same point. In calm weather anglers cast lures in to big calico bass along the western shores of Coronado del Sur. There is also excellent fishing on the "Tijuana Flats," a triangular area between the border, Rosarito, and the Coronados. Work the drop-offs and holes where fish congregate, drifting an anchovy, mackerel, squid, or octopus on the bottom.

Thousands of novice divers have made their first open-water check-out on the east side of Coronado del Norte at a place known as the "Lobster Shack," the shack there having succumbed to the elements a number of years ago. The western side of the island has fine spearfishing, but is exposed to ocean swells. A sea cave cuts across the south tip of Coronado del Norte. The "Slot" between the two middle islands is one of the best dive locations in the vicinity. A reef extending north from Coronado del Sur has rich sea life, including unusual invertebrates like white sea urchin and chestnut cowrie. Eighty-Five-Foot Reef has good spearfishing, but because of its depth it is for advanced divers only. "Five-Minute Kelp," just south of Coronado del Sur, also has fine diving and fishing.

Over 160 species of birds have been observed at the islands, and over 30 species are thought to have nested on them. Today only western gulls, and to a lesser extent brown pelicans, nest in significant numbers, the others having been decimated by egg collectors, feral and domestic animals, and pesticides. Unfortunately, a few goats continue to wreak havoc on Coronado del Sur. The islands are a bird sanctuary and landings are not permitted. There is a sea-lion colony on the western side of Coronado del Norte, and harbor seals can be seen hauled out in several locations, along with an occasional elephant seal.

Most vessels anchor in the lee of Coronado del Sur, which is well protected from the prevailing winds, although it is little more than an open roadstead. While it is very small, Puerto Cueva on Coronado del Sur offers some protection, as does "Moonlight Cove" on the east side of Middle Island. The concrete foundations seen at Puerto Cueva were once part of the

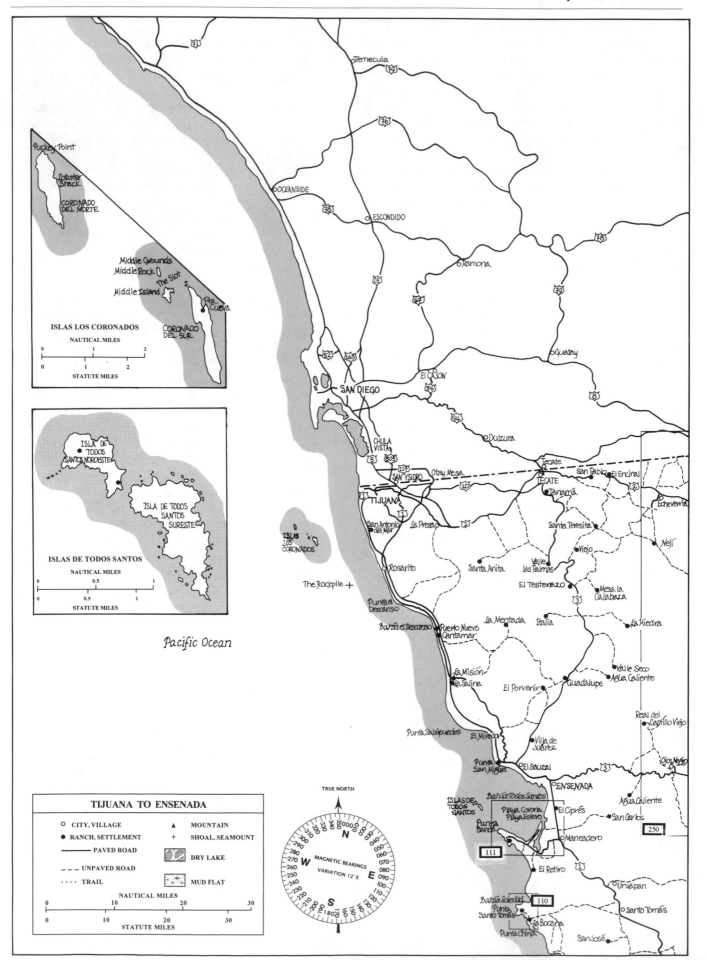

Pacific Ocean

ISLAS LOS CORONADOS
NAUTICAL MILES

STATUTE MILES

Puckey Point
Lobster Shack
CORONADO DEL NORTE
Middle Grounds
Middle Rock
The Slot
Middle Island
Pta. Cueva
CORONADO DEL SUR

ISLAS DE TODOS SANTOS
NAUTICAL MILES

STATUTE MILES

ISLA DE TODOS SANTOS NOROESTE
ISLA DE TODOS SANTOS SURESTE

Temecula
OCEANSIDE
ESCONDIDO
Ramona
Guatay
El Cajon
SAN DIEGO
Dulzura
CHULA VISTA
Tecate
San Pablo El Encinal
SAN YSIDRO   Otay Mesa   TECATE
Echeverria
TIJUANA   Tanamá
San Antonio del Mar   La Presa   Santa Teresita
Neji
Viejo
Rosarito   Santa Anita   Valle las Palmas
The Rockpile   El Testerazo   Mesa la Calabaza
Punta el Descanso   La Mentada   Italia   La Hiedra
Bahia el Descanso Puerto Nuevo Cantamar
La Misión   Valle Seco Agua Caliente
La Salina   El Porvenir   Guadalupe
Real del Castillo Viejo
Punta Salsipuedes   El Mirador   Villa de Suárez   Ojos Negro
Punta San Miguel   El Sauzal   Agua Caliente
ENSENADA
ISLAS DE TODOS SANTOS   Bahia Todos Santos   San Carlos
Playa Corona Playa Estero   El Ciprés
Punta Banda   250
111   Maneadero
El Retiro
Uruapan
Bahia Soledad   110
Punta Santo Tomás   Santo Tomás
La Bocana
Punta China   San José

TIJUANA TO ENSENADA
○ CITY, VILLAGE   ▲ MOUNTAIN
● RANCH, SETTLEMENT   + SHOAL, SEAMOUNT
— PAVED ROAD   DRY LAKE
-- UNPAVED ROAD   MUD FLAT
... TRAIL
NAUTICAL MILES
STATUTE MILES

TRUE NORTH
N
W   E
S
MAGNETIC BEARINGS
VARIATION 12' E

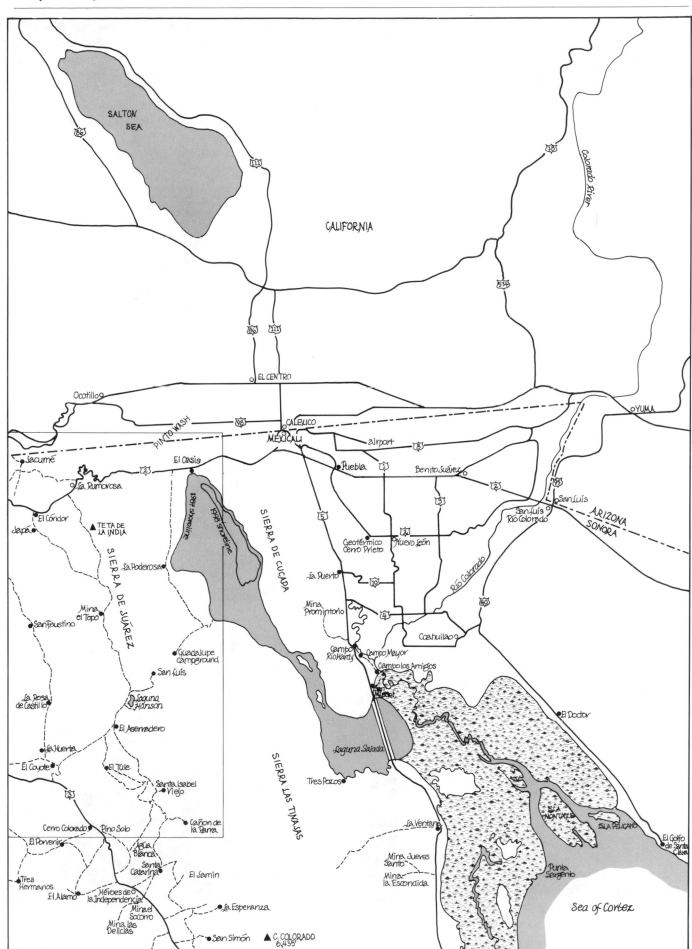

"Coronado Yacht Club," a casino and hideaway for San Diego sinners in the 1930s. The next anchorages to the south are Ensenada and the Islas de Todos Santos. A small commercial harbor is located at El Sauzal, and there is a new marina at the Hotel Coral & Marina at KM 107.

Side trip on the Free Road just south of Rosarito. The KM markers on the Free Road do not match those on the nearby Toll Road, so to avoid confusion, "K" will be used instead of "KM". There are numerous restaurants and hotels along the Free Road until K 61. The coast from Rosarito to a point about 8 miles south of Cantamar has long been famed for surfing. However, access to some of the sites favored by prior generations is becoming difficult due to the construction of private resorts and communities.

KM	Location
19+	Real del Mar Golf Club.
22	**San Antonio del Mar.** KOA campground, east side of the Toll Road with water and electric hookups (some with sewer), dump station, rest rooms, showers, laundry, a small store, views of the Pacific. Many permanents, but space is sometimes available for short-term visitors. Restaurant la Costa, west side of the Toll Road.
25	Oasis Beach Resort and Convention Center. Easily one of the most elaborate, and expensive, RV parks in Baja, with full hookups, rest rooms, showers, beach, beach break, *palapas* (palm-thatched shelters), swimming pools, tennis, volleyball, Jacuzzi, sauna, gym, game room, laundry, restaurant, mini-market, and small putting green. Tent and on-the-ground camping are not permitted (this does not apply to tent trailers).
29+	**Rosarito.** The fast-growing small city of Rosarito is tourist-oriented, with a wide range of hotels, motels, restaurants, stores, Baja Celular office, and services, most of them found along the main street. There are three PEMEX stations (MP at all), information can be obtained from the State Secretary of Tourism, and there is a *Migración* office. A surf shop is located in town, as well as a long beach break at the beach. Fine fishing is encountered a mile offshore, where a 60-to-80-foot drop-off parallels the beach. Jasper is found on the beaches and calcite in nearby hills. Ensenada can be reached from Rosarito in two ways: on the Free Road, described in the following section; and on the Toll Road. If you plan to use the Toll Road, simply turn to the log below at KM 29+.

K	Side trip location
28	Interchange, at which you can choose to take the Free Road or the Toll Road. We will continue along the Free Road.
34	Popotla Trailer Park. This park is the long-term home to many permanents, but space is sometimes available for transient RVers. It has concrete pads, full hookups, and a restaurant, but the beach is little more than cobbles and empty beer cans, there is no place to launch a boat, and the ambiance leaves something to be desired.
36+	Surfing site, parking on the west side of the road.
44	**Puerto Nuevo.** The self-proclaimed "seafood capital" of Baja, restaurants, bars, arts and crafts stalls, musicians. Interchange to Toll Road. Baja California Tours offers a bus trip to Puerto Nuevo for a Mozart concert.
46+	**Cantamar.** Stores, doctor, fruit, bakery, beer distributors, dentists, auto parts, tire repair, pharmacy, and restaurants. Interchange to Toll Road.

Fancy footwork at K 37

48	The rolling "Cantamar Dunes" here are favorites with off-road drivers, parasailors, and the pilots of hang gliders.
49+	Beach access just north of the bridge, RV parking.
54+	RV parking, surfing.
59	Ejidal Trailer Park. RV parking, sand beach.
59+	The beach break here, reached by a road just south of the Hotel la Misíon, is confused and sometimes mushy but often has the largest waves in the vicinity. There is a rough road down the cliffs to a wide sand beach. You may be able to find inexpensive RV parking nearby. Interchange to Toll Road.
61	The Free Road ducks under the Toll Road and turns inland.
64	**La Misión.** Small village with groceries, ice, beer, modest restaurants. On the southern side of the valley are the ruins of a Dominican mission founded in 1787. The road winds up rocky bluffs until K 70, with no grades over 7%. It then crosses rolling hills covered with vineyards, pastures, farm lands, and scattered settlements.
95	Junction with Toll Road, just north of El Sauzal.

■■■■■■■■■■■■■■■■■■

Back on the Transpeninsular at KM 29+

KM	Location
35	Toll booth, rest rooms, refreshments, Red Cross clinic. Exit to Free Road 200 yards north of the KM marker.
49	**Puerto Nuevo.** Already described, interchange to Free Road.
53	**Cantamar.** Already described.
58	Interchange to Free Road.
69	Rest rooms, picnic tables, possible boondocking site (check around to see if it is still permitted), sand beach, beach break.
71	Inexpensive RV parking on the beach at end of sedan road west from the KM marker, just north of the overpass, rest rooms, showers.
72	Baja Seasons. Large, modern RV park with full hookups, rest rooms, showers, restaurant, *cantina*, store, lounge, laundry, swimming pool, Jacuzzi, tennis, volleyball, horseback riding, sand beach, beach break with quirky sandbars, fishing, putting green, miniature golf, and satellite TV hookups. Tent and on-the-ground camping are not permitted (this does not apply to tent trailers).
73	Puerto Salina, an elaborate "Nautical Residential" development now under construction.

77+	Bajamar Oceanfront Golf Resort.
83	"Cueva Huevos."

● ●

66 *Cueva Huevos*

It sounded intriguing; a cave north of Ensenada that swooped down from a plateau to end in the ocean. Based on a short description from a man who claimed to have entered it many years earlier, Reeve and I decided to find it, using our highly scientific, time-tested, state-of-the-art method: asking the natives. We hit the jackpot the first day. In our poor Spanish we announced to a man in a pickup that we were cave explorers, traveling all over Baja hunting for caves, and asked whether he knew of any in Arroyo Cantamar. He looked puzzled for a moment, but his face soon brightened and he announced in Spanish, "Yes, there are many in this area; many, perhaps more than anywhere else in Baja." Our spirits soared—we were about to come up with a major geological discovery! He was obviously pleased at having helped us, and he continued. Pointing to a small rancho, *he said, "Yes, there are some over there, and over there, and there, and there!" We asked about their size and he proudly announced that they were all uniformly large. We marveled at our luck; we had found the most knowledgeable man in all of Baja on our first try! With no prompting he continued, "Yes, we have the finest chickens in Mexico." Confused by his sudden change of direction, we prodded him on, hoping he would return to the subject of caves. With excited jabs, he pointed at each ranch and exclaimed, "There, and there and there! More caves!" It seemed that every tiny* rancho *within sight had been built adjacent to a fine cave. "Yes, fine chickens and many, many big caves." We wondered if the locals could be using the caves for hen houses.*

In a flash our dreams of speleological glory evaporated as we realized we had been asking about cuevas *(caves) and his replies concerned* huevos *(eggs). Our strangely accented Spanish had apparently caused him to believe that we were "egg explorers," driven by a bizarre fetish that caused us to wander ceaselessly throughout the length and breadth of Baja intent on studying the eggs of each region. Once this problem in semantics was cleared up, we found that he knew nothing about caves, in Baja or anywhere else.*

Disappointed but firm in our resolve, we worked our way south, stopping at ranches and asking small boys. As time passed the locals became less and less certain that absolutely no caves were to be found, and soon we started to get a few vague positive responses—the farther south the more positive. We stopped at a road repair camp and were directed to a man who worked as a collector at a toll booth. This man was certain he had been in a cave long ago, but when we followed his directions we found nothing. We returned to see if he could take us there. He could not, but Rafael Aguilera of El Sauzal could.

Just before dark we arrived at what appeared to be

an ordinary hole in the ground. Reeve and I chimneyed down to 70 feet before it leveled out. The air was saturated with water, our camera fogged up, and it became difficult to breathe. We followed a flat, sandy-bottomed corridor, passing through chambers with ceilings 25 feet high. Large boulders lay about, their upper surfaces matching the ceiling configuration, causing a degree of apprehension. We finally came to an abrupt halt at the foot of a cliff. We could see a tunnel 8 feet above us, but when Reeve climbed up, he found it became very narrow and he was unable to see how far it extended. An acute case of "yellow fever" overtook us and we turned back—after all, we owed it to science; if we never returned to the surface the world would be denied knowledge of what we had discovered.

Was this the cave that swooped to the sea? We do not know. Sand and silt may have filled parts of it, perhaps due to changes in the hydrology of the area when the nearby Toll Road was constructed. Ripples in the sandy floor were a sign of flowing water, and they continued right up to the barrier that had stopped our progress. All that water has to go somewhere, and a dedicated caver willing to tunnel through sand below the foot of the cliff might be able to locate chambers farther downstream. We found indications of other underground structures nearby, and there appeared to be a collapse near the entrance. Experienced cavers may find that this area is riddled with caves, and that one does indeed lead to the sea.

Very small, Cueva Huevos is the most accessible cave in Baja. Simply drive north on the Tijuana/Ensenada Toll Road 0.1 mile past the KM 83 marker. The entrance can be found in a flat area 100 yards east of this point. **99**

● ●

Reeve ropes down into "Cueva Huevos"

KM	Location
84	**El Mirador.** Rest stop, restaurant, bar, curios, spectacular views of the coastline. Gray whales occasionally come close enough to be seen with binoculars.
99	Toll booth, refreshments, information, rest rooms. San Miguel Village RV Park, just to the south, has a restaurant, and a few sites with water, sewer, and electric hookups, but most are just places to park. Showers and rest rooms are available, usually in poor condition. This is probably the most popular surfing area in Baja, with a classic right point break that handles almost any wave well. Parking is plentiful, access is easy, and the breaks often crowded.
100+	PEMEX (MD), mini-market.
101+	Route 3 north to Tecate.
104	Ramona Beach Trailer Park. Water, electric, and sewer hookups. Few people will wish to visit the steep cobble beach. Many permanent sites, but there is occasionally room for travelers.
106	LPG yard.
107	The Hotel Coral & Marina offers a fine new marina, with a fuel dock, dockmaster, *Aduana* agent, 30- and 50-amp electrical service, telephone and cable TV hookups, potable water, 24-hour security, rest rooms, parking, a pump-out station, a mini-market, and a steep (19%), wide boat ramp. The ramp fee is also steep, currently $30 in-and-out, payable at the office next to the ramp. Liveaboards are permitted, and a laundry and showers are available. The swanky hotel has a restaurant and all the amenities.
107+	Junction. Contrary to what the signs say, avoid taking the left fork; instead, take the right fork and continue south along the coast until the highway curves left (northeast) in the vicinity of the shipyards, the highway there becoming Av. Azueta in Ensenada. Many drivers have tried to turn Av. Azueta into a short version of the Baja 1000, and the city has responded by installing a series of world-class speed bumps, so keep your speed down. Curve right (southeast) at the stoplight onto Blvd. Cárdenas, just before the PEMEX (MD). To pick up the Transpeninsular again, continue on Cárdenas until Calle Sangines. At this point make a left (east), and continue a half mile to the stoplight, where a right (southeast) turn will put you on the Transpeninsular again.
112	**Ensenada.**

Ensenada

Long an Indian camp and the site of a large ranch during the early 1800s, Ensenada began to develop during the gold rush at Real del Castillo in 1870. Hotels, gambling halls, and restaurants were built, and the new boom town was soon filled with adventurers. Many people were from north of the border, and restaurants served imported ham and eggs at $2.50 a plate, a princely sum in those days. The mines did not prosper, and after the Mexican Revolution in 1910 the town faded into a small fishing village. However, it started to grow again in the 1930s, aided by improved port facilities built to handle agricultural products from the Mexicali area.

Today's Ensenada is a small but bustling city, with an economy largely based on waterfront industries and tourism. It is Baja's largest seaport and a frequent stop for cruise ships. The city is advancing economically, and many new homes have been constructed. Graffiti, cellular phones, junk food, discos, the homeless, and the other trappings of progress are becoming more evident—is Los Angles moving south, or is Ensenada heading north? Despite this, the city retains much of its charm, and the climate is excellent, with mild winters, and summer temperatures held down by sea breezes. With its numerous restaurants, shops, and attractions, many travelers like to stop in Ensenada for at least a day or two before heading south. Dollars are readily accepted, so there is no need to exchange them for pesos if this is as far south as you are going. Many of the attractions are in the waterfront area and along Blvd. Cárdenas and Av. López Mateos, the second of which is now paved with cobblestones and its sidewalks widened.

In the 1930s, the Riviera del Pacifico (24) was a glamorous gambling casino, owned in part by boxer Jack Dempsey, and its clientele included many famous movie stars and prominent civic figures. The *S.S. Catalina* (27), in the harbor southwest of the Riviera, was once a ferry running between Los Angeles and Santa Catalina Island. It carried as many as 2,100 passengers a day on these trips, including Presidents Coolidge and Hoover, actor Robert Mitchum, and jazz musician Lionel Hampton. It was taken out of service in 1975, and showed up in Ensenada 10 years later, where it was to be converted into a floating restaurant. Plans never materialized, and today she is partially sunk and awaiting an uncertain fate.

Plaza Civica (22) has beautiful landscaping, benches, and public rest rooms. The Malecón was renovated recently and paved with cobblestones. López Mateos is Ensenada's primary shopping street, and is chock full of stores selling clothing, T-shirts, native crafts, sea shells, leather goods, jewelry, and curios.

A visit to Hussong's Cantina (6) is almost an obligation to some visitors. Hussong's is undoubtedly the best

*A **perfectly normal Monday afternoon at Hussong's Cantina, just one of about 4,680 Mondays since it opened***

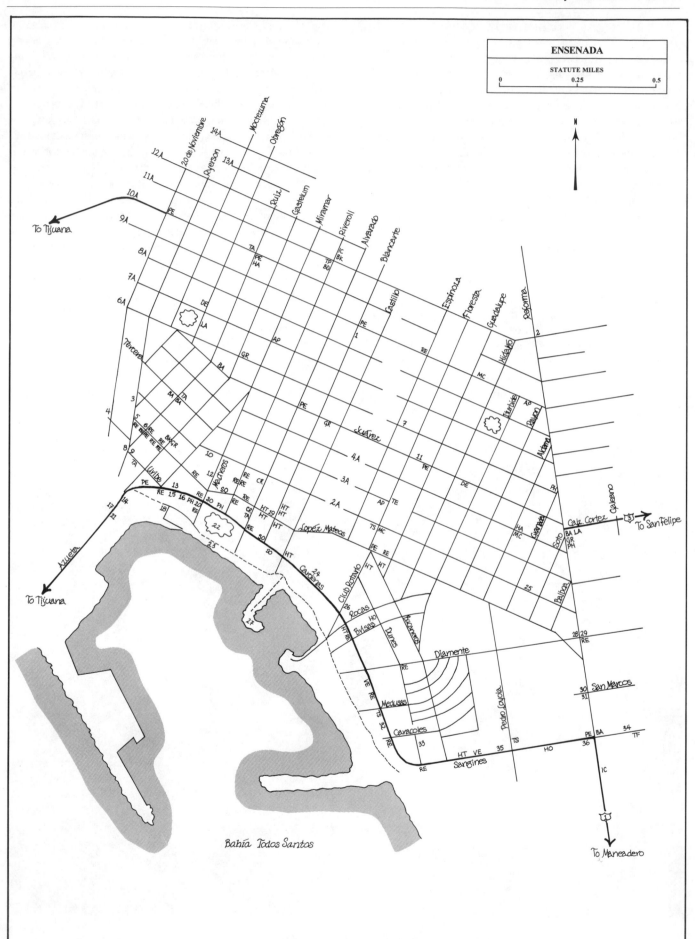

ENSENADA

STATUTE MILES

0   0.25   0.5

N

To Tijuana

To Tijuana

Calle Cortez

To San Felipe

To Maneadero

Bahía Todos Santos

known *cantina* in Mexico and the subject of countless bumper stickers and T-shirt designs, but at first glance, the reason is not obvious: the attraction can't be the decor—yellowed cartoons and hundreds of business cards tacked to peeling walls looming over battered furniture sitting on the sawdust-covered floor. It can't be the beer or the booze, which are standard issue. Rather, the attraction seems to be the sociology of its American patrons, who come to see and be seen doing things no one would think of doing at home.

You won't go hungry in Ensenada. El Rey Sol (19), a French restaurant, is among the best in Baja, although out of the range of the financially-challenged. Try La Cochinita (8) for some sushi. Halitois (34) is a highly recommended seafood restaurant. If your long absence from civilization has produced a hunger that cannot be satisfied in any other way, there are a McDonald's (29), a Pizza Hut (20), a Sanborn's (15), and a Winchell's (28). Don't miss the fish market (18), as much a social institution on weekends and holidays as a place to buy and sell fish, with noisy *mariachis* (bands that play traditional Mexican music), street vendors hawking almost everything imaginable, and throngs of people munching on piscatorial treats.

The big shopping center (36) at the corner of Sangines and Reforma has a bank, a pharmacy, groceries, and a variety of specialty stores. However, it is prudent to leave someone with your vehicle, as there have been instances of theft in the parking lot. There are also American-style shopping centers, Misión Centro Commercial (2) and Plaza Marina (15). There is an Internet café in town, Café Internet de Ensenada (11), as well as a Baja Celular office (16).

Campo Playa RV Park (33) has full hookups, rest rooms, and hot showers. Traffic noise may be a problem, but its location makes it convenient. In addition, there are many parks along the Toll Road to the north and the Transpeninsular to the south, not far from town. If you choose Campo Playa, pay for your stay with cash and get a receipt; there have been recent reports of fraudulent use of credit cards associated with this park. In addition, do not leave gas cans, aluminum chairs, coolers, and other things out where they may disappear.

Fishing is declining due to heavy commercial netting, but it is often better than in Southern California. There are three primary fisheries: yellowtail and bottom species among the rocks at the end of the Punta Banda peninsula; yellowtail, lingcod, and various bottomfish in the cool water immediately west of the Islas de Todos Santos; and albacore 25 miles or so west of Ensenada. In addition, Ensenada party boats often venture south to other locations along the coast, often in pursuit of prized yellowtail. Ensenada has a number of sportfishing boats, ranging from miserable skiffs up to the *Executive Clipper* and the *Clipper Deluxe*. A trip on an Ensenada party boat is great fun. The crews engage in theatrics, cries of "Yellowtail!" greeting every hookup, regardless of species, and multiple hookups rating a Mexican battle cry. The largest operations are Gordo's Sport Fishing and Sergio's Sport Fishing Center, both of which have offices in the lobby of the Hotel Santo Tomás (13), providing tickets, tackle sales, rental equipment, bait, and highly optimistic predictions. They also offer whale-watching trips in the winter months. There are many *pangas* available along the waterfront, and their enterprising skippers make Ensenada the easiest place in the world to rent a boat, or to phrase it another way, they make Ensenada the hardest place in the world to **avoid** renting a boat—they won't take no for an answer. To get rid of one young pest, I told him that I had cancer and was going to die by 2 P.M. He didn't blink an eye, pointing out that half-day boats were available.

The harbor is fairly close to an all-weather anchorage, although it is still uncomfortably open to the south. Locals in *pangas* often meet visiting boats, offering to rent moorings and sell fuel and water. Baja Naval (23) has floating docks with slips with water and 30/50 amp electrical service, a Travelift, boatyard services such as carpentry, fiberglass repair, mechanical overhauls, welding, electronic repairs, topside and bottom painting, fueling, parts and equipment sales, rest rooms, showers, and more. Baja Naval can provide custody and clearance services, and monitors VHF 16 and 77. Reservations are necessary.

There are currently no good locations in Ensenada to launch trailer boats, for the ramp at Gordo's and one just to the north are virtually inaccessible due to construction and heavy traffic in the area, and parking is almost nonexistent. However, Baja Naval will launch boats with its Travelift, and there are ramps along the Punta Banda peninsula to the south, which are described later in this chapter, as well as at the Hotel Coral & Marina. If you get back to Ensenada you may be able to buy live bait from barges anchored in the harbor, although the commercial boats get first call. Frozen bait is usually available at fleet offices.

Ensenada is a port of entry, with a COTP and *Migración* in adjacent buildings (17), and an *Aduana* (4). The *Migración* office is conveniently located for persons heading south and wishing to validate tourist cards, but it is sometimes closed unexpectedly during normal business hours while its staff is attending to cruise ships in the harbor. Inquiries concerning Aero Cedros can be made at the offices of Soc. Coop. de Produccíon Pesquera (3) or the State Secretary of Tourism Office (26).

Diving in the immediate vicinity of Ensenada is poor, and divers head for Punta Banda or Todos Santos. Almar Dive Shop (12) has a compressor and sells fins, masks, spearguns, regulators, and a wide variety of small, hard-to-find parts such as O-rings, spear points, and rubber mouthpieces, and regulator repairs are available. The shop has no rentals, but makes and repairs wet suits; the turn-around time is two to four days. San Miguel Surf Shop (5) sells boards and equipment, makes repairs, and has rentals. A group of surfers could have great fun by chartering one of the large fishing boats for a trip to El Martillo.

If you have vehicle problems, there are many parts stores and mechanics, as well as dealerships for Ford (31), Dodge/Chrysler (30), and Chevrolet (32). A Volkswagen dealer is located on Av. Gral. Clark Flores (the northwest extension of Calle 10, off the map). A Nissan dealer can be found on the Transpeninsular at Mile 1.3, just south of the main part of town. The NAPA auto parts store (1) has just about what you would find in a NAPA store north of the border. Souto Performance and Auto and Truck Repair (7) is a well-equipped and well-staffed vehicle repair facility. If you can't find the parts or services you need, do what you would do in the US; look in the Yellow Pages.

Sales, parts, and service for Johnson/Evinrude outboards and marine supplies, charts, and equipment can be found at Agencia Arjorna (21). Johnson/Evinrude outboard motor sales and service are also available at Equipos TerraMar (35). Industria Mexicana de Equipo Marino (25) is a Yamaha dealer. Aqua Mar de Ensenada (10) sells a wide variety of fishing and boating equipment, handles parts and makes repairs to Yamaha outboard engines, and is a US Divers dealer. Electronica Marina de Ensenada (14) is a modern, well stocked marine store and a dealer for Force and Mercury/Mariner outboards and MerCruiser stern drives. They have a large repair facility across the street, and can make repairs on Mercury/Mariner, Yamaha, Evinrude/ Johnson, and Force outboards, as well as MerCruiser stern drives and Sport Jets. Tecnopesca Mexicana (9) caters mainly to commercial fishermen, but they are a Mercury/Mariner dealer and sell parts for boat trailers, as well as limited sportfishing and snorkeling gear.

Some Baja California Tours bus trips visit the city for wining, dining, and art appreciation There are, of course, many more attractions, including a number of museums, and many restaurants, stores, festivals, winery tours, activities and facilities, too many to describe here. Immense amounts of information can be obtained at the State Secretary of Tourism Office.

If you are headed south of Maneadero, remember that you must obtain a tourist card and that it must be validated, tasks which can be accomplished at the *Migración* office.

■■■■■■■■■■■■■■■■■■■■■■■■■

On the Transpeninsular at the intersection of Sagines and Reforma in Ensenada

This is KM 7 for this section of the Transpeninsular, but since many KM markers are missing, miles will be used until Maneadero. Set odometer.

Mile	Location
0.6	PEMEX (MP), Gigante supermarket.
1.3	Nissan dealer.
2.8	PEMEX (M).
3.3	Joker Hotel & RV Park. Small RV park with

shade trees, electrical, water, sewage and TV hookups, brick barbecues, restaurant, bar, rest rooms, showers, pool.

3.6 El Ciprés airport, departure point for Aero Cedros flights to Isla Cedros and Guerrero Negro. The office is 100 yards south of the control tower. A large ice plant is located across the highway from the airport entrance.

4.7 Road west to beach resorts (signed, stop light). Set odometer. The area is becoming built-up, with a fishing tackle store, a pharmacy, curios, ice, ice cream, car wash, veterinary office, mechanic, groceries, butcher shops, hardware store, and a number of taco stands. If you want a fancy RV park and plan to do some boating, turn left (160°) at Mile 0.8 for the Estero Beach Hotel, an elaborate resort with a hotel and an RV park. The park has full hookups, rest rooms, and showers, and the facilities of the resort are available. Tent and on-the-ground camping are not permitted (this does not apply to tent trailers). Several good paved launch ramps (14%) lead into Estero Punta Banda, where halibut, croaker, sharks, and other fish can be taken. At high tide in calm weather, boats can run the channel into Bahía Todos Santos, but it would be well to discuss this with local residents first, since channels and conditions change frequently. Sailboards and other sports equipment are available for rent. If you would like a more modest park, continue straight ahead at Mile 0.8 until Mile 1.3. At this point, go straight ahead for El Faro Beach Motel & RV Park, with some spaces equipped with water and electricity, a dump station, a fine beach, a small store that carries sodas and snacks, a bar, rest rooms, showers, horseback riding, an area set aside for ATVs, and Leonardo, a very large lion in a very small cage. There are other choices in the area. At Mile 1.3, turn right (340°) for Rancho Playa Monalisa and Corona Beach RV Park, both marked by signs. When approaching Monalisa, watch for the windmill on the property. Monalisa has concrete pads, full hookups, a beach, a small restaurant, and a bar. Corona Beach has a small store selling beer, sodas, and snacks, a recreation room, beach camping, and RV sites with water and electrical hookups. A dump station, showers, and rest rooms are available. The outer beaches in this vicinity have unpredictable breaks.

6.8 Road east to Baja Country Club golf course.
8.0 PEMEX (MP), Baja Celular, bank.
8.5 PEMEX (MP).
8.6 Maneadero. PEMEX (MPD), stores, groceries, meat and vegetable markets, tire repair, bakery,

doctor, dentist, pharmacy, veterinarian, bank, post office, telephone, auto parts, mechanics, chapter of Alcoholics Anonymous, world record speed bumps. The Transpeninsular has KM markers from its intersection with the Punta Banda road, which is KM 21. Junction (signed) with paved road west to the Punta Banda peninsula. Those continuing on the Transpeninsular should turn to page 108.

⬆️➡️ Side trip to Punta Banda, La Bufadora, and the Islas de Todos Santos. The Punta Banda peninsula is one of the most popular fishing, diving, and sightseeing locations in Baja Norte. The side of the road is building up, and many small businesses sell firewood, baked goods, hamburgers, tire repair, art objects, welding services, and fishing trips, and there are a pharmacy, several cafés, and a laundromat. The name of the peninsula, "Banded Point," refers to the many wave-cut terraces that can be seen as you drive west. The KM markers are absent in many places, so miles will be used. Set odometer, turn west on the paved road (signed). Use the inset map on page 111.

Mile	Side trip location
6.0	Loco Lobo Surf and Tackle. Sells and rents surf boards and boogie boards, limited fishing tackle, and snorkeling gear. Modest Loco Lobo RV Park has water and electric hookups, rest rooms, and showers. There is a diver's recompression chamber nearby. Find the dirt road leading south approximately 50 yards east of Loco Lobo and follow it 0.4 miles south. The chamber office is located in a large white building on the east side of the road. The name of the facility is Unidad de Tratamiento Hiperbarico Fanavi, and it is owned by the local sea urchin cooperative. The doctor, Dr. Heriberto Rodríguez, lives in a small white house immediately east of Loco Lobo. Address and phone numbers can be found in Appendix B.
6.1	Laundromat.
7.6	La Jolla Beach Camp. RV sites with water hookups, showers, rest rooms, tennis, horseshoes, ice, a mechanic, a pebble beach, and a restaurant. The steep (17%) one-lane concrete launch ramp requires calm water and high tide. The ramp is getting quite rough, and the bottom is often covered with sand and pebbles. Afternoon winds from the northwest can make retrieving difficult. Villarino Camp, next door, has some full hookup sites, showers, toilets, a small store, a post office, a café, block ice, and a pebble beach. Rental boats and bait can be obtained along the beach

to the west. A geological fault, Falla Agua Blanca, dives into the sea here, and divers will find gas discharges and hot-water springs along a cleft parallel to shore in 30 feet of water.

8.0 Pickup road south (signed COLONEL ESTEBAN CANTU) to Caleta Árbolitos, Kennedy's Cove, and Bahía el Playon. This area, on the southwest side of the Punta Banda peninsula, is very beautiful, and since it is usually quiet and empty, it serves as a good introduction to what Baja has to offer in its more remote areas. The road has been graded up to the crest, but the road down the southwestern slopes has loose rock and grades to 12%. In spite of the signs proclaiming the existence of an RV park, it would not be wise to attempt this road with any but the smallest of trailers. Set odometer, and go left at Mile 0.5 for Árbolitos. If you are heading for Árbolitos and are towing a trailer, you might consider using the grove of trees giving the place its name ("Small Trees") as a boondocking site, and continue on with your tow vehicle, dune buggy, ATV, or motorcycle; the road from this point deteriorates. If you wish to go to Kennedy's or Playon, turn right at Mile 0.5, set odometer. At Mile 0.5 you will encounter a fork at a concrete-block shed; turn left for Kennedy's, right for Playon. The coast in this area is rugged, and you will have to clamber down cliffs to get to the cobble beaches. A davit at Kennedy's can be used with a line to lower portable boats to the beach. The underwater life is typical Southern Californian, and kelp, lingcod, rock cod, lobsters, anemones, and sea urchins abound. The area is well picked over, but good spearfishing and scallops can be found along the coast to the southeast. Visibility averages 20 to 30 feet, but it can get as low as 8 feet and as high as 45. An underwater arch can be found southeast of the two largest islets in Árbolitos, and friendly sea lions may accompany you while you swim through it. There are a number of sea caves, arches, and blowholes along the coast, and a cave near a prominent bird rock a mile east of Kennedy's has an open top that can be entered in calm weather.

8.7 Pickup road north, 17% upgrade coming out, leading 200 yards to a small boondocking site. A steep (22%) concrete launch ramp leads into Bahía Todos Santos. It is badly broken up, exposed, and usually covered with pebbles, but cartop and inflatable boats can be launched in calm weather. Masses of fossilized clams can be seen frozen in the cliffs and scattered among the cobblestones. Thriving 70 million years ago, the species was peculiar, for a clam anyway; its 2 shells were not mirror images. The islands to the northeast are the Islas de Todos Santos.

■ The Islas de Todos Santos

Mother Nature used different specifications for each of these two islands: the northwest one is flat and relatively featureless, the southeast one rugged and much higher. Although the islands are frequently visited by party boats and commercial fishermen, fishing can be good for yellowtail and bottom species. It is still possible to catch large fish, and a few years ago a 260-pound black sea bass was taken west of the northwest island. As is common on most Pacific islands, divers often visit the eastern sides due to calm and protected conditions, but the turbulent western sides have the most prolific underwater life. Visibilities are generally good because of the distance from the coast. Although at least six wrecks have occurred around the islands,

none are of significant interest to divers.

The southeast island is the more interesting, and is visited frequently by yachtsmen, boaters, and kayakers, and both Aqua Adventures and Southwest Sea Kayaks offer trips to the island. A series of small coves on the eastern side provide anchorages, and several pebble beaches permit landings, but the second cove from the north is closed to anchoring due to a large mariculture operation (signed), which is raising abalone for shipment to Japan. Kayakers usually camp on a large flat area over the northernmost cove. The shore is rocky, but there is normally little surge. During periods of extreme tides, kayaks should be carried to the top of the bluff. Hikes are pleasant, and in spring there are masses of wildflowers. A number of birds nest on the island, and many migratory species are also seen. A species of cinnamon-colored rabbit can be spotted from 200 yards away, apparently defying the laws of natural selection. The island is also the home of the rare en-

The start of the Baja Triathlon at La Jolla Beach Camp

Courtesy Bicycling West, Inc.

demic Todos Santos mountain king snake.

Tide pool exploring is excellent around the south end, and a seven-room sea cave can be found. Just to the east at a higher elevation is an egg-shaped relic sea cave. A modest cave system is located 300 yards, 220° from the second cove from the north on the east side. The four-foot-square entrance to one cave is partly obscured by brush at the foot of a north-facing bluff. There is an incipient collapse at the entrance, two more a few yards inside, and a large one in the main chamber. The floor sounds hollow and shakes when struck, so digging might reveal additional chambers. The cave opens on the other side of the bluff into dense brush and boulders. A dozen yards west is a squeeze leading to another cave, which also shows collapse signs. The system is small, and the largest cave is saved from being a grotto (caves go to total darkness, grottos don't) only by a right-angle turn, and then only at high noon, but as is so often true in caving, the mystery of the site is the real attraction: if the geology of the island permits these obvious caves, can there be more?

There are two lighthouses on the northwest island, one active, the other abandoned. The point break southwest of the lighthouses, christened "El Martillo" (The Hammer) by surfers, is both the most talked-about and the least-visited major surfing site between Tijuana and Ensenada. However, a March, 1998, article in *Time* sensationalized the area, claiming that 25 to 35 foot waves were normal, that El Niño had brought 50-footers, and that those of Waimea were puny by comparison. Many more surfers may make the pilgrimage in the future.

There are undoubtedly big waves: in the northwest swells of winter, big rollers from deep water immediately offshore wrap around the rocky peninsula jutting from shore, producing big, booming rights. In the summer, southern swells produce lefts almost their equal. Flexibility in tactics is essential, as the break can be erratic. Sneaker waves are common, so be careful where you operate your boat. The topography of the area produces odd wave patterns, and it is not unusual to encounter point breaks on the north end of the southeast island at the same time these big rights are coming in. Southwestern swells produce long rides in the channel between the two islands, and if conditions are exactly right, waves reflecting off the shores of both islands combine into monumental proportions. Your dainty little tri-fin is likely to be maxed out in this area; think big.

There are lighthouse and naval personnel stationed on the northwest island and a small fish camp. A permit to land on the island is required from the naval commander in Ensenada. The channel between the islands is very shallow and must be avoided by all but the smallest boats and entered only when the sea is calm.

Because of its shallow depths and the profusion of life, the channel also offers excellent snorkeling during calms.

Bahía Santo Tomás is the next satisfactory anchorage south, although Punta Banda can provide marginal protection. Local legend tells that Robert Louis Stevenson used the islands as a model when he wrote *Treasure Island*. Many other islands have also been nominated, but since Stevenson once lived near Ensenada, the legend may be true.

Mile	Side trip location
11.1	Class 1 trail to the top of 1,264-foot Pico Banda, with spectacular views of the peninsula, the Islas de Todos Santos, and Ensenada. An interesting 4-mile loop hike starts by following a trail northwest around the mountain, then paralleling the coastline on top of vertical sea cliffs to the end of the peninsula, where hematite, gypsum, and copper deposits have been reported. There are great views of the surf pounding the many tiny islets and pinnacles extending toward the Islas de Todos Santos. The trail then circles back along

Suzy Peterson emerges from the depths of the small cave on Todos Santos, which we named "Cuevacitas Suzy" to commemorate her speleological accomplishment

the shore of the peninsula past fine sea caves (to be described shortly), returning to the paved road at Mile 11.5.

13.0   **La Bufadora.**

La Bufadora, Bahía Papalote, and the tip of the peninsula

Located on the shore of Bahía Papalote, La Bufadora has restaurants, small visitor businesses, RV parking, and rest rooms. It is the location of a sea spout that sometimes jets a plume of water 100 feet high. The road to the spout is crowded with taco and souvenir stands. The California Current produces upwellings of cold water off Bahía Papalote and Cabo Banda, and anglers will encounter numerous species of bottomfish. Beachcasters willing to do some hiking will find dozens of small coves and beaches along the trail past the sea caves to the point. Stands near the sea spout often sell natural baits. La Bufadora Dive has complete rentals, a compressor, and three *pangas*, and offers guided dive and surfing trips to the islands. The rocky, rough, and very steep (32%) launch ramp ends on a pebble beach, making it unsuitable for launching trailer boats, although it is handy for cartoppers and inflatables. A fee is payable at the dive shop. Be careful of sneaker waves and surge from refracted swell when launching.

Bahía Papalote is one of the better dive sites in Baja, having both close road access and easy beach entries, with mixed bottoms and large areas covered with kelp. Sandy areas are rich in gastropods, and photographers should watch for the dozen species of nudibranch that have been identified. A hot spring area can be found at 70 to 90 feet, venting hot water and gas. Diving along the coast to Cabo Banda is excellent, kelp and sea life becoming denser with each mile. A special treat here and at the Islas de Todos Santos might be an encounter with a Pacific seahorse, near the northern limit of their range. At least four vessels and two multi-engine aircraft have been lost nearby, but the only wreck of interest to divers may be the old steam auxiliary sailing vessel *Santo Tomás*, which sank in 1946. The exact location of the wreck is not known, but old-timers who lived in the area at the time say it sank southeast of Cabo Banda. The end of the peninsula is easily the most interesting dive site in the Ensenada area, with dozens of small islets, craggy pinnacles and rock walls covered with colorful anemones, sponges, algae and hydrocorals. There are many caves and crevices harboring lobsters, which shoot out like Roman candles when they feel trapped. This area is for advanced divers only, for heavy currents can change velocity and direction in minutes.

"Cueva de los Tunels Paralelos," one of the finest and most accessible sea caves in Baja, is located about a mile northwest of La Bufadora, its various chambers, tunnels, and arms extending a total of 300 yards. One narrow chamber extends 80 yards in an almost straight line, and ceiling heights range up to 20 feet. There are many intriguing features, including a natural bridge, arches, an "almost connection," where two chambers fall short of connecting by only a yard

or so, and entrances scattered in unnoticed places. Another nearby sea cave, "Cuarto Con Muchas Ventanas la Mar," is quite different. Instead of having long narrow chambers, it is as wide as it is deep, and half of its area is awash at low tide. Not exceptionally large, Paralelos has 8,000 square feet under the drip line, and Cuarto 6,200. They can be reached by boat from La Bufadora or by a trail from Mile 11.5. More sea caves can be found along the north coast of the peninsula.

Aqua Adventures offers a trip along the southwestern coast of Punta Banda, while Southwest Sea Kayaks offers a trip all the way to Eréndira.

■■■■■■■■■■■■■■■■■■■

Back on the Transpeninsular at KM 21

KM	Location
25	Gentle up- and downgrades to KM 43.
41+	A park immediately on the left (northeast) has spreading oaks, a pavilion, fireplaces, camping, and RV parking. The road to the northeast continues on to Route 3.
43	Spectacular views of the Valle Santo Tomás.
45	Hang on! A branch of the Falla Agua Blanca crosses the road here.
47+	Paved road west (signed) to La Bocana and Puerto Santo Tomás. Those continuing on the Transpeninsular should skip the following section.

Side trip to Puerto Santo Tomás. This trip will take you to the first relatively unspoiled fishing south of the border, as well as excellent diving. The two-lane graded road is capable of handling moderate RVs and trailers, the steepest grade being a modest 12%. Turn west, set odometer.

At Mile 12.7 a pickup road can be seen winding up the hills to the south, passing the vicinity of the old Ink and Marguerita mines and reaching the coast in the vicinity of Punta San José in 8 miles. At Mile 15.2 a road runs south to Punta China, a heavily mineralized area where chalcopyrite, epidote, calcite, and prehnite have been found, along with an abundance of fossils. The shoreline one mile southeast of Punta China is riddled with interesting caves. The road reaches La Bocana ("The Mouth," apparently referring to the river, not the local *delegado*) at Mile 17.1, which has RV parking and a beach. There are right point, beach, and reef breaks nearby. The road then swings north after climbing a short, steep (17%) concrete road. For future reference, note the road headed up the hill at Mile 19.3.

Arrive at Puerto Santo Tomás at Mile 19.8. *Pangas* can be rented, and a steep (21%) concrete launch ramp runs into a small cove, requiring high tides and calm conditions.

Parking is usually no problem. The anchorage provides protection from all but south and west weather, although dense kelp can be a problem. Landings can be made in the lee of the point. To the south, Puntas San José, Cabras, and San Isidro provide marginal anchorages. Cabo Colonet is better, but Isla San Martín is far preferable if heavy weather is expected.

Punta Santo Tomás diverts the California Current and creates a circular countercurrent, pulling up cool bottom water containing nutrients and producing a rich underwater environment and limited visibility in the bay. In spite of local commercial fishing activity, Bahía Santo Tomás has the first relatively unspoiled fishing encountered south of the border, and the vast underwater plain offshore can provide a fine mixed bag of lingcod, calico bass, ocean whitefish, yellowtail, barracuda, bonito, and several species of rockfish and flatfish. Excellent fishing is found in "The Hole" due west of an abandoned concrete building foundation on a finger-like point north of Punta Santo Tomás, where sonar indicates a steep-sided depression at 150 feet. Boats from San Diego take yellowfin and albacore 15 miles offshore, and local boats fish the "22 Spot," 5.5 miles, 189° from the point. Surfers will find a fair beach break at the bottom of the cliffs in the bay.

Rocas Soledad, 1.2 miles west of the point, has sheer walls, caves, crevices, pinnacles, abundant wildlife, and excellent visibility, making it the premier dive site between Punta Banda and San Martín. The deep blue of surrounding depths, red urchins, yellow and red encrusting sponges, and the largest specimens of Pacific green anemone on the Pacific coast, with discs that can expand to 14 inches, provide a field day for photographers. Because of their coating of orange-hued encrusting sponge, it is easy to spot large rock scallops, and abalone hide in deep crevices. Schools of ocean whitefish and sheephead often approach within photographic range. A 500-pound anchor will be found nearby. Depths of over 100 feet prevail close to the rocks, but a shelf extending 40–150 yards south makes it possible to anchor in 40–70 feet.

A trail heads west and then north from the settlement at Puerto Santo Tomás, passing a number of sea caves and a massive rock arch. Camping in almost total solitude can be found on Bahía Soledad's south shore, accessible by the road going north from Mile 19.3. The road gets no maintenance, and with loose rock, ruts, and slopes to 21%, it is for pickups or better.

A prominent sea cave on the western end of this shore shows evidence of a large hidden chamber; heavy surf results in booming repercussions as air and water are expelled from the chamber, producing a violent horizontal geyser hitting the opposite wall. The bay is large and shallow, with depths of 20 to 60 feet, bottoms being boulders, shelf rock, and sand. Visibility in the northern and central parts of the bay tends to be poor, but currents occasionally clear the south end, and visibilities of 40 feet or more can be encountered. Thick kelp beds harbor opaleye, kelp bass, and dense schools of fry, and the beaches along the eastern margin of the bay offer outstanding corbina fishing almost year-round. The bay is too open and exposed for anchoring in anything short of a flat calm, although it should be useful in south weather. Several small vessels and a plane have been lost in the bay, their locations unknown.

■■■■■■■■■■■■■■■■■

Back on the Transpeninsular at KM 47+

KM	Location
51	**Santo Tomás.** PEMEX (M), restaurant, groceries, ice, telephone, doctor, tire repair, LPG sales, ruins of outbuildings of Dominican Misión Santo Tomás (1791–1849). Believe it or not, Santo Tomás was once the capital of the northern territory of Baja California. El Palomar Trailer Park, located in a large olive orchard, has full hookups, barbecues, rest rooms, showers, a volleyball court, two tennis courts, a basketball court, two swimming pools (usually empty), and a small zoo. Use care when leaving the park: the access road is steep and it is difficult to see oncoming traffic. LPG can be purchased at a building 0.6 miles south of the PEMEX. Road south to Punta San José. Those continuing on the Transpeninsular should turn to page 112.

Side trip to Punta San José and Punta San Isidro. Two-tenths of a mile southeast of the PEMEX, turn south and 200 yards later turn right (200°) onto the graded road seen winding up the hills. At KM 23 a sedan road (signed) heads south to Punta Cabras. Turn northwest at the junction at KM 30. A road west of the ranch at KM 38 connects with the Puerto Santo Tomás road mentioned earlier. Arrive at the lighthouse at Punta San José at KM 41. There are fine reef and right point breaks and plenty of room; the Fifth Army could surf here and no one need get burned. The cliffs are high, but a bulldozed ramp makes it easy to carry boards to the beach. The surf and the sloping volcanic shelf-rock beaches make it a poor place to launch a boat, and diving is always bad for the same reasons plus zero visibility. The lee of the point provides a marginal anchorage, completely open to west and south weather. Dense kelp also may be a problem.

Ammonites can be seen frozen in the sedimentary cliffs throughout the area. An interesting scavenger and fossil beach is found below the first arroyo north of the lighthouse, but access is a problem, since it is not possible to follow the beach north around the point.

To get to Punta Cabras and Punta San Isidro, go back to the junction at KM 23, reset your odometer and take the sedan road south. (The old coast road south from the junc-

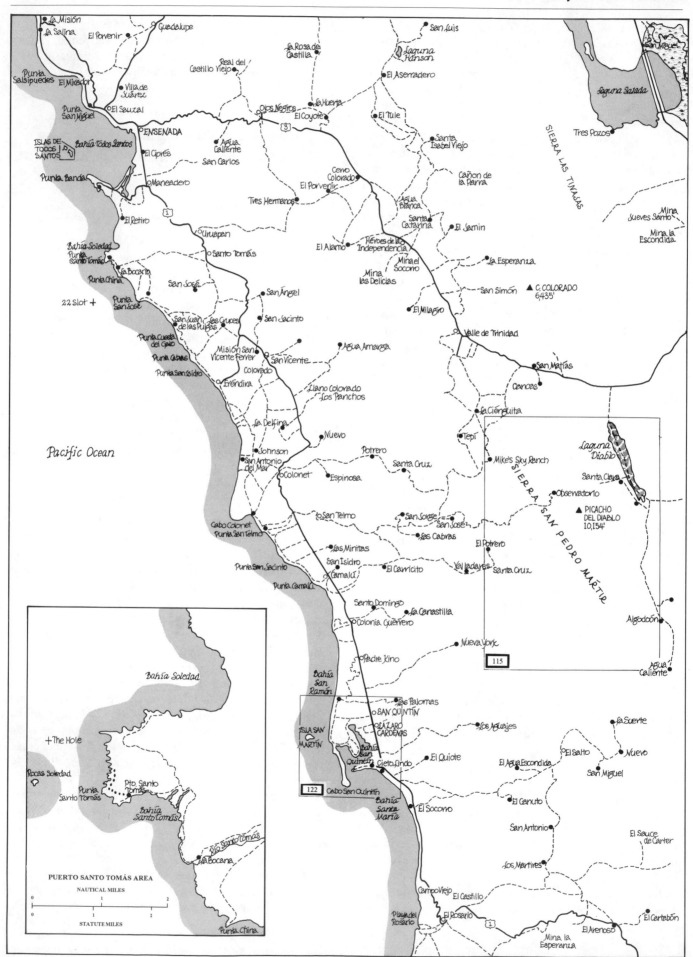

La Misión
La Salina
El Porvenir
Guadalupe
San Luis
San Miguel
Punta Salsipuedes
El Mirador
Villa de Juárez
Castillo Viejo
Real del
La Rosa de Castilla
Laguna Hanson
Laguna Salada
Punta San Miguel
El Sauzal
Ojos Negros
La Huerta
El Coyote
El Aserradero
El Tule
ENSENADA
Tres Pozos
ISLAS DE TODOS SANTOS
Bahía Todos Santos
El Ciprés
Agua Caliente
San Carlos
Cerro Colorado
El Porvenir
Santa Isabel Viejo
SIERRA LAS TINAJAS
Punta Banda
Maneadero
Tres Hermanos
Agua Blanca
Cañón de la Parra
El Retiro
Uruapan
Santo Tomás
El Álamo
Héroes de la Independencia
Santa Catarina
El Jamín
Mina Jueves Santo
Mina la Escondida
Bahía Soledad
Punta Santo Tomás
La Bocana
San José
San Ángel
San Jacinto
Mina el Socorro
Mina las Delicias
La Esperanza
Punta China
San Simón
C. COLORADO 6435'
22 Slot +
Punta San José
San Juan de las Pulgas
Las Cruces
Agua Amarga
El Milagro
Valle de Trinidad
Punta Cuesta del Gato
Misión San Vicente Ferrer
San Vicente
Punta Cabras
Colorado
San Matías
Punta San Isidro
Eréndira
Llano Colorado Los Panchos
Cánoas
La Ciénguita
La Delfina
Nuevo
Tepi
Pacific Ocean
Johnson
San Antonio del Mar
Colonet
Espinosa
Potrero
Santa Cruz
Mike's Sky Ranch
Laguna Diablo
Santa Clara
Observatorio
SIERRA SAN PEDRO MÁRTIR
San Telmo
San Jorge
San José
Las Cabras
PICACHO DEL DIABLO 10,154'
Cabo Colonet
Punta San Telmo
Las Minitas
El Carricito
El Potrero
Valladares
Santa Cruz
Punta San Jacinto
San Isidro
Camalú
Algodón
Punta Camalú
Santo Domingo
La Canastilla
Colonia Guerrero
Nueva York
115
Agua Caliente
Bahía San Ramón
Las Palomas
SAN QUINTÍN
Los Aguajes
La Suerte
ISLA SAN MARTÍN
LÁZARO CÁRDENAS
El Salto
Nuevo
Bahía Soledad
Bahía San Quintín
Cielo Lindo
El Quiote
El Agua Escondida
San Miguel
The Hole
122
Cabo San Quintín
El Canuto
Rocas Soledad
Punta Santo Tomás
Pto. Santo Tomás
Bahía San María
El Socorro
San Antonio
El Sauce de Carter
Bahía Santo Tomás
Río Santo Tomás
Los Martires
La Bocana
Campo Viejo
El Castillo
PUERTO SANTO TOMÁS AREA
NAUTICAL MILES
Playa del Rosario
El Rosario
El Cartabón
0   1   2
El Arenoso
STATUTE MILES
0   1   2
Mina la Esperanza
Punta China

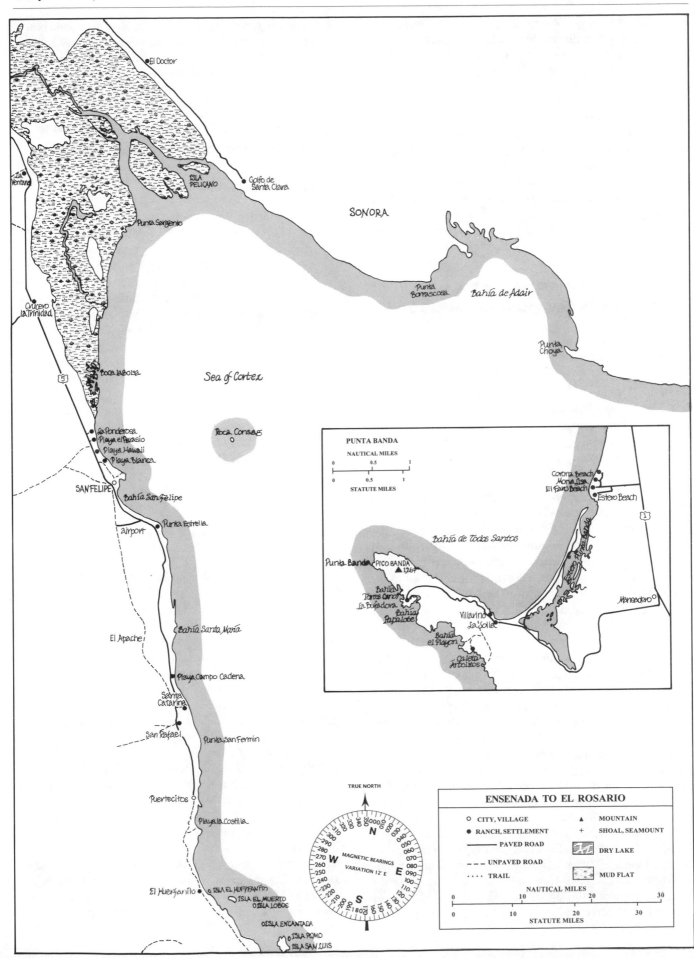

El Doctor

La Ventana

ISLA PELICANO

Golfo de Santa Clara

SONORA

Punta Sargento

Punta Borrascosa

Bahía de Adair

Punta Choya

Crucero la Trinidad

Sea of Cortez

Boca la Bolsa

Roca Consag

La Ponderosa
Playa el Paraiso
Playa Hawaii
Playa Blanca

SAN FELIPE

Bahía San Felipe

Airport

Punta Estrella

Bahía Santa María

El Apache

Playa Campo Cadena

Santa Catarina

San Rafael

Punta San Fermin

Puertecitos

Playa la Costilla

El Huerfanito

ISLA EL HUERFANITO

ISLA EL MUERTO
ISLA LOBOS

ISLA ENCANTADA

ISLA POMO
ISLA SAN LUIS

PUNTA BANDA

NAUTICAL MILES

0   0.5   1

0   0.5   1

STATUTE MILES

Corona Beach
Mona Lisa
El Faro Beach

Estero Beach

Bahía de Todos Santos

Estero Punta Banda

Maneadero

Punta Banda   PICO BANDA
▲ 1264

Bahía Torres Canot
La Bufadora

Bahía Papalote

Villarino
La Jolla

Bahía el Playon

Caleta Arbolitos

TRUE NORTH

N
000/360
340 350   010 020
330   030
320   040
310   050
300   060
W 270 MAGNETIC BEARINGS 090 E
260   VARIATION 12° E   080
250   100
240   110
230   120
220   130
210   140
200 190 180 170 160 150
S

ENSENADA TO EL ROSARIO

○ CITY, VILLAGE   ▲ MOUNTAIN

● RANCH, SETTLEMENT   + SHOAL, SEAMOUNT

——— PAVED ROAD   DRY LAKE

– – – UNPAVED ROAD   MUD FLAT

· · · · TRAIL

NAUTICAL MILES

0   10   20   30

0   10   20   30

STATUTE MILES

tion at KM 30 reaches Rancho San Juan de las Pulgas in 3 miles, where a difficult stream crossing may cause problems for those not in four-wheel-drives.) At Mile 7.7 arrive at Punta Cuesta del Gato. The coast to the north and south is broken by a series of volcanic points, where spectacular blowholes expel great jets of water, and many small coves and beaches provide fine camping and beach-casting. A sandy cove at Mile 8.3 has easy access and occasionally has excellent reef breaks. Punta Cabras at Mile 10.8 provides a marginal anchorage in prevailing weather and has a very small but sandy landing place. At Mile 14.8 encounter Punta San Isidro with good beach and reef breaks. The lee of the point is a suitable anchorage only in the best of conditions. The next anchorage south is Cabo Colonet. At Mile 16.6 arrive at Castro's Fishing Place, described in the following section.

■■■■■■■■■■■■■■■■■■
Back on the Transpeninsular at KM 51

KM	Location
58	Moderate upgrades to KM 63+, then mostly downgrades to San Vicente.
78+	Paved road south to Eréndira (signed). Those continuing on the Transpeninsular should skip the following section.

Side trip to Eréndira and Punta San Isidro. Set odometer. There is a PEMEX (MD), several small stores, groceries, long-distance phone, a motel, tire repair, and a café in Eréndira, beginning at Mile 10.7. At Mile 11.0, the pickup road to Colonet, a key part of the Two Parks Loop Trip, can be seen crossing the river bed to the south. The road swings northwest at Mile 11.6, reaching Castro's Fishing Place at Mile 12.7, which has fishing boats, as well as cabins with bunk beds, stoves, and refrigerators. Boats up to 24 feet have been launched here using the steep (22%), grooved concrete ramp. The ramp ends too soon, placing trailer tires in mud and cobble. If your vehicle is not up to the chore, Castro's usually has a truck equipped for launching. Fishing can be excellent for a mixed bag on local reefs and offshore to 10 miles. Shore-casters will find opaleye, cabezon, sheephead, and calico bass close to the landing. Low-cost RV parking can be found on a bluff a half mile west of Castro's. Copper and iron mines are located nearby. Baja Malibu Sur RV Park can be found south of town. Turn southeast at the sign advertising the park as you enter town, set odometer. At Mile 0.2 cross the river (no problem in years of normal rainfall), at Mile 0.3 turn right (south), and at Mile 0.5 turn left (southeast). Encounter a group of metal agricultural buildings at Mile 1.2. Immediately south of these buildings, turn right (southwest) towards the ocean. The road soon swings south along the shore, passing hundreds of acres of tomato fields. Arrive at the park at Mile 3.1. The park has

full hookups, rest rooms, showers, laundry, and a sand beach. The road south from the park has many fine sand beaches and potentially excellent boondocking sites. However, there are a number of rough stream crossings, with grades up to 27%.

■■■■■■■■■■■■■■■■■■
Back on the Transpeninsular at KM 78+

KM	Location
88+	Sedan road southwest (signed) to ruins of Dominican Misión San Vicente Ferrer (1780-1833), 0.6 mile. There are important copper and iron deposits in the area, and in 1915 a geologist estimated that a hematite deposit 2.5 miles from the mission contained 5 million tons.
90	**San Vicente.** PEMEX (MD), stores, groceries, auto parts, bakery, doctor, dentist, pharmacy, veterinarian, liquor, cafés, post office, motel, fruit stores, butcher shop, *tortilla* factory, ice, hardware, welder, bike shop, tire repair. If your rig finally breaks down completely, there is a used car lot. A small museum of Indian artifacts and local history can be found on the west side of the town square. Bicyclists should top off with water before heading south. Road west to "Cueva Tres Pisos."

●●●●●●●●●●●●●●●●●●●●●●●●●●●
❝ *Cueva Tres Pisos*

The rumor was interesting: after entering the cave above a stony beach, you could follow its spiraling path up to an entrance near the rim of a mesa several hundred feet above the ocean, but no one was certain where it was. After losing a day to false leads, we stopped to ask directions from a group of Mexicans who were roasting mussels and playing guitars on a beach south of Eréndira. They never heard of the cave, but invited us to sample a batch of fresh homemade "red-eye." Encouraged by Jim Smallwood's guitar and a gallon of wine I had brewed before leaving home, the party continued on into the afternoon and loud choruses of La Cucaracha *soon could be heard rising above the booming surf. As darkness fell so did many of the singers, and we found several of our new friends spread-eagled face down in sticky ice plant. By nine the fire was dead and all that could be heard was loud snoring and the surf.*

Jim, Don Nelson, and I quietly stole out of camp at first light the next day and hiked south in hopes of finding the cave. Many waterspouts and blowholes shot into the air, one so enormous we christened it "La Ducha de la Reina." As we rounded a rocky shoulder we knew immediately we

What?! You guys want to hear La Cucaracha *again? Musician Jim Smallwood and singer Pancho Cuosino do not seem too pleased with the latest request*

had found our cave. From a diameter of perhaps 90 feet, the funnel-shaped entrance quickly narrowed down to 6 feet. After following a narrow tunnel into total darkness, we entered a chamber 20 feet high and 30 wide. It continued up for a hundred feet and, as expected, opened into sunlight. A few bats hung upside down, their retinas reflecting an ominous pink color. A chimney spiraled upward in fits and starts, perhaps to another entrance.

We climbed down a steeply pitched tunnel that narrowed to a crawl. On the other side we found increasing signs of speleothems and came on a series of squat columns formed by fusion of stalactites and stalagmites. Large crystals and wide bands of mineralization graced the chamber walls. Wiggling through a squeeze, Don thought he heard a whisper of air rising from the silty soil and we became aware of an extremely faint and low-pitched booming noise—waves—which did not seem to be coming from the entrance, but rather from the floor of the squeeze. As we approached the entrance, Jim stepped into a soft spot and fell into the ground up to his calf, and the ground trembled so much we pulled him out and fled for safety outside. The soft spot was an incipient collapse and our cave was certainly underlain by other chambers.

The entrance to another cave was discovered at a lower elevation 80 yards to the south, and we found that it curved directly under the first cave. We did not explore it fully, but it is possible that a connection exists between the two levels. This still would not explain the wave noises, for even this cave was substantially above sea level. Directly in front of the first entrance the sea had cut a tall, narrow channel in a rocky cliff. The angle did not permit us to see into it very far, but judging by the large amount of water that flowed out on the ebb of each wave, there seemed to be a large tidal

sea cave running directly under us. With Don belaying, Jim rappelled down over the crashing surf and was able to see into a cave running far into the mesa; our cave had three levels, not two. We wanted to explore the sea cave, but the surf and a rising tide made it too dangerous.

To get to the cave, turn southwest in San Vicente just south of the post office. Set odometer. At Mile 0.3 turn half-left (240°) at the intersection, swing south at Mile 0.7, and turn right (265°) at Mile 4.5, signed PLAYAS LOPÉS RAYON. Encounter the Eréndira-Colonet coast road at Mile 12.9, but continue straight ahead, reaching the coast at Mile 14.4. Turn left (205°) and drive to the end of the road at Mile 14.7. Hike southeast along the coast, arriving at a sand beach at Minute 30. Fifty yards up the arroyo, a trail winds up the cliffs south of the beach. The entrance to the cave will be found after 15 more minutes of hiking. **"**

• •

KM	Location
91	Gentle rolling hills to KM 108, then moderate up- and downgrades to KM 117. Bicyclists must often fight headwinds into Colonet.
126	PEMEX (M), grocery stores, bakery, mechanic, liquor, restaurant, telephone.
126+	Graded road west (signed) to San Antonio del Mar, 7 miles, suitable for RVs and most trailers. Set odometer. At Mile 4.5 a road is encountered running north past Rancho Johnson to Eréndira, part of the Two Parks Loop Trip; continue straight ahead for the beach. At the beach there is camping, RV parking, beachcombing, and a beach break, but watch for rocks on the bottom. Surrounding dunes are popular with off-road drivers. Many people return year after year for the excellent surf fishing.
127	**Colonet.** Groceries, doctor, pharmacy, stores, bakery, butcher shops, cafés, *tortilla* factory, beer, auto parts, mechanic, tire repair, telephone. Shore casting is good for croakers and surfperch, but bottomfishing is often poor. There are good reef breaks on big waves. At least a dozen wrecks have occurred nearby, including a twin-engine plane, but diving is poor due to almost-zero visibility. Cabo Colonet's lee provides good protection from prevailing weather, although it can be windy and surgy. The next anchorage to the south is San Martín.
140+	Sedan road east (signed OBSERVATORIO) to Parque Nacional Sierra San Pedro Mártir. Those continuing on the Transpeninsular should turn to page 120.

With Don Nelson on belay, Jim Smallwood investigates the tidal sea cave

Side trip to Parque Nacional Sierra San Pedro Mártir and Picacho del Diablo. High in the mountains to the east of Colonet is a wonderful but little-used national park, the finest in Baja. You will travel at least 125 miles before you return, so make sure you have adequate gasoline. The road is normally well-maintained and can handle sedans. However, there are fairly steep and lengthy grades, and visits with large motor homes and large trailers are probably not a good idea. Set odometer. At Mile 5.7 pass through the village of San Telmo, and at Mile 11.4 through a settlement where groceries and sodas can be purchased.

At Mile 29.7 encounter a fork signed MELING RANCH RIGHT; take the right (080°) fork. (The left (005°) fork goes north to Mike's Sky Ranch. If you decide to take this road look before you leap; a description will be found on page 261.) A right fork at Mile 30.1, signed MELING RANCH RIGHT, will take you to historic Rancho San José. Founded in 1907 by the Meling family, this 10,000-acre cattle ranch has guest facilities and offers horseback riding, swimming, birdwatching, hiking, and trout fishing, plus mule trips to the high country. Some Baja California Tours trips visit the ranch. To continue on to the park, take the left (40°) fork.

At Mile 41.2 park and hike 200 yards north to Mina Socorro. Harry Johnson, father of one of the founders of Rancho San José, made a gold strike here before the turn of the century. Just as he finished constructing a ditch to bring in water from distant Arroyo San Rafael for placer mining,

the Mexican Revolution and new riparian laws brought operations to a halt. The buildings have been dismantled, but aqueducts, holding ponds and an assortment of junk can still be seen. Pegmatite dikes have been reported several miles south, yielding tourmaline. At Mile 45.3 a pipe sticks out of the bank, its waters allegedly good to drink. A concrete horse trough just downhill provides a great place to take a bath. At Mile 45.9, encounter Rancho Manzanos, which has camping areas and three dirt sites for RVs. There are showers and toilets, as well as a dump station, and water is available at the sites. With huge oak trees, and piñon and Jeffrey pine, plus four permanent springs on the property, the setting is beautiful, and the ranch can be a jumping-off point for hiking, climbing, or backpacking trips.

Jesuit Father Baegert complained, "There is no semblance of a forest in [Baja] California, there is also no trace of a meadow or of a green turf," but as you drive upward you will pass through a fascinating biological transition that will prove him wrong on all counts. Leaving the familiar chaparral of the lower regions, you will first enter a pinyon-juniper zone, with pinyon pines, junipers, and oaks, then a zone where the dominant trees are Coulter, Jeffrey, lodgepole, and sugar pine, incense cedar, white fir, and quaking aspen. The rare San Pedro Mártir cypress, endemic to this area, is found in a few isolated locations, the largest known individual having a circumference of 15 feet. As expected, the bird species change with increasing altitude. Birds found in the lower reaches include pygmy nuthatch, pine siskin, red crossbill, mountain quail, and violet-green swallow. Although the upper mountain reaches approximate a Canadian boreal forest, the avian species there include those normally found at somewhat lower elevations, such as western bluebird, pinyon jay, black-tailed gnatcatcher, wrentit, and house finch, along with birds more typical of high mountain areas such as Cassin's finch, dark-eyed junco, and mountain chickadee.

Your arrival at the park entrance at Mile 47.4 may be something of an occasion; during a recent visit Michael and a friend seemed to be the only visitors in the entire 170,000-acre park. Camping is permitted, but there are few formal facilities. Firearms, motorcycles, and off-road driving are prohibited, and fires must be confined to the concrete fireplaces available in some of the campsites. Since much of the park is above 6,000 feet, temperatures average 15° cooler than surrounding lowlands. Hard freezes are common in winter, and snow sometimes blankets higher elevations. The sky is usually bright blue; at night starlight can be so bright it produces shadows, and you can sometimes see a brilliant line of light creep along tree trunks during moonrise. Best of all, you are almost certain to have the silence needed to enjoy this majesty, with no RV generators or rock music to be heard and no rotten kids to distract you, unless you bring your own.

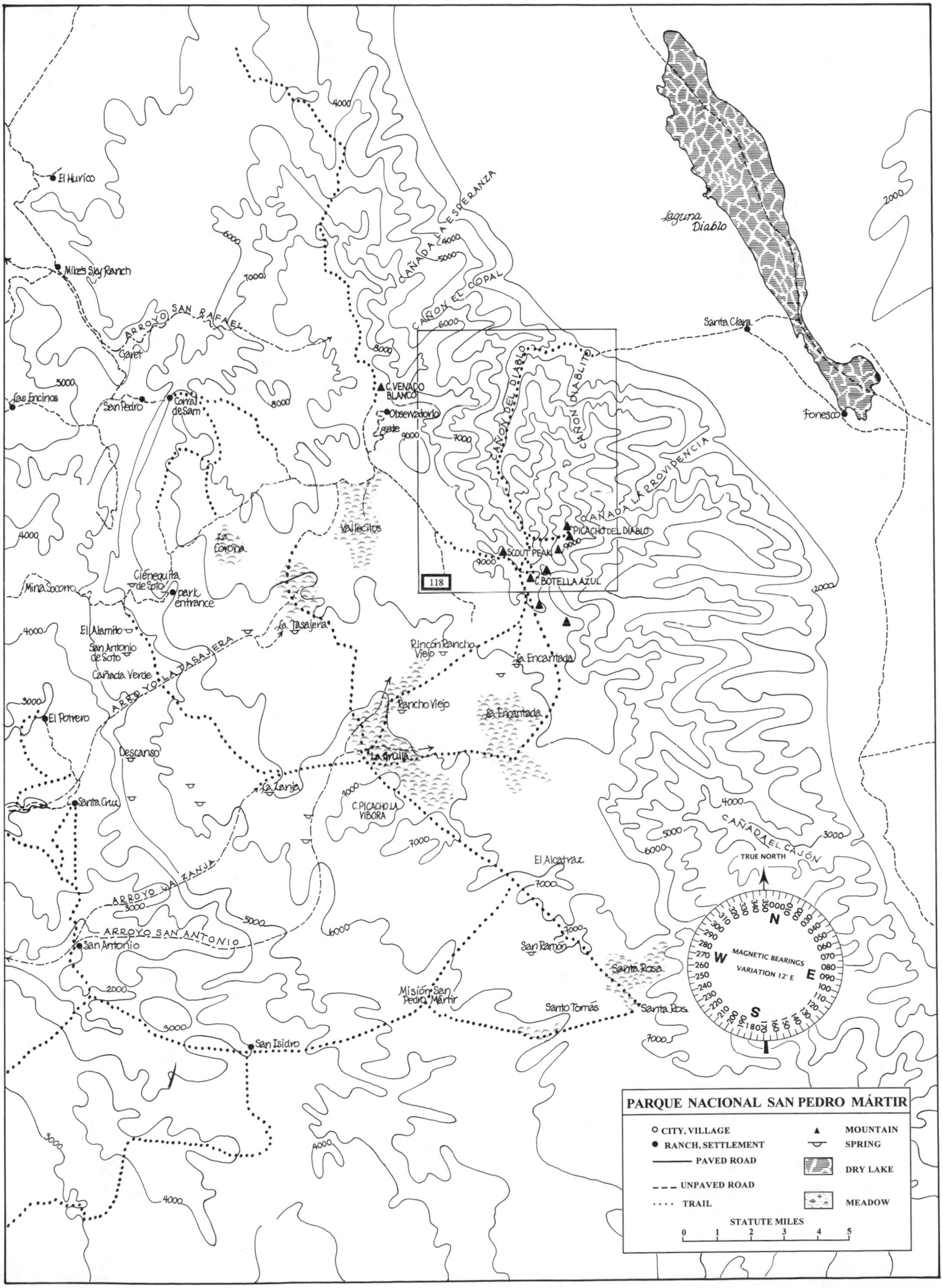
PARQUE NACIONAL SAN PEDRO MÁRTIR
CITY, VILLAGE
RANCH, SETTLEMENT
PAVED ROAD
UNPAVED ROAD
TRAIL
MOUNTAIN
SPRING
DRY LAKE
MEADOW
STATUTE MILES
0 1 2 3 4 5
TRUE NORTH
MAGNETIC BEARINGS
VARIATION 12° E
N
E
S
W
Laguna Diablo
Santa Clara
Fonesco
El Hurico
Mike's Sky Ranch
ARROYO SAN RAFAEL
Gavet
Las Encinos
San Pedro
Corral de Sam
CAÑADA LA ESPERANZA
CAÑON EL COPAL
C. VENADO BLANCO
Observatorio
gate
CAÑON DEL DIABLO
CAÑON DIABLITO
CAÑADA LA PROVIDENCIA
PICACHO DEL DIABLO
SCOUT PEAK
C. BOTELLA AZUL
118
Vallecitos
La Corona
Mina Socorro
Ciénequita de Soto
park entrance
El Alamito
San Antonio de Soto
Cañada Verde
ARROYO LA TASAJERA
La Tasajera
Rincón Rancho Viejo
La Encantada
Rancho Viejo
El Potrero
Descanso
La Grulla
La Zanja
Santa Cruz
C. PICACHO LA VIBORA
CAÑADA EL CAJÓN
El Alcatraz
ARROYO LA ZANJA
ARROYO SAN ANTONIO
San Antonio
San Ramón
Santa Rosa
Misión San Pedro Mártir
Santo Tomás
San Isidro

Set your odometer at the park entrance. At Mile 8.2 a road heads south to La Tasajera meadow, and at Mile 9.2 you pass Vallecitos meadow, with a number of pleasant campsites. At Mile 9.9 a road heads southeast to the place where the approach to Picacho del Diablo begins. At Mile 10.5 a road heads north through a fire fighting camp, ending near Cerro Venado Blanco. At Mile 12.2 a gate may prevent further travel by vehicle. Park and hike up the road, where a number of dome-topped buildings will be encountered which house astronomical telescopes, the largest an 84-inch reflector. No scheduled public tours are offered, but supervisory personnel may be willing to show you around. Views of the lowlands and the Sea of Cortez to the east are wonderful.

The park offers fine hiking and backpacking. A number of meadows will be found scattered south of the road, connected by a web of cattle trails. Some are large, occupying several square miles, including Vallecitos, La Encantada, La Grulla, and Santa Rosa. Some have permanent, year-round water, including La Corona, Santo Tomás, La Encantada, and La Grulla, while El Alcatraz and Santa Rosa usually have water in the spring months. La Grulla often has a running stream and marshy ponds. Four arroyos have year-round streams: San Rafael, La Tasajera, La Zanja, and San Antonio. The arroyo at Misión San Pedro Mártir almost always has water. The accompanying map also shows many small springs, which may or may not have water.

Since there are no signs marking the correct trails, it is easy to become confused, and you must carry a compass and topo at all times. Picacho can be seen from many high points, forming a useful landmark. If you become lost, head directly for the Observatory Road; going in any other direction might result in difficulties. Before you start, inform someone of your intended route, and do not plan on being rescued by rangers or passersby. The best time for a trip is late spring; it is still cool, nature is in bloom, there is plenty of water, and the fire danger is low. Bring warm clothes and a good sleeping bag, for it gets quite cold at night, occasionally down to 40° in the summer. Sources of permanent standing water are few, so carry plenty, and if you do use local water, be sure to treat it—*Giardia* is present.

The trails shown on the map have never been surveyed and their locations are approximations only. Most are pleasant and undemanding, passing through open, park-like country with little or no brush-busting needed and little change in elevation. Other trails undoubtedly exist. A 30-mile loop trip from Vallecitos to La Encantada and La Grulla and back to Vallecitos visits three of the largest meadows, and a side trip could be made to climb Cerro Botella Azul. A round trip from La Grulla to El Alcatraz and Misión San Pedro Mártir and back would add about 22 miles, passing from the pines into the lower chaparral country to the south. The mission, in a narrow and very lonely valley, was founded by the Dominicans in 1794 and operated until about 1806. Little but foundations remains.

A pickup road leading south from Mile 8.2 to the vicinity of La Tasajera passes through some of the finest country in the park. Three of the year-round streams mentioned

earlier—San Rafael, La Zanja, and San Antonio—have a surprise: trout. The climate would seem too hot and the flows of water too low to support them, but there are indeed trout, a few running to 14 inches. A heat-tolerant species closely related to rainbow, they were identified by naturalist E. W. Nelson in 1905. Originally found only in Arroyo San Antonio, they were transported by mule-back into the other streams in the 1930s. In 1937 some were taken to a hatchery in Redlands, CA in an attempt to determine if they could be established in the US, where their ability to withstand heat could be valuable. However, the hatchery and all its fish were wiped out in a flood the next year. Another attempt at a hatchery in Oregon failed when a frog climbed into a pipe and the pond drained. The easiest place to fish for them is in the Río San Rafael near Mike's Sky Ranch, described in Chapter 13. La Zanja and San Antonio are a little tough to get to in the park, but anglers might use the road from Mile 8.2 on the Observatory Road to La Tasajera to hike to the upper reaches of Zanja and San Antonio.

The appropriate Mexican topo is Santa Cruz H11B55. Be prepared to be very isolated—other than the road, some cows, horses, and burros, a possible vapor trail in the sky and, of course, you and your vehicle, you will experience what Mother Nature intended.

At Mile 8.2, the turn to the southeast (150°) is signed La Tasajera 10 km. Set odometer. The sandy road is in fairly good condition, and sedans should have little trouble at first, but since the road is very narrow in places, large RVs will soon encounter difficulty. Go left (170°) at the fork at Mile 2.0. As the road heads in a southerly direction, it winds through grassy meadows. At Mile 3.1, the road drops into an arroyo and then begins a rough 23% upgrade. Mile 3.1 will be as far as most sedans will make it, but if you can conquer the crest, with its fist-sized loose cobbles and pebbles, the road soon gets better.

The road passes through serene meadows and stands of pines with little underbrush, some of the finest country in the park. There are several side roads, but stick to the "main" road. At Mile 6.1 (two hours if you are hiking from Mile 3.1) you will encounter a fork; go right (170°). At Mile 6.6 there is a short, rough upgrade of 27% and then immediate downgrades as the road leaves the trees and enters a deep canyon. If still driving, you should park at Mile 6.6, for a large tree lies across the road beyond the crest, and the combination of the tree and steep grades, deep ruts, and soft sand will defeat virtually all vehicles.

Since there aren't any trees to provide shade, hiking can become very hot in the summer. Passing through large granite boulders, terrain reminiscent of that around Cataviña, the trail can be difficult to follow, although there are occasional ducks. Do not try to head cross-country, for it is impossibly difficult. At Mile 9.2 you will arrive in a flat area graced by many pines. Take careful note of this point, as it may be difficult to relocate on the way back. To the south, there are many small cattle trails. The stream encountered at Mile 9.7 is the north branch of the San Antonio, which flows southeast through Rancho Viejo meadow. It is very small, often no more than a yard across and 3 or 4 inches deep. Camping in the area is pleasant, with few bugs. Although there are cows, horses, and burros wandering around and occasional fences and corrals, you may experience being alone, really alone, for the first time in your life.

Cross the north branch of the San Antonio and continue south until you reach the south branch, which flows west through La Grulla meadow. Hiking is easy, and it is hard to get lost. Total hiking time from Mile 3.1 to La Grulla is about 5 hours, but since you have lost altitude, the hike back will take longer.

There are shallow pools at the west end of La Grulla, Mile 10.6, that have small trout, but the San Antonio is the largest stream in the park, and better fishing is located downstream. Deep pools and a waterfall are reported about 6 miles downstream. The trail to La Zanja crosses the north branch of the San Antonio about 500 yards north of the point where its two branches meet. The upper reaches of La Zanja bear 250°, about 3.5 miles from this point. The trout are a rare species living at the limit of the range of the much admired genus *Salmo*, and are very vulnerable. If you want to try to fool a few of them, use a barbless hook and carefully release them to fight again.

Climbing Picacho del Diablo

Picacho is the highest mountain in Baja California, rising to 10,154 and 10,152 feet. A massive, nearly bare double peak of pale granodiorite, it rises from the escarpment that borders the San Pedro Mártir plateau on the east. From October to May the peak is sometimes covered with snow, and because it can be seen from over 75 miles away, it presents a strange spectacle to travelers driving south from torrid Mexicali. The peak was first climbed in 1911, and many hundreds have succeeded since then. However, Picacho should not be taken lightly, for the climb can be arduous, and novice route-finders may become confused since during the ascent you cannot see the peak until you are almost on top. In 1967 two climbers became lost for a month and narrowly escaped death due to exposure and starvation. The same year a climber had a heart attack and died during an ascent. His friends buried him in a branch of "Slot Wash" and continued on, recording the event in the summit register. Despite these *caveat*s it is an interesting and beautiful class 3 climb within the ability of most persons in good physical condition. Limited technical gear will be welcome if you wish to take one of the more difficult approaches or to traverse between the two summits. A sedan road leads southeast (125°) from Mile 9.9, past Vallecitos meadow. Set odometer. Look for a concrete block shed at Mile 0.4. About 80 yards past the shed you will encounter a **Y**; take the left (080°) fork. At Mile 2.1 pass between two pines close to the road, the left one having a large scar due to missing bark. In about 200 more yards pass a large

aspen on the left, very close to the road. At Mile 2.25 arrive at the parking place. There is little else to distinguish this spot, so make sure you have followed the preceding directions exactly—if the road starts to climb and rough stuff is encountered, you have gone too far. Park, set your altimeter to 8,130 feet, and start hiking southeast up the arroyo, following its meanders. Except for a few short detours, the route follows the arroyo all the way to the eastern rim of the plateau, most of it well ducked.

At Minute 30 the route leaves the arroyo and turns north at a large cairn to miss the dense brush. At Minute 45 you will be back in the arroyo, near a large grove of dense aspen at elevation 8,330. (A trail leads a half mile north from the aspens to the rim of the escarpment, where there is a great view of Cañon del Diablo to the north.) Ducks are scarce until the other side of the grove. Skirt the south margin of the aspens, hiking east to a low saddle. Sight 022° and note "Scout Peak," a striking orange-colored knob, rising 300-400 feet above the surrounding terrain. Cross the saddle, drop into the arroyo at elevation 8,450 and continue east on the south side of the arroyo, which is again well ducked. At Minute 75 arrive at a point south of Scout Peak. This knob should be climbed to get the lay of the land and bearings for the next part of the route. Mineral collectors may find a garnet- and tourmaline-bearing pegmatite dike in the vicinity, a chunk of which is in use as a summit cairn.

Picacho's north peak bears 057° from Scout Peak. A series of bare white peaks runs south from Picacho, swerving west to a rounded, brown, tree-covered 9,450-foot peak, bearing 123°, known as Cerro Botella Azul, which sits on the rim of the escarpment. This crescent-shaped ridge, known as "Pinnacle Ridge," is a difficult and waterless technical route to Picacho. Look for "Blue Bottle Wash," a major wash

The west face of Picacho del Diablo from the escarpment of the San Pedro Mártir plateau

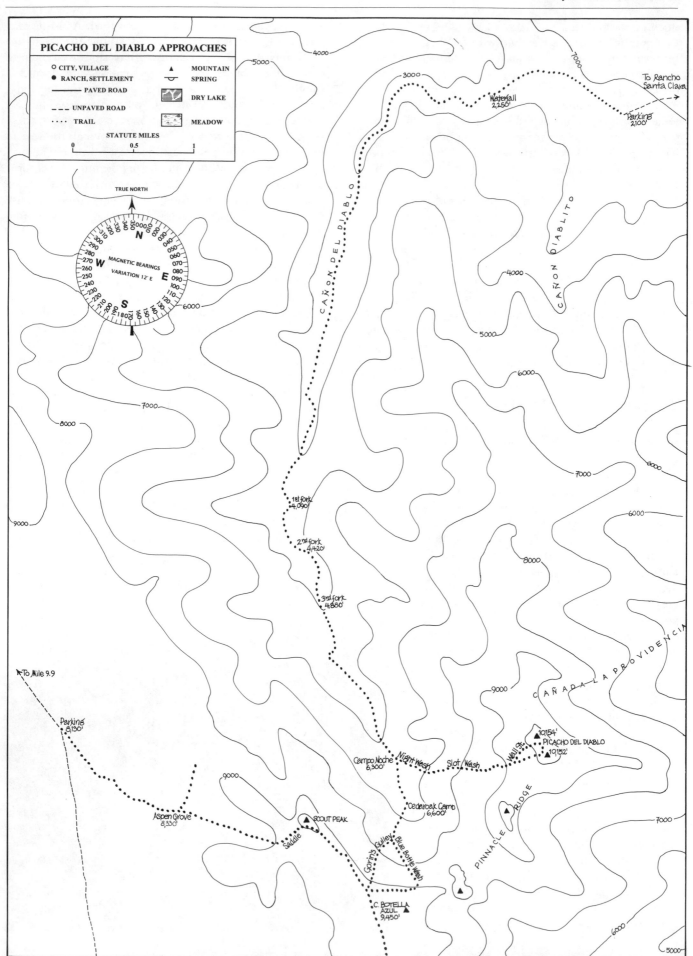

PICACHO DEL DIABLO APPROACHES

○ CITY, VILLAGE
● RANCH, SETTLEMENT
—— PAVED ROAD
– – – UNPAVED ROAD
••••• TRAIL

▲ MOUNTAIN
⚲ SPRING
DRY LAKE
MEADOW

STATUTE MILES
0   0.5   1

TRUE NORTH

MAGNETIC BEARINGS
VARIATION 12° E

To Rancho
Santa Clara

Parking
2,100'

Waterfall
2,250'

CAÑON DEL DIABLO

CAÑON DIABLITO

1st fork
4,090'

2nd fork
4,420'

3rd fork
4,880'

To Mile 9.9

Parking
8,130'

CAÑADA LA PROVIDENCIA

10,154'
PICACHO DEL DIABLO
10,152'

Campo Noche
6,300'

Night Wash

Slot Wash

Well St.

Aspen Grove
8,330'

Cedaroak Camp
6,600'

SCOUT PEAK

Saddle

Gorin's Gulley

Blue Bottle Wash

PINNACLE RIDGE

C. BOTELLA
AZUL
9,450'

strewn with white boulders northeast of Botella Azul, the contact face between brown and white granites and the easiest descent into Cañon del Diablo. The wash is reached by contouring south and then east toward Botella Azul, starting the descent when near its north side. The descent is straightforward with the exception of several detours around waterfalls, ending several hundred yards south of "Cedaroak Camp." Climbers with a hunger for problems may prefer a trying, time-consuming, and extremely steep route known as "Gorin's Gully." It is difficult to see from Scout Peak, but the top can be located northwest of Botella Azul. A rope and a few nuts and carabiners will be required, since several places require a series of 10- to 30-foot pitches of class 5 downclimbing.

Cedaroak Camp will be reached at Minute 315, elevation 6,600 feet. Floods have knocked down many of the cedars, making camping difficult, so boulderhop downstream until you reach "Campo Noche," a large campsite at 6,300 feet. A nice swimming hole will be found nearby.

Start the ascent of Picacho by climbing east up "Night Wash," a large, shallow gully intersecting the main canyon at Campo Noche. Night Wash is well ducked to a headwall at elevation 7,400, from where the route contours left over a small ridge and drops into huge Slot Wash. Water is often found in Slot Wash. Slot Wash is bisected at elevation 8,200 by a granite knob. Take the left fork, and immediately past the knob climb 30 feet up the left

Wayne Campbell rappels past an obstacle in "Gorin's Gully"

side of the wash to a shoulder. A ducked route leads along this shoulder to a steep 200-foot class 3 friction slab at 9,000 feet. At the top of the slab turn north and climb a ducked trail that switchbacks up a brushy slope. After 250 vertical feet, "Wall Street," a narrow passage between steep granite walls, will be reached. Keep climbing, and at 10,154 feet you will have conquered Picacho's north summit. On clear days views are magnificent: to the east lie the lowlands, the sparkling Cortez, and mainland Mexico, 140 miles away; to the west lies the Pacific.

The traverse to the south summit encounters a difficult pinnacle en route, although exhaustive route-finding can keep things down to a highly marginal class 3. In common with many granite peaks, Picacho has numerous knobs, chicken heads, and solution pockets along the traverse. Slot Wash can be reached by dropping directly down from the south summit. Allow 8 to 10 hours for the ascent from and return to Campo Noche. The round trip from the parking area will take a minimum of three days. Spring is the best time to make the climb, while there is plenty of daylight and water, and the weather is still cool.

Mexican topographic maps San Rafael H11B45 and Santa Cruz H11B55 are generally correct except for nomenclature. The mouth of a small canyon 0.75 mile northwest of the mouth of Cañon del Diablo is incorrectly labeled "Cañada el Diablito," while the real Cañon Diablito is not labeled. "Cañada la Providencia," shown east of the observatory, is actually Cañon del Diablo, while a canyon farther east also labeled "Cañada la Providencia" is in fact correct. The "Picaho [sic] el Diablo" shown due east of the observatory is not the "right" one, while the real Picacho is not labeled. Cerro Botella Azul is not identified, and a peak a mile southeast is incorrectly named "Cerros la Botella Azul," and a "C. Pico del Diablo" is shown another half mile southeast. An approach from the mouth of Cañon del Diablo is described in Chapter 13.

There are ominous signs concerning the future of the park. A number of years ago I obtained a copy of a logging plan for San Pedro Mártir, but I could obtain no further information and gathered that my questions were not welcome. Mexican men, especially officials, have been known to resort to a tactic called the *Ley de Hielo* (Law of Ice); to avoid admitting a mistake or dealing with a disagreeable situation, they simply adopt a stern look and refuse to speak. I was greeted with stony silence, and I now recognize that I had experienced a dose of the *Ley*. Recently, there are signs that the worst is about to begin—a sawmill has been erected near the village of San Telmo, and both parks have reportedly been placed under the control of the State of Baja California [Norte]. Why would the national government turn over management to the state? To avoid the controversy that will erupt over the matter and to lay the blame on someone else. Let us

Ted Robertson takes a break near the summit

hope that Mexico comes to its senses before these fragile and irreplaceable parks are destroyed.

■ ■ ■ ■ ■ ■ ■ ■ ■ ■ ■ ■ ■ ■ ■ ■ ■ ■

Back on the Transpeninsular at KM 140+

KM	Location
142	Road west to Punta San Telmo, with several spots difficult for sedans. The turn is hard to find because of missing KM markers, but it is located 0.75 mile south of the Parque road. Set odometer. Turn north at Mile 4.8, and arrive at the point at Mile 6.7. Known to surfers as "Quatro Casas," this place has fine right point and reef breaks. Low cliffs at the point are no problem, and the beaches are pebble and sand with some shelf rock. Mushy beach breaks are found to the south along the sedan road to Punta San Jacinto.
146	Sodas, snacks, groceries, pharmacy, mail, tire repair, mechanics, long-distance telephone.
150	Sedan road west (signed) to Punta San Jacinto, 6 miles. The wreck of the coastal freighter *Isla del Carmen*, driven ashore in 1981, lies near the point. Known as "Freighters" to surfers, even though there is only one, this place has excel-

lent right point breaks on large swells, some a mile from shore. There is plenty of room for boondocking. The road south to Camalú can handle sedans.

157+ **Camalú.** PEMEX (MD), stores, groceries, bakery, fruit and meat markets, cafés, auto parts, mechanics, tire repair, long-distance telephone, post office, doctor, dentist, pharmacy. Turn southwest at the PEMEX for the beach, which has good right point and reef breaks. Sport anglers are rare, but a beach launch is possible, *pangas* are for hire, and thresher sharks and a wide variety of pelagic and bottomfish are taken offshore. Punta Camalú is not too popular with boardsailors, but occasionally good conditions develop, so it's worth a stop to check it out. Diving is poor.

169 Sedan road east (signed) to ruins of Dominican Misión Santo Domingo, 5 miles. Set odometer. History indicates that the good padres said mass in caves at Mile 4.0. If so, it must have been a chummy affair, for the dozen or so grottos are very small. The adobe ruins of the mission constructed later have been badly damaged by treasure hunters. Begun in 1775, the mission was closed in 1839, when epidemics decimated the Indian converts. The bluff above the mission is a source of garnets.

171+ **Colonia Guerrero.** Stores, restaurants, pizza, groceries, fruit stores, butcher shops, bank, post

The Mexican coastal freighter Isla del Carmen, *stranded five miles north of Camalú in 1982*

office, auto parts, hardware, tire sales and repairs, bakery, *tortilla* factory, ice, beer, liquor, long-distance telephone, motel, doctor, dentist, pharmacy, optician, veterinarian.

172+ LPG yard, PEMEX (MD). Sedan road west to Mesón de Don Pepe and Posada Don Diego, both of which are RV parks with some full hookups, rest rooms, showers, and a restaurant. Don Diego has a laundry machine (no dryer, clothes lines provided), and a dump station. The beach several miles west has a long beach break and lots of pismo clams.

178+ Office of State Secretary of Tourism.

188 **San Quintín.**

The San Quintín area

Spread along the highway between KM 188 and KM 196, the San Quintín/Lázaro Cárdenas area has a wide variety of businesses and services, including doctors, dentists, pharmacies, opticians, veterinarians, health clinics, meat, fish and fruit markets, groceries, *tortilla* factories, bakeries, ice cream shops, a camera store, liquor, beer, auto parts, mechanics, welders, laundromat, tire sales and repairs, bicycle repairs, cafés, motels, sporting goods stores, hardware stores, travel agent, bank/ATM, long-distance telephones, post office, cinema, ice manufacturing plant.

The large PEMEX station (MD) has established a consistent, long-term reputation for rip-offs, often achieved by the usual methods: by not clearing the readings from the previous transaction; by clearing the new reading quickly and claiming a larger amount; or by short-changing. Occasionally, though, novel ways are employed: young, self-appointed windshield cleaners descend on a vehicle, climb on the hood, and make a mess of dirt and soapsuds that obscures the view of the pump from within. Complaints to the police have brought no action. If you must patronize this station, get out of your vehicle immediately and stand attentively near the pump with eyes open and calculator in hand. It would be well to carefully scrutinize transactions at the second PEMEX (MP) as well.

Around 1890 the Lower California Development Company, an English concern, sold tracts of land around San Quintín for wheat farming, dredged the harbor, built a flour mill, started construction of a railroad to Ensenada, and instituted weekly steamer service to San Diego. Trial plantings of wheat in 1889 had produced an abundant harvest, and potential investors were invited to witness its grinding in the mill. However, 1889 proved to be an unusually wet year, and local legend has it that the wheat ground into flour in later demonstrations was imported from more productive locations. The scheme soon failed due to inadequate rain-

John Anglin

Will a quarter-inch wet suit keep a horde of angry bees from stinging the author as he smokes out their hive for some breakfast honey?

fall, and the defrauded investors lost their money. A large steam engine from the mill can be seen at the Old Mill Motel (described on page 123), along with artifacts from a fish cannery. The skeleton of a pier lies several miles to the south of the Old Mill, and the old English graveyard can be seen several more miles to the south.

Today, many thousands of irrigated acres are committed to produce, much of which is shipped north of the border. The area is prospering, and satellite TV antennas are seen serving even the most humble abodes. There are a number of computer and video stores, and a bed-and-breakfast is in business. A regularly scheduled local bus line now serves the area, and a rush hour seems to be developing. However, the weather that sealed the fate of the wheat-farming scheme is never far out of mind.

KM	Location
196/0	Start a new KM numbering sequence.
1	*S*edan road west, opposite large electrical station, to Bahía San Quintín. Those continuing on the Transpeninsular should turn to page 125.

Side trip to Bahía San Quintín. Bahía San Quintín is one of the major geological features of Baja's west coast. Five basalt craters mark its location from many miles away (the sixth crater is Isla San Martín). Shallow mud flats that cover much of the bay are nurseries for hordes of fish, mollusks, and crustaceans, and eel grass attracts large numbers of brant and as many as 20 species of ducks and other geese each winter. Many other species like the place as well, and the bay and surrounding land areas are probably endowed with more bird species than any other location in Baja.

The Pacific coast west of San Quintín has sandy beaches alternating with dark volcanic points, with excellent surf fishing and good beach breaks. For a short tour of the area, turn west at the south end of the military base in town, follow the graded road past Pedregal, wind south of Mt. Ceniza, swing past the oyster farm (buy some!) and arrive at the beach at KM 19. The road to this point can handle RVs and trailers, but the coastal road to the north deterio-

rates quickly.

The Bahía San Quintín area is becoming popular with boardsailors, since it offers just about every condition anyone could want, from flat calm inside the bay to long, open Pacific beaches with long waves and good wind, to big refracted rollers wrapping around the point. To take full advantage of this, the well-equipped sailor will head for this area with both a wave and a slalom board. Beginners who have not got their tacking and waterstarts down pat should be aware that a current often sweeps south along the open Pacific beaches.

The area has both relatively unspoiled fishing and a launch ramp capable of handling sizable boats, and an RV park, several motels and restaurants, and other attractions can be found near the head of the bay. To get to the area, turn

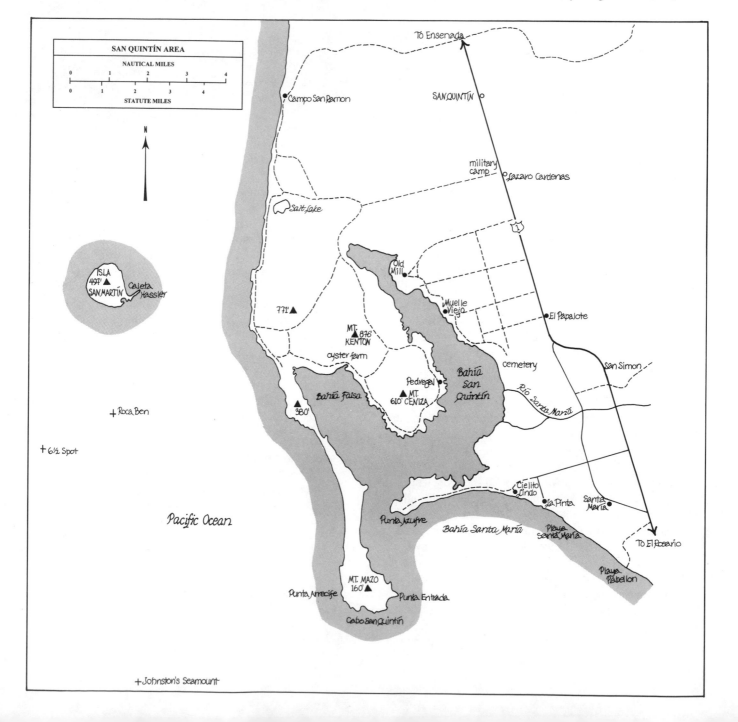

west on the graded sedan road at KM 1, opposite a large electrical station. Set odometer. On the way west, watch for the diver's flags, which lead to Baja Spearfishing Adventures, which offers blue-water hunting trips year-round aboard a 26-foot *Super Panga*, and rental gear such as spearguns, floats, and weight belts.

Arrive at the Old Mill at Mile 3.4. There have been many changes at the Old Mill in recent years. From an antiquated and sleepy backwater, it has developed into a pleasant visitor attraction. Accommodations range from the original brick units to new units with full kitchens and refrigerators. Reservations should be made a week in advance in winter, two weeks in summer. Gaston's Cannery Restaurant is popular. The RV park has full hookups, rest rooms, and showers. Boat charters, with cruisers ranging from 20 feet to 25 feet, are available, as well as rental rods, reels, and other tackle and very limited tackle sales. Tiburon's Pangas Sportfishing, located at the motel, has a 24-foot and several 26-foot cruisers, equipped with bait wells, depth finders, and radios, as well as several *pangas*. Ernesto's Motel, just to the north, offers rooms, a restaurant, and boat charters.

The steep (18%) launch ramp at Old Mill is a dandy, 25 feet wide. Channels running south from the Old Mill and Bahía Falsa join south of Mount Ceniza ("*Ceniza*" means "ashen," in keeping with its volcanic origin) to form a **Y**, then continue on to Punta Azufre (Sulfur Point). Fishing in the "inner bay" north of Punta Azufre is largely for flatfish, although different species of rockfish are found in deeper areas near the entrance. The flatfish can be big, occasionally in the 20- to 30-pound class, and there are reports of occasional giant sea bass. Fishing off Cabo San Quintín can be excellent for a mixed bag of bottom and pelagic fish.

Muelle Viejo (Old Pier) Restaurant serves seafood and steaks. RV parking is available, with showers and rest rooms. It can be reached by turning southwest from the Transpeninsular from KM 3+ on the graded sedan road. If you are at the Old Mill, simply drive south along the eastern shore of the bay.

All-weather anchorages can be found in any of the deeper areas of the inner bay, and the lee north of Punta Entrada is useful in prevailing winds. Breakers and strong rips occur east of Punta Entrada, and the bar here has as little as 6 feet of water at low tide, with sandbars often exposed. Surfing is good over the bar, with a fast inside break, but you need a boat to get there. The "outer bay," Bahía Santa María, provides good protection from prevailing weather, although refracted swells can be sizable. The next good anchorage to the south is Punta Baja.

■ Isla San Martín and the seamounts

Three offshore seamounts to the south of San Martín are among the best fishing and diving locations

Dave Buller kicks out to the end of the old pier in Bahía San Quintín

between San Diego and Isla Cedros. Many of the sport fishing companies out of San Diego offer trips to the area, as does Gordo's in Ensenada. Horizon Charters offers dive trips aboard the *Ocean Odyssey*. It is possible to visit them by trailer boat, and even cartopper in good weather if normal safety precautions are observed. Choose your weather and tides carefully, and while in the inner bay use your depth finder to stay in the channel; for some boaters the run to the seamounts is an easy romp of several hours, while others complain of weed-choked props, heavy tidal rips, and huge waves at the point, and then a long run against heavy wind and waves.

Johnston's Seamount, known to local fishermen as the "240 Spot," is located 6 miles, 240°, from Cabo San Quintín. When you are over the site, Mt. Mazo will bear 052° and the peak on San Martín 340°. It has 2 peaks, 1 of which rises to within 10 feet of the surface, the other to within 55. It is a renowned location for underwater photography. The most unusual feature here and at Roca Ben to the north is the world-class giant mussels which thrive on their southern sides down to 80 feet. In 1964 the 257-ton steel tuna-fishing vessel *Mary S* struck the seamount. She has been examined by insurance-company divers, but since she lies in 220 feet of water she is too deep for sports divers. The seamount has hordes of yellowtail and bottomfish, a few marlin in the warm months, and yellowfin tuna.

Roca Ben, 2.5 miles south of San Martín, is a rocky pinnacle rising to within 12 feet of the surface at low tide. Roca Ben is one of the most colorful dive sites on Baja's Pacific coast. The scenery is magnificent, the deep blue of surrounding depths contrasting with the bright green grass, red sea stars, and blue stony hydrocoral studding sheer volcanic walls. Large lobsters, mussels, scallops, and abalone abound, including huge corrugated abalone. Visibility averages 50 feet and sometimes go to 80, and full wet suits are required. The area is frequented by bonito, yellowtail, and a variety of bottomfish, including lingcod to 30 pounds. At low tide Roca Ben can be found easily, since surf and boils often mark its location. However, at other times it can be elusive and a compass fix may be helpful; when you are over the site, Mt. Mazo will bear 110° and the peak on San Martín 346°. Great care must be exercised while diving and fishing in the vicinity. In 1987 the charter fishing vessel *Fish 'N Fool* out of San Diego was overwhelmed by a huge breaker near Roca Ben and sank with the loss of 10 lives. The swells were only 3 or 4 feet when the vessel went down, but the breaker was reported as being 20 feet high. The vessel is now in 165 feet of water, too deep for sports divers. Do not approach the area unless it is flat calm, and stand off at least a half-hour to determine if there are any "sneaker" waves coming in.

Because it is several hundred yards in diameter, a shallow spot known as the "6 1/2 Spot" to long-range anglers, 1.9 miles southwest of Roca Ben, is easy to locate with a depth finder. Bearings to the landmarks just cited are 099° and 010°, least depth 40 feet, visibility 50 to 70 feet. However, instead of having soaring walls and jagged pinnacles, the area is flatter and less scenic than Roca Ben. Yellowtail are the primary quarry between March and November, when fish migrating along the 100-fathom curve move in to forage (a fathom is 6 feet). Lingcod, ocean whitefish, and calico bass are also caught. Dirty water and rapid changes in water temperature can quickly end the bite, but this instability can also cause conditions to change for the better, and over the long run the area is quite dependable. Long-range boats out of San Diego make frequent trips in season. Yellowfin tuna are often found 15 miles west, primarily in August and September.

San Martín is volcanic, its crater rising to 497 feet. Caleta Hassler, formed by a low, rocky peninsula jutting toward the east, is the first good anchorage south of Ensenada. Aquaculture and lobstering operations are getting in the way, but anchoring conditions are excellent, especially during south and west weather, although northwest swells can refract enough to make it uncomfortable. If this occurs, a move south of the rock wall may help. In spite of Hassler's good reputation, at least eight yachts and small vessels have been lost there, so keep a sharp watch.

If they are not biting at the seamounts, the areas around the island often produce lots of whitefish, lingcod, and barracuda. Sandy bottoms in Caleta Hassler have flatfish and unusually large kelp bass. Although frequently ignored, calico fishing can be excellent, and 20 to 30 hookups a day on bonito are possible. Water condition at San Martín is a good barometer for anglers and divers headed south to Sacramento Reef; if the water is clear at San Martín, it is likely to be clear at the reef.

The island is also a fine dive site, having spider crabs 2 feet in diameter, and diverse and abundant nudibranchs in Caleta Hassler. The south coast has extensive kelp beds, and the jumbled rock bottom drops quickly to 20 feet offshore, then slopes to 100 feet within 200–300 yards. Outer coasts are exposed to full ocean swells and have good populations of fish and lobsters among rocky shelves and caves. A number of wrecks

Exploring one of the great lava tubes on San Martín; clockwise from the upper left, Jeffrey Smith, Don Nelson, Victor Cook, Rick Kremer, and John Williams

have occurred around the island, but none are of significant interest to divers.

San Martín has the only lava-tube caves known in Baja. Dozens of tubes are too small to explore, but there are three major systems. The most accessible can be found by climbing from Caleta Hassler toward the crater. At the first plateau, maneuver so the end of the natural breakwater bears 068° and look for a large collapse. Similar tubes can be found on the north and west slopes. They range up to 25 feet in diameter, but their length has not been determined. Scrambling through them is reminiscent of the movie Fantastic Journey, the smoothly turning and twisting tubes seeming like the bloodless arteries of a giant. Be careful; during their epic kayak voyage in 1933 Dana and Ginger Lamb were almost trapped in the system on the western slope. Divers should keep an eye open for underwater entrances to the lava tubes.

A faint class 2 trail leads to the summit. Near the top look for a large area of jumbled rock, the collapse of a large cave. The western slope has a trail to an old lighthouse. A steady procession of gray whales can be seen passing to seaward in winter, often just outside the surf line. Another trail leads from Caleta Hassler along the eastern shore to the north coast, where sea lions and elephant seals haul out. Harbor seals can be seen in the small lagoon on the south shore, a number of species of birds nest on the island, and it has excellent wildflowers in the spring. Waves on the outer coast are often large and well-shaped, but due to difficult access, steep rocky beaches, cliffs, and thick kelp beds, surfing is poor.

■■■■■■■■■■■■■■■■■■

Back on the Transpeninsular at KM 1

KM	Location
11	Road west to Cielito Lindo RV Park (signed) and the Hotel la Pinta. The road is lined on both sides with tamarisks, almost forming a tunnel in some places. Due to its vigorous growth and toleration of saline soils, this non-native tree was introduced to Baja for use as wind-breaks. The last mile to Cielito Lindo is unpaved and can get very muddy after rains. The management of Cielito Lindo RV Park has apparently abandoned the old RV park near the beach, after years of neglect, and now offers camping near the motel and restaurant, some with full hookups, *palapas*, and concrete windbreaks. The beach break is good on south swells, and excellent surf fishing for barred surfperch is found south to El Socorro. A road heads northwest from the old RV park along the beach to within several hundred yards of Punta Azufre, and a party of anglers, surfers, or divers could

haul in a cartopper or an inflatable, camp on beaches, and work the Cabo San Quintín area 2 miles away. The road becomes very soft near the point. Speedsailing conditions are excellent—boardsailor Frank Hewitt made a broad reach from Punta Azufre to the hotel that averaged 30 knots. If you wish to go to the La Pinta, turn left (south) at the sign for the hotel about 2.8 miles from the Transpeninsular. The hotel has rooms, restaurant, bar, tennis, horseback riding, and a magnificent beach. The wreck of the ex-US subchaser *Scandia* lies off the hotel.

15+	Sedan road west (signed) to El Pabellón Trailer Park, 1.2 miles. Some sites have water and sewer hook-ups, and there are rest rooms, showers, and a beautiful sand beach.
23+	Sportfishing and diving boats for rent, guides.
24	**El Socorro.** Beaches, camping, RV parking, reef breaks. A road leads northeast about 30 miles to the Mina el Morro gold and copper area, where small pegmatite veins with deep emerald-green sphene containing chromium have been reported. The shoreline south from El Socorro for about 13 miles has good surfing, offering shore and reef breaks. The kelp that once congested the area has declined greatly due to the effects of the warm water from El Niño. A number of dirt roads approach the water, allowing solitary camping. However, sleeping on the ground leaves a lot to be desired, for the soil is very fine silt, and a windy night and a heavy dew leave a terrible mess the next morning.
37	The wreck of a large multi-engine aircraft lies in 60 feet west of this point, but it is hard to find due to a dearth of good landmarks and a featureless bottom; ask local divers. The area is loaded with big lobsters.
39	The hills to the east are topped by a weather-resistant Pliocene deposit containing abundant giant barnacles, pismo clams, and sand dollars.
41	Moderate upgrades until KM 51+, then a 14% downgrade to El Rosario, KM 56.
56	**El Rosario.** PEMEX (MD), cafés, stores, restaurants, motels, doctor, bakery, butcher shop, tire sales and repairs, mechanics, auto parts, long-distance telephone, welding, pharmacy. Restaurant Yiyos serves a Mexican menu and is clean and inexpensive. Café Espinosa was the last outpost of civilization in the days before the Transpeninsular was completed, and virtually all travelers stopped to get information, a lobster taco, and one last cold beer before starting out across the wilderness ahead. Many travelers continue the tradition. The restaurant's collection of fossil ammonites is amazing. The supermarket sells groceries, produce (generally of modest quality, but the prices are low), meat, ice, beer, liquor, limited hardware items, and Coleman fuel. A small museum has been estab-

lished in a white building just northeast of the supermarket; ask for the key at Espinosa's. A fish inspection station is often in operation on the Transpeninsular in the northeastern part of town. Sinai RV Park, at KM 57, has water, electric, and sewer hookups. Those continuing on the Transpeninsular should turn to page 129.

↱ Side trip to the Petrified Forest and Playa del Rosario. The Transpeninsular makes a 90° turn northeast in El Rosario. At this point turn southwest onto a pickup road, set odometer, and just short of Mile 0.1 take the right (260°) fork. At Mile 0.9 encounter a **Y**. The left (210°) fork leads to a fish-packing plant which has a diver's recompression chamber. Take the right (270°) fork. At Mile 1.3 encounter a bluff; take the right (290°) fork. The locals have unfortunately been using this area as a garbage dump. The road passes through Baja's "Petrified Forest," a geologically old region of eroded washes and gullies, where branches and entire tree trunks of fossilized conifers and palms can be seen. In the 1960s the fossil bones of a large duckbilled dinosaur that roamed the salt water marshes 79 million years ago were discovered here, as well as bones of amphibians, lizards, snakes, crocodiles, turtles, and several mammals. A terrestrial bird the size of a robin from this location has been termed one of the most important discoveries in avian paleontology in this century. Arrive at the cobble beach at Mile 4.5, which yields petrified wood and dinosaur bones, red jasper, and jasp-agate, some showing red plume and orbicular patterns against a background of white and black agate.

↱ Side trip to Punta Baja and Bahía del Rosario. Starting in El Rosario, set odometer and turn southwest, but take the left (164°) fork just before Mile 0.1 and cross the river at Mile 0.9. This crossing is flat and sandy and is usually no problem, and from this point the road can handle small RVs. Take the right (230°) fork at Mile 1.0, and at Mile 1.5 look on the right for the ruins of Dominican Misión El Rosario (in operation 1774–1832, but these buildings date from 1802). At Mile 2.5 come to a fork and continue straight ahead (245°). Turn left (160°) at the fork at Mile 2.9, signed PUNTA BAJA, and arrive at the settlement at Mile 10.3. Bottomfishing in Bahía del Rosario is excellent, and spearfishermen will find many spots within free-diving range, visibility normally being 15 to 25 feet. Cartoppers can be launched off the beach, and pangas are for hire. The locals have cut a steep dirt ramp with a bulldozer, but it is very steep and rough, and its usefulness for launching trailer boats is questionable. Boats heading for Isla San Jerónimo and Sacramento Reef can avoid the kelp that clogs the bay by staying well offshore. The anchorage off the settlement is satisfactory, although refracted swell is often present. The next anchorage to the south is at Jerónimo. Beach diving is poor throughout the bay, but you might try the lee of the point. On the right waves, thin-walled tubes wrap around the point, providing excellent surfing. Southwest Sea Kay-

aks offers a kayak trip from Punta Baja to Santa Rosalillita, this stretch of coastline being among the finest kayaking areas on Baja's Pacific coast.

The coast between the mouth of the river and the point has been the scene of a number of wrecks, the most famous being the wooden screw steamer *Union*, which hit a reef in calm weather early in the morning of July 5, 1851. The crew and passengers got ashore safely, together with $270,000 in gold coin. When the passengers returned to San Diego the story came out: the crew had celebrated the Fourth of July so enthusiastically that the helmsman was unable to steer. In the early 1960s an old Mexican lady told my friend Harry Wham that she remembered stories from her childhood about the wreck of a vessel named "Hunion" on the beach in "Ensenada Bapoor." Harry's Spanish was not too good, but the wreck was apparently the "Union" in "Steam Cove" (*vapor* is Spanish for steam), and he located large amounts of rusted machinery, visible only at extremely low tides, and a campsite littered with period bottles and chinaware. Gold and silver coins still wash up occasionally, probably from baggage left aboard.

Alcohol figured prominently in another wreck, but this time it was the rescuers, not the crew, who had the hangovers: in 1978 the vessel *Noroeste* went ashore with a cargo of 1,000 cases of beer, leading to a legendary week-long toot in the tiny settlement.

The small fishing camp of Agua Blanca can be reached by taking the left (228°) fork at Mile 2.5. Although it is more exposed than Punta Baja, the flat sand beach is an excellent place to launch a portable boat for diving and fishing in the bay. *Pangas* may be available for hire. Pick your weather carefully, for boats have overturned in the surf. The route to Jerónimo and Sacramento Reef crosses great fields of kelp. Nearby beaches provide outstanding beach-casting for spotfin and yellowfin croaker, to the point that you may not be able to eat them all.

■ Isla San Jerónimo

Ten miles south of Punta Baja, Jerónimo (San Geronimo) has a fair anchorage off the settlement near the southwest point. The island has been disparaged as a "barren pile of bird lime," but you can land at the village, hike to the lighthouse to see its antique acetylene equipment, and visit the sea lions and the shearwaters and other birds at the north end. If you see something that looks like a gray snake with prominent black stripes, it is probably not a snake at all, but the Geronimo Island legless lizard, endemic to the island. In addition, the island is home to the side-blotched lizard, the western patch-nosed lizard, and the endemic white-footed mouse *Peromyscus maniculatus geronimensis*. The remains of the US tuna clipper *Western Sky*, wrecked about 50 years ago, lie on the west side. According to local legend, survivors didn't even get their feet wet, since it was rammed into a narrow cove hardly wider than the vessel itself. Diving around the south end is excellent, and a fine reef extends southwest almost a half mile. Sea lions inhabiting the inner reef are friendly and put on a great ballet. The vessel *Linda* sank here in 1949 while at anchor. The first useful anchorage to the south is Bahía San Carlos, but beware, infamous Sacramento Reef is on an almost direct line between the two.

■ Sacramento Reef

Centered 3 miles southeast of the island, Arrecife Sacramento (Sacramento Reef) has been described as a "seething cauldron of Hell." Since its shallow reaches are exposed to ocean swells, the reef is nothing but white water in anything short of a flat calm. Many vessels have been wrecked, often while blindly coasting north along the 20-fathom curve. Though a place of danger and death to ships and sailors, it pulsates with underwater life, and biologists have termed it a "biological miracle." The most outstanding feature is the dense growth of surf grass, with blades up to 12 feet long, forming homes for great numbers of horn sharks. Gray sponges reach huge proportions, and growths of bryozoans are the heaviest on the Pacific coast. Big black sea bass and large lobsters are common, especially on the eastern margins of the reef. In recent years the visibility has decreased on the reef, possibly caused by runoff from increased farming along the coast to the north. Only time will tell what effect this will have on dive conditions and the underwater life.

The name of the reef comes from the big sidewheel steamer *Sacramento*. Carrying a treasure of gold and silver coins and bullion, she was steaming up the coast in December 1872 when her deck officer smelled kelp. It was too late to do anything, and the ship crashed on the reef. The passengers and crew made it safely to Jerónimo and were soon rescued. The wreck was visible for many years, and as late as 1932 her huge paddle shaft could be seen sticking out of the sea. In the 1950s and 60s Harry Wham, Leonard Bern, and others dove the wreck and found onyx doorknobs, china and silverware, coins, brass valves, large vases, sailor's buttons, and bottles. The gold? Newspapers of the day claimed every penny of the treasure was recovered, variously reported as between $335,000 and $2,000,000, but shipping and insurance companies had a strong self-interest in issuing such proclamations. Today authorities differ, but local sea-urchin divers may reluctantly show you Polaroid photos of small bars, which they claim to be gold taken from the wreck of the "*muy rico yate*" *Goodwill*, lost in 1969. However, the location they describe is that of the *Sacramento*, and they seem to know nothing about how the reef got its name.

Chart 21041 correctly shows a line of small islets along the south margin of the reef. The *Sacramento* is located south of the easternmost islets in this line. If you can't find it, ask one of the locals to take you to "Roca Timón" (Rudder Rock). The wreck is scattered over a large area and is hard to see due to heavy growths of plants and animals. Storms sometimes rearrange things and remove growths, making things easier to identify for a while. Huge timbers are partly buried in sand, and small artifacts lie about the bottom. Her tremendous cylinder, boilers, and walking beam must be out there somewhere.

The 161-foot schooner *Goodwill* is another fine dive. She is located in the northwest reaches of the reef, near the islets shown on 21041. An attempt to recover her bronze towing bitts a number of years ago caused excited rumors about Jesuit church bells to sweep through downtown El Rosario. The wreck shown on 21041 is apparently the US tuna clipper *Countess*, lost in 1949. The site is marked by a large propeller and a monel shaft, so there should be no confusion with the *Sacramento*. There are many other wrecks, and divers often have a hard time figuring out where one wreck

Reeve hits the water at Sacramento Reef, assisted by hose-tender Rob Watson

ends and another begins.

Diveable areas of the reef cover about 2 square miles. It is not safe to dive or fish if swells exceed 2 or 3 feet, even if you can launch safely off the beach at Punta Baja or Agua Blanca. Fishing and diving boats out of San Diego occasionally visit the reef.

● ●

❝ *A voyage in a sea of mud*

Too much rain is more often a problem in the desert than too little. Rob Watson and I once drove our van to Agua Blanca, planning to scout new fishing and diving sites. After several days of exploring Bahía Rosario and a visit to Isla Jerónimo, we returned, loaded our equipment in the van and hoisted the boat onto its roof. It was starting to rain lightly, so we took a skinny-dip in the ocean, using the rain to rinse off the soap and several weeks of accumulated grime. Several locals were standing around laughing, we thought, at our soapy behinds. We looked around and noticed that there wasn't a single pickup left where there had been a dozen when we arrived. Although puzzled, we took our time, and it was raining hard by the time we finally pulled out and headed back for El Rosario. We soon understood why the pickups were gone and what had been so funny to our onlookers— we were in big trouble. The first hundred yards of the road up from the beach was running with liquid mud. Fortunately it was not yet very deep, and our spinning wheels would finally dig down to dry soil. In little jerks and starts, we made it to the crest of the ridge behind the camp.

The countryside ahead of us was a sea of gooey mud, and the nearest pavement was a dozen miles away. Huge clods attached themselves to the wheels until they could hardly turn, and it became almost impossible to steer. We caught up with several Mexicans who had also not left soon enough, and felt a certain solace that at least we were not the only dummies. Everyone got behind a stuck pickup and pushed, but the mud was so slippery that our boots skidded backwards and we fell face-first into the morass. A four-wheel-drive came along, only barely able to make headway. The driver attempted to pull us out of a mud-hole with his winch, but it just dragged his vehicle forward. We tried to jack up the van with our HiLift to put on chains, but it just pumped down into the mud. We didn't have a jack pad or flat piece of wood, and there were no stones about, so we sacrificed the lid to our lobster pot. We finally got the chains on, and they seemed to help us pull out of the goo, but they soon broke and wrapped tightly around the axle. We flipped a coin to see who was going to visit the black purgatory under the van, and I lost. One chain was so tight I had to hacksaw it off.

Just as everyone was becoming resigned to an involuntary week of rest and contemplation, we had an idea. The worst mud seemed to be where earlier drivers had churned everything up, and the soil off the side of the road appeared to be firmer, so I pulled over and immediately got better traction. We were building up a little speed when an agave blocked the way. We could not risk stopping, and with a lurch and a bound the van passed over it. With tires spinning wildly, we slowly made a traverse up the side of a canyon. The van started to skid sideways, but we made the crest and finally got to a reasonably firm road and eventually made it to El Rosario.

As we pulled up to the supermarket, with every surface—human and mechanical—covered with mud, we were greeted with catcalls, hoots, and whistles from the crowd of loafers who had assembled earlier for such purposes. When we came out of the store with a big supply of soap, towels, and alcoholic fortification, there was another torrent of derision—we had two flat tires. The agave we ran over had extracted its revenge. **❞**

● ●

Chapter 10

El Rosario to Guerrero Negro

■ ■ ■ ■ ■ ■ ■ ■ ■ ■ ■ ■ ■ ■ ■ ■ ■

On the Transpeninsular at KM 56 in El Rosario

Until this point, the Transpeninsular has passed through areas that have had paved roads and substantial populations for many years, but the "real" Baja begins here: unfenced ranges, lonely ranches, and miles of almost uninhabited desert. The PEMEX stations at Cataviña, Parador Punta Prieta, and Villa Jesús María sometimes do not have gas, so top off in El Rosario and fill again at every opportunity. The next supermarket is in Guerrero Negro, so get your supplies while you can. Bicyclists will find the highway between El Rosario and Cataviña the most challenging on the entire Transpeninsular, with rolling hills requiring hundreds of gear changes. They will also find that locating a flat campsite away from traffic noise can be difficult in places. Travelers headed "south" early in the day should beware—since the highway runs generally east and southeast for many miles, a blinding sun hovering over the road ahead increases the danger of an already difficult stretch of highway.

KM	Location

71   The strange plants north of the road are boojums (*cirio*). They defy precise description, for the simple reason that analogies fail; there is nothing else like them, although "huge, skinny, up-side-down carrots" comes fairly close. Found only from the southern end of the Sierra San Pedro Mártir south to the Tres Vírgenes area, on Guardian Angel Island, and in a small area in Sonora, boojums reach 60 feet, and are often crowned with a cluster of spindly branches at the top. Apparently the boojums can't decide among themselves on the best form to assume, for some adopt grotesque shapes, sometimes bending down to touch the ground in a living arch, and a boojum "forest" has been compared to "a convention of drunken skywriters." They have no edible fruit and make poor firewood, thus serving no purpose of man other than to amaze and amuse.

76   The plants on the south side of the road that look like giant green porcupines are a species of *agave*. They grow slowly for many years, and then suddenly put up a towering stalk covered with yellow flowers, after which they die, a habit leading to the name "century plant." Some species are used in making mescal, pulque, and tequila.

77+   Pickup road south to Bahía San Carlos. Those continuing on the Transpeninsular should turn to page 133.

Even boojums fall in love

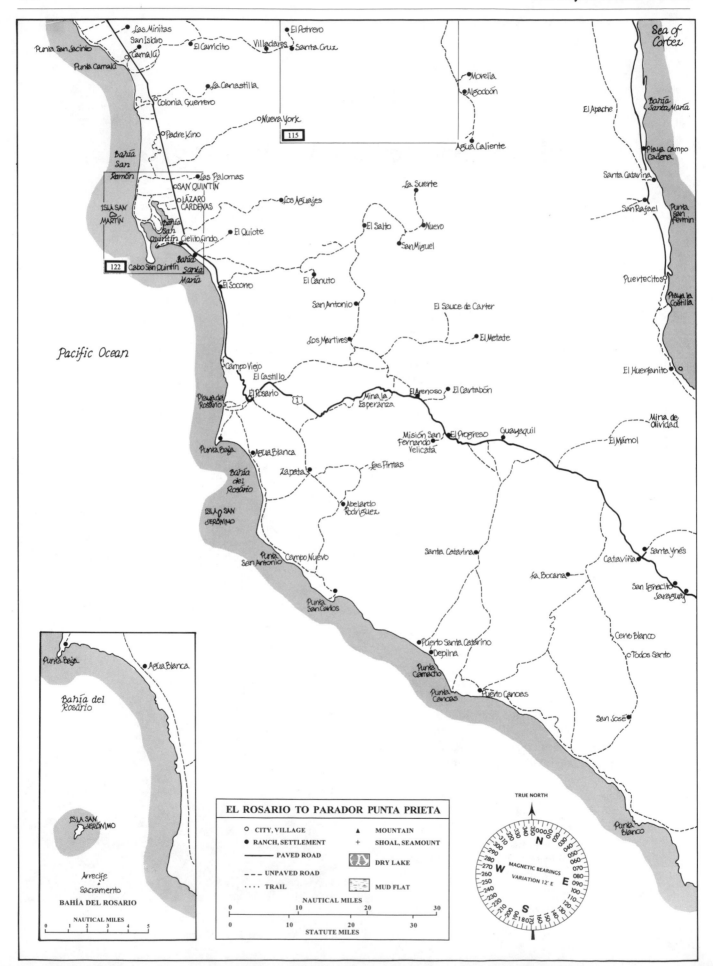

Sea of Cortez

Las Minitas
San Isidro
Punta San Jacinto
Camalú
Punta Camalú
El Camicito
Villadares
El Potrero
Santa Cruz
Morelia
Algodón
El Apache
Bahía Santa María
La Canastilla
Colonia Guerrero
Nueva York
Padre Kino
Agua Caliente
Playa Campo Cadena
Bahía San Ramón
Las Palomas
SAN QUINTÍN
ISLA SAN MARTÍN
LÁZARO CARDENAS
Los Aguajes
La Suerte
Santa Catarina
San Rafael
Punta San Fermín
Bahía San Quintín
Cielito Lindo
El Quiote
El Salto
Nuevo
San Miguel
Cabo San Quintín
Bahía Santa María
El Socorro
El Canuto
San Antonio
El Sauce de Carter
Puertecitos
Playa la Costilla
Los Martires
El Metate
Pacific Ocean
Campo Viejo
El Castillo
El Rosario
Mina la Esperanza
El Arenoso
El Cartabón
El Huerfanito
Playa del Rosario
Misión San Fernando Velicatá
El Progreso
Guayaquil
Mina de Olividad
El Mármol
Punta Baja
Agua Blanca
Zapata
Las Pintas
Bahía del Rosario
ISLA SAN JERÓNIMO
Abelardo Rodriguez
Punta San Antonio
Campo Nuevo
Santa Catarina
La Bocana
Cataviña
Santa Ynés
San Ignacito
Saraguay
Punta San Carlos
Cerro Blanco
Todos Santo
Puerto Santa Catarino
Depilna
Punta Camacho
San José
Punta Canoas
Puerto Canoas
Punta Blanco

Inset map (lower left)

Punta Baja
Agua Blanca
Bahía del Rosario
ISLA SAN JERÓNIMO
Arrecife Sacramento
BAHÍA DEL ROSARIO
NAUTICAL MILES
0   1   2   3   4   5

Legend

EL ROSARIO TO PARADOR PUNTA PRIETA

○ CITY, VILLAGE
● RANCH, SETTLEMENT
── PAVED ROAD
--- UNPAVED ROAD
···· TRAIL
▲ MOUNTAIN
+ SHOAL, SEAMOUNT
DRY LAKE
MUD FLAT

NAUTICAL MILES
0   10   20   30

STATUTE MILES
0   10   20   30

Compass

TRUE NORTH
MAGNETIC BEARINGS
VARIATION 12° E
N E S W

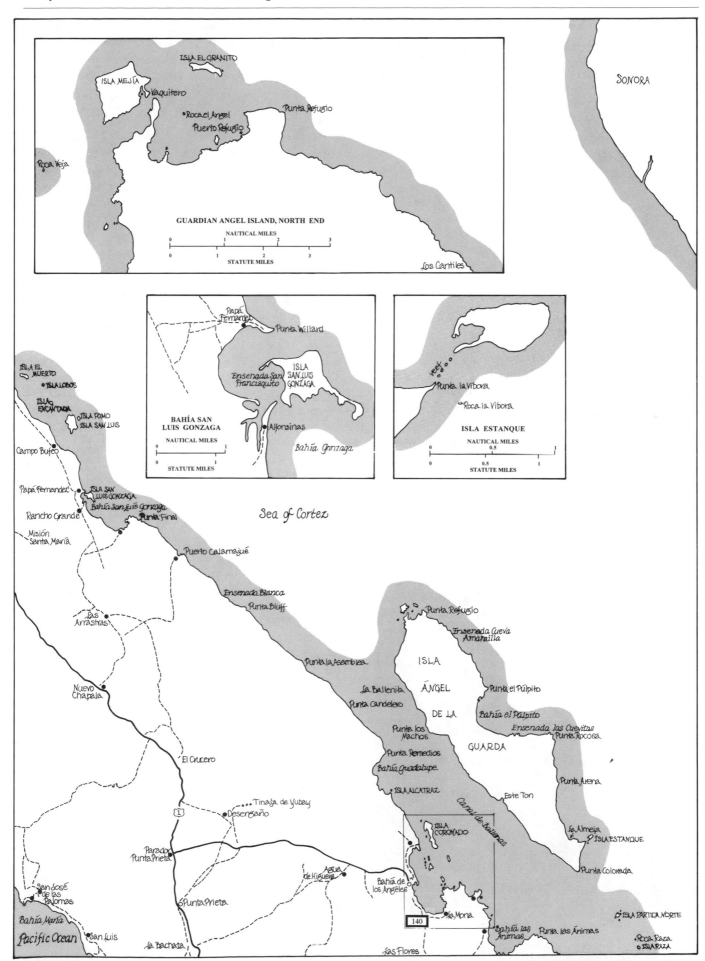

GUARDIAN ANGEL ISLAND, NORTH END

NAUTICAL MILES

0   1   2   3

STATUTE MILES

0   1   2   3

SONORA

ISLA EL GRANITO

ISLA MEJÍA

Vaquitero

Roca el Angel

Puerto Refugio

Punta Refugio

Roca Vieja

Los Cantiles

BAHÍA SAN LUIS GONZAGA

NAUTICAL MILES

0   1

STATUTE MILES

0   1

Papá Fernandez

Punta Willard

Ensenada San Francisquito

ISLA SAN LUIS GONZAGA

Alfonsinas

Bahía Gonzaga

ISLA ESTANQUE

NAUTICAL MILES

0   0.5   1

STATUTE MILES

0   0.5   1

west

Punta la Víbora

Roca la Víbora

ISLA EL MUERTO

ISLA LOBOS

ISLA ENCANTADA

ISLA POMO
ISLA SAN LUIS

Campo Bufeo

Papá Fernandez

ISLA SAN LUIS GONZAGA

Bahía San Luis Gonzaga

Rancho Grande

Punta Final

Misión Santa María

Puerto Calamajué

Sea of Cortez

Ensenada Blanca

Punta Bluff

Las Arrastras

Punta la Asamblea

Punta Refugio

Ensenada Cueva Amarailla

La Ballenita

ISLA ÁNGEL

Punta el Púlpito

Nuevo Chapala

Punta Candelero

DE LA

Bahía el Púlpito

Punta los Machos

Ensenada las Cuevitas
Punta Rocosa

GUARDA

El Crucero

Punta Remedios

Bahía Guadalupe

ISLA ALCATRAZ

Este Ton

Punta Arena

Tinaja de Yubay

Desengaño

La Almeja
ISLA ESTANQUE

(1)

ISLA CORONADO

Canal de Ballenas

Parador Punta Prieta

Agua de Higuera

Bahía de los Ángeles

Punta Colorada

San José de las Palomas

Punta Prieta

La Mona

ISLA PARTIDA NORTE

140

Bahía María

San Luis

La Bachata

Bahía las Ánimas

Punta las Ánimas

Pacific Ocean

Las Flores

Roca Raza
ISLA RAZA

Side trip on the Bahía San Carlos road. Set odometer. A fascinating jumble of rocks named Las Pintas exists east from the road at Mile 11.6. Drive 0.1 mile past a corral and turn northeast on the faint wheel tracks. Follow them 9 miles until they end in a wide arroyo. Las Pintas, not quite visible, is 200 yards upstream. The road to this point can be negotiated by pickups with difficulty, but only four-wheel-drives should attempt to drive directly to the site due to very soft ground. Oyster shells, ammonites, and trilobites by the millions can be seen frozen in various stages of petrifaction at the site, and a stream magically appears from the dry sands of the plateau above and shoots through the air into a sandy-bottomed grotto, a nifty spot for a shower. It then passes through a long, water-carved cleft to disappear into the desert below. To top it off, Indians have graced the place with petroglyphs and small paintings.

Water seeping through fossil beds for millions of years has produced striking orange and white stains and a number of grottos, some of them hollowed-out rocks reminiscent of gigantic sugar Easter eggs. One grotto, formed

Mike takes a badly needed shower in the waterfall at Las Pintas

by an enormous flat-bottomed boulder resting on five stone feet, has a sandy floor—a cool and inviting spot. Graced by total silence and a wealth of natural history, the place is a great spot for loafing and dreaming.

Continuing on the road to San Carlos, cross Cañon San Fernando at Mile 18.3, and at Mile 38.0 turn east at the intersection to go to the fishing village, west to Punta San Carlos. In the past, the road to the San Carlos area has often been one of the better long, unpaved roads in Baja Norte, being well-graded and having only three 14 to 18% grades, all relatively short and smooth. While it should be possible to make the drive with a tent or utility trailer or small RV, it would be inadvisable to bring a trailerboat. Cartop and inflatable boats can be launched with few problems. Divers and anglers will find scattered pinnacles southwest of the point, almost virgin territory. In 1920 the vessel *Newark* sank near the point with a cargo of the sublime and the ridiculous: onyx and guano. Surfers like the reef and right point breaks, and boardsailors make the trek to enjoy good winds and everything from calm inside the bay to waves at the point. The sea caves to the north are worth a visit, and the locals report a large fossil deposit northeast of the village. The anchorage provides satisfactory shelter in moderate prevailing weather, but is swept by heavy swells at times. The lees of a series of points along the coast to the southeast— Escarpada, Canoas, Blanco, Cono, María, and Santa Rosalillita—provide anchorages with modest protection, the last often being the best. Little more than open roadsteads, all are subject to south weather and tend to be uncomfortable. Boats coasting south generally start a "shortcut" at San Carlos and head directly for Isla Cedros, avoiding these relatively poor anchorages and cutting down the distance.

● ●

❝ *A constitutional crisis*

People vary greatly in their tolerance for heat. Will Ashford, Michael, and I once drove off-road to a rock-art site called Las Pintas (see earlier side trip in this chapter), accompanied by Saturñino Diaz, a Mexican gentleman of considerable years. The temperature was at least 90° and as luck would have it our van went down to the axles in deep sand. We started to dig it out, and within minutes Will, Michael, and I were bathed in sweat and feeling faint. Saturñino, dressed in red longjohns and a quilted coat, kept working, showing no signs of stress. After a rest in the shade of a palo verde *we tried it again, and had to quit within minutes, to the barely concealed contempt of our new friend. Finally we remembered our cooler of cold sodas, but a thorn bush prevented us from getting the side door of the van open, and there was no other way to get to it. Using our HiLift, we jacked up the back of the van and gave it a push, causing the jack to tip over and moving the van sideways a foot or so. We then jacked up the front of the van and again pushed it sideways. After 30 of the most awful minutes we had ever experienced, we had moved the van 3 feet and were gulping down cold Cokes. Saturñino said he didn't need a drink and kept working. An hour later we broke free to harder ground, the three of us faint, sick, and almost prostrated by the heat. As we headed back to his ranch Saturñino tried a cold Coke, but when we arrived an hour later it was still half-full.* **99**

● ●

As I pressed the shutter I hoped for a truly spectacular photograph of Victor Cook drinking from the El Volcan geyser, but I had no luck—it erupts only once a month

■ ■ ■ ■ ■ ■ ■ ■ ■ ■ ■ ■ ■ ■ ■ ■ ■ ■ ■ ■
Back on the Transpeninsular at KM 77+

KM	Location
92	The large, solitary cactus standing north of the road is a *cardón*. Found only in Baja from approximately this latitude to the Cape and in a small area in Sonora, these giants may have 20 or more branches and approach 50 feet in height. Perfumed flowers appear in the spring, but the fruit is poor.
99+	Pickup road south to Mina la Esperanza, 4 miles, yielding fair-to-good turquoise. Pickup road north to El Sauce de Carter and Arroyo Grande, signed RANCHO MARTIRES.

Side trip to Arroyo Grande. The trip into Arroyo Grande is one of the most enjoyable and accessible backpacking trips in Baja: not too long, not too short, not too easy, not too hard, and with great scenery. Driving time from San Diego is only about 6 hours plus the time

necessary to conquer 22 miles of pickup road to the jumping-off point, El Sauce de Carter. (The Spanish word *sauce* means willow. History does not seem to have recorded the significance of the name Carter.)

The appropriate topos to get you from the Transpeninsular to El Sauce de Carter are El Aguahito H11B85 and El Metate H11B86. You don't really need them if you carefully follow the road log below, but they might become necessary if you become lost or if a rancher has created a new road and intersection along the way, confusing the road log below. Matomí H11B76 shows the canyon, and El Sauce de Carter is located at longitude 115° 11' west, just off the bottom of the map. Turn north at KM 99+ onto the pickup road, and set odometer.

Mile	Side trip location
2.4	Go left (300°) at the **Y**.
3.5	Continue straight ahead (north) at the intersection. Note the old buildings of Mina el Sausalito. Chrysocolla, malachite, and azurite have been found in the area.
4.8	Cross Arroyo San Juan del Dios. The crossing is rock and sand, and there may be standing water.
5.1	Fork, go right (338°).
5.3	Fork, go right (008°).
8.1	Fork, go right (020°).
9.1	Pass through gate.
9.4	Take either fork.
10.2	Pass through gate. Just past the gate, there are three choices of road; take the center one (048°). A nearby ranch can be reached by taking the left (355°) fork, where someone may be able to provide travel directions should you become lost.
10.5	Short 30% up-grade (going out) in loose rock.
15.4	Keep going straight (048°) at the intersection.
17.0	Fork, go left (028°).
22.2	Arrive at El Sauce de Carter, marked by corrals and a solar panel. Plenty of parking and camping space is available.

The rather unimpressive wash of Arroyo Grande passes just to the north, but the rocky ramparts of the gorge can be seen to the east (082°). After a hike of about 5 miles along the open wash, the main canyon is reached, with its towering pink and orange cliffs. Crystal-clear ponds, some the size of swimming pools, will be found, graced with blue fan palms, willows, and occasional cottonwoods, some of them gigantic. Many idyllic campsites will be found next to the pools. The prints of mountain lions and bighorn sheep will be seen in sandy washes, and a dozen coyotes and a thousand frogs are usually anxious to sing you to sleep. The steepest part of the gorge continues for another 5 miles.

■■■■■■■■■■■■■■■■■■■
Back on the Transpeninsular at KM 99+

KM	Location
104+	The low shrubs with dagger-like leaves on the north side of the highway are *dátillo*, a species of yucca. Up to 15 feet high and having a woody trunk, normally unbranched, and leaves 12-to-19 inches long, they are common in Baja Norte. *Dátillo* can easily be confused with *dátilillio*, another common yucca, which will be seen along the highway at KM 255. Having seen both, you should have little difficulty distinguishing them.
110	Specimens of malachite have been found nearby.
114	Sedan road southwest (signed) to Misión San Fernando Velicatá, 3 miles. In 1769 Franciscan Father Junipero Serra, now a candidate for sainthood despite the fate of his Baja flock and their culture, founded a mission on this site, the name being a Hispanicized version of *Guiricata*, name of the local Indian tribe. Cliffs to the west were quarried to supply stone for an aqueduct. The area is rich in copper and iron, and a half-dozen mines with grand names like Copper Queen and Julius Caesar were established in the early 1900s. Hematite, malachite, chalcopyrite, chalcanthite, bornite, and cuprite can be found nearby.
116+	**Rancho el Progreso.** Food and drink.
127+	**Guayaquil.** Tire repair. Groceries in a small village a half mile north. Pickup road southeast (signed) to Puerto Santa Catarina. Those continuing on the Transpeninsular should skip the following section.

Side trip to Catarina. This road is suitable for pickups, with a few grades to 19%. Set odometer. Pass a ranch at Mile 19.1, and take the right (227°) fork at Mile 21.2. As you bump and bang down this road, reflect on the fact that it was the main route from the onyx mines at El Mármol to the beach at Catarina, and wagons loaded with huge pieces of the stone routinely made the trip, later being replaced by trucks with solid rubber tires (more on El Mármol later). One of the world's finest deposits of fossil ammonites is located at Mile 33.4. Extinct for 70 million years, these cephalopods have only one modern counterpart, the chambered nautilus. Resembling huge snails and ranging in

size from softballs to beach balls, their fossilized remains litter the walls and bottom of the ravine, especially after a hurricane has washed away large amounts of soil. Fist-sized specimens of jasper have been found on the beach at Mile 40.1, some with plume-like formations in several shades of red and a background of red and white jasp-agate, others with concentric circles of black and red on a white agate background. These beauties are hard and unfractured, and cut into fine cabochons. The wrecks of several vessels can be found on the beach. The vessel *Boxer* sank here in the 1920s with 500 tons of onyx aboard.

A side road leads south from the fork at Mile 21.2 to Punta Canoas. Mineral collectors have found malachite at Mina la Fortuna, 5 miles from the fork. Canoas is regarded as only a fair anchorage. Fishermen report the sunken wreck of an old sailing vessel just north of the point.

■■■■■■■■■■■■■■■■■■■
Back on the Transpeninsular at KM 127+

KM	Location
144	Tire repair, café, RV parking. Sedan road northeast (signed) to El Mármol. Those continuing on the Transpeninsular should skip the following section.

Side trip to El Mármol and El Volcán. Turn northeast on a gravel road capable of handling sedans. Set odometer. Just past a corral and windmill at Mile 0.9, take the right (045°) fork and arrive at the site at Mile 9.0. About 1900 Southwest Onyx and Marble, an American company still in business in San Diego, began operations; wells were dug, and homes, a store, and a jail were built. Later a schoolhouse was constructed with onyx walls 30 inches thick, the only one in the world.

Quarried from a deposit 3,000 by 1,200 feet in area and about 40 feet thick, El Mármol onyx was prized for its beautiful veins and subtle shades of brown, tan, red, and yellow. Using wagons and later trucks, it was transported to Catarina. The ruts they left were filled with onyx chips and rolled with a water-filled barrel pulled by a burro. At Catarina the blocks were lightered out from a wooden dock to waiting ships, that carried them to the US, where craftsmen fashioned products ranging from ink pots, doorknobs, and gearshift knobs to the exteriors and interiors of banks, churches, and mansions. A specially selected slab was carved into a bathtub for actress Theda Bara.

Known as Brown's Camp, after the superintendent and his son, who would become superintendent after his father, the busy village grew to several hundred people. Well known to travelers, it was the last source of fuel, water, and supplies for almost 300 miles to the south, and

Huge blocks of onyx at El Mármol. There's a boy in there somewhere

in 1928 Phillip Townsend Hanna compared its strategic importance to Baja travelers to that of Khartoum to travelers between Cairo and the Cape of Good Hope. In its time El Mármol provided a major part of the world's supply of onyx, but with the advent of plastics and inexpensive building materials, demand fell off, and by 1958 the miners and their families had drifted off. El Mármol no longer rings to the sound of air drills, although trucks still come occasionally to haul away stone quarried years ago to be cut into souvenirs and knicknacks.

Today a certain sadness prevails. The homes have fallen down, their lumber has been salvaged, and the famous schoolhouse is slowly succumbing to the elements, its walls cracking and shifting badly. A few people still remember the past; many of the tombstones in the cemetery are graced with plastic flowers. Old-timers tell of a rare hail storm that caused blocks of quarried onyx to ring like a carillon, and of a cavity that was exposed when a block of onyx was cut, the dazzling, crystal-lined prison and palace of a tiny frog.

Mineral collectors will find all the onyx they could ever want, and lesser amounts of mossy jasper and moss agate. A four-wheel-drive road running south offers collecting opportunities. Standing at the schoolhouse, sight 129° and note the road climbing a hill near the horizon. Look for a pegmatite dike at Mile 2.0, and modest amounts of agate at Mile 4.0. Minerals have been found on flat-topped ridges to the south, primarily agate, augite, and andesite. To the east of these ridges is a high basalt-capped mesa nearly a mile in diameter, higher than anything in the vicinity, where large olivine crystals have been collected.

A hike up nearby Arroyo el Volcán is of interest, for there you can visualize the process by which onyx is formed and, if you are lucky, possibly see the only geyser in Baja. A half-dozen bubbling springs deposit thin layers of fresh onyx over a quarter-acre or so. The clear water tastes acidic and faintly sweet. About once a month the geyser shoots up a 60-foot plume of gas and water for several minutes. Immediately south of the springs a dome of onyx has grown to about 30 feet high, causing the tiny spring at its top to reach higher and higher. A hundred yards south, a beautiful layer of striped onyx has been exposed by erosion. Using dry-washing methods, miners used to obtain considerable amounts of gold in the jagged peaks nearby. Good-quality sphene crystals have been found at the mouth of the arroyo near the shores of the Cortez, but since the igneous rocks there are barren, it seems that the sphene must have washed down from somewhere near El Volcán.

To visit the El Volcán onyx dome area sight 040° from the schoolhouse and note the sedan road in the distance. Set odometer. At Mile 4.0 the road crosses the arroyo; the spot will be obvious. Park and hike up the arroyo about 15 minutes. Those with pickups can continue on the road past Arroyo el Volcán. At Mile 7.0 the road passes through areas of heavy mineralization and numerous mining claims. It ends at Mile 10.3 at the La Olividad barite mine, with magnificent views of the Cortez to the east.

■■■■■■■■■■■■■■■■■■

Back on the Transpeninsular at KM 144

KM	Location
146	The strange plants with many whip-like branches on both sides of the highway are *ocotillos*. Common desert plants, they are seen as far south as Bahía Concepción. Often leafless and seemingly dead, these Spartan, no-nonsense plants quickly sprout small green leaves and unexpectedly beautiful mustard-red flowers after a rain. The world record seems to be held by a specimen

157 with 48 whips at the bottom of the Cuesta de la Ley on the El Arco-Bahía San Francisquito road. Entering prime desert scenery, with jumbled boulders, stately *cardóns*, and "forests" of boojums.

160 Modest campsites on both sides of the road.

171+ A small stream crosses the highway, watering a few graceful palms, a great stop for lunch. If you need a bath or a good campsite, sandy areas and deep emerald-colored pools (in wet years) can be found about a half mile upstream. An interesting and easily accessible display of Indian art can be found in a small grotto near here. Red, yellow, and black paintings scattered about its walls and ceiling include abstract designs, humans, and a stylized sun. The bicolor tradition is evident on several figures. The grotto is so small that only a few people can crowd in. In fact, it is on such a small scale and the art so simple that one cannot help imagining that it was a playhouse for Cochimí children—hence its unofficial name, the "Playhouse Cave." Look for dark stains on the ceiling from ancient campfires. The exterior of the site has been vandalized with spray cans, but the art was not damaged. The grotto is easy to locate; park on the north side of the highway and sight 359°. The grotto is located among the largest boulders forming the skyline.

172 The "fat" trees next to the road are *copalquín*, or elephant trees, members of the sumac family. Endemic to Baja and widespread, they seem to prosper in poor conditions, sometimes becoming great prostrate giants on desolate lava beds where nothing else grows. They bear two colors of flowers, some white with touches of pink, others pink to light red. Note that the compound leaves are small, that the branchlets are gray, and that balls of parasitic orange dodder grow on many individuals; these observations will be needed to distinguish *copalquín* from an almost identical species that will be described shortly.

174+ **Cataviña.** The PEMEX (MD) here is very unreliable, and in January, 1998, it was shut down, and the locals were selling gas from drums. Cafés, groceries, tire repair, mechanic. The Hotel la Pinta has rooms, restaurant, bar, pool, tennis court, horseback riding, and local hikes. The RV park has full hookups, rest rooms, and showers, although things almost never work. The park has been landscaped with desert plants, including *copalquín*, just described. However, if you look closely you will note that some of the "fat trees" in the park are not *copalquín*; a few have red-brown branchlets, and their compound leaves are much smaller. These are *torote*, also called elephant trees. Despite being almost indistin-

guishable at first glance and having an overlapping range, they are not even in the same family as copalquín; they belong to the torchwood family. These specimens are transplanted, but the two species can be seen growing side by side in the wild in many locations in this region.

176 Paved road northeast (signed) to Rancho Santa Ynés, 0.7 mile. RV parking, rooms, bunk beds, showers, hot food, and cold beer are available, making it a favorite with motorcyclists, bicyclists, and campers. The highway southeast from this point has long, gentle grades, mostly up, until KM 192, then traverses generally level dry-lake country with only occasional grades to KM 25, south of Parador Punta Prieta. Four-wheel-drive road to Misión Santa María. Those continuing on the Transpeninsular should skip the following section.

Side trip to "Mission Impossible." A four-wheel-drive road runs from Rancho Santa Ynés across a boulder-strewn desert and sandy arroyos to Misión Santa María. Founded in 1767, the mission was abandoned 2 years later when the Jesuits were expelled by royal decree. Graced with plenty of water, the site has many stately palms and pools, and the thousands of frogs never object to a few skinny-dippers. Some adobe walls still stand, and it is not hard to imagine how the Jesuits and their converts struggled to bring "civilization" to this remote region. There is another attraction—the road is one of Baja's worst, so much so that I have dubbed the site "Mission Impossible." Set aside 3 hours for the driving portion of the trip in to the mission. Yes, that's correct, 3 hours; driving faster than 4 or 5 miles an hour will endanger your vehicle and perhaps its occupants.

Start in front of the two large boulders forming the entrance to the restaurant/bunkhouse complex. Set odometer and drive north, make a right (060°) turn in about 100 yards, and another right (140°) in about 200 more yards to get around a fenced corral/storage yard. The road then curves left (060°) and crosses a sandy arroyo. Take the right (050°) fork at Mile 0.7 and the left (030°) at Mile 0.8. At this point you should begin climbing a sandy ridge, and since there are no crossroads from this point on (as of 1998), you can't get too lost. At Mile 1.7 you will encounter a difficult arroyo crossing, with deep holes, loose rock, and an upgrade of 14%. Walk this first—if you are not sure you can cross this arroyo without undue difficulty, turn back while you can. If your vehicle makes this one, you should be able to drive within walking distance of the mission. The road continues, crossing a number of arroyos and a long stretch of fairly flat desert. At Mile 9.7 the Cortez can be seen ahead; the prominent point in the distance is Punta Final. At Mile 12 enter a steep downgrade, with loose rock making it difficult to avoid slipping sideways. At Mile 12.4 stop and note the palm grove ahead—the mission lies ahead twice the distance to the palm grove. This point is the limit most vehicles can go without undue risk. Stop here and walk to the mission, which will take about 40 minutes, one way. If you insist on tempting fate by driving, walk the route first; just ahead lie a number of extremely bad downgrades, with loose rock, huge holes, and bad ruts. You might get in safely, but getting out might be something else again.

■■■■■■■■■■■■■■■■■■■■
Back on the Transpeninsular at KM 176

KM	Location
186	**Rancho San Ignacito.** Food and drink. In September 1973 road crews working north and south met here, completing the construction of the Transpeninsular Highway.
205	Mother Nature stockpiled a large supply of boulders here to spread over the desert just as she did around Cataviña, but the job was never finished.
229+	Road northeast (signed) to Puerto Calamajué, Bahía San Luis Gonzaga, Puertecitos, and San Felipe. See Chapter 13 for a description.
230+	**Rancho Nuevo Chapala.** Food and drink. Laguna Chapala, to the northeast, is dry for years at a time, and its hard, flat surface, marred only by deep polygonal cracks and a thick layer of dust, was a welcome relief for drivers before the Transpeninsular was opened, permitting high speeds and easy driving, if only for a few miles. However, it has no outlet, so when rain finally came a lake formed that could be 3 miles in length and 2 feet deep. As the water dried, mud of unimaginable depths formed. Nothing, neither man nor beast nor vehicle, could conquer the mud, and travelers had to pick their way around the rocky margin of the lake, at the cost of many shredded tires.
255	The trees on both sides of the road with dagger-like leaves resembling the Joshua tree of the US are *dátilillios*. Growing from this region to the Cape, they are often cut into fence posts, many of which take root and produce a living fence. They are very common, sometimes forming great open "forests," especially along the El Arco-San Francisquito road. They can be confused with *dátillo*, noted at KM 104+, but *dátilillios* are generally much taller and may have branches extending anywhere from the trunk.
280	Parador Punta Prieta. The PEMEX (M) here is in a key location, but as noted earlier, do not depend on obtaining gas at this station. In early 1998 the station was closed and the pumps removed, but a local entrepreneur was selling gas from a pickup. The junk yard across the high-

As dusk falls, a Baja 1000 biker races south

way is a good source of emergency parts. Mechanical repairs and towing service may be available. The RV park is not often in operation, but you might be able to park for the night. Paved road east to Bahía de los Angeles. Those continuing on the Transpeninsular should turn to page 148.

 Side trip to Bahía de los Angeles

KM	Side trip location
0	Parador Punta Prieta
11+	Pickup road north to Tinaja de Yubay.

Side trip to Tinaja de Yubay. Known since ancient times, Yubay has played an important part in Baja history. Because it was the only permanent, year-round water hole for many miles, most travelers passing through the region stopped here, including such historical figures as Link, Consag, Crespi, and Serra, and modern adventurers Arthur North and Harry Crosby. Although its drainage is only several hundred acres, impervious rock and the shade from

Mike studiously avoids looking at a broken beam above him while climbing out of Mina Luz de Mexico, east of Desengaño

surrounding bluffs insure that the 40-by-20-foot pond rarely drops below its normal 5-foot depth. The place is beautiful, with white sand and emerald waters surrounded by steep granite walls, and a visit makes an interesting day hike. Since rains sweep the site clean, swimming is fine. Although early travelers complained that it was hard to find, you should have no difficulty. Turn north 0.2 mile east of the KM 11 marker onto a pickup road and set odometer. Take the right (010°) fork at Mile 3.5 and continue north. At Mile 6.0 go east on a little-used sandy road, which ends at a turn-around spot at Mile 8.4. At this point observe the large stony massif to the northeast, capped with a thin, dark horizontal stratum. Yubay is located up an arroyo in the massif, bearing 035°. A round-trip hike takes 2 hours plus exploring and swimming time.

Hikers occasionally find Yubay filled in and showing only a few small pools. Apparently heavy rains carry large quantities of sand into the pool. Based on hundreds of years of recorded history, Mother Nature should soon return it to its former glory. The area is heavily mineralized, and collectors have found pink and green tourmaline. Mina Desengaño, northwest of the fork at Mile 3.5, was a thriving enterprise in the 1930s, planes flying in monthly to carry out the gold.

Back on the road to Bahia de los Angeles at KM 11+

KM	Side trip location
21	Elephant tree forest.
44	Pickup road south (signed) to Misión San Borja. Those continuing on to Bahía de los Angeles should skip the following section.

Side trip to Misión San Borja. Set odometer. Take the right (245°) fork at Mile 2.1 and the left (180°) fork at Mile 4.0. The area is mineralized; note the quartz pavement at Mile 4.7 and the broad band of quartz on the hill at Mile 12.8. Deer, coyote, and many species of birds inhabit this area. Take the left (165°) fork at Mile 15.0 and arrive at the mission at Mile 22.4. Driven at safe speeds, this will take about 3 hours. The handsome stone church, built by the Dominicans in 1801 of stone quarried in the surrounding cliffs and remaining in use until 1818, is the first well-preserved mission building south of the border. Treasure hunters have damaged its walls looking for hidden gold, and its two bells have been stolen (a cow bell now takes their place). A hot spring and a cold spring are located a 5-minute hike, 155°, from the mission, an old kiln can be seen near the graveyards, and stone aqueducts are visible in the orchards. A few people still live in the vicinity, so respect their privacy and don't walk in the gardens. The church is still in use, and you may be asked for a small donation.

Back on the road to Bahia de los Angeles at KM 44+

KM	Side trip location
49	Boojum forest.
52+	Beautiful vistas of the Cortez.
65	**Bahía de los Angeles.**

Bahía de los Angeles

If it was necessary to pick a single location to represent the entire peninsula, there would be little doubt what it would be—Bahía de los Angeles, the quintessential Baja in the eyes of many. Beginning in the 1940s, aviators and four-wheelers returned home to tell of a tiny outpost of civilization that could be found at the foot of a mountain, where friendly fishermen lived in palm-thatched adobe homes, everything dominated by the desert wilderness on one side and the incredibly beautiful blue bay and brown islands on the other. It isn't paradise, for summers can be extremely hot, and in winter katabatic winds funnel down from the canyons to the west at 50 miles an hour for as long as a week, turning inflatable boats into zeppelins and confining visitors to cribbage and Corona. In recent years, the town has not prospered, and is in need of a fix-up, paint-up, and trash-removal program. Still, the natural beauty of the area has endured, and once out on the bay fishing, diving, exploring, boardsailing, kayaking, or whale-watching, you will find that your visit to "The Bay of the Angels" is one of the high points of your trip to Baja.

The RV park situation in town is not inspiring: they are often badly littered, and maintenance ranges from fair to bad, depending on the unpredictable whims of the management. Although you may see water, electrical, and sewage hookups, the chances that they will be operational are poor. Villa Vitta's RV park (6) has a dump station and electric hookups. Guillermo's RV Park (10) has full hookups, but the place is often badly littered. Rest rooms and showers are located in a small building just to the south of the associated restaurant.

There are better choices a short distance out of town. Daggett's Campground (1) has RV parking, rest rooms. showers, BBQ pits, boat trips, fishing, whale-watching, and a beach. At KM 64, set odometer, go north on the two-lane graded road (signed), and follow the signs at each turn, arriving at Mile 1.8. Ruben Daggett, the owner, is a descendent of Dick Daggett, Englishman and pioneer Baja miner. Gecko Campground (14), 4 miles south of town on the road to Las Flores (described later), has RV parking, cabins, showers, and rest rooms. Boondocking and RV parking sites can be found along the northern sweep of the beach from town to Punta la Gringa.

Construction of a new motel, Costa del Sol (5), has just been completed (1998), and it is easily the finest place in town to stay, with large rooms, tile floors, comfortable beds, full baths with tubs, and a satellite telephone. A pool is planned, kayaks and ATVs are for rent, and sportfishing trips can be arranged. The Villa Vitta Motel, just to the south, has a bar, a pool, and a clean and pleasant restaurant. They sell a limited selection of fishing equipment. There are other restaurants, including Casa Diaz (11), Restaurant las Hamacas (4), and one at Guillermo's RV Park (there is a small grocery store and a curio shop in the same building). Cube and block ice can be purchased (7), and there a number of tiny grocery stores.

A new PEMEX station is under construction, and the old one is permanently closed, but in the interim, local entrepreneurs sell gasoline from drums and tank trailers—ask around. LPG, gasoline, and firewood can be purchased at a store (2) on the main drag, which also offers laundry service. There is a telephone office (3) and a health clinic (9). A garage (13) makes mechanical and welding repairs, and sometimes has diesel fuel available. There are a number of other mechanics, but they may not have signs out. There are no auto parts or hardware stores, laundromats, or commercial transportation. Some of the businesses in town keep *siesta* hours from one to three in the afternoon. An interesting museum has been constructed with contributions of money, materials, artifacts, volunteer labor, and donated land (8).

Mineral collectors will find copper minerals at Mina el Toro, reached by taking a pickup road 7 miles north from the vicinity of the fishing cooperative at La Gringa. The volcano on Isla Coronado should provide igneous specimens. "Desert rose," a microscopically crystallized variety of chalcedony quartz, can be found at a site across the bay. Heading south on the "main drag," turn right (west) at the whitewashed concrete fence marking the Casa Diaz compound. Turn left (south) at the first opportunity, and set odometer. Turn east at Mile 4.4 and follow the curve of the bay, eventually turning north near the end of a landing strip. Adjacent to the first group of buildings in the American-owned settlement known as La Mona, north of the end

Even a Trail 90 can't conquer everything

of the airstrip, turn east on the first road encountered. Follow the road to its end; the sites are located in ravines to the north and east.

Popular shelling sites are found along the beach at low tide from Punta Arena to La Gringa. Net fishermen frequently snag unusual specimens in deep water, especially beautiful hard corals and occasional specimens of black coral, which are approaching the northern end of their range, judging by their size. The museum has a shell collection of many local species.

There is a shallow (10%) concrete launch ramp at Villa Vitta, the only one in Bahía de los Angeles that is usable at low tide. It is protected somewhat from north weather by a stone wall. The steep (17%) ramp at Guillermo's is very rough and requires mid- to high tides for larger boats. The steep (19%) Casa Diaz ramp (12) is rough, but a small breakwater offers some protection. Campers at Daggett's Campground can use the shallow concrete launch ramp next door (10%). Gecko Campground has a shallow (7%) concrete launch ramp, but it leads to a pebble area and is usable by larger boats only at high tide.

The best fishing is during the hot months, and in midwinter things slow down considerably. The bay is known primarily for yellowtail, which are present from late April

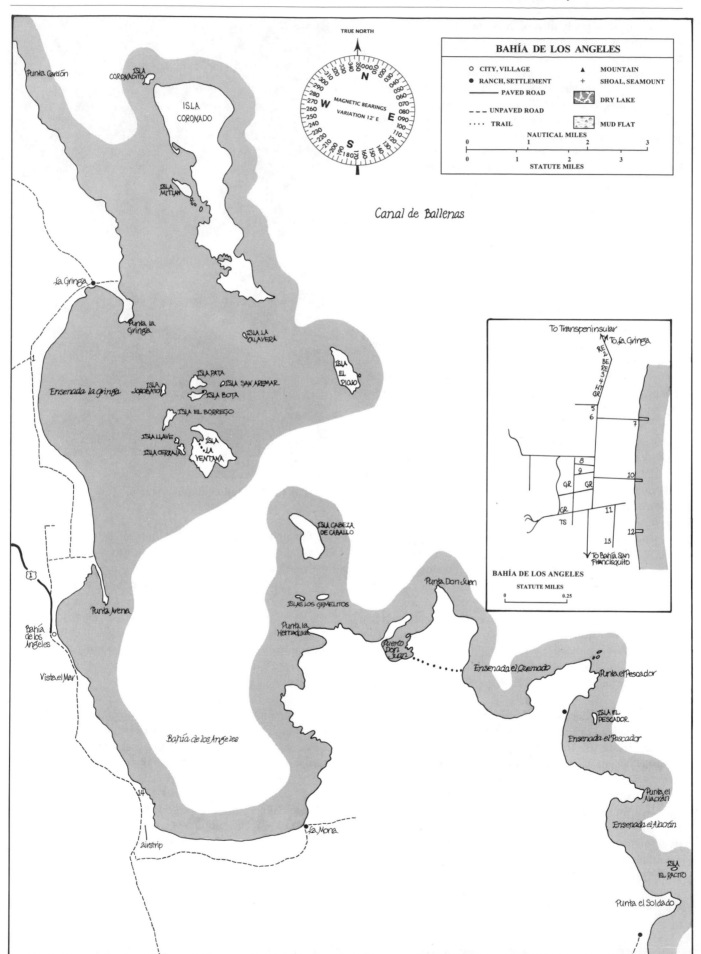

TRUE NORTH

MAGNETIC BEARINGS
VARIATION 12° E

Canal de Ballenas

BAHÍA DE LOS ANGELES

○ CITY, VILLAGE   ▲ MOUNTAIN
● RANCH, SETTLEMENT   + SHOAL, SEAMOUNT
—— PAVED ROAD   ▦ DRY LAKE
--- UNPAVED ROAD
···· TRAIL   ▨ MUD FLAT

NAUTICAL MILES
0   1   2   3

0   1   2   3
STATUTE MILES

Punta Caralón

ISLA
CORONADITO

ISLA
CORONADO

ISLA
MITLAN

la Gringa

Punta la
Gringa

ISLA LA
OLLAVERA

ISLA PATA
ISLA SAN AREMAR
ISLA BOTA

ISLA EL
PIOJO

ISLA
JOROBATO

Ensenada la Gringa

ISLA EL BORREGO

ISLA LLAVE
ISLA CERRAJA

ISLA
LA
VENTANA

1

ISLA CABEZA
DE CABALLO

ISLAS LOS GEMELITOS

Punta Arena

Punta la
Herradura

Punta Don Juan

Puerto
Don Juan

Ensenada el Quemado

Punta el Pescador

Bahía
de los
Angeles

1

Vista el Mar

ISLA EL
PESCADOR

Ensenada el Pescador

Bahía de los Angeles

Punta el
Alacrán

Ensenada el Alacrán

14

la Mona

Airstrip

ISLA
EL PACITO

Punta el Soldado

Inset map

To Transpeninsular
To la Gringa

RE
2
BE
RE
3
4
HT
GR

5
6   7

8
9
GR   GR   10

GR   11

TS   13   12

To Bahía San
Francisquito

BAHÍA DE LOS ANGELES

STATUTE MILES

0   0.25

or early May through October, and dorado are usually available from May through July, white seabass a bit earlier. There are many other species, and the fishery resembles Southern California, with ocean whitefish, various varieties of rockfish, and even sheephead around, the leopard grouper found elsewhere in the Cortez being less common. The result is perhaps the most mixed of "mixed bags" available in Baja, and it is not uncommon to encounter 20 and even 30 species during a week-long fishing vacation. *Pangas* and guides can be arranged at Guillermo's and Casa Diaz. Live bait can be taken with Lucky Joes or snagged with treble hooks near Punta Arena or several miles to the south of the point.

The bay provides good jigging and trolling, especially around the islands. The most productive locations include the east coast of Isla Coronado and the reefs off its north and southeast points, and east of Isla Cabeza de Caballo. The deep water of Canal de Ballenas yields rockfish, various basses, cabrilla, and ocean whitefish, but because of its swift currents, fishing ventures must be planned around the tide tables. Beach-casting with cut bait produces sand bass, triggerfish, guitarfish, and rays. In spring, the shoreline from Punta Arena north to La Gringa is a good place for yellowfin croaker, and halibut to 15 pounds are taken in the inner harbor. Beach-casting equipment is an asset, for it may be the only technique possible during windy periods.

Incidentally, when asking a local fishing guide to take you to Coronado, San Aremar, or El Borrego, you may get a blank look: departing from their official names, local usage has identified these islands as Smith, Rasita, and Flecha, respectively.

Whale- and bird-watchers can remain engrossed for days or weeks. More than a dozen species of whales and dolphins have been seen in the Canal, including blue, finback, gray, Bryde's, Minke, humpback, pilot, sperm, pygmy, killer, and false killer whales, as well as bottlenose and common dolphins. Bryde's whales are the most common, more so than finback whales, for which they are often mistaken. Bryde's whales are seen most frequently in winter, especially January, when they feed on large squid. Finback whales cruise the Bahía de los Angeles area and the Midriff year-round, peaking in the Canal in spring and summer. Sperm whales are less common, and are seen most frequently in February. Grays are encountered only rarely. Dolphins put on a great show for almost any passing boat, and sometimes break into organized groups in Puerto Don Juan, apparently herding forage fish. At least 50 species of birds are seen around the bay and its islands. There are nesting ospreys on Islas la Ventana, Coronado, and El Pescador, a pelican colony on Isla el Piojo, and a frigate resting site on the southeast point of Coronado.

The channel between Coronado and Isla Mitlan offers good snorkeling, and Isla Coronadito has good spearfishing. The east coast of Coronado has fine diving, especially about one-third of the way south from the north cape, where rocks and boulders form caves and small crevices. Many species of fish will be encountered, including Gulf opaleye,

browncheek blennies, triplefins, finescale triggerfish, and Cortez damselfish, as well as sea fans and soft corals. Spearfishermen should find good populations of yellowtail and Gulf grouper. An excellent reef continues from the southeastern tip of the island. Coronadito has fine snorkeling on its north and west sides.

The east coast of Piojo is known for its colorful nudibranchs. I once made 50 free-dives to 35 feet to photograph one of these purple and gold-lamé beauties, and didn't recover from aching Eustachian tubes and palpitating sinuses for 3 days. Although beach diving is generally poor, the reefs north of La Gringa have brilliantly colored sea fans and encrusting sponges, the latter in a dozen hues. Despite the fine diving, there is currently no dive shop and no reliable source of compressed air.

The 50-foot wooden fishing vessel *Marcelo* ran onto the reef between Ventana and Cabeza de Caballo in 1983, and her wreck now makes a fine dive site. Lying approximately 400 yards southeast of the prominent "window" landmark on Ventana, the reef is about 100 yards long. A half-dozen shallow rock pinnacles are barely covered at moderate tides, so take care approaching the site. The bulk of the wreck is about 20 feet from the southeastern pinnacle in 10 to 50 feet of water. Deeper sections of the reef have the most colorful sea life in the bay, and a proposal has been made to make it a national marine park. About 1981 a fishing boat burned and sank off the east side of Isla el Racito, a low, rocky islet 700 yards north of Punta el Soldado, and the wreck presents one of the finest displays of plant and animal life in the Cortez. It lies in 10 to 16 feet of water about 100 feet off the east side, midway between the north and south points.

Boardsailors can have a ball in Bahía de los Angeles. Many just like to explore the islands, while others enjoy getting someone to drive them to La Gringa and making downwind runs to play in the islands, returning directly to town. Still others like to take advantage of every opportunity; when the famous winds are blowing they try speed sailing, when it's calmer they play around the islands, and if it stops they head for Santa Rosalillita. Most avoid the southern part of the bay, since winds are cut off by the surrounding topography and tend to be gusty and erratic.

The best anchorages are inside Punta Arena, or near La Gringa. When these get too choppy or dusty, boaters like to move to Don Juan. This almost-landlocked, all-weather cove has several small sand-and-silt beaches and is a popular jumping-off point for boaters and kayakers headed for the Midriff. A wrecked fishing vessel can be seen near the entrance, and a fine sea cave is located nearby; when anchored in Don Juan, go ashore where the spit forming the north shore joins the "mainland." Hike north across the spit to the bay and then southwest along the shore, and the cave will be found just above sea level. A trail runs between Don Juan and Ensenada el Quemado.

The Bahía de los Angeles area provides small-boat and kayak sailors with a variety of opportunities. There are six popular choices, in ascending order of the distances involved:

stay in the bay; go north to Isla Coronado; visit Bahía las Animas to the south; head south for Santa Rosalía; visit Guardian Angel Island; or visit the Midriff. Guardian Angel Island is ordinarily thought of as part of the Midriff, but will be found in "By water: circumnavigating Guardian Angel," starting in the next column on this page, since most visitors to the island come by way of Bahía de los Angeles. Those using Bahía de los Angeles as a jumping-off place for trips to the beautiful and mysterious Midriff region should turn to Chapter 14.

Cruising Charts publishes a "Paddle Chart of Bahía de los Angeles" and the coast as far south as Bahía San Francisquito, and a Mini-Guide of Bahía de los Angeles and Bahía las Ánimas. Outland Adventures will take kayakers on a paddle to the Midriff from Bahía de los Angeles, and maintains a fleet of kayaks at Bahía de los Angeles for rent to intermediate/advanced kayakers and expert-led groups. Southwest Sea Kayaks offers a trip from Bahía de los Angeles to Ánimas and a circumnavigation of Guardian Angel, and Venture Quest has a trip to Coronado. Aqua Adventures also has trips to the bay. Some Baja Discovery van trips visit the town.

There are over a dozen islands in the bay. Ventana has two small cobble and pebble beaches on the east side, and a steep cobble beach on its northeast side. On the northwest side, a narrow cove provides an anchorage with a sand and mud bottom and excellent protection from all but the infamous west winds, and there is a sand and pebble beach, with a trail to the top of the island. If you get caught by a westerly while in this cove, just move to the lee of low-lying Isla Cerraja, which is surrounded by a sand bottom. The cut between Islas Pata and Bota is well-protected, and there is a beach of crushed shell on Pata. Piojo has pebble beaches on its south, east, and west sides, but it gets few visitors, for it smells of guano and its name might cause concern (a *piojo* is a louse).

Coronado, 2.2 miles from Punta la Gringa, has good campsites, one east of the tidal spit on the southwest side of the volcano, another opposite Isla Mitlan, and a third on the sandy beaches of the cove that almost splits the island in two. The last is good if the weather is unsettled, since an easy portage can be made to the opposite cove, allowing you to "switch sides" if the wind comes up. However, tie down your kayak if you are camping in this spot, for more than one has been carried away by the wind. In periods of west winds, the cove on the east side has a mixed sand and rock bottom and offers good shelter from the waves, but not the wind.

Boaters and kayakers traveling east across the bay and then coasting east and south from Don Juan, Mile 5.8, will encounter open anchorages at Ensenada el Quemado, Mile 8.4, Ensenada el Pescador, Mile 10.5, Ensenada el Alacrán, 12.5, and the southernmost extent of Bahía las Ánimas, Mile 18.8. The sandy beaches in these bays permit easy landings and camping. The northwest side of Quemado, however, is rocky and may provide poor anchoring. Pescador has good camping, and some of the best snorkeling in the Cortez is

found off the point. Isla el Pescador (Isla Rocallosa) is a sensitive bird breeding area, and no one should go ashore. A tourist camp has been constructed on the shore of the bay opposite the island, an unfortunate choice of location. Ánimas has a number of good campsites and places to anchor, mostly on sand bottoms, and offers good local exploring and snorkeling in the mangrove areas.

Instead of camping within Ánimas, some like to head directly east across the mouth of the bay to "The Slot," Mile 19.1, located just east of Punta las Ánimas. This tiny cove is a special favorite of kayakers and those in very small boats. Together with a small island just offshore and a connecting reef, the cove provides some protection from all but east weather, although enough of the waves from the north can make it over the reef that it can be a bit uncomfortable in north weather.

Kayakers and boaters continuing south from The Slot should turn to "By water: coasting to Santa Rosalía," beginning on page 147. Drivers heading for Bahía San Francisquito should turn to that side trip on page 147, and those returning to Parador Punta Prieta and the Transpeninsular should turn to page 148.

By water: circumnavigating Guardian Angel

The big island to the northeast of Bahía de los Angeles is Guardian Angel, 47.3 statute miles from tip to tip. Once a part of the peninsula and now moved 30 miles south by tectonic forces, the island is the result of seafloor spreading about a million years ago, its rocks being of Miocene volcanic and Pliocene sedimentary origin. The geology is colorful, some areas graced with broad layers of gray, white, pink, yellow, green, and red. In spite of being mountainous and second in land area in the Cortez only to Isla Tiburón, it has no permanent surface water. Although there are historical records and archaeological evidence of temporary fishing and sea-lion-hunting camps, it has never been permanently inhabited, and the island and its flora and fauna are in virtually pristine condition. Seemingly completely barren from a distance, it supports small numbers of *agave*, cacti, *cardón*, elephant trees (both kinds—*torote* and *copalquín*) and, on the high peaks inland at the north end, boojum. In all, 199 species of vascular plants, 15 reptiles and amphibians, and 3 small land mammals have been recorded. Birdwatchers might add many sightings to their check lists. The yellow-legged gull nests on the island.

Guardian Angel is slowly being "discovered" by kayakers and boaters. There are many beaches and no excessively long areas of bluffs and steep cliffs to pose an undue danger to slow-moving kayakers should the weather take a turn for the worse and a landing become necessary. However, most of these beaches are something other than the serene, well-protected, glistening stretches of white sand that stir the imagination, for most are fairly steep, consisting of pebbles and cobble, and many are open to prevailing weather.

The most popular route to the island begins at Daggett's Campground, reaches Coronado, and then heads north to Punta Remedios. The route then turns east to Punta los Machos on Guardian Angel, and then heads north to Puerto Refugio. Most return by simply reversing the route, but a few energetic souls venture down the east coast of the island to its south tip and then head west.

A kayak voyage to the island is only for those with open-water experience, but if you don't fit this category, simply hire a *panga* in town to carry you, your kayak, and your gear to the island. Smart voyagers will use their tide tables to plan a trip, using flood tides to push them north and ebbs south. The appropriate Mexican 1:50,000 topos are: Isla Mejía H12C22; Isla Angel de la Guarda Norte H12C32; Punta del Diablo H12C33; Campo Juárez H12C42; and Isla Angel de la Guarda Sur H12C43. These are generally accurate, although a few "phantom" islands and a number of other errors will be noted later. The coverage of the island is incomplete: the 1980 version of H12C42, which is the most current, covers the coast from La Gringa north to a location just short of Remedios, but does not show a 7-mile stretch of Guardian Angel. Also, the 1980 version of Punta las Ánimas H12C53 "ought" to include a small area at the south tip of the island but doesn't, so don't bother buying it. Cruising Charts offers several charts and guides to the area.

The coast north from Coronado consists of rocky bluffs alternating with stretches of pebble beaches, generally providing adequate camping areas. The tides produce swift currents in this area, especially in the vicinity of Isla Alcatraz, 11 miles from Daggett's. (In keeping with the convention used throughout the book, all across-the-water distances are in nautical miles.) As Remedios is approached, 18.2 miles from Daggett's, the beaches give way to sand and pebbles. Remedios is a low rocky point, providing some shelter from the prevailing waves, good anchoring conditions, and adequate campsites.

Colorful Punta los Machos is the closest point on Guardian Angel. The current in the Canal de Ballenas is often heavy and winds can be fierce, so make the crossing at first light, keep a "weather eye" out, and use your tide tables. There is little in the way of striking landmarks to distinguish its location, making a compass bearing essential—it bears 064° from Remedios, 6.9 miles. Machos provides a fair lee in prevailing weather, and the bottom is sand and cobble. There is a small cobble beach just to the east, but the best camping beach will be found a bit further east—see Mile 95.1 on page 146.

Heading north from Punta los Machos, Mile 0, an odd rock formation resembling the Devil's Postpile in California will be encountered at Mile 1.0. At Mile 2.5, a tiny natural breakwater provides a bit of protection, and the steep cobble beach has adequate space for camping. A

fair anchorage and a cobble beach will be encountered in the lee of a tiny cape at Mile 3.5, but there is no good landing for kayaks. The *Escama XXIII*, a steel-hulled fishing vessel, lies at Mile 3.9. It is abandoned and aground, but its hull is apparently intact, and it may eventually be salvaged.

A sand-and-cobble anchorage will be found in the lee of a small cape at Mile 5. However, the cobble-and-boulder beach does not appear too comfortable. There is a stretch of sand beach at La Ballenita, Mile 6.7, with modest protection from north weather. Three-quarters of a mile to the northwest, although the beach is cobble at the north and south ends, there is a sand beach in the middle, offering good camping. It is unfortunately almost completely open to prevailing weather.

There is a long cobble-and-pebble beach at Mile 8.6, but protection and camping areas are limited. A natural breakwater will be found a half mile to the northwest. Although there is good anchoring on a cobble-and-sand bottom, there are no good landing sites. The south end of the beach at Mile 9.7 is cobble, but it gives way to pebbles at the north end, where modest protection and good camping will be found. Mile 10.8 offers a cobble beach and very limited protection. As you near the north end of the island nears, Roca Vela (Sail Rock), its white bird droppings and triangular shape reminding the locals of a sail, can be seen ahead. The large cove at Mile 15.3 provides some shelter and a few fair-to-good campsites.

Boaters and kayakers should enter Puerto Refugio by sticking fairly close to the south shore of Isla Mejía, passing Vaquitero (Mejía Cove), a tiny cove on its eastern shore, at Mile 18.2. Those tempted to take what appears to be a shortcut through the passage between the peninsula forming the southwestern bight of the main bay and what appears to be an island just southeast of Isla Mejía may be greeted by sharp rocks and swift currents. Refugio is the first good anchorage southeast of Bahía Gonzaga, and is one of the most scenic and interesting areas on the island. It is satisfactory in weather from all directions, but you may have to move around to stay out of the chop. Satisfactory anchorages can be made almost anywhere in the main bay where the water is at least 4 fathoms deep, generally on sand bottoms. Landings can be found in a number of small coves along Refugio's southern shore, and sand and pebble beaches provide excellent camping. Many visitors enjoy the southwestern bight the most, where there are sand beaches and good anchoring conditions.

Each of its islands has a distinct character. Mejía is known for lizards, giant cardón, and nesting ospreys, with a reef extending north. Vaquitero is one of the most protected anchorages in the Cortez for small craft. However, beware of its "red beaches." Attractive, smooth, gently sloping, and apparently offering idyllic campsites, they are actually spongy, smelly, and soft, little more than damp bogs of red mush. Another problem is encountered here—

the gulls expend a terrific amount of time and energy squawking all day and part of the night. Perhaps a reader with a background in ornithology can answer the obvious question: What is survival value of all this noise? Isla el Granito (Isla Alcatraz, Isla la Lobera) has brown pelicans and oystercatchers, and divers will find a reef extending from its northwestern tip. Most of the California sea lions that once called this place home have learned that Mexican fishermen are their mortal enemies, and have wisely taken up residence on the eastern side of the island, often at a site to be described later. Granito makes an excellent campsite, but the best areas are often occupied by commercial fishermen. In the past, many kinds of gamefish visited the area, and enormous pileups of yellowtail have been reported, but intensive commercial fishing has reduced the catch.

The trip down the east coast of the island has much the same scenery and conditions as the west side, but has a heightened air of mystery and remoteness. Continuing east from Vaquitero at Mile 18.2, Punta Refugio (Punta Bluff) is passed at Mile 20.6, and the coast temporarily swings sharply south. Pebble beaches with good camping, open to the prevailing weather, will be found at Miles 21.6, 23.3, 23.7, 24.0, 24.7, and 25.0. Heavy currents may be encountered in this area, and the shoreline has lengths of sheer bluffs. A tiny cove at Los Cantiles, Mile 25.8, offers the first minimal shelter from the prevailing weather encountered since Refugio. The pebble beach is only 20 yards wide, but it offers good camping and welcome shade in the afternoon.

The coast at Mile 26.6 provides those possessing the right technique and a little luck an experience that may be one of the highlights of their trip. As mentioned earlier, many of the sea lions that once populated Refugio, the survivors anyway, have moved their base of operations, and this is one of the sites they often choose. The worst way to visit them is to aggressively charge in for a close view, for within seconds the alarm will sound and they will be gone—they are deathly afraid of humans, for good reason. The best way is to stand well off-shore, 50 yards is close enough, and watch them through binoculars, causing as little disturbance as possible. More than a few will be seen carrying fish nets wrapped around their necks, and many of the huge males bear battle scars from masculine disputes. The mighty din of their barking recalls the question about the squawking of the gulls at Refugio—what possible survival value is achieved by this major expenditure of time and energy? Despite their persecution by angry fishermen bent on genocide, the sea lions still

seem to be curious about humans, and once they get used to your presence and lose their nervousness, a half-hour or so, you may be surrounded by dozens of bobbing brown heads, their soft black eyes intently examining the odd creatures invading their domain. They often put on a show of acrobatics, flipping and turning into the air, but whether they do this to please visitors or simply as a sea lion sport is unknown. When you have seen enough, slip away as you came, silently and with as little commotion as possible.

As the trip progresses, minerals slowly turn the soil yellow, almost the color and glint of sulfur by Mile 26.9. The area is labeled "Ensenada Cueva Amarilla" on H12C32, in spite of the facts that there is no cove and there is more than one "cave" (actually just shallow depressions). A hundred yards to the south, a landing on the cobble-and-boulder beach and a short hike are in order. A steep-sided, very narrow arroyo has been carved by water, which has cut the yellow soil into the natural equivalent of a giant waterslide, coursing back and forth in sharp, almost 180°, bends. Why does the water take such a meandering course, when it "ought" to take the shortest distance between two points, a straight line? Scientists tell us that meandering is a manifestation of "a minimum time-rate of potential energy expenditure"; by lengthening its path and thus reducing its rate of flow, the water remains "lazy." A more useful layman's explanation is that the current at natural bends in the stream tends to be swiftest on the outer side, producing greater turbulence and erosion on the outside of the bend than the inside, and eventually leading to a wildly sinuous course. Glints of low-quality quartz can be seen lining the canyon walls, as well as slides of dried yellow mud, ranging from trickles to mighty multi-ton cascades. Because of the torrents of water that occasionally roar through the canyon, the spine-armored plants common to desert regions grow too slowly to survive and reproduce here,

Michael loads up as we continue our circumnativation of Guardian Angel

and the bottom is covered with very delicate and ephemeral flowering shrubs, showing bright shades of red, blue, and yellow, quick to grow, quick to wash away in a flood, and quick to return. After a flood, the mud shrinks as it dries, forming a polygonal pattern reminiscent of a tile floor, giving the canyon a look suggesting that a determined if somewhat disorganized gardener had prepared months in advance for your visit.

The sand-and-pebble beaches on the coast south from Cueva Amarilla give way to cobble and boulders near Punta el Púlpito. There are a number of camping beaches, although none offer much in the way of protection from the waves. The dark, brooding, almost vertical face of Púlpito at Mile 34.2 serves as an excellent landmark. The tidal swamp shown just northeast of Púlpito on H12C32 does not exist. Bahía el Púlpito, south of the point, is subject to heavy and erratic currents, and a sizable chop develops when the currents oppose the wind, so kayakers should plan their day with the aid of their tide tables. The coast from Pulipto, curving south and then east to Ensenada las Cuevitas (Caleta Púlpito West), has a number of campsites, although they are increasingly open to prevailing winds as you turn east.

Cartographers and writers are not immune to wishful thinking. H12C33 would have you believe that there is a tiny, well-protected cove providing kayakers and small-boaters with shelter from winds from any direction at Ensenada las Cuevitas, Mile 43.6, and more than one magazine article has waxed ecstatic over the white sand beach and turquoise water. The truth is more restrained: The small rocky headland riddled with tiny caves that give the place its name divides the cove into two sections; to the west is a small sandy beach, backed by a sand-and-pebble berm, while the east side has an even smaller sand beach backed by a steep cobble-and-boulder berm. The west side provides better camping, the east a bit better protection. The salt marsh in back of the cove is home to many wading birds, as well as hordes of tiny crabs armed with enormous claws, all of whom have waited with anticipation at sharing the warmth and protection of your sleeping bag. It's an interesting place, and because of the area's east-west orientation, there is often good beachcombing. Boaters will find a featureless sand bottom offering good anchoring, but there is no protection from prevailing weather.

Just to the east, there is a small cove with a sand bottom and a cobble-and-pebble beach with little to offer to the kayaker or boater. The western side of "Caleta Púlpito East," at Mile 44.4, has a cobble beach and offers a modest lee from west and south weather, the bottom being largely cobble and sand. The steep beaches on the coast to the east as far as Punta Rocosa (Punta del Diablo) are cobble and boulders, with several very short stretches of pebble.

Punta Rocosa, at Mile 49.8, is a fascinating and challenging place. The prevailing north winds that "bounce" off the northwest-southeast range of mountains forming the spine of the island often oppose a flood tide that can reach 6 knots, turning the area into a maelstrom of white water rating comparison to Patagonia. The deep reefs off the point are noted for big groupers and fine scuba diving, and the unsophisticated cabrilla in close often volunteer to come to dinner. The huge number of forage fish that inhabit the area attract large numbers of pelicans and gulls, and it is not uncommon to encounter the "pileups" of fishy predators that were the subject of so many magazine articles in the "old days." With luck, you may see a yellow-crowned night-heron, an occasional stray from its more southerly range, gingerly catching small fish escaping the melee by fleeing into shallower water. The land masses that can be seen to the east and northeast on clear days are mountains on Isla Tiburón and the mainland. An open anchorage sheltered from prevailing winds can be made south of Rocosa, and there is a pebble beach, making it a good rest stop and camp if the north winds come up.

The bluffs at Mile 53.4 again display the rich, sulfur-like color seen to the north. The short, steep gravel beach here provides poor camping, but could serve as a lunch stop. Punta Arena, Mile 55.2, provides a very modest lee and an excellent camping area. Arena is an undisturbed turtle nesting site, so do your best to keep it that way. The bones of a large whale can be seen at Mile 59.4. The island shown on H12C43 at Mile 61.2 does not exist. The coast in this area consists of bluffs alternating with steep boulder and cobble beaches, and a few sand-and-pebble beaches. The lonely remains of an old house and a concrete boat ramp can be seen at the head of the steep pebble beach at La Almeja, Mile 63.1. The small cove at Mile 64.2 offers a bit of protection from all but north weather and a steep sand beach

Isla Estanque (Isla la Víbora), at Mile 65.4, contains an almost landlocked salt water pond. It makes an excellent all-weather anchorage for shallow-draft boats and has several camping areas, sometimes in use by commercial fishermen (the sandy areas nearby on Guardian Angel are far better, but not so well sheltered). Beware; the island did not get its alternate name for no reason—*víbora* means viper—and the place is home to many rattlers. It has the added attraction of a strange underwater garden. Algae thrive at certain times of the year, and a dive will reveal a world of muted, almost formless brown shapes. A strange stillness prevails; gamefish rarely enter the pond, and what animal life there is moves slowly—it is a noncompetitive world in slow motion. The lack of bright color, especially green, brings on a somber mood and reminds one of Cousteau's television program about Lake Titicaca, without the frogs. The island's east side makes a nice dive, with a steep wall ending in sand, the home of the beautiful spiny oyster, several species of scallop, and large numbers of *chocolates*.

A shallow reef extends southwest from Estanque to Guardian Angel. This reef should be avoided, for the 4- or 5-knot current can easily sweep you into the reef. Those arriving from the south should round the island counter-clockwise and enter the pond from the west, parallel to and north of the reef. The pond goes to 4 fathoms, but we once scraped over the rocky entrance in a sloop drawing 7 feet. Bats inhabit much of Baja, and you may see a special kind near Estanque and south to Isla San José, one that lives on seafood. Watch for ghostly forms skimming over the waves at dusk, catching small fish with their claws. The coast south from Estanque to the south cape of the island has a number of good camping areas, some beaches equipped with sand, others with cobble and pebble. Bottoms are mostly cobble, with patches of sand, and the spearfishing for flatfish can be outstanding. However, there is something you must know: The fish-eating bats don't eat bugs.

● ●

66 *That sinking feeling*

Reeve, John Anglin, and I ran our grossly overloaded 15-foot cartopper out to the beaches at the south tip of Guardian Angel one year. The days were glorious—fine weather and great spearfishing for flatfish, sometimes in water only 4 or 5 feet deep—but the first night was sheer hell. Any thesaurus can provide scores of adjectives that come close—fiendish, ferocious, and frightful are a few—but nothing in English is completely up to the task of describing the jejénes. *They crawled up our noses and ears and we soon had trickles of blood running down our necks. The wind came up the second night and they disappeared, so over the campfire we composed a ditty—inspired, I think, by Janis Joplin: "Please Lord, if you'll keep it blowin' from this point hence, I'll give up gettin' the Mercedes Benz." Divine intervention didn't work, and on the third evening Reeve let out a few favorite Anglo-Saxon curses and stalked out of camp into the darkness up the canyon with his bedroll under his arm. Fifteen minutes later he was back with good news—there were no* jejénes *a hundred feet higher than our camp. He had found the secret, and we slept through the night from then on.*

Three days later we were headed southeast for Isla Partida Norte when our prayers were answered, too late and too well—a fierce north wind came up and the boat swamped and sank. After a few anxious minutes it popped to the surface, minus its cargo. The flotation was not adequate to get the gunnels high enough above the waves to allow bailing, so we emptied two outboard gas tanks and used the anchor line to make a sling between them, lifting the boat. At this point the wind dropped to a flat calm, of course, and after bailing the boat out we paddled back to Guardian Angel with swim fins. It was several hours before we managed to attract the attention of a passing boat, but fortunately our cooler had bobbed to the surface with its vital cargo of beer and

ice, so we had a few cool ones as we contemplated our latest lesson in small-boat seamanship. 99

● ●

At Punta Colorada, the south tip of the island, Mile 69.4, you have the choice of heading directly back to Daggett's, 23.3 miles, 260°, or heading north along the west coast of Guardian Angel to Punta los Machos, crossing the Canal to Remedios, and then heading south. The first route shortens the length of the trip, but will challenge most kayakers—Isla Piojo, the first landfall, is 18.5 miles, 265° from the tip. If you take the direct route back, you will have logged about 118 miles by the time you arrive at Daggett's.

Those heading up the coast will find conditions very much like those encountered earlier on the trip—occasional pebble-and-cobble beaches between steep bluffs, although the stretches of bluffs are a bit longer than those encountered thus far, and the camping areas of some beaches are limited. Este Ton (Caleta Station), at Mile 84.4, is the finest anchorage on the west side of the island. The snug little cove, open to the south, has pebble-and-cobble beaches, and offers good anchoring conditions. It is often occupied by kayakers, boaters, and *pepino* (sea cucumber) divers, but there is usually room for newcomers.

For a number of years, a pair of ospreys has undertaken raising their young in a large nest on top of a conical rock at Mile 85.9. The scene is marvelous—the parents soaring and swooping to pick up fish for their babies. Ensenada los Machos, Mile 92.8, not to be confused with Punta los Machos, is marked by a tumble-down shack and offers good anchoring on a sandy bottom and protection from the prevailing weather. The site is a bit littered, but the hill makes a good windbreak.

The sweep of the coast west to Punta los Machos forms "Humbug Bay." It is deep, but provides a secure anchorage if your anchor can find the bottom. There are many cobble-and-pebble beaches offering good camping, especially at Mile 95.1. Punta los Machos, at Mile 96.8, marks the beginning and the end of the circumnavigation. If you left your rig at Daggett's, went north to Remedios, crossed to the island, circumnavigated it, headed west from Machos and returned to Daggett's by the same route you came, you have logged about 147 miles.

☼ *By water: coasting to Santa Rosalía*

It is 139.0 miles from Bahía de los Angeles to Santa Rosalía. A "Paddle Chart" available from Cruising Charts covers the coast between Bahía de los Angeles and Bahía San Francisquito, and a Mini-Guide covers the coast from Cabo San Miguel to Santa Rosalía. The appropriate Mexican topos are: Bahía de los Angeles H12C52; Puntas las Animas H12C53; Valle San Rafael H12C63; El Progresso H12C73; El Barril H12C74; Los Corrales H12C84; La Trinidad G12A14; El Caracol G12A24; and Punta Santa Ana G12A25. Unless you are a stickler for detail, don't bother to get El Caracol nor El Progresso, which show less than 3 miles and 6 miles of coastline, respectively, and contain no important features. Also, the maps from Punta Santa Ana south to Santa Rosalía are of limited value.

The coast from Bahía de los Angeles to The Slot at Bahía las Ánimas, Mile 19.1 when leaving from town and cutting directly across Bahía de los Angeles and then across Bahía las Ánimas, was described beginning on page 142. There is nothing even approaching an all-weather anchorage along the coast from Don Juan to Bahía San Francisquito. (Chapter 14 describes anchorages at the offshore islands of the Midriff.)

The coast to the south of "The Slot" is very exposed, but has sand beaches at Miles 22.5 and 23.4. The coast tends to be steep from Mile 23.4 to Mile 30.8, but there is a sand beach and a settlement at Mile 37.0, San Rafael. The curve of Bahía San Rafael to the south and east of the settlement has a number of beaches, increasingly sandy and more exposed to the prevailing wind.

Bahía San Francisquito, Mile 55.1, is the best anchorage between Don Juan and Santa Rosalía, and has a white sand beach on the western side for camping (two small coves just to the west of the main bay are popular with kayakers). Deep-draft boats usually anchor in the southwestern part of the bay, shallow-draft boats in the "inner bay" at the south end. You may have to move around a bit to avoid the chop if a north or northeast wind comes up.

Ensenada Blanca, in the lee of Punta Santa Teresa, Mile 57.5, provides good protection from prevailing weather, and there is a sand beach and a resort where meals, fuel, water, and supplies may be available. (See page 162 for more on San Francisquito and the resort.) There is a ranch at El Barril, Mile 64.6, and a sandy beach just to the north, but the anchorage is just an open roadstead. The coast south to Cabo San Miguel is mostly low bluffs alternating with sandy beaches.

The open anchorages on the north and south sides of Cabo San Miguel, Mile 72.8, provide sandy bottoms and limited protection. The small cove just to the south of the point, marked by white cliffs, is inviting, but is rather deep and subject to heavy tidal rips. Kayakers will appreciate the fine white sand beaches north of the point. The coast south from San Miguel tends to be low for many miles. Punta San Juan Bautista, Mile 81.2, and Punta San Carlos, Mile 86.5, are low, with a sand and gravel beaches, and offer little protection. Caleta la Lobera, Mile 92.5, and Punta la Salina, Mile 93.4, are open, sandy anchorages, but one or the other can provide some protection, depending on the direction of the wind. Beware of the rocks off Salina—when arriving from the north, proceed

well past the point, turn west, and approach the anchorage from the south.

Punta Trinidad, Mile 98.4, has a beautiful sand beach and an anchorage with a sand bottom just to the north, offering protection from south and west weather. The area just south of the point offers no anchorage worthy of the name. Islote el Racito, 1.7 miles north of the point, is surrounded by rocky reefs and offers poor anchoring conditions. The coast south of Trinidad is low for about 3 miles, but then steepens until Ensenada Morro Prieto, Mile 106.3.

The waters off Punta Santa Ana, Mile 110.6, are too open to be a useful anchorage in anything more than a flat calm or in southwest winds. Marked by a small grove of palms, the place has beaches that are mostly mixed sand and pebble. The beaches south to Punta Santa María are almost all gravel and pebble, usually found at the mouths of arroyos. Beware of the heavy tidal currents when Isla Tortugas begins to draw abeam to the east. Caleta Santa María, Mile 132.0, is the site of a new industrial pier and breakwater associated with the nearby gypsum mine, offering a sandy bottom and excellent protection from west and northwest weather. However, the place is noisy, the dust is thick, and the lights are often on all night. The coast from Santa María to Santa Rosalía, Mile 139.0, has a number of sandy beaches at the mouths of arroyos, offering good camping but no protection.

Side trip to Bahía San Francisquito. The road to Bahía San Francisquito, 82.6 miles from Bahía de los Angeles, was graded some time ago, making it possible to bring in moderate RVs, small travel trailers, and trailerboats. Recent articles in the Baja newsletters have presented a grim picture of this road, claiming "four-wheel-drive almost required here." During a January 1998 foray, Michael and I found it to be in good condition, with only a few washouts requiring short detours, the steepest grade being 8%. There was one fairly challenging stretch at Mile 34.3, but it was relatively short. To get to San Francisquito, drive south on the main drag in Bahía de los Angeles, and turn right (west) at the whitewashed concrete fence marking the Casa Diaz compound. Turn left (south) at the first opportunity, and set odometer. The road is two-lane dirt and gravel, graded. At Mile 9.6, note the stone building to the west; it is the last remnant of Las Flores, a bustling gold-mining town in the late 1800s. From this point, the road passes through deserted, serene, and almost pristine desert wilderness, the only sign of man being five cows, two rusted auto bodies, a few contrails in the sky, one pickup passing by, and the road itself during our trip, not even a single ranch building marring the landscape. First views of the Cortez appear at Mile 37.9. At Mile 45.4, a road north will be seen, leading to the tiny fish camp of San Rafael. Portable boats could be launched over the sand beach, and *pangas* may be available for fishing and diving expeditions. At the intersection at Mile 70.4 (signed), go straight (060°), and arrive at the turn-off for "inner bay" at Mile 81.6, where boats can be launched easily over the sand beach. To get to the Bahía San Francisquito Resort continue on past Mile 81.6, head southeast, and arrive at the resort at Mile 82.6. The resort and the road southeast to El Arco and the Transpeninsular are described beginning on page 162.

■ ■ ■ ■ ■ ■ ■ ■ ■ ■ ■ ■ ■ ■

Back on the Transpeninsular at Parador Punta Prieta, KM 280

KM	Location
280/0	Start new KM numbering sequence.
13	Punta Prieta. Groceries, café, mechanic, tire repair. Fossilized mammal bones 57 million years old have been found near here, including a hyracotherium, a horse the size of a dog. Arsenopyrite, hematite, gold, and silver and large, well-formed quartz crystals occur at Mina Columbia, 7.5 miles west.
24+	A great deal of low-grade calcite is found nearby, but large, clear 2-inch crystals have been dug up a half mile south of the old buildings at this point.
25	Gentle to moderate rolling hills to KM 75.
38+	Sedan road west (signed) to Santa Rosalillita. Those continuing on the Transpeninsular should skip the following section.

Side trip to Santa Rosalillita and surrounding areas. This area is a favorite with surfers and boardsailors. Set odometer. Note the side road at Mile 8.1 (but don't turn), and arrive at the beach at Mile 9.6. The road is capable of handling RVs, with one 13% grade, and there is plenty of camping and parking along the beach and in the dunes north of the point. Shallow Bahía Santa Rosalillita is a satisfactory anchorage in prevailing seas, the best between Bahía San Carlos and Cedros. There is a small grocery store in the village, and limited supplies of gasoline and water may be available.

The area is rarely visited by sport anglers or divers, but boardsailors like the bay for its strong and reliable afternoon winds, large area, and range of wave sizes, from calm inside to sizable at the point. Many boardsailors rate "Sandy Point" as the best wave-sailing beach in Baja. The right point break here is reputedly the longest in the peninsula, some surfers claiming rides of more than a mile. During frontal conditions an endless succession of perfectly formed 4-to-8-foot waves often sweep around the point. However, storms sometimes rearrange bottom contours and move the bar, resulting in rides that fall short of the glowing reports. If this happens, salvation may not be far away. Punta Rosarito to the south is a "magnet for waves," with a reef break good on almost any swell. There are three more surfing areas to the north, with configurations similar to Santa Rosalillita: Punta San Andrés, Punta Prieta (not to be confused with the town of the same name on the Transpeninsular), and Punta María, each a rocky point forming a small bay open to the south. These five places—Rosarito, Rosalillita, San Andrés, Punta Prieta, and Punta María—are sufficiently different from one another that if the surf is not good in one place, it usually is at one of the others, making this one of the most reliable surfing and wave-sailing areas in Baja.

Although the coastline north from Santa Rosalillita to Punta María is not often visited by kayakers, it has the makings for a fine trip: easy access by road; plenty of scenery, excellent snorkeling, fishing, and foraging; numerous small coves; good campsites with a minimum of litter; and ordinarily plenty of driftwood for evening campfire gatherings. A round-trip involves only about 52 miles, making it a pleasant and undemanding 5-day trip.

A graded road running to the northwest has improved access to these areas, and the wide, white-sand beaches and uncrowded camping along the coast are worth a trip to see, even if you are not a surfer or kayaker. Other than an occasional ranch and several small fish camps, the area is uninhabited, and the beaches and many campsites are almost free of litter. To get to the road, return to the side road at Mile 8.1, reset odometer and turn northwest (320°) on a graded road, signed SAN JOSÉ DE LAS PALOMAS. At Mile 4.0 turn left (180°) onto a sedan road, pass Rancho San Andrés, and arrive at an intersection within 1.5 miles. Continue straight ahead (230°) between the cliffs (if the weather is wet, take the right fork, 280°). The road will cross mud flats, swing north, and arrive at the cove sheltered by Punta San Andrés in another 1.5 miles. This area, known to surfers as "Alejandro's," has good camping, easy access to the sand beach, and a well-shaped but short right point break.

To continue on to Punta Prieta (Punta Negra), return to Mile 4.0, reset odometer, and continue west (280°) until Mile 15.5, where a sharp left turn (160°) onto a pickup road will take you to the beach in a little over 2 miles. There is a wide sand beach, excellent camping, and reef and beach breaks. Anchorage conditions are poor. Continuing on from Mile 15.5, the improved road ends at Mile 20, and the roads beyond require pickups. The surfing potential at Punta Lobos at Mile 22.4 appears low, but there is good camping, and a four-wheel-drive road through deep sand reaches a fine sandy cove to the west.

At Mile 27.6 take the left (275°) fork, and steer for the arroyo dead ahead. The road will climb the arroyo, swing north, then west and then south, arriving in 4 miles at the north coast of Bahía María in the vicinity of a small fish camp. A sandy cove is located west of the camp. The bay has excellent boardsailing, and the point has right point and reef breaks, and good diving. However, the point is 0.75 mile west of the campsite. The locals recommend driving on the beach for 1/3 mile, to where a road can be seen climbing a hill, ending very close to the point. Calculate the tide first and remember that the AAA tow truck is a long way off. The anchorage here is shallow and open, often with refracted swell and surge.

■■■■■■■■■■■■■■■■■■■■■■
Back on the Transpeninsular at KM 38+

KM	Location
52	**Rosarito (Sur).** Groceries, cafés, tire repair. El Marmolito onyx quarry can be reached by driving southeast on the "old," unpaved Transpeninsular and taking the left (066°) fork at Mile 7.4. Although virtually unknown to anglers, the beaches from Punta Rosarito and south to Guerrero Negro are among the finest surf fishing locations in Baja. The prime quarry is migratory white seabass, taken with heavy surf rigs between March and May, although a few are taken as early as January and as late as June. Look for steep drop-offs with sand and cobble bottoms just offshore, and fling out a squid. Throughout the year you might also find yellowfin croakers in the surf line, and barred surfperch a bit farther out. Halibut, although not often considered a surf fish, are also frequently taken here.

■ The lost cave of El Zalate

In his 1895 paper on Indian rock art, Leon Diguet indicated that a site named The Cave of El Zalate was located "near the 29° [parallel of latitude], about fifteen leagues from Calamahi [Camallí] near the road from Calamahi to San Borga [Misión San Borja]." Zalate has never been re-located, and its elusiveness may be caused by varying definitions of a league. In English-speaking countries, a league was 3.0 miles, the old Spanish league used in California was 2.63 miles and the French league (Diguet was French) was 2.5 miles, so the cave could thus be 45, 39 or 37 miles northwest of Camallí. None of these seems likely, since they place the cave very close to or even north of Misión San Borja. However, in 1910 Arthur North provided a more likely definition: a "Mexican league" was the distance you could ride a mule in an hour, about 2 miles. Since Diguet had no accurate way of measuring distances, this may be the definition he used, and the cave may thus be only 30 miles from Camallí. In Diguet's day two Calmallís existed, the mining camp where gold was discovered in 1882, and Camallí Viejo, 10 miles north. El Camino Real,

the "Royal Road" linking the Jesuit missions, ran from Misión Santa Gertrudis northwest past Camallí Viejo to Misión San Borja, and was still in use in the late 1800s. Since maps of the day show no other road in the vicinity, Diguet may have simply followed El Camino Real. These speculations place Zalate about 7 miles east of Rancho San Regis.

The Cochimí Indians of the area were like anyone else; they appreciated well-watered sites with shelter and plenty of food. Zalate is thus not likely to be found on featureless open desert—the place will almost certainly be "somewhere." If the appropriate small-scale topographic map (Isla San Esteban H12-10, 1:250,000) is laid out and the route of El Camino Real plotted, 15 "Mexican leagues," or 30 miles, will indeed take the rider to "somewhere," deep (1,350 feet) and spectacular Arroyo Paraíso. In 1974 Harry Crosby described a descent into awe-inspiring drop-offs, sheer faces, impassable palisades, and the necessity to build a trail with stones to allow the passage of pack animals. In 1975 he described the arroyo as "a place of trees, water, and huge blocks of granite," with sandy flats and a pool "thick with rushes." Cochimí did inhabit the arroyo, and a painting of a deer and a few other simple figures were found.

Nothing more is known about the cave (probably a grotto or an overhang), nor about the art itself, since Diguet described nothing more than its location. Rancho San Regis still exists, and can be reached by driving southeast from Rosarito Sur on the old, unpaved Transpeninsular, turning northeast at Mile 6.3, and arriving at Mile 19.3. There may or may not be a beautiful *zalate* (wild fig tree) marking the mouth of the cave; they are short-lived. See page 202 for a description of the species and page 232 for a photo.

KM	Location
68	Pickup road southwest to El Tomatal (The Tomato Field, signed), 2.9 miles, a large boondocking site behind the dunes. If the wind makes camping uncomfortable, a grove of palms about 100 yards inland can serve as a wind-break. Cobble reefs tend to focus the swells, and the waters off the sand-and-pebble beach often have excellent, if inconsistent, surfing. The constant side-offshore winds provide good boardsailing. As noted earlier, the beaches from here north to Punta Santa Rosalillita and south to Guerrero Negro are among the finest surf fishing locations in Baja. The large island visible in the distance is Cedros.

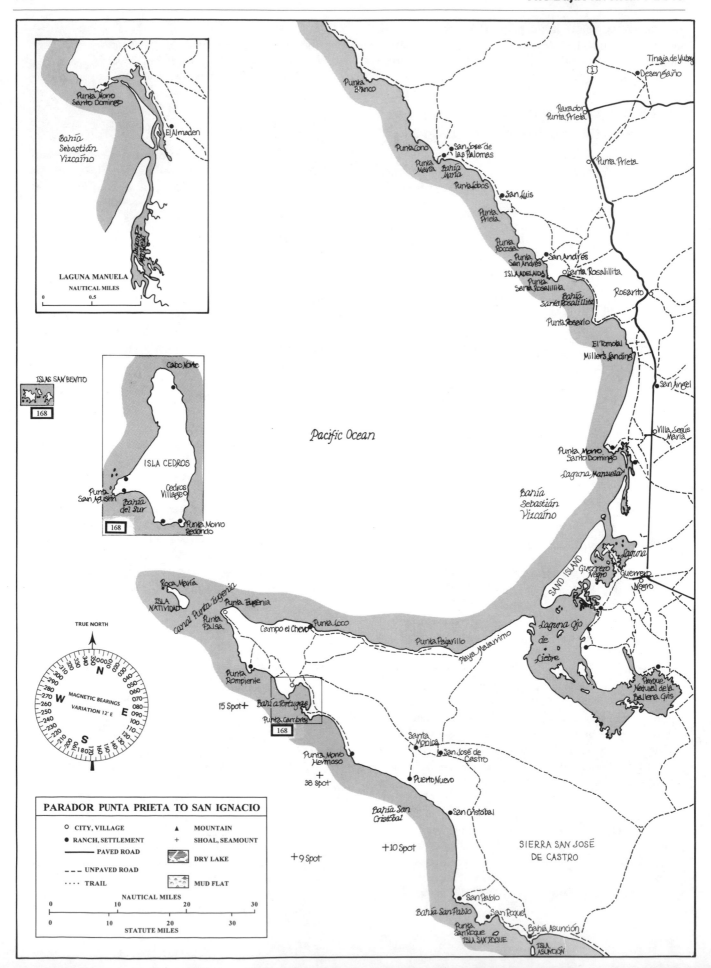

Bahía Sebastián Vizcaíno

LAGUNA MANUELA
NAUTICAL MILES
0   0.5   1

ISLAS SAN BENITO
168

Punta Morro
Santo Domingo

El Almaden

Cabo Norte

ISLA CEDROS

Punta
San Agustín

Bahía
del Sur

Cedros
Village

168

Punta Morro
Redondo

Pacific Ocean

Punta
Blanco

Punta Cono

San José de
las Palomas

Punta
María   Bahía
               María
Punta Lobos
                    San Luis
Punta
Prieta

Punta
Rocosa
Punta
San Andrés   San Andrés
ISLA ADELAIDA   Santa Rosalillita
Punta
Santa Rosalillita
                    Bahía
                    Santa Rosalillita   Rosarito
Punta Rosario

El Tomotal
Miller's Landing

San Angel

Villa Jesús
María

Punta Morro
Santo Domingo

Laguna Manuela

Bahía
Sebastián
Vizcaíno

Tinaja de Yubay
Desensaño

Parador
Punta Prieta

Punta Prieta

1

Laguna
Guerrero
Negro
Guerrero
Negro

SAND ISLAND

Laguna Ojo
de
Liebre

Parque
Natural de la
Ballena Gris

Roca María
ISLA
NATIVIDAD

Punta Eugenia

Punta
Palsa

Campo el Chevo

Punta Loco

Canal Punta Eugenia

Punta Pajarillo

Playa Malarrimo

TRUE NORTH

N
NW   NE
W   E
SW   SE
S

MAGNETIC BEARINGS
VARIATION 12° E

Punta
Rompiente

15 Spot +

Bahía Tortugas
Punta Cambrey
168

Punta Morro
Hermoso
+
38 spot

Santa
Mónica
San José de
Castro

Puerto Nuevo

Bahía San
Cristóbal
                    San Cristóbal

+ 10 Spot

SIERRA SAN JOSÉ
DE CASTRO

+ 9 spot

San Pablo
Bahía San Pablo   San Roque
Punta
San Roque
ISLA SAN ROQUE   Bahía Asunción
                    ISLA
                    ASUNCIÓN

PARADOR PUNTA PRIETA TO SAN IGNACIO

○ CITY, VILLAGE   ▲ MOUNTAIN
● RANCH, SETTLEMENT   + SHOAL, SEAMOUNT
—— PAVED ROAD
- - - UNPAVED ROAD   DRY LAKE
· · · · TRAIL   MUD FLAT

NAUTICAL MILES
0   10   20   30

0   10   20   30
STATUTE MILES

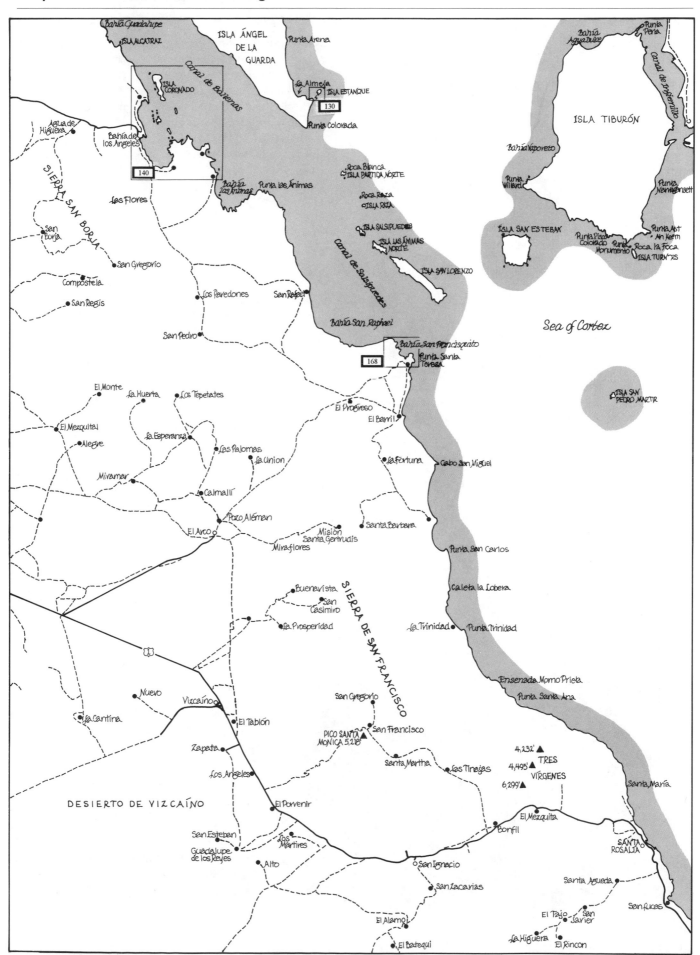

■ Isla Cedros

Because of its two peaks, one 3,950 feet, the other 3,488, Isla Cedros can be seen easily from this area in clear weather, a distance of 61 miles. Not often visited by outsiders except for long-range fishing vessels and passing yachts, the island offers good fishing and diving and some unusual hiking. The island is served by Aero Cedros, with flights from Ensenada and on to Guerrero Negro, as well as Aerolineas California. Cedros is only 13 miles from Punta Eugenia, and it should be possible to launch portable boats there or hire a panga. By way of Isla Natividad, you never need get more than 5 miles from land. Since the run from Bahía Tortugas to the village on Cedros is only 35 miles, the graded road from Vizcaíno also opens up the region to trailerboats (more on this later). Small-boat adventures in this area are for experienced sailors with seaworthy boats only, for fog and wind are common.

Since the island has abundant food and water, Cedros once had a sizable Indian population, estimated at between 500 and 1,000. In 1539 Francisco de Ulloa "discovered" the island, but the Cochimí inhabitants greeted him with stones and clubs, to which he replied with dogs and crossbow bolts. In 1602 Sebastián Vizcaíno found that local attitudes toward strangers had not changed. However, in 1732 Jesuit Father Sigismundo Taraval managed to get in a few words before the clubs and stones started, and the Indians were so impressed with his sweet talk about souls, saviors, and salvation that they agreed to leave the island almost *en masse*

We didn't find any of the five anchors that Francisco Ulloa lost off the water hole at La Palmita on Isla Cedros in 1539, but we did find why he may have lost them: boulders that look like huge popcorn balls lie scattered over the sand bottom and probably chafed through his lines

and settle around Misión San Ignacio. The few who remained died of smallpox, leaving the island uninhabited for the first time in 2,000 years. Yankees and Russians after seals and sea otters often visited the island in the late 1700s, and in the mid-1800s, Chinese and Japanese divers came to take abalone. In 1920 a cannery was built, first specializing in abalone, later in sardines. A lobster fishery became important, the live catch being flown to Ensenada. In the 1960s the island became an important trans-shipment point for the salt produced at Guerrero Negro.

Today the sizable village on the island has a cannery, COTP, *Aduana, Migración*, stores, *cantinas*, cafés, gasoline, diesel, water, a hotel of sorts, a little produce, post office, and a recompression chamber. A new commercial harbor has been constructed at the village. An airstrip and salt-shipment facilities are located at the south end of the island. The primary anchorages are off the village, in Bahía del Sur, and several miles south of the navigation light near the north end. The first anchorage south is Natividad, but Bahía Tortugas is highly preferable.

While this is not virgin territory, fishing is good anywhere on the west side of the island and around the southeast cape for yellowtail, kelp bass, and barracuda. Long-range sportfishing boats out of San Diego occasionally fish the area. Good diving is found at the north point of the island and around the south end, especially in Bahía del Sur. Although at least 25 vessels have gone to the bottom near Cedros, they are either in deep water or on the beach, and the area is not known for wreck diving. A dive on a Cannery Airline plane that crashed into the ocean off the end of the airstrip can be thought-provoking, especially if you plan to leave the island by plane. Spearfishing can be great—in 1997 a woman free-diver bagged a 52-pound yellowtail off the island.

Many thousands of years ago Cedros' climate was wetter than today. As it became dryer the forest of pines died out, except for two small stands, which today depend on moisture from fogs to survive. Early Spanish explorers thought them to be cedars and hence gave the island its name. The cool shade and the smell and rustle of pine needles provide an unusual Baja experience. A trail leads to them from the village, but the most interesting and direct access is found by hiking southwest from the mouth of the Gran Cañon, on the eastern side of the island 7 miles north of the village. The canyon can be identified by watching for the first small grove of pines visible on the crest of the mountains as you travel by boat north

Reeve inches his way up a rock wall on the way to the pine forest

from the village. When this grove is due west you are off the Gran Cañon.

Watch for deer as you hike; an extremely rare sub-species of mule deer found only here still holds out against local poachers. Keeping the pines in view, hike southwest up the main wash. Soon the walls of an arroyo will block the views of the pines, but at Minute 60 they will reappear dead ahead. Stop and make a mental note of the scene at the crest at 252°; the "trail" reaches the crest at this point. Keep hiking up the canyon, and at Minute 80 a prominent fortress-like hill with a number of small caves will be seen on the right side of the canyon, blocking the pines. Just beyond the base of this hill an arroyo will be seen bearing 240°. Hike up this arroyo until Minute 100 and locate a rocky hill 60 feet high with a sharp, cone-shaped tip; it's hard to miss. Pass this to your left, and at Minute 105 the arroyo will divide into two branches. Stop and relocate the spot where the trail reaches the top, now bearing 282°. The right-hand branch of the arroyo is the correct one, but do not enter it yet. Rather, hike up the ridge separating the two branches, bearing 262°, for two reasons: a high and almost impassable rock cliff blocks the right arroyo 200 yards up, and the ridge has a stand of magnificent desert plants you will not want to miss. *Agave* and gnarled shrubs cling to this wind-whipped ridge of sand and rock dust in a seemingly impossible environment. Continue up the spine of the ridge until it levels out, then

swing into the correct (right) arroyo and continue climbing. It will get steep, but good hand and foot holds can be found. At one point it will be necessary to scale a 20-foot cliff, but this should cause few problems. The last 50 yards to the crest will require scrambling up a slope of loose rock and sand on all fours, and you should arrive at the crest at Minute 140, altitude 1,500 feet. The pine forest runs along the rim of the canyon and down the slopes to the northwest toward the incoming fog, many trees being 40 and 50 feet high, some festooned with gray moss. A faint trail follows the ridge, so old that parts of it are worn into the rock, providing grand vistas of the coast and the ocean to the west. Forest fires have decimated a few areas.

A stone shanty supposedly constructed by 19th Century sea-otter hunters can be found in Gran Cañon by returning to the fortress-shaped hill and continuing up the canyon (southwest) for a mile. When you arrive back at the beach at the end of the day, tired, hot, and sweaty, reflect on the fact that the Indians used to fell the pines with crude tools and drag them to the beach to construct rafts.

Mineral collectors should explore slopes of the Gran Cañon south of the otter shack for chromite in yellowish-brown serpentine country rock. A gold-and-copper mine will be found west of the navigation light at the north end of the island, yielding pyrite and minor amounts of chalcopyrite, bornite, covellite, and copper carbonate. There are also reports of manganese minerals. The second grove of pines is located in this vicinity.

Nature-watchers will find much of interest. Goats, cats, dogs, and burros have been released on the island,

Reeve finally gets some use out of his high-school geometry course; the pine was fifty-eight feet high

but their influence on the ecology has not been as drastic as on some other Baja islands, perhaps because miners and fishermen often hunted them for food, and possibly because the goats and burros had to compete with the already established deer. Native mammals include the Cedros wood rat and the Cedros pocket mouse, both endemic to Cedros, while the Cedros brush rabbit and the Cedros white-footed mouse are endemic sub-species. There are seven lizard species and five snakes, the Cedros leopard lizard, Cedros alligator lizard, Cedros horned lizard, and Cedros rattlesnake being endemic to the island. Many bird species are present, but only the Cedros Island wren is endemic. Cedros is also home to a population of Pacific tree frogs, seemingly out of place in the arid climate.

Bernie Eskesen investigates the huge anchor off Benito West

Sue Dippold

■ Islas San Benito

The waters around the three Islas San Benito—Este (East), Oeste (West), and Centro (Central)—16 miles west of Cedros, are the most consistent yellowtail fishery on the west coast of North America. They lie near the 100-fathom migratory path of the fish, and are far enough offshore that they are not plagued with dirty water as is Isla San Martín. The best locations are north of Benito Central, north and east of Benito East, southwest of Benito West, and at Roca Pináculo, just under a mile west of Benito West. Fishing for large kelp bass is also good around all the islands.

Excellent visibility, extensive kelp fields, and many reefs and pinnacles provide the best cool-water diving in Baja, rivaled only by Sacramento Reef and the seamounts south of San Martín, and the best white seabass and yellowtail spearfishing on the Pacific coast. Not a common fish, whites can be found hanging around the outer fringes of the kelp canopy, especially around the south tip of Benito East and along its west coast, and along the north side of Benito West. By early winter, 1997, the current El Niño had devastated the kelp fields around the Benitos, but if history is any guide they will return soon.

After diving the kelp canopy south of the two western islands, Rob Watson marveled at the enormous number of yellowtail. We pooh-poohed him, saying what he saw were bass with yellow tails, but he persisted. After 30 seconds in the water we too became believers; incredible numbers of yellowtail, the correct kind, live under the kelp. The dense canopy is a problem for rod-and-reelers, but provides heart-stopping action for spearfishermen. Big, big, bugs abound. With outstanding spearfishing for yellowtail, Roca Pináculo is an exciting open-water dive. "Yellowtail Alley" between Benito East

and the small islet to the north is another fine spearfishing site. Yellowtail are often too swift to permit a shot—by the time your safety is off, they are long gone. However, they are also curious, so take out your diver's knife and tap on the barrel of your speargun—the noise will often cause them to return. Better yet, if they are still in sight, put your arm out and wiggle your fingers. Nature-watchers will like a pinnacle southeast of the navigation light on the south side of Benito West. When over the site the light will bear 312°, the south tip of Benito East 076°.

Benito West offers several good wreck dives. Just before the newly constructed lighthouse was scheduled to begin operation in 1934, the US tanker Swift Eagle went ashore almost at its foot. She lies in shallow water, her bow section rising to within 6 feet of the surface. The stern is somewhat deeper, but in one place you can stand on a bitt with your head above water. Although her stern is badly damaged, the bow sections are fairly intact. Hull plating is missing in many places, exposing ribs and allowing entry into the hull. Capstans, hausepipes, ports, valves, piping, pumps, anchors, engine blocks, and lengths of chain can be seen. To dive the wreck, head for the north side of Benito West; large boats cannot approach the wreck safely. Look for the lighthouse and turn toward shore when it bears 175°. A second wreck, the Mexican super-seiner Tecapah, run ashore about 1988, lies in the large cove on the west side of the island, southwest of the lighthouse. The lighthouse keeper attributes the wreck to the fact the helmsman was "asleep at the wheel," and the velocity of the encounter was such that she lies in very shallow water.

At least a dozen other wrecks have occurred nearby, but only a few have diving potential. Two are located on the southeast side of Benito East: *Souster*, a tuna boat, and *San Juanico*. Locals say they barbecued survivors from the latter vessel—the cattle she was carrying, that is. Metal wreckage of one wreck can be

Elephant seals like to throw gravel on their backs, perhaps to keep the flies off or for the cooling effect. These females live on Benito East

a shaft, and a 5-foot propeller lie in 3 fathoms. Benito Central's north coast is strewn with all manner of flotsam. An enormous colony of sea lions lives on the island, some so friendly and curious they inhibit spearfishing; you can't shoo them off. A large number of elephant seals inhabit Benito East. Local divers give them healthy respect and stay well clear if they see them in the water. Sea caves are found on Benito East.

Good anchorages are found off the settlement on Benito West and off the south side of the island, but kelp can be dense. No regular source of gas or supplies will be found at the settlement, although emergency assistance might be obtained. Long-range fishing and diving vessels out of San Diego visit the islands, as do some natural-history cruises. Small boats can make the voyage from Cedros, but the route is exposed to ocean waves and currents. There is a good deal of coming and going of pangas between Cedros and the settlement, and it should not be difficult to obtain a ride or hire a boat. Take care; in 1951 an abalone boat turned over en route to Cedros, drowning 23 people.

seen in a cove a half mile north of the south point; the other lies 100 yards north—it is not certain which is which. In the 1970s the tuna vessel Paramount sank north of Benito Central. An angler I met off the Benitos claimed to have seen her go down, and he drew a map placing her about a half mile off the beach, but the truth is that this is pure guesswork, and given the Mexican love for exaggeration, she may be much closer. Other locals also place her a half mile north, but state she is in 100 to 150 fathoms. This cannot be correct since the 100-fathom line is not reached until 2 miles north. She may be in relatively shallow water and is potentially a fine dive site, but there are no reports that she has been located. A $10 bill waved around the village ought to produce a flood of information, some good, some bad. Twenty dollars ought to produce an eyewitness—the wreck is not too old—who should be able to put you very close.

A huge anchor can be found in 50 feet on a sand bottom 200 feet off the southeast point of Benito West. Locals say it was lost by the US vessel *Tatuche* in 1943. When you are over the anchor the north peak on Benito East will bear 056°, the south end of Benito East 090°, and the cross on top of the hill south of the village on Benito West 293°.

A number of bird species nest on the islands, including black, least, and Leach's storm petrels. Beachcombers may find objects of interest in a number of locations. The wreck of the wooden tuna clipper *Southern Pacific* is scattered along the north shore of Benito West, due north of the settlement. Wrecked in 1971, she was equipped with a seaplane. Her engines,

■■■■■■■■■■■■■■■■■
On the Transpeninsular at KM 68

KM	Location
73	A sedan road goes west 0.1 mile south of the KM marker to Miller's Landing, 3 miles. This windblown spot was the shipment point for onyx from El Marmolito, and chunks can still be found scattered over the cobble beach. There is excellent surf fishing at times and reliable reef breaks,

We tried to reassemble a whale we found near Miller's Landing, but there were vital parts missing, and we never did get it working again

75   The highway crosses plains until a few miles
      west of San Ignacio, and the scenery is flat, fea-
      tureless, boring, and often windswept.

84   Note the "living fence" on the east side of the
      road. Ranchers cut down *dátilillios* to make fence
      posts, which sometimes spring to life again.

95   Villa Jesús María. PEMEX (MD), cafés, grocer-
      ies, doctor, mechanic, tire repair, long-distance
      telephone.

96   Sedan road west (signed) to Laguna Manuella.
      Those continuing on the Transpeninsular should
      skip the following section.

Side trip to Laguna Manuela. Although it has excellent fishing and is close to the Transpeninsular, the
Laguna Manuela (Estero Santo Domingo) area is little
known to most *gringo* visitors, in spite of the fact that it has
one of the finest fisheries in Baja close to the Transpeninsular. Set odometer. Follow the paved road to Mile 0.9, turn
left (southwest), and arrive at the beach at Mile 7.0. The
graded sand-and-gravel road can handle RVs and trailers,
but it is often washboarded.

The lagoon was named for the whaling brig *Manuella*,
wrecked on the outer coast of the lagoon in 1871. This desolate spot was once served by regular steamship service to
San Diego. In the heyday of the gold mines in the Camallí
and Alemán areas in the 1800s, the steamer deposited supplies on the beach, which were then hauled to the mines on
mule-back, the steamer heading north with the gold. Although
the lee of Punta Morro Santo Domingo makes a fair anchorage, boats coasting north or south rarely use it, since it is far
off the normal Isla Cedros-points-north-or-south route. The
vessel *Alice* foundered here in 1925, but don't plan to salvage her cargo, for it was ice.

There is plenty of space to park RVs along the beach,
but the shoreline is low, and a high tide can produce surprises. There is no ramp, and trailerboaters will be disappointed unless they are equipped for launching over a
low-slope, soft-sand beach. Those with cartoppers and inflatable boats should not have great difficulty. Boats can enter
and leave the lagoon through the north entrance, but the south
entrance is often unsafe due to heavy surf. The large-scale
inset map on page 150 shows the general topography of the
lagoon, but the mud flat and shallow areas change frequently.

The lagoon extends south about 9 miles or so, and is
very shallow and often choked with eel grass, its bottom
being mixed mud and sand. Surge created by tides and winds
may leave a boat anchored in 3 or 4 feet of water high and
dry 30 minutes later. These conditions make the lagoon a
biological "factory," and the place seems fin-to-fin with yellowfin croaker, corvina, corbina, halibut, and various basses,
especially in its southern reaches.

In suitable weather, the ocean coves just north of Punta
Morro Santo Domingo offer outstanding fishing for corbina,
yellowfin croaker, and halibut, especially in the summer, and
white seabass, giant sea bass, yellowtail, ocean whitefish,
and grouper are also taken. Always guard against sneaker
waves and heavy tidal currents in this vicinity.

Just south of the concrete buildings at Mile 7.0 a road
takes off to the west along the bluffs, passing a series of
beautiful sandy coves. A 25% grade and deep sand will cause
problems for two-wheel-drives. It is usually no problem to
scramble down the cliffs with a surf rod in hand. Northwest
swells march past the point like soldiers, and surfers will
find a long ride. There is good camping on the bluff near the
lighthouse. Surf anglers with a four-wheel-drive with flotation tires or plenty of people to push should drive about a
mile north of the concrete building, where a very poor road
will be found running west. In about two miles this road
arrives at a hard-packed beach on the outer coast. Turn south
at this point and drive a half mile. A series of small coves
from here to about 0.75 mile south are home to hordes of
very unsophisticated halibut, croaker, and corvina.

Aqua Adventures offers an unusual activity at Manuela,
kayak wave-surfing. Taking advantage of the big swells that
wrap around the point, their instructors will get you surfing
in a fraction of the time that it takes to learn surfboarding.
Kayakers have reported rides of almost 2 miles on the crest
of 5-foot swells. The company maintains a camp at the lagoon and will accommodate walk-ins, including both instruction and equipment rental. Also, there are great

*The steep slopes and soft sand of the dunes near Guerrero
Negro make you feel like flying*

whale-watching opportunities just off the point during the winter, and both Aqua Adventures and Southwest Sea Kayaks offer kayaking/whale-watching. Kayakers recently have had the marvelous experience of "playing" with three whales in the surf.

■■■■■■■■■■■■■■■■■■■

Back on the Transpeninsular at KM 96

KM	Location
121+	The magnificent dunes a few miles to the west are spread over 16 square miles.
127+	La Espinita Restaurant, free overnight RV parking. The place is clean, and the food and hospitality are getting rave reviews from travelers.
128	Latitude 28° north, separating the states of Baja Norte and Baja Sur. A new PEMEX station is being constructed. A time zone change occurs here; Baja Sur is one hour ahead of Baja Norte. The Mexican army has constructed a forbidding "fort" here, painted olive-drab and bristling with firearms. Its inhabitants may ask to inspect your vehicle. The Hotel la Pinta has a restaurant and a bar, and whale-watching trips can be arranged at the desk. The dilapidated RV park has full hookups, showers, and toilets, but things rarely work. The birds nesting on the signposts are ospreys. These magnificent fish-eating eagle-like birds have taken to nesting on man-made structures throughout the Guerrero Negro area, often favoring high-tension poles. Their nests are an eclectic mixture of twigs, seaweed, fish nets, tapes from cassette cartridges, rope, surprisingly large pieces of driftwood, fish and bird skeletons, and Bimbo bread wrappers. This point is also KM 221 for the beginning of a new KM sequence.
220	Agricultural inspection for all vehicles. A small *Migración* office will be found here, and you may be asked to produce your tourist card.
218	LPG yard.
217	Guerrero Negro Junction. If you are heading north, it is advisable to gas up in town and at every chance, as gas supplies are unreliable. **Do not depend on getting gas at Parador Punta Prieta or Cataviña.**

Guerrero Negro

Guerrero Negro's odd name came from the whaling bark *Black Warrior*. She was wrecked in 1858 at the entrance to the lagoon that now bears her name while being towed out of the lagoon with a full cargo of oil. The name is also odd for a ship: *Black Warrior* is said to have received it because she had once been engaged in trade with Zanzibar.

The town's economy is based on Exportadora de Sal, S.A. (ESSA), which maintains over 300 square miles of diked ponds south of town and around Scammon's Lagoon, producing 6 million tons of salt a year, making it one of the largest such facilities in the world. Shipped in barges to Isla Cedros, the salt is loaded into bulk carrier ships for shipment to mainland Mexico, Japan, Canada, and the US.

Almost all yachts coasting north or south avoid Laguna Guerrero Negro because changes have occurred in the pattern of commercial shipping and dredging. Older charts and pilots are out of date and reliable information is next to impossible to obtain. Except for those stopping for food and fuel, most people traveling by road also pass the town without slowing down, for the desolate and windblown look of the place does not suggest that it has anything of interest. In fact, there are things to do and see. The town has many supplies and services, including restaurants, motels, liquor, bank, tire sales and repairs, mechanics, welding, auto parts, hardware, groceries, fruit stores, fish market, butcher shops, ice, bakeries, post office, laundromat, *tortilla* factory, long-distance telephone, *Pesca* office, doctors, dentists, pharmacies, opticians, and a hospital. Guerrero Negro is the first sizable town south of San Quintín and the last one before Santa Rosalía, and almost all businesses and services are located along Blvd. Zapata.

Cabañas Don Miguelito offers a motel and RV sites with electric, water, and sewer hookups, showers, and rest rooms. The Malarrimo Restaurant, part of the complex, has been popular with RVers since the construction of the Transpeninsular was completed, especially with those who like seafood. Restaurant Mario's has a seafood and Mexican menu, and a bar. Mercado Ballena carries most of the things you would expect in a small supermarket in *El Norte*. Fresk-Pura sells drinking water purified by reverse osmosis. There is a *Migración* office across the street and a little east of the Malarrimo. A laundromat can be found by driving north on a street immediately east of the Motel el Morro for one block. Fruitería el Triunfo sells a wide variety of fruit and vegetables. The *Pesca* office is located across the street. Can't stand sitting with your spouse in the motor home even one more day? There is an office of Aerolitoral. Supermercado Calimex, smaller than Mercado Ballena, sells basic foods and household items. Farmacia San Martín sells film and can process color prints. There have been recent reports of rip-offs at the first PEMEX (MPD). The second PEMEX has MD. The BANAMEX has an ATM machine. Trips to see the salt-making ponds can be arranged at the ESSA offices

A road running northwest from the ESSA offices leads 7 miles past marshes that are home to many gulls, ducks, herons, and other bird species, ending at the old salt pier. A small number of RVers make this their Baja destination and stay for weeks at a time in spite of its lack of facilities, for on occasion, whales come right up to the pier. Fishing off the pier produces enough cabrilla, sargo, and other species to keep things interesting. Mullet for bait can be snagged with treble hooks, and portable boats can be launched off a sandy area near the pier. During a dive in Laguna Guerrero Negro, you may encounter seahorses, scallops, and several species of nudibranchs. Local scallop divers often return to the dock with interesting shells.

The town is working to improve its image: a new convention center has been built, and many of the streets are being paved. A number of whale-watching excursions are offered, with shiny new mini-busses carrying participants to the old salt pier or to Parque Natural de la Ballena Gris, southeast of town.

■ The mystery of Consag's wreck

Almost two-and-a-half centuries ago a mysterious shipwreck was found on a remote Baja beach and then virtually forgotten. In recent years an incredible find by a party of beachcombers and a lucky series of events have allowed me to weave together a possible explanation as to the identity, location, and circumstances of the wreck.

During a journey in Baja in 1751 Father Fernando Consag encountered a "tongue of sand" that stretched out toward the Pacific. A party of his

A treasure of Pacific flotsam collected by Midge and Wes Hamshaw (left) and Scotty Johnson (right) during a 1962 trip to the island across from the salt pier. The urn Wes is holding was manufactured in Germany between 1690 and 1710!

men set out to explore it and returned two days later with a soup bowl, a cup, a China plate, and a quantity of white wax they had taken from a shipwreck found at the water's edge. The site was littered with baskets of goods similar to what they had brought back, and with large platters and vases, as well as hammered lead and bronze objects. Consag's diary does not provide an adequate map, and most of the place names he used can no longer be identified. However, his description of the "tongue of sand" is unmistakable—it was obviously "Sand Island," visible from the old salt pier at Puerto Viejo.

While doing library research for the first edition of this book, I came across a magazine article by Midge Hamshaw in which she told of a 1962 beachcombing trip to Sand Island in a Second World War "duck" amphibious jeep. Midge, her husband Wes, and their friend Scotty Johnson found a jackpot of modern flotsam, but one item in a photograph attracted my attention, a very unusual clay "urn." It hit me like a lightning bolt—could the urn be an artifact from Consag's wreck? With great good fortune, I was able to locate Midge and Wes. From photographs I took, the Smithsonian Institution was able to determine that the urn was salt-glazed stoneware of German origin, manufactured for the foreign trade between 1690 and 1710 in the Westervald region of the Rhineland. The date, locations, descriptions, geography, everything I knew about the matter, were consistent—Wes, Midge, and Scotty had possibly found a remarkable historical artifact from Consag's wreck!

Assuming it was part of the ship's cargo, the urn and the date of Consag's visit place the wreck between 1690 and 1751. Consag's men described the wreck as old, for iron objects and nails fell into dust when they were touched, and since the urns were not manufactured after 1715 and were somewhat fragile, the earlier years of this range of dates seem more likely. As there were few other ships in this region between these dates, one obvious possibility is that Consag's wreck was a Manila galleon, one of the "black ships" of *Shogun* television fame. These ships sailed between the west coast of Mexico and the Far East between 1565 and 1815. Poor construction, bad navigation, storms, lightning, scurvy, starvation, fire, careless cargo loading, and rotten timbers caused the loss of 30 ships, thousands of lives, and 60 million pesos in property. The goods found by Consag's men were consistent with a such a vessel *en route* to Mexico, and one possibility is that the wreck is the *San Francisco Xavier*, which disappeared after leaving Manila in 1705.

Further research produced a scientific study of carbon-14 dating of sea shells found inland along the same beach. This provided more clues; the beach is advancing, and if the wreck was at the water's edge in 1751, it should now be a hundred yards inland. Remarkably, Wes recalls that the urn was found in the first line of dunes about that distance from the beach! As to the lateral position of the wreck along the beach, little is known, for Consag's account does not contain enough information, and Wes cannot remember exactly where they found the urn (more than 25 years had passed).

There is another odd twist to the story. Why did Consag's men find no items of great value—where was the treasure? The Manila ships carried jewelry, devotional pieces, sword hilts, ornaments made of gold and ivory, gold bells, coins, gems, and at least one "pearle as big as a dove egge," plus such exotic items as artificial noses and alligator teeth capped with gold. The local Indians probably did not haul these things away. Archaeologists have not found such objects at Indian sites anywhere in Baja, and in any event a pot, a knife, an ax, or even a nail would be of infinitely more value to people at the cultural level of the local Indians than, say, a crown. There is, however, a logical explanation as to what happened to the treasure, provided by a "tall tale" known to the people of Guerrero Negro.

Dutch pirates aboard a schooner working the west coast of Mexico about this time supposedly quarreled and began to kill each other, until only one was left alive, the large African helmsman. Unable to manage the ship alone, he ran it ashore on a beach in Bahía Vizcaíno. Since he could not fit all of the ship's treasure into his wooden sea chest, he donned dozens of rings, crowns, and ornaments. Heavily armed, he started across the salt flats, dragging his chest. He soon died of thirst and his skeleton, picked clean by the birds, disappeared into the salt, along with the treasure.

The tale has a certain validity for the local people. Everyone knows that gold flakes can be found on any beach in the vicinity (actually iron pyrites). Also, there is the odd name of the nearby lagoon: Guerrero Negro. Skeptics claim that in the 1950s the *gringo* manager of the salt works made up the tale, keeping his men digging full-speed by offering "finders-keepers," but others say that it had "always" been known to the local people.

This tale has appeared in the literature of Baja a number of times, but whether it still motivates the workers of Guerrero Negro is doubtful. Still, could it have a factual basis; could the ship have been Consag's wreck? Is it possible that someone from the ship actually carried the treasure away? Since no one associated with the wreck survived, the details of the story—the men were Dutch pirates and had quarreled, the only survivor was an African helmsman—could be known to no one, and are probably embellishments added by later storytellers. However, could the core of it—a ship

was wrecked and one man survived, only to die crossing the salt flats carrying a treasure—be an authentic example of oral history, passed down from eyewitnesses through generations of Indians? The tale would also explain why no human bones were reported by Consag's men; all the crew but one were killed at sea and presumably dumped over the side, and the last man alive walked away from the ship.

The operator of a big ESSA scraper may someday set his blade a little too deep and provide the motivation for archaeologists to finally solve the mystery. It will be interesting to find out if the "finders-keepers" offer is still good. Please don't grab your metal detector and head for Sand Island—if Consag's wreck is indeed a Manila galleon, or any wreck that old for that matter, Mexican law allows only professionals working under permits to disturb it.

• •

❝ Ghost story

I was the last to arrive back at camp after a day of exploring Playa María on trail bikes. I had discovered pieces of firewood buried behind the first line of dunes, and it had taken me an hour to pry them loose and drag them back behind my bike. High spirits prevailed, encouraged by glorious weather, good friends, and a lobster dinner. We started a fire, but as the flames spread a sudden change in mood struck all of us simultaneously. For no apparent reason the usual happy chatter was absent, and even the normal Honda versus Kawasaki disputes faded into an uneasy silence. As the embers died we fell into a fitful sleep.

Dawn provided no release from our somber mood. Hoping to obtain more firewood, we returned to the dune with shovels and an ax, and a little digging revealed the source of the wood to be a shipwreck. Large gray timbers soon appeared, embedded with bronze and wrought iron spikes. Hundreds of bronze sheathing nails still protruded from her planking. She was a total wreck and nothing could be determined of her size or shape. Finally we brushed off a timber and found a name burned or scraped into a plank: Jennie Thelin. *We had burned a part of Wolf Larson's ship,* Ghost!

The 91-foot schooner Jennie Thelin *was constructed in 1869 near Santa Cruz, CA. Until her stranding at Playa María in 1912, she had a rowdy career involving poaching and transportation of illegal immigrants, with occasional periods spent carrying lumber and guano, and her loss was possibly an insurance fraud. Such infamy could not go unrecognized, and Jack London used the* Thelin *as the model for the* Ghost *in his novel* The Sea Wolf. *The Thelin's captain, Alexander McLean, inspired the Wolf Larson character, played by Edward G. Robinson in the 1941 movie. (In the 1993 TNT "Original" television movie, Charles Bronson just doesn't have the required menace.)*

The battered bones of the famous ship lying at our feet caused a sense of awe among us. Never destined to take her rightful place in a maritime museum, she will continue to *disintegrate until no trace remains. No matter; we would have no hand in dismantling her. We mounted our bikes and rode off, never to disturb her again.* **"**

• •

The schooner **Jennie Thelin**

Courtesy National Maritime Museum

Chapter 11

Guerrero Negro to Loreto

KM	Location
208	Sedan road to south (signed LAGUNA OJO DE LIEBRE) to Parque Natural de la Ballena Gris. Those continuing on the Transpeninsular should skip the following section.

↱ **Side trip to Parque Natural de la Ballena Gris.** Set odometer. The road crosses a number of salt flats and is badly washboarded over much of its 17 miles, but it can handle most RVs. This whale-watching site on Scammon's is both a disappointment and a joy. The whales are normally far from shore and binoculars are necessary to see any detail, but on a broader scale how many places in the world can you drive to in an ordinary sedan and see three or four whales breaching or spy-hopping simultaneously? Local entrepreneurs sometimes offer whale-watching trips from the park and from the fish camp a mile east.

Most visitors are so entranced by the whales that they do not notice that the lagoon, with its shallow waters, extensive mud flats and marshes, and rich production of fish, mollusks, worms, and other creatures, is prime avian territory. Given its biological and geographical similarity to nearby Laguna San Ignacio, it might be expected that check lists for the lagoon would approach 100 species, but for unknown reasons less than half that appears more realistic, and the species composition differs noticeably. The park is an underwater ecological reserve. A deposit of fossilized shark teeth can be found mixed in the surface gravel northwest of the park.

A very rare creature used to live in the area. Years ago an old man in Guerrero Negro told me about a species of jackrabbit, known locally as *orejas de vela* (sail-ears), that lived along the eastern margin of the lagoon. When the breezes came from the west in the morning the rabbits found they could use their big ears to sail deep into the desert to forage. When the breeze from the east began in the evening they could then sail back to drink at a place known as *Fuente de Liebre* (Jack Rabbit Spring). Those with the largest ears prospered, and as the years passed the species kept evolving

ever-larger ears. However, fishermen in Bahía Vizcaíno began to find them in the stomachs of sharks, and the scenario was obvious: while sailing back to the spring in the evenings they had forgotten to furl their ears in time and were blown into the bay, only to be eaten by the hungry sharks. By now so many have been eaten that the species may be extinct, leaving only jacks with regular ears.

● ●

❝ *The mud flat story*

Occasionally even the most modest of vehicles can triumph over the fancy four-wheelers, at least for a while. John Anglin and I were skirting the east end of Scammon's in my Chevy van, trying a shortcut from Guerrero Negro to the road to Tortugas. As night fell the wheel track we were following disappeared and it became necessary to steer by compass. To liven things up I put on a Vivaldi tape, and John found a bottle of tequila in a duffel bag. The terrain was so smooth and flat we seemed to be flying, and I found I could drive 40 and even 50 miles an hour. This was the way Baja ought to be: no banging and bumping, no clouds of dust, no hot sun! We discovered the secret of drinking tequila; just learn to accept the fact that it tastes like turpentine, and after that it's not too bad. We were thoroughly enjoying ourselves, but finally we picked up the Tortugas road and were soon creeping down a steep, rough grade in a series of hairpin turns toward Malarrimo. Arriving at the beach just as the fifth straight rendition of Four Seasons *finished, we bedded down for the night, very mellow and ready for sleep.*

We awoke the next morning to find three men standing over us, a Jeep and a Power Wagon parked nearby. "How did you get that thing here?" they wanted to know, pointing to the van. I responded that I had driven it. They then wanted to know our route, which I described. As I confirmed that it was indeed a perfectly ordinary battered 250-cube, 3-speed Chevy van with a 15-foot boat on top and a mountain of gear in back, a look of disdain came over their faces, and one of them said, "No way, man." We insisted; the van was right in front of them, wasn't it, and there were no parachutes lying about, were there? Finally one of them blurted out, "You guys claim to have crossed the mud flats in that piece of junk?" Not comprehending his meaning, I replied, "Mud flats? What mud flats?" Only then did we look at the van; an inches-thick layer of gray mud covered the sides, sagging and folding to give it the appearance of a stuffed elephant mounted on little wheels. Apparently we had crossed an extensive mud flat without realizing it during party time the night before, our high velocity saving us from disappearing into the awful ooze. John spoke up instantly. "Mud flats? What mud flats?," he repeated, following it with a knowing chuckle; he wasn't about to let these four-wheel guys with their chrome-plated roll bars, fat tires, and tuck-and-roll upholstery put us down. I caught on, adding with a scoff, "It was nothing. We could hardly tell we were crossing them," without stating the reason why.

We were making progress, for their disdain was obviously melting. "Wow! That's hard to believe. It takes a big four-wheel rig with flotation tires to get through gook like that. You actually made it in that thing without sinking up to your keesters?" Continuing our minimalist approach, we flatly denied that our accomplishment was anything out of the ordinary, subtly implying that only less-than-skilled drivers needed to rely on the advantages of four-wheel-drive, to the obvious discomfort of our audience. We were making rapid progress, for now we had their rapt attention. I discussed several theories on soft-ground driving, not mentioning their recent origin, and John told of the times we had come to the aid of other drivers, creating the impression that some of them might even have been four-wheelers, simply by leaving it unsaid.

Finally, they respectfully thanked us for sharing our knowledge, strode over to their vehicles, and started to drive off—and we had the exquisite pleasure of seeing the Jeep sink to the axles in soft sand. Struggling to hold back the roars of laughter trying to escape, we stoically watched as they rigged a winch line from the Power Wagon, our undeserved triumph complete, if short-lived. Our comeuppance came after breakfast, when we loaded up and started out across the sand, getting perhaps 50 yards before we too sank to the axles. **"**

• •

■ ■ ■ ■ ■ ■ ■ ■ ■ ■ ■ ■ ■ ■ ■ ■

On the Transpeninsular at KM 208

KM	Location
189+	Pickup road northeast (signed) to El Arco and Bahía San Francisquito. Those continuing on the Transpeninsular should skip the following section.

Side trip to El Arco and Bahía San Francisquito. The road through El Arco passes through one of the more heavily mineralized areas in Baja, and it may be useful for making loop trips. The road was once paved,

but maintenance was ignored from the start and it is now a moonscape of potholes. In a thousand years anthropologists may be poking about trying to figure out why a road was built and then immediately allowed to fall into ruin. Sandy trails on each side of the pavement provide good driving.

The road from Bahía de los Angeles is currently in better condition than the El Arco road, but this may not last, for road crews have widened and graded the road to a point 10 miles northeast of El Arco. Until these improvements are completed, the El Arco road has stretches of slopes ranging up to 15%, and a number of rocky and winding areas.

Set odometer. At Mile 25.1, the road passes the northern outskirts of El Arco, where fuel, water, and food may be obtained. In 1882 extensive placers eventually producing over $3 million in gold were discovered at nearby Camallí. Gold was discovered later at El Arco, and in the 1920s, a thousand miners were at work. Today copper and gold mining continues sporadically at a low level. Hopes are high for newly discovered deposits, but little seems to change from year to year. Semi-employed miners sometimes offer samples of quartz, hematite, turquoise, chrysocolla, and malachite. Pseudomorphs of pyrites in scattered crystals have been found nearby.

The road passes through a great *dátilillio* forest beginning at Mile 50.8, and passes the site of La Cuesta de la Ley at Mile 54.7. "The Slope That Rules" has been tamed by bulldozers, but even in years past it was overrated; with its 1 mile of grades, the steepest only 27%, it was no challenge to the "Terrible Three" south of Puertecitos. At Mile 61.1 arrive at Rancho el Progreso, marked by a windmill. Turn left (060°) and at Mile 61.6 join the Bahía de los Angeles-Bahía San Francisquito road, described beginning on page 147. Boats can be launched over the sand beach at the inner harbor.

There is relatively little pressure from sport or commercial fishermen, and sea bass and groupers get very, very large. There is an excellent seasonal fishery for yellowtail, which pass through the area heading south in early November, returning north in late May and early June, as well as a population that hangs around all year. One of the most productive fishing areas is Bahía San Rafael, beginning 5 miles to the northwest of Punta San Francisquito. Whales often are seen in Canal de Salsipuedes. (A description of the anchorages and the coast south to Santa Rosalía will be found beginning on page 146.)

The San Francisquito Resort has cabins, *palapas*, RV parking, restaurant, showers, rest rooms, an airstrip, *pangas*, gasoline, mechanic, and a beautiful sand beach. The resort is a Mecca for spearfishermen in pursuit of the big fish that inhabit the waters around the islands to the east. In the last few years, free-divers have bagged a 70-pound gulf grouper, a 39-pound spotted grouper, and an 80-pound white seabass, in addition to many lesser specimens. For tankers, the resort has an air compressor and a limited number of rental tanks and weight belts; divers should bring all other equipment. Shelling in the area is good, primarily for murex, olive, cowrie, and pearl oyster.

Drivers returning to the Transpeninsular Highway by way of El Arco should set their odometers at the resort. At Mile 33.2, take care at the **Y**; go straight ahead (220°), and avoid the left turn.

■ ■ ■ ■ ■ ■ ■ ■ ■ ■ ■ ■ ■ ■ ■ ■ ■ ■ ■ ■

Back on the Transpeninsular at KM 189+

KM	Location
144	**Vizcaíno.** PEMEX (MPD), restaurants, groceries, auto parts, tire repair, stores, motel, mechanic, ice, liquor, bakery, doctor, pharmacy. The attendants at the PEMEX are magicians, so watch closely. Kaadekamán RV Park has water and electric hookups, and an ambiance score of zero. Sedan road to Bahía Tortugas, Asunción, Punta Abreojos, and on to KM 98. Those continuing on the Transpeninsular should turn to page 166.

Side trip: the Vizcaíno loop trip. One of longest and most interesting "off-road" trips in Baja, the Vizcaíno Loop Trip crosses the Desierto de Vizcaíno to Bahía Tortugas, heads south through Bahía Asunción to Punta Abreojos and returns to the Transpeninsular in the vicinity of San Ignacio. The attraction is not the scenery, for most of the trip is across flat coastal plains, but rather the remoteness and grand scale of the desert. Once you near the ocean the reward is more than 60 miles of the most deserted and pristine beaches in North America, plus fine diving and fishing. With luck, you might see a pronghorn "antelope." One of Baja's rarest animals (only about 90 are still left), the animal is only distantly related to the antelope native to Africa and Asia. The Vizcaíno is not a prime birding area, with relatively low numbers and no species unique to it, but sightings might include sage sparrow, the uncommon LeConte's thrasher, and endemic gray thrasher, as well as birds typically found throughout Baja in similar habitats.

Large areas inside this great loop are covered with a rare type of dune. Called "transverse dunes," they form when winds blow steadily in one direction, causing the surface to look like huge plowed furrows in a farmer's field. Similar dunes have been observed in northern Australia. The central Vizcaíno is among the most inaccessible wildernesses left on the peninsula. However, change is coming; the major roads have been graded, and water and power lines have been extended to the coast. It is now feasible to make the trip in sizable RVs, and adventurous trailerboaters equipped for over-the-beach launches have access to Isla Natividad, Cedros, and the Benitos, and to the south, Asunción and Punta Abreojos.

The road to Tortugas is often washboarded, so plan on at least a six-hour journey, one-way. Gas and supplies may or may not be available in Tortugas, Asunción, and the other villages along the way, so make sure you fill at every opportunity. Set odometer, turn southwest. For the first several miles there are roadside grocery, beer, and liquor stores. The pavement, much of it in poor repair, ends at Mile 18.3 and becomes a graded, two-lane gravel sedan road, damaged in sections by erosion, and badly washboarded.

Cross the first of three salt ponds on an earthen causeway at Mile 36.1. At Mile 46.2 encounter a sedan road south (195°, signed), ending on the coast road east of Asunción. If time is short and you are interested mainly in the beach areas southeast of Asunción, turn south here; otherwise go straight ahead (275°, signed). The pickup road north to legendary Playa Malarrimo will be found at Mile 73.2.

Side trip to Playa Malarrimo. If you have a suitable vehicle, you should plan a side trip to Malarrimo. The road is hard to spot; if you miss it, keep going until you see the sign for Rancho San José de Castro, and go back (east) 200 yards. The 26-mile (one way) road has an 18% grade in one stretch. Because of deep sand, those in two-wheel-drive vehicles should stop a half mile short of the beach and walk in; if you can see the water you are already too close.

Long the most famous beachcombing area in Baja, this beach has yielded US Navy mops and firefighting foam containers, human bodies, palm and redwood logs, hatch covers, enormous numbers of light bulbs and Twinkie wrappers, airplane wings, shipwrecks, both in their entirety and in thousands of parts, prized Japanese glass fishing floats, whale carcasses and bones, a 12-foot torpedo emitting buzzing noises, and a soggy package containing a CD by Hootie and the Blowfish. A statistical analysis of the huge crop of cans and bottles would reveal that humans drink a great deal of alcohol, cover their food with layers of catsup, and are deeply concerned about underarm odor. While you are searching, try to figure out why empty catsup bottles are almost always capped, while alcohol bottles are generally open. The beach is slowly advancing, so it might pay to explore areas as far as 500 yards inland. Spend the night—there is usually plenty of firewood.

Back on the Vizcaíno-Bahía Tortugas road at Mile 73.2

At Mile 75.9 note the intersection with the old road to Asunción to the left (120°). Continue straight ahead (235°) for Bahía Tortugas (Turtle Bay, Port San Bartolome) at Mile 107.3. The ramshackle town has groceries, bakery, restaurants, liquor, ice, purified water, laundromat, clinic, doctors, pharmacy, sporting goods, *pangas* for hire, *Pesca* office, mechanics, auto parts, tire repair, mechanics, several motels, *tortilla* factory, a bank, and a PEMEX (MD). Aerolineas California has an office in town and you can fly to Isla Cedros, Ensenada, and other places on their routes.

There are no organized RV parks, but many sandy locations are available around the bay. Boats can be launched over a sand beach west of the pier in town, at a number of locations along the eastern margin of the bay, or over a hard sand-and-gravel beach near the fishing camp at its southwest end. Fishing in the bay is difficult in some areas due to dense beds of seaweed, but outstanding fishing for sand bass, kelp bass, and ocean whitefish is found outside between Cabo Tórtolo (Cape Turtledove) and Punta Cambrey. The main channel out of the bay, about a mile wide and marked by lighthouses on its north and south margins, offers excellent fishing for bonito, yellowtail, barracuda, and dorado in season, out to 4 miles. There is good offshore fishing at the "15 Spot," 6 miles, 248° from Punta la Cantina, the point forming the north entrance of the bay; at "38 Spot," 12 miles, 150°; at "9 Spot," 22 miles, 176°; and at "10 Spot," 25 miles, 138°. Handliners working from *pangas* account for part of the commercial catch in the area, and they need bait, so gillnets are maintained along the south shore of the bay. This bait is sometimes sold from a boat anchored off the village and might be available—ask around.

Gray whales come close to shore, occasionally entering kelp beds. A friend and I were fishing once near Punta Cambrey when a gray plowed through the kelp like a gigantic bulldozer not 5 yards away, apparently oblivious to our presence. At least 4 fishing vessels have sunk in the bay, but the only known diveable wreck is in 60 feet of water, 2/3 mile southeast of Punta la Cantina. Divers almost acquired a magnificent wreck when the Japanese armored cruiser *Asama* hit a rock at the mouth of the bay while on a First World War patrol, ripping a 15-foot gash in her hull. "Unfortunately," she was refloated three months later and made it back to Japan.

The road to the village near Punta Eugenia is normally passable by passenger cars. Reset your odometer, drive north of town and follow the signs starting near the airport, arriving at Mile 16.5. Portable boats can be launched inside the natural breakwater, and *pangas* are for hire. There is no good place to launch trailerboats. A building in the village houses an inoperative recompression chamber. Due to low visibilities, diving is poor in the immediate vicinity of the village.

Natividad lies 5 miles west. Although it is within easy range of a boat launched from Eugenia or Bahía Tortugas, few sport divers or anglers come to the island. Some surfers consider Natividad one of the best areas on the west coast of North America. The primary break is "Open Doors," a sand-bottom beach break on the east side of the island, off the end of the airstrip. Big swells from July to September bring extraordinary surf, with almost every wave producing stand-up tubes and great rights and lefts. It is only a short paddle to the lineup, and the bottom is reportedly free of obstructions. In winter, northwest swells can wrap around the point into the teeth of the wind, providing fine conditions free of chop. With hollow faces to 15 feet, "Siren Bay" on the southwest side of the island about a mile southeast of the north cape works well in winter. Getting to this site takes about 45 minutes in a boat from the village. Described as "gnarly," it is not for novice surfers, since there is no way to escape

except back the way you came, and a broken leash means a lost board and a long swim. A third major break, "Frijole Bowl," a reef break off the south point, has occasionally seen faces over 20 feet during winter, no place for beginners.

The anchorage off the village at the south end is open and subject to refracted swell, and can be very windy. No regular source of fuel or supplies will be found. A recompression chamber is located in the village. In 1909 the brig *Blakely* was lost along the southeast shore. In addition, villagers report two vessels in about 50 feet 100 yards off the west end of the landing. Chart 21011 shows a wreck on the southwest side.

A sedan road winds south along the shore of the bay and then turns west. The sandy shores here provide good camping and a place to launch boats. At Mile 11.0 (from town) the road ends at Bahía Cambrey (Thurloe Bay). The sandy bottom of the bay is home to astronomical numbers of pismo clams. Stretching east and then south for 5 miles or more, the beds are so dense that the mere act of anchoring can uproot a dinner-load. An oyster farm is in operation nearby. Shell collectors will find specimens of a dozen or more species on the beach, most sea-worn, a few fresh. Vehicles can get near the beach and portable boats can be launched, but a rocky berm makes it difficult to launch trailerboats. The bay provides an open anchorage, the next anchorages to the south being Bahías San Pablo, San Roque, Asunción, San Hipólito, and Ballenas.

Asunción can be reached in two ways from Tortugas: the new route via Mile 46.2, or the old route via Mile 75.9. The distance from Tortugas to Asunción is 90 miles if the new route is taken, 68.8 miles by the new. Both routes are graded, two-lane, although there are a number of arroyo crossings lacking culverts, rendering them vulnerable to rain damage, and in a number of locations the road is reduced to one lane. Asunción has a health clinic, pharmacy, mail, long-distance telephone, hardware, auto parts, mechanics, *Pesca* office, beer, groceries, and a desalinization plant. There is no PEMEX, but several locals sell Magnasin from drums. Diesel might be available at the cannery in an emergency.

After climbing down low cliffs west of town, surfers

Reeve, Rob, and I almost exploded from eating too many lobsters

will find good reef breaks at the point. Boats can be launched over the beach in town and at a steep unpaved area a quarter mile inside the point. Anchorages off the village and at Isla Asunción are usually satisfactory in prevailing seas. Fishing is often excellent on reefs around the island and directly offshore, at "24 Spot," 6 miles, 245° from the south tip of Isla Asunción, and at "6 Spot," 3 miles, 120° from the same place.

Diving near town is limited, but the island has excellent spearfishing. I once fired up my hooka and made a dive off the island. When I reached the bottom, stood up, and looked around, I was stunned to see a dozen, 20, no 40, lobsters within the range of visibility. Had they chosen to act collectively the outcome would have been quite different. Three large US fishing vessels have been wrecked near the island.

A rich deposit of fossilized shark teeth can be seen by hiking from the north end of town on course 343°, aiming for the area between a large red-colored tableland and a row of hills. At Minute 75 you should arrive in a deep and distinctive canyon with a fair amount of tan, chalk-like deposits. Lying in the gravel, the teeth range in size from $1/4$ inch to an inch or more. Also to be seen are assortments of fossilized scallops, whelks, clams, and sand dollars.

San Roque village can be reached by locating the SSA Centro de Salud health clinic in Asunción and driving 9.6 miles northwest on the sedan road (muddy after rains). Good fishing for yellowtail and bottomfish is found northwest of Isla San Roque. Boats can be launched over the sandy beach, and *pangas* are for hire. The anchorage is only fair. Although seldom visited by boaters, Bahía San Pablo to the north offers a deep but otherwise good anchorage. Long-range boats from San Diego sometimes fish San Pablo.

Due to a small navigational error on August 8, 1921, Captain J. C. Zastrow provided future skin divers with an interesting wreck off the island. The steamer *San José* can be found south of its southeast tip, her booms, winches, plates, and ribs scattered over a wide area at depths up to 30 feet. Another wreck lies on a sand bottom east of the island. Originally about 70 feet long, she lies in 40 feet of water. When over the wreck, the aid-to-navigation tower on the island will bear 230°, and the central and largest islet among the small group to the southeast 126°. Large numbers of kelp bass and sand bass frequent the area, and the bugs get so big you can eat their legs like king crab.

The coast between Bahía Cambrey and Bahía San Pablo is penetrated by only a few poor roads, but many reach the beaches southeast from Punta San Roque. This stretch is a surf fisherman's paradise, perhaps the least-stressed and most productive beach fishery in Baja. The beaches between San Roque and Asunción have superb beach-casting for corbina, and the rays of the setting sun passing through the waves often reveal hordes of fish searching for food, a stirring sight to anyone, fisherman or not.

Continuing on the Vizcaíno Loop Trip; reset odometer and drive east from Asunción along miles of beautiful sand beach. At Mile 4.6, encounter the intersection with the "new" road northeast to Mile 46.2 on the Vizcaíno-Tortugas

Bernie Eskesen and Ruben Villa Carmona sort through shark teeth

Road. At Mile 19.6 take the left (125°, signed) fork. (The right fork, 155°, signed, leads to the tiny settlements of Punta Prieta and San Hipólito.) Bahía San Hipólito has a large open anchorage which is satisfactory in prevailing seas, and has a good reef break. The rocky beaches in the area are a favorites with shorecasters, small bits of clam often producing large numbers of yellowfin croakers and sand bass, and there are a number of good boondocking sites.

The town of La Bocana at Mile 49.0, has grocery stores, auto parts, tire repair, small cafés, health clinic, pharmacies, mail, and a desalinization plant. There is no PEMEX, but Magnasin is sold from drums, and diesel may be available at the packing plant. Boats can be launched over the low sand beach south of the packing plant. Large numbers of cabrilla, croaker, corvina, corbina, shark, and halibut are taken inside the lagoon, and although there is an active commercial *panga* fleet, dorado, yellowtail, and black- and white seabass are still numerous offshore.

The road from La Bocana to Punta Abreojos passes close to Estero la Bocana, offering numerous chances to launch portable boats. Many areas in the *estero* are lined with mangroves; see page 208 for some fishing hints. Punta Abreojos, at Mile 60.0, has limited groceries, beer, *Pesca* office, telephone, ice, auto parts, mechanics, tire repair, health clinic, restaurant, and a desalinization plant. No PEMEX again, but locals sell Magnasin out of drums, and diesel may available at the cooperative. The anchorage east of the point is marginally satisfactory, being open to the south, with refracted swell and lots of wind. A number of vessels have been lost due to confusion around the many offshore reefs and pinnacles; they didn't name it "Open-Your-Eyes" for nothing. The point has a fantastic right break in good swells—some fans claim it is the best right point break in Baja. Punta Abreojos is well-known and much discussed among several generations of boardsailors, who capitalize on passing fronts, especially from March to May or June. Fishing is excellent, and shorecasters take corvina, corbina, and croakers. Wright

Shoal, a mile southeast of Punta Abreojos, and Roca Ballena, 4 miles west, produce white seabass and yellowtail, and a dozen grouper and black sea bass would not be too much to hope for during a single trip. Cartop and inflatable boats can be launched northeast of town.

Sailors heading south from Punta Abreojos will find that tidal currents, shoals, and shifting sand bars make the entrance to Laguna San Ignacio dangerous, and the first good anchorages south of Punta Abreojos are shallow Bahía San Juanico and Bahía Santa María.

Leaving Punta Abreojos, reset odometer. At Mile 7.2, a sedan (dry weather) road signed CAMPO RENE leads to the right (110°) 3.4 miles along a sandy peninsula forming the southwestern margin of shallow Laguna Escondida (Hidden Lagoon). Campo Rene will be encountered about halfway to the entrance. RVers and campers are welcome, and cartoppers, inflatables, and small trailer boats can be launched in the lagoon across a hard-packed sand-and-sea-shell ramp at higher tides.

The lagoon offers excellent fishing for spotted bass, grouper, corvina, halibut, sierra, barracuda, and maybe, just maybe, snook. Much of the inside of the lagoon is lined with mangroves, so turn to page 207 for some fishing hints. Various basses, croakers, and groupers are taken in the channel leading to the ocean, and the deep area just inside the entrance can be fantastic, as close to fool-proof fishing as can be found in Baja. The lagoon is very shallow and much of it turns into mud flats in periods of very low tides, so check your tide table before coming. White water is often present on a sandy reef directly south of the channel entrance, and boaters should use great caution when heading for Wright Shoal or Roca Ballena, even in periods of relative calm. Boaters have made it safely around this area by heading south out of the channel for a half mile until they clear the beach breakers, then turning east and running a mile or so until past the white water area. Better yet, watch for local *panga* fishermen heading out and follow them.

The two-lane, graded, sedan road northeast from Punta Abreojos to the Transpeninsular is badly washboarded. At Mile 54.3, the Transpeninsular is reached at KM 98.

■■■■■■■■■■■■■■■■■■

Back on the Transpeninsular KM 144

KM	Location
118	Sedan road northeast to San Francisco (signed). Those continuing on the Transpeninsular should skip the following section.

 Side trip to the Sierra de San Francisco. This side trip will take you to some of the most spectacular mountain scenery in Baja, with the added attraction

of its finest rock-art site closely accessible by car. The new road has no grades over 14% and while it can handle small motor homes, there are sharp switchbacks and few places in which to turn around. At least six hours should be allowed for the trip. Set odometer. After crossing featureless flat desert for 6 miles, the road switches back a number of times to the top of a narrow ridge, climbing toward massive Pico Santa Monica, at 5,218 feet the highest point in the Sierra de San Francisco. There are deep canyons on each side, and although the road closely approaches their edges, it pays to stop occasionally and do some hiking to actually look over the edge— the scenery is dazzling.

After passing several small ranches, the road swings around the upper reaches of Cañon San Pablo at Mile 20.0. One of the most magnificent canyons in Baja—on a par with, but very different from, Cañon Tajo far to the north—this narrow, 1,000-foot-deep, palm-lined gorge is the location of Gardner Cave, the crown jewel of Baja rock art, as well as several other fine sites. With its treasures of man-made and natural art, the entire area should be made into a national park (more on the canyon later in this chapter). At Mile 21.0 arrive at the site of Cueva Ratón (signed). While not of the caliber of the sites farther downstream, this site has a 30-foot-wide mural showing figures of humans, deer, lions, bighorn sheep, and other animals, with examples of the bicolor and overpainting traditions.

Arrangements can be made in the village for three-day burro trips to see Gardner Cave. All visitors to art sites must have a guide, obtained at the village of San Francisco at Mile 22.5, as well as a permit issued in advance at the museum in San Ignacio; see the following page. The local policeman keeps a sharp eye.

Since you were probably intent on the scenery ahead on the way up, the trip back to the Transpeninsular will be an all-but-new treat: canyon walls resembling a vast book with pages 50 feet thick, and vistas of the head of Laguna San Ignacio and the Sierra Santa Clara, over 40 miles away.

■■■■■■■■■■■■■■■■■■

Back on the Transpeninsular at KM 118

KM	Location
98	Road southwest (signed) to Punta Abreojos (already described). Modest café.
90	Rolling hills with gentle to moderate grades until KM 17+.
85	Halfway point between Tijuana and Cabo San Lucas.
77+	Agricultural inspection for north-bound vehicles.
73+	**San Ignacio Junction.** PEMEX (MD), auto parts, tire repair, welding, mechanic. Note the whale skeleton at the intersection. Signs for San Ignacio RV Park, behind the PEMEX, promise full hook-

ups and hot showers. Don't believe a word of it.

San Ignacio

The scenery on the Transpeninsular for more than 100 miles has been flat and featureless, the most boring section of the entire Transpeninsular, and the arrival at San Ignacio, an island of green palms in a sea of brown desert, is one of Baja's most pleasant surprises. Time should be set aside to explore the town, and you should also plan to see what lies outside its boundaries—Laguna San Ignacio, the home of the famous friendly whales, and a number of fine rock-art sites.

The town is rich in history. A Jesuit mission was founded here in 1728, and a system of stone-lined channels and cisterns was built to distribute spring water. Many of the converts were Indians who had been persuaded by the good padres to relocate from Isla Cedros. A wide variety of fruits were grown, and some grape vines were planted so long ago that today they have assumed tree-like proportions. Introduced date palms thrived, and as the years passed, they increased their numbers, crowding out the native fan palms and other less-competitive vegetation, to the point that they now dominate everything, although trees hanging with massive numbers of oranges are gaining rapidly. To protect the agricultural land from floods, Indian converts constructed a gigantic rock diversion wall, which may still be seen today near the town. Constructed of cobbles and mortar, it is 40 feet wide, 10 feet high, and perhaps 3 miles long, making it the largest stone structure on the peninsula.

A more permanent structure than the original adobe church was needed, and construction of a massive stone church with walls of volcanic lava 4 feet thick was begun in the town square in the 1760s. The structure was still without a roof when the Jesuits were expelled from Baja California in 1768, but work began again in 1779, and the building was completed in 1786. The church was renovated in 1976, and it is the most impressive Mission Period church in Baja.

Although there are signs of recent economic progress—construction of a number of buildings and new sidewalks—the village remains amiable, low pressure, and much like it was in the past. Some story telling and loafing go on under the massive Indian laurel trees in the square, and a visit to the church, the new museum, and a walk through the village can occupy several hours. Set odometer at the highway. At Mile 0.1, RV parking is available among the palms, with a good swimming hole and very little litter. Big rigs should not go into the crowded town square; leave them at the flat area at Mile 0.2 and walk the rest of the way—lighted concrete sidewalks have been constructed for this purpose. RV parking can be found at Mile 0.8; look for the sign on the left. Restaurant las Cazuelas at the Hotel la Pinta at Mile 1.0 is beautiful and serves good meals.

The road to Palapa Asadero la Presa goes west just before El Padrino (The Godfather) Trailer Park at Mile 1.1. La Presa has RV parking and a natural swimming hole. The kids can watch for turtles in the pools, and the nightly frog chorus is the best in Baja. The access road may be a little tight for large rigs. In the past, when it was called La Candelaria, the place was kept immaculately clean, and after a shaky start, the new management seems to be succeeding in doing the same. El Padrino has a *palapa* restaurant and bar, and RV sites with water and electricity, as well as rest rooms and showers, and progress is being made at keeping down the litter.

Enter the town square at Mile 1.3. With its golden altar, paintings, carved confessional, and stone construction, marred only by fluorescent lighting, vinyl kneeling pads, and loudspeakers, a visit to the mission church will take you back several centuries. The congregation is still active, and visitors are welcome. The birthday of Ignacio Loyola, the town's patron saint, is celebrated on July 31 each year.

A CONASUPO and several other stores in the square sell basic food and household items, and there are a butcher shop, pay telephones, and public rest rooms. In 1928 Phillip Townsend Hanna worried that the introduction of electricity and cinema would be the "ruination of one of the most engaging spots conceivable," but these evils have had little influence thus far. However, the new video store in the square may soon cause his fears to be realized. Restaurant Rene's, in a new building just east of the southeast corner of the square, serves Mexican food, as does Restaurant Chalita, located in the square. Potable water can be obtained from spigots in the square. An octagonal water reservoir from the days of the Jesuits is still in use, and can be seen by walking 150 yards east from the southeast corner of the town square.

Guided trips to see the whales and nearby art sites can be arranged at Kuyima Servicios Ecoturisticos, which maintains an office in the town square and a camp just south of La Freidera, and Baja Discovery includes the lagoon on some of their van trips—their phone numbers and addresses are in Appendix B. It may be possible to make arrangements to visit Cueva Palmarito in the Rancho Santa Martha area and other rock-art sites to the north; ask at the La Posada Hotel, south of the square several blocks. See page 175 for a bit of the history of the family that owns this hotel.

A new museum, Museo Local de San Ignacio, has been established. Follow the signs from the southwest corner of the square. The stone building contains many beautiful photographs of rock art, information on the history of the Indians, reproductions of art sites and artifacts, and an impressive re-creation of the art at Gardner Cave.

All visitors to archaeological sites in the Sierra de San Francisco must be accompanied by an authorized guide, and must obtain a permit in advance. The permit is free, but it is presently available only at the museum. A form in Spanish and English available at the museum describes a number of requirements concerning assignment and compensation of guides, campsite regulations, reservations, and treatment of the art sites, which should be read prior to departing. For additional information, contact the Instituto Sud Californiano de Cultura in La Paz or San Ignacio.

Sedan road south to Laguna San Ignacio. Those con-

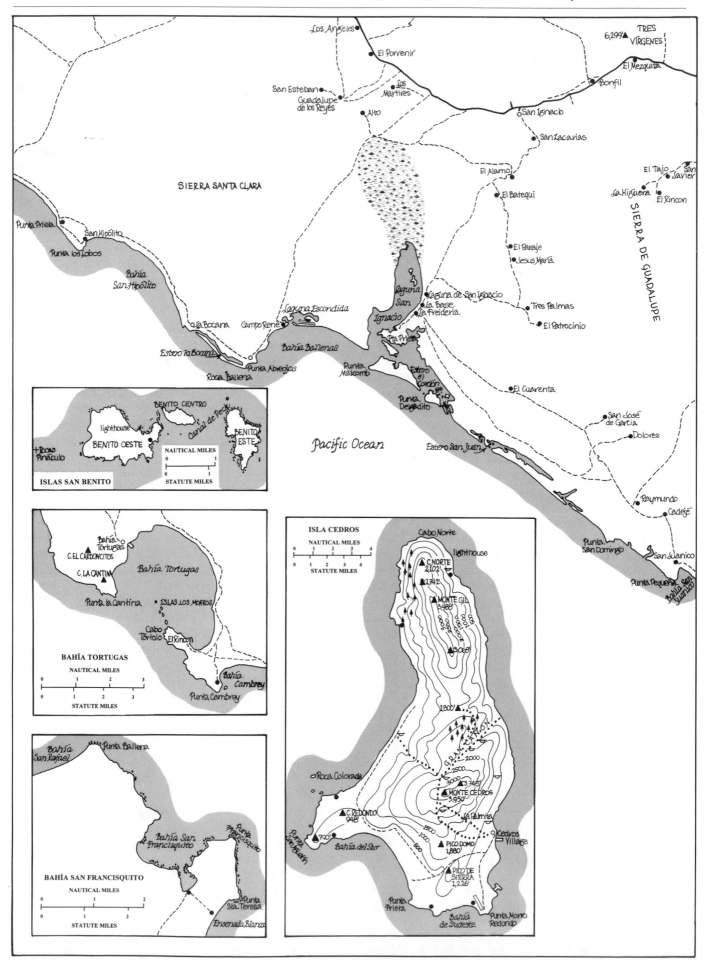

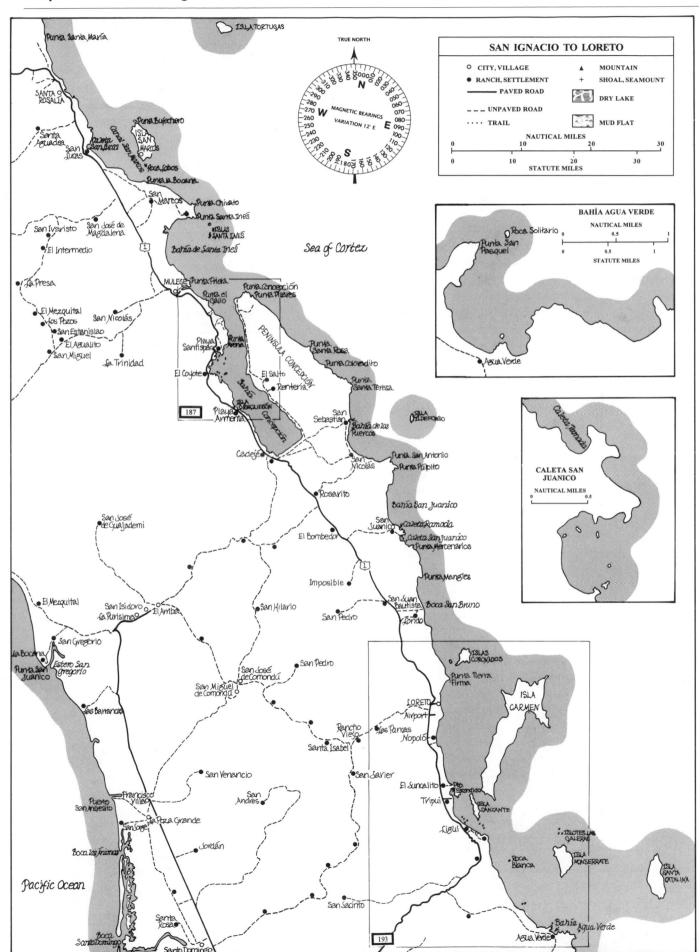

True North

MAGNETIC BEARINGS
VARIATION 12° E

SAN IGNACIO TO LORETO

○ CITY, VILLAGE   ▲ MOUNTAIN
● RANCH, SETTLEMENT   + SHOAL, SEAMOUNT
—— PAVED ROAD
- - - UNPAVED ROAD   DRY LAKE
· · · · TRAIL   MUD FLAT

NAUTICAL MILES
0   10   20   30

STATUTE MILES
0   10   20   30

BAHÍA AGUA VERDE

NAUTICAL MILES
0   0.5   1

STATUTE MILES
0   0.5   1

Roca Solitario
Punta San Pasquel
Agua Verde

CALETA SAN JUANICO

NAUTICAL MILES
0   0.5

Caleta Ramada

Sea of Cortez

Pacific Ocean

Punta Santa María
ISLA TORTUGAS
SANTA ROSALIA
Santa Agueda
Punta Bufechero
ISLA SAN MARCOS
Caleta San Lucas
San Lucas
Roca Lobos
Punta la Bocana
San Ivaristo
San José de Magdalena
San Marcos
Punta Chivato
Punta Santa Inés
ISLAS SANTA INES
El Intermedio
Bahía de Santa Inés
La Presa
MULEGE
Punta Prieta
Punta Concepción
Punta Prieta
El Mezquital
Los Pozos
San Nicolás
Punta el Gallo
Punta Santa Rosa
San Estanislao
El Agualito
San Miguel
La Trinidad
Playa Santispac
Punta Arena
PENINSULA CONCEPCIÓN
Punta Colorodito
El Coyote
ISLA BARGUEDON
El Salto
Renteria
Punta Santa Teresa
Bahía Concepción
San Sebastian
Bahía de los Puercos
ISLA ILDEFONSO
187
Playa Armenia
Cadejé
San Nicolás
Punta San Antonio
Punta Pulpito
San José de Guajademi
Rosarito
Bahía San Juanico
San Juanico
Caleta Ramada
Caleta San Juanico
Punta Mercenarios
El Bombedor
El Mezquital
San Isidoro
La Purisima
El Amba
Imposible
San Hilario
Punta Mangles
San Juan Bautista
Boca San Bruno
San Gregorio
Estero San Gregorio
La Bocana
Punta San Juanico
San Pedro
San Pedro
San José de Comondú
Tordio
ISLAS CORONADOS
Punta Tierra Firma
San Miguel de Comondú
Las Barrancas
ISLA CARMEN
LORETO
Airport
San Venancio
Rancho Viejo
Las Parras
Nopoló
Santa Isabel
Francisco Villa
Puerto San Andresito
San Andres
San Javier
El Suncalito
Pto Escondido
Tripui
ISLA DANZANTE
San Jorge de Poza Grande
Ligui
ISLOTES LAS GALERAS
Jordán
Boca las Animas
Roca Blanca
ISLA MONSERRATE
Santa Rosa
ISLA SANTA CATALINA
Boca Santo Domingo
San Sacinto
193
Bahía Agua Verde
Santo Domingo
Agua Verde

tinuing on the Transpeninsular should skip the following section.

↱ **Side trip to Laguna San Ignacio and on to Villa Insurgentes.** Laguna San Ignacio is one of the world's major gray whale breeding grounds, and one of the few places where friendly whale behavior has been observed regularly. The road from San Ignacio has been graded and improved, and sedans and small motor homes can make the trip. However, be warned—the road is narrow, making it difficult to pass approaching vehicles, and sections of the road have world-class washboard. The drive takes three hours one-way.

Starting in town on the southeast corner of the square, set odometer and drive east, turn right (170°) at Mile 0.3, and left (090°) at the large satellite dish at Mile 0.5. The road will quickly climb a hill, swing right, and head south. Half a dozen ranches will be passed in the first 15 miles, and you will encounter the fish camps of Laguna de San Ignacio, La Base, and La Freidera at Miles 36.0, 37.0 and 40.0, respectively. The last name means "trypot," referring to the means used by shore-based whalers located here in the winter of 1860–61 to reduce their quarry to oil. The scenery is not inspiring, mostly desert scrub, mangroves, and extensive mud flats, and there are no whales to be seen at first, but your disappointment will not last long. Six miles southwest of La Freidera is Punta Prieta, a low-lying point with a rocky margin jutting into the lagoon. The waters surrounding this point and south to the entrance of the lagoon are the winter home of the friendly whales. Due to mud and tidal flats it might not be possible to drive all the way to Punta Prieta, but you should be able to get within walking distance.

Except for the lack of music, the dictionary definition of ballet—a classical dance form characterized by grace and precision of movement and elaborate formal technique—certainly fits the show off the point. Grays look awkward, but they are in fact extremely graceful and have a repertory of movements that would test the skills of the best of ballerinas. Instead of *pirouette, adagio*, or *jeté*, the most frequent move by a whale is the "spy-hop," in which one pushes its flukes against the bottom, or if in deep water, vigorously beats it, allowing the whale to rise vertically about one-third of the way out of the water. Another move is the "breach," in which one leaps almost completely out of the water, often repeated two or three times in a row, landing with great splashes. They often "corkscrew," rolling over again and again as they move through the water. Unromantic people offer sober explanations for such behavior—spy-hopping whales want a better view, and breaching whales are trying to dislodge parasites—but those who have seen it come to believe it is indeed a ballet, or at least a demonstration of their immense power, perhaps a whale sport, that they do it just for fun or simply to show off.

Fishermen at La Freidera and the other fish camps can be hired to take you out in their *pangas* to get a front-row view. A few whales may come closer and spy-hop to get a better look at the curious creatures looking at them. Most whales seem unconcerned by the presence of boats, allowing you to get close to see mothers nursing their babies, mating activity, and the repertory of whale ballet. Some mothers, accompanied by their recently born babies, will come right up to the boat to visit and be scratched and petted.

The motivations of animals can never be known with certainty, and some people insist that grays are not friendly but merely curious. However, based on the experiences Michael and I had during a visit to the lagoon, we have decided they are indeed friendly. Together with several young men we met, we hired a fisherman to take us to Punta Prieta. There were dozens of whales nearby, and as we stopped the boat, a cow and a calf immediately changed course and headed directly towards us. We were soon the recipients of nuzzles and nudges from a 30-ton mother and her 2-ton calf, both intent on being scratched and petted. A person gains a sense of perspective during such an event; the relationship between the weight of a whale and of a human is about the same as that between a human and a rat.

After we had spent 45 minutes with them, we moved to another area, only to quickly gain the attentions of another pair, and later in the day, a third. Each of the three mothers repeatedly swam under her baby and pushed it to the surface, as if urging it to get a better look at the strange creatures peering down at them. The mothers and the babies seemed playful, and as the babies grew more familiar with us they became bolder, one even becoming something of a brat. Michael, then 13 years old, had the wonderful experience of snorkeling for a short time with a mother and baby.

Already guilty of attributing human motivations to animals by stating that the grays are friendly, we will carry it a step further by claiming that they also have a sense of humor. During Gigi's encounter with the *Royal Polaris* (see page 10), she came up very close to one side of the vessel, and when everyone rushed over to see her, she submerged and caused another rush when she came up on the other side. She did this more than a dozen times, and observers came to understand that she was teasing them. During our visit to Laguna San Ignacio, the whale mothers occasionally swished their great flukes under our boat, bouncing it on huge boils of water. One rolled on her side and repeatedly vented spray and smelly breath directly at us as we took photographs. This occurred too often to be mere chance, and each time she would roll over a bit to see that the blast had reached its target. Another mother even played a joke on Steve Prasser. He was sitting with his rear hanging over the side of the boat, when she let out a great blast of bubbles and spray directly beneath him. If this is not humor, what is it?

Like Parque Natural de la Ballena Gris, the whale show rarely gives visitors time to recognize that the lagoon and surrounding areas are prime birding territory.

The map on pages 168 and 169 shows two roads heading southeast from an intersection near La Freidera, the "high road" and the "low road," following the coast to Villa Insurgentes. The intersection can be found as follows: from the center of La

Mike snorkels with a baby

Base camp, drive south on a sandy, one-lane road, staying left at the forks at Miles 0.5, 0.8 and 1.4. Encounter the intersection at Mile 3.0. For the "high road" turn left (102°), for the "low road" continue straight ahead (174°) and make the first left (110°). From this point on, the map is a vast simplification, for there are dozens of impromptu roads; when one becomes too muddy the locals find another way and a new road develops. Accurate maps and road directions are thus impossible, and the trip requires a compass or GPS receiver, patience, and plenty of time. Pickups or four-wheel-drives are advisable on either route.

The "high road" winds past coastal mesas and arroyos and is rough and slow. The "low road" across the mud flats is fast and smooth, but after rains or extreme high tides it can be impassable. Do not stray off the wheel tracks, even in dry weather, for a bottomless pit of gooey muck lies on either side. If you encounter an approaching vehicle on the mud flats, do not pull over to allow it to pass; one vehicle should back down to firm ground.

Approximately 56 miles from La Base by either road the pleasant settlement of Cadajé is reached, where Magnasin may be available from drums, and 9 more miles will take you to San Juanico, located at the head of beautiful Bahía San Juanico. The tiny village has a PEMEX (M), several small stores, a restaurant specializing in fried lobster, and RV parking with hot showers. The head of Bahía San Juanico provides an excellent anchorage, although surf may discourage landings. The highly regarded point breaks at nearby Punta Pequeña are best on south summer swells. Aereo Calafia offers airborne surfing and boardsailing trips to Pequeña from the Cabo San Lucas airport. Nineteen miles southeast of San Juanico, just before the road crosses Arroyo San Gregorio, there is a right (195°) turn, signed LA BOCANA, that leads 9 miles to Punta San Juanico; avoid turns until in the

vicinity of the point. Although less consistent than Pequeña, Juanico also has excellent surfing, especially in southwest to northwest swells. Several intermittent streams empty into the nearby *estero*, causing sanding and frequent changes in bottom contours, and surfers often find things changing day by day. These conditions often make the bay in the lee of the point a poor place to anchor.

Approximately 25 miles southeast of San Juanico (the settlement, not the point) there is an important intersection where you can continue south, arriving at Villa Insurgentes in 68 more miles, or turn northeast through La Purísima and San Isidoro, joining the Transpeninsular at KM 60. This latter road is part of the Mountain Villages Loop Trip, described in Chapter 12.

■■■■■■■■■■■■■■■■■■

Back on the Transpeninsular at KM 73+

KM	Location
53	**Ejido Bonfil.** Cafés, groceries, tire repair. Sedan road north (signed) to Rancho Santa Martha, signed PINTURAS RUPESTRES. Those continuing on the Transpeninsular should skip the following section.

Side trip to the Rancho Santa Martha area. Set odometer, arrive at the ranch at Mile 24.0. Guides can be obtained for a hike to see the rock art at nearby Cueva Palmarito (don't forget to get your permit in San Ignacio). The 2-hour hike is a small price to pay; a great mural is worked across the back wall of a rock shelter 150 feet long and 40 feet high, with figures of red deer, a black mountain lion, and other animals. Over a dozen human figures are shown, many in headdress, some in the bicolor tradition, others in vertical stripes. The ranch can provide horses or burros for those unable or unwilling to hike.

• •

❝ *A trip to Cañon San Pablo*

Although we arrived at Rancho Santa Martha tired from the long drive from Los Angeles, we were excited about the prospect of a burro trip into Cañon San Pablo to see the great Cochimí rock-art murals. Everything was ready, and our guides, Ignacio and Guadalupe Arce, quickly set about loading a mountain of equipment on the sad-eyed burros. Within an hour we were aboard our mounts and following a trail toward a distant ridge. Most of our group were city-

bred and only two or three had ridden before, a fact well known to the burros, who managed a delicate balance between resignation and rebellion, depending on who was aboard. At first the scenery seemed dull, just cactus, scrub, and rock, but we were rapidly gaining altitude. Someone finally looked back and we realized that we had been passing through some fine country, a valley of small green and rose hills rimmed by blue mountains.

The trail became steeper, and we were finally forced to dismount and were soon scrambling on all fours. Each burro was extremely careful where he stepped. If a front hoof successfully found a flat spot on the trail, the little burro brain would direct the rear hoof on the same side to the same spot. If a stone rolled or the burro stumbled, the rear hoof would try a different spot. The pack burros made the last 50 yards to the pass in a series of lunges, their loads swinging precariously, and we entered a broad valley with vistas of the brilliant blue Cortez.

Our first camp was nothing more than a clearing among the thorns, with no food or water for the burros other than cactus lopped off with machetes. Free of their loads, they were soon lying upside down, rolling and kicking in a dust hole like frisky dogs. After a fine supper and a dreamless sleep under a canopy of stars, we awoke and began what became our morning routine: build a fire, make coffee and apply a blanket and saddle to each burro, drink more coffee and pack duffel, eat breakfast and tighten cinches, drink more coffee and load the burros, drink more coffee and start out. Any deviation from this routine upset the burros for the rest of the day.

We found that a definite social order existed among the burros; they had well-developed ideas of who should be first in line, who should be second and so on, and no burro violated that order without fear of retaliatory action by his fellows. These ideas often conflicted with those of the riders, but the burros always won in the long run. We also found that they were very knowledgeable about the route we were following. Using reins, verbal supplications, and body-English, we attempted to turn them toward the route we had chosen when we encountered forks, and they frequently resisted and went their own way. We soon observed that they were almost always correct; with their native ability and years of experience they knew better than we which way was best, and we gave up trying to steer. My burro, though, always wanted to turn to the left. Since he had a snow-white mane and had tried to bite the leader burro, I made a political statement by naming him O'Neill, in honor of the Speaker of the House during Reagan's presidency. We had a similar lack of success in regulating their speed, which was ahead slow, but both cowboys were able to motivate their mules enough to achieve a full gallop. Their secret proved to be the threat of the spur, and we could see the mules roll their wide-set eyes back, watching for the least movement of the cowboy's heels. There were no marks on

their flanks, but the cowboys explained that it is not the rowel that provides the motivation but the noise created by steel jingles hanging from each spur. Pavlov had a point.

Our fascinations were not merely visual. Every day was a concert of a thousand sounds, some soothing and pleasant, others rough and abrasive. Wind and bird songs provided a backdrop for the constant chatter of the riders. Our passage across the desert produced the sound of rolling stones kicked loose, of thorns scraping across leather chaps, and of machetes cutting brush. The cowboys added to the wonderful din with their singing and whistling and piercing screeches, created by pulling a leaf between their fingers. They continually made supervisory noises to the burros, including clucks, sucks, growls, shouts, cries, threats, curses, the crack of whips and the whack of open hands on saddles. The burros added to it all, providing the noise of hooves striking ground, metal shoes scraping rock, whinnies, groans, he-haws, teeth clamping on bits, stomach noises, and—there's no really polite word—farts.

We came to a tiny ranch house with a thatched roof, surrounded by citrus trees and covered with cascades of magenta bougainvillea so bright they seemed to glow from within. The following day we arrived at the village of San Francisco, visited by Erle Stanley Gardner during his expeditions in 1962 (the village can now be reached by road). As we began the steep descent into Cañon San Pablo we entered a different world of palms and pools. Thousand-foot-high walls shaded the bottom of the canyon a good part of the day, a welcome relief from the glare of the high country. How different from the cactus, dry rock, and open vistas we had passed through earlier!

It grew late and we made camp and swam in emerald pools. Our burros loved the place and broke out in a comical chorus of he-haws that went on most of the night and remained funny until ten. Guadalupe had a good knowl-

Burros carry a party of explorers up a steep trail toward the great Cochimí murals in Cañon San Pablo

edge of local herbs and potions, and he treated everyone to a tea reputed to have aphrodisiac properties, a fact he casually mentioned as the last swallow went down. Fortunately for the collective dignity of our group, it didn't work. The fire was almost dead, when both cowboys suddenly became alert, although no sight or sound was detectable to us city folks. Running in a crouch, Guadalupe grabbed a .22 rifle from a scabbard and fired at an unseen target across the camp. Rushing over, he reached into a brush pile and triumphantly hoisted a mortally wounded ring-tail cat, a beautiful creature that looks like a skinny raccoon with a long striped tail. Oblivious to his horror-stricken audience, Guadalupe announced with a golden-toothed grin that ring-tails carry cattle diseases, a fact possibly new to veterinary medicine.

The next day we finally had a chance to see what we had come for, Gardner Cave. After a short hike, we scrambled up a rugged slope to a long, overhung rock shelter. We had seen photographs of the Grand Mural, but they did not evoke a sense of the immediacy and power of the real thing. As we huffed and puffed up the slope, we looked up and there it was—incredible, dramatic, stunning. How could untutored Indians, using simple materials, have created such a scene? Spread along the back of a shallow overhang was a mural hundreds of feet long of larger-than-life deer, bighorn sheep, men, fish, and birds, rendered in black and red. Although painted over 500 years ago, most were bright and well preserved, thanks to the resistant qualities of the rock and the protection of the overhang.

Most Cochimí stylistic conventions could be seen: overpainting, bicolor figures, the outline-and-wash technique. By the standards of a Vermeer the figures were crude, with no fine brush strokes and no subtle shadings of color, but there was no mistaking what the artists hoped to depict: it was power—power over animals, power over men, and power over nature. We spent hours in front of them, and as time passed we found the artist's spell growing on us. Familiarity with this art did not breed contempt; unlike the insipid droolings of a Jackson Pollock painting, the more we saw, the more we appreciated what we were seeing.

Gardner is only one of many art sites in the area, but it drew us back again and again, and we photographed every detail, from every conceivable angle. Days passed and too soon we were aboard our trusty steeds heading back to Santa Martha. As the miles dragged on, they grew tired and cranky, but as we topped the last pass they could see the ranch in the valley, and they suddenly came to life. Instead of a steady, listless plodding, a definite liveliness appeared. As we approached level ground, they abandoned all thoughts of propriety and considerations of social order, and began a pell-mell rush for home. Not that they were galloping, mind you, but compared to the standards of the previous week it seemed as if rustlers at work during the night had substituted unbreakable stallions for our docile donkeys. What had taken hours a week ago now flew by in minutes. O'Neill in his haste brushed me against a thorn tree, inflicting a hundred punctures on my thin gringo skin. With a total lack of dignity, I came thundering up to the ranch and suffered a final humiliation. As I reined O'Neill to a halt and started to swing out of the saddle, the cinch let go and I crashed to the ground at the feet of a laughing eight-year-old. **"**

● ●

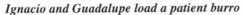

Ignacio and Guadalupe load a patient burro

■ ■

Back on the Transpeninsular at KM 53

KM	Location
41	Tres Vírgenes volcanoes. The Tres Vírgenes are the most recently active volcanoes on the peninsula, Father Consag's diaries describing an eruption that occurred in 1746. Another was reported in 1811, this one accompanied by an earthquake, which apparently killed some of the inhabitants of San Ignacio. In 1857 large volumes of steam were reported, and gas and vapor from fissures have been reported recently near the summit. In 1792 naturalist José Longinos reported that the area was a source of red, yellow, and black ocher pigments used by Cochimí Indians in their grand rock paintings throughout central Baja. He also found a wide variety of minerals, including jasper, sardonyx, a number of types of chalcedony and of spars, sulfur deposits, and even marble. Modern mineral collectors have found zeolites

such as scolecite and heulandite. Sulfur deposits also have been located in surrounding areas, mainly in the valley between the two northern-

A cacophony of figures at Gardner Cave

Ron Smith photographs a herd of deer painted over five hundred years ago

most peaks and in a valley 4 miles northwest of the north peak.

40+ Some of the largest and best-developed specimens of the two species of elephant tree, *copalquín* and *torote*, grow side by side in the lava flows in this area.

35 Eight percent downgrade to KM 31.

17+ First views of the Cortez from the Transpeninsular; begin a 16% downgrade to KM 13+, then moderate up- and downgrades until reaching the shores of the Cortez at KM 7+.

13+ Mina Lucifer. Turn right (southwest), drive 1 mile. The mine was noted for pyrolusite, and specimens of chrysocolla and red jasper with manganese swirls have also been found. Old maps show other mines north of the highway.

12 A massive hill containing gypsum was bisected during highway construction, providing the most accessible mineral-collecting site in Baja, with selenite crystals and sheets, as well as the satin spar variety, some having encrustations of malachite.

11+ LPG yard. Those heading south should fill here, as LPG may be in short supply in the Loreto area.

7+ A sedan road runs north towards an aircraft hangar and then towards a rocky beach, where modest boondocking sites will be found. Avoid parking on the dirt airstrip. Small boats can be launched down a very rough dirt ramp about 200 yards northeast of the dilapidated hangar. The site is becoming littered. Specimens of palm root petrified by red jasper have been found in arroyos to the north. Road north to site of a new gypsum mine near Caleta Santa María, 7 miles, location of several boondocking sites.

6 Isla Tortugas, 23 miles east, is the tip of a 6,000-foot Holocene volcano, rising from 5,000 feet of water. It is not often visited by anglers, but it sometimes has the best grouper fishing in the Cortez. Since it is well offshore and surrounded by deep water, it has the best visibility in the area, a boon to underwater photographers. Described as "barren and useless" by passing yachtsmen, the island is in fact unexpectedly rich in flora and fauna, with 79 species of vascular plants, relatively large populations of lizards and rattlesnakes, one species being endemic, and even an endemic mouse. Small fumaroles show the volcano is still active. Spearfishermen will encounter large and naive fish.

5   Sedan road into mouth of Arroyo de Soledad and Arroyo del Boleo. Those continuing on the Transpeninsular should skip the following section.

Side trip to Arroyo de Soledad and Arroyo del Boleo. Set odometer. Drive west to the fork at Mile 0.1; go left (250°) for Arroyo de Soledad, right (280°) for Arroyo del Boleo. The roads extend 4 or 5 miles into each canyon, passing dozens of old mines, where rare minerals have been found, including crednerite, phosgenite, and remingtonite. Mina Amelia, at Mile 3.7 up Soledad, has yielded cumengite, pseudoboleite, and boleite. The first two are found only here, and boleite at only three other locations in the world. It might be possible to extract samples from the tailings, but I found an easier way: I simply bummed some from an employee at the old mining company office in Santa Rosalía, who had a drawer-full.

Back on the Transpeninsular at KM 5

KM	Location
2	Mouth of Arroyo del Purgatorio, site of a major copper strike in 1868 and now a mineral collecting area.
0	**Santa Rosalía.**

Baja's copper town

Erle Stanley Gardner, in one of his books on Baja, wrote, "Once more I resolved never again to try for detailed information in advance of a trip of exploration. Once let a place get the reputation of being unbeautiful and it's hard indeed to approach it impartially." This seems to apply specifically to Santa Rosalía, for it is unbeautiful, and travel writers have hence given it short shrift. Superficially, the place is gritty and unattractive, an almost comically ugly smelter dominating everything. The town has a distinctly non-Mexican character, with straight streets and buildings constructed of milled lumber instead of crooked lanes and adobe, and in lieu of an historic stone mission, its church is made of cast iron. In spite of this, it is an interesting place, and contrary to Gardner's idea, the key to appreciating Santa Rosalía is understanding its unusual history.

In 1868 José Rosa Villavicencio discovered some odd blue-and-green deposits northeast of his ranch, which proved to be a type of high-grade mixed copper carbonate and ox-

ides known as "boleos" due to their ball-like shape. He decided to take immediate advantage of his good luck and sold his mineral rights for 16 pesos, a decision he would come to regret. A copper mine under German management operated until 1885, when a French company, Compagnie du Boleo, was formed. A mining railroad and piers were built, and equipment for a smelter was transported from Europe in square-rigged sailing ships around Cape Horn. The town was laid out on classic company-town lines: straight streets and virtually identical wooden buildings with corrugated iron roofs, their walls painted in horizontal green and white stripes. Society was highly segregated; French mining company officials lived on Mesa Norte in distinctive French colonial-style homes, Mexican government officials and soldiers dwelt on less-desirable Mesa Sur, and the masses sweltered in the arroyo below.

Soot, gas, and ash from the smelter made the town almost uninhabitable, and there seemed to be only two choices: move the smelter or move the town. Instead, engineers worked out a unique solution; a tall stack was constructed a half mile away and connected to the smelter by a huge horizontal duct. The duct and the stack can be seen best near the Hotel Frances (2) on Mesa Norte.

The mining enterprise was successful from the beginning, and by 1894 production had increased to over 10,000 tons a year. To produce this much copper, the smelter required vast amounts of coke, a fuel produced by heating coal, using twice as much coke by weight as copper produced, and the railroad and the power plant also required coal. Since the coal and transportation industries on the west coast of the US were not well developed, coke was imported from Europe in a large fleet of square-rigged ships. After discharging their cargoes at Santa Rosalía, they often carried lumber and wheat from the US back to Europe. Due to its high value, the copper was shipped out by swift steamer.

By the turn of the century, Santa Rosalía was a major world copper producer, and a parade of square-rigged ships sailed up and down the Cortez. Sailors speaking a dozen tongues walked the streets, seeking the same types of entertainment and social services demanded by sailors everywhere. There was no harbor at the time and no stevedoring services, so the crews had to undertake the hot, stressful, and dirty task of lightering coke ashore, a chore that could take months. The heat was fierce, and other than one brothel and several *cantinas* and restaurants, there was little to occupy their off hours. Rather than face Santa Rosalía, many sailors tried to desert, and one who succeeded was Frank Fisher, a German sailor on the bark *Reinbek*. After a fist fight with the first mate and a short stay in jail, Fisher hiked to the northwest until he came to the village of San Ignacio. He soon established himself as its blacksmith, becoming well known to generations of early Baja travelers suffering from broken springs and axles and inoperative engines. His descendants still operate the La Posada Hotel in San Ignacio.

The German flag became an increasingly common sight in Santa Rosalía after the opening of the Panama Ca-

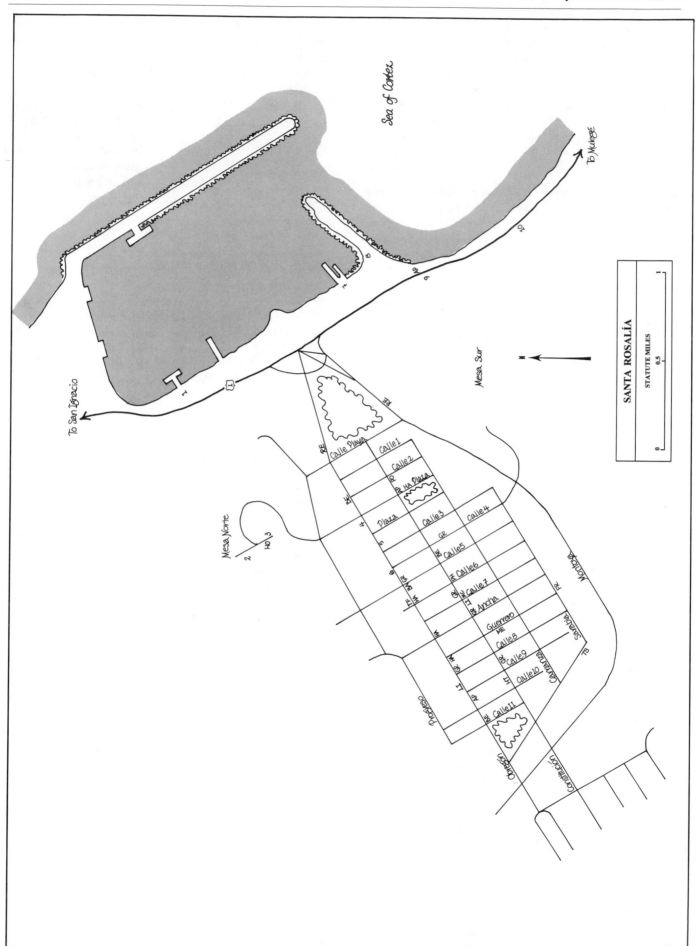

Sea of Cortez

To Mulegé

To San Ignacio

Mesa Norte

Mesa Sur

SANTA ROSALÍA

STATUTE MILES

0   0.5   1

Calle Playa

Calle 1
Calle 2
Plaza
Calle 3
Calle 4
Calle 5
Calle 6
Calle 7
Ancha
Guerrero
Calle 8
Calle 9
Calle 10
Calle 11

nal. However, on August 1, 1914, Germany invaded Belgium. Three days later, England declared war on Germany, and a dozen of the big German square-riggers were interned by Mexico and spent the duration of the war swinging at anchor off the town.

The situation in Santa Rosalía seemed ripe for violence; the staff of El Boleo was French, the town was Mexican, and the crews of the interned ships were German. Coke ships from other countries began to fill the void, and sailors from other nations, especially the US, became more frequent on the streets. In spite of the tensions of the war and their vulnerable position, the German sailors encountered few problems and were generally accepted in the *cantinas* and the brothel. Life on the German ships soon settled down to a deadly routine of blazing heat and dull maintenance work. Weevils procreated happily in the food, the water was poor and rationed, and the sailors were soon reduced to making clothing from flour sacks. Unable to stand the heat and the boredom, some deserted and spread out over Mexico, a few *en route* to the US, some trying to get back to Germany, others settling temporarily or permanently in Mexico, becoming cotton pickers, farmers, prospectors, sailmakers, teachers, circus workers, watchmen, and longshoremen. One even joined the US Army.

The Mexican Revolution also livened up the existence of the sailors. In the Fall of 1914 Pancho Villa's men occupied Santa Rosalía. One day, however, a vessel began firing at the town, and within a day it was in the hands of Carranza's forces. Their flag was hoisted, new money was issued, Villa's commander was shot, and his men given the chance to change allegiance. At intervals, this scenario reversed itself, the town alternately falling to opposing forces. Some of the German sailors found entertainment value in the change-of-allegiance ceremonies and executions, going ashore to view the festivities.

In 1917, hoping to capitalize on the ill-feelings generated by General John Pershing's recent expeditions into Mexico pursuing Villa, Germany tried to enlist Mexico as an ally by offering back the territories in Texas, New Mexico, and Arizona that had been lost to her neighbor. Despite this tempting offer, Mexico wisely remained neutral. On April 6, 1917, the US declared war, blocking the escape of the German sailors to the north. An American consul established offices in Santa Rosalía and developed a blacklist of those supplying the needs of the interned German fleet. The Germans still managed to meet their basic needs through agents and by purchasing food and supplies in Mulegé and Sonora.

Copper production continued after the war. Working for the equivalent of 90 American cents a day, the miners dug 375 miles of tunnels, forming a vast underground network, and more than 18 miles of narrow gauge railroad track were laid. The mines were hot, dirty, and dangerous, where

Santa Rosalía in the days of the great sailing ships

Courtesy Enrique Patron Lara

"men's hearts and bodies wilt almost as rapidly as a bride's corsage," as Phillip Townsend Hanna put it. By the 1920s, ore became scarce, but small-scale operators continued work by removing the pillars of ore left to support ceilings in the old shafts, the mining equivalent of a logger cutting off the branch on which he is sitting. Finally, in the 1950s, production ended.

Other than the physical aspects of the town, little remains of French culture. *Coq au vin* sometimes appears on menus, but it always turns out to be something totally foreign to the mother country, and the question *Parlez-vous français aquí?* will be greeted with blank looks. In excellent condition due to the dry climate, the old smelter, with its furnaces, extractors, a giant air compressor, huge lathes, metal shears, and other machinery, should be made part of a national park. It appears, sadly, that the smelter is being demolished to make way for progress, but all is not lost. A number of locomotives and pieces of mining machinery can be seen in the street on Mesa Norte, near the Hotel Frances. In addition, the old Boleo office on Mesa Norte has been converted into a museum (3), with displays of mining tools, technical apparatus, photographs, and large numbers of ledgers, written in beautiful handwriting with steel pens, describing the ebb and flow of the company. Hopefully, if the smelter is completely demolished, some of the old machinery will be moved to grace the museum.

In 1897 a church (4) constructed from prefabricated cast-iron sections was erected. Designed by Alexandre Gustave Eiffel, of tower fame, it is certainly the most unusual church in Baja. It was designed to be used in France's equatorial possessions, but remained in a warehouse until Compagnie du Boleo purchased it. During the First World War, there was a legendary brawl at the Hotel Central (5), when the crews of several steamers refused to stand when the band played the "Star Spangled Banner." Sailors from two American vessels took exception, and the fight soon spread to the Mexican and German onlookers. The town authorities called in the police and the militia, and the jail was soon filled to overflowing. Smells from the famed El Boleo Bakery (6), established in the days of the French, still make it hard to walk by without stopping for a sample.

A new chapter in the history of Santa Rosalía is unfolding. Several Canadian companies have begun a new mining operation. Copper and cobalt will be produced, some of it from ore from the old mines, some obtained from the slag from the old operation: modern methods of extraction are far more efficient than the old, making such a venture economically feasible. In addition, a new gypsum mining operation has begun to the north of town.

There are many supplies and services in town, including butcher shops, groceries, a *tortilla* factory, liquor and beer, ice, mechanics, auto parts, hardware, tire sales and repairs, pharmacies, doctors, dentists, a health clinic, and banks, as well as numerous pay and credit-card telephones. Due to its narrow and crowded streets, it is inadvisable to drive large motor homes or trailer rigs into the town. If you must drive

into the center of town, be aware that almost all streets are one way, some marked with an arrow proclaiming CIRCULACIÓN, generally posted in the most obscure location available. Lavandería las Burbujas will launder your clothes or you can do it yourself in their machines. It can be found north of town. At KM 2, look for two large silver-colored tanks on the hills just to the west of the highway. Immediately south of the tanks, turn northwest, drive 100 yards, and look for the drinking-water plant. The laundry is in the same building. Motel Sol y Mar (10) is brand new and clean.

There are no RV facilities in town, but trailer parks are located at KM 193 and 182 to the south. There is no paved boat ramp, but portable boats can be launched across the beach at San Lucas Trailer Park at KM 182, and large trailerboats can be launched at Mulegé. Ferries bound for Guaymas leave from the terminal (7). **Remember, temporary import permits are not currently available in Santa Rosalía (see page 84).** There is a COTP (8), and the *Migración* and *Aduana* offices are located in a white building two buildings north of the ferry complex. Santa Rosalía Marina (1) has a dozen modern slips, and offers diesel and gas, telephone and fax, mechanical and electrical services, showers, LPG, and boat washing and polishing. They permit liveaboards. The next satisfactory anchorage to the south is Caleta San Lucas, 9 miles. Divers will find little of interest locally.

There is only one PEMEX (9, MPD) in town, and in recent years travelers have found it advisable to (1) keep all vehicle and trailer windows and doors locked or attended at all times, (2) insure that the gas pump reading is zeroed before filling begins, (3) know approximately how much fuel will be needed to fill the tanks, and the price per liter, and (4) to have a calculator ready to insure that all mathematical maneuvers involving volume and price are on the up-and-up. Also, make sure that your gas comes out of the same pump used by the locals.

■ ■ ■ ■ ■ ■ ■ ■ ■ ■ ■ ■ ■ ■ ■

On the Transpeninsular at KM 0

KM	Location
0/197	Start new KM numbering sequence.
195+	Motel el Morro. Restaurant, bar.
193	Las Palmas RV Park. Full hookups, *palapas*, rest rooms, showers, laundry machines, small restaurant, bar.
189+	Place where litterbugs, despoilers of archaeological sites, and those exceeding bag limits may end up.
182+	Restaurant.
182	**San Lucas.** Sedan road west to Caleta San Lucas, 0.4 mile. This cove has excellent fishing for snap-

per, grouper, and halibut. A deep hole at the entrance has immense numbers of bass, and outside lurk leopard grouper, corvina, sierra, barracuda, yellowtail, gulf grouper, skipjack, pargo, roosterfish, amberjack, snapper, dorado, and a dozen or so other species. The best fishing is within a radius of 5 miles from the entrance, and that's a lot of territory! This area is near the juncture of the northern Cortez, with its cool waters, and the more tropical southern Cortez, and migrant species and year-round residents from both are often present. Good fishing is thus possible all year, usually becoming excellent between May and October. A prime fishing area is a half mile east of a solitary hill at the northern end of the rocky arm forming the eastern side of the cove; you can't miss the hill. A wreck near the entrance offers good snorkeling. Outside the cove, divers will find the bottom loaded with numerous mollusks and lobsters. Mangroves at the north end are home to many birds. The cove is a good all-weather anchorage for shallow-draft boats. The next anchorages are at the south end of Isla San Marcos, 8 miles, and at Punta Santa Inés, 20 miles. San Lucas Trailer Park, near the north end, is becoming increasingly popular. It has *panga* rentals, rest rooms, showers, *palapas*, and a dump station, but no hookups. The water from their well is brackish. The best launching location is over the beach (no paved ramp) at the park, since most other beaches in the cove turn into mud flats at low tide. A narrow channel running south from the park winds through the shallows to the entrance.

178　Sedan road northeast to cobble beaches and modest boondocking sites, 0.7 mile. Once at the beach, a marginal sedan road leads right (southeast) to additional secluded sites, some shaded by palms.

176　Isla San Marcos, 5 miles to the northeast, was once the bed of an ancient lake. In it, huge amounts of gypsum precipitated out, and the island is now the site of a large mine. Huge amounts of gypsum are shipped to the US and other countries to make drywall. There are three coves along the northwest shore, providing shelter from south and east weather. Bottoms are sand with rocky patches. One of them, about a mile southwest of the north point of the island, is a favorite with many visitors, and *panga* trips to see it can be obtained by contacting local fishermen or Orchard Vacation Village in Mulegé. There are a series of caves, some on land, some being sea caves, as well as several rocky arches. The waters from here to the north point have excellent fishing and spearfishing for yellowtail,

barracuda, and grouper, and the best underwater photography in the area. The eastern point of the island has a shallow sloping reef loaded with mollusks and several species on nudibranchs. The south end of the island has some of the best tide pools in the Cortez. The anchorage at the south end has good protection from north weather. Sand and cobble bottoms and shallow rocky reefs are found from San Marcos south 0.75 mile to Roca Lobos. This diversity of habitat produces fish to match, and it is not uncommon to catch two dozen species in a day. Launch at Mulegé or Caleta San Lucas, but if you want to save running time camp on Lobos. The waters surrounding the tiny island are loaded with yellowtail, barracuda, and snapper, and divers will find foraging excellent. A 3-fathom reef, located 1 mile, 060° from Lobos, has produced groupers to 100 pounds.

156　Sedan road 300 yards north of the KM marker southwest to Rancho de San Baltizar, 17 miles, signed RUPESTRIAN CAVES SAN BORJITAS. Gruta San Borjitas, located on the ranch, is among the better known and most studied Cochimí rock-art sites in Baja. Due to the number and quality of its figures and to being both well preserved and closely approachable by vehicle, it is the subject of continuing interest. The grotto is on private property, and since it is a registered archaeological site, you will need a guide. Trips can be arranged in Mulegé; inquire at any of the hotels or RV parks.

156　Sedan road northeast (signed PUNTA CHIVATO) to the Punta Chivato/Santa Inés area. Those continuing on the Transpeninsular should skip the following section.

↱　***Side trip to the Punta Chivato/Santa Inés area.*** For many miles to the north, most RV facilities have been places to stay overnight en route to other places, but the Punta Chivato/Santa Inés area, 14 miles to the east of the Transpeninsular, is a place to stay and play. With its sparkling beaches and good fishing, diving, and boardsailing, it is the Baja destination for many. The Hotel Punta Chivato, located west of the point, has a restaurant with a grand view to the south and west, bar, pool, gift shop, and beach, plus fishing boats with guides. A small grocery store can be found nearby, and golfers have not been forgotten: there is a desert course (no turf) northwest of the hotel. The shallow (9%) concrete launch ramp, found just west of the hotel, ends abruptly and is best used at high tide. The best anchorages are in the lee of the point and west of the hotel. The next anchorage is the estero at Mulegé, 10 miles south. Since the estero is limited to small boats, larger craft should head for Santispac, inside Bahía Concepción.

A beach with camping and RV parking can be found by turning east through an area of homes near the hotel—follow the signs saying PLAYA. The beach has *palapas*, water, showers, and pit toilets, but there are no hookups. Portable boats can be launched over the sandy beach, and some protection from waves is provided by small, rocky fingers at some east-facing sites. The beach is prime real estate, and there are plans to use the area for the construction of new homes, relegating the campground to a lesser location. A dump station can be found just south of the trailer and boat storage area, west of the hotel.

Fishing can be good, especially for yellowtail near the aid-to-navigation light tower on Punta Santa Inés. Ladyfish action can be found in the hot months by casting small chrome spoons, feather jigs, or soft plastic lures from the shore with light spinning gear at dawn or dusk. Roosterfish are sometimes taken along the beach in front of the hotel and along the beach to the southwest. Tuna, billfish, and dorado are offshore in the warm months, and close-in there are reefs everywhere with lesser species. Seven miles, 040° from Punta Santa Inés, the water begins to get very deep, in excess of 400 fathoms, and yellowfin tuna are often present in the summer months. The Islas Santa Inés, especially the southernmost island, are good for yellowtail, snapper, pargo, and amberjack.

A good diving reef extends east from Punta Santa Inés. Mexican divers have found gold coins the diameter of a US silver dollar but twice as thick, in a small bay northwest of Punta Chivato with the intriguing name of Caleta Muertos (Dead Man's Cove). The locals report that a large sailboat sank north of Punta Chivato in 1981. A shipwreck can be found in the cove south of Punta Chivato, name and date unknown. The Mexican fishing vessel *Britania*, lost in 1980, lies 150 feet east and 300-400 feet south of the northern tip of the south island in 5 to 15 feet of water. The historic schooner *Abel Miranda* lies somewhere in the vicinity. Built in 1859, she was the oldest vessel in the Mexican merchant-marine register and the last merchant sail in the Cortez when she was lost in 1957. According to Socorro Real Rocha, the captain's sister, she sank near the south island. The wreck of a private plane can be found in 3 fathoms a half mile southwest of the hotel.

Shelling is outstanding, especially at "Shell Beach," which is the western curve of the shore as it begins to swing south; the shallow bay must be wall-to-wall mollusks. Also, the cliffs in this area are loaded with fossils.

Boardsailors will find excellent winds in the December through February season. The bay west of the hotel offers speed sailing in flat conditions, with winds accelerated by the venturi effect of the hills to the north, and reaches are measured in miles. Beginners will not be left out; on non-wind days there is often a light breeze around noon, picking up toward evening, and the south beach is sandy and the bottom shallow. The camping area provides advanced sailors with a sandy launch, often with breaking waves and strong sideshore winds outside.

■ ■ ■ ■ ■ ■ ■ ■ ■ ■ ■ ■ ■ ■ ■ ■ ■ ■ ■ ■
Back on the Transpeninsular at KM 156

KM	Location
143	Moderate up- and downgrades into Mulegé.
136+	Auto parts store. One hundred yards to the north, on the west side of the highway, will be found El Alémán, which has very limited marine parts such as propellers, water pump impellers, fuel line hose and fittings, gear oil, two-cycle oil, and a few RV parts, such as waste line fittings, holding tank chemicals, and mirrors. Pickup road west to ice plant at Mile 0.5, and on to Rancho la Trinidad, 15.5 miles. Those continuing on the Transpeninsular should skip the following section.

Side trip to Rancho la Trinidad art sites. Several arroyo crossings near the ranch involve 21% grades and loose rock. Set odometer. Turn west from the Transpeninsular opposite the auto parts store. At Mile 1.2 swing left (southwest). There is a **Y** at Mile 2.9; go right (260°). Go straight ahead (240°) at the intersection at Mile 3.0, cross a cattle guard at Mile 5.3, and immediately swing right (180°). At Mile 7.8 there is a sign, SAN ESTANISLAO, and a **Y**; take the right (290°). At Mile 8.6, you have a choice: straight ahead, left, or right; take the right (230°). As you approach the ranch, the scenery ahead becomes beautiful, with massive, deeply eroded bluffs, the skyline accented by palo blanco trees clinging to their summits. Pass a sign, LAS TINAJITAS, at Mile 12.4, and at Mile 13.2 look for a sign, LA TRINIDAD, and at the first **Y**, take the left (160°). At Mile 14.1, pass through a barbed wire fence, make an immediate right (190°), and arrive at the ranch at Mile 15.5. Since this is private property and an archaeological site, you will need a guide, who can be obtained at the ranch for a small fee. The canyon is the upper reaches of Arroyo Mulegé, which supplies water to the "Río Mulegé," although it disappears underground for a good deal of the way.

A hike of about 20 minutes is required to the first site, over relatively flat country, except when clambering over a stone dam, a feat which requires a certain degree of agility. The art figures include a white, upside-down deer, an "x-ray" fish shot with an arrow, a standing man done in white, and other figures. If the dozen or so white hand prints were those of adults, the Cochimí were a rather small people.

The second site requires a swim through a high-walled canyon. Yes, that's correct—a swim. You must be in reasonably good condition and dressed for the occasion. If you want to bring a camera, it should be a submersible model or you should have some means of floating a non-submersible safely, such as an inflatable beach mat or an innertube with cloth or plywood covering the center. You must have at least six hours available for the round trip from the ranch to the second site.

The Trinidad sites have been known for many years, and were number 13 on the list in Leon Diguet's paper. The two art sites are not spectacular (a third site lies further upstream), but the drive and the hike are well worthwhile, and the swim will certainly be a Baja experience to remember.

■■■■■■■■■■■■■■■■■■■■
Back on the Transpeninsular at KM 136+

KM	Location
135+	Mulegé.

Baja's tropical village

Although well north of the Tropic of Cancer, Mulegé is Baja's stereotypical tropical village, with thousands of graceful palms, thatched roofs, and masses of bougainvillea, an unexpected green oasis in a drab brown desert. The Jesuits founded a mission here in 1705 at the site of an old Indian settlement, and in 1719 the sailing vessel *El Triunfo de la Cruz* was launched, built of wood cut in the mountains. The original mission building was destroyed by a *chubasco* in 1770. Misión Santa Rosalía de Mulegé (19) was completed in 1766, and although it was abandoned in 1828, it has been remodeled a number of times and is now in active use. US troops occupied the town for one day in 1847 during the Battle of Mulegé. During the *chubasco* of September 9, 1959, nearby arroyos carried as much as 60 feet of water, and boulders 12 feet in diameter were swept away.

Despite its ups and downs, the town is now fairly prosperous and manages to maintain a languid, slow-bell approach to life that attracts many repeat visitors; few Americans and Canadians encountered in the streets have been to Mulegé only once. It is the first town south of Ensenada where tourism is a major industry, and there are gift and curio shops, grocery stores, mechanics, tire repair shops, several doctors, a veterinarian, a dive shop, and a number of restaurants, RV parks, and hotels. Despite the fact that it is largely a resort town, most RV parks and local restaurants are rather inexpensive, and even the hotels and their restaurants are moderately priced.

As noted in Chapter 1, the local Chamber of Commerce would have you believe that a river courses through the town, but the "Río Mulegé" is actually an *estero*, a brackish arm of the Cortez, although it does receive small amounts of fresh water from springs above a dam. (Its official name is Estero Mulegé, and some people also call it the Río Santa Rosalía, referring to the nearby mission.) Level areas nearby are used to sort and process the date crop. Due to the narrow streets, large motor homes and vehicles towing trailers should avoid using the PEMEX in town, heading instead to the one at KM 130+, just to the south. There is no tourism office,

and the American Consular Office that was once here has closed.

Restaurant la Cabaña (12), a tiny *palapa* at the entrance to town, serves inexpensive Mexican food. The money-changing office (10) will change dollars to pesos, and cash personal and traveler's checks. The PEMEX (8, M) is being renovated. Casa Yee (7) is the best stocked grocery store in town, can provide information on local attractions, and may or may not have LPG. Hotel las Casitas (9) has a restaurant and arranges rock-art tours to Ranchos Baltizar and La Trinidad. There is often a guitarist to liven things up at Restaurant el Candil (11). Many locals consider Restaurant las Equipales (5) the best in town.

The town is blessed with a modern laundromat (3). Saul's Tienda (1) is a well-stocked grocery store, and English is spoken. The top of the navigation light at El Sombrerito provides a great view of the area. Despite the exterior appearance of the place, the tacos and seafood at Café la Almeja (13) are highly thought of by visitors and locals alike.

The celebrated Mulegé Territorial Prison (2) was in operation from 1907 to 1975 and provided a unique chapter in the annals of penology. At dawn each day, two soldiers would hike up from their barracks, one carrying a conch shell, the other a massive brass key. Upon reaching the prison one would blow a signal while the other opened the massive gate and let the prisoners out! At six in the evening, the gate clanked shut to the sound of the conch, and the prisoners lost their freedom until dawn. Apparently prison officials believed that no one would want to escape from the charm of a town like Mulegé, something certainly believable. A small museum has been established at the prison, which contains historical artifacts from the prison and the town. The museum is sometimes open 9 to 5 every day except Sunday, sometimes not.

There are a number of RV parks along the river south of town (some are completely filled by permanents and are hence not described). Orchard Vacation Village (15) has clean, litter-free, palm-shaded sites with full hookups, showers, rest rooms, *palapas*, and a dump station. The rough, steep (19%) concrete launch ramp needs high tides. A long-distance phone can be found at the office, and canoe rentals and boat and trailer storage are available. Poncho's RV Park (16) is dirty and ill-kept, and the full hookups are not likely to function. Villa María Isabel RV & Trailer Park (17) has full hookups, *palapas*, showers, rest rooms, a laundry, a swimming pool, and an American-style bakery (sweeter, more fillings than Mexican). The steep (17%) ramp has limited parking and maneuvering room, and is best suited for small boats. The Hotel Serenidad (18) is the scene of famed Mexican fiesta banquets on Wednesdays, complete with *mariachis*, as well as a Saturday night pig feed (referring to the entrée, not the diners). The RV park has full hookups, rest rooms, and showers. The ramp (12%) is often covered with so much sand and mud that it is hard to tell where it is.

Shallow-draft boats can anchor in the mouth of the

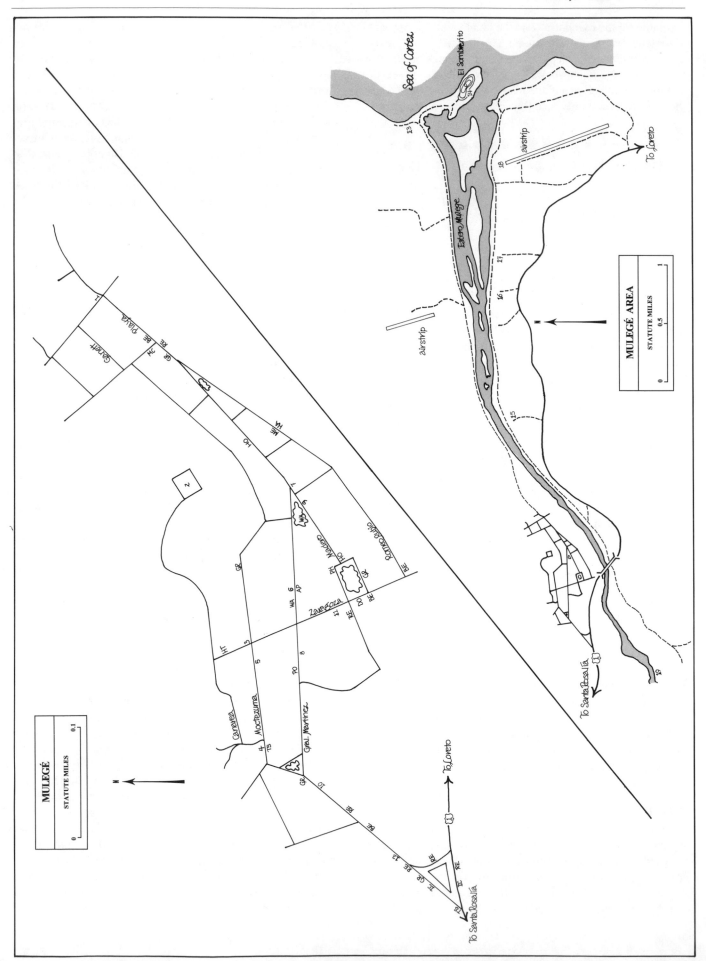

Sorting and drying the Mulegé date harvest

estero, but it has many shoals and is best entered at high tide. The "outside" anchorage north of El Sombrerito is unprotected. The next good anchorage south is Santispac in Bahía Concepción, or Bahía de los Puercos (Pig Bay) on the "outside coast" of Peninsula Concepción. There is a COTP office (14), but no *Aduana* or *Migración*. All the ramps in Mulegé require high tides. In addition to the ramps already mentioned, boats can be launched near the lighthouse at El Sombrerito on a hard-packed sand and dirt beach. If your boat is sizable and you wish to leave it in the water overnight at the docks there, check with the COTP.

Ray Cannon's story of a titanic struggle with a snook established Mulegé as the place in Baja to try for snook, but Ray never succeeded in actually catching a Mulegé snook and neither have many others. Yellowtail, roosters, and a dozen other varieties can be taken by shorecasters off the beaches on either side of the mouth of the *estero*, especially from early fall to midwinter. Anglers with boats usually concentrate their efforts on yellowtail, amberjack, pargo, and grouper at Punta Hornitos, Punta Concepción, Punta el Gato, and the "outer coast" of Peninsula Concepción. Farther out in the Cortez yellowfin tuna, dorado, marlin, and sailfish are found in the hot months. Boats and guides can be arranged at Villa María Isabel, at most of the hotels, and at the landing near El Sombrerito. Live bait may be available between April and June.

Mulegé Divers was recently separated into two enterprises, The Shop and Cortez Explorers. The Shop (6), retaining the previous location, offers diving and snorkeling equipment sales and rentals, as well as books, T-shirts, fishing tackle, and other items. Cortez Explorers (4) offers scuba and snorkeling excursions on a custom dive boat, guides, compressed air, and a scuba resort course. Most divers head for Bahía Concepción, Punta Concepción, the east coast of Peninsula Concepción, or the Islas Santa Inés. In keeping

with its "almost tropical" status, divers in the waters off Mulegé often see species such as king angelfish, Cortez rainbow wrasse, giant damselfish, and green moray. Locals report a large wrecked sailboat in 4 fathoms 150 yards southeast of Punta el Gallo, located 3 miles southeast of the mouth of the *estero*.

There have been reports of a dozen different minerals from mines in the area, mostly copper-bearing, but the reports are too vague to be useful in relocating the sites. The beautiful spiny oyster is found along the coast south of town.

Those continuing on the Transpeninsular should turn to page 185.

By water: coasting to Loreto

The 84-mile kayak and small-boat trip from Mulegé to Loreto is one of the most beautiful and enjoyable in Baja. The shoreline is generally steep and rocky, cliffs and bluffs alternating with pebble and cobble beaches. Except between Rancho San Nicolás and Punta San Antonio, there are few sand beaches. Some landings are steep and exposed, making them difficult in anything short of a flat calm. As fate would have it, the best camping spots are often less than or more than a kayaker's normal 10-to-20 mile daily run apart, and trips require flexibility and careful planning. Water can sometimes be obtained at the ranches at San Sebastián, and San Nicolás, and yachts are frequently found at anchor at Caleta San Juanico. Vehicles and trailers can be left at one of the RV parks along the "river." Those with only short vacations can shorten the trip by launching at San Sebastián. The appropriate 1:50,000 topos are: Mulegé G12A57; San Nicolás G12A68; Santa Rosa G12A78; and Loreto G12A88. One of Cruising Charts' Paddle Charts covers the coast from Bahía Concepción to Isla Carmen. Southwest Sea Kayaks offers trips along this stretch of coast.

The crossing of the mouth of the bay is best made by way of Punta el Gallo to Punta Hornitos, a distance of 6 miles. The beach south of the aid-to-navigation tower at Hornitos is shelf rock giving away to sand, and is often used by kayakers and small-boat sailors as their first overnight stop. Shelling along the beach is excellent, and the point has good diving and fishing. The anchorage is well-protected from all but southerly and westerly winds.

The coastline from Hornitos, Mile 6, to Gavilanes, Mile 11.3, is mostly low cliffs alternating with pebble-and-cobble beaches. Gavilanes, marked by a number of concrete building foundations and mining excavations, has an exposed pebble-and-cobble beach. The mine was once a prominent source of manganese, but it has not operated since the Second World War. Look for numerous thin veins of pyrolusite an inch wide spaced at intervals of 10 to 15 feet, and small deposits of vanadinite, quartz, limonite, dolomite, calcite, aragonite, and manganiferous travertine. Manganese cobbles can be found on the beaches. Divers will find numerous small reefs and large boulders on a sandy bottom, and the waters to the east offer good fishing.

The coast south to San Sebastián is generally rocky cliffs, although there are a number of narrow pebble-and-cobble beaches in the mouths of arroyos. The first sizable flat area south of Gavilanes is at Mile 18.2, marked by the stone foundation of a building. The lee of Punta Santa Rosa, Mile 20.5, provides very marginal protection and a pebble beach. Punta Coloradito (Punta Colorado), Mile 24.4, can be recognized by its bands of rust and yellow. The first sand beaches south of Punta Concepción are found at Mile 27.6. However, the first really good sandy campsite is found at the head of a tiny bay immediately northwest of Punta Santa Teresa, Mile 29.5. The bay is too shallow for anything but kayaks and small boats, but it does provide a marginal lee which facilitates landings and there is a great campsite.

Punta Santa Teresa is rocky and has poor anchorage and landing conditions. The coast from Teresa to San Sebastián, Mile 34.5, is primarily cliffs alternating with steep pebble beaches. The cove at San Sebastián, known as Bahía de los Puercos, provides a good anchorage, protected from all but east winds. See page 189 for more on San Sebastián.

Isla Ildefonso, 8 miles to the east, has no good beaches, although it is possible to land in tiny coves in calm weather. Anchorage conditions are poor. Since it is free of land predators, several dozen species of birds live on, nest on, or pass by the island. The Cortez endemic fish-eating bat is also present. The tide pools are among the best in the Cortez. The reefs at the north and south points are the best dive locations, their great pinnacles and walls being covered with sessile marine life. Green and jewel morays are common, and jawfish can be seen peeking out of their burrows. There are large populations of lobsters, and three species can be found in close proximity: California, pinto, and slipper. Black coral can be seen in deep water off the island. Bonito, grouper, snapper, and cabrilla are taken year-round. In warm months trolling feathers work well for dorado in the deep water to the east. One June a friend was snorkeling off the island with a pole spear, when he came face-to-face with a large sailfish. Eyeing each other warily, each saw that the other was equally well-armed and they mutually decided to back off and swim away.

The coast immediately south of San Sebastián is cliffs, but the terrain gradually becomes lower, giving way to sloping plains. There are a ranch and a sand beach at San Nicolás, Mile 39.4. The coast east of San Nicolás is sand-and-pebble beaches backed by low dunes, all very exposed to prevailing winds. The lee of low Punta San Antonio, Mile 44.5, provides modest protection and a sand beach.

Punta Púlpito, Mile 46.6, is a rocky massif visible for many miles. However, it is an indifferent anchorage subject to surge. Camping is poor, since the beach is almost entirely steep cobbles, with only a small sandy area. The water off the point is deep and cold, and big gamefish sweeping in provide exciting fishing and diving. The climb to Púlpito's 500-foot summit offers spectacular views.

The shoreline between Púlpito and Caleta Ramada (Ensenada Puerto Almeja) is largely cliffs with narrow pebble beaches, although there is a good campsite in a rocky cove at Mile 47.6, and sand beaches are encountered in the vicinity of Rancho San Juanico. The ranch is up the arroyo, unseen from the beach. Ramada, Mile 56.1, is open to the north and has a sand beach at its south end. A small sand beach on its east side gets some shelter from prevailing seas and may be useful to kayakers and small-boaters, although Caleta San Juanico (Ensenada San Basilio) is much preferable.

The north anchorage in Juanico, Mile 58.0, is one of the best in the Cortez, providing protection from all but southeast weather, and it is not uncommon to see as many as a dozen yachts at anchor. Juanico has clean sand beaches and good camping, hiking in the surrounding canyons and hills is interesting, and shelling is excellent. The cape forming the east side of the north anchorage provides a small, shallow cove, containing a campsite with a sand beach. A rocky hill provides shade from the sun in the afternoon, and fossils and quartz crystals can be found in the bluffs. At times the population of small fish in the cove is so dense that there seem to be more fish than water, and squadrons of pelicans put on the best diving show in the Cortez just yards off the camp. Snorkeling is excellent, with clear, calm water and dozens of species to observe. The south anchorage is excellent in west and south weather, but provides surprisingly little protection from southeast weather, during which Ramada would be the best choice. Good shelling will be found on the beaches. Quartz crystals can be found just west of a small 50-foot-high islet about half way between the north and south anchorages. A road has been constructed from KM 40+ on the Transpeninsular to the north shore of Juanico (see page 189).

The coast from Juanico to Punta Mangles, Mile 66.1, is high, with only a few cobble beaches in front of steep cliffs. Mangles is a fair anchorage in north weather, although it can be surgy. Camping ashore is only fair, with a sand-and-gravel beach in front of a stagnant mangrove lagoon. The coastline lowers south of Mangles, giving way to low plains and sandy beaches near Boca San Bruno, Mile 70.0. The coast south of San Bruno quickly becomes steep again, with only a few cobble-and-pebble beaches until Punta Tierra Firma, where it becomes lower again, with long stretches of low cliffs and pebble beaches until Loreto. Camping along this stretch of coast is generally poor, so boaters and kayakers often stop at the Islas Coronados, Mile 79.0 (the name is plural because of a tiny islet nearby). The sand bottoms on either side of the spit sticking out to the southwest of the island provide good anchorages in almost any weather, and there is excellent camping. Loreto will be found at Mile 84.0.

■ ■ ■ ■ ■ ■ ■ ■ ■ ■ ■ ■ ■
On the Transpeninsular at Mulegé, KM 135+

KM	Location
130+	PEMEX (MD), small café, mini-market, telephone. An excellent boondocking site can be found by following a marginal sedan road from a point just south of the PEMEX.
130	Some of the most dramatic scenery in all of Baja lies along the west shore of Bahía Concepción from this point south, with unexpected panoramas of brilliant blue coves, brown islands, and white sand beaches. The shallow bay is the largest protected body of water in the Cortez, and water temperatures in summer can rise to over 90°. The water stays warm throughout the rest of the year, making it a fine place to swim, water ski, and sail dinghies, Hobies, and sailboards during a winter vacation. Winds often spring up in the afternoon, so divers and anglers can plan an early day, sailors a late day. There are no marinas and only two paved launch ramps open to the public, although sizable trailerboats have been launched across the sand beaches at Santispac and Posada Concepción. Serious anglers tend to avoid the bay, but it can yield pan-sized sierra and cabrilla for the kids, with an occasional surprise like a barracuda, pargo, or

John Anglin put the last of our fresh water to good use before we left Janico for Loreto

snapper to keep things interesting. Cruising Charts offers a "Paddle Chart" that includes the bay and the area south to Isla Carmen, as well as a guide to the bay.

126	Gentle-to-moderate up- and downgrades with stretches of level road until KM 98, south of Loreto. Note the microwave tower ahead. A rocky cove between two cliffs on the beach east and a little south of the tower is a reported source of "moonstones," 2-inch translucent-to-milky chalcedony nodules with color inclusions of red, orange, and yellow. It can be reached safely only by boat. The jumbled boulder bottom in this vicinity has good fishing for pargo, cabrilla, snapper, corvina, and heavy-duty grouper.
121	Sedan road northeast 1.5 miles to Ricky's. The private launch ramp here may be used for day-trips (no overnight camping). The fishing vessel *Bonito* sank in 3 fathoms, 3,000 yards off Punta San Pedro in 1963.
118+	Sedan road east to Playa los Naranjos and Playa Punta Arena. Set odometer. At Mile 0.5 encounter intersection; go straight ahead (east) for Naranjos (1.5 more miles), or turn right (south) for Arena (1.6 more miles). Both places are low and windswept, with sand-and-pebble beaches. Boats can be launched over the beaches. Naranjos has a restaurant, toilets, and showers, Arena a desert golf course but no toilets or showers, and both have cabin-like *palapas*. There are huge numbers of shellfish offshore, many *chocolate* clams feeling so secure that they do not take the trouble to bury themselves in the sand. Boardsailors like the wide range of conditions, from waves east of the point to calm in the lee. The surrounding land is low, so the winds are often the heaviest in the bay.
114+	**Playa Santispac** (signed). Beach, pit toilets, showers, *palapas*, RV parking, dump station. Ana's Restaurant, serving Mexican and seafood, is popular, and has a bar, a bakery, and a grocery store. Truckers sometimes sell block ice and vegetables, fishermen hawk shrimp and scallops, and the "tamale lady" comes around each morning. The beach is jammed on holidays, with dozens of jet-skiers and water-skiers tearing around offshore. Hills break up the breezes, but many boardsailors and Hobie sailors visit the place anyway. Excellent snorkeling can be found among the islands. The old wooden shrimper *San Gabriel*, home to hordes of small fish, lies in 3 fathoms 250 feet northeast of Isla la Pitahaya. Pitahaya has a tiny sand beach that is a favorite with snorkelers and kayakers. (There are differences in the

Bonnie Wong

The hand-laid rock pavement on the old road south of Mulegé sees little traffic today

names applied to the islands in the bay by different charts.)

112   Posada Concepción. RV Park with full hookups, showers, rest rooms, a game room, and tennis. Most sites are occupied by permanents, but you may get lucky.

111+   EcoMundo, the home base of Mulegé Kayaks/ Baja Tropicales, is easy to locate since the buildings are constructed of ecologically-sustainable straw bales. Guided day-long "paddle, snorkel, dive, and dine" kayak trips in the bay are offered, visiting beautiful coves, hot springs, a shipwreck, etc. The scenery is beautiful, the bay is normally calm, and the locations visited are interesting. They are also a full-service kayak outfitter. The coffee house offers minimalist, health-conscious meals. They are developing an admirable natural-history educational center and a youth hostel, and future plans include a book store and a sports retail store.

111   **Playa los Cocos** (signed). RV parking on one of the best beaches in the bay, but no facilities are available except for pit toilets, trash barrels, a dump station, and a few *palapas*. The area is popular with boardsailors, although the surrounding hills tend to keep things gusty and unpredictable.

109   **Bahía Burro.** RV parking, beach, *palapas*, trash barrels, anchorage. An airplane wreck lies 200 yards off the south point in 2 fathoms.

108   **El Coyote.** Restaurant Estrella del Mar.

107+   El Coyote RV Park; drinking water, solar-heated showers, trash barrels, and pit toilets, but no hookups. A road south along the shore leads to a nicer RV parking area, with *palapas* and trees to provide some shade. Fishing is often good along the rocky beaches and cliffs from here south to Playa Requesón, primarily for cabrilla, pargo, and snapper, plus an occasional barracuda. Isla Blanca has the best diving in the area, with lots of marine life and caves on the southwest side. Locals take their children on picnics here and look for a pirate ship supposedly wrecked somewhere to the south. The arroyo to the east on the other side of the highway has a number of Indian petroglyphs,

106   Site of "The Unhappy Coyote." One of the more engaging examples of Indian rock art in Baja, this painting is of a lop-eared coyote, his mouth open and tail sticking straight astern, his back humped up and his left front paw swollen. At first glance this simple portrait, mottled and indistinct due to aging, hardly seems to rate a second glance, but it seems to grow on most people, at least those with some imagination. The Cochimí artist not only created a coyote but even managed to convey something of its physical and mental state—he is obviously hassled and dejected, perhaps due to a thorn in his paw. In addition to the coyote there are over a dozen other painted figures including seven fish, a man, and something that looks like a very pregnant pussycat. The Unhappy Coyote can be visited by stopping at KM 106. At the marker sight 101° and note the 3 small rock shelters. Do this quickly and watch for traffic—the shoulder is narrow. Drive one-quarter mile north and park on the east side of the road. The shelters can then be reached by hiking about 400 yards south along the old unpaved highway.

94+   **Playa Buenaventura.** Motel, restaurant, bar, RV parking, showers, rest rooms, *palapas*, beach. The concrete launch ramp (12%) is usable by big deep-Vs only at high tide.

92+   **Playa Requesón** (signed). Beach, RV parking, *palapas*, pit toilets, trash barrels, anchorage for small boats. The configuration of this area allows novice boardsailors to find side-shore conditions no matter which way the wind blows. A wreck dating from about 1940 lies 4 miles southeast, its top 6 feet from the surface. The plants that look like they are stand-

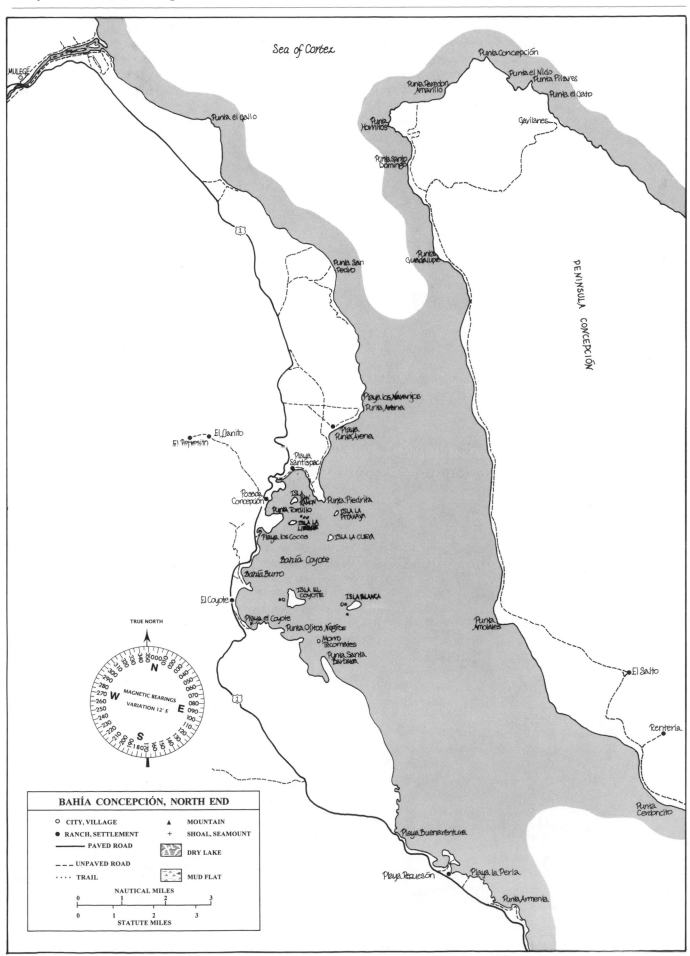

Sea of Cortez

Punta Concepción
Punta Paredón Amarillo
Punta el Nido
Punta Pilares
Punta el Gato
Punta Hornitos
Gavilanes
Punta Santo Domingo

PENINSULA CONCEPCIÓN

Punta el Gallo

Punta Guadalupe

Punta San Pedro

Playa los Naranjos
Punta Arena

El Llanito
El Pedregosito
Playa Punta Arena

Playa Santispac

Posada Concepción
ISLA SAN RAMÓN
Punta Piedrita
Punta Tordillo
ISLA LA PITAHAYA
ISLA LA LIEBRE
Playa los Cocos
ISLA LA CUEVA

Bahía Coyote

Bahía Burro

ISLA EL COYOTE
ISLA BLANCA
El Coyote

Playa el Coyote
Punta Amolares
Punta Ositos Negros
Morro Tecomates
El Salto
Punta Santa Bárbara

Rentería

Punta Cerdoncito

Playa Buenaventura

Playa Requesón
Playa la Perla

Punta Armenia

TRUE NORTH

N
W E
S

MAGNETIC BEARINGS
VARIATION 12° E

BAHÍA CONCEPCIÓN, NORTH END

○	CITY, VILLAGE	▲	MOUNTAIN
●	RANCH, SETTLEMENT	+	SHOAL, SEAMOUNT
	PAVED ROAD		DRY LAKE
	UNPAVED ROAD		MUD FLAT
	TRAIL		

NAUTICAL MILES

0   1   2   3

0   1   2   3

STATUTE MILES

ing on stilts at the edge of the water are mangroves. Forming dense thickets in saline locations avoided by other vegetation, they serve important ecological functions. Their roots offer shelter to hordes of fry and other small creatures, and tend to trap particles, causing the mud flats to extend, in turn providing homes for countless worms and mollusks. Their branches and leaves attract many species of birds, whose droppings enrich the environment below. Several species of mangrove are found from Bahía las Ánimas south in the Cortez and in many lagoons on the Pacific side, as well as on some Cortez islands from Isla Coronado south. The greatest mangrove lagoon in the Cortez is located at Bahía Amortajada at the south tip of Isla San José.

91+   Sedan road east to Playa la Perla (signed), 0.4 mile; RV parking, sand beach.

90+   Sedan road east to Punta Armenta (signed). The road reaches the beach in 0.5 mile and then turns south. Sandy cove, RV boondocking, pit toilets, *palapas*. Fishing camps along the beach to the south sometimes have scal-

Boardsailing action at Bahía Concepción

lops for sale.

88   Boondocking beach.

81   The area on the west side of the road has some plants common to similar habitats throughout much of Baja. The trees with green trunks are *palo verde*; those with white trunks are *palo blanco*; those having slender, leathery leaves with rolled margins, 2 to 5 inches long, are *palo San Juan*; and the straggling, almost shapeless trees with sharp thorns that resemble cat's claws are *palo fierro*. Despite sharing the common name "*palo*" and having overlapping ranges, they are not closely related. *Palo fierro*, also known as ironwood because of its dense wood, was widely used for carvings and tool handles, while *palo verde* bark was once popular for tanning leather, so much so that both species became rare in parts of their ranges. The distinctive "bearded" cactus is *garambullo*, found widely in lower elevations throughout much of the peninsula.

76+   Pickup road east to Peninsula Concepción and San Sebastián. Those continuing on the Transpeninsular should skip the following section.

Side trip to Peninsula Concepción and San Sebastián. A road runs east and then north to the vicinity of Punta Hornitos. The shores on the east side of the bay are less scenic than those on the west side, but there are many fine sand-and-pebble beaches, and good camping, exploring, shelling, mineral collecting, fishing, and diving are to be found. Best of all, the crowds encountered at Santispac and other west-side locations during holidays are absent—in fact, most campsites are usually deserted. The road crosses coastal plains and there are no major grades, although several arroyos and places where the road follows the upper margins of pebble beaches may cause problems for sedans. At KM 76+ turn east and set odometer. Pass an abandoned RV park at Mile 0.5. Shells to be found at the south end include *Dosinia ponderosa, Oliva spicata, Murex elenesis, Strombus gracilior*, variegated auger, and giant egg cockle. In addition, enormous numbers of *chocolate* clams live in the sandy shallows along this stretch of beach. Divers will find them in as little as 3 feet of water. Don't bother looking for a vent hole—the really big vents are giant egg cockles—but look instead for a small, suspicious-looking indentation in the sand. Just plow your thumb through the loose sand. *Chocolates* have a smooth, vitreous, light brown shell.

At Mile 5.5 take the left (020°) fork, and at Mile 5.6 take the left (345°) fork. Note the second fork well; it may be important later. The wreck of a wooden sailboat lies in shallow water west of this point. The sandy arroyo at Mile 6.1 is the severest test of vehicles for the next 14 miles. Watch for frigate birds sitting on tall cactus, quail, and several species of hawks. There are many campsites with pebble, shell, and sand beaches along the road, and the shallow waters offshore are loaded with clams. At Mile 15.2 a road leads east to Rancho Renteria; continue straight ahead. Take the left (350°) fork at Mile 17.1; the right leads to Rancho el Salto. Punta Amolares at Mile 20.0 has excellent shelling. There is an onyx deposit in Cañon Amolares, 2.25 miles, 059° from the point. Poor road conditions will probably keep sedans from going much farther north. Quartz, calcite, and barite are found in the mouth of Arroyo Minitas de Guadalupe, passed at Mile 27.3. The beaches from here to Punta Hornitos are prime shelling areas.

At Mile 30.5 arrive at an important intersection. The left (290°) fork leads about 2 more miles to the vicinity of Punta Hornitos. The right (110°) fork goes east up an arroyo through highly mineralized areas, the earth bright with shades of tan, mustard, and rose. At Mile 34.7 the road ends at Gavilanes, described earlier. Most of the building foundations are in the next cove to the north.

Isolated and still relatively unknown, San Sebastián provides an idea of what things were like in Baja in the "old days" before the Transpeninsular was completed. A number of years ago, a party made up their collective mind to bring a big fifth-wheeler into San Sebastián. It took days of digging down humps in the road, clearing brush, and cutting tree limbs, and the holding tank and much of the plumbing under the rig was wiped out. However, they made it, and spent a happy month at the beautiful little bay recalling the experience. Since then, the place has become home to almost a dozen "permanent" trailers. Still, there are a number of steep slopes with loose rock, and the road cannot be recommended to those with trailers or motor homes (a road from KM 62 will be described later). To drive to San Sebastián, drive to Mile 5.6, take the 045° fork and arrive at the beach in 9 miles.

San Sebastián has no tourist facilities, stores, or launch ramp, just a few ranch buildings, parked trailers, pigs, goats, and chickens, a pebble beach, and shaded campsites, although you might be able to hire a *panga*. The cove in front of the settlement, known as Bahía de los Puercos, is a Baja rarity— a snorkeling site with excellent beach access, protected waters, and unspoiled conditions, with huge morays, groupers, parrot fish, and possibly a dozen other species. Roosterfish show up in April or May and stay for several months, and in the hot months large numbers of dorado are present. Yellowtail from the north migrate past the area in November and return in June, and grouper, bonito, and barracuda stay all year, although the best months are the hot ones. A large variety of shells can be found, including coffeebean, several species of *Thais*, and unusually large tent olives.

■■■■■■■■■■■■■■■■■■■■■■■

Back on the Transpeninsular at KM 76+

KM	Location
68	The first of the wild and beautiful Sierra de la

Giganta can be seen to the south.

62	Road north (signed) to San Nicolás and San Sebastián. This newly constructed road is passable by almost any vehicle as far as San Nicolás, the main challenge being several 23% grades and a number of deep *vados* (dips), where closely-coupled trailers may have problems. Set odometer. At Mile 9.8 intersection, go right (075°) for San Nicolás, or left (025°) for San Sebastián. San Nicolás, 0.8 more miles, has a small settlement, palm groves, plenty of boondocking sites, and lots of goats and pigs that may pay a visit. The dark sand beach appears too soft to permit launching trailer boats. The road to San Sebastián is much poorer, and should be limited to pickups or better. Reset odometer. At Mile 3.7, encounter a fish camp, and at Mile 6.4, enter San Sebastián.
60	Road southwest (signed) to La Purísima and the Comondús. This road is part of the Mountain Villages Loop Trip, described beginning on page 199. See page 206 for an easier route to the Comondús.
40+	Pickup road northeast to Caleta San Juanico (for a description of Juanico, see page 184). Set odometer. In early 1998 the road was newly graded, but it lacked slope stabilization and culverting and will not necessarily stay good. The maximum grade is 17% and there are stretches of loose rock and sand. At Mile 6.7, go straight (025°) at the intersection. At Mile 7.7 arrive at a closed but normally unlocked gate. The land around the bay is private property; read the sign—you may be asked for a fee. Arrive at the beach at the north end of the bay at Mile 8.6. There is a sand beach and plenty of room for boondocking.
0	**Loreto.**

Loreto and Isla Carmen

Loreto's neighbors to the north, Santa Rosalía and Mulegé, are in a sense opposites, one once a bustling industrial town, the other a sleepy, stereotypical "tropical" village. Loreto seems to fit somewhere between the two; it caters to visitors from the north, but at the same time it is a busy center for ranching, construction, and commerce.

Loreto was the first permanent Spanish settlement in the Californias, being founded by Jesuit Father Juan María Salvatierra in 1697. The mission building was completed in 1752, using bricks made in Italy and brought to Loreto as ballast in sailing ships. The town thrived at first, serving as a political capital, a military center, and a base for Jesuit operations. A shipyard and a school to teach Indians to handle sailing vessels were established. However, fate was not to be kind. A *chubasco* wrecked the town in 1829, and in 1830 it lost its political status when La Paz was made the capital. In 1877 the town was badly damaged by an earthquake, perhaps generated by the movement on the same geologic fault that created the Cortez. Coupled with an inadequate economic base, these disasters caused Loreto to decline into a backwater for more than three-quarters of a century.

Today, Loreto is fairly prosperous again, due in part to the construction of a hotel complex to the south at Nopoló. The international airport brings in tourists intent on tennis and lounging in the pool at local hotels, and shuttle busses cruise the streets. Father Salvatierra would probably not approve, but part of the street named in his honor has been turned into a shopping mall.

Loreto is blessed with some good street signs, an almost unique asset among Baja towns; not every street, mind you, but enough that you can get around reasonably well. Of the RV parks now in operation, Villas de Loreto (31) is the nicest. This is the old Flying Sportsmen's Lodge, one of the original fly-in fishing resorts in Baja, then operating its own DC-3. Refurbished and under new management, it has full hookups, rest rooms, showers, a laundry, a pool, and a marginal beach. Kayak rentals are available, as well as fishing and diving trips. The park is also home to several kayak companies, and on a space-available basis, they will rent equipment to experienced paddlers and provide instruction to those who are not. Loreto Shores Villas & RV Park (32) has a beach, pull-through spaces, full hookups, laundry machines, rest rooms, showers, and *palapas* along the pebble beach. El Moro RV Park (8) has no beach, but is within walking distance of the central part of town, with full hookups, rest rooms, and showers. It does not always operate year-round. Los Peregrinos RV Park, across the street from El Moro, has full hookups, rest rooms, showers, and BBQs.

There is a variety of good restaurants in every price range, including El Nido (28), Rochin's Palapa (26), Tiffany's Pisa Parlor (18), Playa Blanca (17), La Palapa (16), Loreto Grill (3), and Café Olé (10). La Fuente (21), a modest, inexpensive café, is popular with the locals, and there is an ice cream shop (14). Jorge's Cool-Off Place (12) is a juice bar serving a wide variety of fresh-squeezed juices, smoothies, and milkshakes. Taking an unusual course in the history of advertising, Anthony's Casa de la Pizza (30) offers the "world's worst pizza," apparently suffering from undue modesty or trying to attract the curious. Should the worst occur after a slice of the worst, there is a funeral parlor in the plaza. There are a number of hotels in town, each with a restaurant, a bar, an excursions reservations desk, and other facilities that may be of interest, including La Pinta (1), Oasis (29), Hotel Plaza de Loreto (20), and Hotel Misión (6).

Finding what you need should be no problem. The new but smaller (23) and the old but larger (22) El Pescador supermarkets have almost everything you could wish for in the way of food and household items. Pescadería Davis (2) is a retail fish market. There are two PEMEX stations (25, MD) and (7, M). Commercial Marina de Loreto (24) has Johnson/Evinrude sales, parts, and service. The 7-11 Liquor (27) sells spirits, beer, and racy T-shirts. Due to recent difficulties with credit card fraud, the bank and some merchants will no longer accept credit cards—ask first. In early 1998 the bank was requiring a surcharge for cashing traveler's checks.

In early 1998 the informal LPG yard west of the highway at KM 2 was refusing to fill the small cylinders found on RVs and campers, and in fact there was no place in the entire town to fill tanks. Until this problem is remedied, travelers should fill at Ciudad Constitución or Santa Rosalía.

There are things to see and do. Misión Nuestra Señora de Loreto (11), constructed between 1704 and 1752, is still in use, repairs and renovations being funded in part by 500,000 (old) pesos won by its priest in the national lottery a number of years ago. An inscription carved over the main door reads CABEZA Y MADRE DE LA MISIÓNES DE BAJA Y ALTA CALIFORNIA (Head and Mother of the Missions of Baja and Upper California.) There is an interesting museum next door. The pleasant Malecón (9) has brick paving and benches, half of them facing east for the sunrise, half to the west for the sunset. Las Parras Tours, next door to Café Olé, offer trips to San Javier, whale-watching at Bahía Magdalena, an expedition to the art sites at Rancho la Trinidad, and others, plus mountain bike and kayak rentals and tours, sailing, and horseback riding. Many people like to visit the Islas Coronados, a small volcanic island and a tiny islet about 5 miles north of Loreto. A cove with a white sand beach will be found, an ideal place for picnics, and the warm and clear water invites snorkelers. On the north side of the island, a reef of massive boulders is home to gorgonians, puffers, morays, and triggerfish, and large numbers of *chocolates* will be found on the sandy bottom.

Loreto is home to almost all the species of fish that anglers come to Baja to pursue. As the town changed over the years, so did the anglers; Rather than a relatively small number of dedicated anglers, new facilities have brought in large numbers of tourists, to whom fishing may be an incidental activity, to be squeezed in between a day on the tennis courts and a day in the pool. Their sheer numbers, together with increased commercial netting, have resulted in a decline in the fishery. A few years ago many would-be anglers at a beachfront hotel watched in horror as a commercial boat netted a reported 10 metric tons of fish directly off the hotel. The new complex to be constructed at Puerto Escondido, with its hundreds of boat slips, and the "fisherman's pier" planned for the Nopoló area will certainly accelerate this trend. Mexican President Zedillo recently signed a decree establishing the "National Marine Park, Bay of Loreto," which is about 37 miles long from north to south, and ranges seaward an average of 25 miles from the coastline. The Islas Coronados to the north and Isla Catalina to the south are the rough limits of the proposed boundaries. However, there is no funding attached, and powerful commercial fishing interests are in opposition, and the park, or at least enforcement of conservation laws, may be years in the future.

In spite of it all, there are still plenty of fish—the netters proved that—and it's the trend more than the actual num-

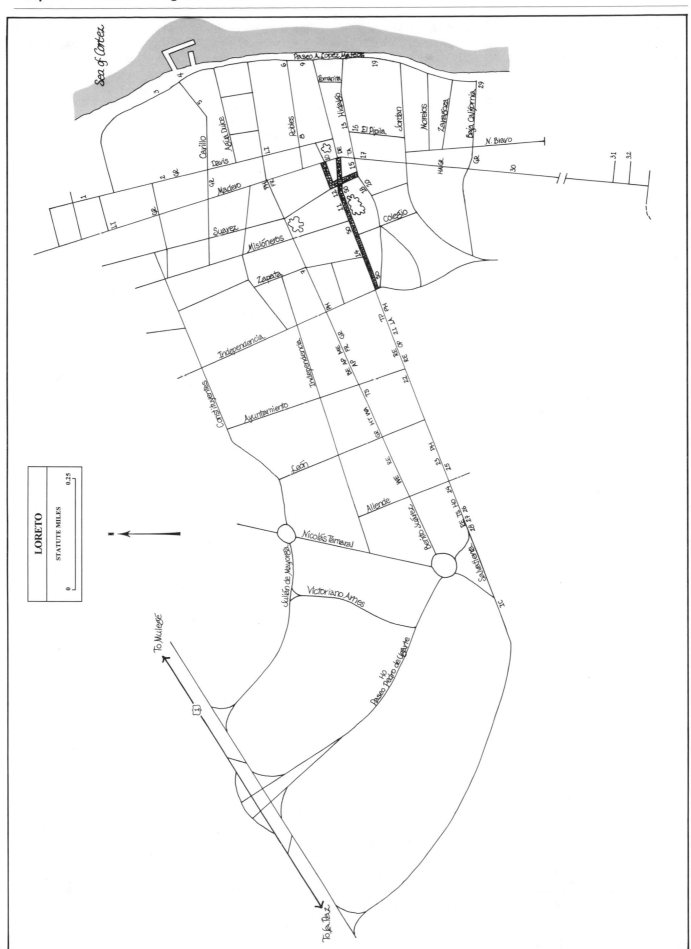

Sea of Cortez

Paseo A. López Mateos

Romanita
Hidalgo
El Pipila
Jordan
Morelos
Zaragoza
Baja California
N. Bravo

Carrillo
Abila Dulce
Davis
Robles
Madero
Suarez
Misióneros
Zapata
Colegio

Independencia
Independencia
Ayuntamiento
León
Allende

Constituyentes

Nicolás Tamaral
Julián de Mayorga
Victoriano Ames

Benito Suárez
Salvatierra

Paseo Pedro de Ugarte

LORETO

STATUTE MILES

0   0.25

To Mulegé

To La Paz

bers of fish taken that is the worry. Many people still find excellent fishing, especially those with a boat big enough to get well out into the Cortez. The action is quite seasonal, with the warm months best. In July the area east of Isla Carmen outside the 100-fathom line, reached about 2 miles east of both Punta Lobos and Punta Baja, provides some of the hottest dorado action in Baja. The waters between the Islas Coronados and Carmen sometimes have excellent runs of yellowtail and dorado. Other favorite fishing spots include the areas south and east of the Coronados, the deep water between Loreto and Carmen, and a rocky shelf leading east from Punta Lobos, the last of which often has the largest congregation of leopard grouper, cabrilla, and large gulf grouper in the Cortez.

The grooved concrete public ramp (4, 12%) leads into the small man-made harbor. The parking near the ramp is limited. Portable boats can also be launched over the sand beach at the north end of town, and just south of Loreto Shores, where there is plenty of parking. Large trailer boats should be launched at Puerto Escondido, about 15 miles south. Daily, weekly, monthly, and annual fishing licenses available at Deportes Blazer (15), which also sells fishing tackle and sporting goods, and makes limited repairs to rods (tips and guides). *Pangas* and cruisers are available at Arturo's Sport Fishing Fleet (13), which also sells tackle. *Pangas* can also be rented at offices on the beach in the north part of town. Fishing International offers package trips to the area.

During periods of north weather, Carmen's chain of mountains—some in excess of 1,500 feet, extending over its entire 20-mile length, plus its northeast-southwest orientation, tends to funnel heavy winds past Loreto, and with lots of fetch and plenty of wind, the channel is often choppy. Skippers of small boats should give careful thought about trips to Carmen; a safer choice would be Danzante. The anchorage off Loreto is nothing more than an open roadstead and the harbor is very small, so plan to bring your boat ashore each night. The first good anchorage to the south is Escondido. There is a COTP in town (5), and an *Aduana* and a *Migración* at the airport.

Baja Outpost (19) offers full dive rentals (no sales), air, and a number of *pangas*. A number of NAUI and PADI certification and specialty courses are available. They also operate an inexpensive bed-and-breakfast. Deportes Blazer has compressed air, limited sales, and complete rentals of diving equipment, and has a supply of hard-to-find gadgets like wishbones, sling rings, speargun points, and snorkel tabs. Arturo's has full equipment rentals (no sales), compressed air, and dive excursions to the islands aboard *pangas*. There is also a dive shop at the Eden Loreto Resort south of town.

Most divers head for Isla Carmen or Isla Danzante, although those with adequate boats often choose Isla Monserrate or Isla Santa Catalina. Divers will find *chocolates* to be abundant on shallow sandy bottoms off the western shores of Carmen. The best diving is off the north end and along its east coast. Also, a reef about 1,500 yards south of the south cape comes to within 12 feet of the surface and offers outstanding snorkeling. Divers should watch for the Pacific razorfish, which grows to 10 inches and has a blunt head, a bluish-gray body, and three indistinct vertical bars. Near the northern end of its range in the Cortez, the razorfish does not rush into rocky crevices when fleeing its enemies as do its wrasse cousins, but rather dives head-first into the sandy bottom, almost magically disappearing. The water is alive with fry and tiny mysids, and large barracuda, leopard groupers, pargo, and snappers are common, along with king angels and several species of grunts. Underwater photographers should stay alert for colorful nudibranchs. There are at least 9 sea caves on the north shore near Punta Lobos and as far west as Isla Cholla, the longest stretching more than 150 feet. All except one are in a limestone cliff, bordering on a fine sand beach. The last one, near the point, is in volcanic rock and has a 30-foot underwater passage to another entrance. At least two others have extensive air chambers, as evidenced by large volumes of air expelled during periods of heavy surge.

Carmen has two good anchorages, Puerto Balandra on the west side and Bahía Salinas on the east. Composed of marine sedimentary and Holocene volcanic rock, Carmen is the site of a large volcano, its crater the source of exceptionally pure salt. The salt operation is now closed, but about 40,000 tons a year used to be shipped from the pier in Bahía Salinas. The 120-foot vessel *Engenada* sank in 1981 and can be found a half mile directly off the salt pier in the bay. Although the visibility is often limited, divers like the wreck for the profusion of fish it has attracted. It lies in 35 feet of water. Many years ago salt was carried by burros from Salinas to Balandra, and a hike on the trail might provide mineral-collecting opportunities. An old miner's map shows numerous copper claims near a landing spot 1.5 miles north of Balandra. The waters around the island are among the best in the Cortez for encountering blue and finback whales, and those to the south have blue, fin, Minke, and Bryde's whales.

The coast between Loreto and La Paz is one of the most interesting areas in the Cortez. South of Ensenada Blanca roads penetrate in only a few places, including Bahía Agua Verde and San Evaristo, and the area is unspoiled and almost deserted. There is a great deal to do here, including hiking and exploring, nature-watching, fishing, diving for edibles, and making friends with manta rays. Some of the islands are home to unusual wildlife, such as black jackrabbits and silent rattlesnakes, and the waters surrounding them are alive with hundreds of species of fish. With adequate planning, drinking water should not be a problem, for there are a number of permanent ranches and settlements along the coast, and two settlements on the islands offshore, and yachts frequent the area. A trip by kayak or small boat down the coast can assume either of two basic forms: offshore island-hopping (below) or a coasting trip (following the island-hopping trip).

Those continuing on the Transpeninsular should turn to page 199.

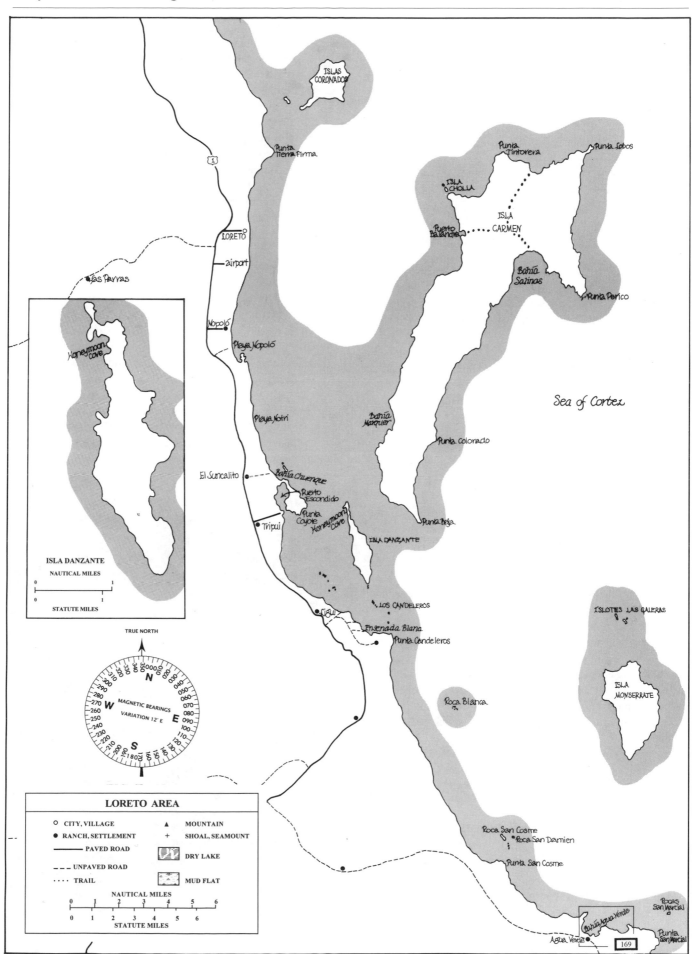

ISLAS
CORONADOS

Punta
Tierra Firma

1

LORETO

airport

Las Parras

Nopoló

Playa Nopoló

Punta
Tintorera

Punta Lobos

ISLA
O'CHOLLA

ISLA
CARMEN

Puerto
Balandra

Bahía
Salinas

Punta Perico

Sea of Cortez

Playa Notri

Bahía
Marquer

Punta Colorado

HONEYMOON
COVE

ISLA DANZANTE

NAUTICAL MILES

0   1

0   1

STATUTE MILES

El Juncalito

Bahía Chuenque

Puerto
Escondido

Punta
Coyote

Honeymoon
Cove

Tripui

Punta Baja

ISLA DANZANTE

TRUE NORTH

MAGNETIC BEARINGS
VARIATION 12° E

ISLOTES LAS GALERAS

LIGUI

LOS CANDELEROS

Ensenada Blana

Punta Candeleros

ISLA
MONSERRATE

Roca Blanca

LORETO AREA

○ CITY, VILLAGE   ▲ MOUNTAIN

● RANCH, SETTLEMENT   + SHOAL, SEAMOUNT

—— PAVED ROAD

- - - UNPAVED ROAD   DRY LAKE

· · · TRAIL   MUD FLAT

NAUTICAL MILES

0   1   2   3   4   5   6

0   1   2   3   4   5   6
STATUTE MILES

Roca San Cosme

Roca San Damien

Punta San Cosme

Rocas
San Marcial

Bahía Agua Verde

Agua Verde

169

Punta
San Marcial

By water: island-hopping

Those in adequate vessels may wish to island-hop from Loreto to La Paz by way of Islas Danzante, Monserrate, Santa Catalina, Santa Cruz, San Diego, San José, San Francisco, Partida Sur, and Espíritu Santo, a trip of about 145 miles. A Paddle Chart offered by Cruising Charts provides a great deal of useful information on the islands in this area.

It is 16 miles from Loreto to the south tip of Danzante. (More information on Danzante will be found later in this chapter.) A group of small rocky pinnacles known as Los Candeleros are found 1.5 miles southeast of Danzante. These are fine deep-dive sites, with plenty of large fish and shellfish. Low-lying Monserrate is 10.5 miles from Los Candeleros. Its surface looks largely barren, but surrounding waters teem with fish and lobsters. The north end has an anchorage useful in south weather and a sand beach where landings can be made, and reefs off the north points provide fine diving and fishing. In prevailing weather boats can be anchored off the southeast side, although it is very exposed. Islotes las Galeras, a small group of islets 2 miles north of the island, are seldom visited but have excellent fishing and diving on a jumbled bottom, with numerous rocky ledges, as well as a sea lion colony.

Twelve miles east of Monserrate is Isla Santa Catalina (Isla Santa Catalan), one of the most famous islands in the Cortez. Home of the "rattle-less" rattlesnake, the island is visited by many natural-history tours. Unlike ordinary rattlesnakes, these small, docile, and very rare snakes shed their terminal scales with each molt and thus never develop rattles. First described in 1953, their days are probably numbered, since feral cats prey on them. A question for visitors to the island: do rattle-less rattlesnakes still shake their tails when disturbed, and if so, why? Another curiosity is an unusually large barrel cactus which often reaches 10 feet in height and 3 feet in diameter, named *Ferocactus diguetii*, after Leon Diguet of rock-art fame, who discovered it. Equally strange is the torchwood plant, which bears two distinct types of flowers. Several coves on the south end provide good anchorages, and landings can be made. There are a number of sandy campsites on the west side. Diving is excellent all around the island, with numerous rock walls, caves, and crevices, but beware of strong currents. A mysterious wreck, possibly two, has been reported on the east side near the south end, but no details are available.

Isla Santa Cruz, 19 miles from Catalina, is steep and barren, the best camping being near the light at the southwest end. Surrounding waters are deep, and the only good anchorage is on the east side, where there is a pebble beach. A sea cave large enough to enter with a boat can be found at the north end of this beach. The southwest reef also offers good fishing and diving, but the best diving and fishing are encountered at the north end, with huge boulders and rocky ledges that are home to grou-

pers and bottomfish. Spearfishermen have had outstanding hunting where the north ledge suddenly drops off into deeper water, especially for tuna up to 65 pounds.

Isla San Diego, 4 miles from Santa Cruz, has an anchorage in an open bight on the northwest side. The shoreline is almost entirely steep cliffs, but a landing can be made on the southwest side. The island has a large population of scorpions, mice, and lizards. The southwest reef is an outstanding dive site, with intricate lava formations honeycombed by grottos. An especially fine grotto system can be found in 30-to-40 feet of water near 2 pinnacles awash at the end of the reef. Huge groupers and large populations of lobsters are often seen here, along with corals and red, gold, and white sea fans.

While it is off the route of the Island-Hopping Trip, anglers and divers, especially underwater photographers, should visit Isla las Ánimas Sur, 9 miles east of Punta Calabozo on Isla San José. Seen from the west, the island resembles a whale chasing a fish, the aid-to-navigation tower on the island being the whale's spout and a small islet being the fish. Ánimas Sur is one of the premiere deep dives in the Cortez, its sheer sides plunging almost vertically to about 300 feet. So steep is the area that it is very difficult to anchor safely, although in calm weather small boats may be able to anchor in 80 feet off the south side. The water is deep blue, indicating its depth, and visibilities can reach 100 feet. Upwellings of cold, nutrient-rich water promote spectacular growths of gorgonians on

John Anglin pops a purple-lip off Candeleros

the steep walls. Because of the variety of micro- and macro-habitats available, few locations in the Cortez have such a range in the size of fish present, from clouds of tiny fry to colorful reef fish to heavy-duty gamefish, including grouper, marlin, dorado, and shark. Watch for the rare longnose butterfly fish. There are a number of caves, including one on the east side at 60 feet, which you can enter and chimney up through passages, and another large one at 80 feet on the northeast side. Although this is scuba country, free-divers might get a shot at large groupers and jacks around the pinnacles on the east side.

Isla San José, 7 miles south of Isla San Diego, is the largest island in the chain, about 18 miles long. The principal island rocks are mixed Miocene volcanic and Pliocene and Pleistocene marine, the island itself the product of fault-block uplift in the Pliocene. With a sizable area and some

Steve Salas and his 102-pound roosterfish taken while free-diving north of La Paz

surface water, the island supports a wide variety of wild-life, including deer, ring-tailed cats, and coyotes. Scorpions up to 6 inches long wait to terrorize campers. There are 21 species of reptiles and amphibians, of which 1 is endemic, and 138 vascular plants, none of which are endemic. The low rate of endemics is due to the close proximity of the peninsula. Birders will be kept busy, with at least 40 species being present at least part of the year.

The island was the home of Pericú Indians until the mid-1700s. Gold, silver, copper, lead, and calcite occur on the island. There is good diving off the north tip, where diveable depths extend more than a mile from shore, and at Punta Colorada. A sea cave so large it can be entered with a dinghy will be found near this point. There is relatively little commercial fishing along the east side, so sportfishing and spearfishing are good. A salt works has been in operation at Punta San Isidro (Punta Salinas) on the west shore, and fuel and water might be obtained at the settlement. The anchorage south of the point is suitable in prevailing weather. Bahía Amortajada, west of the south end of the island, provides a good anchorage in south weather, but is completely open to west and northwest winds, and the *jejénes* can be miserable; Lynn and Larry Pardey of *Seraffyn* fame complained about the "flying teeth." Kayakers will find good camping on the west side of the island, especially on the beaches just south of Punta San Isidro. Just west of the bay, the waters around Isla Cayo have good diving, much of it within free-diving range, and sections of it are loaded with shellfish. Garden eels can be seen in sandy areas.

The entrance to a large mangrove lagoon is on the shore of the beach forming the margin of Bahía Amortajada. It is the largest mangrove area in the Cortez, and a dinghy trip is worthwhile. There are many small channels off the main waterway, and once in the mangroves it's a whole new Baja experience. Large numbers of birds inhabit the thickets, including the big and obvious ones like herons, egrets, and ibises, and others so small and reclusive you may not be aware of their presence unless you stop the engine and sit quietly for a while. The waters are filled with large numbers of fish, and oysters can be seen clinging to mangrove roots. The visibility is often surprisingly good, and a snorkeling venture will an experience to remember. Bottoms range from clean sand to the blackest of gooey mud. For the stout-of-heart, a snorkeling foray at night ought to be fantastic!

Between San José and Isla San Francisco is tiny Isla Coyote (Isla Pardito), site of a prosperous fishing settlement, with neat homes and a well-cared-for look. It might be possible to obtain emergency gas and water here. Diving is especially colorful among the rock islets to the west and at the solitary rock to the north, all of which have huge orange and red sea fans and many reef fish.

Isla San Francisco, 2 miles south of San José, was worked for pearls from the late 1500s to the early 1900s, and between 1881 and 1886 a German operated a one-

Our sloop Azabache *was too large to get in close at Las Ánimas Sur, so Reeve and Mike loaded the hooka in the dinghy*

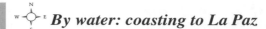

By water: coasting to La Paz

Marine charts of this coast are inadequate for kayaking and small-boat cruising, but the following 1:50,000 Mexican topographic charts are useful: Ligui G12C29; San José de la Noria G12C39; Timbabichi G12D31; Los Burros G12D41; and San Pedro de la Presa G12D51-52. The last will carry you as far south as Punta el Mechudo, and the remaining maps in the series have so little useful data that they are not worth buying. A Paddle Chart offered by Cruising Charts covers the coastline from Isla Carmen to La Paz, and several of their guides cover the same area. Baja Expeditions, Baja Outdoor Activities, Aqua Adventures, Outland Adventures, and a number of other companies offer this trip or shorter versions of it.

The distance by water from Loreto to La Paz is either 147 or 151 miles, depending on the route you take. The coast from Loreto, Mile 0.0, to Ensenada Blanca, Mile 22.0, is described beginning on page 194. A small cove at Mile 24.1, south of Punta Candeleros, provides a sand beach and a small anchorage, good in all but north and east weather. The rocky coast gives way to sand near Bahía Agua Verde, Mile 40.9. Bahía Agua Verde is formed from numerous small coves, one or another of which will provide protection from weather from any direction except northeast. The largest black-coral "forest" in the Cortez can be found in 80–130 feet of water off the rocky pinnacle of Roca Solitario, a 115-foot-high pinnacle at the mouth of the bay. Solitario serves as an excellent land-

man gold mine on the island. There are good anchorages on both sides of the spit extending to the south, and in south weather a bay on the northwest end is usually satisfactory. The end of the spit provides good diving with fine visibility in periods of north weather. Watch for garden eels and jawfish on the sandy bottoms. The sand beach on the west side of the spit has good shelling if you like your shells small, including the olive, pearly top, venus, hoof, sea button, and bean families, and four or five species of tiny clams. Marine life on the east side is very different, and pearl oysters, nerites, cowries, and arks are found on the rocky beach. Quartz pebbles also can be found in quantity. The deep water to the east has good fishing for dorado and yellowfin tuna in season.

The next island in the chain is Partida Sur, 17 miles from Isla San Francisco. Because Partida Sur and Espíritu Santo are close to La Paz and because many diving and fishing trips to them begin in that port, they are described in the next chapter—see page 219.

The unfortunate photographer was sinking rapidly in the slime and expecting attack by swamp creatures as he took this photograph of Judy, Suzy, and Mike exploring the Amortajada lagoon

mark for those arriving from the north and east. A road, described beginning on page 203, connects Agua Verde with the Transpeninsular. Punta San Marcial, Mile 44.2, has a fine sand beach and forms a good anchorage on its south side, protected from north weather. Large catches of yellowtail, dorado, and roosters are common in season, and excellent diving is available just to the south of the point. A small but interesting sea cave south of the point can be entered by boat.

The coast from Marcial to Puerto Gato is mostly bluffs, with a few sand beaches. Puerto Gato, an open bight just north of Punta Botella (Punta San Telmo), Mile 54.8, is celebrated as the most colorful anchorage in Baja, with a backdrop of rocky layers in red, white, and black. Its beautiful sand beaches permit easy landings, but the anchorage is open to the east and can be surgy. Diving on the reef in the southern part of the bay is outstanding, and shelling is good on the beach. Although there are no deep underwater canyons to draw tuna in as there are at East Cape, they sometimes approach shallow water nearby. Punta Botella, the site of a multimillion-ton deposit of high-grade phosphate with a uranium content, has several sand beaches.

The coast from Puerto Gato to Nopoló is mostly bluffs, with small beaches at the mouths of canyons. Bahía Timbabichi, Mile 57.5, (Bahía San Carlos), marked by a two-story abandoned stone building just to the south, is protected from north weather. Landings can be made on the fine sand beach, and there is a sizable mangrove lagoon worthy of exploration. Several families live nearby, and water may be available.

Rancho los Dolores, located just north of Punta los Burros, Mile 73.6, has a sand beach and irrigated gardens of citrus, figs, and grapes. Water is usually available, fruits can be purchased in season, and it may be possible to obtain fuel in an emergency. The anchorage is poor, and usable only in west and south weather. Immediately south of the point is Rancho los Burros, which has an open anchorage and a beach, and may have water. Nopoló, Mile 79.9, is a small settlement with an anchorage open to the east. Pebble beaches here alternate with sand beaches. The villagers are friendly, and gas and water may be available.

The coast from Nopoló to Bahía San Evaristo, Mile 87.0, is mostly bluffs, with a few beaches. Evaristo is an excellent all-weather anchorage, and a settlement just to the north has water and possibly emergency gasoline. Fine sand beaches provide many campsites, and snorkeling at the point is excellent, with many small reef fish inhabiting the cobble and boulders down to a sand bottom at 20 feet. A night dive will reveal large numbers of a sea cucumber with a worm-like body up to 4 feet long, uncommon in the Cortez. The following chapter describes the road between Evaristo and La Paz.

There are few good campsites and rather featureless terrain along the coast to the south, and during periods of

Rob Watson claimed to have seen glowing eyes looking back at him while exploring a sea cave near San Francisquito

calm, stable weather, boaters and experienced kayakers sometimes head from Evaristo to Isla San Francisco, Mile 95.2, described on page 195, and then directly to Isla Partida Sur, Mile 112.8. Partida Sur and Isla Espíritu Santo, just to the south, are two of the nicest camping and loafing islands in the Cortez and are described on page 219. La Paz is reached at Mile 147.1.

For those continuing along the coast, a ranch will be found near Punta Salinas (Punta Arena), Mile 89.1 (continuing the numbering system from Evaristo). Punta el Mechudo, Mile 94.1, is a headland of 300-foot cliffs. There are a number of sand beaches between Evaristo and Mechudo. Between Mechudo and San Juan de la Costa, Mile 122.1, there are more beaches and a few small fish camps and ranches. The phosphate-mining town of San Juan de la Costa, a healthy walk from the beach, has a public restaurant and water from spigots. Since there is easy road access, some kayakers and small-boat sailors end their trip here rather than going on to La Paz. The road from La Paz to Evaristo is described on page 213. There are occasional fish camps and ranches along the beach to the south, with cliffs alternating with pebble beaches and cobble beaches, slowly giving way to sand. There are no good anchorages, but the beaches and low points provide campsites, and it is often possible to scout up driftwood for a fire. La Paz is reached at Mile 151.

> ❝ *Necessity is the mother of invention*
>
> *We had learned much about botany, ornithology, and marine biology during a long day of diving and exploration near Amortajada, but little did we realize as we bedded down for the night that we were about to undergo a required course in entomology! As the moon rose, a primordial urge descended on the resident* jejéne *population. Blood! Human blood! In seconds the air was full of horrid little black flies. Rather than sticking you with a tube like an honest mosquito seeking a square meal, they are "pool feeders;" using scissor-like mouth parts they slash your skin and greedily lap up the oozing blood. They are found in salt marshes, mangroves, and decaying seaweed, the prime locations being the coast south of Puertecitos, Guardian Angel Island, especially the north and south ends, Isla Partida Norte, Isla Turners and, you guessed it, Amortajada. The best defense is avoidance, and moving your camp or boat as little as a mile can put you out of range. An increase in elevation of only 100 feet also helps; sleep up a canyon, not on the beach.*
>
> *We didn't know these things at the time, and desperation drove us to don all available clothing, pull plastic bags over our hands, and climb into our sleeping bags, in spite of the warm night. This helped, but many succeeded in finding tunnels and crevices. We wondered if we would be sucked dry, leaving three mummies to be prodded and photographed by passersby. About four in the morning I was forced out of my sleeping bag by a call of nature and was bitten in an extremely sensitive location. My dignity destroyed, I dashed back to the safety of my sleeping bag, my chore unfinished. We lay on our air mattresses stifling in the heat and fighting off swarms of insect invaders, watching the moon travel on its westward journey, inch by inch. Just before dawn an idea hit all three of us simultaneously and there was a rush for our duffel bags. Dawn found three exhausted skin divers asleep on the beach in full wet suits, masks in place and breathing through their snorkels, surrounded by hordes of frustrated insects angrily trying to penetrate the neoprene.* ❞

Kayakers explore a remote coast

Will Waterman

Chapter 12

Loreto to Cabo San Lucas

■■■■■■■■■■■■■■■■■■■■■■■■
On the Transpeninsular at Loreto, KM 0

KM	Location
0/120	Start new KM numbering sequence.
118	Road west (signed) to San Javier, 22.1 miles. Those continuing on the Transpeninsular should turn to page 201.

↱ ***Side trip: the mountain villages loop trip.*** This trip passes through fine mountain scenery and visits a number of interesting villages, the first of which, San Javier, has one of the finest Jesuit mission churches in Baja. The road as far at San Javier is improved, being almost completely graded and having many stream crossings paved with concrete. However, it is subject to weather problems and has grades to 19%, and if there is doubt that your vehicle can handle it, any of the hotels in Loreto can arrange a van trip. Storms often damage the road north from San Javier to San José de Comondú, and it is usually a long time until they are completely repaired, so you will need a pickup or better for the remainder of the loop trip. This trip is a favorite with off-road bicyclists, but due to steep grades some walking will be necessary, and brakes should be in top condition. There are ranches along the way where extra water may be obtained, but since these sources are not dependable, the amount carried by bicyclists needs to be adequate to get from village to village. If your objective is only to visit the Comondús, a much easier route is described beginning on page 206.

Set odometer. Starting at Mile 1.4, commence moderate up- and downgrades, soon followed by a steady climb. Water may appear in canyon bottoms starting about Mile 8.7, sooner if the weather has been wet, and it might be possible to find a swimming hole. As the road switches back and forth the scenery becomes more spectacular, with *zalates* clinging to almost vertical canyon walls and palms lining the bottom of the canyon.

El Pilón de Parras, a huge pyramid of rock next to the road, is an excellent climb. A number of approaches are avail-

able, starting at about Mile 11.1. Its summit is at 3,477 feet, and since the altitude of the road at its closest approach is 1,330 feet the total climb is over 2,100 feet. The climb is class 3, with a good deal of traversing necessary to avoid technical sections. It is strenuous, and a long day should be planned, but the views of the deeply eroded Sierra de la Giganta and the blue waters of the Cortez are smashing. Rock climbers will find a technical climb on a sheer rock face at Mile 11.6. After a 50-minute class 2 and 3 approach, the face will be encountered at elevation 2,100 feet. About three pitches in length, it is crossed by a large diagonal crack, and

Jim Smallwood top-roping on the rock face at El Pilón, camera-shy Don Nelson unseen

the closer you get the more impressive it looks. The rock is strong and there is plenty of placement. Once above the approach, the climb is lower- to upper-class 5.

At Mile 11.9 encounter Rancho las Parras (Grapevine Ranch), with a stone chapel, small dam, and citrus and olive trees. At Mile 13.0, the road reaches the summit at 1,700 feet, offering fine views of the canyon below and of the Cortez. Occasional small streams and ponds may be found from here to San Javier. Pass Rancho Viejo (signed) at Mile 16.6, and at Mile 18.0 note the road to the right (295°, signed COMONDÚ); you will need it later.

Arrive at San Javier at Mile 22.1. In 1699 Jesuit Father Francisco Píccolo founded a mission at Rancho Viejo, but in 1707 the site of the present village was developed as a garden and visiting station by Father Ugarte, and in 1720 the mission was moved here. In 1744 the stone church was started, taking 14 years to complete. The golden altar and its paintings were carried by burro and ship from Mexico City. The church has 3 bells, 2 dated 1761, one 1803. The church is still in use, and on December 2 and 3 of each year the almost-deserted village is filled with people from surrounding ranches, there to celebrate Saint Javier's birthday. A tiny *palapa* café sells Mexican food and cold sodas, there is a small grocery store, and you can buy oranges from the children. Drinking water can be obtained from spigots along the divided parkway serving in lieu of the traditional plaza.

To continue on the trip, return to the intersection at Mile 18.0, reset your odometer, and turn left (295°). The road will immediately swing right along the old route of the Loreto-San Javier road. At Mile 0.4 turn left (020°) at a concrete marker. The rough road has seen some improvements like culverts and concrete causeways, but many have been swept away by floods. At Mile 9.5 start a major upgrade, 2 miles of loose rock, bumps, and slopes up to 21%. Bicyclists will walk this one.

Good campsites are difficult to find at the top of the mesa, as almost everything is cobbles and boulders, so start looking early. There are great views of the canyons to the west, making the area a fine sunset spot. At Mile 13.3, start a mile of switchbacks, loose rock, and downgrades of 23% into a canyon. The strange structure at Mile 15.4 is a lime kiln, built without the benefits of cement. The rough road levels out a bit, with no major grades until Mile 19.7, where a mile of 19% upgrades is begun, and Mile 24.7, where a mile of 21% downgrades ends at the village of San José de Comondú.

The twin villages of San José and San Miguel occupy the bottom of a fertile, well-watered canyon. Suddenly you enter a cool sea of green so dense with oranges, sugar cane, figs, corn, grapes, palms, bougainvillea, and a dozen flowering plants that there doesn't seem room for the people. Most of the buildings are traditional adobe, and except for the electric lines, the vehicles, and a satellite TV dish, it could be a scene from the previous century. The small plaza in San José will be encountered upon entering the village. The stone building is a missionary house from Misión Comondú, the

bell in front dating from 1708 (the church was torn down).

To get to San Miguel, continue on a third of a mile from the plaza and note the road right (335°), but do not turn (you will need this road if you decide to travel on to La Purísima). Continue straight ahead, and 2.25 miles from the plaza, turn right (253°), cross the canyon bottom and enter San Miguel de Comondú. San Miguel was established in 1714 by Father Ugarte to supply food for Misión San Javier. Look for antique sugar-cane presses, operated by burros walking in circles. San Miguel has a store that sells groceries, and you can buy gas at a house on the southeast side of the road—look for the piles of drums.

It appears that despite the new graded road into the villages from the west, the tranquillity and beauty of the villages, and the wealth of food made possible by Mother Nature, the Comondús are dying. Their populations are half those of 10 years ago, the handful of businesses has declined to 2 or 3, and most of the faces seen are wrinkled and the hair gray. One wonders—is the decline related to the construction of the new road, or did the road keep it from dying altogether?

At this point, you have two choices, continuing on to La Purísima and returning to the Transpeninsular at KM 60, or going west from San Miguel on the newly graded gravel road to Villa Insurgentes and then back to Loreto on the Transpeninsular; the Villa Insurgentes route is described beginning on page 206.

To continue on the loop trip by way of La Purísima and KM 60, return to the intersection noted previously, reset your odometer and turn left (335°) through a corridor of palms, encountering an 18% upgrade on the other side of the canyon. At Mile 0.75 take the left (335°) fork and pass a cemetery on the right. Once on top of the mesa, the road improves, but there are many gentle-to-moderate grades. Campsites are hard to find, so start looking early. The great Arroyo de la Purísima can soon be seen ahead, and the road begins to descend. Note the road going right (010°) at Mile 18.8; you may need it later. At Mile 19.7 you will arrive at El Arriba, a small community of palm-thatched homes and citrus groves. An aqueduct cut through stone cliffs and crossing fields parallels the palm-lined road for miles. San Isidoro, with a general store, cold beer, and water from spigots, is reached at Mile 21.2.

There are great views of the village and the surrounding palm groves and ponds at Mile 22.7. At first glance El Pilón, the massive rock formation towering over the village, might look like a volcano, but it was actually formed because a cap of weather-resistant rock shielded it while the rest of the valley eroded away. A local climber fell from the top some years ago, and a cross was erected there in his honor. La Purísima is reached at Mile 23.3, with a food store, cold beer, water from spigots, ice plant, liquor, doctor, dentist, and post offices. The road continues about 5 miles southwest down the canyon to an important intersection, from where you can go north to San Ignacio, or south to Villa Insurgentes.

El Pilón and the countryside near La Purísima

To return to the Transpeninsular, go back to the intersection at Mile 18.8, reset your odometer and turn left (010°). The road has been improved, with some grading and culverting, but is less scenic and interesting than earlier parts of the trip. At Mile 21.6 go straight ahead, arriving at KM 60 on the Transpeninsular at Mile 33.0.

■■■■■■■■■■■■■■■■■■■■■■■■■
Back on the Transpeninsular at KM 118

KM	Location
117	Paved road east (signed) to Loreto International Airport.
111	**Nopoló.** Sedan road east (signed) to the Eden Loreto Resort (ex-Loreto Inn, ex-El Presidente Hotel). If you are seeking silence and solitude, this is the place—it has one of the highest vacancy rates of any hotel on the continent. Aqua

Sports de Loreto, based at the hotel, offers full dive rentals (no sales), air, and guided trips to Carmen, the Coronados, Danzante, and other hot-spots in the hotel's *pangas*. NAUI resort, certification, and specialty courses are available, as well as whale-watching, fishing trips, and water sports equipment rentals.

107+	They don't rival the Golden Gate, but the only two suspension bridges in Baja can be seen here. They allow golfers to pass over an inlet.
103	**Playa Notrí** (signed). Public beach, no facilities. The beach is a source of several species of cowrie shells.
98	The road levels out until KM 83.
97+	Sedan road east (signed) to El Juncalito. Those continuing on the Transpeninsular should skip the following section.

 Side trip to El Juncalito. This palm-lined little cove is a favorite with many travelers, offering camping, trash cans, and a pebble beach with stretches of sand.

The road in can handle almost any RV. A small fee is charged. Parking on the beach south of the grave of Bad José is restricted. Launching cartoppers and inflatables over the sandy beach is easy. There is fine beach-casting for yellowtail along the south shore of the bay from December to April, and jack crevalle and roosters are taken in the spring. Divers will find purple-lips among large rocks below the cliffs outside the cove to the south, also the habitat of many sizable snapper, grouper, pargo, and cabrilla. The cove is a fair anchorage in all but north or northeast weather.

The strikingly beautiful tree on the beach with creamy-yellow bark and bright-green deciduous leaves is a *zalate*, or wild fig. Found from San Ignacio south, *zalates* often choose exposed locations where no other large trees are able to survive, sometimes clinging to sheer cliff faces, their root systems taking advantage of every available crack. The tree can be seen from the highway at KM 99, but a better (and safer) look can be obtained by driving to the shore and heading north around the curve of the bay past the small rocky headland. While *zalates* are fairly common, this will be your only chance to see a mature tree close to the Transpeninsular until south of La Paz.

Divers will find the wreckage of a large twin-engine plane in 22 feet of water on a gently sloping cobble bottom 75 yards south of Isla Chuenque, the only island in the bay. When you are over the wreck the central peak on the island will bear 342°. The 2 large air-cooled radial engines are easy to locate, each with 14 cylinders. The area is littered with large quantities of aluminum wing sections, ribs, sheet, and structural parts, stainless hose, plastic sheet from the windows, and the landing gear. Based on the engines (Wrights), the plane was probably a DC-3.

● ●

❝ *An epistle on Evinrude*

We were heading back to camp after a day of diving, when the outboard engine suddenly acted up. The symptoms were puzzling; it would start and run momentarily, backfire, and then quit, with gas spraying out of the air intake. It obviously could not be fixed in situ *and it was not until after midnight that we got back with the aid of another boat. With abundant advice from an audience of several locals from the nearby settlement, I tore the engine apart the next morning and found that one of the four leaf valves had broken. These consisted of flat metal springs fastened at one end to a metal plate, each covering a hole in the plate. This assembly allowed the air-fuel mixture to pass from the carburetor into the crankcase, but not the other way. My audience soon grew to 5, and they began to offer their best advice: drive the 150 miles to the nearest dealer, order the part, and pick it up 2 weeks later. This didn't sound too attractive, so I had to devise a repair. I cut two pieces of sheet aluminum slightly larger than the hole in the metal plate behind the broken*

leaf, and fastened them together with a small machine screw. By blocking the hole I hoped that the three remaining valves would allow the engine to operate satisfactorily. As I worked in the hot sun my audience grew to seven, all of whom soon started shuffling about and making clucking noises—sure signs, I feared, of disapproval. Finally, one of them could restrain himself no longer; "It would never work, never," he said, to the obvious approval of the crowd, who responded with grins, head shaking, smirks, and finger wagging.

The repair completed, I reassembled the engine and carried it down to the boat, pursued by a group of jeering children. I got no help from my critics, none of whom wanted to be associated with such an obviously futile endeavor. With every eye on me I squeezed the fuel bulb, gave the starter a yank, and the engine roared to life—the first time, as best I can remember, that it had ever started on the first pull. Unfortunately, the engine was in gear—the interlock that normally stopped it from starting while in gear was not adjusted properly—and the sudden acceleration threw me aft towards the engine, and I lost my footing. Draped across the engine on my stomach, feet up, nose almost in the water, it took me half a minute to regain my balance. As the boat sped away I finally looked back; the beach was deserted, my critics apparently having decided that the pain of being wrong was greater than their amusement at my predicament.

The spectacle did not end without comment, however; my fellow divers had arrived back in camp from a supply run to town at just the right moment. Around the campfire that night my valve-repair triumph was forgotten and the central topics of conversation were endless commentary on how silly I looked draped over the engine, countless recreations of the event, and abundant speculation as to how far the boat would have gone before running out of gas had I been pitched into the water. **❞**

● ●

■ ■

Back on the Transpeninsular at KM 97+

KM	Location
94+	Paved road east (signed) to Puerto Escondido. Those continuing on the Transpeninsular should skip the following section.

↱ **Side trip to TRIPUI, Puerto Escondido, and Isla Danzante.** TRIPUI Resort RV Park, a half mile east of the highway, has full hookups, rest rooms, showers, laundromat, restaurant, bar, grocery store, gift shop, pool, and tennis courts. Puerto Escondido is the best all-weather anchorage for larger boats in the Cortez, completely surrounded by land except for its 65-foot-wide, 10-foot-deep (at zero tide) channel. Tidal current flows through this channel at up to 4 knots. A steep (17%) concrete launch ramp is available inside the harbor entrance, suitable for even large trailerboats, although the concrete is cracking and spalling badly. Instructions for use of the ramp are posted at the ramp. Obtain a ramp permit at the office in a stone building with a metal roof, 100 yards south of the ramp. It is allegedly open Monday through Friday (except Mexican holidays), but if there is no one there, it may be necessary to contact the Captain of the Port in Loreto. Construction has been underway for a number of years on a major development of the area, which may eventually provide a yacht club, markets, sports club, beach, condominiums, residential subdivisions, and other facilities. Construction is now at a standstill, but rumors persist that things are to get going again. Yachts may still anchor in the harbor and trailerboats can be launched, but RVs may no longer be parked in the area. Dinghy and boardsailors will find calm and safe conditions inside the bay.

The outer harbor area, known as the "Waiting Room," is also a good anchorage. Divers will see garden eels and might be able to ride whale sharks, which occasionally visit the area. In 1932 the 101-ton yacht *Aimee* sank here. Several massive black coral "trees" can be seen in deep water off Punta Coyote, the easternmost extension of the peninsula forming the bay. Divers report that dense schools of yellowtail inhabit this area year-round at depths of 100-120 feet, a fact not known to many visiting anglers.

The island 3 miles to the southeast is Isla Danzante. There is an excellent anchorage in tiny "Honeymoon Cove" on its west shore, just south of the north tip, often used by antisocial boaters wishing to escape crowded Escondido. The tiny sand beach at the head of the cove attracts many kayakers—far too many—but there is good camping in small, open coves just south of Honeymoon, as well as other locations along the island's west coast. There is a good deal of commercial netting in the area, but fine fishing is still available, the productive locations for it including the reefs and small islands from Danzante south to Punta Candeleros and the water outside the 100-fathom line, 5 miles east of Danzante.

Diving is best on Danzante's east side and on the reef at the south cape, where garden eels have been seen in the sand at 65 feet, and black coral in deeper water. The south cape is also excellent for fishing and spearfishing for barracuda, yellowtail, leopard grouper, and snappers. Fishing and diving are good near a rock visible from the surface 4 miles, 072° from the south cape of Danzante. When you are over the site the south cape will bear 252°, Punta Perico on Carmen 011°.

■ ■

Back on the Transpeninsular at KM 94+

Although mostly just steep cobble, the beaches from here south to Ensenada Blanca are favorites with pickup-

campers and those with small trailers and motor homes, as well as bicyclists, and many anglers prefer them to any other in the Loreto area. There are a number of faint, almost unnoticeable trails that lead to the beach, permitting camping with some degree of privacy and ready access to Danzante and the other islands. Diving around the small islets just offshore is excellent.

KM	Location
94+	Opposite the road to Escondido, a sedan road heads southwest 0.7 mile to the mouth of Cañon Tabor, a fine hiking location. At one point there is a huge boulder wedged in the narrow canyon, making it necessary to scoot under it and then climb a notched log. There are palms and surface water in some places. Bighorn sheep have been seen in the canyon.
85	**Rancho Ligui.** A sedan road (signed) heads east to a boondocking beach, no facilities. One-half mile from the highway, a sedan road heads right (110°) to shallow, sandy Ensenada Blanca (Bahía Candeleros). Several spur roads along the way lead to seaside campsites, one with a fine sand beach. Ensenada Blanca is well protected from all but north winds. The beaches are sand and silt, with some rocky areas. The tiny settlement has a small store.
83	Seven percent upgrades and many switchbacks to KM 77, then ups-and-downs to KM 45.
63+	Road southeast (signed) to Bahía Agua Verde, 26 miles.

Side trip to Bahía Agua Verde. This road is important in that it opens the Bahía Agua Verde (Green Water Bay) area to anglers and divers having cartoppers and inflatables, who would otherwise have to run over 20 miles from the beaches near Danzante. Set odometer. For the first dozen miles, the road is graded, culverted, and equipped with concrete paving at most of the stream crossings, and there are no major grades. However, the road then begins a series of hairpin turns, with fairly steep (16%) grades. Several of the hairpin turns are blind: a driver going down and a driver coming up cannot see each other until only a dozen yards apart, and there are few places to pass and virtually nowhere to turn around. The road reaches beach level at Mile 14.4, opposite two small islands on the shores of the Cortez, and continues southeast along the shore. The beaches are mostly steep cobble, although short stretches of sand can be found near Agua Verde. The road closely parallels the water, but side roads leading to the beaches are limited, making it important to find a place to park before nightfall. The scenery alone is worth the trip. The Sierra de la Giganta assume wildly improbable shapes—lopsided

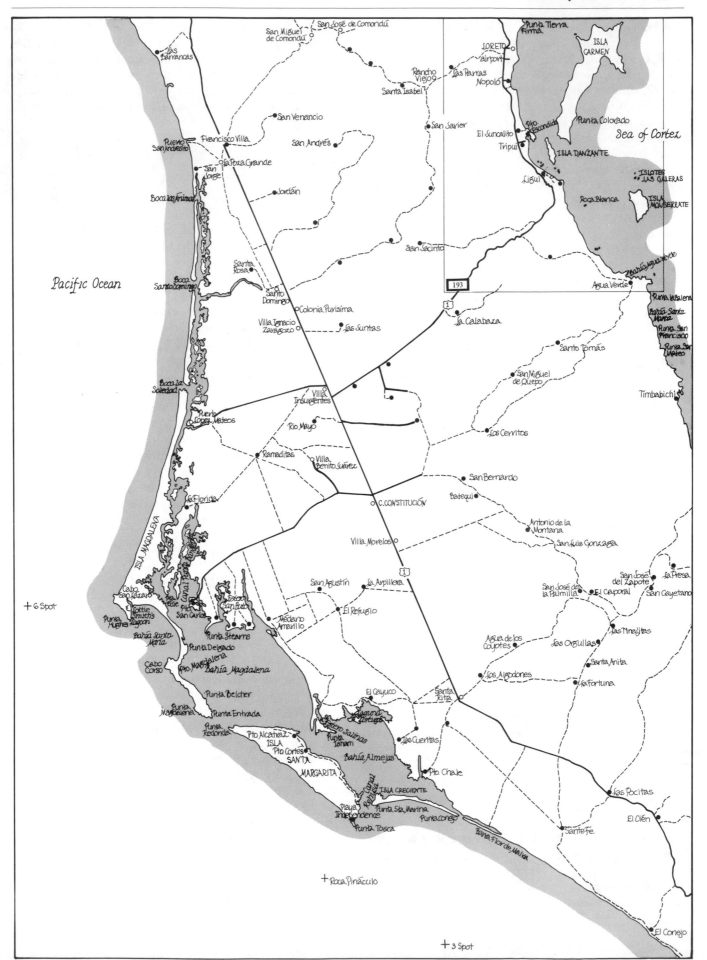

Pacific Ocean

Sea of Cortez

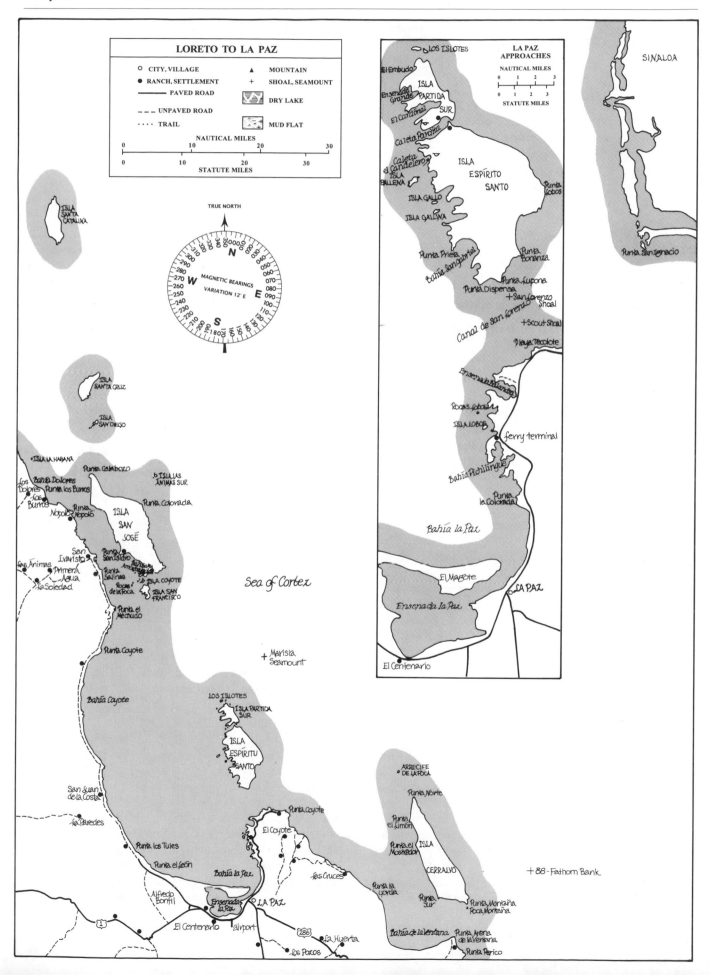

LORETO TO LA PAZ

○	CITY, VILLAGE	▲	MOUNTAIN
●	RANCH, SETTLEMENT	+	SHOAL, SEAMOUNT
—	PAVED ROAD		DRY LAKE
– – –	UNPAVED ROAD		MUD FLAT
· · · ·	TRAIL		

NAUTICAL MILES
0   10   20   30

STATUTE MILES
0   10   20   30

LA PAZ APPROACHES

NAUTICAL MILES
0   1   2   3

STATUTE MILES
0   1   2   3

TRUE NORTH

MAGNETIC BEARINGS
VARIATION 12' E

SINALOA

ISLA SANTA CATALINA

ISLA SANTA CRUZ

ISLA SAN DIEGO

Sea of Cortez

LOS ISLOTES
El Embudo
Ensenada Grande
ISLA PARTIDA SUR
El Cardonal
Caleta Partida
Caleta el Candelero
ISLA BALLENA
ISLA GALLO
ISLA GALLINA
ISLA ESPÍRITO SANTO
Punta Lobos
Punta Prieta
Bahía San Gabriel
Punta Bonanza
Punta Lupona
Punta Dispensa
San Lorenzo Shoal
Canal de San Lorenzo
Scout Shoal
Playa Tecolote
Ensenada Balandra
Rocas Lobos
ISLA LOBOS
ferry terminal
Bahía Pichilingue
Punta la Colorada
Bahía la Paz
El Mogote
LA PAZ
Ensenada la Paz
El Centenario

ISLA LA HABANA
Punta Calabozo
Bahía Dolores
Los Dolores
Punta los Burros
Los Burros
Nopoló
Punta Nopoló
ISLA LAS ÁNIMAS SUR
Punta Colorada
ISLA SAN JOSÉ
San Evaristo
Punta San Isidro
Las Ánimas
Primera Agua
Punta Salinas
La Soledad
Rocas de la Foca
ISLA SAN FRANCISCO
ISLA COYOTE
Punta el Mechudo
Punta Coyote
Marisla Seamount
Bahía Coyote
LOS ISLOTES
ISLA PARTIDA SUR
ISLA ESPÍRITU SANTO
San Juan de la Costa
La Paredes
Punta los Tules
Punta el León
Bahía la Paz
Alfredo Bonfil
Ensenada la Paz
LA PAZ
El Centenario
airport
La Huerta
Los Pozos
El Coyote
Punta Coyote
Las Cruces
ARRECIFE DE LA FOCA
Punta Norte
Punta el Limón
Punta el Mechudo
ISLA CERRALVO
Punta la Gorda
Punta Sur
Punta Montaña
Roca Montaña
Bahía de la Ventana
Punta Arena de la Ventana
Punta Perico
88-Fathom Bank

domes, fantastic plunging cliffs, strange valleys, and great battlements from ancient days, all worked in red and purple rock, disproving Father Baegert's claim that there is no scenery to please the eye in Baja California. At Mile 23.1 the road climbs a hill, providing a sweeping view of the coastline to the northeast and southwest, allowing some scouting for places to camp. The village is reached at Mile 26.1. Some time ago, the wells turned saline and the place seemed doomed, but water is now piped in from the back country. There are two small grocery stores and a blaze of bougainvillea and hollyhock. As noted earlier, the largest black-coral "forest" in the Cortez can be found in 80 to 130 feet off the rocky pinnacle of Roca Solitario, a pinnacle rising 115 feet out of the Cortez at the mouth of Bahía Aqua Verde. Large catches of yellowtail, dorado, and roosters are common in season, and excellent diving is available.

■■■■■■■■■■■■■■■■■■■■■■■■

Back on the Transpeninsular at KM 63+

KM	Location
60+	Road south (signed RANCHO HUATAMOTE) to a clearing with some camping sites and a bit of shade.
45	On top of a mesa, mostly gentle downgrades or level from here to KM 123, south of Ciudad Constitución. Headwinds are frequent in the afternoon.
17	PEMEX (MD), sodas, and food.
0	**Villa Insurgentes.** PEMEX (MD), bank, stores, groceries, bakery, meat and fish markets, restaurants, beer, tortilla factory, ice, auto parts, tire sales and repair, health clinic, pharmacy, veterinarian, optical, telephone, mail, and Baja Celular office. Road north to Puerto Lopéz Mateos, the Comondús, and San Ignacio. Those continuing on the Transpeninsular should skip the two following sections.

↱ **Side trip to Puerto Lopéz Mateos.** The town of Puerto López Mateos can be reached by driving northwest through Villa Insurgentes and taking a left (262°, signed) on the paved road 1.4 miles north of the Transpeninsular. The town, at KM 35, has groceries, butcher shop, *tortilla* factory, restaurants, beer, liquor, ice, long-distance telephone, health clinic, pharmacy, and a *Pesca* office. Gasoline is available from drums at a place 100 yards northeast of the church. The areas near the lighthouse and north of the cannery have largely been appropriated by whale-watching organizations, and there are rest rooms and taco stands nearby. The best camping and launching areas can be found a mile east of town—turn south at the water tower.

López Mateos would normally be of little interest, except for one thing—the whales. During the winter months, especially February, the whales cruise by in the narrow waterway that passes the town, within easy viewing distance, and *pangas* can be hired to get even closer. The best viewing location is at Curva del Diablo (The Devil's Bend), a sharp bend in the waterway where the tides from the north and south tend to meet, located 17 miles south of town. A number of local organizations provide whale- and birdwatching tours; watch for the signs.

↱ **Side trip to the Comondús.** This trip will take you to the Comondús, described earlier. Begin by turning north through Villa Insurgentes. At KM 16, the road will pass through Villa Zaragoza, which has tire repair, groceries, ice, auto parts, liquor, beer, a fish market, and a PEMEX (MD). The arrow-straight road then passes through orchards and fields of corn and wheat. At KM 64, turn half-right (north, signed COMONDÚ) onto the graded two-lane road. The Comondús are no place for a trailer, so if you are towing one, leave it here, hopefully manned by a volunteer to maintain security. A new KM sequence begins at this point. There will be 3 stream crossings (wet weather) and several 19% grades, but the new road is smooth and the traction good. At KM 33, arrive in San Miguel de Comondú.

■■■■■■■■■■■■■■■■

Back on the Transpeninsular at Villa Insurgentes, KM 0

KM	Location
0/236	Start new KM numbering sequence.
221+	LPG yard. Those heading north should fill here, as LPG may be in short supply in the Loreto area.
214	PEMEX (MD), auto parts.
213	Chevrolet and Johnson/Evinrude parts, service, and repairs. Manfred's Trailer Park; full hookups, rest rooms, showers, Austrian restaurant.
212+	**Ciudad Constitución.**

Baja's Indiana

Dozens of wells tapping huge underground aquifers have converted the surrounding areas into Baja's equivalent of Indiana, and the town appears to be thriving. (The city is sprawled along the Transpeninsular, and the facilities noted below are easy to locate.) There are hospitals and doctors, dentists, pharmacies, opticians, veterinarians, PEMEX (two, MD at both), mechanics, auto parts, welding, locksmith, long-distance telephone, new tire dealers and tire repairs, a Yamaha outboard dealer, post office, department stores, restaurants, butcher shops, beer, hardware, travel agents, banks, hotels, laundromat, sporting goods, bike shops, a Baja Celular office, an ice manufacturing plant, a yoga parlor, and a psychiatrist. There are several stores which are close approximations of American-style stores, and there is a homeopathic pharmacy. The restaurants in Ciudad Constitución cater to the locals, but they are quite inexpensive and there are a number of choices. Campistre la Pila Trailer Park, at the south end of town has a dump station, water and electric hookups, a pool, tent sites, toilets, and showers. Drive south from the downtown area and watch for the large electrical substation on the east side of the road. Turn west at this point and watch for signs in about a half mile.

Those continuing on the Transpeninsular should turn to page 212.

↱   ***Side trip to the Bahía Magdalena area.*** Commencing at Boca las Ánimas, a series of narrow barrier islands stretches south for over 130 miles. Two of them, Islas Magdalena and Santa Margarita, form Bahía Magdalena and its southern extension, Bahía las Almejas. Although this vast area has a great potential for fishing, diving, kayaking, and other activities, it is seldom visited by outsiders. Access and facilities are limited; there is only one paved road to the bay, and only one paved launch ramp. Commercial fishermen tell of 60-pound snook netted in the hundreds of miles of mangrove-lined waterways and small bays, but ordinary techniques common to Baja fishing simply do not work. Storms often cut new channels and silt up old ones, changes which are not reflected on the marine charts. However, unfamiliarity and mystery are the stuff of adventure, and there is a great deal to see and do.

The bay is best reached by driving west from Ciudad Constitución from the signed intersection at the north end of town. Trailer Park la Curva at KM 56 advertises sewer, water, and electric hookups, rest rooms, and showers, but appears to be closed, although RV parking and a mud beach are available. San Carlos, at KM 58, is a deepwater port, with a COTP, *Aduana*, and *Migración*. The small town has a PEMEX (MD), *Pesca* office, restaurants, ice manufacturing plant, beer, liquor, mechanics, laundry service, tire repair, doctor, dentist, pharmacy, health clinic, grocery stores, butcher shop, post office, and long-distance telephone. The new Museo de la Ballena (Whale Museum) has artifacts and machinery from the old whaling station at Punta Belcher. A recompression chamber has been installed in the Productos Pesquera de Bahía Magdalena plant, but its operational status is unclear.

The town lacks RV and camping facilities, but many flat parking spaces can be found. The old Flying Sportsman's Lodge once operated a fishing camp south of town. It is now out of operation, but RV parking is available. It is found by driving 0.2 mile, 060° from the PEMEX, then 120° for another 1.5 miles. Boats as long as 28 feet have been launched from the rough, shallow (7%) concrete ramp, but tides of at least 3.5 feet are required.

Bay and blue-water fishing

Bahías Magdalena and Almejas are shallow, half their area averaging 60 feet or less, and large areas are exposed at low tide. However, the bay east of the shoreline between Punta Entrada and Puerto Magdalena is fairly deep, some locations being over 140 feet, especially north and east of Punta Belcher. In these areas, you can catch cabrilla, grouper, yellowtail, and black sea bass. Favorite spots outside the entrance include the area between Punta Magdalena and Cabo Corso, and off Punta Hughes. Surf fishing can be excellent on the beaches north of Cabo Corso. If it's too rough to land, pull up on the protected beach several miles north of Puerto Magdalena on the "inside" and hike over the dunes.

Larger boats have access to world-class big-game fishing offshore. The 100-fathom line is 9 miles off Punta Entrada, but sailfish and dorado are caught within 5 miles, marlin preferring it a bit deeper. Banco Thetis, a favorite with long-range boats from San Diego, and known for marlin, yellowfin, wahoo, and giant sea bass, is 18 miles, 290° from Cabo San Lázaro, least reported depth 6 fathoms. Thetis has been fished by trailerboats using the launch ramp at Puerto San Carlos. When water temperatures and wind are favorable, boats often get into boils of wahoo so bold that they will attack baitfish seeking refuge in the shadow of the boat. Anglers have been known to complain that they can't get their baits past the marlin to the other species of fish. Another fine location is "6 Spot," 16 miles, 266° from Punta Hughes. A large rig could make productive daily runs to these locations for as long as fuel permitted, anchoring in the lee of Punta Hughes at night. Live bait is no problem, for mackerel can be caught by the ton near Punta Entrada. For those with adequate range a little-fished 22-fathom spot known as Roca Pináculo, 8 miles, 192° from Punta Tosca, offers the same species as Thetis. In addition, "3 Spot," 22 miles, 133° from Tosca, offers good fishing. Cortez Yacht Charters offers trips to these locations. To date no one seems to have mustered the courage, but spearfishermen should note that several of these locations are within easy diving depth.

The best months for bay fishing tend to be in the summer and fall, although there are reports of good catches as late as early February, depending on water temperatures and currents. Frequent northwest winds and fog may cause problems. It is common to be able to fish only one or two days a week, and wipeouts of two weeks are possible. April, May, and June are usually the windiest months, September, October, and November the calmest. Alternating shore and sea breezes often push fog back and forth, creating clear and foggy periods sometimes only hours apart. If it's a total wipeout, cheer up—Puerto Escondido is only 109 road miles away and La Paz 166, and the Cortez will probably be calm.

Fishing in a green jungle

A wide variety of fish can be caught in the mangrove areas fringing much of the eastern coastlines of both bays and the inland waterways to the north, including but certainly not limited to cabrilla, corvina, snook, mangrove snapper (red bass), yellowtail, and halibut. The variety of fish present is so large that something is usually biting. The best boat is a cartopper or an inflatable, since larger rigs will have trouble with the extensive shoals. If you insist on using your big cruiser, be sure to have a length of line and a video camera—you will be able get some great shots of your crew doing Bogart/Hepburn *African Queen* routines if you stray from the channels. The outside of a bend in a waterway will probably be deep and hold more fish, so anchor on the inside and cast across to the other side, giving you the advantage of playing the fish directly away from the cover. Trolling or casting parallel to the outside perimeter of the mangroves allows you to cover more territory, at the cost of letting some fish get into their roots when hooked. If you can't cast to an enticing location, use the current to drift a bait into place. Fish at high water, for at low tide some of the big fish have left for deeper water. An incoming tide is usually better than the outgoing, because the previous low has concentrated fish in deeper spots and the water is clearer. If you are after snook, drift or anchor; they are spooked by even the small-

Fishing action at Banco Thetis

est motors. Watch for large fish working mullet. Rays often can be seen "flapping" on the bottom to dislodge small organisms, and other species often rush in to join the feast.

The wreck of the Independence

The outer shores of Islas Magdalena and Santa Margarita have been the scene of more major shipwrecks than anywhere else in Baja California. The first was a tragedy, the greatest maritime disaster in Baja history. Early on a February morning in 1853 the 211-foot sidewheel steamer *Independence* rammed a submerged pinnacle north of Punta Tosca with 400 passengers and crew jammed aboard. The situation was deadly, for heavy surf was breaking at the foot of dark perpendicular cliffs, and no one would survive if the ship broke up in this location. The captain backed the ship off the pinnacle, turned northwest and slowly ran her along the coast. Steam pressure was falling rapidly, the ship was soon turned toward a small beach and run aground. Flames roaring out of the furnaces soon touched wood and spread rapidly. Terrified people began to jump overboard and struggle in the sea, clinging to flotsam. A woman attempting to climb overboard snagged her full skirts on a davit and was left swinging until she was consumed by the flames and dropped into the sea. Rather than let their children burn, parents threw them overboard to an almost certain but less painful death by drowning. Swimmers were sucked under when the ship rose and settled in the waves, and others clinging to chicken coops were swept out to sea. On the beach men were seen looting corpses and quarreling over the spoils. About 150 people died and were buried in shallow graves high up on the beach and in the canyon beyond. The survivors were soon rescued by whaling ships at anchor inside the bay.

Over 145 years of surf and storm have not succeeded in erasing all traces of the *Independence*, and a visit to the beach will teach you all you want to know about ghosts. The two 10-inch-diameter iron shafts that carried her great paddlewheels lie among the rocks on the beach, and several anchors, a capstan, booms, and twisted iron parts can also be seen. Above the beach, numerous shards of pottery and thousands of rusted iron objects lie about, mingled with human bones. Magnetometers have failed to reveal the presence of sizable metal objects outside the surf line, but her huge boilers, massive walking beam, and paddlewheels must be out there somewhere. As with all Baja wrecks, look but don't touch.

"Playa Independence" can be reached in several ways. In Canal Rehusa a sand spit forms a shallow, sandy lagoon 3 miles north of the lighthouse. An arroyo heading southwest from the south end of this lagoon climbs to a pass and then drops down to the beach, a hike of about 3 miles one-way. Allow 6 hours for a round trip, including several hours at the site. In calm weather a boat can be landed on the beach: proceed northwest along the outer coast from Punta Tosca for 2.5 miles and look for a sandy beach fronting an arroyo, the first substantial sand beach northwest of the point. A broad stripe of green rock runs diagonally up the hill forming the northwest shoulder of the arroyo.

A nautical comic opera

Seventeen years after the *Independence* disaster, the sidewheel steamer *Golden City*, one of the largest and finest wooden oceangoing ships ever constructed, went aground 11 miles north of Lázaro in a fog. The actions of her captain, crew, and passengers provide the great comic opera of Baja shipwrecks. As the lifeboats went over the side, a passenger became involved in a shouting match with Captain Comstock and several officers over whether he or the treasure of gold bars should go ashore first. The choice was easy, and they triced him up by tying his hands behind him and connecting the rope to a spar above, leaving him lurching about the heaving deck, standing on tiptoes. Blustering, cursing, waving a saber in one hand and a revolver in the other, the captain began bullying everyone in sight. Once ashore, a number of steerage passengers got into a fight over a cask of liquor that had washed up, which the captain ended by striking one of them in the face with his saber. A cow that swam to the beach was promptly slaughtered and boiled in a huge pot of sea water. At first light the next day it was found that the steamer had broken in half aft of her paddleboxes, discharging a flotsam of 43,000 chests of tea, hundreds of bales of silk, and more liquor. The steerage passengers began drinking and quarreling, and Captain Comstock found it necessary to strike Mr. James Murphy over the head with a pistol and kick him in the face. Drunken passengers continued to stagger around the beach, Mr. Murphy later having a "fit."

Some time later the steamer *Colorado* appeared off the beach. Since the surf was too rough to permit safe embarkation, Captain Comstock asked that the ship anchor in Bahía Santa María. He then assembled the passengers and ordered them to "go down the beach," waving his saber toward the south, swearing and threatening to shoot. With no guidance as to the route to be taken, and without adequate food or water, groups of people started out, a number of old or invalid passengers being carried on litters. One elderly gentleman was carried seated upright in a chair. Everyone

Salome Hiquera and Reeve Peterson measure the paddlewheel shafts from the **Independence.** *Salome is a lighthouse keeper at Punta Tosca*

The **Golden City** *in 1867, three years before her loss on Isla Magdalena*

finally arrived, safe and reasonably sober. A small lagoon at the north end of the bay was named "Lottie Smith's Lagoon," after the first woman rescued from the ship. The *Colorado* made steam for San Francisco, leaving Captain Comstock, a small crew, and a number of volunteer passengers, duly fortified with a large supply of wine, to guard the treasure and baggage. Two days later the unfortunate Mr. Murphy was seen jumping over the rail of the *Colorado*. The ship was stopped, but no sign of him could be found. Captain Comstock and the others were picked up several weeks later by the steamer *Fideliter*, treasure intact and bottles presumably empty. Spielberg should look into this!

The most beautiful shipwreck that ever happened

The next wreck was the antithesis of the *Independence* tragedy. About 7 in the morning of April 13, 1909, the lookout on the US cruiser *West Virginia* saw distress signals near Punta Tosca. They proved to be from the 343-foot steamer *Indiana*, which had run aground in a fog in calm seas and was resting easily. Because of their shallow draft the naval vessels *Navaho* and *Fortune* were able to come almost alongside, and all passengers and their luggage were taken off without so much as a pair of wet feet. Transferred to the cruiser *California*, they were treated royally as the ship headed for San Francisco. Officers gave up their cabins so the "survivors" could be comfortable, and the band played on deck each evening. One happy woman wished "... Mother had been wrecked with us; she would have enjoyed every hour of it." Another found it "... the most beautiful shipwreck that ever happened." Passengers pleaded unsuccessfully with Captain Cottman to slow the *California* down to give them another day, and it was with regret that they finally reached San Francisco, arriving a day earlier than if the *Indiana* had not been wrecked.

Although nothing can be seen of her above water, large sections are still intact, and she makes a fine spearfishing site, since the hull is home to many large groupers. She lies on the east side of Punta Tosca 300 yards north of the lighthouse in 18 to 24 feet of water on a sand bottom. There are heavy tidal currents coming from Canal Rehusa, but usually only refracted swell. Visibility averages about 10 feet.

A submarine mystery

The US submarine *H-1* was underway in the darkness early on March 12, 1920. Seeing what appeared to be the entrance to Bahía Magdalena, the captain ordered the helmsman to turn northeast. Suddenly a rending shock hit the vessel and she listed violently and began taking water through the conning-tower hatch. Deceived by a long, low stretch of coast opposite Puerto Cortés with high hills on each side, her captain had run her aground on Santa Margarita. Sea water hitting the batteries caused a dense cloud of chlorine gas and forced the skivvie-clad crew to don life jackets and jump into the huge breakers. The wreck was seen by an accompanying ship and the survivors were picked up the next morning, but four men were dead, including the unfortunate skipper.

The weather remained rough, but crew members from the *USS Vestal* finally got aboard several days later, and found a profound mystery; someone had looted the boat. Her magnetic compass, gyro repeaters, rifles, pistols, ammunition, bombs, and detonators had been stolen. The lock on the safe had been torn off, and her signal books and confidential publications were gone. On March 24 the *H-1* was towed off the beach and promptly sank. Due to the hazards and expenses involved in re-floating her, she was abandoned and stricken from Navy records.

Although pilots have not been able to see the outline of the wreck from the air, there seems to be no further record of her fate, and the Navy Historical Center is of the opinion she was never salvaged. If the sea has not completely destroyed her, she is one of the greatest prizes in Baja diving. Lying on a flat bottom in a known location, she should be relatively easy to locate with a magnetometer. She sank in 9 fathoms at 24° 24' 54" north latitude, 111° 50' 45' west longitude, 9^3/4 miles northwest of Punta Tosca. On March 24, after the *H-1* sank, the following was recorded in the *Vestal*'s log: "Rt. peak 100° true. Gorge Rock 315° true." The *USS Brant*'s log for March 23 shows her position as "Outer Twin Sisters bearing 119° true, Point Toscok [Tosca] 130° 30 minutes true..." Most of these names and locations appear on marine chart 21121, "Rt. peak" apparently being the 1,631-foot peak and "Gorge Rock" one of the rocks at the foot of the white bluff. To convert true bearings to magnetic, subtract 11 degrees to account for local variation.

Four tiny guardians

The next wreck was the 5,643-ton vessel *Colombia*, which went aground at Punta Tosca in a heavy gale on September 13, 1931, carrying 234 passengers and crew, and $850,000 in gold and silver bars. The steamer *San Mateo*, the first vessel to arrive at the scene, found her a total wreck. Lifeboats were scattered over an angry sea, but everyone was rescued without injury. The *Colombia* had survived a series of mishaps since she had been launched in 1915, including a mutiny and being torpedoed once, grounded once, and driven ashore twice. This time, however, her luck ran out and she was declared a total wreck and abandoned to her underwriters, with the gold still aboard. Some believed that Mexican law held that a ship was abandoned only when "every living

Charles Velton

The USS H-1 *on the beach at Isla Margarita, 1920*

thing" had been removed, and that such a vessel belonged to the first person who got there and established himself in command. Captain Oaks, possibly foreseeing this, had left an alley cat and a mongrel dog on board, and it was found later that passengers had also left two monkeys. There was some doubt whether this quartet met the letter of Mexican law, and even greater doubt as to whether the "lawless ranchers and coast pirates" of the region would honor their presence, so a salvage tug was sent racing to protect the treasure. Boats were reported swarming around the wreck by the night of the 14th, and it seemed only a matter of time until the treasure was discovered. The tug arrived late in the afternoon of the 15th, and it was found that people had been aboard. However, they were unaware of the treasure, which was now reported in the newspapers to be worth only $185,000. Salvage divers cleared a path to the vaults with dynamite.

Today she lies on a sand bottom in about 50 feet of water, 20 yards east of the last wash rock south of Punta Tosca. Surge and currents can be a problem, but exploring her is great fun, and large jewfish, cabrilla, and lobsters abound. The wreck is badly broken up, huge metal plates and ribs lying about. The gold? As was usual in such circumstances, the owners and insurance companies wanted it believed that everything was recovered, and a photo of Miss La Vina Harper sitting on a large stack of gold and silver bars was prominently displayed in the newspapers. However, many believe that a substantial amount was not recovered, and several diving expeditions have been organized over the years. Harry Rieseberg salvaged $2,000 in gold, but a later group, working for almost 2 months, recovered nothing of value. Who knows, even if there is no gold left perhaps Mrs. Arthur Vaughn's $35,000 necklace still lies on the bottom.

A few more wrecks

The fishing vessels *West Point* and *Liberty Bell* will be found in Bahía Santa María, 1 mile, 054°, and 1.6 miles, 047°, respectively, from Punta Hughes. The 424-foot Canadian dry cargo ship *Westbank Park* was driven ashore by a storm outside Punta Entrada on October 6, 1945. She was a prominent landmark for a number of years, but she has slowly succumbed to the sea, until today only a rusty bow section is visible above water. She can be found by locating a striking lopsided, cone-shaped hill a mile west of Punta Entrada, saved from becoming an island only by a tiny sandspit. The wreck is 200 yards east of this hill. The fishing vessel *Shasta* was lost in 1965 in Canal Rehusa off the west end of Isla Creciente. Loaded with huge lobsters, she was once a popular dive site, but several years ago her mast fell over and she is now difficult to find. If you do locate her, watch out for sharks; Dave Buller had to scramble up the mast to escape a hungry mob of them.

Other activities

Fishing, diving, and visiting wrecks are not the only activities the area provides. The vast expanse of the bay and its breezes make it an excellent location for boardsailing. The downwind ride from Lopéz Mateos to Puerto Chale is one of the longest protected runs—70 miles—in Baja. Vast quantities of clams lie scattered all over the bottom of the bay. Gray whales can be seen in winter months, and whale-watchers in a boat anchored inside Punta Entrada are apt to see a magnificent ballet of breaching and spy-hopping. Whales frequently use Boca la Soledad, and up to a hundred of them can be seen cavorting in the narrow channel. *Panga* fishermen at Lopéz Mateos are often willing to take out whale-watchers. Those without a boat can see them from the beaches near town. Baja Expeditions, Wilderness: Alaska/Mexico, and NOLS offer kayak trips to the area, some involving whale-watching.

Surfers rarely visit the area because of the difficulty in getting to the outer beaches, but Punta Hughes has a long point break on south or west waves.

Mineral collectors will find magnesite, amphibole asbestos, and tremolite on Santa Margarita. The many miles of flat sand beach north of Lázaro contain a jackpot of flotsam, but a motorcycle or an ATV is required to inspect it completely. An enormous variety of birds inhabit the area, either permanently or seasonally. A complete check list might go to a hundred species, second only to the Bahía San Quintín area in numbers.

Camping in mangrove areas leaves something to be desired, as they can be boggy, buggy, and damp, so try the east side of Isla Magdalena, where sandy areas are to be found, or better yet, camp at the *bocas* leading to the ocean north of Lopéz Mateos. Here you have the best of two worlds: clean sand, lots of firewood, ocean surf fishing, with the mangroves close by. Santa Margarita also has many fine sandy beaches. If camping on the "inside," bring a stove, since mangrove wood makes a lot of smelly smoke. A tent will be appreciated unless you like to wake up wet with dew and covered by wind-blown sand. If you park in the mangrove areas be careful of the tides; we once returned to Puerto Chale from a wreck dive to find our vans on an island, surrounded by salt water and gooey mud. Kayakers and small-boaters should use care in the vicinity of Boca la Soledad and the other openings between the barrier islands—strong tidal currents can sweep the unwary out to sea to a certain capsize and an uncertain future in the breakers.

Anchorages and additional access

The bay and waterways can also be reached by unpaved roads leading to López Mateos, Puerto Chale, and several other points. Small boats can be launched at López Mateos and at the settlement at Puerto Chale.

The best anchorages for boats coasting north or south or fishing the offshore banks are at Bahía Santa María, inside Punta Entrada, around Punta Belcher, and off Puerto Magdalena. The anchorage at Punta Tosca is convenient, although surgy and sometimes rough. Good anchorages also can be found almost anywhere between San Carlos and López Mateos, and boats can use Boca la Soledad to gain access to the ocean in good weather. Canal Rehusa is too shallow for all but the smallest boats, and there are heavy currents and sand bars. It may be possible to obtain limited fuel, water, and emergency assistance at the small naval base at Puerto Cortés, at Puerto Alcatraz, and at Puerto Magdalena. The next anchorage south of Punta Tosca is at Cabo San Lucas.

● ●

❝ *A boating/biking/beachcombing adventure*

One bright winter day Reeve, Michael, and I decided to see what we could find in the way of treasures and wrecked ships on the outer beaches of Isla Magdalena. As we loaded our two motorcycles into our cartop boat, the word spread through López Mateos, and within minutes we were surrounded by a mob of incredulous schoolboys, each insisting on helping. Hoping that we could land on the crescent of flat beach at Boca la Soledad, we headed north through the calm waterway separating Magdalena and the mainland. Floating very low in the water, we passed a pod of gray whales, which seemed to swim closer to see the unusual sight. Several Mexican fishermen were taken aback at the motorcycle-equipped whale-watchers, and we could see them shaking their heads in wonderment.

Landing with no problems, we pulled the boat high up on the beach, mounted our bikes, rounded the point, and headed south along the magnificent Pacific beach. Within a few miles we found the fantail of a large wooden vessel and then the ribs and timbers of another. Within 20 minutes a beautiful 40-foot sloop appeared ahead, intact, unmarked and ready for sea except for its sails and electronics (don't rush to the scene; it was later salvaged). The next wreck was a Catalina 27 sailboat, inspiring some deep thought by Reeve, who owned an identical boat and had been considering a trip to Baja in it. An intense feeling of exhilaration prevailed as we sped down the deserted beaches at 50 miles an hour. The breakers put up a low mist which limited our view of the beach ahead to a mile or two, heightening the mystery of the place. Large flocks of sea birds scrambled for a takeoff, accurately bombing us with tokens of their displeasure at being disturbed. Secure in their isolation, dozing seals scarcely knew we were there until we had already passed. Soon, we found a small sloop, and then a capstan and a keelson from a large vessel, and then another unattached fantail and sev-

eral winches. Five miles north of Cabo San Lázaro a 450-foot ship lay parallel to the water's edge. She was heavily damaged, but firebricks from her boilers were still lined up in neat rows, some missing sections forming nesting sites for ospreys. Close to Lázaro was the vessel Jupiter, *of similar size and construction. After riding about 38 miles, we arrived at the lighthouse and inspected its extensive collection of flotsam and nautical trash.*

With great anticipation, we set our odometers and headed north for the highlight of the adventure, an attempt to locate the Golden City. *The accounts of the survivors in the newspapers of the day placed the wreck 11 miles north of Lázaro, so we simply headed north along the beach, and when our odometers said 11, we stopped our bikes and started searching. With almost magical luck, we found her in minutes, just beyond the first line of dunes. Massive timbers 16 inches square and up to 40 feet long lay everywhere, along with thousands of bronze and iron fastenings. Mysterious buried objects lay just below the surface, each having length, width, and height, but a consistency of little more than iron-stained sand. Planking that once sheathed the hull was studded with hundreds of small bronze nails that held her copper sheathing. Huge amounts of broken ceramics and glass bottles lay over an area of several acres, apparently marking the location of the ship's dining and cooking areas. There was no sign of her massive boilers, of her giant steam cylinder, with its 8-foot, 9-inch bore and 12-foot stroke, nor of her 40-foot paddle wheels. We took nothing except for a small sample of wood, which I later sent to the University of Arizona Dendrochronology (Tree-Ring Analysis) Laboratory. The lab identified the wood as red pine, of East Coast origin, about 1862. Right on, U of A; she was built in New York in 1863!*

By dusk we were back in camp, trying to tell a crowd of Mexican boys about what we had found. To our surprise, some of them knew a little of the history of the Ciudad de Oro. *Over a campfire they told us tales of other shipwrecks and pirate treasures that lay on the outer beaches, and named several vessels that I had never heard of before, providing reason enough for our next boating/biking/beachcombing adventure.* **❞**

● ●

■ ■ ■ ■ ■ ■ ■ ■ ■ ■ ■ ■ ■

On the Transpeninsular at Ciudad Constitución, KM 212+

Except in its final miles, the highway between Ciudad Constitución and La Paz is the second most boring drive in Baja, and the only boondocking sites are little more than side roads away from traffic noise. Since it is 131 miles long, bicyclists will spend a night on the road.

KM	Location
198	**Villa Morelos.** Groceries, restaurant, long-dis-

Will Waterman

Bruce Barrus provides the music while Elizabeth Wolfe and Scott Wright do the paddling on a trip to Bahia Magdalena

tance phone, beer.

157 **Santa Rita.** Tire repair, limited auto parts, restaurant, groceries, pickup road southwest (signed) to Puerto Chale, 15 miles.

154 Boondocking site, north side of road, traffic noise may be a problem. Hematite and malachite are found nearby.

135 Road southeast, modest boondocking site.

130 One hundred yards southeast of the KM marker another dirt road leads south to several other boondocking areas.

127+ Groceries, restaurant.

127 Start gentle ups and downs until KM 34, becoming a little steeper as you continue.

122+ Tiny café.

112 **Las Pocitas.** Tire repair, mechanic.

110+ Café.

100 **El Cién.** Cafés, stores, beer, tire repair, PEMEX (MD).

80 Sedan road southwest (signed) to El Conejo, 10 miles. Long a favorite with surfers, Conejo has easy access and excellent lefts and rights on a small rocky point, working well in almost any swell, although best when they are from the northwest. The place is windswept, with frequent cross-onshore winds, making it popular with heavy-weather boardsailors, especially during frontal conditions. In summer, it can be a blow-out all day. Be careful of a strong current paralleling the shore and of frequent sneaker waves. Driftwood sometimes can be found for campfires, and there is good surf fishing. Lobsters and oysters may be purchased from the locals. Diving potential is almost zero. Secluded beaches and sandy campsites can be found for many miles to the south.

55+ Sedan road southwest to campsites. This road, which leads to the Punta Bentonita area, is graded but washboarded. Go right (200°) at the side road at Mile 0.8. Don't expect too much here; it's just a few flat places with no scenery to speak of, but at least it's out of sight, road noise should not be a problem, and you won't be impeding traffic on the main dirt road. The side road continues on a short distance and loops back to the main dirt road, but large rigs may have trouble turning around.

34 Magnificent views of La Paz and Isla Espíritu Santo. Generally moderate downgrades and then level road into La Paz.

21+ Agricultural inspection station.

17 Road northwest to Evaristo, signed SAN JUAN DE LA COSTA. Those continuing on the Transpeninsular shoiuld skip the following section.

 Side trip to San Evaristo. As noted earlier, the highway from Ciudad Constitución is the second dullest section on the Transpeninsular. However, the dullest, between Guerrero Negro and San Ignacio, had a gem waiting near the end (San Ignacio), and this section is no different. The trip to Evaristo is best made early in the morning in clear weather. Set odometer. Turn at the sign and drive northwest. The washboard gets bad past the end of the pavement, but since the road is graded, sedans and motor homes can continue. The road follows the shoreline, and there are a number of places to camp. Most beaches are pebble and cobble, but sand will be found at Miles 20.0 and 22.8. At Mile 23.8 take the right (010°) fork (the left fork leads to San Juan de la Costa, a phosphate mining town with a public restaurant and water from spigots).

Mother Nature soon begins the most colorful display of sedimentary showmanship in all of Baja. Some layers of sandstone are graced with easily described colors, such as black, purple, gray, and pink, and there are three shades each of green and beige. Others require physical analogy: persimmon, cinnamon, coffee, guacamole, salmon, and grape Popsicle. Up close, each color is muted, just touches of pastel in otherwise ordinary rock, but the "big picture," from a distance, is stun-

ning. Erosion has carved strange shapes; there is a turtle with a green shell spotted with brown, and a salmon castle with green battlements. At Mile 29.0 the road squeezes between the blue Cortez and a cliff of brick-red, green, and tan rock, the most colorful half mile drive in Baja. Past the cliff, add olive drab, burnt umber and salmon-tan to the list of colors.

Only pickups and four-wheel-drives should continue beyond Mile 31.2. There is another beautiful display just ahead; the road winds up a huge wedge of rock, and near its top is a castle seemingly molded out of sand, perched on a green cliff plunging into the blue sea. When just past the sand castle, stop and peek over the edge for another visual treat. The road soon winds inland to avoid Punta el Mechudo, with loose rock, switchbacks and grades to 27%. The waters immediately off Mechudo may not strike you as a promising fishing area, but it is often one of the better in the Cortez, and dorado and billfish are found a mile from shore in the hot months. At Mile 33.5 the road gets its turn; ordinary gray to this point, it becomes green, not just faintly green but green. The road returns to the coastal plain and to ordi-

We found this beautiful yacht stranded on Isla Magdalena. It was later salvaged unharmed

nary desert colors at Mile 37.4, and arrives at Evaristo at Mile 45.6, described in the previous chapter.

■■■■■■■■■■■■■■■■■■■■■

Back on the Transpeninsular at KM 17

KM	Location
14+	Oasis los Aripez Trailer Park. Full hookups, showers, rest rooms, laundry, restaurant, bar, pool.
14	Cafés, auto parts, *tortilla* factory, pharmacy.
9	Road south (signed) to La Paz International Airport.
6	Junction; turn right (south) for the Cape region. Those headed south should turn to page 222.
5+	The offices of the State Secretary of Tourism are located on the south side of the road. To the north, there is a small marina adjacent to the Crowne Plaza Resort with a shallow (10%) launch ramp, but it is not yet in operation.
4+	Casa Blanca RV Park. Full hookups, shade trees, laundry, pool, tennis, showers, rest rooms, small store, long-distance phone—a nice park, clean and litter-free. Hospital, pharmacy, and motel nearby.
4	PEMEX under construction. El Cardón Trailer Park; full hookups, showers, rest rooms, dump station, laundry, pool, *palapas*, shade trees. A laundry service will be found 75 yards east of El Cardón. La Paz RV Park, found by turning north just west of the VW dealer, has concrete pads, full hookups, pool, laundry, rest rooms, showers.
0	**La Paz.**

La Paz

While Santa Rosalía was a copper town, and Mulegé and Loreto were founded by the Jesuits for religious reasons, La Paz started out as an outpost for men with a more adventurous quest in mind, the pursuit of treasure. In late 1533 or early 1534 Hernán Cortés, conqueror of Mexico, sent 2 ships to explore the west coast of Mexico, looking for a shorter way from "New Spain" to the sources of the spices so highly prized in Europe and, of course, for gold and pearls. The crew of one ship mutinied and sailed into a large bay, where most of them were killed by the local Indians. However, the few survivors told of pearls, and in 1535 Cortés himself founded a colony, which failed in less than 2 years. In 1596 Sebastián Vizcaíno attempted to found a colony in the area, which he named La Paz (The Peace), since the Indians were now found to be friendly. However, the stockade soon burned down and the place was abandoned.

In 1683 another colonizing expedition journeyed to the area, this one led by Jesuit Father Eusebio Kino and accompanied by Admiral Otondo y Antillión and a group of marines. The Indians had changed their minds again, shooting arrows and carrying on, so the admiral invited a group of them to a feast, which ended when he fired a cannonball into their midst. By 1720 the cannonball had been forgotten, and a Jesuit mission was established by Fathers Jaime Bravo and Juan de Ugarte. However, there were further uprisings, which ended only after epidemics had killed most of the Indians. With few souls left to save, the mission was abandoned in 1749, and it was not until 1811 that a permanent settlement was established. In 1829 Loreto, the territorial capital, was severely damaged by a *chubasco*, and the growing village of La Paz was named the capital the following year. It was captured by American forces in 1847 during the war with Mexico, and was held until passage of the Treaty of Guadalupe-Hidalgo ended the fighting in 1848. Adventurer William Walker tried to take over the city in 1853, but failed. By the 1950s, La Paz had become famed for its fine fishing and as a vacation destination for Americans and mainland Mexicans. Baja California Sur gained Mexican statehood in 1974, and La Paz was named its capital.

Compared to the rest of the peninsula, today's La Paz seems to be a place of extremes, with the prettiest women in the shortest skirts, the ugliest dogs, the most flowers—a riot of color at every part of the spectrum—the least visible one-way signs, and the most shoe stores per capita on the peninsula. The growing number of ice cream shops and *dulcerías* (candy stores) is surely considered a blessing by the town's many dentists. The place is growing up, cellular phone service is available, and you can get a computerized horoscope. As a town modernizes, things tend to become more specialized, and La Paz is no exception: there are a number of health food stores, and even a vegetarian restaurant (9). La Paz is advancing economically, and the tree-shaded streets are being paved, new homes are being built, and the cars plying the streets are of more desirable makes and models than in some American towns.

Despite these changes, La Paz does not seem to be in danger of losing its Mexican identity by assuming a homogenized culture like Cabo San Lucas—it is distinctly Mexican and is staying that way. Many private businesses observe *siesta* between 1 P.M. and 3 P.M. The weather is fine from November to May, with warm days and balmy nights, and a breeze called the *coromuel* keeps the place cool in the summer.

The "downtown" area, roughly bounded by Av. Allende, Hildalgo, Prieto, and the bay, holds many of the town's attractions. (The inset on the accompanying map describes this area.) There are many souvenir and crafts shops selling T-shirts, sea shells, carvings, paintings, *serapes*, posters, jewelry, music cassettes featuring all the latest tunes from Mexico City, *sombreros* large enough to make the most discriminating *bandido* proud, and just about anything else you could need or want. The beautiful Malecón has sand beaches, *palapas*, and palm-shaded benches, and vendors hawk snacks and cold beverages from carts. The Los Arcos Hotel (18) has a coffee shop, bar, and gift shop, as well as an activities desk where fishing and dive trips can be arranged. The Restaurant Bermejo at the hotel is excellent. There are a number of good restaurants, including El Camarón Feliz, a *palapa* just northwest of the hotel, Carlos 'n Charlie's (5), Restaurant Kiwi (2), and Restaurant Adriana (1). Although the pizzas produced by La Fabula (3) bear little resemblance to those of Palermo, they are good in their own way.

Baja Outdoor Activities (6) offers the most imaginative and eclectic array of Baja adventure activities available, including a sea-kayak trip that circumnavigates Espíritu Santo, shorter trips to the island, mountain-bike/sea-kayak combos, a trip which includes fly fishing from kayaks, a boardsailing/sea kayaking combo, kayaking trips from Loreto to La Paz, and trips combining sea kayaking and whale-watching. If this doesn't leave you exhausted, there is a trip combining sea kayaking, snorkeling, hiking, island exploration, and whale-watching. Rentals, day trips, comprehensive outfitting services, and a beginner kayak certification course are available. Kayak rentals include plastic to fiberglass, single or double, closed-cockpit or sit-on-top. Walk-ins are welcome. Scuba Baja Joe (14) has full rentals, air, and a number of *pangas* with engines up to 200 horsepower (most La Paz dive boats are equipped with large engines because the best dive sites are some distance away), and offers trips to all local dive sites, including night dives, plus NAUI and PADI instruction. Deportivo La Paz (7) has sales (no rentals) of diving equipment such as suits, gloves, masks, spear guns, regulators, goody bags, and small, hard-to-find parts like mask and fin straps, spear points, tank valves, rubber slings, and wishbones, as well as fishing tackle and T-shirts. Deportes Calafia (10), Deportes America (8), and Deportes Ortiz (17) are close approximations to north-of-the-border sporting-goods stores.

There are a number of attractions outside the downtown area you may wish to visit. The Museo de Anthropologia (19) has photographs and exhibits on Indian life and rock art, the history of Baja California Sur, folk art, minerals, and fossil shells. Artesanias Cuauhtemoc (34) sells fabrics, place mats, tablecloths, tapestries, bed spreads, and clothing of cotton and wool. All in-house products are made on foot-powered looms, the only electricity being utilized by the lights.

You should have little trouble finding food and supplies. There are two large, well-stocked department stores, Dorian's and La Perla de La Paz, (11, 13). The large MAS store (16) is the rough equivalent of a Target store. The CCCs (31, 38) are well-stocked supermarkets, every bit as good as anything in the US. Both have ATM machines, which are also to be found at most banks. Stop at Baja Celular (26) if you need to establish roaming service. Baja Net (4), a computer services office, has Pentium PCs, a scanner, B&W and color printers, and Internet access. Ace Hardware (20) contains just about what you have come to expect at home. Help is not far away should you encounter mechanical difficul-

ties, for there are a number of dealers with parts and repair facilities: Dodge (32), Dodge/Chrysler (25), Nissan (36), Volkswagen at KM 3, west of town, and Ford/Lincoln, also at KM 3. The large Chevrolet dealership (30) handles parts and service for Chevys, as well as other GM makes, Johnson/Evinrude outboard parts and repairs, some trailer items (hitches, bearings), and marine accessories like pumps and anchors. Baja California Motors (39) handles parts for Nissan, Dodge, Ford, and Toyota, as well as Chevrolet and other GMC makes. There are numerous other parts stores, mechanics, radiator, clutch, and brake shops, and new tire sales and repairs. Agencia Arjona (23) is a Johnson/Evinrude dealer, and sells tools, hardware, camping equipment, and Coleman stoves. Mercury/Mariner parts and repairs are available (35). They can repair sterndrives; parts not in stock can take 3 to 7 days. There is a Yamaha dealer (40), which also has a very small supply of Mariner parts. An LPG yard is located at KM 203, south of town. There are a number of PEMEX stations: (12, MD), (24, M), (27, M), (37, MD), and (41, MPD), and several new ones are under construction.

In addition to the RV parks on the southwestern outskirts of town, there is a nice one in town. Aquamarina RV Park (28) is the most beautiful RV facility in La Paz, and has sites with full hookups shaded by trees, bougainvillea, and other flowering plants, rest rooms, showers, laundry machines, a pool, boat and trailer storage, and a concrete launch ramp (14%). Ask to see the orchid garden. During the hot months call the park before you go: they accept guests only by reservation for stays of more than three days at this time of the year.

The accompanying map shows the location of many other restaurants, stores, and other attractions that may be of interest. There are a number of travel agencies in town that can arrange fishing, diving, and whale-watching trips, horseback riding, ATVs, boardsailing, water-skiing, and so forth. In addition, the hotels catering to visitors from the north have reservations desks. Additional information on restaurants, hotels, stores, night spots, and such can be obtained from the State Secretary of Tourism office, located at KM 5+ west of town, as well as an office across the street from Carlos 'n Charlie's.

The waters north and east of La Paz have long been among the most prominent fishing locations on the continent, and a number of world records for sailfish, roosterfish, and amberjack have been set here. The best fishing is in deep water off the east sides of Islas Espíritu Santo and Partida Sur, primarily for wahoo, yellowfin tuna, and dorado from June to November, marlin in the hot months, and sailfish from July through October. Yellowtail migrate from the upper Cortez and are found in large numbers in winter and early spring off rocky points, reefs, and headlands throughout the region. The Jack Velez Fleet operates a fleet of cruisers and *pangas*, and fishes Espíritu Santo, Isla Cerralvo, and the La Paz area—they have a desk at the Los Arcos. Fisherman's Fleet offers trips to Ensenada los Muertos, fishing the prolific waters around Cerralvo out of *pangas*. Reservations can be made at the Los Arcos or by telephone.

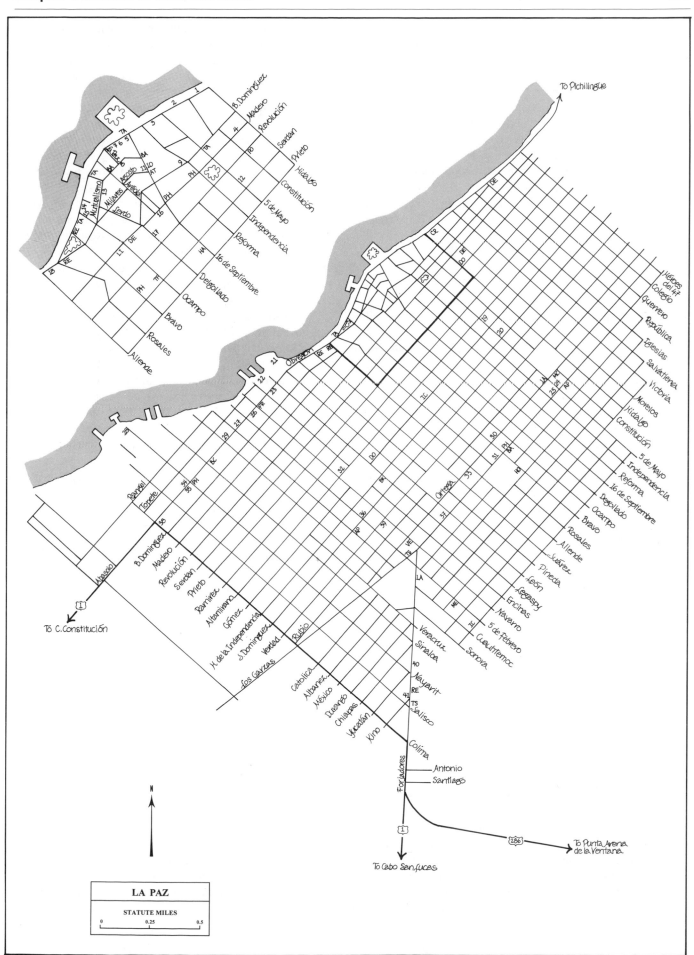

To Pichilingue

B. Domínguez
Madero
Revolución
Serdán
Prieto
Hidalgo
Constitución
5 de Mayo
Independencia
Reforma
16 de Septiembre
Degollado
Ocampo
Bravo
Rosales
Allende

Obregón

Héroes del 47
Colegio
Guerrero
República
Iglesias
Salvatierra
Victoria
Morelos
Hidalgo
Constitución
5 de Mayo
Independencia
Reforma
16 de Septiembre
Degollado
Ocampo
Bravo
Rosales
Allende
Suárez
Pineda
León
Legaspy
Encinas
Navarro
5 de Febrero
Cuauhtémoc
Sonora

Ortega

Rangel
Topete

B. Domínguez
Madero
Revolución
Serdán
Prieto
Ramírez
Altamirano
Gómez
H. de la Independencia
J. Domínguez
Verdad
Los Garzas
Rubio

Católica
Albáñez
México
Durango
Chiapas
Yucatán
Kino

Veracruz
Sinaloa
Nayarit
Jalisco
Colima

Antonio
Santiago

Utpesso

To C. Constitución

To Cabo San Lucas

To Punta Arena de la Ventana

Forjadores

N

LA PAZ

STATUTE MILES

0   0.25   0.5

Information on other fleets and boats is available from any hotel or travel office in La Paz. Jonathan Roldan's Sportfishing Services, another prominent fishing fleet, will be described shortly. Tony Reyes Fishing Tours offers trips out of La Paz that range between the Mulegé area and the Bancos Gorda, and Fishing International has package trips.

Most divers head for Espíritu Santo, Partida Sur, Los Islotes, the wreck of the *Salvatierra*, or Marisla Seamount, which are described in later sections. The best months are generally April through June for spearfishermen, June through October for photographers and nature-watchers. *Marisla II*, operated by La Paz Diving Service, offers dive expeditions throughout the southern Cortez; she docks at Marina Marisla in front of the Aquamarina RV Park. Owners Richard and Mary Lou Adcock are pioneers in Cortez diving, and have operated La Paz Diving Service since 1957. The boats *Don José* and *Río Rita*, operated by Baja Expeditions (29), offer a wide variety of diving and natural-history trips.

Centro de Buceo Carey (21) has full dive sales and rentals, compressed air, a portable rental compressor, and several *pangas* equipped with Biminis and radios, and offers day-trips to Los Islotes, *Salvatierra*, Marisla Seamount, and other attractions. SSI classes are available, and liveaboard trips are offered aboard the 73-foot *Muy Pronto*. Scu-Baja Dive Center is the newest dive operation in La Paz, with an office (15), boats, and rental equipment. Full equipment sales and rentals and compressed air are available. Trips are offered to Marisla Seamount, Los Islotes, *Salvatierra*, Cerralvo, and Isla San Francisco aboard 2 26-knot dive boats (3 more are on order), each carrying 12 divers. Package trips and night dives are offered, and PADI instruction includes a resort course through various levels of certification, as well as a number of specialty courses. Trips to Agua Verde and a "Camp-and-Dive" trip to Espíritu Santo can be arranged. ATVs and kayaks are for rent, and walk-ins are welcome. There are also new dive shops at the Cortez Club, the Club Hotel Cantamar, and Tecolote, all described shortly.

With its fine harbor and many services and attractions ashore, La Paz is a sailor's city, and often over a hundred foreign yachts are swinging at anchor in the bay at the height of the cruising season. The "La Paz Waltz" requires good anchoring equipment and technique because tidal currents of up to 6 knots swing the anchored boats first one way and then the other. A local summer breeze called the *coromuel* was supposedly named after the pirate Cromwell when locals observed that he sailed out with the strong breeze that sprung up from the south in the afternoon and arrived back with the northwesterlies early the next day. The *coromuel* is often felt as far north as Evaristo and as far south as Muertos, providing welcome relief from the heat, but plaguing boaters and yachtsmen in exposed anchorages. La Paz is a port of entry, with a COTP, *Aduana*, and *Migración* (inquire at the State Secretary of Tourism for their current locations). The Moorings maintains an office at Marina Palmira, located at KM 2.5 on the road to Pichilingue, and offers a wide variety of yacht charters. Inquire at the marinas or at the office of the State Secretary of Tourism about other yacht charters.

The marina situation in La Paz is vastly better than in the past. Marina de La Paz (22) offers the full range of facilities and services you would expect at a marina in the US, including slips having potable water and electrical service, fueling facilities, maintenance services, and mechanical repairs. Their marine store carries a variety of maintenance materials, parts, and accessories with familiar brand names, and an inventory of trailer parts, including seals, bearings, hubs, springs, couplers, V-blocks and rollers, roller shafts, hitch balls, lights, and U-bolts, most of it oriented toward boat trailers but possibly useful on other types as well. There are also a shower room, a laundromat, public rest rooms, and a long-distance telephone. The Dock Restaurant at the marina serves good meals attuned to American tastes. The concrete launch ramp (14%) leads to protected waters, although maneuvering room and parking are limited. There are also two other marinas, which will be described shortly.

A trip to Tecolote can occupy several pleasant hours. Marina Palmira, at KM 2+, is one of the finest in Baja, offering slips, utilities, storage, gasoline, diesel, repair, and painting, and the marine store has items that may be of interest to travelers, such as small trailer tires and hitches, wheel bearing assemblies, water pumps, ice, beer, fishing tackle, and a variety of hardware and electrical items. The steep (17%) concrete launch ramp leads to protected water, there is plenty of parking, and your rig will be watched by guards while you are away.

The La Concha Beach Resort at KM 5 has a restaurant, several bars, a gift shop, and a reservation desk. The Cortez Club, next door to the resort, offers water- and jet skiing, boardsailing, Hobie cats, kayaking, and bicycling, and walk-ins are welcome. The dive shop has complete rentals and sells equipment and compressed air, and PADI instruction is available. A fleet of 12 dive boats with multi-lingual crews will take you to dive sites throughout the southern Cortez, and liveaboard trips, wreck dives, and night dives can be arranged. Jonathan Roldan's Sportfishing Services at the club offers fishing expeditions to such hot spots as Cerralvo, Muertos, Ánimas, and Espíritu Santo, and fly-fishing and ultra-light tackle trips are available. A weekly fishing report on the Cortez Club Internet site will tell you how things have been going.

The boat yard at KM 7+ has a marine railway and does repairs, bottom jobs, etc. There is a restaurant and beach at KM 10, and a boondocking site at KM 11. Playa de Tesoro, at KM 13, has a fine beach, a café, and *palapas*. Ferries from the terminal at KM 17 provide service to Topolobampo and Mazatlán.

Club Hotel Cantamar, just north of the terminal, is a sports lodge catering to divers and kayakers. The lodge has rooms, a dockside café, a laundry, and a pool, Full dive equipment sales and rentals are available, as well as compressed air and PADI instruction. Eleven boats, ranging from 22-foot *pangas* to a 42-foot cruiser, carry divers as far north as Isla San Francisco, and east and south to Cerralvo. The lodge has a rarity, an installed recompression chamber, one of only three privately-owned chambers on the peninsula, and they can make hydrostatic tests of tanks. Ask to see the huge compressor, the largest in Baja. The lodge rents kayaks for day use, provides full kayak outfits for longer jaunts, and has rental waverunners, jet-skis, and paddle boats. Adjacent to the lodge, Marina Pichilingue has slips, water, electricity, sewage, fuel, dry storage, and a boat ramp (14%). The ramp is open to the public, a small fee being charged, and parking is available on the premises.

In January 1998 my son and I were at Cantamar and witnessed a wonderful event—3 humpback whales repeatedly breaching, sometimes almost clear of the water, over a period of 10 minutes or so, all within 50 yards of a cabin cruiser. The people in the cruiser will surely treasure the memory.

The public launch ramp in the cove north of Cantamar can be found by turning left (west) at the *palapa* restaurants at KM 18. The shallow, rough concrete ramp (10%) is protected from waves, but there is no security for your rig when you are gone. However, there is adequate parking, and they are the closest ramps to the great fishing and diving to the north and east. At KM 23, a **Y** is encountered; the left (250°) curves around the north shore of Ensenada Balandra (Sloop Cove), where a beautiful sand beach, *palapas*, and toilets will be found. Watch for herons, egrets, and other marsh birds in the coves in this area.

The right (055°) fork continues for several more kilometers to Playa Tecolote (Owl Beach). There is RV parking, a number of *palapas*, a few equipped with barbecues, public rest rooms, several restaurants, and one of the finest sand beaches in Baja. Beach Club El Tecolote has basic dive equipment rentals (no compressor, but filled tanks are available), and offers local dives on a 22-foot *panga*, as well as renting kayaks, jet skis, and water-sports equipment. *Jejénes* are sometimes present. Portable boats can be launched over the beach, but the place is exposed and waves can make it difficult. Boardsailors will find exposed onshore conditions.

■ The coast to the north and the Salvatierra

Three good anchorages, Bahía Pichilingue, Caleta Lobos, and Ensenada Balandra, will be found 5, 8, and 10 miles north of the east tip of El Mogote. All are easily accessible by road, and hence fishing is generally poor. Pichilingue is an all-weather harbor and the location of the ferry terminal. The preferred anchorage is at the south end of the bay, where a US coaling station was active during the First World War. A large anchor and the wreck of a wooden vessel sheathed with copper lie in 2 fathoms off the pier. Isla Lobos, recognizable by its white coating of guano, and Roca Lobos, a rocky islet to the north, have fair diving. Caleta Lobos, east of Roca Lobos, is open to the southwest, but provides good protection from other directions. Sandy Balandra is scenic, and its beaches are often compared to powdered

sugar. Novice boardsailors love the place, but yachties should beware—the bay tends to be shallow, especially in its eastern reaches. Pichilingue beaches leave a lot to be desired as campsites, but kayakers will find clean sand beaches and good camping at both Lobos and Balandra. The first good anchorage along the coast to the south is Muertos, described in the next chapter.

Salvatierra, an ex-US Navy Second World War LST, sank in Canal de San Lorenzo in 1976, and is now one of the premiere dive sites in the La Paz area. Colorful photographic subjects abound, including yellowtail surgeonfish, grunts, goatfish, angelfish, morays, rays, and several species of large parrot fish. Her propellers and rudders are easily accessible, and large schools of fish hide under her stern, often so dense you literally have to brush them aside to swim through. The ship was carrying a cargo of trucks and trailers, and many still can be seen scattered over the sandy bottom.

The wreck is relatively easy to find. There are two aid-to-navigation structures in Canal de San Lorenzo: the southernmost, Scout Shoal Light, is a concrete tower, while the northernmost, San Lorenzo Shoal Light, is a metal pipe structure. The wreck is located 1 mile east of the latter structure. When you are over the wreck Scout Shoal Light should bear 206°, San Lorenzo Shoal Light 267°. If visibility is good, the wreck can be seen from 200 yards away as a large dark patch. Local fishing boats frequent the vicinity. She lies in 57 feet, her highest part rising to within 23 feet of the surface. Tidal currents in excess of 3 knots are possible in the channel, requiring divers and kayakers to plan their activities using the tide tables.

■ Isla Espíritu Santo

Dramatically and unexpectedly beautiful, with deeply indented coves along its west coast and high bluffs formed from folded strata of pink, red, white, yellow, and black, Espíritu Santo is a favorite with divers, sailors, and kayakers. Excellent campsites can be found on the sand beaches in most of the coves on the west side, and north of Punta Bonanza on the east side. A hot spring is reported at Punta Bonanza. Kayakers should be able to scrounge drinking water from the numerous yachts normally at anchor, enabling lengthy stays. Water for washing and bathing can sometimes be obtained from a well found about 150 yards up the canyon from the building on the beach at the north end of Caleta el Candeleros. The surface of the water in the well is normally about 16 feet below ground level, so you will need a bucket and a line. The slightly saline water might serve as drinking water in an emergency (boil or treat before use). This well, as well as the one mentioned shortly, often goes dry, so don't rely too heavily on it.

Bahía San Gabriel is only a fair anchorage, being a bit too shallow and open to *coromuel* winds. A small coral reef will be found near its north shore, readily seen due to its dark color. A hike ashore is worthwhile. Stone basins and building foundations of the old oyster farm can be explored along the southeast shore, and millions of fiddler crabs skitter through the mangroves. Birding is excellent, with a full complement of shore and sea birds. Espíritu Santo is home to one species of ground squirrel, two of mice, one rat, ring-tailed cat, and the famous black jackrabbit. Twenty species of reptiles and amphibians inhabit Espíritu Santo and Partida Sur. Fine shelling can be found near Punta Lupona and Punta Bonanza.

Diving and snorkeling around Islas Gallo and Gallina are good, and the north side of Isla Ballena has good scuba diving and serves as a fair anchorage during *coromuel* winds. There are several dive-through caves on the island, one with a pocket of air allowing you to surface. Candeleros is a fair anchorage, also open to the *coromuel*.

Caleta Partida, separating Espíritu Santo and Partida Sur, is the best anchorage in the area, its roughly circular shape giving fair protection from the *coromuel*, and the low spits jutting from each island allowing fresh breezes on hot nights. If you anchor near the northwest shore, the bluffs bring welcome shade in the afternoon. Dinghys and kayaks can transit the shallow channel between the islands. There are several fishing settlements in the vicinity.

■ Isla Partida Sur

Although very narrow and tending to be hot, El Cardóncito, located just south of El Cardónal, is a fair anchorage, and the surrounding rocks are interesting. The reef extending to the southwest from its mouth is one of the best snorkeling sites in the area. Large groupers inhabit its outer reaches, but they seem thoroughly checked out as to the intent of spearfishermen. A masonry well will be found about 150 yards up the canyon from the small sand beach, its depth and water quality being about the same as those of the well on Espíritu Santo. It is not dependable, and is often dry. The trail to the well continues to the top, providing nice views of Caleta Partida. The next cove to the north, El Cardónal, almost cuts the island in half, and the low profile of the land to

the east allows breezes. Ensenada Grande, with lots of scenery and sandy beaches, is a favorite anchorage with many people, although it is open and sometimes surgy. Just an open roadstead, El Embudo provides protection from south weather, and there is an excellent camping beach. A wreck lies in the cove.

■ Los Islotes

Los Islotes are islets north of Partida Sur. The surrounding waters have the best diving in the area, and are often visited by La Paz dive boats. The greatest attraction is a colony of friendly sea lions, who put on a wonderful show of underwater acrobatics, often doing barrel rolls around divers and indulging in a one-sided game of "chicken," rushing in and veering off at the last second. The best diving is among the boulders on the north and east sides. In general the site tends to be deep, although there is limited snorkeling close in. Many

We anchored our sloop Gypsy *in El Cardoncito during a 1982 trip*

species of fish can be seen, most notably mantas, sharks, king angelfish, and yellowtail surgeonfish, along with many octopuses. A reef abounding with gamefish and gorgonians will be found starting 800 yards southwest. Scuba is required over most of its area.

■ Marisla Seamount

As described in Chapter 2, manta rays and hammerhead sharks have made Marisla Seamount (El Bajo) the most famous dive site in Baja California. The seamount is located 8.2 miles, 032° from Los Islotes. When you are over the site the largest of the Islotes will bear 212°, the highest point of Isla San Francisco 287°, and the left tangent of Espíritu Santo 166°. Local commercial fishermen often anchor a buoy on the seamount, and in calm weather they fish the area in *pangas*. There are 3 distinct underwater peaks arrayed along a 300-yard line running 120–300°, the northernmost rising to within 83 feet of the surface, the central peak to 52 feet, and the southern to 69 feet. The central peak, with its shallow depths and relatively flat top, is the primary dive site and anchoring location.

Don't get your hopes too high on the mantas; the friendlies are rare. In the past, the best months have been August and September. Marlin, tuna, and jacks have been seen nearby. John Riffe tells of a group of divers who came up from their first dive raving about the huge fish. One man, though, complained that he had seen nothing. After his second dive he still had seen nothing, so John followed him down on the third dive. The scene

Mike frolics with friends at Los Islotes

was priceless: the diver was found annoying a tiny moray in a pile of boulders, all the time being observed by a huge jewfish not more than 3 feet away. The hammerheads seem to prefer the north peak. The best way to dive it is to note the direction of the current and set up a drift dive.

• •

❝ *Cloudburst*

As we headed home we were jabbering happily about our diving trip to the islands north of La Paz, when we found our eyes struggling to focus on the terrain ahead. The familiar desert brush, the sere plains, the dark clouds, all had disappeared into a gray veil—rain! We soon passed into a torrent; it was not mere rain but a cloudburst, and for an instant the front of our VW van was immersed in a waterfall while the rear was dry. We were forced to drive at a crawl, and after a mile or two my brother slammed on the brakes so hard we were thrown against our seatbelts; two figures were standing in the middle of the road. They proved to be that species of young American known to the locals as "heeeepies," complete with backpacks, bedrolls, combat boots, and a drooping cardboard sign announcing their destination, Los Angeles. Impressed with the effectiveness of their hitchhiking technique, we slid the side door open and they jumped in. Although thoroughly soaked and shivering, they were cheerful and began to reiterate their experiences with an astounding variety of tidal waves, earthquakes, typhoons, and tornadoes.

Villa Insurgentes was awash in 2 feet of water, and as we turned east toward Loreto we drove up to a number of Mexican drivers sitting in their trucks in front of a large pond extending across the road. Against much generous advice, we started across, assuring them of the invulnerability of German engineering. Exactly at the point of no return the engine gasped, steamed a bit and died. Amid joyous honking from our audience we got out and pushed the van to shallower water ahead. Ten minutes of drying the ignition system revived the engine, and we pulled slowly away, our hippie friends displaying a well-known Italian street gesture to our detractors through the rear window.

The rain moderated, but many low spots were deeply flooded and the engine quit three or four more times. At one point, a torrent of water once again killed the engine, and the van was slowly pushed sideways, the wheels skidding sideways in tiny hops. Through a small miracle we got the engine started again before we went sideways into a morass of mud, and we finally reached shallower water. As night fell we began to encounter boulders *and rocks which had slid onto the road, forcing us to stop and clear the debris in the light of our headlights. Finally, the long hours and heavy work made sleep essential. The rain had stopped and our headlights illuminated two thatch-roofed* palapas*, erected at the bottom of a steep slope. A boulder larger than the span of my arms had rolled down the slope and punched a huge hole through one of them. Too tired to give it much thought, we blew up our air mattresses under the other* palapa *and crashed. After several hours we found we were all still wide awake, waiting for the sound of the next boulder, so we hurriedly packed up and left. Dawn found us speeding past Loreto, a golden sun rising into a clear blue sky.* ,,

● ●

■ ■

On the Transpeninsular in La Paz, KM 0

The road starts out level, with only minor ups-and-downs until KM 169. Fence-building ranchers are making it increasingly difficult to find good campsites.

KM	Location
0/216	Start new KM numbering sequence.
213	Route BCS 286 to Punta Arena de la Ventana and Ensenada los Muertos. Those continuing on the Transpeninsular should turn to page 224.

➤ **Side trip to La Ventana, El Sargento, Ensenada los Muertos, Punta Arena de la Ventana, and Isla Cerralvo.** Turn east at KM 213, about 2.5 miles south of the waterfront in La Paz. At KM 37, a paved road heads north to the tiny village of La Ventana, 4.6 miles, and to El Sargento, 1.9 more miles. There are beautiful sand beaches in this vicinity, and great boardsailing conditions. From early November to mid-April the area offers warm water, good wind, and a variety of sailing sites well suited to anyone from beginning waterstarters to expert sailors. The curve of the beach acts to catch sailors who are having problems staying upwind. Ventana Windsurf is a bed-and-breakfast—look for the signs. In addition to living accommodations and two meals a day, they offer package trips, equipment rentals, instruction, and video critiques of technique. Sea kayaks and snorkeling gear are available. The informal *ejido* campground at Ventana has palms, toilets, showers, fresh water, a restaurant, and a beautiful sand beach over which boats can be launched, but no hookups. Virtually everyone at the campground is a windsurfer. El Sargento has grocery and hardware stores and a health clinic. There is little doubt that the area's natural assets and close proximity to La Paz and its airport will bring development.

Continuing on Route 286 from KM 37; at KM 40, note the road south to San Antonio—you may need it later. Enter the town of Los Planes at KM 43, which has groceries, tire repair, long-distance telephone, *tortilla* factory, auto parts, a Red Cross clinic, and a restaurant. Magnasin is sold from drums at a lot just west of the Supermercado del Pueblo. At KM 46+ the road swings north. At KM 48+ pass a small grocery store selling gasoline from drums, and immediately encounter an intersection; take the fork signed ENS DE MUERTOS. Set trip odometer. The pavement ends at Mile 0.2, the road becoming graded, two-lane. At Mile 3.7, encounter a **Y**; go straight (080°) for Muertos, arriving at Mile 5.5. There are numerous RV parking sites along the beach, but no facilities are available. Diving is limited, but a huge anchor, metal rails, and ore carts will be found scattered over the bottom, mementos of a silver-mining operation in the 1920s. Boardsailing conditions are good, with calm water and offshore breezes along most of the shoreline, and waves outside. This shallow, sandy bay is the only good anchorage between Balandra and Bahía Frailes, 48 miles north and west, and 52 miles south, respectively.

The beach is soft sand with steep cobbles above it, but local fishermen have cleared paths, and it might be possible to launch small trailer boats. Cabrilla and pargo are taken in the immediate vicinity, "big fellows" in deeper water. The outside waters are the finest roosterfish grounds in the world, and Canal de Cerralvo has excellent striped marlin, wahoo, sailfish, and dorado, and merely fine amberjack and grouper. Although there are fish to be caught all year, May through October are the best months, peaking in the last two weeks of July and the first two of August. Fisherman's Fleet, based in La Paz, offers *panga* fishing trips out of the bay.

Cerralvo, 12 miles north, is the southernmost island in the Cortez and is much larger than it appears from the Muertos area; you are seeing only the south coast. For a number of reasons, both oceanographic and icthyological, many of the fish that migrate in and out of the Cortez pass on each side of the island, often very close to shore. The close-packed schools produce some of the hottest fishing action imaginable, peaking in mid-May and again in October. The fish must be fin-to-fin around Roca Montaña, a pinnacle coming to within a fathom of the surface about 1,200 yards south of Punta Montaña. (The rock got its name when the steamer *Montana* struck it in 1874. "Unfortunately" for divers, it did not sink.) Wahoo are often thick offshore. The bottom is crowded with invertebrates, including crown of thorns, sponges, hydroids, gorgonians, cowries, conches, spindle cones, nudibranchs, lobsters, arrow crabs, urchins, sea stars, brittle stars, and several species of coral. There are vast beds of garden eels in sandy areas, and black coral can be seen in deep water. Spearfishing for large gamefish is excellent. A reef about 1.5 miles north of Punta Montaña on the east side also has excellent diving.

The west coast of the island is marked by white fossil deposits of oysters, corals, scallops, and an echinoid. Two miles north of Punta Sur is the prominent white stripe of such a deposit. The mouth of a canyon lying several hundred yards south of the deposit has pristine and spectacular

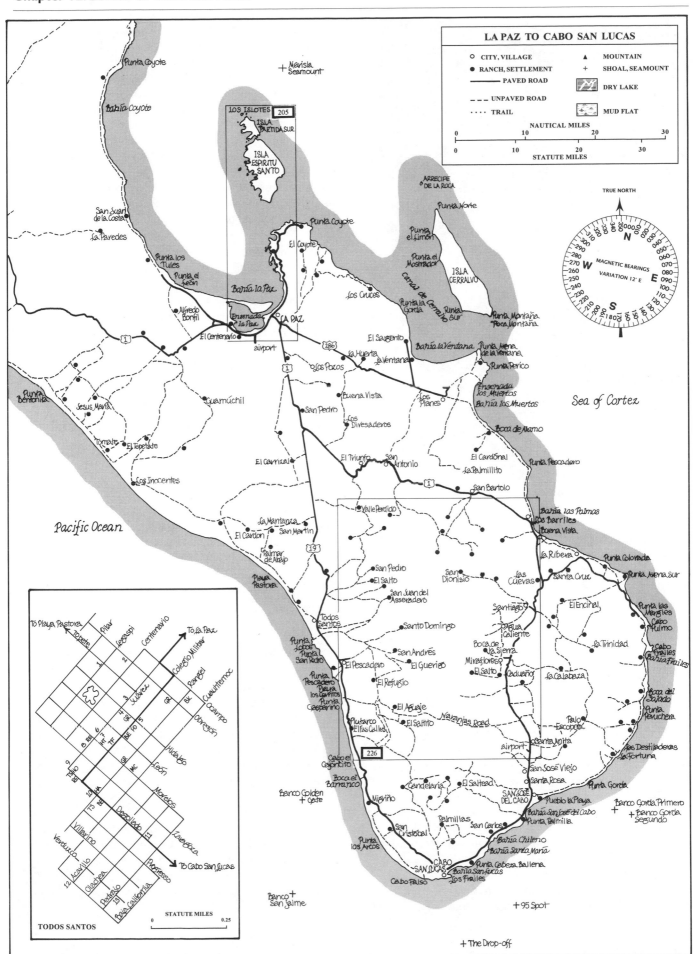

LA PAZ TO CABO SAN LUCAS

○ CITY, VILLAGE ▲ MOUNTAIN
● RANCH, SETTLEMENT + SHOAL, SEAMOUNT
——— PAVED ROAD DRY LAKE
– – – UNPAVED ROAD MUD FLAT
· · · · TRAIL

NAUTICAL MILES
0   10   20   30
STATUTE MILES
0   10   20   30

TRUE NORTH

MAGNETIC BEARINGS
VARIATION 12° E

Punta Coyote
Bahía Coyote
San Juan de la Costa
La Paredes
Punta los Tules
Punta el León
Alfredo Bonfil
Ensenada la Paz
El Centenario
airport
Bahía la Paz

+ Marisla Seamount
LOS ISLOTES 205
ISLA PARTIDA SUR
ISLA ESPIRITU SANTO

Punta Coyote
El Coyote
LA PAZ

ARRECIFE DE LA ROCA
Punta Norte
Punta el Limón
Punta el Moshrador
ISLA CERRALVO
Los Cruces
Punta la Cerralvo Gorda
Punta Sur
Punta Montaña Roca Ventana

El Sargento
La Huerta
La Ventana
Bahía la Ventana
Punta Arena de la Ventana
Punta Perico
Ensenada los Muertos
Bahía los Muertos

Sea of Cortez

286
Los Pocos
Buena Vista
San Pedro
Los Divesaderos
Los Planes
Boca de Álamo

Guamúchil

El Carrizal
El Triunfo
San Antonio
El Cardonal
La Palmillito
Punta Pescadero

Punta Bentonita
Jesus Maria
Tomate
El Topetate
Los Inocentes

San Bartolo

Valle Perdido
Bahía los Palmos
Los Barriles
Buena Vista

La Mantanza
San Martin
El Cardon
Palmar de Abajo
Playa Pastora

19

La Ribera
Punta Colorada
Las Cuevas
Santa Cruz
Punta Arena Sur
Punta las Margies
Cabo Pulmo
Cabo Frailes
Bahía Frailes

San Pedro
El Salto
San Juan del Assenadero
San Dionisio
Santiago
El Encinal
La Trinidad

Pacific Ocean

Todos Santos

Punta Lobos
Punta San Pedro
El Pescadero
Punta Pescadero
Playa los Cerritos
Punta Gasparino

Santo Domingo
San Andrés
El Guerigo
Agua Caliente
Boca de la Sierra
Miraflores
El Salto
Caduaño
La Calabaza

Boca del Salado
Punta Peruchera

El Aguaje
El Saltito
Naranjas Road
Palo Escopeta

Las Destiladeras
La Fortuna

Plutarco Elías Calles
Cabo el Cejoncito
Boca el Barranco

Santa Anita
airport
San José Viejo
Santa Rosa
Punta Gorda

226

Banco Golden + Gate

Migriño
Candelaria
El Saltead
SAN JOSÉ DEL CABO
Pueblo la Playa
Banco Gorda Primero
+ Banco Gorda Segundo

San Cristóbal
Palmillas
San Carlos
Bahía San José del Cabo
Punta Palmilla

Punta los Arcos
Bahía Chileno
Bahía Santa Maria

CABO SAN LUCAS
Punta Cabeza Ballena
Bahía San Lucas
Cabo Falso
Los Frailes

Banco + san Jaime

+ 95 Spot

+ The Drop-off

TODOS SANTOS

To Playa Pastora
Topete
Pilar
Legaspi
Centenario
To La Paz
Colegio Militar
Juárez
Rangel
Cuauhtemoc
Ocampo
Obregón
Hidalgo
León
Morelos
Zaragoza
To Cabo San Lucas
Villarino
Degollado
Verduzco
Acaxuilo
Olachea
Carabajal
Ocampo
Progresso
Baja California

STATUTE MILES
0   0.25

Bernie Eskesen checks out an old mining cart at Muertos

desert vegetation, largely untouched by domesticated animals. Diving at the north end is excellent, with a maze-like reef at 60 feet, home to turtles, coral heads, barracuda, morays, and huge numbers of sergeant majors. A wreck lies 200 yards south of Arrecife de la Foca in 70 feet on a sand bottom, the name "Mazatlán" showing on her steel stern. The engine, boilers, propellers, and stern section can be seen, and the area is strewn with debris. The area is loaded with large fish, and a reef at 80 feet is home to a colorful community of corals, gorgonians, rays, and jewel, green, and zebra morays. There are no good anchorages at Cerralvo, although boats sometimes use the area off the navigation light at Punta Sur and a small cove at Punta el Limón.

For those with adequate boats, outstanding fishing can be found east of Cerralvo at "88-Fathom Bank," 15.5 miles, 040° from the light at Punta Arena de la Ventana. When over the bank, the north end of Cerralvo will bear 298°, the south end 246°. This bank gets little traffic from La Paz or the hotel boats from East Cape, and the chances are good that you will be alone. The fish are prolific and unsophisticated—there is a record of a triple hookup on a blue marlin, a striped marlin, and a sailfish! If that isn't enough, there are dorado in the 40-pound class, and wahoo to 60.

To get to Punta Arena, go back to the fork at Mile 3.7 and take the fork heading north. Set odometer. Due to the

maze of roads, exact driving instructions are not possible; steer for the white lighthouse, keeping clear of the salt ponds, arriving at the beach at Mile 3.9. The point is low and flat, with a fine sand beach over which portable boats can be launched. The only anchorage, north of the point, is an open roadstead sheltered from south weather. Boardsailors will find exposed onshore and cross-onshore conditions and good winds. The waters close to the point are shallow out to a thousand yards or so, with rocky fingers crossing sandy areas, but snorkeling is not too exciting, unless you are a spearfisherman. Shelling along the beach can be rewarding, and an exploration with mask, snorkel, and fins will reveal deep, sandy pockets between coral heads which trap many shells. Most are sea-worn, but some are fresh, and it would not be unusual to find 20 species in an hour of snorkeling. Unimproved RV boondocking and camping can be found just west of the navigation tower. A wrecked ship lies at the water's edge to the west.

Those heading south towards the Cape from the Muertos/Punta Arena area should return to the road to San Antonio noted at KM 40. It is graded and will handle any vehicle. Arrive at San Antonio in 13.3 miles.

■■■■■■■■■■■■■■■■■■■■■■■
Back on the Transpeninsular at KM 213

KM	Location
203	LPG yard.
190	**San Pedro.** Restaurant, groceries, beer, pottery, long-distance telephone.
185	Route 19 south to Todos Santos.

■ The Sierra de la Laguna

The intersection of Route 19 and the Transpeninsular Highway marks the approximate northern limit of the rugged Sierra de la Laguna. This granitic range has a roughly north-south axis, the Pacific slope being much steeper than the Cortez side. Each side is cut by a series of parallel canyons having an east-west orientation. So rugged is the terrain that only a few flat areas of any size exist in the entire range, the largest and best-known being La Laguna, a meadow about a mile long and a half mile wide, located at 5,600 feet between Picacho la Laguna and Cerro las Casitas. Temperatures below freezing are possible, fog and heavy dew are fairly common, and the sound of thunder is frequent. Rainfall is much heavier than in any other part of Baja, up to 30 inches in some micro-climates, most of it occurring between July and November. Small streams and springs can normally be found in the upper regions of virtually all the larger canyons. However, in addition to the seasonal variation, rainfall varies widely from year to year, and in some years hikers in Cañon San Bernardo have found its emerald-colored swimming holes reduced to "puddles of cow wee-wee," while in other years, they have marveled at the "jungle" created by recent heavy rains.

The region is a wilderness much different from anywhere in the US, a great deal of it highly isolated and inaccessible even by foot due to difficult terrain and dense vegetation. Except in the northernmost part, there is no well-defined crest, and steep canyons make it difficult to hike in a north-south direction. However, a geographic peculiarity makes it possible to hike considerable distances in an east-west direction without undue difficulty: some of the canyons on opposite sides of the Sierra de la Laguna almost meet. Two of these situations provide the primary backpacking routes in the area: from Rancho San Dionisio up Cañon San Dionisio to La Laguna and then to San Juan del Aserradero (La Burrera), 15 miles; and from Boca de la Sierra up Cañon San Bernardo and then to Santo Domingo, 14 miles. These routes once had trails used by the locals to visit friends and relatives on opposite sides of the sierra, but with the advent of motor travel they have fallen into disuse and have almost disappeared. However, floods keep canyon bottoms fairly free of brush, and backpackers and hikers will encounter emerald-green pools, massive rock formations, and fine, unspoiled scenery. Six days should be set aside for the Dionisio hike, and 5 days for San Bernardo. The best time of year is generally November to February, when the wet season is over, water is plentiful, and everything is green. Because it is often the best-watered, has the easiest access and is the most suitable for day hikes and short backpacking forays, the San Bernardo route is described beginning on page 232.

La Laguna is a popular destination for backpackers and natural history buffs. It was once the bed of a lake, but erosion cut through its rim about 1870, leaving a grass-covered meadow. It was used as a potato farm in the heyday of the silver mines at El Triunfo. Two small streams flow through it, one toward the Cortez, the other toward the Pacific. Several rangers watch for fires and tend a small weather station in an old farm building.

Baja was once cooler and wetter than today. As the climate became hot and dry, the flora and fauna of the surrounding lowlands changed dramatically, but in small "island" environments high in the mountains, especially around La Laguna, a wonderful mix of the rare, the ordinary, and the seemingly out-of-place remains. An all-inclusive list would be impossibly long, but you will find pinyon pine, mosses, prickly-pear cactus, jewel lichen, algae, oak, madrono, fern, marigold, monkey flower, evening primrose, willow, rose, geranium, palmita, straw-berry, sorrel, wild grape, watercress, deer, coyote, pocket gopher, water beetle, mosquito, band-winged grasshopper, walkingstick, waterstrider, dragonfly, caddisfly, Pacific tree frog, and the exotic-looking *sotol*, with its yucca-like leaves perched on top of a tall, thin trunk. With luck, you might see a mountain lion. Birders will encounter a strange mix due to the area's isolation and many microenvironments, including the endemic Xanthus hummingbird and the uniquely plumaged endemic sub-species San Lucas robin. Sober-faced naturalists can undoubtedly provide very objective explanations for all this diversity, noting La Laguna's high altitude, generous rainfall at high elevations, the aridity of the surrounding regions, the influences of the nearby Pacific and Cortez, and its position just north of the Tropic of Cancer, missing being "tropical" by less than 4 miles. Still, it seems certain that there is at least a bit of magic involved. Backpackers often visit La Laguna using the trail northeast from San Juan del Aserradero, described on page 244. NOLS and Wilderness: Alaska/Mexico offer backpacking trips to La Laguna.

There are a number of interesting class 3 climbs in the Sierra de la Laguna, including 6,264-foot Cerro Salsipuedes, 5,528-foot Cerro Zacatosa, and 5,215-foot Picacho San Lázaro. The Naranjas Road, the closest approach to all three, is described beginning on page 233. The only good technical climb in the area is Cerro Blanco, accessible from Cañon San Bernardo. Cerro Blanco, Salsipuedes, Zacatosa, and San Lázaro are plainly visible from the Transpeninsular, and bearings are provided in later sections, but due to a lack of established trails nothing in the way of specific approach information can be given.

The following 1:50,000 scale topographic maps are available for the Sierra de la Laguna: San Antonio F12B13, El Rosario F12B23, Las Cuevas F12B24, Todos

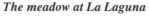

The meadow at La Laguna

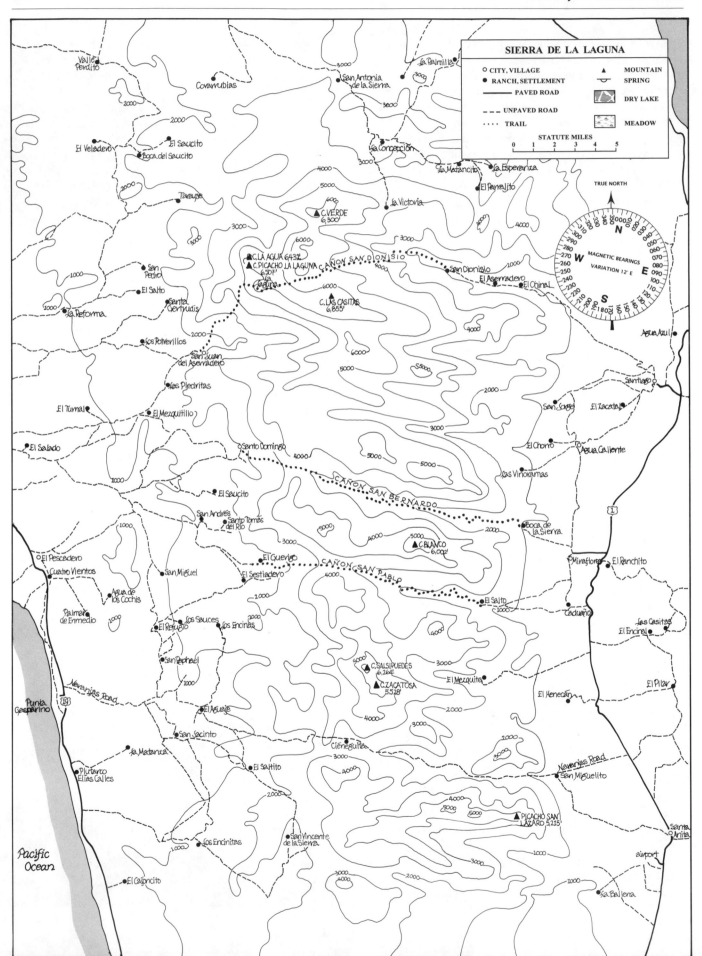

SIERRA DE LA LAGUNA

○ CITY, VILLAGE   ▲ MOUNTAIN
● RANCH, SETTLEMENT   ⊽ SPRING
──── PAVED ROAD
── ── UNPAVED ROAD   DRY LAKE
· · · · TRAIL   MEADOW

STATUTE MILES
0   1   2   3   4   5

TRUE NORTH

MAGNETIC BEARINGS
VARIATION 12° E

Santos F12B33, Santiago F12B34, La Candeleria F12B43, and San José del Cabo F12B44.

Backpackers and hikers in the Sierra de la Laguna face challenges, and the area is not likely to appeal to the weak of spine or limb. However, the area is both highly interesting and largely unspoiled, qualities that are becoming very difficult to find in today's world.

Collectors have found many different minerals in the areas surrounding the Sierra de la Laguna, but nothing has been reported in the range itself, except for vague reports of spessartine garnet at its southern end, pyrite at La Aguja, and molybdenite at "Cerro de las Cabras, west of Santiago." No map I am aware of shows a "Cerro de las Cabras" west of Santiago, although there is a peak named Pico Azufrado, which translates to "Sulfur-like Peak," located just north of Cañon San Bernardo. Molybdenite is dull gray, but forms secondary minerals through weathering, some of which are yellow. This analysis is pure speculation, but collectors might have fun checking it out.

Joe Farrell leads a group up Cerro Blanco

Will Waterman

■■■■■■■■■■■■■■■■■■■
On the Transpeninsular at KM 185

KM	Location
169	Rolling hills to KM 103, with moderate grades and numerous blind curves.
164	**El Triunfo.** In 1862 the Triunfo Gold and Silver Company began operations and El Triunfo soon had a population of 10,000, the largest mining town in Baja California. Today the town is little more than a collection of time-worn adobe buildings. Only the huge chimney, constructed of brick in 1905 and still in good repair, helps it cling to the name "The Triumph." Nature was generous to mineral collectors at El Triunfo, in variety if not quantity, for in addition to silver and gold, 33 other minerals have been found, second only to Santa Rosalía. The simple sulfides and sulfosalts predominate, but carbonates, halides, silicates, oxides, and other groups also are represented. Fine garnets to a half-inch in white rock have also been reported. There are several small grocery stores and a long-distance telephone, and water is available from spigots.
156	**San Antonio.** When mining boomed in the region during the mid-1800s, San Antonio and El Triunfo were great rivals, but San Antonio failed to keep up. Today the tables have turned and it is distinctly the more clean, pleasant, and prosperous town, with a PEMEX (M), library, grocery and gift stores, doctor, post office, liquor, beer, and cold sodas. The architecture of its church, built in 1825 and remodeled a number of years ago, may be the most unusual in Baja, a massive concrete amalgam of the features of a railroad locomotive and a river steamer. Road north to the Muertos/Punta Arena area.
141+	Rancho Verde, a new RV park, offers 22 sites with sewer and water hookups (no electric), rest rooms, showers, horseback riding, hiking, four-wheel-drive trails, and nature walks.
129	A beautiful *zalate* lives on the rocks on the north side of the road.
127	**San Bartolo.** Café, groceries, fruit, sodas, beer, long-distance telephone, famous springs of exceptional purity.
108+	Paved road east to the shores of Bahía las Palmas, signed LOS BARRILES. Those continuing on the Transpeninsular should turn to the following page.

■ **Bahía las Palmas**

Stretching from Punta Pescadero south to Punta Arena Sur, Bahía las Palmas is world-famous for its gamefish. In one recent year anglers were complaining that hordes of dorado and sailfish made it difficult to catch blue marlin! For over 10 miles the 100-fathom line averages less than a mile offshore, the closest lengthy approach anywhere in the Cape region, which may account for the fine fishing and many successful resorts. Blue and black marlin and sailfish are taken from May to October, sometimes by astonished anglers in cartoppers. Roosters are caught year-round, but fishing for them is best from May to October. Yellowtail are best from January to April, and striped marlin, dorado, tuna, wahoo and lesser fish inhabit the area all year, although the warm months are the most productive and December through March can be slow. Four miles south of Punta Pescadero is the famous "Tuna Canyon," where Ray Cannon found depths of 50 fathoms a hundred yards from shore and a year-round population of large yellowfin tuna. Roosters can also be caught from the beach at Tuna Canyon, and at the beach north of Punta Pescadero. Fishing International offers a number of package trips to the area. Diving is pleasant, with large sandy areas broken by reefs. Gunning for pelagic gamefish should be great.

The bay is the most popular boardsailing location in Baja, with clean, sandy beaches, and pleasant weather, the Los Barriles area being the center of Baja boardsailing. Winds are often in the 18- to 25-knot range from mid-November through mid-March. Winds during this period blow for three to eight days, with two to four days of light breezes in between. They are normally from the north, producing side-shore conditions from Punta Pescadero to the Buena Vista area. The beach from Buena Vista to Punta Colorada is often sandy and the launch easy, but the shoreline curves eastward to the point that boardsailors may begin to encounter onshore winds. Winds are normally light in the morning, but they build up as the day passes, and riders in the afternoon should have previous high wind experience or the ability to learn quickly, and be able to make confident water starts. In most locations there is usually enough chop that uphauling doesn't work out. A number of boardsailing operations are located along the shores of the bay.

There are no protected anchorages from Muertos to Cabo Frailes, Bahía las Palmas being little more than an open roadstead, although Punta Arena Sur provides marginal protection, and there are no marinas or fuel docks. Although a number of concrete ramps have been built in the area through the years, most have been destroyed by waves or deeply buried by sand. All beach launches open into unprotected waters and can be used only in calm conditions.

 Side trip to beach resorts and Los Planes. A number of resorts and RV parks on the beaches along the coast to the north are reached by driving east on the

sedan road at KM 108+. Those in large RVs and those towing trailers should not attempt the road north to El Cardónal and Los Planes. Set odometer.

Mile	Side trip location
0.0	Leave highway at KM 108+, drive east on the paved road. Immediately encounter a small mall having money exchange, ice cream, arts and gifts, café, fish smoking, jewelry, and a cantina. There is a supermarket just to the east.
0.3	Entrance to the Hotel Palmas de Cortez, which has a restaurant, a fleet of sportfishing boats, rental tackle, live bait, fishing licenses, diving and certification courses, kayak rentals, and a boat launching service, all open to walk-ins on a space-available basis. The Playa del Sol next door to the north has a fleet of cruisers and pangas, live bait, rental tackle, and snorkeling gear, and is also open to walk-ins. Vela Windsurf Resorts, located at the Playa del Sol, has equipment, instruction, and clinics. Bicycles and kayaks are available for rent. All facilities are available to walk-ins on a space-available basis (unlikely between Christmas and New Year's). Vela is open from Thanksgiving to early March, and package trips are available. Tío Pablo's Restaurant, across from the hotel entrance road, is pleasant and clean, and there are a few small grocery stores, a Baja Celular office, a motel, a laundromat, several restaurants, auto parts, beer, a mechanic, a post office, and a hardware store in this vicinity.
0.5	Martín Verdugo's Motel and Trailer Park has full hookups, showers, rest rooms, a laundry facility, a restaurant, and a motel, as well as boat charters and a swimming pool. The launch ramp (14%) leads to a sand beach, with very limited maneuvering room, but the park provides a launching service. Full rentals are available, and the company will accommodate walk-ins. Blue-water hunters are welcome if arranged in advance. Make inquiries at the desk at Verdugo's. Juanito's Garden RV Park, across the street from Verdugo's, has full hookups, a number of large palapas, rest rooms, showers, and a laundromat. Sites available to transients are limited.
1.0	Pavement ends, sedan road continues north.
9.1	Hotel Punta Pescadero. No facilities for RVers or campers.
12.0	El Cardónal Resort. Full hookups, showers, rest rooms, sandy beach, water purification system, motel, and store selling limited basic groceries, sodas, and snacks. The resort offers diving, snorkeling, kayaking, fishing, and visits to nearby rock art sites. Diving off the settlement is excellent, with many small tropical fish and jewel, green, and zebra morays. The road continues

northwest, winding through deep coastal canyons with many sharp turns and switchbacks and few if any areas to pass.

28.0 **Los Planes.**

■ ■
Back on the Transpeninsular at KM 108+

KM	Location

107+   PEMEX (MPD), groceries, newly constructed East Cape RV Park. Baja Adventures is found by driving east on the sedan road across from the PEMEX and following the dive flags. Sailboard rentals and instruction are offered, and transportation is available to other sailing sites and for downwinders. Their dive shop offers rental equipment, local trips, and certification ranging from a resort course through full certification. Hobies, mountain bikes, and sea kayaks are for rent, and snorkeling and kayak day-trips are available. Package trips are offered, and walk-ins are welcome, subject to first call by guests. Several hotels having restaurants and bars are within easy walking distance.

104+   Rancho Buena Vista is one of the best-known fishing resorts in Baja, with probably more fishing world records than any other place in the world. It offers cottages with baths, pool, tennis courts, dining room, bar, cruisers, rental tackle, live and frozen bait, and a sand beach.

103+   Buenavista Beach Resort (signed), which has a restaurant, cruiser and *panga* fleets, live and frozen bait, tackle rental, and snorkeling gear. Boat and trailer storage can be arranged, and dive excursions and rental kayaks are available. Vista Sea Sports, near the hotel, offers dive trips ranging from Cerralvo to the Bancos Gorda, and the owners are very knowledgeable about the best dive sites. They have three dive boats (a fourth will be acquired in the near future), a compressor, full rentals, and limited sales, and offer PADI instruction from resort/refresher courses to full certification and specialty courses. They are US Divers-certified for repairs and warranty on regulators and can do VIP inspections on scuba tanks. To locate them, turn east at KM 103+ on the sedan road, pass the hotel, turn right (south) at the two white buildings, and look for a white house with green trim sporting the diver's flag. Information on Vista can be obtained at any of the hotels in the area.

102   Sedan road east to La Capilla Trailer Park and Rancho Leonero (signed). Set odometer. At Mile 0.8, go straight ahead (005°, signed) for La Capilla at Mile 1.1, which has full hookups,

showers, and rest rooms. The beautiful sand beach is only 100 yards north, and portable boats are easily launched. To go to Rancho Leonero, turn right (120°) at Mile 0.8, follow the signs and arrive at the ranch at Mile 4.3. Although the sandy sedan road has some bumpy areas and several 20% grades, it is passable by almost any RV. The ranch has fishing cruisers and *pangas*, licenses, live bait, and tackle rental and sales, and offers kayaking, boardsailing, Hobies, and snorkeling. Diving is excellent right in front of the resort

101+   The road levels out, with only occasional arroyo crossings and gentle grades until Cabo San Lucas.

91+   **Las Cuevas.** Grocery store, paved road northeast (signed) to La Ribera and Arricefe Pulmo. Those continuing on the Transpeninsular should turn to page 231.

➤ ***Side trip on the "East Cape Coast Road."*** Part of the Cape Coast Loop Trip, this road passes Pulmo Reef, one of Baja's natural wonders, some good diving wrecks, and dozens of miles of the finest and most pristine beaches imaginable. The road has been paved to a point just short of Pulmo, and will someday be completed all the way to San José del Cabo. Improved and graded, the unpaved parts of the road can handle sedans and moderate RVs throughout its length, although washboard, washouts, and rough sections are common. Spur roads to the beaches have been slow to develop, but campsites can be found at places where the road dips into arroyos near the water and along lengthy stretches of beach approaching San José del Cabo. Bicyclists will find no dependable natural sources of water, but it should be possible to bum a supply along the way.

Turn northeast at Las Cuevas, and pass through Santa Cruz at KM 3+, which has a restaurant and groceries. At KM 10+, continue straight ahead (northeast) at the intersection, and arrive at La Ribera, which has groceries, tire repair, *tortilla* factory, restaurants, long-distance telephone, cold sodas and beer, ice, doctor, and pharmacy. To find the PEMEX (MD), continue straight ahead (northeast) until you are forced to turn right or left. Turn right (east) on the sedan road, and find the station in 0.6 mile.

To go to Correcaminos Trailer Park, turn left (west) at the intersection just noted. The graded dirt road leads to the park entrance in 0.3 miles. Located in an old mango orchard (the crop is ripe for picking in summer), the park has full hookups, showers, and rest rooms. The sand beach 0.2 mile to the north is prime boardsailing country, with good winds and frequent cross-onshore conditions. Portable boats can be launched across the beach.

To head for Pulmo, go back to the intersection at KM 10+ and turn southeast at the intersection. Set odometer. At Mile 5.3, note the road left (045°, signed, one 14% grade with loose rock), which leads 2.3 miles to Hotel Punta Colorada. The hotel has fishing cruisers, *pangas*, rental tackle, and bait, which are available to walk-ins. Boardsailors will find lots of wind and cross-onshore conditions in front of the hotel. This is one of the more challenging areas in Baja, and if you are looking for logo waves, this may be the place. A number of sandy shallow bars about 100 yards out have the reputation of being the best place in Baja for wave-jumping. In the past, the hotel has allowed RVers to park overnight at the beach just to the southeast of the hotel.

At Mile 7.1, a pickup road left (north, signed) leads to Punta Arena Sur. Set odometer. At Mile 0.7, turn right (100°), at Mile 2.8 go half-left (050°) between several ranch buildings, and at Mile 7 arrive at the beach. This area is the scene of fine beach-casting for roosters. Inshore are jack crevalle, sierra, and ladyfish, and out several miles dorado, skipjack, yellowfin tuna, sailfish, and black, blue, and striped marlin in season. The water east of the lighthouse is a top location for high-wind and wave boardsailing. The lee of the point is excellent for speed sailing, with lots of sand beach and cross-offshore conditions. The bay, known as "Bahía Rincón" to boardsailors, is a good place to practice jibes and water starts. There are many boondocking locations, but beware of soft sand.

Back on the Pulmo road at Mile 7.1; the pavement ends at Mile 10.4, and the graded, washboarded road begins. Arrive at Pulmo at Mile 16.3. The name is derived from *pulmón*, the Spanish word for lung, apparently adopted during the days of the pearl divers.

The tiny animals that build coral reefs are among the world's most industrious creatures, being responsible for building Australia's Great Barrier Reef and other immense public works around the world. These animals, jelly-like carnivorous polyps encased in a "skeleton" of calcium carbonate, are delicate and require a strict set of environmental conditions, one of which is being far from the fresh-water discharges of rivers. In addition, the polyps need water temperatures above 72°. In spite of these requirements, their colonies are found over 80 million square miles of the Earth's surface, an area 22 times that of the US, generally between 32° north and 27° south latitude. Corals have managed to establish reefs in only four locations along the west coast of North America—one in Panama, one in Costa Rica, one in mainland Mexico, and Pulmo. (There are, however, coral heads in many Cortez locations, as well as a very small reef in Bahía San Gabriel at Isla Espíritu Santo.)

The corals of Pulmo, shielded from the cold Pacific and finding other conditions to their liking, have constructed a sizable reef. Starting near shore just south of Cabo Pulmo and running in a northeasterly direction, 3 broad rows of coral heads of 2 dominant species continue, ending in depths of 70 feet. The row pattern is caused by the geology of the area—the corals are cemented to elongated ridges of basaltic rock protruding from the sandy bottom. The astronomical number of nooks, crannies, and cavelets formed by the reef are home to huge numbers of creatures. In his book *The Log From the Sea of Cortez*, John Steinbeck recounted a visit to Pulmo during a 1940 boat trip to collect biological specimens: "The complexity of the life-pattern on Pulmo Reef was even greater than at Cabo San Lucas. Clinging to the coral, growing on it, burrowing into it, was a teeming fauna. Every piece of the soft material broken off skittered and pulsed with life—little crabs and worms and snails. One small piece of coral might conceal 30 or 40 species, and the colors on the reef were electric." Let us hope that development in the area does not destroy this marvel.

Pulmo is one of the most famed diving locations in the Cortez. The water is warm and the visibility is often 30 to 50 feet, occasionally 75. Since the innermost coral heads can be found in only a few feet of water immediately off the beach, neither scuba nor a boat is essential. As you enter the water, be ready for a surprise; at some times of the year small *sardinas* are so numerous that they may envelop you in a silver cloud, bringing on vertigo. Once, in deeper water, I was approached by a school of goatfish, which turned and began making endless circles, placing me at the center of a living carousel, its leader apparently having come to the conclusion that he was at the end of the procession rather than at its beginning. Certainly, do not miss a night dive.

El Cantil, a dive site on the outermost rows of corals, lies 084°, 0.7 miles from the beach due east of the dive shop/restaurant area, least depth 45 feet. Bajo el Pulmo, another excellent dive site, lies north of the main coral reefs. With a least depth of 32 feet, it is located 1.7 miles, 035° from the same beach. You should be able to see it as you approach. With coral heads, deep caves, many species of sea fans, colonies of yellow colonial tulip corals, dog and yellow snappers, grunts, giant hawkfish, bicolor and bumphead parrot fish, sea bass, broomtail grouper, turtles, and an occasional jewfish, the place is throbbing with life. The small white islet at the south end of the bay is also a fine dive, with sea fans, cup corals, pargo, and numerous other species.

There are several shipwrecks in the area. In 1941 the old 107-foot steel auxiliary sailing vessel *Colima* sank with a cargo of beer and general merchandise, the cause being "...the poor state of the bottom of the ship" according to the newspapers of the day. Lying in about 35 feet of water, what is left is now scattered across a sandy bottom and can sometimes be seen from the surface. To visit her, maneuver until Cabo Pulmo bears 154° and the rounded peak having the greatest apparent height on the western skyline bears 250°, a point 1.25 miles from the cape. As of early 1998 the wreck was completely hidden by sand, but it may reappear.

The large Mexican purse seiner *Vencedor* sank in the vicinity in 1980. The extensive collection of junk, excellent visibility, bright sand bottom, easy accessibility, and almost artistic setting make the *Vencedor* a fine dive site. Start just east of Cabo Pulmo and note the dark, cone-shaped rock at the end of the Cape. When this rock bears 209°, put it astern and proceed on course 029°. Look to the south and locate the rocky massif forming Cabo Frailes. When its central peak bears 174° and the water depth is 45 feet, you will be very close to the wreck site.

Pulmo is a National Marine Park, and fishing, spearfishing, foraging, and shell collecting are not permitted. The northern boundary of the marine park is an east/

west line 3.75 miles north of Cabo Pulmo, the southern an east/west line 0.5 mile south of the south shore of Cabo Frailes, the eastern boundary being a north/south line 2.5 miles east of Cabo Pulmo. To play it safe and simple, just stay east of a north/south line 2.5 miles east of Cabo Pulmo.

Sailfish are numerous in the deep water offshore, sometimes producing two or three per boat per day. There is a concrete launch ramp (14%), but it has limited maneuvering room and ends abruptly in rather shallow water, making it a high-tide proposition for larger boats. To find the ramp, drive from Tito's Restaurant 0.75 mile northeast, parallel to the shore, to a stone building near a rocky headland. Check at the restaurant about fees and rules. Pulmo is a poor overnight anchorage, and yachtsmen will be far happier at Bahía Frailes. Avoid anchoring on the reef, for you can cause severe damage to the coral. There is often a good afternoon breeze, and the bay is popular with boardsailors. In winter, the prevailing north winds often exceed 20 knots, providing excellent cross-onshore conditions.

Pepe's Dive Center has rental equipment, guided scuba and snorkel tours, night dives, snorkeling, two *pangas*, compressed air, full PADI certification, and a resort course for beginners. Package trips are available. Edgardo Ochoa, the manager, will provide visitors with an orientation on the ecology of the reefs and measures necessary for their protection. He is knowledgeable and speaks excellent English. Cabo Pulmo Divers, located near the beach, offers rentals, air, guides, boat dives, and snorkeling. Fiesta Sportfishing & Diving offers dive excursions to Pulmo.

Tito's Restaurant has no official menu, but usually has fish, scallops, tacos, and beer available. Nancy's Restaurant serves meals, cocktails, and snacks, under a *palapa* roof. Restaurant el Caballero also offers good meals, if somewhat limited in choice. Cabo Pulmo Beach Resort offers rental homes, *casitas*, and bungalows. There are many boondocking sites on the beach to the north of the settlement.

Continuing on the East Cape Coast Road; reset odometer. Arrive at Bahía Frailes at Mile 4.7. A deep submarine canyon winds into the bay, having depths of over 400 feet within 400 yards of shore. The closest approach of the canyon to the shore is at that point on the beach where the right tangent of the shoreline at Cabo Frailes bears 055°. The bay is part of the National Marine Park. There are a few boondocking locations along the shore. The Hotel Bahía los Frailes offers a restaurant, fishing, hiking, rock climbing, snorkeling, scuba diving, and kayaking, and caters to walk-ins.

A fairly secure anchorage can be made south of the point, the next satisfactory anchorage to the south being Cabo San Lucas, 45 miles. The lee of the point is too well protected from wind to be a good boardsailing site, but by the time it has reached the south end of the bay the wind is strong and steady, providing good speed-sailing conditions. You can't get any farther east on the Baja peninsula than Frailes, and in some respects this marks the southernmost extent of the Cortez—the beaches to the south start to show ocean swell and surf. If north winds start to blow and your engine refuses

to run, don't worry—Easter Island is only 2,735 miles south.

Because it is the first place where the sweep of the coast begins to face the south swells of summer, the vicinity of Punta Peruchera (Boca de Tule) at Mile 15.2 is ordinarily the first place in the Cortez where hope begins to stir in the hearts of surfers. The point itself isn't much, but there are a number of reef and beach breaks. These tend to be a bit small and mushy most of the year, but can assume heroic proportions during the summer hurricane season. At Mile 20.3 you will encounter one of the greatest *zalates* in Baja, a giant of a tree in a typically nontypical recumbent pose. A steel tuna vessel can be found 50 yards off the beach in about 25 feet of water at Rancho las Destiladeras, Mile 23.4. Beachcombers may enjoy investigating a wreck on the beach 300 yards southwest of the above vessel. The wreck of the Mexican freighter *Morelia* can be seen at Mile 25.6. The US fishing vessel *Waldero*, stranded in 1949, is buried in the dunes 200 yards northeast of the *Morelia*. This general area, known as "Shipwrecks," is well regarded by boardsailors. Punta Gorda at Mile 30.6 has point and reef breaks, and storms sometimes deposit many shells on the beach. A 165-foot vessel, name and date unknown, is reported in 45 feet of water off Punta Gorda.

The wreck of a large steel ship lies 800 yards off the beach at Mile 34.9. When you are close to the wreck, the lighthouse east of San José del Cabo should bear 255°. Now look for three low hills north of the coast road. When you are facing north, the left one is the most pointed, the right one is slumped over, and the center hill is rounded. The peak of the center hill should bear 318°. The left and center hills are obvious from the road. The wreck is in about 35 feet of water on a sand bottom and usually can be seen from the surface. The Greek refrigerator ship *Anastacios*, lost in 1980, is home to squadrons of fish, some quite sizable.

At Mile 36.9 pass a lighthouse on the left, and at Mile 37.2, shortly after passing a grocery store, go straight (260°) at a fork. A maze of crossroads develops as you approach San José del Cabo, but continue west, steering for the north end of the large grove of palms surrounding the freshwater *estero*. At Mile 37.5 pass the road to Pueblo la Playa fishing village, and at Mile 38.8 cross a stream. Arrive at the intersection of Avs. Benito Juárez and Antonio Mijares at Mile 39.0. Use the city map on page 236 to continue.

■ ■ ■ ■ ■ ■ ■ ■ ■ ■ ■ ■ ■

Back on the Transpeninsular at Las Cuevas, KM 91+

KM	Location
83+	Groceries. Paved road west to Santiago (signed). Set odometer. This small town has a PEMEX (MD), groceries, stores, clinic, doctor, pharmacy, long-distance telephone, mail, cold beer and sodas, ice, small zoo. Pleasant Restaurant Palomar can be found by following the signs from the

The great zalate *in the East Cape Coast Road*

southwest corner of the town square for about 75 yards. The road to Rancho San Dionisio, jumping-off point for the Cañon San Dionisio-La Laguna backpack/burro trip, is found by turning right (355°) at Mile 1.5, then half-right (320°) at Mile 1.9 and then continuing straight ahead (300°) at the intersection at Mile 2.4. The ranch is reached at Mile 14.4. The road is capable of handling sedans. The mouth of the canyon can be seen at 300° from KM 84+.

80 Tropic of Cancer. Those heading south are officially in the tropics.

70 PEMEX (MD). Sedan road west (signed) to Miraflores, which has groceries, stores, medical, dental, cold beer, *tortilla* factory, long-distance telephone, water from spigots, leather shop. Those continuing on the Transpeninsular should skip the following section.

Side trip to Cañon San Bernardo. An interesting day hike or backpacking trip can be made up Cañon San Bernardo. Stop and sight 272° from KM 70; the mouth of the canyon can be seen in the distance. If you plan to climb Cerro Blanco, sight 260° and study the domed summit. Set odometer and turn west on the paved road to Miraflores, at Mile 1.4 enter town, and turn right (345°) at Mile 1.7. At Mile 1.9 go half-left (310°), and at Mile 4.9 arrive at the tiny settlement of Boca de la Sierra. The road can handle sedans.

The approach to the canyon begins on the road several hundred yards southeast of the settlement. A dam in the lower

reaches of the canyon provides water to the surrounding farms. Either follow the aqueduct upstream or follow the trail to the west over the hills to the dam. Past the dam the canyon soon becomes rugged and beautiful, with massive rock formations and emerald-colored swimming holes, some of which can get to 30 feet across and 15 feet deep if the rainfall has been normal. The stream occasionally forms low waterfalls, and there are many fine *zalates* and palms. Firewood is plentiful and there are numerous places to camp.

Five miles from the dam, Cerro Blanco lies 2 miles south, offering rare technical challenges. Careful scouting will reveal long fingers of bare granite which run from the bottom of the canyon far up the slope, greatly reducing the amount of brush-busting required. Climbs on the south face range from easy class 5 on up, and the summit dome has numerous cracks of varying degrees of difficulty. Continuing up the canyon, you will reach the crest about 12 miles from the dam, at approximately 3,000 feet. West of this point, a fairly well-defined cow trail runs down to Santo Domingo and the roadhead. The appropriate topos are: Santiago F12B34; and Todos Santos F12B33. If you are not going all the way to Santo Domingo you don't need the second one.

■■■■■■■■■■■■■■■■■■■■■■■

Back on the Transpeninsular at KM 70

KM	Location
61	Clear views of Cerros Zacatosa and Salsipuedes, bearing 254° and 259° respectively, approxi-

mately 10 miles away.

53+ Naranjas Road (signed). Those continuing on the Transpeninsular should turn to page 235.

Side trip on the Naranjas Road. Less energetic explorers can visit the Sierra de la Laguna by vehicle on a road which crosses to the vicinity of Punta Gasparino on the Pacific side. Before you leave the Transpeninsular at KM 53+, sight 223°, 273°, and 275° to San Lázaro, Zacatosa, and Salsipuedes, respectively. Set odometer. The pickup road meanders through brush-covered hills and scenic canyons, with dark emerald ponds shimmering in light-colored rock. There are very few signs of civilization—just a few cows, small flocks of goats, and an occasional ranch. Soon after you start, zalate and oak trees will be seen, somehow out of place amid the palms. At Mile 5 San Lázaro lies 2 miles south. This white granite knob provides a difficult class 3 climb and marvelous views of the sierras and the plains to the south. There are no established trails, so it is a compass-and-bushwhacking proposition until you are high on the slopes. Zacatosa and Salsipuedes lie 3.0 and 3.5 miles north from Mile 14, both difficult class 3.

The crest of the range is reached at Mile 13, elevation about 3,400 feet, from where the Pacific can be seen. The road east of the crest is graded, but to the west it is poor, with switchbacks and slopes to 30%. Turn right (004°) at a small cluster of buildings marked "El Aguaje" at Mile 23.1. The road quickly swings west, and a power line will be seen paralleling it almost all the way to Route 19. Take the left (252°) fork at Mile 24.7, and at Mile 30.8 arrive at Route 19.

The Naranjas Road is a civil engineering disaster-in-the-making, with poor culverting and steep, unstabilized grades, so go now before nature makes it impossible.

● ●

❝ Cutting it close

When the Naranjas Road was still under construction Reeve and I drove up into the Sierra de la Laguna from the Pacific side. Angling up the steep mountain grades, the road continued to narrow until only inches kept us from plunging down extraordinarily steep slopes that continued for hundreds of feet, ending in boulder-strewn creek bottoms. The van was heavily loaded with camping and dive gear,

The south face and summit dome of Cerro Blanco

and there was a 15-foot boat on the roof, so we frequently smelled burning clutch. We encountered a section blasted through solid rock where the fit was so tight we had to fold in the left outside mirror. The door on that side could not be opened, and the right led to thin air, so if it became necessary to get out of the van to fix a flat we would have had to burrow through the equipment in back to get to the rear door. Finally we came to a point where a huge boulder lay 6 feet away from a rocky cliff. Two Mexican road workers smiled as we pulled up, knowing that we would never be able to squeeze between the cliff and the boulder. They said they were working on the problem, but it was too hot for such heavy labor and they were about to head home for several days of rest. Perhaps the boulder would be out of the way by April.

We didn't like the prospect of backing down the narrow road for perhaps 5 miles; the slightest inattention, the smallest jerk of the steering wheel, even an untimely hiccup, and we would be history. I got out and spanned the opening between the boulder and the cliff with my arms. No way, it was too narrow! Reeve, not so ready to give up, pulled a length of line off a fishing reel and we measured the width of the inside of the van and compared it to the opening. It still did not look like we could make it; the opening seemed to be exactly the width of the van.

We measured again, more carefully this time. The line was stretchy, but there might be perhaps an eighth of an inch of clearance. With big grins, the men assured us that the gap was too narrow, but I pulled ahead, backed down, moved over, pulled ahead, and kept repeating the process with Reeve coaching me until there was equal space on each side of the van. Both outside mirrors were folded back, but it looked like we going to have to unbolt and remove their mounts from the doors.

Luck was with us; as I crept forward each mount passed through small cracks and crevices in the rock. Walking slowly backward in front of the van, Reeve made signs to turn right and then left, but finally his hand went up; the men were right—the van was wider than the gap. Their grins gave way to beaming smiles, and their body-language—legs crossed, leaning jauntily on their picks—signaled certainty and anticipation of the upcoming spectacle. After 5 more minutes of backing and filling, the van was repositioned slightly and I pulled ahead at a creep. There was a faint sound, like the tearing of a piece of paper, but the van was finally on the other side, much to the disgust of our audience, who suddenly lost interest and got back to work, swinging their picks and studiously looking the other way. Reeve jumped in, and when we had made it around the next bend and were out of sight, we

Nils Green and Linda Redman survey the Victorias from the summit of Cerro Zacatosa

got out and found a shallow scratch on one side of the van extending 3 or 4 feet, and a scratch in the protruding bumper on the other. We did not return to congratulate them, but the men had been right—the van was wider than the gap, by the thickness of a layer of paint and a little chrome! **"**

• •

■ ■
Back on the Transpeninsular at KM 53+

KM	Location
51	Sedan road southwest 0.2 miles to LPG yard, entrance 100 yards southeast of KM marker, marked by green gates.
45+	**Santa Anita.** Grocery stores.
43	Los Cabos International Airport. Start divided highway.
39+	**San José Viejo.** Groceries, tire repair, fish market, bakery, auto parts, long-distance telephone.
36+	**Santa Rosa.** PEMEX (MD), Volkswagen dealer, car rental, tire repair, fruit stores, butcher shops, café, grocery stores, pharmacies, liquor, new shopping center, Baja Celular office.
33	Ice manufacturing plant, hardware.
32+	**San José del Cabo.**

San José del Cabo

Beginning in 1566 the galleons coming from Manila, the "black ships" of *Shogun* fame, stopped at San José del Cabo to obtain water and fresh provisions *en route* to Acapulco. A Jesuit mission was founded in 1730, but epidemics quickly killed most of the Indians. In 1822 English sea lord Thomas Cochrane attacked the town, and in 1847 the American frigate *Portsmouth* landed a company of marines to occupy the town during the Mexican-American War. Mexican patriots besieged them for several months, almost wiping them out before reinforcements arrived. Today's Av. Antonio Mijares is named for a Mexican lieutenant killed in an attack. The mission church was destroyed in the battle, and the present one (4) was built in the 1940s.

Today, San José del Cabo is one of the most beautiful towns in Baja. The pace is slower and more mature than at Cabo San Lucas, and the town does not attract as many collegians on spring break. The raunchiness of the T-shirts for sale is several orders of magnitude less than Cabo, and there are fewer people hawking time-share condos and trinkets along the streets. The town caters to hotel inhabitants rather than RVers and campers, but there are many restaurants, beaches, and other attractions that bring such vagabonds into the area.

There are numerous restaurants in many culinary traditions and price ranges, and you should be able to find almost anything you need. Almacenes Grupo Castro (11) is a large store, selling groceries, meats, cold cuts, wine, liquor, fruit, and vegetables. Aramburo's Supermarket (6) has meats, groceries, household items, and good produce. Pescadería San Marcos (12) sells fresh fish and fish bait. The Mercado Municipal (13) has many stands selling fresh produce, meat, and fish, and has large baskets of hot peppers, and there are small food stands and a juice bar. Plaza los Cabos (23) has mini-markets, travel agents, handicraft and T-shirt shops, restaurants, airline offices, and long-distance telephone. The PEMEX (1) sells MPD.

There are many shops selling jewelry, pottery, leather goods, folk art, and other items. The Regional Museum (16) contains just a dozen or so paintings. However, there are plans to include exhibits on fossils, whales, antiques, and the Pericú Indians, as well as gift and snack shops. There are a number of hotels in the area that have restaurants, reservations desks, sportfishing fleets, and other things of interest, including: the Aquamarina (21), Fiesta Inn (24), Howard Johnson Plaza Suites (18), Posada Real Best Western (20), Presidente Intercontinental (17), Posada Terranova (7), and the Tropicana Inn (10). If you wish to take a break from RVing or camping, the last is the best bargain in the Cape region in terms of quality, amenities, appearance, comfort, plumbing, and price. Information is available at the municipal tourist office (5).

A large lagoon is found just east of town, where more than 180 species of birds have been spotted. The Presidente Intercontinental has canoes and paddle boats available for birding ventures on the lagoon. If you are a golfer, try Campo de Golf San José (19). A long stretch of sand beach, known as the Costa Azul, one of the most magnificent in Baja, sweeps past the town, providing fine swimming and loafing. However, the water immediately offshore is very deep, and when swells are present, especially in summer, a booming surf renders water activities difficult. Although some individual combinations of bottom contour and wave direction permit surfing along the Costa Azul, the waves sometimes go from crest to crash in 6 seconds or less, and most surfers head east for the Punta Gorda or Shipwrecks areas, or for "Zippers," " The Rock," "Old Man," and points west. Killer Hook Surf Shop (8) sells and rents surfing equipment, makes repairs, offers surfing instruction and charters, and sells beach equipment.

There are no launch ramps nor a harbor in the area, and the sportfishing industry is not as well developed as in Cabo San Lucas. Most hotels have a reservations desk, where *pangas* and cruisers can be hired for fishing and diving trips. Victor's Sportfishing, with offices at the Posada Real and next to the Tropicana, can book fishing trips in *pangas* and cruisers. In addition, *pangas* can be booked at Pueblo la Playa, a settlement on the beach just east of the main part of town. Since the only harbor and trailerboat launch facilities in the area are at Cabo San Lucas, a description of the Bancos Gorda and other Cape fishing areas will be found later in this chapter. A COTP will be found in town (9), *Aduana* and *Migración* at the airport. Señor Diver (22) offers full rentals and day-trips to local diving attractions.

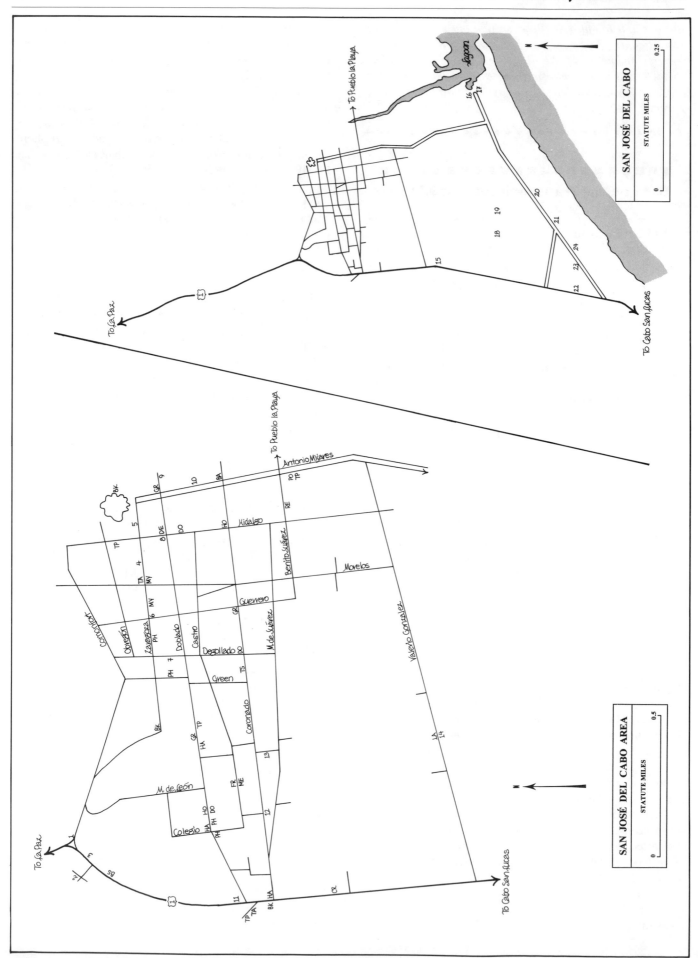

CITEC (Ciencias Technicas Computacionales (3)) is a computer services office, where six PCs and a color/B&W printer are available, and you can access e-mail and the Internet. There is also a Baja Celular office (14).

Wahoo RV Center (2) offers a wide variety of services, including plumbing, electrical, awning, refrigeration, toilets, hot water heaters, and LPG refrigeration (no engine, mechanical, or brake work). They stock a large inventory of RV parts, and sell sewer hoses, gas regulators, hitches, hitch balls, toilet chemicals, water pumps, deep-cycle batteries, electrical equipment, and many other items. A stock of standard springs is maintained, but if nothing fits, custom-made springs can be obtained in three days. They make "house calls" within a 50-mile radius, can take special orders, and can ship anywhere in Baja by bus. There is also a Nissan dealer (15).

■■■■■■■■■■■■■■■■■■
On the Transpeninsular at KM 32+

KM	Location
29+	Brisa del Mar RV Resort. Full hookups at many sites, motel, rest rooms, showers, pool, recreation room, restaurant, bar, laundry, bicycle and water sports equipment rentals, volleyball, horseshoes, fishing trip arrangements, and a beautiful beach.
28+	Zippers. Short, fast inside break. Costa Azul Surf Shop sells clothing, as well as selling, renting, and repairing surfing equipment and snorkeling gear.
28	Zippers Restaurant, RV parking, groceries, liquor, beer. The Rock is the middle break, and Old Man is the long outside break. Across the highway is Cabo Pulmo Eco-Tours, which offers kayaking, diving, and snorkeling at Pulmo.
26+	**Punta Palmilla.** The luxurious Hotel Palmilla has several restaurants and a reservations desk, offering fishing, snorkeling, and sailing excursions. Tío Sports has a reservations desk at the hotel, offering scuba diving and water sports equipment rentals. *Pangas* and fishing cruisers can be rented at the beach. The Palmilla Golf Club is located north of the highway. The small bay is used as an anchorage, but is very exposed. In south swells several point and reef breaks off the hotel provide good surfing; not too reliable, but when they work they work well.
25	Restaurant Da Giorgio; up-scale Italian
24+	PEMEX (MP).
23+	Westin Regina Hotel.
20	Casa del Mar Hotel, Cabo Real Golf Club.
17+	Centro Nacional de Artes Popular combines a restaurant with a number of small shops selling Mexican art.
15	Hotel Cabo San Lucas. Located on 2,500 acres, the luxury hotel has rooms, apartments, and villas with baths, dining room, bar, pool, horseback riding, tennis, fishing cruisers, rental tackle, and bait. The point off the hotel has a long right break.
14+	**Bahía Chileno.** The beach here (signed) is public, with fenced daily parking and a rest room. The bay has rocky reefs alternating with sandy areas and shoals of colorful tropical fish. A night dive here is a special treat. Cabo Acuadeportes, at the western end of the bay near the parking lot, has compressed air, and wet suit and dive equipment rentals and limited repairs. A full array of scuba courses is available. Scuba and snorkeling trips with bilingual guides are available for trips to the Sand Falls (described shortly), the Bancos Gorda, Pulmo, and other prime locations, as well as night dives in Bahía Chileno and the Cabo area. Whale-watching trips can be made from January through March.
12+	**Bahía Santa María.** Public beach with fine diving on coral heads, loaded with brilliant tropical fish. Drive 0.3 mile south on the sedan road, park at the gate, and walk 5 minutes to the beach. Fair anchorage in fair weather.
12	Twin Dolphin Hotel. Pickup road 0.4 mile to Playa las Viudas (Widow's Beach); look for a sign immediately southwest of entrance to the hotel. The beach alternates between sandy and rocky areas, and is open from 7 A.M. to 7 P.M.
9+	Cabo del Sol Golf Club.
5+	El Arco Trailer Park; full hookups, showers, rest rooms, ice, restaurant, bar, palm-shaded patio with pool and a view of the ocean.
4	Cabo Cielo RV Park; some full hookups, rest rooms, showers, mini-market, ice, some sites shaded by palms.
3	Vagabundos del Mar RV Park; full hookups, pool, showers, rest rooms, laundry machines, bar, café, long-distance telephone. This is one of the most popular RV facilities in the Cabo San Lucas area. Ice manufacturing plant, Cabo San Lucas Country Club Golf.
0	**Cabo San Lucas.** This is it, the end of the Transpeninsular! You made it!

Cabo San Lucas

There seems to be a greater percentage of Americans and Canadians in the day-to-day population of Cabo San Lucas than any other town in Baja. Crews from the vast fleet of yachts wander the streets at all hours, wearing studied uniforms of faded T-shirts emblazoned with the logos of ritzy handball emporiums, frayed shorts, and rotted running shoes. Subconsciously wishing to call public attention to the fact that they have survived the perilous voyage from San Diego, they walk slowly through town with a slight but still rakish swagger, faint whiffs of alcohol and pretended massive indifference permeating the air. Hemingway would have understood. An almost continuous parade of vans, daisy-painted ex-school buses, and magnificent motor coaches clogs the narrow lane-and-a-half streets, their occupants often pouring out to invade the Giggling Marlin (22) in search of burgers and beer.

Time is not being kind to those who love the place for what it was. In an effort to make a good first impression, officials have caused several hundred yards of new four-lane, mercury-lighted highway to be built into the eastern outskirts of town, only to plunge traffic abruptly into its densely crowded center. Construction of hotels and condominiums threatens to overwhelm the place and will certainly change its character. A gigantic hotel now looms over the marina, no structure in North America less suited architecturally to its surroundings. Its exterior color, previously unknown to all but professors of optical physics, can only be described as "shocking terra cotta." A garish Planet Hollywood adds to the feeling of unease. Even so, Cabo San Lucas is still the most lively and thoroughly amiable town in Baja, although one wonders how long it can last, for the growing hustle and bustle must someday bring gridlock.

A tour of the downtown district is best made on foot. Besides the traffic, there is one hazard to watch out for: people selling time-share condos. This is a high-pressure enterprise, and dozens of men stand outside tiny offices, performing the same function as the doormen at houses of ill-repute—get the customers inside. You may be negotiating for the rental of an ATV, or even buying an ice cream cone, and suddenly find yourself contemplating a catalog of condos. Total nonrecognition is the best tactic, and few salesmen will persist in an obnoxious way.

There are a number of American-style malls. Plaza las Glorias (43) is a large hotel and shopping complex, and is home to many businesses. Five dive companies currently have offices there: Baja Dive Expeditions, Land's End Divers, Neptune Divers, Pacific Coast Adventures, and Underwater Diversions, offering a wide spectrum of resort, certification, and specialty courses, local scuba and snorkeling excursions, trips to Pulmo and Gorda, equipment sales, rentals, and repairs, and compressed air. For the well-heeled, Aereo Calafia provides flying nature and adventure tours out of the Cabo San Lucas airport. The tours involve whale-watching at Bahía Magdalena, snorkeling with the sea lions at Isla Espíritu Santo, kayaking in Bahía Concepción, surfing and boardsailing at Punta Pequeña, viewing Indian cave paintings in the Sierra de San Francisco, diving with the whale-sharks at Gorda aided by a spotter plane, snorkeling and kayaking at Pulmo, and much more. Dollar Moto Rent rents ATVs and offers tours to El Faro Viejo (The Old Lighthouse), and there is even a miniature golf course. There are, of course, many restaurants, including Dairy Queen and Kentucky Fried Chicken, and those specializing in Mexican and Japanese cuisine, as well as many shops selling art ob-

jects, clothing, souvenirs, and other such things.

Among its many businesses, Plaza Nautica (40) has a Domino's Pizza, whose products are indistinguishable from those of higher latitudes, and a Subway. Motos Karlsa rents ATVs. If there has been too much partying, the plaza has a gym with a pool and aerobics equipment. Plaza Bonita Mall (6) houses numerous boutiques, T-shirt stores, and knick-knack shops, and you will not go hungry or thirsty; La Trattoria is an upscale Italian restaurant, Restaurant la Terraza offers sushi and teriyaki, and Olé-Olé specializes in Spanish and Mediterranean food, and there are several cantinas.

There are perhaps 50 other restaurants in town, ranging from humble to haughty, offering almost every food preference possible, including seafood, steaks, pizza, L.A.-deli, Japanese, Chinese, German, Swiss, Italian, American, French, Spanish, and even Mexican. Restaurant Romeo and Julieta (46) serves excellent Italian. El Galeón (51) is one of the finest, and most expensive, in town. There are four establishments that defy simple explanation and have no common denominator except that they are designed to appeal to the college crowd and passing yachties. The Giggling Marlin is in competition with Hussong's in Ensenada as to which will be the most famous bar in Baja, and serves burgers, beer, mixed drinks, and a heavy dose of ersatz funk. El Squid Roe (10) is skillfully decorated to look like a dump, but it turns out to be a rather good restaurant. Carlos 'n Charlie's (20) has a large menu, with lots of beef and beer, and a gift store selling "fresh" T-shirts, although it is uncertain whether this refers to their age or their design. Cabo Wabo (33) is a spring-break hangout, but a substantial number of students in Cabo must be on 12-month breaks, for they are encountered throughout the year, lured by loud music, almost-obscene dancing, and suicidal, all-you-can-drink specials.

There are many small shops scattered around the center of town selling jewelry, colorful belts, figurines, clothing, handicrafts, carvings, rugs, huaraches and serapes, glassware, and pottery, as well as T-shirts, each shop competing to see which can provide the raunchiest. The open air market (49) may be the best place, in terms of price, to buy ironwood carvings, huaraches, T-shirts, or knickknacks. The silver jewelry seems to be as good in quality as that in the shops, and with some bargaining, you may be able to get a better price.

Playa el Médano (Sand Dune Beach), to the east of the harbor entrance), is the best swimming beach in the Cape region. Tío Sports (28) has rentals of ATVs, waverunners, sea kayaks, Prindle 18 cats, and mountain bikes, trips on a semi-submersible and a glass-bottom boat, and para-sailing, as well as scuba and snorkeling excursions and courses similar to those of the shops noted earlier. The Activity Center (29) and Pisces Tidal Sports (25) offer a similar cornucopia of things to do and toys to play with. There are a number of fast-food and refreshment stands at Médano, as well as some excellent restaurants, including Peacock's (23), Jennifer's (21), Las Palmas Lobster House (32), and Edith's (31).

Los Frailes, the rocks that seem to form the "end" of

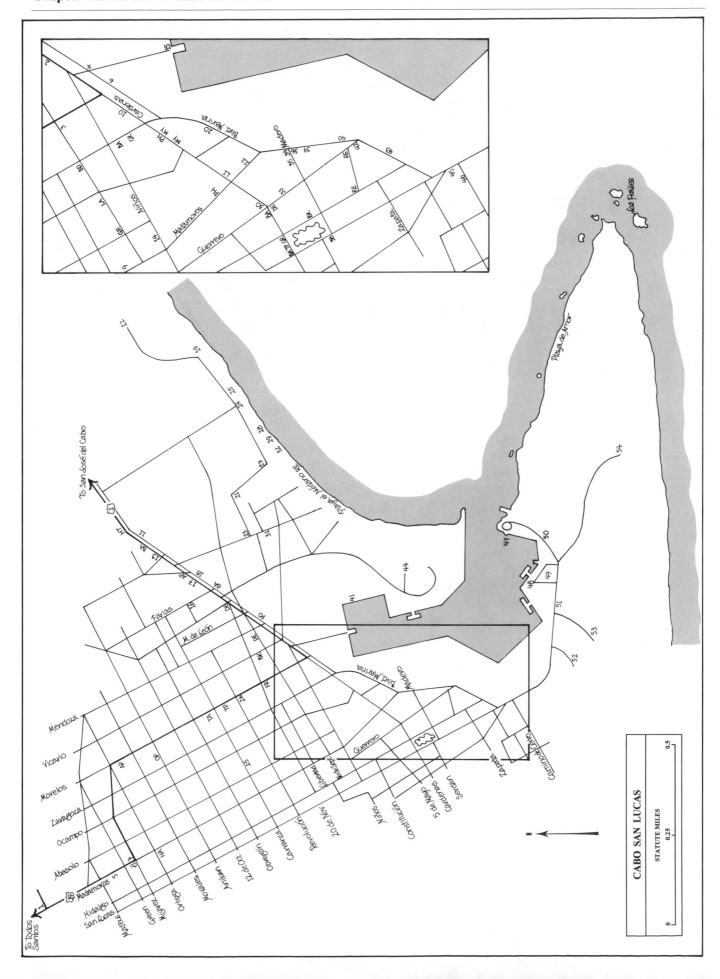

CABO SAN LUCAS

STATUTE MILES

0   0.25   0.5

Cabo San Lucas and Los Frailes

the peninsula, are an attraction for climbers. So picturesque are these rocks that they were used to film a scene in the recent climbing movie *Everest*. The easternmost rock is 222 feet high, the western 291 feet. Dotted with weird dikes and pockets, these solid, high-friction miniature mountains offer practice in face, crack, and chimney climbing in an unusual setting, with routes at almost every skill level. El Trono Blanco it's not, but Frailes has something no other climb in Baja can claim—should you become prostrate from too much exertion, your buddies can carry you to the bar at the nearby Hotel Solmar (54) for replenishment and rejuvenation. That thin vertical spire ("Neptune's Finger") nearby rising 80 feet out of the water off Playa de Amor has been conquered, the climber taking the fast way down—he dove.

The waters around Cabo San Lucas provide some of the finest fishing in the world. During a recent visit, every fishing cruiser I saw returning to the harbor was flying a billfish flag, indicating a catch, most with two or more, and one with seven. On a typical day in April or May, it is not uncommon to see 5 or 6 finning striped marlin within a circle 100 yards across, and anglers often report active competition among the fish over which will be first to take the bait. There is year-round fishing for stripers and sailfish, the warm months being best. Four of the best marlin areas are Banco San Jaime, 18 miles, 252° from Cabo Falso; Banco Golden Gate, 19 miles, 293° from Falso; Banco Gorda Primero, 8.5 miles, 095° from the San José del Cabo lighthouse; and Banco Gorda Segundo, 11 miles, 095° from the San José del Cabo lighthouse. Run 23 miles, 056° from Cabo San Lucas for Gorda Primero. The "95 Spot" and "The Drop-off," 9 miles, 106° and 12 miles, 160°, respectively, from Los Frailes are

also good, but harder to find. Many marlin are also caught between Falso and Frailes, where the 100-fathom line comes within a mile of shore. Yachtsmen coming from Mazatlán report large numbers of sailfish at Cabrillo Seamount, 26 miles, 110° from the San José del Cabo lighthouse.

There are, of course, numerous other species in Cape waters. Dorado are often taken incidentally by those pursuing marlin. Fishing very deep at night, anglers have taken swordfish. Bancos Gorda Primera and San Jaime produce many fine wahoo, and when water temperatures are normal (non-El Niño years) they may come close to shore between Chileno and Santa María, and between Frailes and Falso. The area south of "Red Hill," just west of Punta Palmilla, is also excellent for wahoo, often in water less than 200 feet deep. Trollers sometimes work roosters right in front of the Hotel Solmar, but be careful of the waves, for more than one boat has been tossed here. Excellent fishing for wahoo and dorado can be found in 125 to 300 feet of water along the beach from Falso to Frailes. The beach immediately west of Frailes can be a hot spot for shore-casters, and yellowtail, roosters, and even dorado are possible.

Don't worry too much about locating a fishing boat; it is probably the least difficult thing you will do in Cabo San Lucas. A large and ever-growing fleet is available, the prominent ones including the Hotel Hacienda Beach Resort Fishing Fleet (44), the Solmar Fleet (50), Ursula's Sport Fishing Charters (42), Pisces Fleet (34), Juanita's Fleet (37), and Gaviota's Sportfishing Fleet (2), as well as the Los Dorados Fleet in the Plaza las Glorias. Fiesta Sportfishing & Diving Co. offers fishing trips to such hot spots as the Bancos Gorda, San Jaime, and Golden Gate, and fly and light-tackle fish-

The Plaza Las Glorias and other commercial buildings now dominate the marina district in Cabo San Lucas

ing are available. Fishing International offers a number of package trips to the Cape. Cortez Yacht Charters has fishing charters ranging from *pangas* to a 57-foot motor yacht; information and reservations can be obtained at the Gaviota office. Several others operate out of offices at the fishing docks, including Rafael's Sport Fishing Fleet. Freelance boat operators will also be found at the docks. They often promote high expectations, one claiming "Jacques Cousteau asks our guys where the fish are." Baja Anglers, located adjacent to the Plaza las Glorias, specializes in light-tackle and fly fishing. They operate 26-foot sea-going catamarans specially designed for such fishing, powered by twin 150-horsepower engines. Their shop offers a wide variety of flies, tackle, equipment, clothing, and gifts. Minerva's Baja Tackle (35) stocks a complete line of rods, reels, line, leader, artificial baits, and other needs, plus lunches, snacks, licenses, and boat permits. *Minerva 3*, a Bertram 31, released 13 marlin in 3 days in early March 1995.

Marina Cabo San Lucas (4) offers floating docks, electrical service, potable water from a desalinization plant, a TV system, storage boxes, holding-tank pump out, trash disposal, security system, rest rooms, laundry, a pool, a launch ramp, maintenance services, a haul-out yard (70-ton), showers, and check-in with the COTP, *Aduana* and *Migración*. The chandlery is among the most complete in Baja, and has a selection of parts that may be of interest to people towing trailers, including rollers and shafts, hitch balls, and U-bolts. Parts not in stock can often be ordered and are usually received within a few days.

The steep (16%) Marina Cabo San Lucas launch ramp (15) has no major tide problems, but maneuvering room is becoming more limited with each passing year. Ask at the office where you should park your rig. There is a public ramp

(48, 14%), but a fee is being charged and parking and maneuvering room are limited. There are a Captain of the Port (9), *Migración* (17), and *Aduana* (38) offices, as well as a new fuel dock (47) sporting the PEMEX logo. The inner harbor is often crowded, especially from December to May, and the docks are almost always jammed. Live bait is usually available from *pangas* in the dock area.

Although weather at the Cape is usually benign, at least during the non-*chubasco* months from mid-November to mid-May, occasional freak weather is possible. On December 8, 1982, a sudden southeast gale caught the fleet of yachts anchored off Playa el Médano unprepared, wrecking 22 of them. Boaters headed for areas west of Falso should take care, for weather there is often very different—usually worse—from that observed off the harbor. Unofficial weather reports are broadcast on VHF channel 22 each morning.

There are other dive shops in addition to those already mentioned. Amigos del Mar, next door to the Solmar Fleet office, has rentals, sales, courses, local excursions, and scuba trips similar to the other shops in town. The company operates 2 large trimarans, and a 25-foot twin-engine *panga*. In the winter, they offer whale-watching trips. They also manage diving operations for the *Solmar V*, a luxurious 112-foot, compressor-equipped liveaboard based in Cabo that makes dive trips to Isla Socorro, Isla Clarion, Pulmo, and the Sea of Cortez. Cabo Acuadeportes, at the Hacienda, has the same basic equipment, instruction, rentals, and services as their facility at Chileno, described earlier. In addition, waverunners, canoes, catamarans, kayaks, and sailboards are for rent, and parasailing and water-skiing are available. J & R Baja Divers in the Plaza Bonita Mall has full rentals and limited sales, air, and two dive boats. A wide variety of dives at local attractions are avail-

Mark Wilford

Barbara Busse climbs Los Frailes, undoubtedly the most southerly climbing location in Baja

and Frailes. Starting with a rather modest slope, the canyon begins to descend at an average of 75% within a few hundred feet. It then levels off to a slope of 10%, which it maintains until the water is 6,000 feet deep. Granite walls tower over the bottom of the canyon, and at a depth of 5,400 feet, the walls are over 3,000 feet high. Long rivers of excess sand from the beach flow down the tributaries of the canyon at a rate of 0.1 mile an hour, forming sandfalls when they reach cliffs. The sandfalls should be visited only by certified divers with some deep water experience. The best place to start a dive is half-way between the mouth of the inner harbor and Frailes, where an islet with a flat top will be seen 60 yards from shore. Follow the slope down and start watching for falls at 100 feet. Most are intermittent, but the chance of seeing at least one cascading over the cliffs is good. Rocky areas are covered with lush growths of corals and gorgonians, and there are many species of fish to be seen, but touch nothing, for the bay is an underwater ecological reserve.

Banco Gorda Primero is another excellent dive site, although it is too deep for all but experienced divers, since its shallowest areas are about 110 feet. Nautical charts show one area at 8 fathoms, but experienced local divers insist it does not exist. The primary diving attractions at Gorda are the large numbers of heavy-duty gamefish, plus the chance to see black coral. In addition, Gorda is frequented by whale sharks. Some gray whales continue past the Cape during their annual migration, and divers have occasionally been able to swim with them. Marisla Seamount is not the only place that has been graced by friendly mantas: in early 1995 divers just outside the harbor entrance encountered friendlies for a period of almost 3 weeks. Fiesta Sportfishing & Diving offers diving excursions to Gorda, as do all the local dive shops.

There are other, less demanding dives in the area. An interesting wreck can be found in 50 feet of water on a sand bottom just southwest of the most southerly rock

able, as well as PADI certification and specialty courses. The president of the company, Jorge Schultz Harp, has discovered a "secret site," where lots of very large and trusting fish congregate. Being an excellent underwater photographer, he can take you to the best sites for that purpose.

A recompression chamber is located in the Plaza las Glorias. Local dive shops collect a $2 donation on all dives ($4 on a two-tank dive). This donation goes to the recompression facility, and entitles the diver to free hyperbaric chamber treatments if necessary, a wise and inexpensive investment. Also, the medical clinic operated by Dr. Alfonso Nájar (25) has a chamber. He speaks English and has credentials in hyperbaric medicine.

One of the most interesting scuba dives in Baja can be made in the outer harbor. The narrow strip of land leading out to Frailes is overtopped by waves during storms, carrying sand into the bay. Several tributaries of an enormous underwater canyon begin between the mouth of the inner harbor

Mike's first marlin, taken at Banco Gorda after a ninety-minute fight. It was released unharmed

at Frailes. It is badly disintegrated, but is home to a number of unusual fish, including an occasional longnose butterfly fish. Be careful diving here, for sightseeing and fishing boats studiously ignore diver's flags. The wreck is often festooned with fishing lures, some quite expensive, small treasures for the taking. Big jewfish occasionally visit the wreck in the summer months, and sea lions living nearby often accompany divers.

In addition to the RV parks on the Transpeninsular already mentioned, there are a few in town. Club Cabo Motel and Campground Resort (12) has suites, many shaded RV sites with full hookups, showers, rest rooms, laundry, ice, pool, hot tub, trampoline, ping pong, a hammock lounge area with color TV, and a kitchen cleaning station where campers can do their dishes. El Faro Viejo Trailer Park (7) has palm-shaded sites, full hookups, showers, rest rooms, and a restaurant/bar. There are numerous hotels having bars, restaurants, reservations desks, fishing fleets, and other facilities that may be of interest, including the Finisterra (52), Mar de Cortez (30), Solmar, Hacienda, Plaza las Glorias, Club Cascades de Baja (24), Marina Fiesta Resort (41), Meliá San Lucas (27), Terra Sol Beach Resort (53), and Villa de Palmar (19).

Obtaining food and supplies will not be a problem. Almacenes Grupo Castro (26) sells groceries, meats, cold cuts, wine, liquor, fruit, and vegetables. Sanliz Supermarket (36) sells imported foods from the US, as well as local meats and vegetables. Panadería San Angel (3) sells bakery goods, pastries, cold drinks, and dairy products. Pollos y Carnes Lizarraga, just north of Panadería San Angel, is a butcher shop. Fresh fish is available at El Pescadería el Dorado (14). There are, of course, many other small grocery stores and beer distributors throughout the town. Wetsun (16) sells water purified by reverse-osmosis in large quantities, and can fill RVs. There are two PEMEX stations (1, MD) and (13, MPD). Proveedora Agricola Automotriz California (11) is a Chevy dealer, and offers parts, service, and repairs. Refaccionaria López Cinco (5) sells auto parts, and has a machine shop. Celis Automotriz, a few doors southwest of Wetsun, has parts and service for Volkswagen.

There are several laundromats, including Lavandería Evelyn (8), and many doctors and dentists. An American Consular agency (45) has been established. LPG can be obtained at a yard at KM 111, north of town on Route 19. NetZone, located across the street from the PEMEX on the Transpeninsular, is an Internet café, offering computers, and e-mail and Internet access, as well as beer, mixed drinks, and light food. They have PC stations, color/B&W printers, and scanners. Baja Celular has an office in town (18).

Side trip on Route 19 to Todos Santos and KM 185 on the Transpeninsular. Although this paved road crosses many arroyos, most grades are gentle and only a few are very long. There are many spur roads to fine beaches and good camping. Bicyclists will find the trip to Todos Santos enjoyable and undemanding. Birders should keep a sharp eye out, for there are a number of unusual and interesting species. Begin by driving northwest from KM 2 of the Transpeninsular on the road signed TODOS SANTOS. In just under 2 miles, you will encounter a junction with Route 19, marked by a large Coca-Cola sign, where you should turn right (northwest).

KM	Side trip location
111	LPG yard, southwest side of road.
102	Marginal sedan road to Playa las Margaritas. Turn southwest (240°), arrive at the beach in 1.5 miles. Don't attempt to climb the last dune—it is too soft for most vehicles, and driving on the beach is prohibited. There is a large boondocking area behind the dune, and miles of pristine sand beach.
97	**Migriño.** Sedan road to a beautiful public beach. Set odometer. Turn off the highway and make an immediate right (320°) turn. At Mile 0.1, turn left (255°), arrive at the beach at Mile 0.6. Short beach break, good right point break on the right waves.
90+	Sedan road southwest (200°) to Boca el Barranco, a sandy boondocking beach. Be sure to camp on high ground, for the water offshore is deep, and the sand beach is exceptionally steep. Waves thus break within yards of the beach, occasionally driving water inland, and many an unsuspecting camper has been flooded out. For these reasons, the surfing is poor, since waves close out in seconds, and swimming is dangerous. The heavy and persistent winds make it a fine heavy-weather boardsailing site.
81	RV parking, southwest of highway.
77	**Plutarco Elías Calles.** Settlement, restaurant.
73+	**Punta Gasparino.** Good right point breaks on large waves.
71+	Western end of the Naranjas Road.
64	Sedan road southwest (255°) 1.6 miles to Playa los Cerritos. Public beach, point and beach breaks. As you approach the beach you will encounter a **Y**; go left (145°) for the abandoned RV park, go right (205°) for a beach. Although the RV park here has a few sewer and water hookups, the facilities are minimal. However, many independent-minded people choose to stop anyway. A small fee is charged, the money going to the town of El Pescadero. Boondocking is available at the sandy beach northwest of the park. Informal Cerritos Surf Shop, operating out of a trailer, offers surf board, Boogie board, and skimboard rentals.
62	**El Pescadero.** Cafés, groceries, fruit store, *tortilla* factory, water, long-distance telephone. The main part of town lies east of the road. The reef and beach breaks in this vicinity consistently produce fine surfing, with steep faces and short, fast

rides. Boardsailors also love the place. Road east to Santo Domingo. Those continuing on Route 19 should skip the following section.

↱ Side trip to Santo Domingo. As noted earlier, the roadhead at Santo Domingo is the end point of the Cañon San Bernardo backpack trip. Turn east (095°) 0.4 mile northwest of the KM 62 marker. Set odometer. At Mile 0.4 take the left (070°) fork near the village stadium, take the right (056°) fork at Mile 0.8, and the left (006°) fork at Mile 5.8. Take the left (320°) fork at Mile 6.1, turn right (065°) at Mile 6.8, and right (074°) at Mile 7.5. The grading ends here and the road requires a pickup or better. Take the left (058°) fork at Mile 9.2, and go straight ahead (107°) at Mile 12.3, and straight ahead (030°) at Mile 12.9, arriving at the settlement at Mile 13.3.

Back on Route 19 at KM 62

KM	Side trip location
59	Sedan road southwest to San Perdito RV Park (signed). The park has full hookups, rest rooms, *palapas*, showers, pool, bar, restaurant, laundry service, sand beach, good beach break on northwest swells. Playa las Palmas, a fine boondocking beach, can be found by turning southwest at KM 59. Set odometer, and turn right (310°) at Mile 0.1 on the sedan road. At Mile 0.4 take the left (255°), at Mile 1.2 the left (225°), and arrive at the beach at Mile 1.6 (the last 200 yards get a bit bumpy). There are numerous campsites in the palm groves just inland from the beach. The sandy half-mile beach is bounded at each end by rocky headlands.
55+	Sedan road east to Rancho San Juan del Aserradero. Those continuing on Route 19 should skip the following section.

↱ Side trip to San Juan del Aserradero. This ranch is a popular starting point for backpacking and mule forays to La Laguna. Although steep, the trail is only about 7 miles long and it may be cooled by fogs and winds off the ocean. The trip up by mule will take only about 4 hours, making it a temptation to try to make the trip a one-day affair, but you should make it an overnighter, for there is much to see. A round-trip afoot should take at least 3 days, including exploring time. To get to the ranch, turn northeast (059°) 0.3 mile north of the KM 55 marker. Cross a cattle guard and set odometer. The steep face seen at 045° from this point is Cerro la Aguja. Go straight ahead (140°) at Mile 2.2, pass a forest-fire tower at Mile 2.7, go left (043°) at Mile 3.9, straight ahead (030°) at Mile 8.8, left (015°) at Mile 10.8, straight ahead (090°) at Mile 12.7 and arrive at the ranch at Mile 13.5. The road can handle sedans, although a 21% downgrade at Mile 12.3 may cause problems on the way out.

The trail departs the ranch in an easterly direction, quickly swinging north and continuing up the north side of Cañada San Matías. At the half-way point, a water source may be encountered. On the ridge above Cañon el Frijolar, Picacho la Laguna can be seen just over a mile to the north. As the altitude gets higher oaks and then pines appear, providing welcome shade. The Mexican 1:50,000 topos—Las Cuevas F12B24, and El Rosario F12B23—show a close approximation of the route, the first also showing the route from Rancho San Dionisio. "El Rosario" shows the ranch on its lower margin; the next topo to the south, Todos Santos F12B33, shows the roads and intersections on the way to the ranch from Route 19, as described above.

Back on Route 19 at KM 55+

KM	Side trip location
51+	Todos Santos.

Todos Santos

A pleasant agricultural town, once the site of a Jesuit mission, Todos Santos is now the home of a number of painters, potters, woodcarvers, and other artists, plus a growing community of American expatriate retirees, artists, surfers, and loafers. With its old brick buildings, tranquillity, and leisurely ways, the town is in dramatic contrast to "go-go"

A near-miss at Pescadero

Cabo San Lucas. One claim to fame for the place is that it is located directly on the Tropic of Cancer.

When entering town from the southeast, keep a sharp eye for a red stop light, dangling at an unusually high location over the road. The local police have been known to operate a scam here, ticketing *gringo* drivers not seeing the light, a transgression costing 450 pesos, 300 if the police "pay the fine for you."

There are a dozen or so restaurants, in every price range, often having unusual hours and days of operation. Almacenes Grupo Castro (11) has groceries, meats, cold cuts, wine, liquor, fruit, vegetables, and household items, and there is a laundromat (13). Tienda ISSSE (8) has basic food and household items. Cristalina (7) sells ice and purified water. There is a bank (2), and the PEMEX (10) sells MD. A new mini-mall and motel (5) are available. The book store (3) carries a wide variety of books about Baja and magazines in English. El Litro RV Park (12) has a few sites with full hookups, rest rooms, and showers.

The Old Casa Cultura (1) has red-dyed skulls of Pericú Indians, pottery, baskets, and other local crafts, historical displays, photos of the old sugar days, and a small collection of rocks and minerals. The remains of an old sugar cane processing mill (9) can be seen. A number of the artists mentioned earlier work out of their homes, and some small shops sell locally made furniture, Mexican clothing, local handicrafts, hand-woven upholstery fabrics, and hand-made pottery. These shops come and go, and some are open only erratically, so locating them requires some driving around and asking questions. Fishing trips can be arranged at the Hotel California (6). The quarry are marlin, wahoo, yellowtail, and dorado, but a trip is not for the faint-hearted, for there is no harbor and boats must negotiate the surf. Good surf-casting is available at all local beaches. If you don't connect, you need not lose face— there is a fish market in town (4).

There is fine boondocking and surfing at Playa Pastora. Set odometer, drive northwest on Topete onto a graded sedan road. Turn left (235°) at Mile 0.2, bear right (250°) at the **Y** at Mile 0.5, turn left (260°) at the intersection at Mile 0.6, pass two stores at Mile 0.8, and at Mile 0.9 bear right (320°). The road continues northwest, paralleling the beach, about a half mile inland. Pass through a large grove of palms at Mile 4.2. Continue straight ahead until Mile 4.3, where you will turn left (205°), towards the beach. Arrive at Mile 4.5. The beautiful sand beach provides numerous boondocking opportunities, and the area is famous among surfers for its point and beach breaks, with surf up to 12 feet on northwest swells.

KM	Side trip location
29	Liquor store, restaurant.
8	Cafeteria, swimming pool, *palapas*.
0	Junction with the Transpeninsular Highway at KM 185.

● ●

❝ *Las Cuevas de los Indios*

A number of years ago I stopped at La Ciéneguita, a tiny settlement on the newly bulldozed Naranjas Road across the Sierra de la Laguna. The local people were having a volleyball game, but as I drove up the women and children ran in terror and the adult men formed a small arc and approached my van with grim looks. The place had been almost totally isolated until the road was constructed, and it was obvious that the inhabitants were not used to strangers and had no intention of becoming so. They appeared to be rather unsophisticated, almost the image of the traditional American hillbilly. Some of the men had dental work that appeared homemade, with equal amounts of tooth enamel and gold showing, the latter worked into fleur-de-lis and other heraldic devices.

I was scouting for "new" caves, and when I asked whether there were any in the vicinity they said no, rather too emphatically. Hoping to pry out the information with an ancient device, I opened a large cooler full of Dos Equis and a gallon of home-made wine, and within minutes I had their rapt attention and full cooperation. There was perhaps a small cave of little consequence up the road, they admitted, and as the alcohol flowed the cave assumed grander proportions. There were actually three of them, known as "Las Cuevas de los Indios," and they were so large that entire tribes of ancient Indians used to gather in them for magic ceremonies. When I announced, just at the end of the fifth six-pack, that I wanted to explore the caves and needed a guide, there was a rush for the van and before I could protest it was jammed with the entire male population of La Ciéneguita. The weight was so great that we barely made it up the first small grade, a problem somewhat relieved when half of my guides demanded a stop for a call of nature. Singing and joking, we continued on our journey, but there was soon a call for another stop and the other half relieved themselves. This place, however, was also the closest approach to the caves.

None of my guides were in any condition to perform their duties, but two of the more sober got out of the van, promising the grandest of all caves. However, as we climbed down a steep gorge I began to notice that it was increasingly hard to keep them on the subject of caves; they wanted to talk about deer hunting. As we approached the caves the reason became apparent—the tribes must have been elves. Instead of the grand Cuevas de los Indios I had been promised, we found several small grottos, distinguished only by the presence of a few emaciated bats hanging dejectedly from the ceilings. The third grotto could be approached only by rappelling down from above, but given the diluted state of the blood of those who would be on belay, I was not about to stretch my luck.

As we hiked up the gorge toward the sound of music coming from the van, my guides sheepishly turned the conversation back to deer hunting. When that didn't work they started a short seminar on native medicine. Every few yards they dismantled a bush or uprooted a shrub, assuring me that the sap, leaf, or bark was good for cancer, rheumatism, piles, and/or impotence, apparently hoping that I suffered from one or more and thereby gaining my attention. I was surprised to find that one medicine actually did work, rather dramatically in fact. When I scraped my hand on a thorn they gleefully broke a branch from a low, woody shrub with reddish bark they called lomboy colorado *and rubbed the clear astringent sap on the wound. Within seconds the bleeding stopped and by the next day the scrape could hardly be seen. When we reached the van the medical seminar ended and one of my guides returned to the subject of caves. With a golden grin he said that it was a shame that I had chosen not to explore the third cave, for it was the one the Indians really had used. A real shame! With everyone singing raunchy songs, we returned to La Ciéneguita, party-time continuing until the cooler was empty. My new friends were perhaps a bit unsophisticated and given to exaggeration, but they proved to be friendly, intelligent, and well-informed about their small part of the world.* **"**

● ●

Chapter 13

Tecate to San Felipe

By necessity, the organization of this chapter will be more complex than its predecessors. First, we will follow both Route 2D, the new Tijuana/Mexicali Toll Road, and Old Route 2 from Tijuana to Tecate, and then follow Old Route 2 from Tecate to La Rumorosa, where we will again be on Route 2D, which becomes Route 2 again 11 miles east of Mexicali, and then on to the intersection of Routes 2 and 5. We will then return to Tecate to cover Route 3 to Ensenada. Returning to Mexicali, we will head south on Route 5 to Crucero la Trinidad. From this point we will return to Ensenada and cover Route 3 back to Route 5, then travel south on Route 5 south to San Felipe, and then on to KM 229+ on the Transpeninsular. Use the regional map on pages 110 and 111 and that on pages 130 and 131.

■■■■■■■■■■■■■■■■■■■

At the Otay Mesa border crossing, preparing to head east to Tecate and Mexicali

Once across the border, there are *Migración* and *Aduana* offices. Set odometer, and head south. This stretch of road is blessed with abundant road signs. There are two choices of route. To use Route 2D, the new Tijuana/Mexicali Toll Road, follow the signs TECATE CUOTA. At Mile 1.0, turn left (east, signed) and you will soon be on the Toll Road. There are no gas stations or facilities on the Toll Road as far as Tecate. A Toll Road exit at KM 123 allows travelers to exit to Tecate. In early 1998 the Toll Road ended at KM 118, where traffic was diverted to Old Route 2 until La Rumorosa, where the Toll Road begins again, and Old Route 2 "disappears," only to reappear again at KM 18.

If you wish to take Old Route 2 from Tijuana to Tecate, continue past Mile 1.0 and follow the signs TECATE LIBRE. You will soon swing east and be headed for Tecate on Old Route 2.

KM	Location
157	PEMEX (MPD).
156	LPG plant.
154	PEMEX (MPD).
153	PEMEX (MPD).
132	Tecate.

Tecate

Tecate is a small, tourist-oriented city with a variety of supplies and services, including a number of banks and ATMs. The border crossing to the US is generally uncrowded, at least by Tijuana standards, and is open from 6 A.M. to midnight. There is a *Migración* office where tourist cards can be obtained and validated, but it is sometimes closed on Sundays. Local information can be obtained from the office of the State Secretary of Tourism on the south side of the park at the corner of Route 3 (Av. Benito Juárez) and Av. Ortiz Rubio. A Baja Celular office is located on the north side of Juárez, two blocks east of the park. Route 3 south to Ensenada.

Although many miles of pavement have been laid, and numerous overpasses constructed, the Toll Road from Tecate to La Rumorosa was still not operational in early 1998, so Old Route 2 must be utilized.

■■■■■■■■■■■■■■■■■■■

In Tecate, headed east on Old Route 2

KM	Location
122	**San Pablo.** PEMEX (MD). An old caver's publication noted a large gypsum cave in this vicinity, but it seems to have become "lost" in recent years.
112	Rancho Ojai RV Park. Full hookups, some sites with patio and group areas, rest rooms, showers, shade trees, club house, barbecue area, volleyball, horseshoes, hiking and nature-watching trails, playground, horseback riding, small store, working ranch.
109	PEMEX (MD), tiny cafés, groceries, tire repair.
104	Club Campestre Eréndira RV Park; shade trees, brick barbecues, playground equipment, rest rooms, potable water, several small lakes for fishing and swimming, but no hookups.

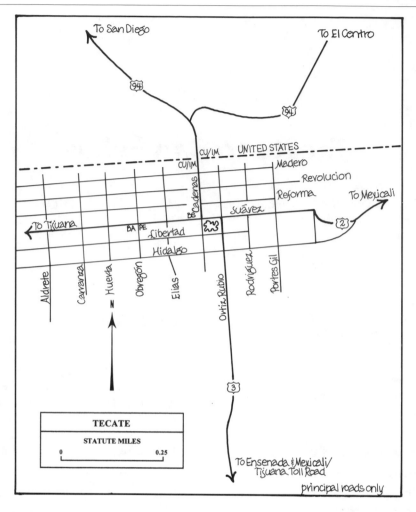

To San Diego

To El Centro

UNITED STATES

CU/IM

CU/IM

Madero

Revolucion

Reforma

To Mexicali

Suárez

To Tijuana

BA PE

Libertad

Hidalgo

Aldrete

Carranza

Huerta

Obregón

Elias

Ortiz Rubio

Rodríguez

Portes Gil

Cadenas

N

TECATE

STATUTE MILES

0   0.25

To Ensenada & Mexicali/
Tijuana Toll Road

principal roads only

98   **Ejido Luis Echeverria Alvarez**. Sedan road south to Ojos Negros. Those continuing on Route 2 should skip the following section.

![] *Side trip to Ojos Negros.* This pleasant trip crosses fine rolling chaparral country dotted with pine-rimmed meadows and groves of oaks. The area is heavily mineralized, and collectors could look for pegmatite dikes. The road is generally in good condition, with no bad grades, not much change in altitude, and only two sizable stream crossings, both of which are sandy and flat, so almost any vehicle except low-slung sedans can make it. Although there are many minor forks and intersections, the correct road is usually obvious, and there is little danger of becoming lost.

The road starts south 0.1 mile east of the KM 98 marker. Set odometer. The road passes a bakery, a *tortilla* factory, a laundromat, mechanic, auto parts, and a number of grocery stores, but the pavement (rough and potholed) ends at Mile 4.5. At Mile 5.6 go straight ahead (130°). (The right—190°—fork is a sedan road leading 1 mile to Hacienda Santa Veronica. This beautiful park has spreading oaks, open meadows, some hookups, rooms, a swimming pool, tennis courts, mountain bike and motorcycle courses, camping areas, a nice dining room, bar, rest rooms, and showers.

RV facilities may be closed during the winter months, but RV parking—no hookups—is permitted.) At Mile 8.8 continue straight ahead (183°) at the fork. Rancho Nejí is reached at Mile 11.3. Continue straight ahead (125°) at Mile 12.4, and at Mile 18.8 turn right (140°), passing through El Compadre, a small settlement graced by enormous oaks. The road then crosses several streams, passes through large meadows and by several ranches at San Faustino at Mile 29.0, and then runs through a series of majestic oak groves, offering fine boondocking sites. At Mile 36.7 wheel tracks lead 2 miles north to a tungsten deposit.

After you pass more oak groves, La Rosa de Castilla, a tiny ranching community, is reached at Mile 42.6. The tailings of Mina el Fenónemo can be seen on the ridge to the west. As its name implies, the mine was a phenomenon of its time, producing over 2% of the world's supply of tungsten during its short working life. By 1943 the 100,000-ton ore body was exhausted, and today the mine is a totally deserted and fascinating place. The west flank of the ridge has cool, mysterious mine shafts. Look for thousands of cast iron balls used in the mill to crush scheelite. Minerals to be found include apophyllite, garnet, calcite, quartz, malachite, azurite, schorl, actinolite, arsenopyrite, bismuth, pyrite, chalcopyrite, clinozoisite, diopside, scheelite, hedenbergite, idocrase, pyrrhotite, axinite, epidote, and prehnite. Surrounding areas contain many mine shafts, tailing dumps, and signs of pegmatite dikes. A pegmatite dike on a ridge about 500 yards east has yielded small yellow-to-lavender tourmaline crystals, and sapphire has been found to the southwest.

La Huerta, a small settlement, is reached at Mile 50.8, and at Mile 52.1, El Coyote, an important junction, unmarked except for a barbed-wire fence with metal posts, a rarity in Baja. To continue on to Ojos Negros, drive straight ahead (255°), arriving at Mile 61.1. If you intend to head for Parque Nacional Constitucíon de 1857 turn left (110°), and you will encounter the KM 55+-Parque 1857 road in 3 miles.

■■■■■■■■■■■■■

Back on Old Route 2 at Ejido Luis Echeverria Alvarez, KM 98

KM	Location
89+	The La Jollita pegmatites, an extension of well-known mineral deposits in the US, are located to the north. Turn onto the road signed Jacumé, use the overpass to cross the Toll Road, and park at the first opportunity. Hike 0.2 of a mile east to a low ridge. The light-colored rocks on the hillsides are remnants of pegmatite dikes, yielding green tourmaline, blue topaz, cleavelandite, muscovite, beryl, microcline, apatite, and lots of schorl.
83	**El Cóndor.** PEMEX (MPD), restaurant, pickup road south to Parque 1857. Those continuing on Route 2 should turn to page 255.

↱ *Side trip to Parque Nacional Constitucíon de 1857.* An ever-changing maze of roads from El Cóndor to the park makes a compass useful, and there are enough rough spots that sedans are not recommended. The road running north from KM 55+ on Route 3 into the park is often in better condition, allowing those in sedans easier access.

The road from El Cóndor heads south next to the PEMEX station. Set odometer. Take the left (145°) fork at Mile 11.4. The surrounding areas are among the most heavily mineralized in Baja, with many gold, tungsten, manganese, and cobalt mines. Collectors have found clinozoisite, quartz, axinite, grossularite garnet, blue tourmaline, and epidote. Keep left (123°) at the intersection at Mile 12.0. La Mesquita, near Mile 13.0, is known for beryl, aquamarine, and apatite mined from vugs in a pegmatite dike. At the crossroads at Mile 17.0 note the sign EVITE INCENDIOS and continue straight (141°) ahead. (The right (179°) fork leads to the Las Margaritas and Gavilanes mineral areas.) Take the left (128°) fork at Mile 17.5, and at Mile 18.0 join the La Rumorosa-Parque 1857 road; continue southeast (125°). The side road

east at Mile 20.0 leads to the Rancho San Ignacio-La Milla area, jumping-off point for hikes into Cañon Tajo. Those continuing on the road to Parque 1857 should turn to page 252.

↱ *Side trip to Cañon Tajo.* The upper reaches of Cañon Tajo approach this point. Largest canyon in the Juárez escarpment, Tajo is also the most colorful, with broad bands of white, green, black, red, brown, beige, and tan frozen into its rocks. Thousands of palms line the canyon, firewood is plentiful, and there are many campsites, some next to fine swimming holes. El Trono Blanco, Baja's supreme technical climbing challenge, lies at the head of the canyon at the confluence of its northwest and south forks.

The easiest approach to El Trono Blanco and into the main canyon is by way of "Bell Dome" campground. Turn east at Mile 20.0 onto a pickup road signed RANCHO SAN IGNACIO-LA MILLA, set odometer and turn right (160°) at Mile 1.1. You will pass a tiny ranch on the right, and the road will begin to meander. Stay left at every fork, and at Mile 3.8 you will arrive at the small, clean campground (no facilities). A canyon will be noted bearing 095°, with a bell-shaped dome on the left, a steep rock cliff on the right. The uphill foot route east from the campground soon passes through an area of massive boulders requiring a great deal of scrambling and even some travel on hands and knees through dark passages. In fact, if you need some bouldering practice, this is the place to do it. After about 45 minutes the pass is reached, and there are glimpses of what lies ahead, the bottom of a gigantic canyon 2,300 feet below and a great wall of rock to the left. The canyon ahead is Tajo's south fork, about a mile from its junction with the main east-west canyon. As you drop into the canyon it becomes steeper, and although the brush grows thicker, little heed will be given to it as the proportions of the awesome 1,600-foot wall become more apparent. Composed of lightly weathered granite with large feldspar crystals, it provides excellent climbing conditions, so much so that one San Diego climber has made 50 ascents at last count. The descent from the campground will take about 3 hours.

An eagle's-eye view of Tajo can be found by hiking from the La Milla campground to a ridge overlooking the canyon. Return to the fork at Mile 1.1, reset your odometer and drive northwest (320°). The road will meander north and then east toward the Juárez escarpment. Swing right (090°) at the forks at Miles 0.6 and 0.7, left (090°) at Mile 0.8, and arrive at the campground at Mile 1.7 (no facilities). There is no trail to the ridge, but the country is fairly open and hiking is easy. Simply head east from the campground for about an hour, avoiding dropping too deeply into the northwest fork of the canyon, which approaches the campground.

Backpackers wishing to experience one of Baja's most challenging trips can drop down into the main canyon by way of the northwest fork. This trip is shorter but more difficult than that through Cañon del Diablo, described begin-

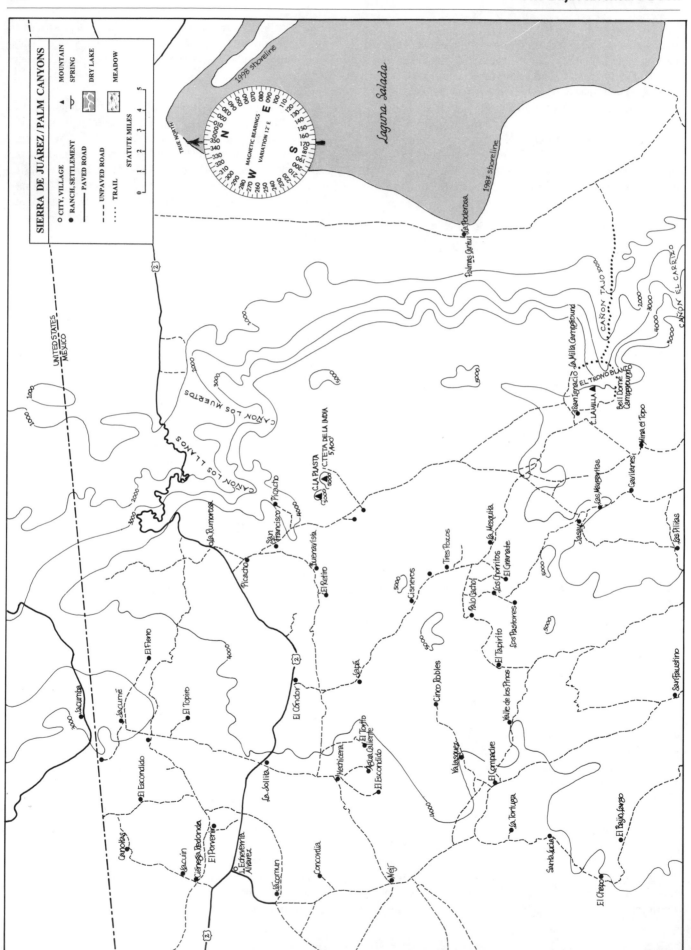

SIERRA DE JUÁREZ / PALM CANYONS

O CITY, VILLAGE
● RANCH, SETTLEMENT
▲ MOUNTAIN
⚡ SPRING
DRY LAKE
MEADOW

——— PAVED ROAD
– – – UNPAVED ROAD
········ TRAIL

STATUTE MILES
0 1 2 3 4 5

MAGNETIC BEARINGS
VARIATION 12° E

N E S W

TRUE NORTH

UNITED STATES
MEXICO

Laguna Salada

1998 shoreline
1987 shoreline

CAÑON LOS MUERTOS

CAÑON LOS LLANOS

CAÑON TAJO

CAÑON EL CARRIZO

Palms Cantu
La Poderosa

San Ignacio La Milla Campground
EL TRONO BLANCO
EL LA VILLA
Bell Dome
Campground
Mina El Topo

Los Maravillas
Cavilanes
Jose

La Mesquita
Los Chorritos
El Granate
Las Pilitas

Picacho
San Francisco
Picacho

LA PLASTA
LA TETA DE LA INDIA

Buenavista
El Retiro

Tres Pozos
Cisneros

Palo Cacho
Los Pastores

San Faustino

Rumorosa

El Fierro
Jacumé
El Topito

El Cóndor
Jalé

Cinco Robles

El Tapirito
Valle de los Pinos

El Compadre

Valasquez

Jacumba

El Escondido

La Jollita
Hechicera
El Torito
Agua Caliente
El Escondido

La Tortuga
El Bajio Largo

Capolas
Jacuin
Cienega Redonda
El Porvenir
J. Echeverría Álvarez
Jacomun

Concordia

Nejí

Santa Lucía

El Chapo

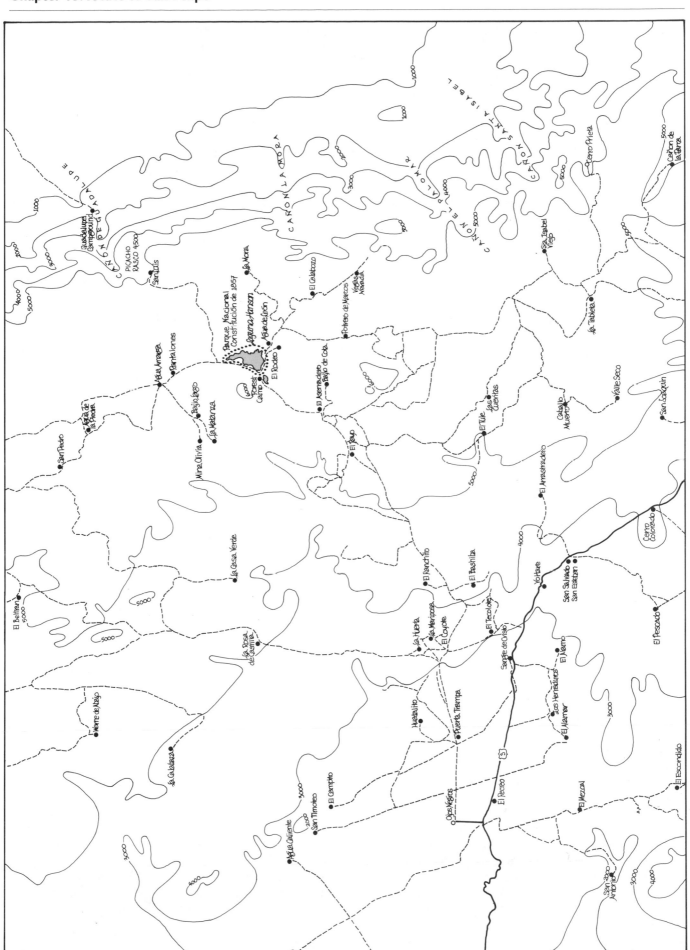

Stephen Peterson

Climbers work their way up El Trono Blanco

by the time you see the first palms you will be wishing you had taken the route from Bell Dome. Horizontal progress is irrelevant; it's the vertical that matters. Great boulders lie jumbled, one on top of the other, and the term "boulder-hopping" becomes meaningless—you don't hop but rather struggle from one down to the next, sliding on seat bottoms, securing hand- and footholds as they present themselves, and skidding your pack along. The first pools will be encountered within an hour. There are rewards for all this work; a number of beautiful, thready waterfalls drop into crystal-clear pools, some a dozen feet deep, slowing the progress of those who can't resist a skinny-dip in each of them. Working around the first 30-foot waterfall is a real challenge, but greater ones lie below, including a 60-footer. Watch for tourmaline crystals. Incredibly, it will take a long, hard day to arrive at the bottom of the main canyon, less than 1.5 miles from the campground.

The main canyon, lying east of El Trono Blanco, is less steep than the northwest fork but is still challenging. Great numbers of palms continue for the next 3 miles, amid huge piles of boulders and pools of water, after which the canyon floor becomes broader and more sandy. Fill all canteens, for the stream soon disappears under the sand, and no surface water will be found to the east. Considerable effort can be saved by hiking on cattle trails along the south side of the canyon. You will arrive at the roadhead sore, sweating, and thoroughly tired, but happy with a new experience.

Back on the Parque 1857 Road at Mile 20

A tungsten mine was once located southeast of Mile 20.0. Starting at this point there are great views of "Picacho Row," a line of miniature granite spires rising up to 500 feet above the tableland, with many spires, chimneys, and domes (one of which is Bell Dome), some offering fine rock climbing. Continue straight ahead (150°) at the intersection at Mile 24.0. Mina el Topo, near Mile 24.5, produced gold and cuprite. "Rough stuff" is encountered between Miles 25.5 and 28 as the road climbs a ridge. Take the left (114°) fork at the intersection at Mile 30.6.

At Mile 34.5 a pickup road leads 3.5 miles southwest to Mina Olivia, producing scheelite. In 1964 an odd spherical formation of axinite was uncovered there, and within several months 1,200 pounds had been removed. Fifty pounds were of gem quality, and one crystal, cut into a beautiful flawless gem of almost 24 carats, is in the National Museum in Washington, DC. The mine owner estimates the crystals sold for $400,000 at retail, but laments that little was realized by him or the lucky miners. When news of this world-class find reached the outside world a mob of collectors and opportunists headed for the mine, but no more crystals were

ning on page 262. Since the return trip back to the campground involves stretches of technical climbing, virtually everyone making the trip arranges to be picked up at the mouth of the canyon. The horizontal distance involved, about 8 miles from the campground to the head of the road leading west from the Laguna Salada area, is deceptive, and at least 3 days should be set aside for a one-way trip, including some time for loafing and exploring. Careful route finding will keep it a marginal class 3, and it would be well to bring a rope to allow lowering backpacks down chasms. The appropriate 1:50,000 Mexican topo is La Poderosa I11D74. Though not labeled, the canyon is shown along the bottom margin.

The northwest fork of the canyon is entered by hiking 165° from the campground. The open, relatively level terrain during the first half-hour will instill undue confidence, but the moment of reckoning will soon approach. The terrain quickly becomes steeper and the underbrush denser, and

Reeve Peterson

A Cañon Tajo swimming hole

found and the excitement quickly died out. However, small amounts of axinite and clinozoisite are found nearby.

At Mile 35.5 encounter an abandoned forest-fire camp, and at Mile 37.3 a pickup road (signed) northeast to Rancho San Luis, 7 miles. This ranch is near the upper reaches of Cañon Guadalupe, only 4 miles from the Guadalupe campground as the crow flies. Since there are no established trails, a trip into the canyon is strictly a compass-and-topo proposition. The reward at the end will be a soak in a hot tub. See Arroyo del Sauz I11D84 for this and other hikes in the vicinity of Laguna Hanson.

Much of the park is above 4,000 feet, and the chaparral of lower regions has given away to the cool pine forests and dry meadows of the Sierra de Juárez. Shallow and muddy Laguna Hanson, at Mile 38.9, and just over a mile across, is home to many water birds. Campsites are available around the shores of the lake, a few with rustic tables. Potable water can be obtained from a tiny seep at the forest camp a half mile southwest. You will rarely see more than a half-dozen campers, but during Easter vacation it can become a scene from Hell: hundreds of people sitting in pickups, swilling beer, and roasting chunks of meat over fires, with ATVs and trail bikes splitting the blue air. A week later all is quiet again.

■ A pot of trouble

Most place names in Baja California are, of course, in Spanish, and many are after saints—the index lists over 150 names beginning with "San..." and "Santa..." Place names in English are unusual, and one that immediately strikes the eye is "Laguna Hanson." "Lake Hanson" got its name from a strange incident in the minor history of Baja.

The discovery of gold at Real del Castillo, located east of Ensenada, in 1870 attracted a horde of international adventurers to northern Baja and the Sierra de Juárez. However, not everyone there was gold-crazy. In 1872 an American named Hanson drifted into the area. Twenty-four years old and something of a dreamer, he was attracted to the beauty of the forest and its wildlife, and he "discovered" the lake that now bears his name (the local Indians knew it well, of course). Popular with the locals, he assumed the management of Rancho el Rayo, located on the southwestern outskirts of what is now the national park.

One morning in 1880 the local people awoke with a sense of foreboding—during the night the livestock had broken out of the corrals, and a white calf had been seen running into the woods, a bad omen to the superstitious people. They soon noticed that Hanson was not to be found, although a fire was still burning beneath a huge iron caldron near his home. Inexplicably, an American friend of Hanson's named Harvey appeared. He was uncharacteristically friendly and generous, distributing gifts of clothes and *huaraches* to the adults, and passing out handfuls of sugar cubes to the children. Scarcely noticed was a strange odor coming from the cauldron.

Several weeks passed and concern for Hanson faded—the locals simply assumed he had suddenly decided to leave Baja and return home. One afternoon mounted police arrived, tied and gagged Harvey and dredged up the contents of the cauldron into a bag. The human bones found there were to be used as evidence in his trial. However, Harvey was too rich not to be able to buy his freedom, evidence or not, and within several months he was freed and fled to the US.

Because of its altitude, the park is cooler than surrounding areas, and there is little underbrush, making hiking enjoyable. There are no marked trails and no maps are available from rangers. The 6-mile hike around the lake through the pines and meadows is pleasant. A number of granite peaks offer excellent climbs, and slabs, cracks, and beautifully carved chimneys abound. You can see much of the surrounding country from class 3 formations rising to several hundred feet 500 yards northwest of the buildings at Mile 39.4. Picacho del Diablo, 78 miles away, bears 140°. East is the Juárez escarpment, dropping precipitously to the desert floor. The escarpment can be approached on either of two roads south of the lake. Rolling waves of rock are passed before the sudden

Will Ashford

A peaceful scene on Laguna Hanson

drop. Views from the top of the sharp-pointed peaks 6 miles east of the lake are smashing. The highest peak in the Juárez is 6,435-foot Cerro Colorado, somehow out of place in much lower tablelands 42 miles southeast. As might be expected, the Laguna Hanson area provides fine birding.

The road south to Route 3 starts near the buildings at the southwest end of the lake. Set odometer. At Mile 0.4 pass the forest camp and another small lake, at Mile 1.1 a tree farm, at Mile 2.5 a ranch, and at Mile 3.9 arrive at El Aserradero (The Sawmill). The place is almost deserted, but you may be able to buy a meal, and collectors can purchase mineral samples. The road from here on is in good condition, with many long downhill stretches. At Mile 6.6 pass more ranches and a small lake. A fine shaded campsite will be found at Mile 14.8.

Encounter a fork at Mile 16.5. Mina Verde, famous for huge crystals of danburite, among the largest in the world, is located less than a mile southeast of this point. Although the fork is important, it is unmarked and looks like just another place where drivers have made parallel roads to avoid bad spots, and if you don't look sharp it is easy to miss. If you are headed south (including those on the Two Parks Loop Trip), take the left branch, which immediately turns southeast to a fork reached in 0.8 mile. Take the right (180°) turn here and arrive on Route 3 at KM 55+.

Those on the Laguna Hanson Loop Trip and those headed for Ojos Negros should go straight ahead at the fork at Mile 16.5. The road immediately swings west, then drops through a canyon and arrives at El Coyote, another important intersection, at Mile 19.4. Those on the Laguna Hanson Loop Trip should turn right (065°). The route north from this point to KM 98 on Route 2 is described beginning on page 248. Those heading for Ojos Negros should turn left (255°).

■■■■■■■■■■■■■■■■■■■■■■■■■

Back on Old Route 2 at El Cóndor, KM 83

KM	Location
72	Pickup road south to Cerro Teta de la India and

Parque 1857. Due to recent construction, there are no reliable landmarks to show the correct road—inquire locally. Those continuing on Route 2 should look just below.

> ### Side trip on the La Rumorosa-Parque 1857 Road.
> Turn southeast 0.2 mile east of the KM 72 marker. Set odometer. Stop and sight 125°; Mexican cartographers gave the mountain 6.5 miles southeast the name "Cerro Teta de la India" (Indian Tit Hill) because of its shape, but less delicate locals call it simply "Chi Chi." The mountain serves as a useful landmark throughout the northern Sierra de Juárez. At Mile 1.9 encounter a park owned by the local *ejido*, with trees, fireplaces, and a pavilion. Unfortunately it is often badly littered, and the water and sanitary facilities are usually inoperative. A pickup road runs east from Mile 7.3, shortening the approach to Chi Chi. After a class 2 scramble, a climber will be greeted with the best views in the Juárez. A naive friend of mine once set out to climb it, but the photos he produced upon his return showed he had chosen the less shapely mountain just to the west, apparently oblivious to the meaning of Chi Chi's official and unofficial names. A number of minerals have been reported nearby, including quartz, tourmaline, jasper, and chalcedony. Arrive at the intersection with the El Cóndor-Parque 1857 Road at Mile 16.0, previously described.

■■■■■■■■■■■■■■■■■
Back on Old Route 2 at KM 72

KM	Location
71	**La Rumorosa.** PEMEX (MD), food stores, bakeries, mail, restaurants, cafés, mechanics, welder, auto parts, tire repair, Red Cross, mini-mart.
67	Begin Toll Road, Route 2D, toll booth (Old Route 2 has ceased to exist from here east). There are 15 miles of twisting downgrades averaging 5% between here and KM 44, with wonderful views.
40	Pinto Wash, well known to US mineral collectors, crosses the border into Baja north of this point.
28	Road south to the Palm Canyon area (signed CAÑON GUADALUPE). Those continuing on Route 2D should skip the following section.

> ### Side trip to the Palm Canyon area. A series of
> wildly beautiful canyons are eroded into the Juárez escarpment in this area. The road west of Laguna Salada passes through typical desert scrub, but in the canyons California fan palms, blue fan palms, smoke trees, cottonwoods, and elephant trees can be found. The largest canyons, Tajo, El Carrizo, Guadalupe, La Mora, and El

Palomar, have surface water, often inhabited by such unlikely Baja creatures as tree frogs, water striders, and giant water bugs. Large emerald pools make fine swimming holes. Indians used the canyons as routes between the desert and the pine forests above. Virtually all portable artifacts were carried off long ago, but petroglyphs, pictographs, chipping waste, *metatès*, and pottery shards are common in the palm groves and around watered sites.

A two-lane sedan road heads south at KM 28. Set odometer. At Mile 14.7 encounter Rancho la Poderosa, at Mile 20.7 shacks and a water tank, and at Mile 21.4 a road leading west toward the mouth of Cañon Tajo. El Trono Blanco is in plain view, looking deceptively close because of its massive size; it is actually over 8 miles away. Pickups can get 1.5 miles west on this road before it becomes too soft, four-wheel-drives somewhat farther.

Continue southeast to Mile 26.8 and turn southwest between irrigated fields. Note the pointed peak dominating the skyline ahead, Picacho Rasco, 4,500 feet, and the sharp spire, which is the Virgin of Guadalupe, named for a fancied likeness to the Madonna.

Arrive at the campground in Cañon Guadalupe at Mile 34.6. There are a number of RV sites, with natural tubs fed by hot springs. *palapas* cover some of the sites, and a large pool holds 1,500 gallons under 2 enormous boulders, forming a cave of sorts. Some sites also have barbecue pits and tables. A year-round cool-water stream cascades through hundreds of palms and disappears in the alluvial fan below. Views from the ridge above are well worth the climb; the view of the canyon is breathtaking. The Pool of the Virgin can be found 2 miles upstream. Bounded on three sides by white granite cliffs, surrounded by cottonwoods, willows, ferns, and mosses, and fed by a slender waterfall, it seems out of place. Hikers can also get into the canyon from the vicinity of Rancho San Luis, as noted earlier in this chapter.

The best time to visit Cañon Guadalupe is from early November to the end of May. Holding tanks should

El Trono Blanco from the floor of the canyon

Reeve Peterson

be dumped prior to arrival at the campground. The hot mineral water is safe to drink, but has a mild sulfur odor, so it may be best to bring your own water for cooking and drinking. There is no electricity or telephones, but a small store sells canned food, snacks, soda, beer, motor oil, and firewood. A restaurant serves Mexican dishes on weekends, and off-road tours to a number of Indian sites are available. Stop at the store for site assignment. The minimum stay is two nights. Reservations are required, which can be made by calling Rob's Baja Tours. It is best to call again just before departure to learn about road conditions.

■■■■■■■■■■■■■■■
Back on Route 2D at KM 28

KM	Location
26	Restaurant, rest rooms, swimming pools (open April through September).
24	El Oasis. Refreshment stand. Laguna Salada can be seen far to the south. In 1987, when the first edition of this book was completed, the lake was at a much higher level due to heavy flows of the Río Colorado. A road led a short distance to a camp on its shores, where anglers could rent boats to pursue bass, crappie, carp, and huge catfish. The continuing drought has reduced the size of the lake to where the shoreline is today; the change is remarkable.
18	Route 2D ends, becoming Route 2.
7+	PEMEX (MPD).
4+	PEMEX (MD).
	Continue driving east until signs note the intersection of Routes 2 and 5. Go left (north) for Mexicali, right (south) for San Felipe.

Mexicali

Mexicali is the capital of the state of Baja California [Norte] and has most supplies and services. No driver in the city's history has ever yielded the right-of-way to another vehicle, and travelers should expect sulfurous fumes, suicidal pedestrians, supersonic taxis, and sado-masochistic truckers. There are now two border-crossing stations in the Mexicali area, Calexico West (the old one) and Calexico East (the new one, 6.5 miles to the east). Calexico West is open 24 hours a day, Calexico East from 6 A.M. to 10 P.M., both 7 days a week.

South-bound drivers headed for Baja via Calexico West will find route signs directing them onto Calzada Lopéz Mateos at the first stoplight encountered after entering Mexico. Signs noting the location of the *Migración* and *Aduana* offices will be seen immediately south of the border crossing. Set odometer. Lopéz Mateos is the "main

drag" running southeast through town, crossing Calzada Benito Juárez at Mile 5.0. At this point, make a half-right (160°), and continue on to Mile 5.5, the intersection of Routes 2 and 5.

Drivers headed south for Baja via Calexico East should drive to the intersection of Routes 98 and 7 east of the town of Calexico, and turn south on Route 7. The new border crossing will be encountered in about a mile and a half. *Migración* and *Aduana* offices are available, and there is a bank and a money-changing office, all with plenty of parking. Drive south from the border station, turn right (west) at the first stop sign onto Av. Cristobal Colón, a one-way, west-bound street immediately south of the border fence. Set odometer. At Mile 3.7 turn left (south) onto Calzada Justo Sierra. At Mile 4.8 turn half-left (147°) onto Calzada Benito Juárez and proceed to the intersection of Routes 2 and 5, Mile 8.1.

North-bound drivers headed for the US via Calexico West should drive to the intersection of Routes 2 and 5, set odometer, and head northwest on Calzada Benito Juárez (the extension of Route 5). At Mile 3.3 turn half-right (north) onto Calzada Justo Sierra, and at Mile 4.4 turn left (west) on Av. Cristobal Colón, arriving at Calexico West at Mile 7.2.

North-bound drivers headed for the US via Calexico East should drive to the intersection of Routes 2 and 5, set odometer and head northwest through Mexicali on Calzada Benito Juárez (the extension of Route 5). At Mile 3.3 turn half-right (north) onto Calzada Justo Sierra, and at Mile 4.4 turn right (east) on Av. Argentina, a one-way, east-bound street one block south of the border fence. At Mile 8.1 turn left (north) and arrive at the border station.

■■■■■■■■■■■■■■■
Tecate to Ensenada via Route 3

This route is very scenic, with rolling hills and large boulders. Bicyclists will find it challenging, with headwinds and long grades. There are many small stores, and thirsty bikers will find everything from tequila to orange juice, but increased fence-building is making it difficult to find places to camp.

KM	Location
3	Interchange to Tijuana/Mexicali Toll Road, Route 2D. In early 1998, travelers joining the Toll Road at this point could only travel west towards Tijuana, the eastern section being incomplete as far as La Rumorosa—see page 247.
10	Tecate Resort and Country Club. RV parking, no hookups.
10+	**Tanamá.** Pyrites have been found nearby.
27+	**Valle las Palmas.** PEMEX (MD), tire repair, cafés, groceries, ice, doctor.

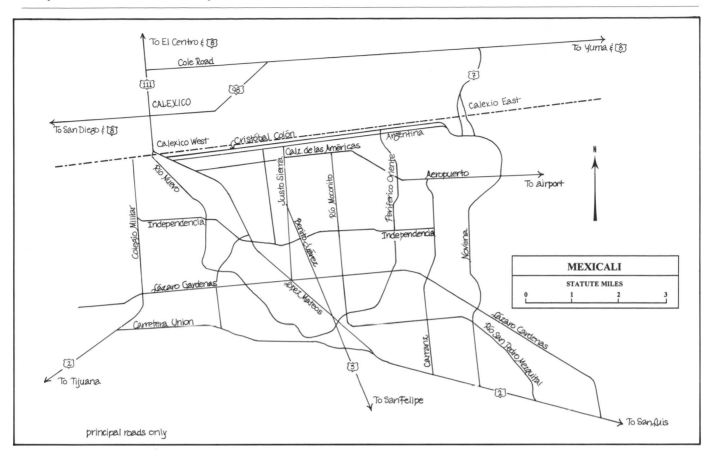

35 Begin moderate upgrades, averaging 7%.

40 Highest point on this section of Route 3, 2,130 feet. Begin downgrades to KM 47.

49 **El Testerazo.** Groceries, tire repair.

73 Domecq Winery. Tours are available Tuesday through Sunday, 9:30 A.M. to 1:00 P.M. Pickup road east to Rancho Agua Caliente. Those continuing on Route 3 should skip the following section.

Side trip to the Cuevas de Agua Caliente. The area surrounding Rancho Agua Caliente consists of plutonic rocks, but the ranch itself is on limestone and is the site of two fine solution caves. In recent years a locked gate has often blocked the way, and permission to visit the caves has sometimes been refused when requested at the ranch (to be noted shortly). There is no way to determine this in advance, and no phone where current information can be obtained, so the only course of action is to try to get in and see what happens.

Turn east opposite the Domecq winery. Set odometer. At Mile 1.1 turn north, at Mile 1.9 east, and at Mile 4.0 encounter a stream, which most vehicles should be able to ford safely in dry weather. Gate at Mile 4.8. At Mile 5.2 another crossing has soft sand where even four-wheel-drives sometime have problems. Park, ford the stream, and hike up the canyon. At Minute 30 arrive at the ranch, identified by meteorological and hydrological apparatus. Stop, pay your re-

spects and ask permission to continue, while simultaneously jutting forth a cold six-pack.

At Minute 20 (from the ranch) encounter a cliff on the south side of the stream. A tributary stream in a small arroyo above the cliff sometimes forms a fine waterfall. The caves are in this arroyo. Continue up the main stream 150 feet past the cliff, scramble up the steep, rocky slope, and hike up the tributary stream for 15 minutes. The first cave is 30 feet above the stream bed on the right side. A climb down through a 2-by-3-foot entrance leads to a multilevel maze cave several hundred feet long. This cave has chambers up to 30 feet high, and hidden passages, squeezes, breakdown blocks, ledges, drops, flowstones, ceiling domes, and a number of natural bridges. Cavers have sometimes found it necessary to dig through breakdown clogs. The second cave is on the right side 90 feet farther upstream, 100 feet above the stream bed. A 3-by-4-foot entrance leads to an L-shaped chamber 125 feet long, 20 feet wide, and 10 feet high.

■ ■ ■ ■ ■ ■ ■ ■ ■ ■ ■ ■ ■

Back on Route 3 at KM 73

KM	Location
74+	Rancho Sordo Mundo Trailer Park; some full hookups, showers, rest rooms. The park's odd name, "Deaf World," comes from its association

Modest Mike insisted that his dad take this photograph of him skinny-dipping in a tiny pool above the Rio Gudadalupe from a **long** *distance away*

77   **Guadalupe.** Tire repair, café, groceries, liquor. Set odometer. The paved road right (210°) leads into the village, where a mechanic, bakery, auto parts, doctor, pharmacy, post office, butcher shop, and hardware store will be found. The ruins of Dominican Misión Nuestra Señora de Guadalupe can be seen by continuing on through the village, turning left (130°) where the pavement ends, and driving about 200 yards on the very marginal sedan road. Dating from 1834, it was one of the last missions constructed in Baja California and was in operation for only 6 years. Fleeing persecution in Russia, a religious sect called the Malakans founded a colony here in 1905, but today little differentiates the village

other than an occasional head of blond or red hair. A small museum, Museo Comunitario del Valle de Guadalupe, has been opened at Mile 1.5, devoted to community history, including the Russians.

82+   Rancho Mother Teresa Trailer Park; full hookups, *palapas*, BBQs, rest rooms, showers, two pools, grass lawns, and flowers, surrounded by vineyards and orange groves.

93   Mechanic, tire repair, restaurant. Pancho's RV Park; full hookups, rest rooms, showers, large oak trees, pool. Beautiful specimens of pearly, silver-green talc have been found in the vicinity.

94   **Villa de Juárez.** Groceries, beer. Cuprite, silver, and gold have been found nearby.

98   Long downgrades to Route 1.

105   Junction with Transpeninsular at KM 101+. Those traveling on to Ensenada should turn to page 100.

■ ■ ■ ■ ■ ■ ■ ■ ■ ■ ■ ■ ■ ■ ■ ■

At intersection of Routes 2 and 5 south of Mexicali, headed south on 5 to Crucero la Trinidad

KM	Location
0	Start KM numbering sequence.
2+	PEMEX(MD).

Members of Baja's Club Pedal y Fibre swing past Guadalupe

10+	PEMEX (M).
27	The steam clouds to the east come from a geothermal electrical generating station.
31	PEMEX (M), small auto parts store.
49	Pickup road west to the Mina Promontorio sulfur area. Set odometer. At Mile 1.0 a grade of 15% is encountered, the most difficult obstacle. At Mile 6.3 take the north fork, and arrive at Mile 9.4. The mine is fenced, but deposits are found throughout area, largely small crystals on rocky substrates. Quartz thundereggs have been reported in the surrounding Sierra de Cucapa.
52	A number of very modest RV camps are found along the Río Hardy for the next few miles. The road passes extensive marshes, with immense populations of pelicans, coots, cranes, egrets, and a dozen or more species of ducks. It is not uncommon to see thirty egrets solemnly surveying a single pond 20 yards across.
57	Groceries, cold sodas, tiny museum.
65+	The road starts across Laguna Salada on a causeway. In recent years this end of the lake has been dry, with no water to be seen for miles, but in 1987 it was the scene of a thriving freshwater fishery, with large numbers of catfish to 20 pounds and other fish being taken by dozens of commercial fishermen, whose trucks and camps crowded the highway.
87+	South end of Laguna Salada. The low, dark mountains to the west are the Sierra las Tinajas.

■ Too little and then too much

In the early part of this century two strange tragedies occurred in northeastern Baja, one caused by too little water, the other by too much.

In the summer of 1902 a group of 42 Chinese laborers arrived in San Felipe aboard the small steamer *Topolobampo*. They found no work, but heard rumors of vast irrigation projects that were underway to the north. No transportation existed, so they hired a Mexican guide and on August 26 set out on foot for Mexicali, 130 miles of sand, stones, and 120° heat away. They had virtually no equipment and little food. Some did not even have shoes or hats, and the only water they had was carried in cans and old liquor bottles. They headed for a well 30 miles to the north in the vicinity of a volcanic butte now called Cerro el Chinero (Chinese Hill). One man died on the way, but panic did not set in until it became certain that the well was not where the guide said it was. Pressing on, they turned northwest toward the optimistically named Tres Pozos (Three Wells), located to the west of this point. Thirty-three men died *en route*. No water could be found and two more men promptly

died of shock. Nine days after leaving San Felipe, the guide and five Chinese reached the Río Hardy and were rescued. Another man was subsequently found safe.

Although the area where the Chinese died is the hottest and driest on the continent, the nearby Río Colorado provided one of nature's great phenomena involving the movement of water: the great Colorado River Tidal Bore. When the 31-foot tides of the Cortez met the swift current of the Colorado, a huge wave called a tidal bore was produced that moved far upstream. It had been first reported by Francisco Ulloa in 1539 and had been seen by explorer James Pattie in 1826, and by Joseph Ives of the Corps of Topographical Engineers in 1857. In 1864 the schooner *Victoria* was damaged by the bore, and in 1893 R.E.L. Robinson and a party of adventurers witnessed the bore, claiming it was 15 feet high and 20 miles wide. Their sailboat was swept along and deposited on the mud flats far inland.

With the completion of Laguna Dam the river's current was reduced, but apparently the bore still retained much of its power. On the evening of November 18, 1922, 20 years after the Chinese tragedy, the captain of the *Topolobampo*, the same ship involved in the earlier incident, decided to stop for the night and ordered anchors set fore and aft near La Bomba, many miles north of the mouth of the river. The steamer had departed Guaymas with 125 Mexican workers and their families bound for Mexicali, where work was available in the cotton fields. All seemed secure, and the crew and passengers made their meals and dozed off—after all, what could happen on a tranquil moonlit night on the muddy Colorado? A number of hours later, no one really knows when, a deafening roar brought a stampede of sleepy people to the deck. Stunned, they saw a gigantic wall of water approaching them from downriver. Before anyone could react, the ship rolled over and sank. Days later rescuers were still finding bodies and half-crazed survivors, their skins blistered by the sun, riddled by hordes of mosquitoes, and blasted by a sandstorm. Eighty-six people lost their lives. New dams and silting of the now-slowly-moving river have tamed the bore and it is now little more than a ripple lost among the wind-driven waves.

KM	Location
105	**La Ventana.** PEMEX (M), cold drinks, small store, beer distributor.
113	The hill to the east is a source of Apache tears.
123	Sedan road west to Mina la Escondida. Set odometer. Take the left (270°) fork at Mile 2.7, and arrive at the mine at Mile 4.1. The area is highly mineralized with gold, silver, lead, and

copper. To visit Mina Jueves Santo, return to the fork at Mile 2.7, take the right (305°) fork, drive as far as possible and walk the trail to the mine, where an American company has been taking gold out of a quartz vein.

140   **Crucero la Trinidad** (Crucero el Chinero). Restaurant.

■ ■ ■ ■ ■ ■ ■ ■ ■ ■ ■ ■ ■ ■ ■ ■

In Ensenada on Calzada Cortez (the extension of Route 3), headed east for Crucero la Trinidad

KM	Location

0   Start new KM numbering sequence. Once out of town the road makes a moderate and nearly unbroken climb to near the Ojos Negros turnoff. The sides of the road are fenced almost continuously for the next 100 miles, and campsites are scarce. Those mentioned in later sections are modest indeed, most of them little more than places to pull off the road.

11   LPG yard.

13   Great 13 Recreation Park; playground equipment, restaurant, pool, showers, rest rooms, *palapas*, RV parking spaces, some with water hookups.

26   Pickup road to Rancho Agua Caliente, signed. With its restaurant and bar (open warm months only), pools, rest rooms, showers, hot springs, shade trees, and RV parking spaces, this recreation area is popular with the locals. However, the maintenance and cleanliness of the place have varied over the years from satisfactory to awful. Unfortunately, you must pay your toll at the gate, which is out of sight of the facilities, and you either pay or don't get in. Short stretches of 23% upgrades going in and out.

39+   Paved road (signed) north to Ojos Negros, 1.3 miles, which has groceries, restaurants, post office, limited auto parts, tire repairs, doctor, and pharmacy. The Los Casian Trailer Camp will be found 0.7 mile east of the end of the pavement. It has shaded campsites (no hookups), a large swimming pool, brick barbecues, rest rooms, showers, and a small pond. The place is dirty, ill-maintained, and badly littered, and the rest rooms and showers have not seen monkey wrench, paintbrush, nor PineSol for many years. However, the place seems to be improving slowly over the years. To drive north on the Alvarez-Ojos Negros road or to Parque 1857, set odometer at the end of the pavement and drive east. There is a tiny gas station along the road—follow the signs. At Mile 4.0 note the road ahead winding into the hills and steer for it, arriving at El Coyote junction at Mile 7.7, described earlier.

52   Moderate upgrades to KM 69.

55+   Sedan road north to Parque 1857, signed LAGUNA HANSON (for a description, see page 249). About 0.6 mile to the north the fencing ends and camping is possible.

62   From a point 100 yards southeast of KM marker a bulldozer road leads south to possible campsites.

69   Gently rolling hills, low to moderate up- and downgrades to KM 114.

71+   **Rancho Cerro Colorado.** Pickup road southwest to Rancho el Porvenir, 6 miles, known for pale yellow labradorite, and Rancho Tres Hermanos (Santa Clara), 11 miles, known for chiastolite.

75   **Pino Solo.** The small tree at 250 yards, 222° is the new replacement for a famous pine that used to inhabit the spot. This is a celebrated pegmatite dike area, yielding ilmenite, quartz, tourmaline, and gem-quality epidote, and some believe it to be the most important sphene area in the world. The dikes start 20 yards south of the tree.

85   A dirt road leading southwest to campsites will be found 0.3 mile southeast of the KM marker.

86   Sedan road southwest (signed) to El Alamo, 11 miles. Those continuing on Route 3 should skip the following section.

↱ *Side trip to El Alamo.* The nearby Santa Clara gold placers were discovered in 1888, and El Alamo soon had more than 5,000 inhabitants, a newspaper, a pool hall, and a *cantina*. Unwashed miners had another source of entertainment: the first captured louse to scurry out of a circle won a poke of gold dust for his handler. Gold seemed unlimited, and a one-ounce nugget was found in the gizzard of a chicken. Famous mystic Eilley Orrum, the Washoe Seeress, soon appeared. In earlier years, aided by a crystal ball, she had provided Nevada miners with advice on where to stake their claims, and which way and how deep to dig. Her advice had made her and a number of miners wealthy. At one point she owned a mansion in Virginia City, but when she arrived in El Alamo she was an elderly widow down on her luck. Pitching her tent and polishing her ball, she went into business again. Her first "seeing" demonstrated that she knew the commercial value of positive thinking; the ball showed El Alamo's gold fields to be extensive, spreading all the way to San Diego, and the specifics could be known for a price. Finding gold in Nevada was one thing, in El Alamo another, and even Eilley's talents could not sustain the boom, and today El Alamo is almost a ghost town. Mineral collectors have found magnetite, specularite, pyrrhotite, sphalerite, chalcopyrite, galena, pyrite, marcasite, and, of course, gold and gold inclusions in quartz. A few miners still are at work, and gold can be purchased at market prices.

■■■■■■■■■■■■■■■
Back on Route 3 at KM 86

KM	Location
92	**Héroes de la Independencia.** Gas station (MD), cafés, auto parts, tire repair, groceries, fruit market, stores, doctor, pharmacy.
95+	Pickup road south. Those continuing on Route 3 should skip the following section.

Side trip to Minas El Socorro and Las Delicias. Two of the most famous mineral sites in Baja are located nearby. Turn southeast 0.2 mile east of the KM marker and you will immediately encounter a **Y**. Set odometer, take the left (200°) fork, stop at Mile 1.3 and sight 230°. The light-colored hill 1,000 yards away is El Socorro. The mine is cut into a classic pegmatite dike, and schorl, mica, biotite, beryl, topaz, muscovite, quartz, and green, blue, rose, and watermelon tourmaline have been found.

The old direct route to Las Delicias has been cut by washouts and by fence-building farmers. If you are willing to do some exploring, take the right (240°) fork at the **Y**. The road will begin to meander radically in a southerly direction. Take the left forks at Miles 1.9 and 2.0. From this point explicit directions are impossible. Using your compass, try to head south when you can. At Mile 3.0 start looking for a prominent rock-strewn hill with sparse vegetation. At Mile 4.0 a road will be found at the north end of this hill, running east-west and turning south along the hill's western side. At Mile 5.1, stop and hike south up the trail to the mine. A deep canyon running roughly east-west lies a third of a mile to the south of the mine, and the highway lies 5 miles to the north, so you should not get really lost. Forming a complex and beautiful pegmatite dike, the area's light-colored rocks are shot with fan patterns of black schorl, and quartz, garnet, sphene, beryl, topaz, epidote, aquamarine, and blue, pink, green, and watermelon tourmaline have been found. So much mica lies about that reflections can be dazzling.

■■■■■■■■■■■■■■■
Back on Route 3 at KM 95+

KM	Location
110	Cattle guard, dirt road northeast to modest campsites.

114	Downgrade to KM 125.
121	**Valle de Trinidad.** PEMEX (MD, located south side of town), mechanic, auto parts, tire repair, stores, groceries, meat, restaurants, doctor, dentist, post office, bakery, ice.
138	Sedan road south (signed) to Mike's Sky Ranch, 20 miles. Those continuing on Route 3 should skip the following section.

Side trip to Mike's Sky Ranch and the Observatory Road. Set odometer. Located at Mile 20, at 4,000 feet elevation near the northwestern outskirts of Parque Nacional Sierra San Pedro Mártir, Mike's Sky Ranch is perhaps the most unusual resort in Baja; it is the highest in elevation, the only one with a trout stream, and the only one catering largely to motorcyclists and off-road racing enthusiasts. Although graded and generally fairly smooth, the road has up- and downgrades to 26% and there are some rough stretches. People get trailers and motor homes in here, but it takes time, patience, and some very low gears. The route is signed all the way. Perched on a knoll above the year-round Río San Rafael and surrounded by pine-covered mountains, it offers very modest motel accommodations, bar service, family-style meals, and shaded campsites. Using worms dug along the riverbank, less mechanically inclined visitors can try to catch extremely wary trout. Good hiking can be found up and down the river among the pines and interesting rock formations, and there are a number of swimming holes upstream.

Guadalupe Ruiz works a small gold claim near the historic town of El Alamo

A road heads west immediately in front of the resort buildings, climbs precariously out of the canyon, and joins the Observatory Road, making it a key section in the Two Parks Loop Trip. The road is best driven in a four-wheel-drive, although lightly loaded two-wheel-drive pickups can make it with some difficulty. Other than shortness of breath and sweaty brows, bicyclists should have no undue problems.

Mile	Side trip location
0.0	In front of resort buildings. Set odometer.
0.1	Fork, take left (195°), begin 21% upgrade in loose rock.
1.6	On top.
5.1	Fork, go right (280°). The next mile has excellent shaded campsites among the oaks, possible streams in wet years.
11.3	Rough stuff, 34% downgrade into canyon.
12.2	Gate in barbed wire fence.
12.8	Gate in barbed wire fence.
13.5	Junction, go right (242°).
14.3	Junction, go left (180°), cross cattle guard.
14.6	Junction, go straight (190°).
19.2	Junction, go right (200°).
19.4	Junction with Observatory Road at Mile 29.7. Go left (090°) for Parque Nacional Sierra San Pedro Mártir, right (240°) for the Transpeninsular.

■ ■ ■ ■ ■ ■ ■ ■ ■ ■ ■ ■ ■ ■ ■
Back on Route 3 at KM 138

KM	Location
142	**San Matías.** Tiny store.
147	Unfenced area, possible campsites. Begin moderate-to-gentle downgrades to KM 164+.
152	Soft, sandy road west to flat spots, best campsites in area.
164+	The road from here to Crucero la Trinidad is generally unfenced, with numerous side roads leading to camping areas. Upgrades to KM 168, then gentle ups-and-downs to KM 187, followed by downgrades to Crucero. Road south to Laguna Diablo, signed COL. SAN PEDRO MÁRTIR. Those continuing on Route 3 should skip the following section.

Side trip to Laguna Diablo and Cañon del Diablo. A road south crosses Laguna Diablo and eventually swings east, joining Route 5 at KM 179. Except for a few stretches of sand and minor washboard, the road is easily passable by sedans in normally dry years, and is an inter-

esting and adventurous way to get to San Felipe. The road also permits driving to the mouth of Cañon Diablito, the jumping-off place for backpacking ventures up Cañon del Diablo and an alternate approach to the ascent of Picacho del Diablo, described in Chapter 9.

Set odometer and close your windows. At Mile 4.0 take the left (170°) fork. At Mile 6.5 the road starts across the dry lake. The bed of the lake is so hard and flat that drug smugglers have been known to land their 4-engine DC-4s here after flights from Colombia. The road will begin to rise out of the dry lake at Mile 18.7. At Mile 19.5 encounter a ranch building; take the left (110°) fork. At Mile 21.4 go left (100°) at the fork, at Mile 27.3 go straight (040°), arriving at Route 5 at Mile 40.7.

Those headed for Cañon del Diablo should stop at Mile 14.3 (from KM 164+) and locate the observatory perched on the rim of the mountains. Continue on until it bears 240°. At this point the observatory will be right over the mouth of Cañon del Diablo, and Picacho will bear 204°. Sight 232°: this is the mouth of Cañon Diablito and the roadhead where you will park. Continue on to Mile 15.4 and look for wheel tracks leading west. Set odometer. At Mile 0.9 pass a corral and ranch building, and at Mile 1.2 take the right (226°) fork. Arrive at the roadhead at Mile 6.5, elevation 2,100 feet, marked by a plywood shack. The local rancher has indicated he will close the area if the parking area is littered or vandalized, or if access is blocked by parked vehicles.

The most musically talented coyotes in all Baja live nearby. During a trip a number of years ago, we were treated to a concert of glorious howling at dusk. Later that night the members of the chorus paid a visit, and there was a great deal of snarling and snapping over food we had left out. Secure in my van, I thought the event was hilarious, but Rick Tinker and Will Ashford didn't appreciate the humor from the confines of their pup tents.

After crossing a boulder-strewn wash, contour northwest to Cañon del Diablo, an easy 45 minute hike across fairly smooth and open desert. Turn west into the canyon and after about a half mile you will encounter what is often the most difficult single obstacle on the entire journey: a beautiful waterfall at elevation 2,250 feet cascading through steep, smoothly curving granite walls into a pool with a sandy bottom. Sand carried by storms sometimes fills the pool, allowing one to clamber up the falls with few problems. At other times you can almost see over the top but can't quite make it, for the walls are smooth and lack handholds; so near and yet so far! Creative climbers have improvised ladders out of tree branches and even constructed human pyramids. A number of years ago, someone installed an expansion bolt and a wire rope, allowing climbers to hand-over-hand up the wall and pendulum over the falls. If this is gone and nothing else works, simply climb the north ridge.

At Mile 1.0 (from the waterfall), elevation 2,660 feet, the canyon turns south. Stay left at the major forks encountered at Mile 4.5, elevation 4,090, at Mile 5.0, elevation 4,420, and at Mile 5.8, elevation 4,880. Cañon del Diablo is much larger than any of its tributaries, so the choice is usually obvious. After the first fork the canyon again swings left, to about 140°. In its lower reaches fantastic water-carved granite sculptures surround deep, sandy-bottomed swimming holes and fine waterfalls. The changes in vegetation are striking, starting with *palo verdes* and *cardóns* at lower elevations and going through *agaves* and barrel cactuses to willows, aspens, oaks, and cedars as you climb. The route is well ducked, but waterfalls may require creative route-finding. At Mile 7.0, elevation 6,300, you will find Campo Noche. The ascent from this point was described in Chapter 9. Two days should be allowed for the climb to the camp, and 1.5 days for the return to the roadhead.

■ ■ ■ ■ ■ ■ ■ ■ ■ ■ ■ ■ ■ ■ ■ ■ ■
Back on Route 3 at KM 164+

KM	Location
173	Picacho del Diablo, Baja's highest mountain, dominates the skyline at 196°. In winter, the crest is often covered with snow. Look carefully along the ridge (204°) and you will see a white dot. This is the astronomical observatory in Parque Nacional Sierra San Pedro Mártir, described on page 116.
197	**Crucero la Trinidad.**

Will Ashford and Rick Tinker enjoy a beautiful pool in Cañon del Diablo

■ ■
On Route 5 at Crucero la Trinidad, KM 140, headed south to San Felipe

KM	Location
141+	PEMEX (MD). Except for the pumps, no valve, pipe, tank, nail, board, or brick in this station seems to have started its career as part of a gas station. There ought to be a place in Guinness for it. Note the antique glass-barrel gas pump. Many beach camps and RV parks are located between here and San Felipe.
176	El Dorado Ranch. 200 RV sites, full hookups, beach, tennis, pool, rest rooms, showers, sailing, *cantina*, restaurant, store, laundry, kayak rental.
178	Sedan road east to Pete's el Paraíso Camp, 1 mile, offering a beach, a restaurant and bar, rest rooms, a laundry, and showers. This is one of the more better-established RV parks north of San Felipe, but it tends to be inhabited by people with partying, fireworks, ATVs, and dune buggies on their minds, and the din can be terrific. An impromptu desert golf course is available.
179	Road to Laguna Diablo and KM 164+ on Route 3 (see page 262). Take the right (230°) fork 13.5 miles west of this point. Rather Spartan, Cachanillia's RV Camp, providing full hookups, showers, rest rooms, dump, vehicle and boat storage, will be found 0.3 mile west of Route 5.
191	PEMEX (MP), convenience store.

San Felipe

Santa Rosalía was founded by the French, who were interested in copper, and San Felipe was also founded by foreigners, but this time it was Germans interested in fish. In the early part of this century, Chinese living in Guaymas, a port opposite Santa Rosalía on the eastern shore of the Cortez, discovered that the dried swim bladders of the large bass-like *totuava* had a ready market in China, where they were used in soups. However, the fishermen in their dugout canoes were too successful, and the catch soon declined. A group of German seamen, possibly from the great sailing ships that were interned in Santa Rosalía during the First World War, did some scouting and located virgin fishing grounds in the northern Cortez. Below a rocky headland, they founded a settlement.

The fishermen had apparently learned nothing from the conservation lessons taught off Guaymas, and their dugouts came back heavily loaded with *totuava*. As had been customary, the swim bladders were removed and the rest of the fish discarded, thus wasting up to perhaps 200 pounds of excellent food from each. The profits were sizable at first, and the settlement grew rapidly. Rumors spread, and several American truckers from Calexico made the hazardous trip across the salt flats and sand dunes, to arrive safely in San Felipe. Buying fresh *totuava* carcasses at the rate of one American cent for 20 pounds, they loaded their trucks and headed north to the markets of Southern California. Aided by this new financial incentive, the fishery thrived, and in the 1927-28 season, over 1.8 million pounds of fish were landed. Roads from the US were soon paved, and large numbers of sport anglers began to arrive. It couldn't last, and by the late 1960s, the *totuava* were almost gone.

Today, San Felipe is almost completely dependent on tourism, a place where people from Arizona and Alta California can have an inexpensive beach vacation without a long drive. No one knows with certainty, but the RV parks in the vicinity must total at least 45 or 50, making it the RV capital of Baja. With its numerous restaurants and curio shops, and miles of beautiful sand beaches, the town is lively and pleasant, with a fascinating mix of sights and sounds: vendors walking through the RV parks, hawking everything from ironwood carvings to fresh shrimp; gentle old Mom and Pop, spending the day sitting under the awning of their Winnie, talking about their previous trip and planning the next; boardsailors flitting along the beach like a covey of bright marine butterflies; a fat woman with enormous breasts bouncing around an improvised slalom on an ATV, unaware that the combined effects of gravity, inertia, and centrifugal force are making her the center of attention.

Locating a suitable RV park among the multitude is worth a bit of research, for each tends to cater to a specific clientele. Playa de Laura RV Park (11) has full hookups, a beach, rest rooms, showers, ice, and *palapas*. Campo San Felipe Trailer Park (8) has full hookups, a beach, showers, ice, and *palapas*. Victor's El Cortez RV Park (17) offers full hookups, a beach, rest rooms, showers, *palapas*, and the use of the El Cortez Motel facilities next door, but only a few spaces are usually available for transients. Club de Pesca Trailer Park (19) has RV sites (many permanent) with electrical and water hookups, dump station, tent sites, rest rooms, showers, recreation room, store, ice, and a beach. La Jolla RV Park (10) has full hookups, showers, rest rooms, a pool, a laundry, and *palapas*.

Further afield, Mar del Sol RV Park (21) has full hookups, showers, rest rooms, laundry, pool, a small store, and *palapas*, with tennis courts available at the hotel just to the north. San Felipe Marina Resort and RV Park (22) is the most elaborate RV park in town, offering full hookups, a clubhouse, pool, bar, showers, rest rooms, and satellite TV at the pads. Tenting and on-the-ground camping are not permitted.

Ruben's Trailer Park (2) is one of the most popular RV parks in San Felipe, offering full hookups, showers, two-story *palapas*, restaurant, bar, ice, and a beautiful beach. The park caters largely to exuberant young visitors from the north, who are out to have a ball and who have a taste for incred-

ibly loud and uninterrupted rap music, something the management seems to encourage. The din is awful, but if you are an exuberant young visitor from the north out to have a ball and have a taste for incredibly loud and uninterrupted rap music, this is the place. Playa Bonita (1) has full hookups, showers, rest rooms, sun shelters, *palapas*, and a beach. Marco's RV Park, across the street from Playa Bonita, has full hookups and sun shelters, but, of course, no beach.

If you want a break from your RV or camping, the Hotel Riviera (15) has rooms with bath, pool, restaurant, and bar. Hotel las Misiónes (20) offers rooms and suites with baths, most with a view of the Cortez, plus pools, tennis, basketball, restaurant, bars, gift shop, and a beach. El Cortez Motel (14) has rooms with baths, some two-bedroom units, pool, picnic area, gift shop, restaurant, bar, and *palapas* on the beach.

"Restaurant Row" is a section of Av. Mar de Cortez with numerous restaurants offering fish, shrimp, clams, lobster, steaks, chicken, and almost anything else you could possibly want to eat, even frog's legs and quail. Along the Malecón, the street next to the beach paralleling Av. Mar de Cortez, there are a number of restaurants and open-air cafés. Most of the hotels and some of the RV parks have restaurants, and there are many inexpensive cafés spread throughout the town. There are public rest rooms and showers at each end of the Malecón, both charging small fees.

There is much to see and do. Long stretches of beautiful sand beaches invite swimming and loafing; Hobies, sailboards, and jet skis are for rent; and banana boat rides are available. You can drive up to the top of the headland at Punta el Machorro (Punta San Felipe) to get a good look at the town and the surrounding desert. If you want to try your hand at piloting an ATV, the dune area (18) is great fun. A number of discos will be found around town—look for the signs. Rockodile (4) is one of the most popular, offering a bar and lots of music, in terms of quantity if not quality. Some Baja California Tours bus trips visit the town during the *Cinco de Mayo* holiday.

Enchanted Island Excursions (12) offers trips on a well-equipped 37-foot motor-sailer to Gonzaga and the Islas Encantada, as well as trips on a *"Super Panga"* equipped with a Bimini, sonar, radio, live bait tank, and fighting chairs. Charters Mar de Cortez (9) offers sailing trips; dune buggy excursions; fishing trips; kayak, sailboard, and Hobie rentals; and horseback riding.

Interesting dive trips can be made along the coast to the south, including Puertecitos and Gonzaga. Due to the extreme tides, visibility ranges between 3 and 30 feet. The best diving occurs from the end of April through June, and in September and October, the summer air temperatures being too hot for most people, the winter water temperatures too cold. San Felipe has only one dive operation. Information and reservations can be made by contacting Charters Mar de Cortez or El Dorado Ranch. Compressed air and full equipment rentals (no sales) can be obtained, and PADI instruction is available. Day trips by van to Puertecitos and

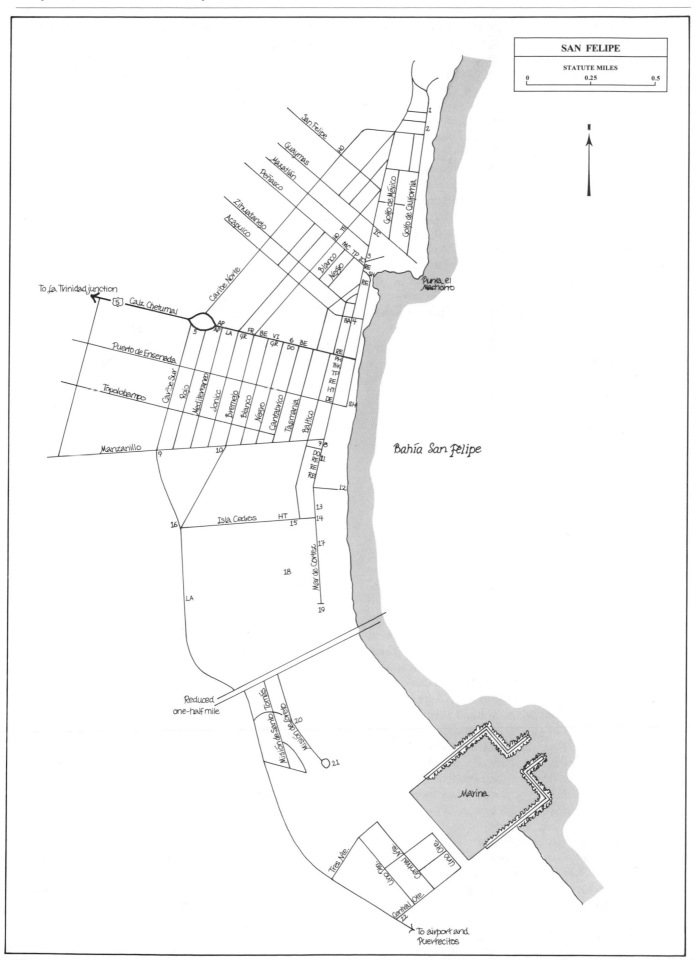

SAN FELIPE

STATUTE MILES

0   0.25   0.5

San Felipe

Guaymas

Mazatlán

Peñasco

Zihuatanejo

Acapulco

Caribe Norte

Golfo de México

Golfo de California

Blanco

Negro

Punta el
Machorro

To La Trinidad junction

⑤ Calz. Chetumal

Puerto de Ensenada

Caribe Sur

Topolobampo

Manzanillo

AP
AP LA FR BE VI 6 BE
        GR GR DO BE

Rojo

Mediterráneo

Jónico

Bermejo

Blanco

Negro

Cantábrico

Tasmania

Báltico

Bahía San Felipe

Isla Cedros   HT

Mar de Cortez

LA

Reduced
one-half mile

Misión Santo Tomás

Misión de Loreto

Marina

Tres Mte.

Uno Pte.

Central Nte.

Uno Ote.

Central Ote.

To airport and
Puertecitos

points south are available on two days notice, and multi-day trips can be arranged. Spearfishing is not encouraged, and shell collecting not permitted. Divers planning to visit the area should make inquires at least a month in advance to obtain tide information, which is vital to the success of a dive trip in this area.

Through the years, many world fishing records have been set at San Felipe, but the fishery continues to decline, and only small corbina, cabrilla, and sierra are found in most coolers. Even corvina, mainstay of San Felipe fishing until the late 1970s, can be scarce. Roca Consag, seen on the horizon to the east, 17 miles, 062° from the lighthouse on Punta el Machorro, used to be one of the fabled Baja hot spots. Today, the fishing there is only fair, with a mixed bag of cabrilla, triggerfish, and sierra. There may be some hope—anglers have recently pulled in some very nice white seabass, ranging up to 72 pounds. There are numerous *pangas* for rent, and limited tackle is available at hardware stores and sportfishing offices. Yes, climbers, Consag has been conquered.

There are two usable concrete launch ramps in San Felipe. The ramp at the El Cortez Motel is fairly shallow (11%) and rough, but wide and generally in good condition. The ramp at Club de Pesca (13%) is missing a chunk of concrete at its foot, reducing the usable width to about 8 feet. You may or may not be charged a fee, usually depending on whether you are staying at the park—ask at the office. As might be expected, parking your tow vehicle and boat trailer can be a problem during holidays. Because of the enormous tides, the shoreline can extend a half mile at low tide, and these ramps are thus usable at high tide only. Since they lead to unprotected water, afternoon wind and waves can cause difficulty, and guide-boards are an asset. The ramp at Ruben's has been undermined and broken up, but they have special vehicles for across-the-beach launches. Winds tend to blow in the afternoon, so head out early. A hardware store (3) has service and some parts for Johnson/Evinrude outboards.

The office of the State Secretary of Tourism (7) has many brochures, fliers, and maps to give away. **At present there is no *Migración* office in San Felipe, and those headed south will not find it possible to obtain tourist cards or to have them validated; get the job done at the border.** The three PEMEX stations (5 and 16, Magnasin only; the station at KM 191 has Magnasin and Premium) have been known to run out of gas during holidays, resulting in lines at every station all the way to Ensenada. Diesel is available at the commercial marina south of town, but you must bring a funnel, since the nozzle is too large to fit an automotive tank. There are a number of places to buy food, including a small supermarket (6) carrying most of the items you would find in a similar establishment in *El Norte*. The Net Cyberservices is a computer service office, and their office (13) is open between 9 and 12 daily except Sundays. They can provide access to the Internet and you can send and receive e-mail. They have most of the latest upgrades of word processing and spreadsheet programs, and both PCs and Macs are available, as well as a laser printer, scanners, and a fax machine.

San Felipe is not often visited by cruising yachts because of its distance from the Cape, although some are now being berthed at the commercial harbor. The harbor has not been dredged adequately, and areas go dry at low tide. It was badly damaged by a recent *chubasco*, but repairs are underway. Because of its proximity to the border and excellent road access, the town is often the starting point for the 160-mile cruise to Bahía de los Angeles and the Midriff, the first anchorage south being Puertecitos, 40.5 miles away. Kayakers and small-boat sailors will find numerous camps and homes where water may be available, and there are many sand beaches and pebble beaches for landings en route to Puertecitos.

● ●

66 *Wind in the rigging*

Reeve, Perry Studt, and I had launched a small sail-boat in San Felipe, and arrived at Bahía de los Angeles after five enjoyable days. Anchored off the village on the last night before heading north, there was a great deal of philosophizing and story telling as we sat in the cockpit. This was our first cruise in the Cortez, and things could not have gone better; fine weather, excellent fishing and diving, interesting hikes ashore, and a close-up view of a finback whale. It was flat calm, and our only complaint was that it looked like we would have to listen to the engine as we worked our way north the next morning. About midnight we went below, and as we began to doze off we could hear wind in the rigging, and we smiled to ourselves—a heck of a cruise, one heck of a cruise!

By 2 A.M. the wind was a full gale from the west, and the boat was surging heavily back and forth on the anchor line. About 4 there was a sudden shout from topside, "We've got to get my boat!" We had towed Perry's small outboard boat behind us, using it for fishing and explorations ashore, but the painter had chafed through during the night, and the boat was nowhere to be seen. By the time Reeve and I got topside, Perry had tied a float to the anchor line and was about to uncleat it, but we rushed forward in the nick of time. To get underway in the heavy winds and inky darkness would be nearly suicidal, for we would probably end up wrecked on one of the numerous islands to leeward.

By dawn the wind had moderated, and we calculated that the wind and tidal currents would have carried the outboard on a vector of about 070°, assuming it got past the islands. Within an hour we found it, undamaged and still afloat. As we started north under bright blue skies, the wind was driving us along at 5 knots and seemed to be swinging to the northwest and increasing. The waves began to bounce the boat around, so we steered closer to shore and were soon tearing along in almost flat-calm water. By noon we were again in a full gale, with the gunnel in the water under a reefed main sail. An hour later the wind had swung more to the north, to the point we either had to steer more offshore or use the engine. The horizon to the east was lumpy, indicating very large waves, so we took in the sails and started the engine.

By 2 in the afternoon, we were in trouble. The wind was almost dead ahead and the full power of the engine was only inching us along. Perry came up with a good idea; the sailboat's 6-horse outboard engine was clamped on a bracket on the transom, but the boat also had a well in the cockpit where the 4-horse engine from his boat could be installed. The second engine helped us make some progress for an hour or so, but the wind continued to increase and was soon ripping off the surface of the water. We could not face the stinging spray for more than a few seconds, and Perry's boat was swinging wildly back and forth on the painter and frequently looked like it was about to go airborne.

It was a bizarre situation: bright blue skies, 100 yards from shore, no waves more than an few inches high, the wind roaring through the rigging, spray stinging us like hailstones, two engines straining at full throttle, and we were almost dead in the water. No one could come up with a good scheme—our fuel was getting low, the deep water and rocky bottom along the beach limited our chances of getting an anchor to hold, and if either engine stopped or the wind increased any more we would surely be driven to leeward and be swamped by the huge waves. Our decreased velocity through the water had made the helm unresponsive, and if our heading were driven even a few degrees to starboard, the increased wind pressure on the hull might make it impossible to turn back, and a turn to port would drive us on the rocky beach. Hoisting sail would be dangerous, since there was only one set of reef points, and a port tack would quickly put us into the big waves. Nothing we could remember from Knight's Seamanship described anything like this, and there seemed to be nothing we could do to help ourselves.

Twenty minutes later a line of sight past two cactuses ashore provided more bad news; we were at a standstill, and only the wash of Perry's engine across the rudder was allowing us to control the boat. After a half-hour of anxious staring at the cactuses, we saw that they were finally starting to move apart. There was no apparent decrease in the wind at first, but within 30 minutes the boat was speeding along in a flat calm, our clothes were drying in the sun, and we were toasting our latest escape from the jaws of death. **"**

San Felipe to KM 229+ on the Transpeninsular Highway

The road south to Puertecitos and Bahía San Luis Gonzaga ending on the Transpeninsular is one of the most interesting in Baja. Bicyclists will find it a fairly demanding six- to eight-day ride, January and February often being the only months cool enough to be really enjoyable for bicyclists. Water is not difficult to obtain from homes and camps along the way, and many beach campsites will be found. The road as far as Puertecitos was paved a number of years ago, but the job was done so poorly that it quickly deteriorated into a moonscape of potholes—in places it is hard to tell that it was ever paved at all. The road was recently damaged by a recent hurricane, but it can be negotiated by almost any vehicle. Start south at the intersection of Calzada Chetumal and Av. Caribe Sur. Set odometer. At Mile 6.1 encounter a junction; take the left (090°) fork (the road otherwise goes to the airport).

KM	Location
7	El Faro Beach Trailer Park has full hookups, rest rooms, showers, pool, bar, tennis, and ice. A "hole" a mile east of the point in 80 feet of water is the first outpost of good fishing south of San Felipe, mostly for a mixed bag of cabrilla, corbina, sierra, grouper, and an occasional white seabass. Just after slack tide, when the currents are moving but not roaring along, the fishing in a shallow area 200 yards offshore can be excellent. There are numerous private homes and inexpensive RV camps along the beach for many miles to the south, and it appears that someday they will stretch wall-to-wall all the way to Puertecitos.
64+	A four-wheel-drive road meanders west far into Arroyo Matomí, which bears 255°. Marine chart 21008 and Mexican 1:500,000 topo Ensenada 11R-II show the "Cuevas de Santa Rosa," placing them about 5 miles northwest of the ranch. A reconnaissance geology map of the area suggests volcanic rock can be expected; could they be lava tubes? There are also sedimentary areas in the vicinity; could they be solution caves? Although large-scale topos do not show references to caves and nothing further is known, cavers could have a fine time searching. The appropriate 1:50,000 topos are: Bahía Santa María H11B67; and Puertecitos H11B77.
72+	A dense outcropping of quartz crystals up to 8 inches long has been found near the first foothills to the west.
73	Speedy's Camp. RV parking, sand beach.
75	**Puertecitos.** This small village has a PEMEX (M, not always open during business hours, closed Wednesday), a few RV parking sites, some with *palapas* and occasional electricity, a *cantina*, several stores with limited produce, ice maybe, the world's smallest public library, and many retired Americans living in ramshackle homes. Diving is limited, but fishing is a noticeable improvement over San Felipe. A steep (16%) and rough

launch ramp leading into semiprotected waters can be found at the south point of the peninsula forming the harbor. Although the ramp extends into fairly deep water, the tidal range here is still extreme, so use your tables. There are several natural hot tubs in the rocky beach near the point, each having a different temperature. To try them out, locate the launch ramp, turn around, and drive about 100 yards north. The tubs are on the Cortez side of the peninsula, marked by a scalloped stone fence and a rough concrete path. The anchorage, some of it a mud flat at low tide, is protected from all but south and southeast winds. Commercial fishing vessels like to anchor behind a spur of land 0.75 mile south. The next anchorages south are Isla San Luis and Gonzaga. Kayakers and small-boat sailors will encounter numerous sand beaches and pebble beaches along the 39-mile coastline to Gonzaga.

■■■■■■■■■■■■■

On the road to Gonzaga, south of Puertecitos

The road south from Puertecitos has been improved, although washouts, rough spots, and washboard can be expected. There are no upgrades over about 14% going north or south, but underpowered, three-speed vehicles, especially those with heavy loads or towing trailers, may encounter difficulty. Many people drive far too fast along this stretch—a man recently bragged to me that his wife had made the 45-mile run between Puertecitos and Alfonsina's in an hour in her "hot-rod sand rail." There have been a number of accidents, so take your time and drive defensively. Use the regional map on pages 130 and 131; set odometer.

Mile	Location
4.3	**Playa la Costilla.** Camping and boondocking, sand beach with stretches of gravel for several miles to the south.
8.8	The dark hill to the east is Volcán Prieto ("Black Volcano"). The shallows offshore are great for leopard grouper, and the small indentation in the shoreline just to the south has excellent corvina, pargo, and snapper. Cartoppers can be launched at Costilla or at Mile 10.6, trailerboats at El Huérfanito, Mile 16.3.
10.6	Access to a sand-and-cobble beach with a natural breakwater. Beware of the 25% grade coming out.
15.7	Site of infamous grade in the "old" road.

■ The "Terrible Three"

Steep grades, loose rock, sharp turns, and yawning chasms made the 11-mile stretch in this area a bane to travelers and an attraction to the daring for many years, the most celebrated "off-road" road in Baja. Three of the worst grades, the "Terrible Three" (some insist there were a "Terrible Six"), tested the metal and mettle of every vehicle and driver. No one seems to know the least-capable type of automobile to ever survive the trip to Gonzaga before improvements were made, but the dividing line seems to be somewhere between the levels of a Corvair and of a Gremlin; the rusted remains of a Corvair still lie at the bottom of one grade, but I met a man who claimed to have made it in a Gremlin, with considerable damage. Many years ago Reeve and I drove it in a VW van, but at the bottom of the most terrible of the "Terrible Three" we had to unload and carry everything to the top; the van didn't have the power to make it any other way. With burning rubber, flying stones, and screaming engine we barely made it to the top. The road has now been graded, greatly easing the difficulty of passage, but also reducing its character and the feeling of accomplishment in survival. The accompanying photo was taken on the worst of these grades, seen today by looking south from Mile 16.6.

Mile	Location
16.3	**El Huérfanito** ("The Little Orphan," Nacho's Camp). There are just a few homes here, opposite a tiny island. A rough concrete launch ramp (12%) leads to a pebble beach. Kids will have a ball with the hordes of small spotted bass. The most northerly of the Islas Encantada lies offshore.

■ Enchanted Islands

The Islas Encantada are a group of 6 small islands stretching along the coast for 18 miles, the most northerly lying offshore at this point. Their collective name stems from the facts that mirages are often seen, currents on their eastern and western sides run in opposite directions, some of the beaches are black (lava sand), some rocks float (pumice), and others are made of glass (obsidian). The first four, El Huérfanito, El Muerto, Lobos, and Encantada (El Huérfanito, Miramar, Lobos, and El Muerto, respectively, on some charts) were formed by fault blocking of Miocene volcanic rock during the Pleistocene epoch. Huérfanito, Lobos, and Encantada provide little shelter for boats, but Muerto has several small coves on its southwestern side (keep the DEET handy). Although kayakers will find no adequate place to camp on Huérfanito or Lobos, Encantada has a rocky beach on its southwest end with adequate camping, and San Luis, the most southerly of the Encantadas, has a number of good locations.

The area east of Encantada is the focus of fishing in the area. About 700 yards to the east of the island is a tiny islet, covered with bird droppings and unworthy of a name, and even farther to the east is a large reef. Studded with pinnacles, this reef is loaded with gulf grouper, yellowtail, cabrilla, and moderate numbers of white seabass. The reef is generally too deep for free-divers, so spearfishing is very limited. The eastern margin of the reef is marked by a wash rock that bares to 3 feet at low tide.

San Luis (Encantada Grande, Isla Salvatierra), the largest of the islands, is also the most interesting. As you near the island, its western side gives few hints as to its violent volcanic birth during the Holocene epoch, but as you round the southern coast, layers of ash and pumice are encountered, and the east side proves to be far more dramatic than the west. Even those without a graduate degree in geology will recognize that the semi-circular bluff encountered there is the inside curve of a volcano, and that the 50-foot cone of dark, rough lava in the center is a vent plug, formed as volcanic activity ended. The eastern half of the volcano is missing, blasted into oblivion when it exploded. The coast on both sides of the volcano is a fantastic sculpture of volcanism and erosion.

Boaters and kayakers should set aside a day to explore San Luis and its companion, Isla Pomo. A long sand spit sticks out from the southwestern side of San Luis, providing exposed anchorages on either side, as well as a place to land and camp. The volcano site, with its sloping beach of pumice and pebbles, also provides a good place to camp, the looming bluffs providing welcome shade in the afternoon. The aid-to-navigation tower here, askew on its foundation, has been dubbed "The Leaning Tower of Pumice." A pebble beach on the east side, just south of the north tip of the island, provides another place to camp. Rounding the north tip counterclockwise, you will soon see a snug little harbor, but beware—the entrance may be awash at low tide, the rocks are sharp, and the place stinks to high heaven because of its popularity with sea birds. Just to the south, sun will be seen glinting off huge boulders of low-grade obsidian. Nearby is a "lunch cave," a small sea cave providing a cool, dark place to take a break if tidal conditions permit. There are numerous sand beaches and pebble beaches along the west coast which provide good camping.

Isla Pomo, just to the northeast, also of Holocene

The worst of the "Terrible Three" as it was in 1967. The surface had been firmed up by dumping bags of cement. Any help was welcome

volcanic origin, has another lunch cave on its south side, but there are few good places to land and camp. Above and adjacent to the cave is a mystery—are those white objects cactus covered by bird droppings, natural sculptures created by artistic birds using the same material, or stalagmites produced by an as-yet unknown geologic process? The cove on the east side is less protected than it may appear, but camping might be possible in periods of low tides.

Fishing is good around the islands, and trollers working yellowtail may have trouble keeping the numerous cabrilla off their bait. Try the south and east sides of San Luis, the shallow channel across to Pomo, and several reefs a half mile or so north of both San Luis and Pomo. Diving is uninspiring, the bottom being generally featureless cobble and gravel, but spearfishing might prove rewarding. Visibilities range between 6 and 25 feet, varying widely in only short distances. Mineral collectors will find all the obsidian they could ever want. The islands are home to many sea birds, including ospreys, Heermann's gulls, frigates, and brown- and blue-footed boobies. Hundreds of pelicans often inhabit the sand spit on San Luis. There are large deposits of guano on both islands, and during a recent circumnavigation, most of the guano flies left their normal habitat and landed on my brother, a week from his last bath. Did they know something?

Mile	Location

20.2   Arroyo el Volcán. Good quality sphene crystals, possibly washed down from the El Mármol area, have been found at the mouth of the arroyo.

23.0   Water, food, sodas.

26.9   Boondocking site.

34.2   **Las Encantadas.** Sportfishing, food, drink, sand beach.

35.7   **Campo Bufeo** (signed). Restaurant, RV parking, cabins, hot showers, gas, diesel, mechanic. The long sand beach here is a good jumping-off place for visits to San Luis and Pomo.

40.5   Campo el Faro. Sportfishing.

40.8   Papa Fernández', 1 mile east (signed), may have gas, oil, food, drink, and rental boats. Launch over a fairly hard sand-and-pebble beach. The twin bays of Ensenada San Francisquito and Bahía Gonzaga provide an excellent all-weather anchorage, although you may have to move around to keep out of the chop. Fishing, diving, and shelling continue to improve as you go farther south from San Felipe. Fishing can be good from spring to fall for grouper, sierra, snapper, and spotted bass, and the area is frequently the northernmost range of significant numbers of migratory yellowtail. Hot spots include the waters off Punta Willard and along the shoreline just to the north. Commercial boats anchored in the bay may have fresh shrimp for sale. The next all-weather anchorage south is Puerto Refugio on the north end of Guardian Angel Island, 52 miles. Kayakers and small-boat sailors following the coast will find that the 78-mile trip to Bahía de los Angeles requires caution, for the coastline has long stretches of high bluffs. The coves just west of Punta Final are good anchorages in south weather, but the one at Puerto Calamajué is suitable only in calm weather. It has a sand beach, and the camp here may be the last source of water until Bahía de los Angeles. Ensenada Blanca is an open roadstead, with a gravel beach. Punta Bluff provides a bit of protection from prevailing weather, and there is a sand beach. Short stretches of sand-and-pebble

beaches will be found near Remedios, giving way to pebble beaches and rocky bluffs as you near Bahía de los Angeles. Remedios is a low rocky point, providing some shelter from the prevailing waves, and good anchoring conditions. Tidal currents in the Canal de Ballenas can be heavy. See page 143 for more information on the coast between Remedios and Bahía de los Angeles.

43.2   **Campo Rancho Grande.** Gasoline, small store, mechanic, tire repair, and *agua purificada*. A new PEMEX is being built nearby. Road east (signed) to Alfonsina's, 2 miles. This resort has modest rooms, restaurant, gas, water, limited supplies, rental boats, and possible mechanical repairs. Boats can be launched easily over the beach. There is a growing community of Americans. The newly constructed Rancho Grande RV Park, south of the Alfonsina's complex, has RV parking, *palapas*, showers, rest rooms, and a beautiful beach. In early 1998 it was not yet in operation.

Reeve with a dandy white seabass, caught off a rocky point near Isla San Luis

48.0	Junction, take the right (210°) fork. The other fork leads to Punta Final.
58.5	Pickup road southwest to a turquoise and chrysocolla site. You can drive 5 miles, but the last mile must be hiked.
60.8	**Las Arrastras.** Mechanic, cold sodas, tire repair.
64.2	Coco's Corner. RV parking, sodas, water, very modest café. Intersection (signed), go left (045°) for Puerto Calamajué or right (164°) for the Transpeninsular.
76.3	Arrive at the Transpeninsular Highway at KM 229+.

Staggering out of the van, we found it sunk to the axles, exactly 57 feet from the end of the pavement. During the next four hours we reorganized the shambles in the back, collected our scubas, and dug away tons of sand in an attempt to build a road to firmer ground. Every 20 minutes or so a car or pickup would whiz by about 50 yards ahead of our excavations. We finally got underway, pulling onto the freshly graded road to Puertecitos that we had missed earlier. **99**

• •

66 *Off-road adventures*

Having read of the vast and mysterious wasteland to the south, Reeve and I finally mustered enough courage to take our first trip to Baja. The broken axles and shredded tires plaguing other drivers would not catch us unprepared! We visited a Volkswagen dealer and bought so many spare parts we could have almost built a new van. Enough insect repellent, first-aid supplies, aerial flares, emergency water, shovels, and sunburn glop to support a platoon of Marines were then collected. The van became so packed that we were forced into a difficult choice; something had to stay, our cooler of ice and beer or our half-dozen scuba tanks. A neighbor saved us by offering a roof rack.

Scubas on the roof, beer at the ready, we pulled out of San Diego rehearsing what action we would take in every conceivable emergency situation. The scorching flats south of Mexicali shimmered in the heat, reminding us that this was the real Baja, where people actually died from unpreparedness or even from simple mistakes like turning the wrong way at a fork. We passed through San Felipe and knew that the first of the Terrible Three was just 60 or 70 miles ahead. We could not find the road to Puertecitos shown on our maps, but finally we approached the end of the pavement. The road ahead certainly looked like what we imagined a Baja road should look like: deep sand and ruts. Having read that speed and power were necessary to overcome such a situation, I shifted into a lower gear and pushed the accelerator to the floor. Slightly overestimating the required velocity, we shot across the first dip and ricocheted over a rise with such force that my head hit the ceiling of the van, momentarily stunning me. The van swerved violently left, its spinning steering wheel almost tearing off one of my thumbs. The van then hit a bump so hard that the roof rack collapsed, scattering scuba tanks in every direction, and causing Reeve's door to fly open, his seat belt saving him from ejection. The violent deceleration threw me against the dashboard, and there was an avalanche of equipment from the rear of the van. Fortunately nothing was hard or sharp.

Bill Gibson quenches a mighty thirst during a trip south of San Felipe

Bonnie Wong

National Aeronautics and Space Administration

The complex geology of northeastern Baja; the Sierra de Cucapa, the mouth of the Río Colorado, and the northern Sea of Cortez.

Chapter 14

The Midriff Region

The "Midriff," the most exotic, remote, mysterious, and interesting region of the Cortez, has been saved for last. It contains about 55 islands, islets, and pinnacles, the most interesting being Guardian Angel, Partida Norte, Raza, Salsipuedes, Las Ánimas Norte, San Lorenzo, San Esteban, Turners, Tiburón, Patos, and San Pedro Mártir. (To promote a smoother and more useful flow of information, Guardian Angel was described in Chapter 10.) Remote and unspoiled, all are uninhabited except for fishermen and guano collectors living in temporary camps, plus a few game wardens. The Cortez is less than 60 miles wide at this point, and enormous tidal currents race by, forming giant whirlpools and pulling up nutrients from deep waters, which support vast quantities of plankton. These in turn provide food for animals higher in the food chain, and the area is alive with birds and marine mammals, especially dolphins. Fin and Bryde's whales are seen year-round, and blue whales visit the area from late winter to late spring. Gamefish, primarily yellowtail, grouper, cabrilla, and white and black sea bass, are abundant, and provide one of the least-stressed fisheries in the Cortez. In warm months yellowfin, marlin, and dorado migrate into the area. Tony Reyes Fishing Tours offers trips from San Felipe which fish the Midriff.

 By water: the Stepping-Stones Trip

The waters of the Midriff offer some of the world's finest small-boat cruising. Although there are no all-weather anchorages, a boat crossing from Bahía de los Angeles to Bahía Kino in Sonora never needs to be more than 8 miles from land, and some shelter from weather from almost any direction can be found. There are no marinas, parts stores, or villages, and there is little chance of getting help from passing vessels in case of emergency. Writers pursuing literary effect have given the area an aura of danger and mystery. Ray Cannon's description of a crossing was titled a "Voyage of Terror," due to a storm he encountered. Actually, the weather is normally tranquil, and a well-equipped and seaworthy cruiser or small sailboat, operated in a conservative manner, can make the voyage safely. I have explored much of the area and crossed the Cortez twice in a 15-foot cartop outboard (not a recommended activity). However, this is not to say that it is always tranquil. Southern *chubascos* can reach the

Midriff from mid-May to mid-November, peaking in August and September, and abnormal water temperatures occasionally cause them to form in other months. During the fall and winter months, passing cold fronts and stagnant high-pressure areas in the southwestern US can cause wipeout conditions in the Midriff, and it is not unheard of for kayakers and small-boaters to have to "hole-up" for up to a week. Reliable weather reports are not available, and every traveler must have adequate food and water and avoid the temptation to travel if there are any doubts; keep a "weather eye" at all times. Cruising Charts offers a guide to the area, as well as a map of Bahía Kino and the eastern shore of Tiburón. If you get into trouble remember that Club Deportivo Bahía Kino monitors CB channel 11 and VHF channel 16.

The nearest paved launch ramps in Baja are at Bahía de los Angeles. Many people launching there spend the first night at Puerto Don Juan, sorting out gear and getting things shipshape before starting the crossing the next morning. An alternative is to drive the road from Bahía de los Angeles (or the road through El Arco) to Bahía San Francisquito, where boats can be launched over the beach. You could, of course, start in Kino.

Twenty-three miles from Don Juan is Isla Partida Norte (Isla Cardinosa), the first in a chain of islands running southeast to San Lorenzo. Partida has an anchorage in a small bay on the northwestern side, and another off a sand beach on the southeastern side. The island has the largest concentrations of petrels in the Cortez. The *jejénes* can be fierce, so be prepared to move. Fishing is best north of the island, and south half-way to Raza. Diving is excellent, especially around Roca Blanca, 1,200 yards north.

Your first impression of Raza, 5 miles from Partida Norte, is apt to be "ho-hum." Only 150 acres in area and less than 100 feet high, with sparse vegetation and abundant guano, it seems to be just another tiny, lifeless, rocky island. Not so, for Raza is the scene of a spectacular pageant of conflict, disaster, death, and renewal. In March or April vast numbers of Heermann's gulls arrive and begin to scratch out nesting sites. Since every square foot of available land is occupied by these noisy, aggressive birds, it would seem foolhardy for another species to attempt a beachhead. However, elegant terns and, to a lesser ex-

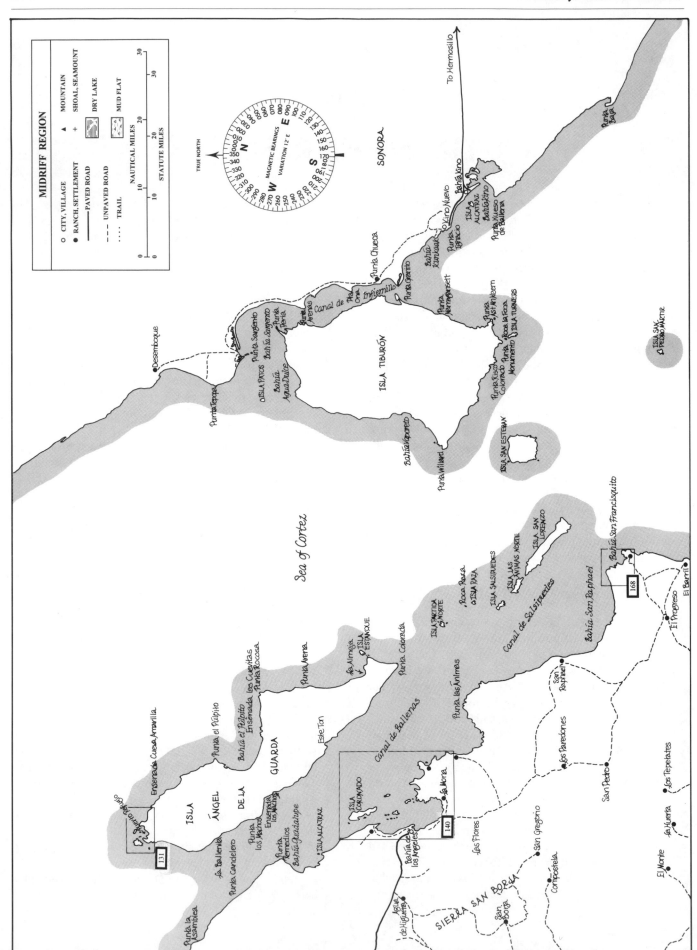

MIDRIFF REGION

○ CITY, VILLAGE   ▲ MOUNTAIN
● RANCH, SETTLEMENT   + SHOAL, SEAMOUNT
——— PAVED ROAD   ▦ DRY LAKE
- - - UNPAVED ROAD   ▨ MUD FLAT
· · · · TRAIL

NAUTICAL MILES
STATUTE MILES

TRUE NORTH

MAGNETIC BEARINGS
VARIATION 12° E

SONORA

To Hermosillo

Punta Baja

Bahía Kino
Punta Vino Nuevo
ISLA ALCATRAZ
Bahía Kino
Punta Hueso de Ballena

Punta Chueca
Bahía Kunkaak
Punta Granito

Canal de Infiernillo
Punta Arena

Punta Kamargeet
Punta Ast-Ankeem
Roca la Foca
Punta Monumento
ISLA TURNERS

Desemboque

ISLA PATOS
Punta San Gento
Bahía la Sargento
Punta Perla
Punta Arena

ISLA TIBURÓN

Punta Riesco Colorado

Punta Tepopa

Bahía Agua Dulce

ISLA SAN PEDRO MÁRTIR

Bahía Vaporeta

Punta Willard

ISLA SAN ESTEBAN

Sea of Cortez

Bahía San Francisquito

Roca Rosa
ISLA Raza
ISLA SAN LORENZO

ISLA PARTIDA NORTE
ISLA SALSIPUEDES
ISLA LAS ÁNIMAS NORTE

168

El Barril

Canal de Salsipuedes

Bahía San Raphael

El Progreso

Punta Arena

La Almeja
ISLA ESTANQUE
ISLA ROCOSA
Ensenada los Cuevitas
Punta Rocosa

Punta Colorada

Punta las Ánimas

San Raphael

Los Paredones

San Pedro

Ensenada Cueva Amarilla

Punta el Púlpito
Bahía el Pulpito
Ensenada

Este Ton

GUARDA

Canal de Ballenas

Los Flores

San Gregorio

La Huerta
Los Tepetates

Puerto Refugio

ISLA

ÁNGEL

DE LA

Punta la Ballena
Punta los Machos
Ensenada los Machos
Bahía Guadalupe
ISLA ALCATRAZ

ISLA CORONADO

La Mona

140

Bahía de los Ángeles

San Pedro

San Gregorio

Compostela

El Monte

Punta Candelero

Punta Remedios

131

Punta la Asamblea

Agua de Higuera

San Borja

SIERRA SAN BORJA

tent, royal terns soon begin to arrive with high strategy and nesting on their minds. Several hundred thousand birds may be on the island at one time.

After walking about for a while, preening themselves with an air of massive indifference, one night the terns suddenly fly into a dense formation, alight in a predetermined location, and force the gulls away. By dawn they have assumed a circular defensive formation 30 or 40 feet in diameter surrounded by outraged gulls. You could say the gulls were "terned out," but they soon counterattack, strutting about, engaging in rowdy behavior, and pecking open freshly laid eggs. By evening many terns have been frightened off and the circle has shrunk by half, but during the night the missing terns return and the circle widens. As days pass, some eggs hatch and a few chicks manage to survive the seesaw battle, enough to insure a stable population.

In addition to this natural spectacle, Raza offers a man-made mystery. Piles of stone, some as high as 5 feet, are scattered throughout the island. Aerial photographs show an amazing 1,100 of them. Theories differ on their purpose and origin. Some people claim the piles were made by egg gatherers, who discovered that by piling up stones the tern-versus-gull land grab could be eased and egg production increased. Others insist they were constructed by guano collectors who cleared the area to facilitate deposition and collection of the valuable fertilizer. Some say Seri Indians from Tiburón used Raza as a burial ground and the piles are monuments. A Seri once told me this was not true, that Raza was used as a penal colony, where prisoners stacked rocks to hold up canvas sun shades. A few claim that there *are* graves on the island, but for guano collectors who expired due to the hot sun and the stench.

Indians collected eggs on Raza for centuries, doing little permanent damage, but by the early 1900s the copper mines at Santa Rosalía developed and the hungry miners had to be fed. Raiders measured the freshness of eggs by their specific gravity; fresh eggs sank in a bucket of water, old ones floated. If there were too many old ones they simply smashed every egg in sight, and the bereaved parents would promptly lay replacements. By

The mysterious stone "monuments" on Raza

the 1960s outboard motors had greatly increased the efficiency of the operation, causing a drastic decline in bird populations, so in 1964 President Lopéz Mateos declared the island a wildlife preserve. Although closed to casual visitors, the "big picture" of the annual nesting spectacle can be seen from a boat. Wardens on the island may provide an escorted tour if you can attract their attention from the lagoon and determine the current regulations before going ashore.

Raza has a fair anchorage on the south side, but Partida Norte and Salsipuedes are close and provide more secure conditions. Diving around Raza is good, but not up to the standards of the other islands, although Roca Raza, 1 mile north, is excellent. Local divers have attempted to locate the end of a huge metal chain found off the northeast tip, but it is so long that the water becomes too deep for their hookas.

Salsipuedes, 4 miles from Raza, is 1.5 miles long and is almost pinched in half two thirds of the way south, forming 2 coves, 1 opening north, 1 south, both providing good anchorages. Fishing is best on the northeast side, where the bottom is steep and has numerous ledges and small caves harboring black sea bass. Fishing is also excellent for yellowtail, cabrilla, and sierra. Diving is good almost anywhere, especially at the pinnacles off the northwest end and on the south reef.

Las Ánimas Norte (Isla San Lorenzo Norte), a little over a mile from Salsipuedes, has several small anchorages, one on the northeastern side, the other at the south end, both open and surgy. The east end is known for large grouper and black sea bass in water up to 500 feet deep, and feeding frenzies of yellowtail sometimes cover 3 or 4 acres. Diving is good, but the island should not be confused with Isla las Ánimas Sur, several hundred miles to the south.

San Lorenzo, the southernmost island in the chain, is separated by a narrow channel from Las Ánimas Norte and is high and steep, with a few narrow gravel beaches. Two small coves on the southwestern side provide anchorages with marginal protection from prevailing winds. Small sand beaches will be found on the western coast 3 miles from the northwest end and at the southeast tip. Although the island appears to be barren, zalate, elephant trees, and copalquín flourish in the canyons. San Lorenzo, Las Ánimas Norte, and Salsipuedes collectively have the world's largest colony of nesting brown pelicans. Although the yellow-legged gull tends to nest alone or in small groups, the largest number of nests in the world is found on the island. The bottom drops to 2,000 feet within a half mile of shore. Fishing is usually best on the northeast side and to the south.

The Canal de Salsipuedes, between the chain of islands and the Baja coast, is deep, running to over 800 fathoms in places, and swift tidal currents form huge whirlpools. In the early 1700s Jesuit Father Juan de Ugarte tried to sail his sloop up the channel, but had to give up after 20 days of continuous effort. Modern sailors and kayakers are apt to be equally frustrated unless they time their schedules to the tides.

San Esteban is 16 miles east of the north tip of Salsipuedes and can be seen easily, since it rises to 1,771 feet. Its coast consists primarily of sea cliffs, except for a large gravel beach on the east side. Boats can anchor off the southwest spit. Diving is excellent, especially on the reef extending a half mile off the northeast tip, although there are reports of aggressive sharks. Yellowtail fishing is fine all around the island, including the reef just mentioned. Few thrills in fishing can equal letting down a bait into a horde of silvery shapes streaking erratically through the clear blue water of this reef.

Esteban was formed of volcanic rock extruded as a result of sea-floor spreading during the Pliocene epoch. Being somewhat more remote than most of the larger Cortez islands, and about midway between the Baja peninsula and the mainland, it has the distinctive flora and fauna that might be expected. Birds include the endemic black-throated sparrow, Amphispiza bilineata cana, and the curved-billed thrasher sub-species Toxostoma curvirostre insularum, found only on Esteban and Tiburón. In addition, there are 117 species of vascular plants, 5 of which are endemic to the island, 8 amphibians and reptiles, 4 of which are endemic, the gigantic blotched chuckwalla Sauromalus varius, and the small rattlesnake Crotalus molossus being the most distinctive.

Although Esteban has no permanent potable water, bands of Seri Indians used to maintain camps on the island, traveling there from the mainland and Tiburón in their reed boats. Other than one endemic species of white-footed mouse, the island has no native land mammals, and the Seri diet was mainly sea lion, fish, shell fish, chuckwalla, and edible native plants. (There are recent reports of introduced rats "big as cats" on the island.) The San Esteban people were known as great gamblers, and they sometimes engaged in games where the stakes were life and death. Seri legend indicates that the men would challenge each other to a game of "chicken." Climbing to the top of a steep gravel slope that ended at the edge of a cliff high over a rocky beach, each would take his turn sliding down the slope in a large turtle shell. At the last possible moment before plunging over the cliff, each would leap out, and whoever came the closest to the edge was the winner. If someone misjudged his timing and went sailing over the edge, the first man to yell "Your wife is mine" obtained the right to marry the widow-to-be, even if he already had a wife. The cliff can be seen on the east side of the island, a short distance north of the main canyon.

I have camped on Esteban, equipped with several large coolers full of ice, vegetables, fresh milk, meat, and vast quantities of beer, a nylon canopy to keep the sun off, a radio to keep me entertained, a sleeping bag and an air mattress to allow me to sleep comfortably, and an aluminum boat driven by an outboard engine to take me anywhere I wished to go with little effort. I found the experience rather demanding, and knew I would be dead in several days should I be deprived of my comforts. One can only marvel at the remarkably hardy people who once lived out their lives on this tiny scrap of rock and appreciate the unique culture that made it possible. Seri legend indicates that in the 1800s Mexican troops rounded up and deported the entire population of the island.

● ●

❝ A sharp problem at hand

Reeve, Dick Mandich, and I had risen before dawn, anticipating another tussle with the big yellowtails off our camp on Esteban. Cold "C" rations were quickly washed down with cans of Coke, and as the sun rose we were trolling through the calm waters. The horizon revealed nothing, not a panga, not a shrimper, and there wasn't even a vapor trail in the sky—we seemed to be the only people on Earth. The yellowtail were temporarily absent so we decided to jig for some bottom dwellers. I snapped on a large metal jig, dropped it to the bottom, and commenced pumping the rod. Several fish fell for our inducements and were hoisted to the surface, their eyes and bellies bulging. Unhooking a fish, I looked away as I dropped it in the cooler. I felt something odd and when I looked back I found that a very large and stout treble hook had rammed through my thumb just below the nail. Reeve reacted with sympathy pains and Dick seemed a little pale, but everyone soon calmed down. Recalling our Red Cross first aid classes, we decided not to try to back the hook out—the large barb would drag a considerable amount of flesh with it—so I pushed the hook point the rest of the way through the thumb. The old fly-fisherman's trick of wrapping a piece of line around the shank under the barb would not work; the ball of line would have been almost a half-inch in diameter. Reeve dug through the tackle box and found a large pair of side-cutting pliers which should have made short work of the hook, but try as he might, he could do no more than put several small dents in the tempered metal.

The situation began to look serious. I had gotten a tetanus shot recently, was losing only a small amount of blood, and was feeling no intense pain, but I obviously could not go around for the remaining 10 days of our trip with a large lure dangling from my thumb. The nearest permanent settlements were Kino, 35 miles to the east and Bahía de los Angeles, 55 miles to the northwest, long trips in a 15-foot aluminum cartop boat. As we motored back to camp Reeve remembered that we had a tool kit with a hacksaw and a pair of ViseGrip pliers. Dick calmly squeezed the ViseGrips until he had the shank of the hook in an iron grip. With Dick bracing the pliers on a large rock, Reeve began sawing off the protruding end, producing the same effect as a thousand fingernails dragging across a hundred black-

boards. After 10 minutes the blade broke, with only half the diameter cut. We had no spares, so Reeve gripped a section of the broken blade in a rag and kept sawing. The blade sections kept breaking until all of them were too small to hold. Remembering that the metal in the hook was very hard, Reeve took pair of pliers and started to bend the hook back and forth at the cut. After a few minutes the metal finally fatigued and broke, and I applied a little iodine and slowly backed out the shank of the hook. Ten minutes later a dressing had been applied and we were speeding away from camp in pursuit of the yellowtail. The wound healed uneventfully. **❞**

● ●

From San Esteban, boaters usually head for Isla Turners (Isla Dátil) off the southern tip of Tiburón, 13 miles east. Turners is high and rocky, but landings are possible on pebble beaches on the east and west sides. Although exposed, anchorages can be made on mixed bottoms. The Ensenada Chamber of Commerce likes to tout that city as the "Yellowtail Capital of the World." Not so! The title belongs to a small wash rock just west of the north tip of Turners. Spearfishing is excellent, especially around Roca la Foca (Isla Cholludo), between Turners and Tiburón.

With an area of 385 square miles, Tiburón is the largest island in Mexico, extending 33 miles north-south and 18 east-west. Good anchorages can be found between Punta Monumento and Punta Risco Colorado, and in a bight just north of Punta Ast Ah Keem ("Dog Bay"). Fishing is good all around the island, especially along the northwest coast and at the south tip. Spearfishing can be world-class; Don Barthman's 550-pound jewfish came from Tiburón waters. Persons wishing to land on the island must request advanced permission from the chief of

Lloyd Rice and Jim Purvis fill a goody bag off Tiburón

the Seri tribe through the Instituto Nacional Indigenista, which is listed in Appendix B. No one at the Instituto is currently (1998) fluent in English. Southwest Sea Kayaks offers a kayak trip around the island, beginning and ending at Punta Chueca.

The channel between the island and mainland Sonora is shallow, with shifting sandbars and currents so swift that it is known as Canal de Infiernillo (Channel of Little Hell). Fishing in the Canal can be good all year for cabrilla, corvina, sierra, pargo, grouper, and halibut, as well as sea bass to 40 pounds, and shelling and clamming are excellent. With due care for the currents, especially at the north and south entrances, the Canal can be safely navigated by cartoppers, and there is a fair amount of traffic from local divers and fishermen who might be able to render assistance if things go wrong. There is an unpaved area near Punta Chueca where boats can be launched, and local Seri Indians offer *panga* rentals and guide services, as well as ironwood carvings, baskets, and other arts and crafts. The Seri have their own feelings about being photographed, and it is customary to ask permission and make a monetary offer first.

● ●

❝ High wind in Little Hell

Reeve, Dick Mandich, and I were once sentenced to an involuntary stay on Tiburón during a period of bad weather, but our supply of beer and ice finally failed us and we decided that the time for our departure was at hand, no matter what the weather. Reeve volunteered to shuttle the equipment across the Canal in our cartopper, and even to this day—20 years later—the memory is chilling; the 40-knot winds from the north rammed against a heavy tidal current rushing the other way, and every square foot of the Canal was lashed to a froth. Reeve headed into the melee and within seconds disappeared, only to reappear airborne every minute or two. They were not waves in the conventional sense; churned into monumental proportions by the opposing forces of wind and tidal current, they reflected back off points and shores and combined into freakish sharp-pointed peaks that looked like ice cream cones and seemed to violate the laws of physics, only to have their tops ripped off by the wind. Ominously, Reeve did not appear for several minutes, but finally through binoculars we could see the boat leap above the spray, going sideways, only to disappear again. Ten minutes passed, then 20, and after an hour we thought he was a goner, when the bow of the trusty Gregor nosed through the waves and spray to slide up on the beach in front of us, its skipper having the biggest grin even seen by man.

We made it back safely, but when I returned home I found we had all drowned! It seems that a camper who had seen us depart 10 days earlier had decided that no one could possibly survive all that weather and had telephoned the California Highway Patrol with the license number of our van. My wife Judy just laughed when she got the unhappy call from Sacramento, and said, "You couldn't hold those guys under with a sack of bricks." ❞

● ●

Not all mariners are so lucky and the Canal is alleged to be the scene of many shipwrecks, some carrying treasure. Chico Romero, a famous Seri Indian leader, now dead, told my friend Tom Crutchfield that Spanish sailing vessels coming up the Sonora coast in periods of strong southwest winds would be driven helplessly into the Canal. Having limited speed and poor tacking ability, they were swept north by the current and eventually went aground. The tribe would then kill survivors and strip the copper sheathing off the hulls to make arrowheads. There may be some truth to this, for several collections of Seri artifacts include arrowheads made from copper sheet. During a trip in the Canal in the 1960s, Tom's boat was disabled and he drifted over 2 wrecks in 4 fathoms north of Punta Chueca. The Seri knew of the wrecks and later told him that their ancestors had followed their "usual" procedure with the survivors. Some treasure hunters believe that gold removed from Mexico City after its capture by Hernán Cortés was aboard a schooner later wrecked in the Canal.

The Canal de Infiernillo is also the scene of a strange natural phenomenon. In the winter green turtles partially bury themselves in the mud and sand, and begin a dormant period that may last for up to three months. Situated about 10 to 15 feet apart, they lose weight and accumulate thick coats of algae on their shells. They rarely surface for air, and no one has found out how they manage to survive for so long without oxygen. The Seri hunted for them with long spears at low tide, limiting the take to their immediate needs. However, in the late 1950s commercial fishermen joined in the slaughter, with the usual devastating outcome. In 1990 President Salinas declared a total and permanent ban on turtle hunting in Mexico, hopefully insuring that the turtles can slumber in peace.

Several books on shipwrecks indicate that a Dutch frigate named *Draecke* foundered June 12, 1689 in 10 fathoms 1 mile off the south tip of Tiburón with $1 million in gold and silver bullion, specie, and pearls. No historical records of such a ship seem to exist, and except for one hint, *Draecke* appears to be a figment of someone's imagination. Seri oral history says that about the year 1900 children in foraging parties found Dutch coins on a beach between Punta Risco Colorado and Punta Monumento. No one seems to know whether this is authentic oral history or a modern extension of a fairy tale told to the Seri by outsiders.

Two more attractions

Two more islands attract boaters having adequate time and range, Patos and San Pedro Mártir. Patos, north of Tiburón, is not known for ducks, as its name implies, but for pelicans; its population in 1966 was estimated to be between 50,000 and 100,000 of the birds. The island has a thick coating of guano, and in the mid-1800s great sailing ships came to load the rich fertilizer. To boost production the island was cleared of vegetation and Peruvian guanay birds were introduced. The guanay died out and the big ships are gone, but today a few men continue to haul away the smelly material in *pangas*. The sandy-bottomed southern anchorage is excellent, but fishing is not exceptional and there is little to see except birds, rocks, and guano. Diving is only fair, although there are a few wrecks, including a large wooden wreck 130 yards west of the southwestern point, and another one 500 yards southeast of the island. There is, however, a great attraction in the south anchorage.

In 1858 the full-rigged ship *John Elliott Thayer* burned at anchor while loading guano at Patos, the victim of arson by a disgruntled crew member. Seri oral history indicates that many years ago the tribe supplied meat, fish, water, and firewood to large sailing ships at Patos, and that one of them burned and sank. Ramona Blanco, a Seri woman now dead, could remember its masts sticking out of the water at the turn of the century. In 1982 I located the *Thayer* and found her to be a dandy wreck; huge wooden timbers and thick planking still formed the recognizable outline of a sailing ship. The site was littered with debris, obviously of mid-19th Century American origin, including many types of glass bottles, silverware, three types of ceramic plates, bronze spikes and copper sheathing, a huge iron capstan, anchors, an iron object that was perhaps a gaff-jaw, a large metallic ring, brass sailor buttons, and iron harpoons.

About 1964 an American treasure hunter recovered a dozen gold coins from a wreck in the vicinity, apparently Lima Mint 1780 Charles III 8-escudo coins. He obtained permits from the Mexican government enabling him to explore the wreck, but various problems arose, and he was not able to continue. He later turned over his information to CEDAM, the Mexican/American diving archaeology organization, stating that his research in a mission archive in Mexico City had revealed that the gold had come from 1 of 3 Spanish ships wrecked in 1780, carrying 10 million similar coins. Making no effort to verify the story, in spite of obvious inconsistencies, and aware that the *Thayer* would have to have miraculously landed on top of the "treasure ship" in a manner similar to the movie *The Deep* (I told them so), CEDAM nevertheless announced an expedition. Gathering in Hermosillo in June 1983 unwary members traveled to Desemboque, on the Sonora coast north of Patos, to begin diving operations.

You guessed it: the alleged treasure ship proved to be the *Thayer*. How could Lima Mint Charles III 8-escudo coins dated 1780 come to be aboard a US sailing vessel sunk in 1858? Easy; by an act of Congress this coin was legal tender in the US for many years, and it was often carried by ships to pay locals suspicious of paper money, in this case the Seri who brought water and firewood. How could CEDAM swallow a whopper about a Spanish treasure ship carrying the greatest treasure in world history, hook, line, and sinker, with no effort at verification, even after they had been warned? No one knows.

Ten million gold coins or not, the *Thayer* is a fine dive. When over the wreck, the aids-to-navigation light on Patos bears 320°, it is 283° to a rocky outcrop forming its southwest cape, and the left tangent of the small island south of Punta Sargento bears 053°. Depth averages 45 feet and currents can be swift; during the CEDAM clown-show one diver was swept away and almost drowned, and Lloyd Rice and I were at the limits of our endurance as we arrived back at the boat with the sodden diver in tow. On exceptional days visibility can approach 60 feet, and she can be seen from the surface. And who

Cardón *poke out of a bountiful supply of fertilizer on San Pedro Mártir*

Courtesy Peabody Museum of Salem

The full-rigged ship **John Elliott Thayer**

knows, could Captain Pousland have anticipated paying more than 96 escudos to the Seri?

You might have some difficulty in developing enthusiasm for a remote, smelly, noisy chunk of guano-covered volcanic rock jutting out of a cold sea swept by heavy currents, and you would not be alone, for San Pedro Mártir is among the least-visited islands in the Cortez. Upon closer inspection, you will find it to be a beautiful and wonderful place, pulsing with life. About 1 square mile in area and 1,000 feet high, it is located 22 miles south of Turners. Since the island is surrounded by deep water and subject to heavy currents, tidal mixing causes plankton to thrive, and they support an extensive food chain. The island is home to myriad sea birds, primarily blue-footed and brown boobies, frigates, brown pelicans, cormorants, red-billed tropicbirds, and yellow-legged gulls.

Blue-footed boobies are the most numerous birds. Their comical and not-too-bright appearance and demeanor are responsible for the name, which comes from the Spanish *bobo*, meaning clown or dunce. They are, however, skilled flyers and plunge divers, and groups of blue-footed boobies sometimes make synchronized dives when they see food near the surface. Unlike most diving birds, they seize prey from below and swallow before reaching the surface. Boobies examine trolled lures intently and sometimes make the wrong decision, to the consternation of anglers. In pairing off for mating pur-

poses, boobies go through an elaborate courtship ritual. After a period of waddling, goose-stepping, and showing off its bright blue feet, a bird of either sex may "skypoint," stretching its neck, bill, and tail feathers vertically and canting its wings. Skypointing is accompanied by honks if the bird is a female, whistles if a male. Ceremonies after mating are limited to "foot-showing" when the male lands near the nesting site. Two or three eggs are laid on bare ground. Plunge diving is difficult to learn, and young birds receive food from their parents long after they have learned to fly at seven or eight months. The easiest way to tell male from female is to look at their eyes; a female's black pupil appears to be larger than a male's. Actually they are the same size, but females have a ring of black pigment around the iris.

Red-billed tropicbirds, which look like large white terns with two long sweeping tail feathers and red beaks, also breed on the island. They too are plunge divers, feeding on fish and squid. Although not gregarious, they can be seen nesting together on cliffs, their shrill cries cutting the air.

Since rainfall averages only 3 inches a year, guano collects year after year, giving the island the appearance of an iceberg. Protruding through the deep white riches is a forest of dwarf *cardón* cactus and lesser numbers of chollas, *zalates*, and a mallow having seasonal orange flowers. In fact, 24 types of higher plants have adapted to the exotic high-nitrogen, low-rainfall environment. Two species of lizard, both found nowhere else on Earth, scurry over the white surface. They are bold and even show a streak of curiosity—a number of them watched intently and moved closer to get a better view as I changed film in my camera. No land mammals have been found except introduced rats. In the 1880s more than 135 Yaqui Indians and their families lived on the island, mining guano for an American company, a remarkable, and perhaps unique, setting for a human settlement.

Due to a steep and rocky bottom, boaters may encounter some difficulty anchoring. Given suitable winds, the anchorage of choice is a small sandy area off the eastern side. The place can be noisy, for numerous sea lions inhabit small ledges and contribute their barking to the fearful din of the birds. A series of fine sea caves invites examination with an inflatable dinghy. Diving areas are limited, since depths in excess of 200 feet are encountered within a dozen yards around much of the island, although a sizable area with depths of 20 to 60 feet is located around two islets at the south end. Visibility is usually 30 to 60 feet, and the bottom is jumbled cobble, boulders, and shelf rock. Another small dive site can be found along the western shore. I have always found a full wet suit to be needed, but there are reports of warm-water Moorish idols and garden eels. Large numbers of heavy-duty gamefish will be encountered by divers.

Schools of crazed yellowtail so large that estimates were phrased in terms of acreage have been seen around the island. Bottomfishing is excellent, and commercial hand-line boats come from La Paz to work the area. Try fishing in 200–250 feet of water several hundred yards south of the island and off its northeast side. The western side drops steeply and has a series of ledges and caves loaded with grouper. Typical catches include yellowtail, bonito, cabrilla, black sea bass, white seabass, and yellowfin, and dorado "pile-ups" have been reported, but most anglers come for big grouper. Catches are seasonal, with March and April tops for white seabass, black sea bass and cabrilla, May through July for yellowtail, and August to October for grouper, dorado, and yellowfin.

People on the Stepping-Stones Trip often head for Bahía Kino to refuel and resupply or to pull their boats out, making it a one-way trip. Club Deportivo Bahía Kino operates an all-tides launch ramp, which is available to all, and has a clubhouse with a meeting hall, library, barbecue, arts-and-crafts center, and cooking and recreation facilities. The club offers group insurance for boats and vehicles, fishing licenses, boat permits, mailbox, and other services, as well as the search-and-rescue service noted earlier.

● ●

❝ *Cannibals!*

The hair on the back of their necks rose at the mention of the word, and the darkness beyond the circle of light from our campfire on Tiburón intensified, I hoped, the mood of fear. Reeve and Dick Mandich listened intently as I continued with my repertory of Seri Indian stories.

The accounts of Cabeza de Vaca in 1536, Padre Gilg in 1692, and R. W. H. Hardy in 1829 revealed that a "primitive" tribe lived on Tiburón and on a narrow strip of coast between today's Desemboque and Guaymas. By the mid-19th Century Mexican cattle ranches began to appear in their arid territory, made possible by the construction of deep wells. The Seri resented the intrusion and considered cows, horses, and burros fair game. Conflict soon broke out, and the following years were bad ones for the Seri, as constant warfare and epidemic diseases caused a drastic decline in their numbers. No one could find anything good to say about them, and stories of unrestrained violence and even cannibalism began to circulate, and in the newspapers of the day referred to them as "stinking savages," and their faces as

A proud boobie father shows off his babies

"nasty," their brains "coarse," their music and dancing "insipid, monotonous, and boringly sad." The Seri were reputed to make poison for their arrows by pressing the points into a cavity in a chunk of liver, within which a repulsive mass of centipedes, tarantulas, and rattlesnakes had been placed and encouraged to attack each other until all were dead and then allowed to putrefy. A weaver of tales named J. Bulwer Clayton published a newspaper account claiming that in 1867 he had been shipwrecked on Tiburón and every survivor had been killed and eaten but him, and that he had been spared only because he had been emaciated by scurvy. He said his captors decided that he would be more appetizing if he were healthier, and started to cure him with herbs. "Probably the only man who ever put his foot on Tiburón Island and lived to tell about it," Clayton reported that after being held for 18 months he escaped to Sonora on the back of a turtle.

Magazines and newspapers liked to publish such stories well into the 1930s. Most were either outright fabrications like Clayton's or simply rank speculation about travelers who had disappeared, but all were given a degree of credibility by a few real incidents. In 1893 2 treasure hunters disappeared, and although their bodies were never found (or perhaps because they were never found), it was reported that the Seri had mashed them to a pulp with stones and eaten them. In 1896 a newspaper reporter was stoned to death after landing on Tiburón, his companion narrowly escaping. Captain George Porter, who had participated in several of the earliest natural-history expeditions to Lower California, sailed his junk to Tiburón in the summer of 1897 to collect sea shells and curios. When he failed to return, Mexican soldiers searched the island and found a shoe, the remains of a large campfire, and the junk's stern plank. Although there were no signs of a struggle and no human bones gnawed clean, it was assumed that Porter and his crewman had been barbecued over the coals of their own boat.

Anthropologists have shown that the Seri were in fact a remarkable people. Living in a harsh and demanding environment, they were great hunters and sailors, voyaging throughout the Cortez in reed boats, and had achieved considerable artistic skill with finely woven baskets and thin, hard pottery. While there was undoubtedly violence, I knew there was never a shred of reliable evidence that anything unusual had ever ended up in Seri stew pots, but I wasn't about to ruin the spell by telling Reeve and Dick. The night

had grown even darker, and the world seemed to end outside the circle of our campfire, so I began another story.

It seems that in 1904 2 Yaqui bandits had been causing trouble in Sonora, but pursuing soldiers finally caused them to flee to Tiburón. Governor Izabal sent a message to the Seris, "Bring in the Yaquis with their hands tied to a pole and you will receive a reward." However, the Seri did not speak Spanish and the messenger was forced to communicate in sign language. The Seris got the idea, or most of it anyway. In due time, a group of Seri women, led by a woman named Manuela, appeared to collect their reward, carrying a pole to which eight Yaqui hands were tied, still dripping blood while dangling below two protective straw hats. The incident was duly reported in National Geographic and the Guaymas newspapers.

I was silently congratulating myself for reducing my audience to a quivering, jelly-like state of fear when we heard the faint whisper of an outboard motor. Our eyes strained to adjust to the darkness and we could finally make out the slim shape of a panga. It stopped just off our camp and for no apparent reason the two men in the boat sat watching us for perhaps an hour, not moving a muscle. Reeve, Dick, and I sat equally motionless, hoping that the men were not Seris planning their menu, and even I became apprehensive. Finally, the motor started and they slowly disappeared. The mood didn't seem ripe for more cannibal stories, so we inflated our air mattresses and settled down for the night. No one said a thing, but each knew the others were lying awake, listening for the sound of knives being sharpened and the clank of pots. We had just dozed off when there was a pistol shot and a scream, and someone raced across the campsite. Leaping out of our sleeping bags, Dick and I prepared to defend ourselves from attack, stark naked and shivering in the cold. Reeve was screaming for help, but as I gathered my wits I realized they weren't screams—he was laughing, howls of laughter, at Dick and me! A resinous knot in the fire had exploded, waking Reeve, who saw a coyote stealing food from our packs, so he had yelled and thrown a stick.

After the uproar died down we knew there was to be no sleep that night, so we stoked up the fire and I started another story. It seems that a party of four American gold prospectors led by Tom Grindell disappeared in Seri country in 1905, so his brother went to find out what happened, and... **99**

● ●

Appendix A

Map Key, Distances, Measurements, Peso/Dollar Calculator

Town/City Map Key

Auto/truck parts	AP	Hotel/motel	HT	Photography	PT
Bakery	BK	Ice	IC	Post office	PO
Bank/ATM	BA	Immigration	IM	Rest rooms (public)	RR
Beer	BE	Laundry	LA	Restaurant/café	RE
Bus depot/stop	BD	Liquor	LI	RV park/campsite	RV
Butcher shop	BU	LPG	LP	Souvenirs/gifts	SO
Car rental	CR	Mechanic	MC	Sporting goods	SG
Customs	CU	Money exchange	MY	Telephone	TP
Dentist	DE	Motorcycle shop	MS	Tire sales/repair	TS
Doctor	DO	Optical	OP	*Tortilla* factory	TF
Ferry/ferry office	FE	Outboard parts/repairs	OB	Travel agency	TA
Fruit/vegetables	FR	*Pangas*, cruisers, guides	PA	Veterinarian	VE
Groceries	GR	PEMEX	PE	Water (potable)	WA
Hardware	HA	*Pesca* (fishing license) office	PS	Welding	WE
Hospital/clinic	HO	Pharmacy	PH		

Mileage Between Points—Transpeninsular Highway

	Tijuana	Ensenada	San Vicente	San Quintín	El Rosario	Cataviña	Parador Punta Prieta	Guerrero Negro	Vizcaíno	San Ignacio	Santa Rosalía	Mulegé	Loreto	Ciudad Constitución	La Paz	San José del Cabo	Cabo San Lucas
Tijuana																	
Ensenada	69																
San Vicente	125	56															
San Quintín	186	117	61														
El Rosario	226	157	101	40													
Cataviña	299	230	174	113	73												
Parador Punta Prieta	365	296	240	179	139	66											
Guerrero Negro	447	378	322	261	221	148	82										
Vizcaíno	492	423	367	306	266	193	127	45									
San Ignacio	536	467	411	350	310	237	171	89	44								
Santa Rosalía	581	512	456	395	355	282	216	134	89	45							
Mulegé	619	550	494	433	393	320	254	172	127	83	38						
Loreto	703	634	578	517	477	404	338	256	211	167	122	84					
Ciudad Constitución	792	723	667	606	566	493	427	345	300	256	211	173	89				
La Paz	923	854	798	737	697	624	558	476	431	387	342	304	220	131			
San José del Cabo	1037	968	912	851	811	738	672	590	545	501	456	418	334	245	114		
Cabo San Lucas	1057	988	932	871	831	758	692	610	565	521	476	438	354	265	134	20	

Measurements

1 pound	= 0.454 kilogram		1 inch	= 2.54 centimeters
1 kilogram	= 2.2046 pounds		1 centimeter	= 0.393 inch
1 gallon	= 3.784 liters		1 kilometer	= 3,280.8 feet
1 liter	= 0.264 gallon		1 kilometer	= 0.621 statute mile
1 liter	= 1.057 quarts		1 kilometer	= 0.53 nautical mile
1 quart	= 0.946 liter		1 statute mile	= 1.61 kilometers
1 meter	= 39.37 inches		1 nautical mile	= 6,076.1 feet
1 meter	= 3.281 feet		1 nautical mile	= 1.15 statute miles
1 foot	= 0.305 meter		1 nautical mile	= 1.85 kilometers

Peso/Dollar Calculator

The following diagram can be used to convert pesos to dollars at any normal exchange rate. Simply place a straight line (the edge of a piece of paper will do fine) between the number of pesos and the current exchange rate, expressed in pesos/dollar, and read the dollars scale. An example is shown on the diagram: 40 pesos at an exchange rate of 10.0 pesos/dollar equals $4.00. If the peso amount is between 100 and 1,000, simply divide the number of pesos by 10, enter the diagram, determine the dollar amount, and multiply that by 10. In the example below, 400 pesos at 10.0 pesos/dollar equals $40. If the amount of the transaction is between 1,000 and 10,000 pesos, divide and multiply by 100: 4,000 pesos at 10.0 equals $400.

Converting dollars to pesos is equally simple: Place a straight line between the number of dollars and the current exchange rate and read the peso scale. Using the example below, $4.00 at an exchange rate of 10.0 pesos/dollar equals 40 pesos. If the dollar amount is greater than 10, use the divide-and-multiply-by-10 or 100 rule described above: $40 at 10.0 pesos/dollar equals 400 pesos, $400 at 10.0 pesos/dollar equals 4,000 pesos.

In a similar manner, the diagram can be used to calculate exchange rates. If an item you wish to purchase is marked 40 pesos, and the shopkeeper asks for $4.00, you will know he is using a rate of 10.0 pesos/dollar.

DOLLARS   PESOS   EXCHANGE RATE

PESOS ÷ EXCHANGE RATE = DOLLARS
40 PESOS @ 10/1 = $4.00

Appendix B

Directory

Businesses and organizations often change phone numbers, e-mail addresses, and/or Internet Service Providers, or move to new locations. If those you seek seem "lost", the most efficient way to relocate them is by use of the Yellow Pages or one of the search engines on the Internet.

If you are in the US and need a number in Baja, you won't have the Yellow Pages directories for Baja available, but there is a simple solution—access them on the Internet at:

www.seccionamarilla.com.mx

This site is available (partially) in English and you can search by business name, by town, by category, etc. If you need to search by category, say for outboard engine dealers, you will need to know the Spanish word for outboard or engine, or at least the first few letters. This should be available in any Spanish/English dictionary, but if not, there are ways to get around the problem. For instance, search on the brand name, say Evinrude, since the name will be the same in English and Spanish. If you are in Baja, you can access the site at any of the Internet cafés or computer service offices.

If you don't have access to the Internet, call your telephone information operator, or contact the Secretary of Tourism of the state involved. Telephone numbers in Baja California can also be obtained from US phones by dialing 00-0. The international operator of your long distance carrier will route your inquiry to a bilingual information operator. Be warned: there is an almost astronomical fee for this service. If you are not using Netscape or Internet Explorer, be sure to add http:// at the beginning, and the slash at the end of the Internet addresses shown below.

Activity Center
Playa Médano
Apdo. Postal 444
Cabo San Lucas, BCS, México
011-52-114-33093 phone
011-52-114-30928 fax

Aereo Calafia
Blvd. Marina
Plaza las Glorias, Local 4-A
Cabo San Lucas, BCS, México
011-52-114-34302 phone
011-52-113-34255 fax
aerocalafia@cabonet.net.mx
www.aerocalafia.com

AeroCalifornia
1960 East Grand Ave.
El Segundo, CA 90245
310-322-2644 phone
800-237-6225
011-52-114-30827 Cabo San Lucas

Aero Cedros

Soc. Coop. de Produccíon Pesquera
Av. Ryerson 117
Ensenada, BC, México
011-52-61-782084 and 61-783808
cedmex@compunet.com.mx

El Ciprés Airport
Ensenada, BC, México
011-52-61-766076

Aerolitoral
800-237-6639
www.aerolitoral.com (provides e-mail link)

Aeromedical Group, Inc.
21893 Skywest Dr.
Hayward, CA 94541
510-293-5950 phone
510-293-5972 fax
800-854-2569 from the US
95-800-01-00986 from México

AeroMexico
800-237-6639
www.wotw.com/aeromexico

Airstream, Inc.
419 West Pike St.
Jackson Center, OH 45334-0825
513-596-6111 phone
513-569-6092 fax

Alaska Airlines
800-426-0333
011-52-114-21016 Los Cabos
www.alaskaair.com

AllCoast Sportfishing Magazine
www.sport-fish-info.com

Almar Dive Shop
Av. Macheros 149
Ensenada, BC, México
011-52-61-783013 phone

American Airlines
800-433-7300
webmaster@americanair.com
www.americanair.com

American Cetacean Society
Box 1391
San Pedro, CA 90731-0943
310-548-6279 phone
310-548-6950 fax
www.redshift.com/~estarr/acs/baja.htm

American Continental Travel
4492 Camino de la Plaza, Suite 1120
San Ysidro, CA 92173
888-712-2294 phone and fax
amcontinental@compunet.com.mx

America West Airlines
800-363-2597
www.americawest.com

Amigos del Mar
Apdo. Postal 43
Cabo San Lucas, BCS, México
011-52-114-30505 phone
011-52-114-30887 fax
310-454-1686 fax
800-344-3349
www.amigosdelmar.com

Aqua Adventures
4901 Morena Blvd., Suite 1102
San Diego, CA 92117
619-272-0800 phone

800-269-7792
www.webvmall.com/aqua.htm

Aqua Sports de Loreto
Apdo. Postal 194
Loreto, BCS, México
011-52-113-30700 phone
011-52-113-30377 fax
aquasports@hotmail.com
www.loreto.com

Aquamarina RV Park
Calle Nayarit 10
Apdo. Postal 133
La Paz, BCS, México
011-52-112-23761 phone
011-52-112-56228 fax
marisla@balandra.uabcs.mx
www.pe.net/~marisla

Arcos, Hotel los
Av. Obregón 498
Apdo. Postal 112
La Paz, BCS, México
011-52-112-22744 phone
011-52-112-54313 fax
800-347-2252
arcoslap@balandra.uabcs.mx

Arco Trailer Park, El
Apdo. Postal 114
Cabo San Lucas, BCS, México
011-52-114-31686 phone
011-52-114-33998 fax

Arturo's Sports Fishing Fleet
Paseo Hidalgo s/n
Apdo. Postal 5
Loreto, BCS, Mexico
011-52-113-50766 phone
011-52-113-50022 fax

Backroads
801 Cedar St.
Berkeley, CA 94710-1800
510-527-1555 phone
510-527-1444 fax
800-462-2848
goactive@backroads.com
www.backroads.com

Bahía de los Angeles
(Town satellite phone service)
011-52-665-0-3206 and 3207 phone

Bahía los Frailes, Hotel
Apdo. Postal 230
San José del Cabo, BCS, México
011-52-114-10122 phone
800-934-0295
losfrailes@bajalife.com
www.losfrailes.com

Baja Adventures
Apdo. Postal 50
Buena Vista, BCS, México
011-52-114-10271 phone and fax
800-533-8452 reservations from US and
Canada
mrbill@windriders.com
www.windriders.com/baja

Baja Anglers
Box 6065
Marble Canyon, AZ 86036
888-894-3474 phone
info@baja-anglers.com
www.baja-anglers.com
    or
Marina 8-6, Darsena
Cabo San Lucas, BCS, México
011-52-114-34995 phone

Baja California Tours, Inc.
7734 Herschel Ave., Suite O
La Jolla, CA 92037
619-454-7166 phone phone
619-454-2703 fax
bajatour@aol.com

Baja Discovery
Box 152527
San Diego, CA 92195
619-262-0700 phone
800-829-2252

Baja Dive Expeditions
Plaza las Glorias, Local 1-4
Cabo San Lucas, BCS, México
011-52-114-33830 phone
011-52-114-87579 cell phone
bajadive@cabonet.net.mx
www.caboland.com/bajadive/index.html

Baja Expeditions
2625 Garnet Avenue
San Diego, CA 92109
619-581-3311 phone
619-581-6542 fax
800-843-6967
travel@bajaex.com
www.bajaex.com

Baja Life
Box 4917
Laguna Beach, CA 92652
714-376-2252 phone
714-376-7575 fax
www.bajalife.com

Baja Naval, S.A. de C.V.
Av. de la Marina 10
Apdo. Postal 1408
Ensenada, BC, México
011-52-61-740020 phone
011-52-61-740028 fax

    or
2630 E. Beyer Blvd., Suite 1037
San Ysidro, CA 92143-9011
mexico-travel.com/estados/e02/191hb1.htm

Baja Net
Madero 430 Centro
La Paz, BCS, México
011-52-112-59380 phone
webmaster@baja.net.mx
www.baja.net.mx

Baja Outdoor Activities
354 Madero, Centro
Apdo. Postal 792
La Paz, BCS, México
011-52-112-55636 phone
011-52-112-53625 fax
boa@kayactivities.com
www.kayactivities.com

Baja Outpost
Apdo. Postal 52
Blvd. López Mateos s/n
Loreto, BCS, México
011-52-113-51134 fax and phone
888-649-5951
bajaoutpost@bajaoutpost.com
www.bajaoutpost.com

Baja Seasons
1177 Broadway, Suite 2
Chula Vista, CA 91911
619-422-2777 phone
800-754-4190

Baja Spearfishing Adventures
Apdo. Postal 333
San Quintín, BC, México
011-52-616-52535 fax
011-52-617-13087 cell phone

Beach Club El Tecolote
Dominguez y 5 de Mayo
La Paz, BCS, México
011-52-112-28885 phone
011-52-112-54971 fax
011-52-112-64454 cell phone

Bicycling West, Inc.
Box 15128
San Diego, CA 92175-5128
619-583-3001 phone
www.adventuresports.com/asap/bike/rosarito/
    ensenada.htm

Bodegas de Santo Tomás
Av. Miramar 666
Ensenada, BC, México
011-52-61-782509 phone

Brisa del Mar Trailer Park
Apdo. Postal 45

San José del Cabo, BCS, México
011-52-114-22828 phone and fax

Buenavista Beach Resort, Hotel
KM 105, Carretera al Sur
Buena Vista, BCS, México
011-52-114-10033 phone
or
Apdo. Postal 574
La Paz, BCS, México
or
100 West 35th St., Suite U
National City, CA 91950
800-752-3555
hotelbvbr@aol.com
www.hotelbuenavista.com

Bufadora Dive, La
Dale Erwin
Apdo. Postal 102
Maneadero, BC, México
011-52-615-42092 phone
www.labufadora.com

Cabo Acuadeportes, S.A. de C.V.
Apdo. Postal 136
Cabo San Lucas, BCS, México
011-52-114-30117 phone and fax
011-52-114-86404 cell phone
cabo@sierra-computers.com
xenon.sierra-computers.com/~cabo

Cabo Cielo RV Park
KM 3.8, Carretera Transpeninsular
Apdo. Postal 109
Cabo San Lucas, BCS, México
011-52-114-30721 phone
011-52-114-32527 fax

Cabo Pulmo
(Town radiotelephone service)
011-52-114-10001 phone

Cabo Pulmo Beach Resort
Box 3344
Hailey, ID 83333
888-997-8566 US phone
208-788-8823 fax and international calls

Cabo Pulmo Divers
011-52-114-71804 phone

Cabo San Lucas, Hotel
Box 48088
Los Angeles, CA 90048
213-655-2323 phone
213-655-3243 fax
800-733-2226
www.hotelcabo.com

Café Internet de Ensenada, S.A. de C.V.
Av. Juárez 1449 10 y 11
Centro Commercial EME

Ensenada, BC, México
011-52-61-761331 phone
011-52-71-762923 fax
riva@compunet.com.mx
www.compuclub.com.mx

California Baja Rent-A-Car
9245 Jamacha Blvd.
Spring Valley, CA 91977
619-470-7368 phone
619-479-2004 fax
888-470-7368 phone
info@cabaja.com
www.cabaja.com

Campistre la Pila Trailer Park
Apdo. Postal 261
Ciudad Constitución, BCS, México
011-52-113-20562 phone

Campo Playa RV Park
Apdo. Postal 789
Ensenada, BC, México
011-52-61-762918 phone
011-52-61-783767 fax

Canadian Consulate
German Gedovius 10411-101
Condominio del Parque
Tijuana, BC, México
011-52-66-840461 phone
011-52-66-880301 fax
rencinas@bbs.cincos.net

Canadian Department of Foreign Affairs and International Trade
125 Sussex Dr.
Ottawa, Ontario
Canada K1A 0G2
613-944-4000 phone
800-267-8376 (in Canada)
www.dfait-maeci.gc.ca/english/menu.htm

Cardónal Resort, El
El Cardónal, BCS, México
011-52-114-10040 phone and fax

Cardón Trailer Park, El
Apdo. Postal 104
La Paz, BCS, México
011-52-112-40078 phone

Casa Blanca RV Park
KM 4 1/2, Carretera Transpeninsular
Apdo. Postal 681
La Paz, BCS, México
011-52-112-25109 phone

Casa Diaz
Bahía de los Angeles
Apdo. Postal 579
Ensenada, BC, México

Casitas, Hotel las
Fco. Madero 50
Apdo. Postal 3
Mulegé, BCS, México
011-52-115-30019 phone
011-52-115-30340 fax

Castro's Fishing Place
Apdo. Postal 974
Ensenada, BC, México
011-52-61-762897 phone

Cavas Valmar
Ambar 810 esq. Riveroll
Apdo. Postal 392
Ensenada, BC, México
011-52-61-786405 phone
011-52-61-786405 fax

Centro de Buceo Carey
Marquez de León y Topete 2415-A Loc. 17
Col. El Manglito
La Paz, BCS, México
011-52-112-32333 phone and fax

Charters Mar de Cortez S.A. de C.V.
Av. Mar Caribe 325
San Felipe, BC, México
011-52-657-71278 phone
011-52-657-71779 fax
or
355 W. 2nd. St., Suite 310
Calexico, CA 92231

Chevrolet dealers south of the border cities

Motores de Ensenada
Blvd. Cárdenas y Caracoles
Ensenada, BC, México
011-52-61-760208 phone
011-52-61-770580 fax

Proveedora Agricola Automotriz California
Ciudad Constitución, BCS, México
011-52-113-22180 phone
011-52-113-20343 fax

Proveedora Agricola Automotriz California
Bravo 1220
Apdo. Postal 242
La Paz, BCS, México
011-52-112-22313 phone

Proveedora Agricola Automotriz California
Lázaro Cárdenas, Camino al Médano
Cabo San Lucas, BCS, México
011-52-114-32087 phone
011-52-114-32088 fax

Ciencias Technicas Computacionales, S.C.
Plaza Dorada's, Local 11-12
Blvd. Mauricio Castro
Col. 5 de Febrero
San José del Cabo, BCS, México
011-52-114-22520 phone

Club Cabo Motel and Campground Resort
Apdo. Postal 463
Cabo San Lucas, BCS, México
011-52-114-33348 phone
www.mexonline.com/clubcabo.htm

Club Hotel Cantamar
Apdo. Postal 782
La Paz, BCS, México
011-52-112-21826 phone
011-52-112-28644 fax
bajadiving@lapaz.cromwell.com.mx
www.clubcantamar.com

Club de Pesca Trailer Park
Apdo. Postal 90
San Felipe, BC, México
011-52-657-71180 phone
011-52-657-71888 fax

Club Deportivo Bahía Kino
Apdo. Postal 84-83340
Bahía Kino, Sonora, México
011-52-624-20321 phone and fax

Concha Beach Resort, La
KM 5, Carretera a Pichilingue
Apdo Postal 607
La Paz, BCS, México
011-52-112-16544 phone
011-52-112-16218 fax
or
619-260-0991 phone
619-294 7366 fax
800-999-2252
laconcha@juno.com
www.laconcha.com

Continental Airlines
800-523-3273
www.flycontinental.com

Coral & Marina, Hotel
KM 103, Carretera Ensenada y Tijuana
Numero 3421, Zona Playitas
Ensenada, BC, México
011-52-61-750000 phone
800-826-9020
or
2385 Shelter Island Dr., Suite 202
San Diego, CA 92106
619-523-0064 phone
619-523-0069 fax
800-946-2746

mcuriel@sprynet.com
www.surfernet.com/coral

Cortez Club
KM 5, Carretera a Pichilingue
La Paz, BCS, México
011-52-112-16120 phone
011-52-112-16123 fax
thecortezclub@lapaz.cromwell.com.mx
www.cortezclub.com

Cortez Explorers
Moctezuma 75A
Mulegé, BCS, México
011-52-115-30500
www.bajaquest.com

Correcaminos Trailer Park
La Rivera, BCS, México

Cortez, Motel el
Box 1227
Calexico, CA 92232-1227
011-52-657-71056 phone

Cortez Yacht Charters
7824 Longdale Dr.
Lemon Grove, CA 91945
619-469-4255 phone
619-461-9393 fax
www.sport-fish-info.com/cortez2.html

Costa Azul Surf Shop
KM 29, Carretera Transpeninsular
San José del Cabo, BCS, México
90-114-70071 cell phone
costazul@1cabonet.com.mx
www.1cabonet.com.mx

Costa del Sol Motel
KM 66, Carretera Parador-Bahía
Bahía de los Angeles, BC, México
011-52-515-1-4195 phone
or
9602 Adoree St.
Downey, CA 90242
562-803-8873

Critical Air Medicine
4141 Kearny Villa Road
San Diego, CA 92123
619-571-0482 phone
619-571-0835 fax
800-247-8326
criticalair@msn.com

Cruise America
11 West Hampton Avenue
Mesa, AZ 85210
602-464-7300 phone
602-464-7302 fax
800-327-7799
travel@cruiseamerica.com
www.cruiseamerica.com

Cruising Charts
Box 976
Patagonia, AZ 85624
520-394-2393 phone

Dagget's Campground
% J. L. Ortega
Apdo. Postal 83
Guerrero Negro, BCS, México
011-52-665-03206 phone

Dawson's Book Shop
535 North Larchmont Blvd.
Los Angeles, CA 90004
213-469-2186 phone
213-469-9553 fax
dawsonbk@ix.netcom.com

Deportes Blazer
Paseo Hildalgo 23
Loreto, BCS, México
011-52-113-50911 phone

DHL Worldwide Express
www.dhl.com/dhl/index.html
Offices in Baja California:

DHL International de México
Av. Abasolo Edificio 78
Locales 4 y 5 Esq. Nayarit
Col. Pueblo Nuevo
La Paz, BCS, México
011-52-112-56150 phone

DHL International de México
Calz. Cuauhtemoc (Antes Aviación)
Numero 10 Casi Esquina con Justo
Sierra Col. Cuauhtemoc Norte
Mexicali, BC, México
011-52-65-681760 phone

DHL International de México
Paseo Delos Heroes 9105
Esq. Francisco Javier Mina
Zona del Río
Tijuana, BC, México
011-52-66-842993 phone

Discover Baja Travel Club
3089 Clairemont Dr.
San Diego, CA 92117
619-275-4225 phone
619-275-1836 fax
800-727-2252
discovbaja@aol.com
www.discoverbaja.com

Dodge/Chrysler dealers south of the border cities

Autoproductos de Tijuana
Av. Reforma y San Marcos
Ensenada, BC, México
011-52-61-770204 phone
011-52-61-765063 fax

Nueva Automotriz del Toro
Isabel la Católica 1315
La Paz, BCS, México
011-52-112-22557 phone
011-52-112-21534 fax

Domecq Winery
KM 73, Carretera Tecate y El Sauzal
Apdo. Postal 987
Tijuana, BC, México
011-52-66-232408 phone
011-52-66-232414 fax

Dorado Ranch, El
101 Inverness Dr. East, Suite 130
Box 3088
Englewood, CO 80155-9861
303-790-1749 phone
303-705-1958 fax
800-404-2599
011-52-657-71278 phone
patbutler@eldoradoranch.com
eldoradoranch.com

Enchanted Island Excursions
Apdo. Postal 50
San Felipe, BC, México
011-52-657-71431 phone and fax
somers@canela.sanfelipe.com.mx
or
Box 952
Calexico, CA 92232-0952

Estero Beach Hotel
Apdo. Postal 86
Ensenada, BC, México
011-52-61-766225 phone
011-52-61-766925 fax
or
482 W. San Ysidro Blvd., Suite 186
San Ysidro, CA 92173

Faro Beach Motel & RV Park, El
Apdo. Postal 1008
Ensenada, BC, México
011-52-61-774630 phone
011-52-61-774620 fax

Faro Beach Trailer Park, El
Apdo. Postal 107
San Felipe, BC, México

Faro Viejo Trailer Park, El
Mijares e/ Matamoros y Abasolo
Apdo. Postal 64
Cabo San Lucas, BCS, México
011-52-114-34211 phone

Fiesta Inn
Blvd. Malecón s/n
San José del Cabo, BCS, México
011-52-114-20701 phone
011-52-114-20480 fax
800-343-7822
www.fiestamexico.com

Fiesta Sportfishing & Diving Co.
Box 1555
Gilbert, AZ 85299
602-814-0414 phone
602-813-0011 fax
800-839-2021
bajafish@earthlink.net
worldwidefishing.com/b166.htm

Finisterra, Hotel
Apdo. Postal 1
Cabo San Lucas, BCS, México
011-52-114-33333 phone
011-52-114-30590 fax
800-347-2252

Fisherman's Fleet
Av. Alvaro Obregon 670 y Allende
La Paz, BCS, México
011-52-112-21313 phone
011-52-112-57334 fax
david@lapaz.cromwell.com.mx

Fisherman's Landing
2838 Garrison St.
San Diego, CA 92106
619-221-8500 phone
619-222-0799 fax
619-224-1421 hot line
www.fishermanslanding.com

Fishing International, Inc.
1825 Fourth Street
Santa Rosa, CA 95404
Box 2132
Santa Rosa, CA 95405
707-542-4242 phone
707-526-3474 fax
800-950-4242 reservations
fishint@wco.com
fishinginternational.com

Ford dealers south of the border cities

Automotriz de Ensenada
Av. Reforma y San Marcos
Ensenada, BC, México
011-52-61-763668 phone
011-52-61-760844 fax

Automotriz Baja California
Carretera Transpeninsular al Norte 3565
La Paz, BCS, México
011-52-112-28870 phone
011-52-112-28877 fax

Frances, Hotel
Col. Mesa Francia
Santa Rosalía, BCS, México
011-52-115-22052 phone

Gaviota's Sportfishing Fleet
Blvd. Lázaro Cárdenas e/ Morelos y Vicario
Cabo San Lucas, BCS, México
011-52-114-30430 phone
011-52-114-30497 fax
www.sport-fish-info.com/gaviota.html

Good Sam Club
Box 6888
Englewood, CO 80155-6888
303-792-7306 fax
800-234-3450
www.goodsamclub.com

Gordo's Sport Fishing
Apdo. Postal 35
Ensenada, BC, México
011-52-61-783515 phone
011-52-61-740481 fax

Green Tortoise Adventure Travel
494 Broadway
San Francisco, CA 94133
415-956-7500 phone
800-867-8647
info@green tortoise.com
www.greentortoise.com

H & M Landing
2803 Emerson St.
San Diego, CA 92106
619-222-1144 phone
619-222-0784 fax
619-224-2800 hot line
hmmail@hmlanding.com
www.hmlanding.com

Hacienda Beach Resort, Hotel
Playa el Médano
Cabo San Lucas, BCS, México
011-52-114-30122 phone
011-52-114-30666 fax
800-733-2226
hacienda@1cabonet.com.mx
www.haciendacabo.com

Hacienda Santa Veronica
Blvd. Agua Caliente 4558, Piso 1, Desp. 106B
Tijuana, BC, México
011-52-66-817428 phone
011-52-66-817429 fax
or
2272 Iris Avenue
San Diego, CA 92154
619-423-3830

Horizon Charters
4178 Lochlomond St.
San Diego, CA 92111
619-277-7823 phone
619-560-6811 fax
divesd@aol.com
www.earthwindow.com/horizon

Hyperbaric Technology, Inc.
200 W. Arbor Dr.
San Diego, CA 92103
619-543-5222 (24 hours) phone

Instant Mexico Auto Insurance Services
223 Via de San Ysidro
San Ysidro, CA 92143
619-428-4714 phone
619-690-6533 fax
800-345-47012

Instituto Nacional Indigenista
Ruta de Correos 124
Apdo. Postal 154
Bahía de Kino, Sonora, México
011-52-624-20105 phone

Instituto Sud Californiano de Cultura
La Paz office
Av. 16 de Septiembre 1520
La Paz, BCS, México
011-52-112-27389 phone and fax

San Ignacio office
San Ignacio, BCS, México
011-52-115-40222 phone and fax

Jack Velez Fleet
Apdo. Postal 402
La Paz, BCS, México
011-52-112-22744, ext. 608
011-52-112-15577 home
011-52-112-55313 fax

J & R Baja Divers
Plaza Bonita Mall #48
Cabo San Lucas, BCS, México
011-52-114-31545 phone
011-52-114-85063 cell phone
j&rbajadivers@cabotel.com.mx
www.cabotel.com.mx/j&rbajadivers/home.htm

Jolla Beach Camp (Punta Banda), La
Apdo. Postal 102
Punta Banda, BC, México
011-52-61-542004 phone

Jolla RV Park (San Felipe), La
Box 978
El Centro, CA 92243
011-52-65-77122 phone

Juanita's Fleet
Plaza Karina Local 1, Blvd. Marina
Apdo. Postal 29
Cabo San Lucas, BCS, México
011-52-114-30522 phone and fax
800-421-8925

Juanito's Garden RV Park
Apdo. Postal 50
Los Barriles, BCS, México
011-52-114-10024 phone and fax

Killer Hook Surf Shop
Calle Hidalgo s/n, e/ Zaragoza y Doblado
Apdo. Postal 346
San José del Cabo, BCS, México
011-52-114-22430 phone and fax

Kuyima Servicios Ecoturisticos S.A de C.V.
Apdo. Postal 53
San Ignacio, BCS, México
011-52-115-40070 phone and fax

La Paz Diving Service See **Aquamarina RV Park**

La Paz RV Park
Brecha California 120
Apdo. Postal 482
La Paz, BCS, México
011-52-112-28787 phone
011-52-112-29938 fax

Land's End Divers
Plaza las Glorias, Local A-5
Cabo San Lucas, BCS, México
011-52-114-32200 phone and fax
011-52-114-75981 cell phone
800-675-3483
bajatec1@cabonet.net.mx
www.mexonline.com/landsend.htm

Las Parras Tours
Fco. 1 Madero s/n
Loreto, BCS, México
011-52-113-51010 phone
011-52-113-50900 fax

Lee Palm Sportfishers
2801 Emerson St.
San Diego, CA 92106
619-224-3857 phone
619-224-2201 fax

Loco Lobo Surf and Tackle
011-52-62-542144 phone

Loreto Shores Villas & RV Park
Apdo. Postal 219
Loreto, BCS, México
619-223-8562
011-52-113-50629 phone
011-52-113-50711 fax

Los Dorados Fleet
Hotel Plaza las Glorias, Local 31630
Cabo San Lucas, BCS, México
011-52-114-31630 phone and fax
619-427-1214 phone
800-272-6263

Manfred's Trailer Park
KM 213, Transpeninsular
Apdo. Postal 120
Ciudad Constitución, BCS, México
011-52-113-21103 phone and fax

Manzanos, Rancho los
Box 3055
National City, CA 91951-3055
619-417-1133 cell phone
011-52-61-701527 phone

Map Centre, Inc.
2611 University Avenue
San Diego, CA 92104-2894
619-291-3830 phone
619-291-3840 fax
gayla@mapcentre.com

Map World
123-D N. El Camino Real
Encinitas, CA 92024
760-942-9642 phone
760-942-3229 fax
800-246-6277
maps@mapworld.com
www.mapworld.com/maps

Marco's RV Park
Av. Golfo de California 788
San Felipe, BC, México
011-52-655-72579 phone

Mar de Cortez, Hotel
Cárdenas y Guerrero
Cabo San Lucas, BCS, México
011-52-114-30032 phone
011-52-114-30232 fax
    or
17561 Vierra Canyon Road, Suite 99
Salinas, CA 93907
408-663-5803 phone
408-663-1904 fax
800-347-8821

Mar del Sol RV Park
San Felipe, BC, México
011-52-657-71280 phone
800-336-5454

Marina Cabo San Lucas
Lote A-18 De la Dársena de C.S.L.
Apdo. Postal 371
Cabo San Lucas, BCS, México
011-52-114-31251 phone
011-52-114-31253 fax

Marina de La Paz, S.A. de C.V.
Topete 3040 y Legaspi
Apdo. Postal 290
La Paz, BCS, México
011-52-112-52112 phone
011-52-112-55900 fax

Marina Palmira, S.A. de C.V.
KM 2.5, Carretera a Pichilingue
Apdo. Postal 34
La Paz, BCS, México
011-52-112-16338 phone
011-52-112-16142 fax
marinapalmira@baja.net.mx
www.trybaja.com/marinabroch.html

Marina Pichilingue *See* **Club Hotel Cantamar**

Marisla II See **Aquamarina RV Park**

Martín Verdugo's Motel and Trailer Park
Apdo. Postal 17
Los Barriles, BCS, México
011-52-114-10054 phone and fax
martinv@lapaz.cromwell.com.mx

Meliá San Lucas, Hotel
Playa el Médano s/n
Cabo San Lucas, BCS, México
011-52-114-34444 phone
011-52-114-30420 fax
800-336-3542
www.solmelia.es

Mesón de Don Pepe RV Park
Apdo. Postal 7
Colonia Vicente Guerrero, BC, México
011-52-616-62216 phone
011-52-616-62268 fax

Mexicana Airlines
011-52-114-20943 Los Cabos phone
800-531-7921
www.mexicana.com

Mexican Consulate General
1549 India St.
San Diego, CA 92101
619-231-8414 phone
619-231-4802 fax

Mexican Consulates and Consular Agencies in other cities

Albuquerque, NM	505-247-2139
Atlanta, GA	404-266-1913
Austin, TX	512-478-9031
Boston, MA	617-426-4942
Brownsville, TX	512-542-2051
Calexico, CA	619-357-3863
Chicago, IL	312-855-1380
Corpus Christi, TX	512-882-3375
Dallas, TX	214-630-7431
Del Rio, TX	512-775-9451
Denver, CO	303-331-1110
Detroit, MI	313-567-7709
Eagle Pass, TX	512-773-9255
El Paso, TX	915-533-3644
Fresno, CA	209-233-3065
Houston, TX	713-524-2300
Laredo, TX	210-723-6369
Los Angeles, CA	213-351-6800
McAllen, TX	210-686-0243
Miami, FL	305-716-4977
Midland, TX	915-687-2334
New Orleans, LA	505-522-3596
New York, NY	212-689-0456
Nogales, AZ	520-287-2521
Oxnard, CA	805-483-4684
Philadelphia, PA	215-625-4897
Phoenix, AZ	602-242-7398
Sacramento, CA	916-363-3885
Saint Louis, MO	314-436-3233
Salt Lake City, UT	801-521-8502
San Antonio, TX	210-227-9145
San Bernardino, CA	909-889-9836
San Diego, CA	619-231-8414
San Francisco, CA	415-392-5554
San Jose, CA	408-294-3415
Santa Ana, CA	714-835-3069
Seattle, WA	206-448-6819
Tucson, AZ	602-882-5595
Washington, DC	202-736-1000

Mexican Ferry System

Guaymas Office
011-52-622-23390 phone
011-52-622-23393 fax

La Paz Office
Guillermo Prieto and 5 de Mayo
011-52-112-53833 phone
011-52-112-54666 fax

La Paz, Pichilingue Terminal
011-52-112-54440 phone
011-52-112-26588 fax

Mazatlán Office
011-52-698-17020, ext. 21 phone
011-52-698-17023 fax

Santa Rosalía Office
011-52-115-20013 phone
011-52-115-20014 fax

Topolobampo Office
011-52-686-20141 phone
011-52-686-20035 fax

Mexican Government Tourism Offices

70 East Lake St., Suite 1413
Chicago, IL 60601
312-606-9015 phone
312-606-9012 fax

2707 North Loop W, Suite 450
Houston, TX 77008

713-880-1833 phone
713-880-5153 fax

1801 Century Park E, Suite 1080
Los Angeles, CA 90067
310-203-8191 phone
310-203-8316 fax

405 Park Avenue, Suite 1401
New York, NY 10022
212-755-7261 phone
212-753-2874 fax

1911 Pennsylvania Avenue NW
Washington, DC 20006
202-728-1750 phone
202-728-1758 fax

One Place Ville Marie, Suite 1526
Montreal, Quebec
Canada H3B 2B5
514-871-1052 phone
514-871-3825 fax

2 Bloor St. West, Suite 1801
Toronto, Ontario
Canada M4W 3E2
416-925-0704 phone
416-925-6061 fax

1610-999 West Hastings St.
Vancouver, BC
Canada V6C 2W2
604-669-2845 phone
604-669-3498 fax

Mexico Ministry of the Environment, Natural Resources, and Fisheries
2550 Fifth Avenue, Suite 101
San Diego, CA 92103-6622
619-233-6956 phone
619-233-0344 fax

Minerva's Baja Tackle
Apdo. Postal 156
Cabo San Lucas, BCS, México
011-52-114-31282 phone
011-52-114-30440 fax

Misiónes, Hotel el
Av. Misíon de Loreto 148
San Felipe, BC, México
011-52-657-71280 phone
011-52-657-71283 fax
800-336-5454

Monte RV Rentals & Sales, El
12818 Firestone Blvd.
Santa Fe Springs, CA 90670
562 404-9300 phone
562 909-8008 fax
800 367-3687
reservations@elmonte.com (within the US)
international@elmonte.com (outside the US)
emrvtour@elmonte.com (for guided Baja RV tours)
www.elmonte.com

Moorings, The
19345 US Highway 19 North, Forth Floor
Clearwater, FL 33376
800-535-7289
813-535-1446 outside US and Canada
yachts@moorings.com
www.moorings.com

Moro RV Park, El
Rosendo Robles 8
Loreto, BCS, México
011-52-113-50542 phone
011-52-113-50788 fax

Mulegé Kayaks/Baja Tropicales
Apdo. Postal 60
Mulegé, BCS, México
011-52-115-30409 phone
011-52-115-30190 fax

Nájar, Dr. Alfonso
Venustiano Carranza 11, e/Abasolo y
Ocampo
Cabo San Lucas, BCS, México
011-52-114-31218 phone
011-52-114-75919 cell phone
011-52-114-35050, ext. 1501 pager

NAPA Auto Parts
Ave. Blancarte y Calle 9 1026
Ensenada, BC, México
011-52-61-782420 phone

National Outdoor Leadership School
288 Main St.
Lander, WY 82520
307-332-6973 phone
307-332-1220 fax
admissions@nols.edu
www.nols.edu

Natural Habitat
2945 Center Green Court, Suite H
Boulder, CO 80301
303-449-3462 phone
303-449-3712 fax
800-233-2433

Neptune Divers
Plaza las Glorias, Local A-14
Cabo San Lucas, BCS, México
011-52-114-31110 phone and fax

Net Cyberservices, The
Av. Mar de Cortez s/n
Plaza Canela, Local 1
San Felipe, BC, México
011-52-657-71600 phone and fax
info@canela.sanfelipe.com.mx
www.sanfelipe.com.mx

NetZone
Edificio Posada Local 5
Blvd. Lázaro Cárdenas s/n

Cabo San Lucas, BCS, México
011-52-114-35390 phone
011-52-114-33944 fax
netzone1@cabonet.net.mx
www.mexonline.com/netzone.htm

Nissan dealers south of the border cities

Comercio Automotríz
KM 111, Carretera Transpeninsular
Ensenada, BCS, México
011-52-61-766118 phone

Grupo VAPSA Autocompactos
5 de Febrero 1050
La Paz, BCS, México
011-52-112-22277 phone
011-52-112-54100 fax

Vehiculos Automotríz
Blvd. San José 2000
San José del Cabo, BCS, México
011-52-114-21666 phone
011-52-114-21667 fax

Northwest Airlines
800-225-2525
www.nwa.com

Oasis Beach Resort and Convention Center (north of Ensenada)
KM 25, Carretera Tijuana y Ensenada 14010
Rosarito, BC, México
011-52-66-313250 phone
011-52-66-313252 fax
    or
Box 158
Imperial Beach, CA 91933
888-709-9985
www.oasisbaja.com

Oasis los Aripez Trailer Park
KM 15, Transpeninsular Norte
La Paz, BCS, México
011-52-112-46090

Oceanic Society Expeditions
Fort Mason Center, Building E
San Francisco, CA 94123
415-441-1106 phone
415-474-3395 fax
800-326-7491
www.oceanic-society.org

Old Mill Motel
619-271-1304
800-479-7962 phone

Orchard Vacation Village
Apdo. Postal 24
Mulegé, BCS, México
011-52-115-30300 phone
mulegecyn@aol.com

Outland Adventures
Box 16343
Seattle, WA 98116
206-932-7012 phone and fax

Pacific Coast Adventures
Plaza las Glorias, Local H-6
Cabo San Lucas, BCS, México
011-52-114-31070 phone
011-52-114-31560 fax
pcatemo@cabonet.net.mx
www.pacificcoastadv.com

Pacific Sea Fari Tours
2803 Emerson St.
San Diego, CA 92106
619-226-8224 phone
619-222-0784 fax
divesd@aol.com
www.spectrav.com/—10309.html

Palmas de Cortez, Hotel
Box 9016
Calabasas, CA 91372
818-222-7144 phone
818-591-1077 fax
800-368-4334
011-52-114-10050
bajafishing@pacificnet.net

Palmilla, Hotel
San José del Cabo, BCS, México
011-52-114-45000 phone
011-52-114-45100 fax
    or
4343 Von Karman Avenue
Newport Beach, CA 92660-2083
714-833-3030 phone
714-851-2498 fax
800-637-2226
sebriggs@ix.netcom.com
www.palmillaresort.com

Pepe's Dive Center
Cabo Pulmo
Apdo. Postal 532
Cabo San Lucas, BCS, México
011-52-114-10001 phone and fax
011-52-114-82711 cell phone
310-379-0846 fax
800-246-6226
pepe@crossadventure.com
www.crossadventure.com/pepe

Pisces Fleet Sportfishing
Blvd. Marina y Madero, Local 2
Apdo. Postal 137
Cabo San Lucas, BCS, México
011-52-114-31288 fishing hot line
011-52-114-30588 fax
pisces@1cabonet.com.mx
www.mexonline.com/pfleet1.htm

Pisces Tidal Sports
Club Cascadas de Baja
Apdo. Postal 508
Cabo San Lucas, BCS, México
011-52-114-87530 phone
011-52-114-86519 fax

Playa Bonita RV Park (San Felipe)
475 E. Badillo St.
Covina, CA 91723
818-967-8977 phone and fax

Playa de Laura RV Park
Av. Mar de Cortez
San Felipe, BC, México
011-52-657-71128 phone

Playa del Sol, Hotel
Box 9016
Calabasas, CA 91372
818-591-9463 phone
800-368-4334
011-52-114-10050
www.captnmikes.com/cmplaya.html

Point Loma Sportfishing
1403 Scott St.
San Diego, CA 92106
619-223-1627 phone
619-223-1591 fax
619-223-0451 hot line
info@PointLomaSportfishing.com
www.pointlomasportfishing.com

Point South RV Tours, Inc.
11313 Edmonson Avenue
Moreno Valley, CA 92555
909-247-1222 phone
909-924-3838 fax
800-421-1394

Posada Concepción
Apdo. Postal 14
Mulegé, BCS, México
011-52-61-783329 phone
mexico-travel.com/states/s03/76eu6.htm

Posada Don Diego
Apdo. Postal 126
Colonia Vicente Guerrero, BC, México
011-52-616-62181 phone

Posada Real Best Western, Hotel
Malecón s/n, Zona Hotelera
Apdo. Postal 51
San José del Cabo, BCS, México
011-52-114-20155 phone
011-52-114-20460 fax
800-528-1234

Presidente Intercontinental Hotel
Blvd. Mijares s/n
Apdo. Postal 2
San José del Cabo, BCS, México

011-52-114-20211 phone
011-52-114-2-0232 fax
800-447-6147
loscabos@interconti.com
www.interconti.com/pages/l/losprea.html

Punta Chivato, Hotel
Apdo. Postal 18
Mulegé, BCS, México
011-52-115-30188 phone
011-52-115-20395 fax

Punta Colorada, Hotel
Box 9016
Calabasas, CA 91372
818-591-9463 phone
818-591-1077 fax
800-368-4334

Rafael's Sport Fishing Fleet
Apdo. Postal 5
Cabo San Lucas, BCS, México
011-52-114-30018 phone and fax
91-114-75324 cell phone

Rancho Buena Vista
Box 1408
Santa Maria, CA 93456
805-928-1719 phone
805-925-2990 fax
800-258-8200
011-52-114-10177 phone
011-52-114-10055 fax

Rancho Leonero
Apdo. Postal 7
Los Barriles, BCS, México
011-52-114-10216
        or
Box 698
Placentia, CA 92871
714-524-5502 phone
714-524-1856 fax
800-334-2252
www.rancheroleonero.com
rancholeonero@worldnet.att.net

Rancho Ojai RV Park
Box 280
Tecate, CA 91980
011-52-66-544772 phone
011-52-66-544772 fax
ibanez@telnor.net

Rancho Playa Monalisa
Apdo. Postal 607
Ensenada, BC, México
011-52-61-775100 phone
011-52-61-774920 fax

Rancho San José
3415 McLaughlin Avenue 109
Los Angeles, CA 90066
310-390-7449 phone

        or
Apdo. Postal 1326
Ensenada, BC, México

Rancho Verde
Box 1050
Eureka, MT 59917
406-889-3030 phone
406-889-3033 fax
888-516-9462
011-52-112-57570 fax
www.mexonline.com/verde.htm

Recreation Industries Co.
9011 SE Jannsen Road
Box 1840
Clackamas, OR 97015-9629
503-655-9443 phone
503-655-9469 fax
800-937-3433

Rescue One *See* **Club Deportivo Bahía Kino**

Riviera, Hotel
Av. Mar Baltico s/n
San Felipe, BC, México
011-52-657-71185 phone

Rob's Baja Tours
Box 4003
Balboa, CA 92661
714-673-2670 phone and fax

Ruben's Trailer Park
Golfo de California 703
San Felipe, BC, México
011-52-657-72021 phone

Safety Seal Tire Repair Products
800-888-9021

San Felipe Marina Resort and RV Park
San Felipe, BC, México
011-52-657-75069 phone
011-52-657-75066 fax
619-558-0295
800-291-5397

San Francisquito Resort
667 Twining Avenue
San Diego, CA 92154
619-690-1000 phone

San Lucas Trailer Park
Apdo. Postal 50
Santa Rosalía, BCS, México

San Miguel Surf Shop
López Mateos 335 at Plaza Hussong 2
Ensenada, BC, México
011-52-61-782475 phone
011-52-61-770695 fax

or
Box 432947
San Ysidro, CA 92173

San Perdito RV Park
Apdo. Postal 15
Todos Santos, BCS, México
011-52-112-24520 phone
011-52-112-34643 fax

Santa Rosalía Marina
Angel Jesus Rodríguez G., Dock Master
Santa Rosalía, BCS, México
011-52-115-20011 phone and fax

Señor Diver
Apdo. Postal 37
San José del Cabo, BCS, México
011-52-114-22285 phone and fax

Scuba Baja Joe
Av. Alvaro Obregón 460
Apdo. Postal 361
Admon. Correos 1
La Paz, BCS, México
011-52-112-24006 phone
011-52-112-24000 fax
011-52-112-62274 cell phone

Scu-Baja Diving Center
Bravo e/ Mutualismo s/n
Col. Centro
La Paz, BCS, México
011-52-112-32381 phone
011-52-112-27423 fax
    or
Sun and Adventure
900 Wilshire Blvd., Suite 522
Los Angeles, CA 90017
213-891-9202 phone
213-624-0545 fax
888-868-3483
sal@sunadv.com
www.sunadv.com/diving.html

Sea Trek Ocean Kayaking Center
Box 561
Woodacre, CA 94973
415-488-1000 phone
415-488-1707 fax
paddle@seatrekkayak.com
www.seatrekkayak.com

Serenidad, Hotel
Apdo. Postal 9
Mulegé, BCS, México
011-52-115-30530 phone

Sergio's Sport Fishing Center
2630 E. Beyer, Suite 676
San Ysidro, CA 92143
011-52-61-782185 phone

Shop, The
Gral. Martinez s/n
Mulegé, BCS, México
Mailing address: Same
011-52-115-30059 phone and fax

Soc. Coop. de Produccíon Pesquera *See*
Aero Cedros

Solmar, Hotel
Av. Solmar 1
Apdo. Postal 8
Cabo San Lucas, BCS, México
011-52-114-33535 phone
011-52-114-30410 fax
800-344-3349
caboresort@aol.com
www.solmar.com

Solmar Fleet *See* **Hotel Solmar**

Solmar V See **Amigos del Mar for information and reservations**

Southwest Sea Kayaks
2590 Ingraham St.
San Diego, CA 92109
619-222-3616 phone
619-222-3671 fax
kayaked@aol.com
www.swkayak.com

**Souto Performance and Auto and
Truck Repair**
Av. Espinoza 541, Zona Centro
Ensenada, BC, México
011-52-61-770807 phone

Special Expeditions, Inc.
720 Fifth Avenue
New York, NY 10019
212-765-7740 phone
212-265-3770 fax
800-762-0003

Spirit of Adventure Charters
1646 Willow St.
San Diego, CA 92106
619-226-1729 phone and fax

**State Secretary of Tourism of Baja
California [Norte]**

Ensenada Office
Edificio Centro de Gobierno
Blvd. Lázaro Cárdenas 1477
Ensenada, BC, México
011-52-61-723022 phone
011-52-61-723081 fax

Mexicali Office
Plaza Baja California, Local 4
Calzada Independencia y Calle Calafia
Mexicali, BC, México
011-52-65-554950 phone and fax

Rosarito Office
Blvd. Benito Juárez, Centro Comercial
Villa Floresta 2000, Local 8
Rosarito, BC, México
011-52-661-20200 phone and fax

San Felipe Office
Av. Mar de Cortez y Calle Manzanillo 300
San Felipe, BC, México
011-52-657-71155 phone and fax

San Quintín Office
KM 178.3, Carretera Transpeninsular
San Quintín, BC, México
011-52-616-62498 phone

Tecate Office
Callejon Libertad 1305
Tecate, BC, México
011-52-665-41095 phone and fax

Tijuana Office
Blvd. Diaz y Av. el Americas
Edificio Plaza Patria, 3er. Piso, Zona "K"
Tijuana, BC, México
011-52-66-812074 phone
011-52-66-819579 fax
ralvarez@icanet.com.mx
    or
Box 2448
Chula Vista, CA 91912

**State Secretary of Tourism of Baja
California Sur**
KM 5 1/2, Carretera Transpeninsular
(FIDEPAZ)
Apdo. Postal 419
La Paz, BCS, México
011-52-112-40100 phone
011-52-112-40722 fax
turismo@lapaz.cromwell.com.mx

Surf Check
714-840-3800 fax
714-840-4943 phone
800-445-1099
cyberkahuna@surfcheck.com
www.surfcheck.com

Surfline
800-940-7873 information
900-976-7873 toll hotline

Tiburon's Pangas Sportfishing
011-52-616-52768 phone and fax
011-52-617-14730 cell phone
619-479-3476 phone

Tijuana Tourism and Convention Bureau
Box 434523
7860 Mission Center Court 202
San Diego CA 92143-4523
619-298-4105 phone
619-294-7366 fax
800-522-1516 CA, AZ, NV
800-225 2786 US & Canada
011-52-66-840537 phone
011-52-66-847782 fax
impamexicoinfo@worldnet.att.net
www.tijuana-net.com/cotuco.htm

Tío Sports
Playa Médano
Apdo. Postal 37
Cabo San Lucas, BCS, México
011-52-114-32986 phone
011-52-114-31521 fax
or
98 18th Street
Hermosa Beach, CA 90254
310-379-5126 phone
310-379-0896 fax
800-246-6226
tiosport@cabonet.net.mx
www.tiosports.com/menu.html

Tony Reyes Fishing Tours
133 S. Yorba St.
Orange, CA 92869
714-538-8010 phone
714-538-1368 fax

Tracks to Adventure
2811 Jackson, Suite K
El Paso, TX 79930
915-565-9627 phone
800-351-6053

TRIPUI Resort RV Park
Apdo. Postal 100
Loreto, BCS, México
011-52-113-30818 phone
011-52-113-30828 fax

Tropicana Inn
Blvd. Mijares 30
San José del Cabo, BCS, México
011-52-114-21580 phone
011-52-114-21590 fax

Underwater Diversions de Cabo
Plaza las Glorias Local F5
Marina Blvd. s/n
Cabo San Lucas, BCS, México
011-52-114-34004 phone and fax
or
Box 545
San Juan Capistrano, CA 92078
714-728-1026 phone
714-728-1046 fax
800-342-3143
divecabo@sure.net
www.divecabo.com

Unidad de Tratamiento Hiperbarico Fanavi
Ejido C. Esteban Cantú
KM 10, Carretera La Bufadora
Punta Banda, BC, México
011-52- 615-42050 phone of urchin processing plant
011-52-61-716281-17 doctor's cell phone

United States Coast Guard Command Center
Coast Guard Island
Alameda, CA 94501-5100
510-437-3700 phone

United States Consular Agency
Blvd. Marina y Calle de Cerro
Cabo San Lucas, BCS, México
011-52-114-33566 phone and fax

United States Consulate General
Av. Tapachula 96
Col. Hipódromo
Tijuana, BC, México
011-52-66-817400 phone
011-52-66-818016 fax
or
Box 439039
San Ysidro, CA 92143
619-585-2350 24 hour answering service

United States Customs Service
Box 7407
Washington, DC 20044
202-566-8195 phone
www.customs.ustreas.gov

United States Fish and Wildlife Service
Department of Interior
Washington, DC 20240
202-208-5634 phone
www.fws.gov

United States State Department
Citizen's Emergency Center
202-647-5225 phone

University of Arizona
Printing & Publishing Support Services
Box 210058
Tucson AZ 85721-0058
520-621-2571 phone
520-621-6478 fax
lewalskr@u.arizona.edu

Ursula's Sport Fishing Charters
Hidalgo y Blvd. Marina
Cabo San Lucas, BCS, México
011-52-114-31264 phone and fax

Vagabundos del Mar Boat and Travel Club
190 Main St.
Rio Vista, CA 94571
707-374-5511 phone
707-374-6843 fax

800-474-2252
vags@compuserve.com
ourworld.compuserve.com/homepages/vags

Vagabundos del Mar Trailer Park
Apdo. Postal 197
Cabo San Lucas, BCS, México
011-52-114-30290 phone
011-52-114-30511 fax

Vela Windsurf Resorts
16 E. Third Avenue 6
San Mateo, CA 94401
415-373-1106 phone
415-373-1111 fax
800-223-5443
info@velawindsurf.com
www.velawindsurf.com

Ventana Windsurf
Topete 2730-A El Manglito
La Paz BCS, México
011-52-112-53829 fax
800-782-6037
ventanaws@hotmail.com
www.ventana-windsurf.com

Venture Quest Kayaking
125-A Beach St.
Santa Cruz, CA 95060
408-427-2267 phone
venture@cruzio.com
members.cruzio.com/~venture

Victor's Sportfishing
Hotel Posada Real Best Western
Zona Hotelera, Malecón s/n
San José del Cabo, BCS, México
011-52-114-21092 phone
011-52-114-21093 fax
800-528-1234
victors@1cabonet.com.mx
www.worldwidefishing.com/b116.htm

Victor's el Cortez RV Park
San Felipe, BC, México
011-52-657-7-1056 phone
or
Box 1227
Calexico, CA 92232

Villa Marina, Hotel
Av. Lopéz Mateos y Blancarte 1024
Ensenada, BC, México
011-52-61-783351 phone
011-52-61-783321 fax

Villa María Isabel RV & Trailer Park
KM 134, Carretera Transpeninsular
Apdo. Postal 5
Mulegé, BCS, México
011-52-115-30246 phone and fax
www.mexico-travel.com/states/s03/76eu7.htm

Villarino Camp
Apdo. Postal 1
Punta Banda, BC, México
011-52-61-542044 phone

Villas de Loreto RV Park
Antonio Mijares y Playa
Colonia Zaragoza
Apdo. Postal 132
Loreto, BCS, México
011-52-113-50586 phone and fax

Villa Vitta Hotel Resort
509 Ross Dr.
Escondido, CA 92027
011-52-665-03208
760-741-9583

Vista Sea Sports
Apdo. Postal 42
Buena Vista, BCS, México
011-52-114-10031 phone and fax
800-368-4334

Volkswagen dealers south of the border cities

Concesionario Volkswagen
Av. Jesus Clark y Miguel Aléman
Col. Moderna
Ensenada, BC, México
011-52-61-744676 phone
011-52-61-744625 fax

Automotriz Transmar de Cortés
KM 4, Carretera al Norte
La Paz, BCS, México
011-52-112-22054 phone
011-52-112-50939 fax

Automotriz Transmar de Cortés
KM 36, Carretera Transpeninsular
Santa Rosa, BCS, México
011-52-114-20854 phone
011-52-114-20880 fax

Wahoo RV Center, S.A. de C.V.
Col. Chula Vista
San José del Cabo, BCS, México
011-52-114-23792 phone and fax
www.mexonline.com/wahoo.htm

Wilderness: Alaska/Mexico
1231 Sundance Loop
Fairbanks, AK 99709
907-479-8203 phone
wildakmx@polarnet.com
www2.polarnet.com/~wildakmx

Appendix C
A Baja Fishing Calendar

	Jan.	Feb.	Mar.	Apr.	May	June	July	Aug.	Sept.	Oct.	Nov.	Dec.
Ensenada, Isla de Todos Santos												
albacore						▓	▓	▓	▓	▓		
barracuda				▓	▓	▓	▓	▓	▓	▓	▓	
bass, kelp				▓	▓	▓	▓	▓	▓	▓	▓	
bonito					▓	▓	▓	▓	▓	▓	▓	
cod, rock	▓	▓	▓									▓
croaker					▓	▓	▓	▓	▓	▓	▓	
perch, barred	▓	▓										▓
yellowtail					▓	▓	▓	▓	▓	▓		
Bahía San Quintín, Isla San Martín, Sacramento Reef												
albacore						▓	▓	▓	▓	▓		
barracuda				▓	▓	▓	▓	▓	▓	▓	▓	
bass, calico	▓	▓	▓	▓	▓	▓	▓	▓	▓	▓	▓	▓
bass, kelp				▓	▓	▓	▓	▓	▓	▓	▓	
bonito						▓	▓	▓	▓	▓	▓	
cod, rock	▓	▓						▓	▓	▓	▓	▓
croaker					▓	▓	▓	▓	▓	▓	▓	
dorado							▓	▓	▓	▓		
halibut			▓	▓	▓	▓	▓		▓	▓	▓	
perch, barred	▓	▓	▓	▓	▓	▓	▓	▓	▓	▓	▓	▓
tuna, yellowfin				▓	▓	▓	▓	▓	▓	▓	▓	
yellowtail				▓	▓	▓	▓	▓	▓	▓	▓	
Bahía Tortugas												
albacore					▓	▓	▓	▓	▓	▓	▓	
bass, giant sea					▓	▓	▓	▓	▓	▓	▓	▓
cabrilla												
corvina	▓									▓	▓	▓
croaker			▓	▓	▓	▓	▓	▓	▓	▓	▓	▓
dorado						▓	▓	▓	▓	▓		
halibut			▓	▓	▓	▓	▓		▓	▓	▓	
tuna, yellowfin						▓	▓	▓	▓	▓	▓	
yellowtail			▓	▓	▓	▓	▓	▓	▓	▓	▓	
Bahía Magdalena												
bass, giant sea					▓	▓	▓	▓	▓	▓		
cabrilla												
corvina	▓	▓	▓							▓	▓	▓
dorado						▓	▓	▓	▓	▓	▓	
halibut			▓	▓	▓	▓	▓	▓	▓	▓	▓	▓
sailfish						▓	▓	▓	▓	▓		
snapper				▓	▓	▓	▓	▓	▓	▓		
tuna, yellowfin						▓	▓	▓	▓	▓	▓	▓

	Jan.	Feb.	Mar.	Apr.	May	June	July	Aug.	Sept.	Oct.	Nov.	Dec.
Bahía Magdalena (continued)												
wahoo						X	X	X	X	X	X	X
yellowtail			X	X	X	X	X	X	X	X	X	X
San José del Cabo, Cabo San Lucas												
cabrilla					X	X	X	X	X	X		
dorado	X	X	X	X	X	X	X	X	X	X	X	
marlin, blue							X	X	X	X	X	X
marlin, striped	X	X	X	X	X	X	X	X	X	X	X	X
roosterfish	X	X	X	X		X	X	X	X	X	X	
sailfish	X	X	X	X	X	X	X	X	X	X	X	
sierra	X	X	X								X	X
snapper						X	X	X	X	X		
swordfish					X	X	X	X	X	X	X	X
tuna, yellowfin					X	X	X	X	X	X	X	
wahoo												
yellowtail	X	X	X	X	X							
Puertecitos, Bahía Gonzaga												
cabrilla					X	X	X	X	X	X		
corvina			X	X	X	X	X	X	X			
croaker	X	X	X	X	X	X	X	X	X	X	X	X
seabass, white			X	X								
sierra					X	X	X	X				
Bahía de los Angeles												
bass, giant sea			X	X	X	X						
cabrilla				X		X	X	X	X	X	X	
corvina			X	X	X	X	X	X	X	X	X	X
dorado						X	X	X				
grouper				X	X	X	X	X	X	X		
seabass, white				X	X	X						
sierra					X	X	X	X	X			
yellowtail					X	X	X	X	X			
Mulegé												
cabrilla			X	X	X	X	X	X	X	X	X	
corvina					X	X	X	X	X	X		
dorado						X	X	X	X	X		
grouper				X	X	X	X	X	X	X		
marlin, striped						X	X	X	X			
sailfish					X	X	X	X				
sierra	X	X	X	X	X							X
tuna, yellowfin							X	X	X			
yellowtail	X										X	X

	Jan.	Feb.	Mar.	Apr.	May	June	July	Aug.	Sept.	Oct.	Nov.	Dec.
Loreto												
bonito	■	■	■	■						■	■	■
cabrilla			■	■	■	■	■	■	■	■	■	
corvina				■	■	■	■	■	■	■		
dorado				■	■	■	■	■	■	■	■	
grouper				■	■	■	■	■	■	■	■	
marlin, striped					■	■	■	■	■			
roosterfish					■	■	■	■	■			
sailfish					■	■	■	■	■			
sierra	■	■	■	■						■	■	■
snapper				■	■	■	■	■	■	■		
tuna, yellowfin					■	■	■	■	■	■		
yellowtail	■	■	■	■						■	■	■
La Paz, Isla Espíritu Santo												
cabrilla				■	■	■	■	■	■	■	■	
crevalle, jack							■	■	■	■	■	
dorado					■	■	■	■	■	■	■	
grouper				■	■	■	■	■	■	■	■	
marlin, black							■	■	■	■	■	
marlin, striped					■	■	■		■	■		
roosterfish					■	■	■	■	■	■		
sailfish					■	■	■	■	■	■		
sierra	■	■	■	■			■		■	■	■	■
snapper					■	■	■	■	■	■		
tuna, yellowfin						■	■	■	■	■	■	
wahoo						■	■	■	■	■	■	
yellowtail	■	■	■	■						■	■	■
East Cape, Punta Arena de la Ventana, Isla Cerralvo												
amberjack					■	■	■	■	■	■		
cabrilla				■	■	■	■	■	■	■	■	
crevalle, jack				■	■	■	■	■	■	■		
dorado					■	■	■	■	■	■	■	
grouper					■	■	■	■	■	■	■	
marlin, black					■	■	■	■	■	■	■	
marlin, blue					■	■	■	■	■	■	■	
marlin, striped					■	■	■	■	■	■	■	
roosterfish					■	■	■	■	■	■	■	
sailfish					■	■	■	■	■	■	■	
snapper				■	■	■	■	■	■	■	■	
tuna, yellowfin				■	■	■	■	■	■	■		
wahoo					■	■	■	■	■	■	■	■
yellowtail	■	■	■	■								

Appendix D

A Baja Bookshelf

So you have made your first trip to Baja and were fascinated and want to read more? If so, the first book to consider is Walt and his son Michael's highly praised book on RV travel and natural history, available from your bookseller or directly from Wilderness Press:

Peterson, Walt, and Michael Peterson, *Exploring Baja by RV*. Berkeley: Wilderness Press. 1997.

If you like to dive or snorkel, don't miss Walt's new book, to be published in 1998:

Peterson, Walt, *Diving and Snorkeling Guide to Baja*. Lonely Planet. 1998.

The following books cover a diversity of interests and are highly recommended:

Baegert, Johann Jakob, *Observations in Lower California*. Translated by M. M. Brandenberg and Carl L. Bauman. Berkeley: University of California Press. 1979.

Behrens, David W., *Pacific Coast Nudibranchs—A Guide to the Opisthobranchs, Alaska to Baja California*. Monterey (CA): Sea Challengers. 1991.

Browne, John Ross, *Explorations in Lower California*. Studio City (CA): Vaquero Books. 1966.

Brusca, Richard C., *Common Intertidal Invertebrates of the Gulf of California*. Tucson (AZ): University of Arizona Press. 1980.

Cannon, Ray, *The Sea of Cortez*. Menlo Park (CA): Lane Books. 1967.

Crosby, Harry, *The King's Highway*. Salt Lake City: Copley Books. 1974.

——, *Last of the Californios*. Salt Lake City: Copley Books. 1981.

——, *Antigua California*. Albuquerque: University of New Mexico Press. 1994.

——, *The Cave Paintings of Baja California*. Salt Lake City: Copley Books. 1997.

Gordon, David, and Alan Baldridge, *Gray Whales*. Monterey (CA): Monterey Bay Aquarium. 1991.

Gotshall, Daniel W., *Marine Animals of Baja California*. Los Osos (CA): Sea Challengers. 1987.

——, *Guide to Marine Invertebrates—Alaska to Baja California*. Monterey (CA): Sea Challengers. 1994.

Henderson, David A., *Men and Whales at Scammon's Lagoon*. Los Angeles: Dawson's Book Shop. 1972.

Huycke, Harold D., *To Santa Rosalía: Further and Back*. Newport News (VA): Mariners Museum. 1970.

Mackintosh, Graham, *Into A Desert Place*. New York: W. W. Norton Co. 1995.

Minch, John, and Thomas Leslie, *The Baja Highway*. San Juan Capistrano (CA): John Minch and Associates, Inc. 1991.

North, Arthur W., *Camp and Camino in Lower California*. Glorieta (NM): Rio Grande Press. 1977.

Roberts, Norman C., *Baja California Field Plant Guide*. La Jolla (CA): Natural History Publishing Co. 1989.

Romano-Lax, Andromeda, *Sea Kayaking in Baja*. Berkeley: Wilderness Press. 1993.

Steinbeck, John, and Edward R. Ricketts, *The Log from the Sea of Cortez*. New York: Viking Penguin. 1995.

Thomson, Donald A., Lloyd T. Findley, and Alex N. Kerstitch, *Reef Fishes of the Sea of Cortez*. New York: John Wiley & Sons. 1979.

Wiggins, Ira L., *Flora of Baja California*. Stanford (CA): Stanford University Press. 1980.

Wilbur, Sanford R., *Birds of Baja California*. Berkeley: University of California Press. 1987.

Zwinger, Ann, *A Desert Country Near the Sea*. New York: Harper & Row Publishers. 1983.

In addition, Dawson's Book Shop offers books on such disparate Baja subjects as history, ethnology, linguistics, Indian art, whales, pirates, the Gold Rush, railroads, and cattle drives and brands, and publishes a number of books under their own imprimatur. They will send a book list upon request. There is also a fine magazine, *Baja Life*. Filled with articles on such subjects as golf, whales, Bahía Magdalena, the desert's seasonal show of colorful plant blooms, volleyball, a whale shark encounter, La Paz, and Misión San Javier, and complemented by excellent color photographs. It also contains departments on yachting, retirement and living in Baja, ecological matters, fishing, and other subjects.

Index

abalone 8, 31, 75, 106, 109, 124, 152, 155
Abreojos, Punta 8, 18, 21, 47, 51, 71, 73, 89, 163, 165, 166
Activity Center 238
Aduana See Mexican Customs Service
Aero Cedros 83, 103, 104, 152, 273
Aerolineas California 152, 163
Aeromedical Group 89
agaves 6, 13, 65, 66, 74, 90, 128, 129, 142, 153, 263
Agencia Arjona 79, 104, 216
Agua Blanca 126, 128
Agua Verde, Bahía 18, 29, 55, 78, 192, 196, 203, 204, 218
Aguja, Cerro la 227, 244
airlines, airports 48, 51, 52, 72, 74, 79, 81, 83, 95, 103, 104, 152, 157, 162, 163, 164, 171, 174, 190, 192, 201, 215, 235, 238, 267
Airstream 62
Alacrán, Ensenada el 142
Alcatraz, Isla (Sonora) 44
Alcatraz, Isla *See* Granito, Isla el
Alejandro's *See* San Andrés, Punta
Alemán 156
Alfonsina's 268, 270
Almar Dive Shop 103
Almejas, Bahía las 19, 71, 207
Alta California (US state) 7, 264
American 1, 7, 13, 14, 15, 77, 78, 83, 84, 85, 86, 87, 88, 95, 103, 134, 139, 177, 178, 181, 207, 215, 218, 221, 235, 237, 238, 243, 244, 245, 253, 260, 264, 267, 270, 279, 281, 282
American Cetacean Society 14
American Continental Travel 77
Amigos del Mar 14, 22, 241
Amolares, Cañon 189
Amolares, Punta 189
Amortajada, Bahía 188, 195, 198
amphibians 7, 13, 116, 126, 134, 135, 136, 142, 145, 154, 167, 195, 220, 225, 255, 276
Amphispiza bilineata cana 276
anchorages 6, 98, 103, 106, 107, 109, 112, 113, 123, 124, 126, 127, 132, 134, 141, 142, 143, 145, 146, 147, 148, 149, 152, 155, 156, 162, 164, 165, 166, 171, 178, 179, 181, 183, 184, 185, 186, 192, 194, 195, 196, 197, 202–03, 208, 212, 218, 219, 220, 224, 228, 231, 237, 266, 268, 269, 270, 273, 276, 277, 279, 281
Angeles, Bahía de los 6, 8, 15, 18, 29, 38, 39, 48, 51, 55, 56, 57, 58, 60, 62, 68, 71, 76, 77, 78, 82, 87,

137, 138–142, 146, 147, 162, 266, 270, 273, 277
Ánimas Norte, Isla las 273, 276
Ánimas Sur, Isla las 13, 15, 18, 22, 39, 194, 218, 276
Ánimas, Bahía las 55, 142, 147, 188
Ánimas, Boca las 207
Ánimas, Punta las 142
antelopes 7, 163
Aqua Adventures 14, 58, 74, 106, 108, 142, 156, 196
Aqua Sports de Loreto 201
Aquamarina RV Park 216, 218
Árbolitos, Caleta 105
Arena de la Ventana, Punta 28, 71, 222, 224, 227
Arena Sur, Punta 71, 227, 228, 230
Arena, Punta 139, 141, 145, 197
Argentina 11
Arizona 79, 177, 212, 264
Armenta, Punta 188
Arrecife de la Foca 224
Arroyo Mulegé 180
arroyos *See* canyons
Arturo's Sport Fishing Fleet 192
Ast Ah Keem, Punta 277
Asunción 18, 19, 38, 51, 64, 68, 82, 89, 163, 164, 165
Asunción, Bahía 164
Asunción, Isla 165
ATVs (all-terrain vehicles) 104, 105, 139, 211, 216, 218, 237, 238, 253, 263, 264
Australia 59, 163
automatic teller machines (ATM) 81, 121, 157, 216, 247
autos/pickups 21, 24, 39, 41, 47, 59, 60, 63, 64, 65, 66, 68, 70, 75, 80, 83, 84, 85, 86, 99, 105, 109, 112, 114, 116, 117, 120, 123, 126, 133, 134, 135, 138, 139, 148, 155, 161, 163, 165, 166, 170, 174, 179, 181, 185, 188, 203, 214, 228, 229, 230, 232, 244, 245, 249, 252, 253, 255, 262
  dealers 86, 103, 104, 206, 215, 216, 235, 237, 243
  parts 65, 85–86, 98, 104, 105, 112, 113, 120, 121, 125, 139, 157, 163, 164, 165, 166, 178, 180, 206, 213, 215, 216, 222, 228, 235, 243, 248, 255, 258, 259, 260, 261
Azufrado, Pico 227
Azufre, Punta 123, 125

backpacking 46, 48, 52–55, 58, 75, 114, 116, 133, 225–27, 232, 244, 249–52

Backroads 52, 58
Baegert, Johann Jakob 76, 114, 206
Baja 1000 52, 100
Baja Adventures 52, 72, 229
Baja Anglers 241
Baja California Tours, Inc. 14, 50, 62, 98, 104, 114, 264
Baja Celular 82, 83, 87, 98, 103, 104, 206, 207, 216, 228, 235, 237, 243, 247
Baja Discovery 14, 58, 62, 142, 167
Baja Dive Expeditions 238
Baja Expeditions 14, 18, 22, 57, 196, 211, 218
Baja Malibu Sur RV Park 112
Baja Naval, S.A. de C.V. 41, 103
Baja Net 216
Baja Norte 32, 38, 62, 74, 76, 80, 83, 87, 105, 132, 134, 157
Baja Outdoor Activities 14, 52, 58, 72, 196, 216
Baja Outpost 192
Baja Seasons 99
Baja Shuttle 71
Baja Spearfishing Adventures 22, 123
Baja Sur 7, 22, 38, 48, 80, 83, 87, 157
Baja, Punta 57, 73, 123, 126, 128, 192
Bajo el Pulmo 230
Balandra 71
Balandra, Ensenada 219
Ballena, Isla 220
Ballenas, Bahía 164
Ballenas, Canal de 141, 143, 270
Banda, Cabo 108
Banda, Pico 53, 107
Banda, Punta 15, 19, 20, 22, 53, 58, 74, 103, 105, 107, 108, 109
banks 34, 81, 103, 104, 105, 120, 121, 157, 163, 178, 190, 206, 216, 245, 247, 256
Barranco, Boca el 243
bats 77, 113, 146, 184, 245
batteries 21, 61, 64, 86, 93, 210, 237
Beach Club El Tecolote 219
beachcombing 113, 145, 155, 158, 163, 212, 231
beaches 9, 15, 18, 19, 20, 24, 28, 29, 32, 33, 39, 46, 51, 52, 53, 55, 59, 60, 66, 67, 68, 71, 73, 74, 75, 90, 91, 92, 93, 98, 99, 104, 105, 106, 108, 109, 112, 113, 120, 121, 122, 125, 126, 128, 134, 139, 141, 142–43, 144, 145, 146, 147, 148, 149, 152, 153, 155, 156, 158, 159, 161, 162, 163, 164, 165, 166, 174,

178, 179, 180, 183, 184, 185, 186, 188, 189, 190, 192, 194, 195, 196, 197, 198, 201, 202, 203, 207, 208, 209, 210, 211, 212, 213, 214, 215, 218, 219, 220, 222, 224, 228, 229, 230, 231, 235, 237, 240, 242, 243, 244, 245, 263, 264, 266, 267, 268, 269, 270, 273, 276, 277, 278
Belcher, Punta 207, 212
Bell Dome 53, 249, 252
Bentonita, Punta 213
Bering Sea 10, 11
bicycling 46, 47, 48–52, 56, 58, 68, 83, 92, 95, 112, 113, 121, 129, 136, 163, 165, 189, 190, 199–201, 203, 207, 212, 216, 218, 228, 229, 237, 238, 243, 248, 256, 262, 267
Bicycling West, Inc. 52
bighorn sheep 7, 74, 134, 166, 173, 203
bird-watching, birds *See also* species name 7–8, 13, 14, 31, 37, 74, 80, 91, 92, 93, 95, 106, 114, 122, 125, 126, 138, 141, 142, 143, 145, 146, 154, 155, 157, 161, 163, 170, 173, 179, 184, 188, 195, 206, 211, 212, 219, 220, 225, 235, 243, 253, 254, 259, 269, 273, 275–76, 279, 280, 281
Black Volcano *See* Volcán Prieto
Blanca, Ensenada 147, 192, 196, 203, 270
Blanca, Isla 186
Blanco, Cerro 54, 225, 232
Blanco, Punta 132
Blue Bottle Wash 117, 119
Bluff, Punta 144, 270
boardsailing 5, 52, 71–72, 74, 104, 120, 122, 125, 132, 138, 141, 148, 149, 165, 171, 179, 180, 185, 186, 203, 211, 213, 216, 218, 219, 222, 224, 228, 229, 230, 231, 238, 241, 243, 244, 264
boating 8, 11, 12, 13, 15, 18, 20, 21, 24, 26, 27, 31–32, 33, 34, 38–45, 55, 58, 62, 65, 69, 74, 77, 79, 80, 83, 84, 85, 86, 89, 90, 91, 92, 103, 104, 105, 106, 107, 108, 109, 122, 123, 125, 126, 138, 139, 141–47, 152, 154, 155, 156, 162, 163, 164, 165, 166, 170, 174, 179, 180, 181, 183–85, 186, 190, 192, 194–97, 202, 203, 207, 208, 211, 212, 216, 219, 222, 224, 228, 229, 234, 235, 237, 238, 240, 243, 245, 263, 264, 266–67, 268, 269, 270, 273–81
  boat trailers 68, 104, 218
  launching services *See also* launch ramps 112

marinas *See also name* 41, 44, 85, 86, 98, 100, 103, 178, 185, 215, 218, 219, 228, 241, 266, 273
marine parts *See also* Agencia Arjona 41, 180, 218, 241
  outboard engines 13, 41–42, 77, 78, 104, 190, 202, 206, 216, 266, 276, 282
  sterndrive engines 42, 104, 216
  yachts 19, 38, 40, 41, 48, 91, 95, 124, 152, 157, 183, 192, 203, 218, 219, 237, 241
Bocana, Estero la 165
Boleo, Arroyo del 175
Bon Voyage, But... 80
Bonanza, Punta 219, 220
boobies 31, 37, 269, 280
boojums 48, 129, 136, 138, 142
boondocking *See* RVing, RVs, boondocking
borders, border crossings 1, 24, 34, 35, 36, 49, 74, 76, 79, 80, 81, 82, 83, 84, 85, 86, 87, 89, 94, 95, 100, 109, 138, 247, 256, 266
Bota, Isla 142
Botella Azul, Cerro 116, 117, 119
Botella, Punta 197
brakes 49, 51, 66, 68, 86, 87, 199, 237
Brant 210
Bravo, Jaime 215
breach 8, 11, 12, 17, 161, 170, 211
Brisa del Mar RV Resort 237
British Columbia 12
Brown's Camp *See* El Mármol
Browne, J. Ross 15
Buena Vista 228
Burro, Bahía 186
burros 62, 75, 87, 116, 117, 153, 154, 171, 172, 192, 200, 232, 281
Burros, Punta los 197
bus tours 14, 50–51, 62, 75, 98, 114, 264
bus transportation 14, 48, 50, 51, 55, 62, 83, 95, 190, 237
butane *See* liquefied petroleum gas (LPG)

Cabeza de Caballo, Isla 141
Cabeza de Vaca, Alvar Nuñez 281
Cabo Acuadeportes, S.A. de C.V. 14, 237, 241
Cabo Cielo RV Park 237
Cabo Pulmo 28, 51
Cabo Pulmo Beach Resort 231
Cabo Pulmo Divers 231
Cabo Pulmo Eco-Tours 237
Cabo San Lucas 1, 5, 8, 9, 14, 15, 16, 18, 19, 20, 22, 24, 25, 26, 28, 29, 31, 34, 36, 38, 40, 41, 48, 51, 54, 55, 59, 60, 63, 71, 72, 73, 74, 78, 82, 83, 86, 88, 89, 92, 133, 137, 166, 171, 199, 212, 215, 224, 229, 230, 231, 235, 237–43, 245, 266
Cabras, Cerro de las 227
Cabras, Punta 7, 68, 109
Cabrillo Seamount 240

Cabrillo, Juan Rodríguez 9
Cachanilla's RV Camp 263
cactus 13, 48, 50, 62, 65, 69, 90, 91, 133, 142, 172, 188, 194, 225, 263, 269, 280
Cadajé 70, 171
Café Internet de Ensenada, S.A. de C.V. 103
Calabozo, Punta 194
Calexico 79, 256, 264
Calexico East 79, 95, 256
Calexico West 95, 256
California 210
California Current 1, 5, 6, 108, 109
Camallí 149, 156, 162
Camalú 76, 120
Camalú, Punta 120
Cambrey, Bahía 164, 165
Cambrey, Punta 164
camping 14, 42, 46–48, 50, 52, 54, 55, 56, 58, 64, 73, 78, 92, 93, 98, 99, 104, 106, 108, 109, 112, 113, 114, 116, 117, 119, 125, 129, 133, 134, 136, 142, 143, 144, 145, 146, 147, 148, 149, 156, 164, 166, 167, 179, 180, 183, 184, 185, 188, 189, 194, 195, 197, 200, 201, 203, 206, 207, 211, 213, 214, 216, 219, 220, 222, 224, 229, 233, 235, 243, 248, 249, 252, 253, 254, 255, 256, 260, 261, 262, 264, 267, 268, 269
Campistre la Pila Trailer Park 207
Campo Bufeo 270
Campo el Faro 270
Campo Noche 119, 263
Campo Playa RV Park 103
Campo Rancho Grande 270
Campo Rene 166
Campo San Felipe Trailer Park 264
Canada, Canadians 19, 59, 60, 78, 80, 82, 84, 86, 89, 91, 94, 114, 157, 178, 181, 211, 237
Canadian Department of Foreign Affairs and International Trade 80
Canal de Ballenas 146
Candeleros, Caleta el 219
Candeleros, Punta 196, 203
Cannery Airline *See* Aero Cedros
Cannon, Ray 24, 32, 183, 228, 273
Canoas, Punta 132, 134
Cantamar 98, 99
Cantamar Dunes 99
Cantamar, Arroyo 99
Cantina, Punta la 164
canyons *See also* name 1, 7, 46, 48, 53, 93, 99, 109, 113, 114, 116, 117, 132, 133, 135, 136, 138, 144, 146, 147, 148, 149, 153, 166, 171, 174, 175, 180, 181, 184, 188, 189, 197, 198, 199, 200, 208, 219, 222, 224, 225, 229, 231, 232, 233, 242, 243, 249, 252, 255, 257, 262, 276
Cape Coast Loop Trip 51, 68, 229
Cape Expeditions 228
Cape region 1, 6, 7, 15, 18, 20, 22, 24, 25, 27, 30, 35, 52, 55, 58, 215, 228, 238
Captain of the Port 12, 41, 43, 103,

152, 178, 183, 192, 203, 207, 218, 235, 241
Cardinosa, Isla *See* Partida Norte, Isla
cardóns 6, 133, 136, 142, 143, 263, 280
Carmen, Isla 13, 38, 53, 78, 79, 183, 185, 189, 192, 196, 201, 203
Carranza, Venustiano 177
Carrizo, Cañon el 255
Casa Blanca RV Park 215
Casa Diaz 139, 141
Casitas, Cerro las 1, 224
Castro's Fishing Place 112
Catalina, Isla 190
Cataviña 75, 85, 87, 116, 129, 136, 137, 157
cats 7, 80, 153, 194, 211, 276
cave exploring, caves *See also* lava tubes 39, 46, 77, 95, 99–100, 105, 107, 108, 109, 112–13, 120, 125, 132, 141, 149, 155, 179, 194, 195, 197, 220, 245–46, 247, 257, 267, 281
Cayo, Isla 195
CEDAM 279
Cedaroak Camp 119
Cedros, Isla 4, 5, 7, 9, 22, 34, 38, 43, 53, 82, 83, 104, 123, 132, 148, 149, 152–54, 155, 156, 157, 163, 167
Ceniza, Mount 122, 123
Centro de Buceo Carey 218
Cerraja, Isla 142
Cerralvo, Canal de 222
Cerralvo, Isla 22, 27, 216, 218, 222, 224, 228, 229
Cerritos Surf Shop 243
certification *See* diving, certification
cetaceans *See also* species name 8, 9
Chapala, Laguna 67, 137
Charters Mar de Cortez S.A. de C.V. 264
charts *See* maps, charts
checks 35, 80, 81, 83, 84, 85, 181, 190
Chileno, Bahía 237, 240, 241
China 152, 238, 259, 263
China, Punta 108
Chinero, Cerro el 259
Chinero, Crucero el *See* Trinidad, Crucero la
Chivato, Punta 5, 71, 179–80
Cholla, Isla 192
Cholludo, Isla *See* Roca la Foca
chubascos 5, 181, 189, 241, 266, 273
Chueca, Punta (Sonora) 278
Chuenque, Isla 202
Chukchi Sea 10
churches *See* missions, churches
Ciencias   Technicas Computacionales, S.C. 237
Cinco de Mayo 264
Circumnavigating Guardian Angel Trip 38, 55, 142–46
cirio See boojums

Ciudad Constitución 14, 82, 86, 89, 190, 206–07, 212, 213
clams 31, 32, 35, 47, 75, 105, 121, 125, 164, 165, 185, 188, 189, 196, 211, 264, 278
Clarion, Isla 22, 241
Clayton, J. Bulwer 282
climate *See also* weather 4–6, 50, 54, 60, 92, 101, 116, 154, 178, 225
climbing 46, 52–55, 58, 114, 116, 117, 119, 153, 184, 199–200, 225, 231, 232, 233, 240, 249, 252, 253, 255, 262, 263, 266
Clipper Deluxe 103
clothing 46, 91, 101, 116, 177, 198, 216, 237, 238, 241, 245
Club Cabo Motel and Campground Resort 243
Club Campestre Eréndira RV Park 247
Club Cascades de Baja 243
Club de Pesca Trailer Park 264, 266
Club Deportivo Bahía Kino 43, 44, 273, 281
Club Hotel Cantamar 41, 58, 218–19
Coasting to La Paz Trip 38, 55, 56, 196–97
Coasting to Loreto Trip 38, 55, 56, 183–85
Coasting to Santa Rosalía Trip 38, 55, 142, 146–47
Cochrane, Thomas 235
Colombia 19, 210–11
Colonet 68, 90, 112, 113, 114
Colonet, Cabo 112, 113
Colonia Guerrero 120–21
Colorada, Punta 29, 71, 146, 195, 228
Coloradito, Punta 184
Colorado 209, 210
Colorado River Tidal Bore 259
Colorado, Cerro 254
Colorado, Río 1, 4, 7, 38, 79, 256, 259
Comondús 7, 51, 60, 68, 189, 199, 200, 206
Compagnie du Boleo 175, 178
compasses 48, 52, 54, 64, 79, 116, 124, 143, 161, 171, 210, 233, 249, 253, 261
computers *See also* Internet, Internet cafés and computer service offices 60, 82, 83, 87–88, 237, 243
Concepción, Bahía 19, 47, 55, 58, 71, 75, 76, 78, 79, 135, 179, 183, 185, 238
Concepción, Punta 183, 184
Cono, Punta 132
Consag, Fernando 137, 158–59, 173
conservation 36–37, 91–93, 119–20, 190, 263
Consulate General of the US, Tijuana 88, 94
copalquín 6, 136, 142, 174, 276

coral 8, 15, 18, 52, 60, 91, 139, 141, 184, 194, 196, 203, 206, 220, 222, 224, 230, 231, 237, 242
cordonazo 5
corkscrewing 16, 170
coromuel 5, 215, 218, 220
Corona Beach RV Park 104
Coronadito, Isla 141
Coronado Yacht Club 98
Coronado, Isla 55, 139, 141, 142, 143, 188
Coronados, Islas 184, 190, 192, 201
Coronados, Islas los 9, 15, 27, 36, 95, 98
Correcaminos Trailer Park 229
Corso, Cabo 207
Cortés, Hernán 215, 278
Cortez Club 22, 218
Cortez Explorers 183
Cortez Yacht Charters 34, 44, 207, 241
Cortez, Sea of 1, 4, 5, 6, 7, 8, 9, 10, 13, 15, 16, 18, 19, 21, 22, 24, 25, 27, 30, 31, 33, 37, 38, 41, 42, 43, 44, 46, 48, 52, 53, 55, 56, 58, 71, 72, 75, 76, 78, 79, 92, 93 *passim*
Costa Azul 235
Costa Azul Surf Shop 237
Costa del Sol Motel 139
Costa Rica 230
courses 13–14, 44, 54–55, 57–58
Cousteau, Jacques 11, 145, 241
Coyote, Isla 195
Coyote, Punta 203
coyotes 7, 13, 47, 57, 134, 138, 186, 195, 225, 262, 282
crabs 35, 77, 124, 145, 220, 222, 230
Creciente, Isla 211
credit cards 80, 81, 82, 83, 84, 85, 103, 190
Critical Air Medicine 89
Crosby, Harry 137, 149 276
Crowne Plaza Resort 215
Crucero la Trinidad 263
Cruise America 62
Cruising Charts 43, 56, 78, 142, 143, 146, 183, 185, 194, 196, 273
Cuarto Con Muchas Ventanas la Mar 108
Cucapa, Sierra de 259
Cuesta del Gato, Punta 112
Cueva Amarilla, Ensenada 144, 145
Cueva de los Tunels Paralelos 108
Cueva Huevos 99, 100
Cueva Palmarito 51, 53, 75, 167, 171
Cueva Pintada *See* Gardner Cave
Cueva Ratón 75, 166
Cueva Tres Pisos 112
Cuevas de Agua Caliente 257
Cuevas de Santa Rosa 267
Cuevitas, Ensenada las 145
cultural property 19, 91
currents 4, 5, 6, 17, 21, 23, 33, 42,

55, 56, 71, 72, 79, 83, 84, 92, 108, 109, 122, 123, 141, 143, 144, 145, 146, 147, 154, 155, 156, 166, 194, 203, 207, 208, 210, 211, 212, 218, 219, 221, 259, 266, 267, 268, 270, 273, 276, 278, 279, 280
Curva del Diablo 206
Customs Hints for Visitors (Non-residents) 91

Daggett's Campground 139, 143, 146
Danzante, Isla 38, 55, 192, 194, 201, 202, 203
Darwin, Charles 13
Dátil, Isla *See* Turners, Isla
dátilillios 134, 137, 162
dátillo 134
Davidson Current 1–2
deer 7, 13, 74, 138, 149, 153, 154, 166, 171, 173, 180, 195, 225, 245
delegación municipal 82, 89
delegado 89
dentists 90, 98, 105, 112, 120, 121, 157, 178, 200, 206, 207, 215, 232, 243, 261
department stores 206, 216
Deportes Blazer 192
Desemboque (Sonora) 279, 281
deserts 6, 7, 13, 46, 48, 52, 54, 58, 65, 70, 86, 91, 128, 129, 132, 136, 137, 144, 147, 149, 153, 161, 163, 166, 167, 170, 172, 179, 181, 215, 221, 224, 253, 255, 262, 264
Devil's Postpile 143
DHL Worldwide Express 85–86
Diablito, Cañon 119, 262
Diablo, Cañon del 53, 117, 119, 249, 262–63
Diablo, Laguna 58, 68, 262, 263
Diablo, Picacho del 1, 6, 53, 114, 116, 117–20, 253, 262, 263
diarrhea 48, 89, 90
diesel 24, 85, 139, 152, 164, 165, 178, 218, 266, 270
Diguet, Leon 75, 149, 181, 194
Dionisio, Cañon 53
Discover Baja Travel Club 35, 41, 60, 61, 80, 84, 91
diving 5, 8, 9, 12, 15–23, 36, 38, 39, 40, 52, 58, 60, 70, 75, 76, 77, 78, 79, 80, 83, 95, 103, 104, 105, 106, 107, 108, 113, 120, 123, 125, 126, 127, 128, 132, 138, 141, 142, 145, 146, 148, 152, 154, 155, 162, 163, 164, 165, 170, 179, 180, 181, 183, 184, 185, 186, 188, 189, 190, 192, 194, 195, 196, 197, 198, 201, 202, 203, 206, 207, 210, 211, 213, 216, 218, 219–21, 222, 224, 228, 229–31, 233, 235, 237, 238, 241–43, 264, 266, 267, 269, 270, 276, 278, 279–81
  boats 20, 22, 123, 218, 241
  certification 20, 22, 192, 201, 216, 218, 228, 229, 231, 238, 242, 264
  recompression chambers 21–22, 105, 126, 152, 164, 207,

219, 242
  spearfishing 9, 18–19, 22, 95, 105, 123, 126, 141, 146, 152, 154, 155, 162, 165, 175, 179, 194, 195, 203, 207, 210, 218, 220, 222, 224, 228, 230, 266, 269, 277
doctors 22, 90, 98, 105, 109, 112, 120, 121, 125, 156, 157, 163, 178, 181, 200, 206, 207, 227, 229, 231, 243, 256, 258, 260, 261
dodder 136
Dog Bay 277
dogs 62, 69, 80, 148, 152, 153, 211, 215
dolphins 8, 9, 141, 273
Domecq Winery 257
Dominicans 99, 109, 112, 116, 120, 126, 138, 258
Don José 22, 218
dorados 24, 29, 30, 34, 141, 164, 179, 180, 183, 184, 189, 192, 195, 196, 197, 206, 207, 214, 216, 222, 224, 228, 230, 240, 245, 273, 281
Drop-off 240
drugs 41, 84, 88, 90, 91
Ducha de la Reina 112
dune buggies 105, 263, 264
dunes 57, 99, 113, 148, 157, 159, 163, 184, 207, 212, 231, 243, 264
Dutch 75, 159, 278

e-mail 32, 44, 83, 237, 243, 266
East Cape 5, 19, 22, 24, 25, 28, 29, 34, 41, 52, 71, 72, 197, 224
East Cape Coast Road 229–31
East Cape RV Park 229
Easter Island 231
ecology 12, 36, 61, 154, 161, 186, 188, 231, 242
EcoMundo *See* Mulegé Kayaks/ Baja Tropicales
Eden Loreto Resort 192
Eiffel, Alexandre Gustave 178
85-Foot Reef 95
Ejido Bonfil 171
Ejido Luis Echeverria Alvarez 248, 249
El Aguaje 233
El Alamo 76, 77, 260–61
El Alcatraz meadow 116
El Arco 51, 68, 76, 77, 136, 137, 148, 162–63, 163, 273
El Arco Trailer Park 237
El Arriba 200
El Aserradero 77, 254
El Bajo *See* Marisla Seamount
El Barril 147
El Borrego, Isla 141
El Camino Real 149
El Cantil 230
El Cardón Trailer Park 215
El Cardónal 220, 228
El Cardónal Resort 228
El Cardóncito 220
El Cién 213
El Ciprés 83, 104
El Compadre 248
El Cóndor 51, 68, 249, 254, 255

El Conejo 38, 71, 73, 213
El Cortez Motel 264, 266
El Coyote 51, 68, 186, 249, 254, 260
El Coyote RV Park 186
El Dorado Ranch 263, 264
El Embudo 220
El Faro Beach Motel & RV Park 104
El Faro Beach Trailer Park 267
El Faro Viejo 238
El Faro Viejo Trailer Park 243
El Huérfanito 268
El Huérfanito, Isla 268
El Juncalito 201–02
El Litro RV Park 245
El Mármol 62, 134–35, 270
El Marmolito 149, 155
El Martillo 73, 74, 103, 107
El Mirador 100
El Mogote 219
El Monte RV Rentals & Sales 62
El Moro RV Park 190
El Niño 4, 10, 16, 27, 31, 107, 125, 154, 240
El Norte 157, 266
El Oasis 256
El Pabellón Trailer Park 125
El Padrino Trailer Park 167
El Palomar Trailer Park 109
El Pescadero 243–44
El Pilón 200
El Pilón de Parras 53, 54, 199–200
El Rosario 6, 22, 24, 32, 48, 75, 76, 82, 88, 93, 94, 125–26, 127, 128, 129
El Sargento 222
El Sauce de Carter 133
El Sauzal 95, 98, 99
El Socorro 125
El Sombrerito 181, 183
El Testerazo 257
El Tomatal 149
El Triunfo 76, 77, 225, 227
El Triunfo de la Cruz 181
El Trono Blanco 53, 240, 249, 252, 255
El Volcán 53, 134, 135
electricity 60, 61, 65, 87, 93, 98, 99, 100, 103, 104, 105, 109, 112, 121, 123, 125, 126, 136, 138, 157, 163, 166, 167, 178, 181, 186, 190, 200, 202, 206, 207, 215, 216, 218, 219, 227, 228, 229, 237, 241, 243, 244, 245, 256, 257, 258, 259, 263, 264, 267
elephant seals 9, 95, 125, 155
elephant trees *See also copalquín; torote* 136, 138, 142, 174, 255, 276
emergencies, emergency assistance *See also* Green Angels; United States Coast Guard; police 22, 39, 43–44, 54, 55, 64, 80, 82, 83, 85, 89, 95, 137, 155, 164, 195, 197, 212, 219, 273, 278, 281
Emergency Center *See also* emergencies, emergency assistance; Green Angels; United States

Coast Guard 88
Encantada Grande, Isla 269
Encantada, Isla 268, 269
Encantada, Islas 264, 268–70
Enchanted Island Excursions 264
endemic species 6, 7, 9, 13, 106, 114, 126, 136, 154, 163, 175, 184, 195, 225, 276
England, English 19, 25, 44, 81, 83, 87, 89, 90, 121, 146, 149, 167, 177, 181, 231, 235, 242, 245, 253, 278
Ensenada 9, 14, 15, 19, 20, 22, 31, 34, 38, 41, 42, 43, 46, 50, 54, 57, 58, 59, 62, 72, 73, 74, 75, 77, 79, 82, 83, 85, 86, 88, 89, 94, 95, 98, 99, 100, 101, 103–04, 107, 108, 121, 123, 124, 152, 163, 181, 216, 238, 247, 253, 256, 258, 260, 266, 277
Entrada, Punta 123, 207, 211, 212
environment 1, 7, 8, 15, 46, 109, 153, 188, 225, 230, 281, 282
Eréndira 32, 57, 68, 108, 112, 113
Escarpada, Punta 132
Escondida, Laguna 166
Espíritu Santo, Isla 13, 15, 27, 38, 55, 57, 194, 196, 197, 213, 216, 218, 219–20, 221, 230, 238
Estanque, Isla 145
Este Ton 146
Esteban, Isla San 276
Estero Punta Banda 104
Eugenia, Punta 1, 6, 11, 74, 152, 164
Executive Clipper 103
Exportadora de Sal, S.A. 157, 159

Falla Agua Blanca 105, 108
Falsa, Bahía 123
Falso, Cabo 26, 38, 240, 241
feral animals 7, 95, 194
ferries, ferry transportation 24, 44, 48, 51, 79, 83, 84, 178, 218, 219
Fideliter 210
Fiesta Inn 235
Fiesta Sportfishing & Diving Co. 22, 34, 231, 240–41, 242
15 Spot 164
Final, Punta 136, 270, 271
fires 42, 47, 64, 66, 83, 84, 90, 92, 93, 108, 112, 114, 116, 148, 153, 158, 159, 163, 172, 173, 197, 213, 225, 232, 253
firewood 54, 90, 105, 129, 139, 159, 211, 249, 256, 279
Fish 'N Fool 124
Fisher, Frank 175
Fisherman's Fleet 34, 216, 222
Fisherman's Landing 34, 78
fishing 5, 8, 21, 24–37, 38, 39, 46, 47, 52, 55, 57, 62, 78, 79, 80, 83, 84, 92, 93, 95, 98, 99, 103, 104, 105, 106, 108, 109, 112, 113, 114, 117, 120, 122, 123, 124, 125, 126, 127, 128, 132, 138, 139, 141, 143, 145, 148, 149, 152, 154, 155, 156, 157, 158, 161, 162, 163, 164, 165–66, 170, 174, 178–79, 180,

183, 184, 185, 186, 188, 189, 190, 192, 194, 195, 196, 197, 201, 203, 207–08, 211, 212, 214, 215, 216, 218, 219, 221, 222, 224, 227, 228, 229, 230, 231, 235, 237, 240–41, 243, 245, 256, 259, 261, 263, 264, 266, 267, 268, 269, 270, 273, 276, 277, 278, 279, 280, 281
fishing cruisers 5, 24, 31, 32, 34, 38, 78, 123, 192, 216, 229, 235, 237, 240
Fishing International, Inc. 34, 192, 218, 228, 241
Five-Minute Kelp 95
Flecha, Isla 141
food 47, 50, 51, 54, 56, 60, 64, 70, 77, 80, 90, 91, 92, 95, 99, 103, 104, 109, 112, 113, 114, 120, 121, 125, 134, 136, 137, 139, 148, 149, 152, 154, 156, 157, 162, 163, 164, 165, 167, 171, 177, 178, 179, 181, 185, 190, 197, 200, 202, 203, 206, 207, 212, 213, 215, 216, 222, 224, 227, 228, 229, 231, 232, 235, 237, 243, 245, 247, 248, 255, 256, 258, 259, 260, 261, 262, 263, 264, 267, 270, 273
forests 6, 51, 54, 93, 114, 153, 253
Fortune 210
fossils 105, 108, 109, 125, 126, 132, 134, 148, 161, 165, 180, 184, 216, 222, 235
Frailes, Bahía 222, 231
Frailes, Cabo 71, 228, 230, 231
France, French 75, 103, 149, 175, 177, 178, 238, 263
Free Road 95, 98, 99
Freighters *See* San Jacinto, Punta
Frijolar, Cañon el 244
Frijole Bowl 164
fuel *See also* diesel; gasoline; PEMEX 40, 41, 42, 47, 62, 85, 86, 100, 103, 125, 134, 147, 157, 162, 164, 195, 212, 218, 219, 228, 241

Galapagos Islands 13
Galeras, Islotes las 13, 194
Gallina, Isla 220
Gallo, Isla 220
Gallo, Punta el 183
Gardner Cave 75, 166, 167, 173
Gardner, Earle Stanley 62, 75, 172, 175
gasoline *See also* PEMEX 40, 46, 47, 62, 63, 64, 65, 66, 81, 85, 86, 87, 89, 93, 114, 129, 136, 137, 139, 146, 148, 152, 155, 157, 162, 163, 164, 165, 171, 178, 195, 197, 200, 202, 206, 218, 222, 247, 260, 261, 263, 266, 270
Gasparino, Punta 233, 243
gastropods 108
Gato, Punta el 183
Gavilanes 183, 184, 189, 249
Gaviota's Sportfishing Fleet 240
Gecko Campground 139
Germany, Germans 158, 175, 177, 178, 195, 221, 238, 263

geysers 8, 109, 135
Giardia lambia 48, 116
Giganta, Sierra de la 1, 6, 189, 203
Giggling Marlin 238
Gigi 10, 170
Gilg, P. Adamo 281
goats 7, 50, 87, 95, 154, 189, 233
Golden City 19, 209–10, 212
Golden Gate, Banco 240
golf, golfing 80, 98, 99, 104, 179, 185, 201, 235, 237, 238, 263
Gonzaga, Bahía 58, 143, 270
Good Sam Club 60, 62
Gorda Primero, Banco 240, 242
Gorda Segundo, Banco 240
Gorda, Bancos 18, 22, 26, 27, 34, 218, 228, 229, 235, 237, 238, 240
Gorda, Punta 231, 235
Gordo's Sport Fishing 34, 74, 103, 123
Gorge Rock 210
gorgonians 18, 190, 194, 221, 222, 224, 242
Gorin's Gully 119
GPS 171
Gran Cañon 53, 152, 153
Grand Canyon (Arizona) 4
Grande, Arroyo 53, 133–34
Grande, Ensenada 220
Granito, Isla el 143, 144
Great Barrier Reef 230
Greek 231
Green Angels 89
Green Tortoise Adventure Travel 62, 75
Grey, Zane 31
Gringa, Punta la 139, 142
gringos 50, 156, 159, 173, 245
Gruta San Borjitas 75, 78, 179
Guadalupe 258
Guadalupe, Cañon 53, 253, 255–56
Guadalupe, Isla 34
Guadalupe, Sierra de 1, 74
guano 13, 132, 142, 159, 219, 270, 273, 275, 279, 280, 281
Guardian Angel Island 9, 13, 78, 92, 129, 142, 143, 145–46, 198, 270, 273
Guayaquil 134
Guaymas (Sonora) 38, 43, 83, 178, 259, 263, 281, 282
Guerrero Negro 1, 12, 14, 32, 48, 62, 74, 75, 79, 82, 83, 89, 104, 129, 149, 152, 157–58, 159, 161, 214
Guerrero Negro, Laguna 10, 157, 158
guides 25, 32, 41, 42, 43, 75, 78, 125, 141, 143, 167, 171, 179, 180, 183, 185, 196, 231, 245, 259, 273, 278
Guillermo's RV Park 138, 139, 141
gulls 8
   Heermann's gull 13, 269, 273
   yellow-legged gull 7, 13, 142, 276, 280
gypsum 13, 107, 147, 174, 178, 179, 247

H & M Landing 34, 78
H-1 210
Hacienda Santa Veronica 70, 248
Hanna, Phillip Townsend 63, 135, 167, 178
Hanson, Laguna 4, 51, 53, 68, 77, 253, 254
harbors 26, 36, 98, 101, 103, 121, 141, 152, 162, 175, 192, 203, 218, 219, 235, 238, 240, 241, 242, 245, 266, 268, 269
Hardy, R. W. H. 281
Hardy, Río 259
Hassler, Caleta 124, 125
health 85, 89–90, 186
Héroes de la Independencia 261
highways *See also* Transpeninsular Highway 48, 50, 68, 74, 95, 100, 108, 222, 224, 233, 243, 244, 247, 248, 249, 254, 255, 256, 257, 260, 261, 262, 263
hiking, hikes 29, 46, 52–55, 58, 64, 70, 75, 77, 93, 106, 107–08, 109, 113, 114, 116, 117, 125, 126, 133, 135, 137–38, 141, 142, 144, 149, 152, 153, 165, 166, 171, 173, 180, 181, 184, 186, 192, 203, 207, 208, 216, 220, 224–27, 231, 232, 233, 247, 249, 252, 253, 255, 257, 260, 261, 262, 266
HiLift 64, 68, 128, 132
Hitting the High Spots Trip 68
Hobies 38, 43, 44, 185, 218, 229, 264
Honeymoon Cove 203
Horizon 22, 123
Horizon Charters 14, 22, 123
Hornitos, Punta 183, 188, 189
horses 52, 99, 104, 114, 116, 117, 125, 136, 171, 190, 216, 227, 237, 247, 264, 281
hospitals, clinics 90, 99, 121, 139, 157, 163, 164, 165, 178, 206, 207, 215, 222, 231, 242, 255
Hotel Aquamarina 235
Hotel Bahía los Frailes 231
Hotel Cabo San Lucas 237
Hotel California 245
Hotel Casa Mar 237
Hotel Central 178
Hotel Coral & Marina 41, 98, 100, 103
Hotel Estero Beach 104
Hotel Finisterra 243
Hotel Frances 175, 178
Hotel Hacienda Beach Resort 241, 243
Hotel Hacienda Beach Resort Fishing Fleet 240
Hotel la Pinta 125, 136, 157, 167, 190
Hotel La Posada 175
Hotel las Casitas 181
Hotel las Misiónes 264
Hotel Los Arcos 216
Hotel Mar de Cortez 243
Hotel Meliá San Lucas 243
Hotel Misión 190

Hotel Oasis 190
Hotel Palmas de Cortez 228
Hotel Palmilla 237
Hotel Playa del Sol 228
Hotel Plaza de Loreto 190
Hotel Plaza las Glorias 243
Hotel Posada Real Best Western 235
Hotel Posada Terranova 235
Hotel Presidente Intercontinental 235
Hotel Punta Chivato 179
Hotel Punta Colorada 229
Hotel Punta Pescadero 228
Hotel Riviera 264
Hotel Serenidad 181
Hotel Serenidad RV Park 181
Hotel Solmar 240, 243
Hotel Terra Sol Beach Resort 243
Hotel Twin Dolphin 237
Hotel Villa de Palmar 243
Hotel Westin Regina 237
hotels, motels, and resorts *See also* name 20, 21, 22, 31, 34, 36, 41, 44, 52, 58, 60, 70, 74, 75, 78, 80, 81, 82, 89, 94, 98, 99, 100, 103, 104, 112, 121, 122, 123, 125, 136, 139, 147, 148, 152, 157, 162, 163, 167, 175, 178, 179, 181, 183, 186, 190, 192, 199, 201, 202, 206, 215, 216, 218, 222, 228, 229, 231, 235, 237, 238, 240, 243, 245, 256, 261, 262, 264, 266, 270
Howard Johnson Plaza Suites 235
huaraches 238
Hughes, Punta 207, 211
Humbug Bay 146
hummingbirds, Xanthus 7, 225
Hussong's Cantina 101–02, 238
Hyperbaric Technology, Inc. 22

ice 50, 66, 90, 99, 104, 105, 109, 112, 121, 125, 139, 146, 156, 157, 163, 165, 178, 180, 185, 200, 206, 207, 218, 229, 231, 235, 237, 243, 245, 256, 261, 264, 267
Iceland 11
Ildefonso, Isla 78, 184
Independence 19, 208, 209, 210
Indiana 19, 210
Indians 46, 55, 62, 74, 75, 80, 101, 112, 120, 132, 134, 136, 149, 152, 153, 159, 167, 171, 173, 180, 181, 186, 189, 195, 215, 216, 235, 238, 245, 246, 253, 255, 256, 275, 276–77, 278, 279, 280, 281, 282
Infiernillo, Canal de 278
inspections 79, 126, 157, 166, 213
Instant Mexico Auto Insurance Services 84
Instituto Nacional Indigenista 278
Instituto Sud Californiano de Cultura 167
insurance 5, 39, 41, 79, 80, 83, 84–85, 159, 211, 281
International Game Fish Association 31
Internet, Internet cafés, and computer service offices *See also*

computers 32, 44, 71, 74, 78, 79, 80, 83, 86, 91, 103, 216, 218, 237, 243, 266
ironwood *See palo fierro*
Island-Hopping Trip 38, 194–97
Italy, Italians 189, 237, 238
Ives, Joseph 259

J & R Baja Divers 241
Jack Rabbit Spring 161
Jack Velez Fleet 216
jacks 60, 64, 65, 67, 132
Japan 12, 13, 19, 36, 75, 106, 152, 157, 163, 164, 238
jejénes 55, 90, 146, 195, 198, 219, 273
Jesuits 75, 76, 114, 127, 136, 149, 152, 167, 181, 189, 199, 200, 215, 235, 244, 276
jet-skis 219, 264
John Elliott Thayer 19, 279–80
Johnson Ranch 68
Johnson, Harry 114
Johnston's Seamount 15, 18, 38, 123
Johnston, Bill 36
Jonathan Roldan's Sportfishing Services 218
Juanita's Fleet 240
Juanito's Garden RV Park 228
Juárez, Sierra de 1, 4, 6, 7, 46, 53, 54, 58, 249, 253, 255

katabatic 5, 71, 138
kayaking, kayaks 5, 12, 14, 17, 41, 42, 46, 47, 48, 52, 55–58, 62, 72, 74, 79, 80, 91, 92, 106, 125, 126, 138, 139, 141–47, 148, 156, 183–85, 186, 190, 192, 194–97, 197, 203, 207, 211, 216, 218, 219, 220, 222, 228, 229, 231, 237, 238, 241, 263, 264, 266, 268, 269, 270, 273–78
kelp 4, 11, 15, 21, 30, 105, 108, 109, 124, 125, 126, 127, 154, 155, 164
Kennedy's Cove 105
Killer Hook Surf Shop 235
kilometers, kilometer markers 52, 56
Kino, Bahía (Sonora) 38, 43, 44, 273, 277, 281
Kino, Eusebio 215
Know Before You Go 91
Kuyima Servicios Ecoturisticos 167

La Almeja 145
La Ballenita 143
La Base 170, 171
La Bocana 89, 108, 165, 171
La Bomba 259
La Bufadora 55, 105, 108
La Bufadora Dive 108
La Capilla Trailer Park 229
La Ciéneguita 245, 246
La Concha Beach Resort 58, 218
La Corona meadow 116
La Cuesta de la Ley 51, 136, 162

La Encantada meadow 116
La Freidera 167, 170
La Gringa 139, 141, 143
La Grulla meadow 116, 117
La Huerta 249
La Jolla Beach Camp 105
La Jolla RV Park 264
La Jollita 249
La Laguna meadow 7, 53, 55, 224, 225, 232, 244
La Mesquita 249
La Milla 48, 53, 249
La Misión 95, 99
La Mona 139
La Olivilad mine 135
La Paz 1, 5, 6, 7, 9, 14, 15, 16, 17, 18, 19, 20, 22, 24, 25, 28, 30, 32, 34, 38, 41, 42, 43, 48, 50, 51, 52, 55, 57, 58, 60, 63, 68, 71, 72, 75, 77, 78, 79, 82, 83, 84, 86, 88, 89, 167, 190, 192, 194, 196, 197, 202, 207, 212, 213, 215–18, 220, 221, 222, 224, 281
La Paz Diving Service 22, 218
La Paz RV Park 215
La Purísima 51, 68, 171, 189, 200
La Ribera 68, 229
La Rosa de Castilla 248
La Rumorosa 51, 76, 77, 247, 249, 255, 256
La Tasajera 116
La Tasajera, Arroyo 116
La Ventana 71, 72, 222, 259
La Zanja 116, 117
La Zanja, Arroyo 116
Laguna Hanson Loop Trip 51, 254
Laguna, Picacho la 224, 244
Laguna, Sierra de la 1, 6, 7, 46, 53, 54, 55, 224–27, 233, 245
lakes 4, 67, 95, 136, 137, 179, 225, 253, 254, 256, 259
Land's End Divers 238
Las Arrastras 271
Las Cuevas 51, 229, 231
Las Cuevas de los Indios 245
Las Encantadas 270
Las Flores 139, 147
Las Margaritas 249
Las Palmas RV Park 178
Las Parras Tours 190
Las Pintas 75, 132
Las Pocitas 213
launch ramps 40–41, 100, 103, 104, 105, 108, 112, 122, 123, 126, 139, 145, 156, 166, 174, 178, 179, 181, 183, 185, 186, 189, 192, 203, 207, 215, 216, 218, 219, 228, 231, 235, 241, 266, 268, 273, 281
launching service 228, 266
laundry, laundromats 89, 98, 99, 100, 105, 112, 121, 139, 157, 163, 178, 181, 190, 202, 207, 215, 216, 218, 228, 237, 241, 243, 244, 245, 248, 263, 264
lava tubes 38
laws, regulations 13, 19, 21, 31, 36, 75, 78, 79, 80, 83–84, 88, 89, 90, 91, 114, 159, 167, 190, 210, 276

Lázaro Cárdenas 121
Lázaro, Cabo San 209, 212
Leaning Tower of Pumice 269
Lee Palm Sportfishers 34
Ley de Hielo 119
licenses 35–36, 41, 75, 79, 80, 83–84, 192, 228, 229, 241, 281
Limón, Punta el 224
liquefied petroleum gas (LPG) 42, 47, 61, 70, 85, 89, 100, 109, 121, 139, 157, 174, 178, 181, 190, 206, 216, 224, 235, 237, 243, 247, 260
Lobera, Caleta la 147
Lobera, Isla la 144
Lobos, Caleta 219
Lobos, Isla 219, 268
Lobos, Punta 148, 192
Lobster Shack 95
lobsters 23, 31, 35, 47, 50, 74, 92, 105, 108, 124, 125, 127, 152, 154, 159, 165, 171, 179, 184, 194, 211, 213, 222, 264
Loco Lobo Surf and Tackle 105
lomboy colorado 246
Longinos, José 173
Lopéz Mateos 211, 212
Lopéz Mateos, Adolfo 276
Loreto 16, 18, 19, 25, 28, 34, 38, 48, 51, 55, 56, 57, 58, 68, 71, 76, 77, 82, 83, 87, 89, 93, 161, 174, 183, 184, 185, 189–92, 194, 196, 199, 200, 203, 215, 216, 221, 222
Loreto Shores Villas & RV Park 190, 192
Los Barriles 228
Los Candeleros 18, 194
Los Cantiles 144
Los Casian Trailer Camp 260
Los Dorados Fleet 240
Los Frailes 1, 54, 238, 240, 242, 243
Los Islotes 9, 22, 218, 220–21
Los Peregrinos RV Park 190
Los Planes 222, 228, 229
Lost Cave of El Zalate 149
Lottie Smith's Lagoon 210
Lower California Development Company 121
Loyola, Ignacio 167
Lupona, Punta 220

Machorro, Punta el 264, 266
Machos, Ensenada los 146
Machos, Punta los 143, 146
Magdalena, Bahía 1, 4, 7, 9, 10, 11, 12, 14, 19, 24, 25, 27, 28, 29, 30, 32, 34, 38, 55, 57, 71, 190, 207–12, 238
Magdalena, Isla 207, 208, 211, 212
Magdalena, Punta 207
mail 35, 78, 81–82, 83, 84, 105, 112, 113, 120, 121, 152, 157, 164, 165, 200, 206, 207, 227, 228, 231, 255, 258, 260, 261
Malakans 258
Malarrimo 68
mammals 7, 8, 9, 10, 13, 17, 91, 126, 142, 148, 273, 276, 281
Maneadero 79, 82, 86, 104–05

Manfred's Trailer Park 206
Mangles, Punta 184
mangroves 7, 55, 56, 142, 165, 166, 170, 179, 184, 188, 195, 197, 198, 207, 211, 220
Manila galleons 158
manta rays 8, 15–16, 192, 221, 242
Manuela, Laguna 57, 58, 74, 156–57
Map Centre, Inc. 78
Map World 78
maps, charts 42, 43, 52, 54, 56, 63, 64, 68, 71, 76, 77, 78–79, 80, 85, 104, 116, 119, 127, 133, 142, 143, 146, 147, 149, 155, 156, 157, 158, 164, 170, 174, 183, 185, 186, 192, 194, 196, 207, 225, 227, 231, 232, 242, 244, 252, 253, 266, 267, 268, 273
Mar del Sol RV Park 264
Marco's RV Park 264
María, Bahía 148–49
María, Punta 148
Marina Cabo San Lucas 41, 86, 241
Marina de La Paz, S.A. de C.V. 41, 86, 218
Marina Fiesta Resort 243
Marina Marisla 218
Marina Palmira, S.A. de C.V. 41, 86, 218
Marina Pichilingue XE "Club Hotel Cantamar" See Club Hotel Cantamar
Marisla II 22, 218
Marisla Seamount 15, 16, 18, 22, 218, 221, 242
marlin 18, 24–27, 29, 30, 31, 34, 38, 83, 123, 183, 195, 207, 216, 221, 222, 224, 228, 230, 240, 241, 245, 273
Martín Verdugo's Motel and Trailer Park 228
Matomí, Arroyo 267
Mazatlán (Sinaloa) 24, 43, 83, 218, 240
Mazo, Mount 123
meadows 7, 51, 53, 114, 116, 117, 224, 225, 248, 253
mechanics 49, 62, 66, 85, 86, 93, 104, 105, 113, 120, 121, 125, 136, 139, 148, 156, 157, 162, 163, 164, 165, 166, 178, 181, 206, 207, 213, 216, 228, 248, 255, 258, 261, 270, 271
Mechudo, Punta el 196, 197, 214
Mejía, Isla 13, 143
Meling Ranch See Rancho San José
Mesa Norte 175, 178
Mesa Sur 175
Mesón de Don Pepe 121
Mexicali 4, 6, 48, 54, 82, 83, 86, 89, 95, 101, 117, 247, 256, 258, 259
Mexican Consulate 79, 84, 91
Mexican Customs Service 41, 90, 91, 100, 103, 152, 178, 183, 192, 207, 218, 235, 241, 247, 256
Mexican Government Tourism Of-

fices 79, 91
Mexican Navy 43
Mexican Office of Immigration 41, 79, 94, 98, 103, 104, 152, 157, 178, 183, 192, 207, 218, 235, 241, 247, 256, 266
Mexico Ministry of the Environment, Natural Resources, and Fisheries 18, 31, 35, 41, 157, 163, 164, 165, 206, 207
Middle Grounds 95
Middle Island 95
Middle Rock 95
Midriff 4, 8, 9, 13, 15, 18, 19, 21, 25, 29, 30, 34, 38, 39, 42, 43, 78, 141, 142, 147, 266, 273–82
Migración See Mexican Office of Immigration
Migriño 243
Mike's Sky Ranch 53, 68, 70, 114, 116, 261–62
Miller's Landing 155–56
Mina Amelia 175
Mina Columbia 148
Mina Desengaño 138
Mina el Fenónemo 248
Mina el Morro 125
Mina el Sausalito 133
Mina el Socorro 261
Mina el Topo 252
Mina el Toro 139
Mina Jueves Santo 260
Mina la Escondida 259–60
Mina la Esperanza 133
Mina la Fortuna 134
Mina las Delicias 261
Mina Lucifer 174
Mina Olivia 252
Mina Promontorio 259
Mina Socorro 114
Mina Verde 254
mineral collecting, minerals 13, 53, 70, 76–77, 98, 107, 108, 112, 113, 114, 117, 120, 125, 126, 133, 134, 135, 138, 139, 144, 148, 149, 153, 155, 162, 173–74, 175, 183–84, 185, 188, 189, 192, 196, 197, 211, 213, 214, 216, 227, 245, 248–49, 252–53, 254, 255, 256, 258, 259–60, 261, 267, 268, 269, 270, 271
Minerva's Baja Tackle 31, 78, 241
Minitas de Guadalupe, Arroyo 189
Miraflores 232
Miramar, Isla 268
Misión Nuestra Señora de Guadalupe 258
Misión Nuestra Señora de Loreto 190
Misión San Borja 138, 149
Misión San Fernando Velicatá 134
Misión San Ignacio 152
Misión San Javier 200
Misión San Pedro Mártir 116
Misión San Vicente Ferrer 112
Misión Santa Gertrudis 149
Misión Santa María 66, 136–37
Misión Santa Rosalía de Mulegé 181
Misión Santo Domingo 120

Misión Santo Tomás 109
Mission Impossible See Misión Santa María
missions, churches See also name 66, 80, 99, 109, 112, 116, 120, 126, 127, 134, 136, 138, 149, 152, 167, 175, 178, 181, 189, 190, 199, 200, 206, 215, 227, 235, 244, 258
Mitlan, Isla 141, 142
Mitsubishi Corporation 12
mollusks 35, 75, 76, 122, 161, 179, 180, 188
money 35, 78, 80, 81, 177, 181, 256
Monserrate, Isla 13, 192, 194
Montaña, Punta 222
Monumento, Punta 277, 278
Moonlight Cove 95
Mora, Cañon la 255
mordida 78
Morro Prieto, Ensenada 147
Morro Santo Domingo, Punta 156
Motel el Morro 157, 178
Motel Sol y Mar 178
motor homes See RVing, RVs, motorhomes
motorcycling 58, 62, 68, 69–70, 80, 83, 84, 86, 90, 91, 105, 114, 136, 159, 211, 212, 248, 253, 261
mountain lions 7, 74, 134, 166, 171, 225
Mountain Villages Loop Trip 51, 171, 189, 199–201
mountains 1, 5, 6, 7, 46, 53, 54, 55, 89, 113, 114, 116, 117, 119, 142, 145, 152, 155, 166, 167, 181, 189, 192, 199, 221, 225, 245, 253, 254, 255, 259, 261, 262
Muerto, Isla el 268
Muertos, Caleta 180
Muertos, Ensenada los 34, 216, 218, 219, 222, 224, 227, 228
Mulegé 4, 9, 15, 18, 19, 20, 29, 30, 34, 38, 43, 55, 57, 58, 60, 62, 63, 71, 75, 82, 88, 177, 178, 179, 180, 181–83, 185, 189, 215, 218
Mulegé Divers 183
Mulegé Kayaks/Baja Tropicales 58, 186
Mulegé Territorial Prison 181
Mulegé, Estero 180, 181
Mulegé, Río See Mulegé, Estero
murrelet, Craveri's 13
museums 75, 76, 77, 104, 112, 125, 139, 160, 166, 167, 178, 181, 190, 207, 216, 235, 245, 258, 259
Muy Pronto 218

Nájar, Dr. Alfonso 242
Naranjas Road 225, 233–34, 243, 245
National Marine Park, Bay of Loreto 190
National Marine Park, Pulmo 230–31
National Oceanic and Atmospheric Agency (NOAA) 79
National Outdoor Leadership School (NOLS) 14, 44, 54, 57–

58, 211, 225
Natividad, Isla 22, 73, 74, 152, 163, 164
Natural Habitat 14
natural history 1, 4–14, 18, 55, 77, 132, 153–54, 174–75, 186, 194, 218, 225, 282
Navaho 210
Nelson, E. W. 116
Neptune Divers 238
Neptune's Finger 240
NetZone 243
New Zealand 48
Night Wash 119
9 Spot 164
95 Spot 240
Nopoló 190, 197, 201
North American Plate 1
North, Arthur 137, 149
nudibranchs 23, 108, 124, 141, 158, 179, 192, 222

Oasis Beach Resort and Convention Center 98
Oasis los Aripez Trailer Park 215
observatory 116, 119, 262
Observatory Road 68, 116, 261, 262
Ocean Odyssey 22, 123
Oceanic Society Expeditions 14
ocotillo 6, 135–36
octopus 24, 95, 221
off-road driving 51, 52, 62–69, 74, 89, 99, 113, 114, 147–48, 161–62, 163–66, 170–71, 175, 179–80, 188–89, 199–201, 203, 204, 213–15, 228–31, 233–35, 243, 244, 248–49, 256, 261, 262, 267–71
oil 10, 11, 41, 64, 65, 70, 85, 89, 91, 92, 93, 157, 170, 180, 256, 270
Ojo de Liebre, Laguna See Scammon's Lagoon
Ojos Negros 68, 248–49, 254, 260
Old Man 235, 237
Old Mill 121, 123
Old Mill Motel 121
Old Route 2 247
onyx 62, 132, 134, 135, 149, 155, 189
Open Doors 74, 164
opticians 121, 157, 206
Orchard Vacation Village 179, 181
Orrum, Eilly 260
ospreys 57, 141, 143, 146, 157, 212, 269
Otay Mesa 79, 95, 247
Otondo y Antillión, Admiral 215
outboard engines See boating, outboard engines
Outland Adventures 58, 142, 196
oysters 35, 122, 145, 164, 195, 196, 213, 220, 222

Pacific Coast Adventures 238
Pacific Ocean 1–2, 4, 5, 6, 7, 8, 9, 15, 18, 19, 21, 22, 24, 27, 30, 32, 38, 43, 44, 47, 52, 53, 55, 56, 71,

73, 74, 75, 77, 78, 98, 106, 119, 122, 123, 126, 127, 154, 158, 188, 212, 225, 230, 233
Pacific Plate 1, 12
Pacific Sea Fari Tours 14
Palapa Asadero la Presa 167
palapas 98, 125, 167, 178, 179, 180, 181, 185, 186, 188, 190, 200, 215, 218, 219, 231, 244, 255, 258, 260, 264, 267, 270
palm canyons 255–56
Palmas, Bahía las 71, 227–28
Palmilla, Punta 237, 240
palms 7, 98, 126, 133, 136, 147, 163, 166, 167, 172, 174, 179, 181, 199, 200, 201, 203, 215, 222, 231, 232, 233, 237, 243, 244, 245, 249, 252, 255
palo blanco 6, 180, 188
palo fierro 91, 188, 238, 264, 278
palo San Juan 188
palo verde 6, 132, 188
Palomar, Cañon el 255
Panama 55, 230
Panama Canal 175
Pancho's RV Park 258
pangas 31, 32, 38, 74, 78, 103, 108, 123, 126, 141, 143, 147, 152, 155, 163, 164, 165, 166, 170, 179, 189, 192, 201, 206, 211, 216, 218, 219, 221, 222, 228, 229, 231, 235, 237, 241, 264, 266, 277, 278, 279, 282
Papa Fernández' 270
Papalote, Bahía 108
Parador Punta Prieta 62, 85, 87, 129, 136, 137, 142, 148, 157
Paraíso, Arroyo 149
Pardito, Isla *See* Coyote, Isla
Parque Nacional Constitución de 1857 53, 249–54, 255, 260
Parque Nacional Sierra San Pedro Mártir 48, 53, 68, 76, 93, 113–20, 261, 262, 263
Parque Natural de la Ballena Gris 12, 158, 161, 170
Partida Norte, Isla 13, 30, 146, 198, 273, 276
Partida Sur, Isla 53, 55, 194, 196, 197, 216, 218, 220
Partida, Caleta 220
Pata, Isla 142
Patos, Isla 13, 273, 278, 279
Pattie, James 259
pearls 15, 159, 162, 195, 196, 215, 230, 278
Pedregal 122
pelicans 31, 95, 141, 144, 145, 184, 259, 270, 276, 279, 280
PEMEX *See also* diesel; fuel 41, 78, 85, 86, 87, 98, 100, 104, 109, 112, 113, 120, 121, 125, 129, 136, 137, 139, 156, 157, 163, 164, 165, 166, 171, 178, 181, 185, 190, 206, 207, 213, 215, 216, 227, 229, 231, 232, 235, 237, 241, 243, 245, 247, 249, 255, 256, 258, 259, 261, 263, 266, 267, 270
Península Concepción 183, 188–89

Pepe's Dive Center 22, 231
Pequeña, Punta 72, 73, 74, 171, 238
Perchuera, Punta 231
Perico, Punta 203
permits 12, 13, 19, 41, 79, 80, 84, 88, 89, 90–91, 107, 159, 167, 171, 178, 203, 241, 279, 281
Pershing, John 177
Peruchera, Punta 231
Pesca office *See* Mexico Ministry of the Environment, Natural Resources, and Fisheries
Pescadero, Punta 5, 33, 227, 228
Pescador, Ensenada el 142
Pescador, Isla El 141, 142
pesos 80, 81, 82, 101, 158, 175, 181, 245
Pete's el Paraíso Camp 263
Petrified Forest 126
pets 8, 57, 80, 91
Pets, Wildlife 80
pharmacies 80, 82, 88, 89, 90, 98, 103, 104, 105, 112, 113, 120, 121, 125, 157, 163, 164, 165, 178, 206, 207, 215, 229, 231, 235, 258, 260, 261
photography 16, 21, 22, 23, 42, 44, 45, 62, 77, 78, 100, 108, 109, 121, 123, 127, 141, 158, 167, 170, 173, 174, 178, 179, 180, 192, 194, 208, 211, 216, 218, 242, 275, 278
Picacho Row 252
Píccolo, Francisco 200
Pichilingue 218
Pichilingue, Bahía 219
pigs 7, 189
pines 114, 116, 126, 244, 248, 253, 260, 261
Pinnacle Ridge 117
pinnipeds *See also species name* 9, 93
Pinto Wash 255
Piojo, Isla el 141, 142, 146
Pisces Fleet Sportfishing 78, 240
Pisces Tidal Sports 238
Pitahaya, Isla la 185
plastics 47, 66, 85, 91, 92, 135
Playa Bonita RV Park 264
Playa Buenaventura 186
Playa Buenaventura Motel 186
Playa Bufeo 66
Playa de Amor 240
Playa de Laura RV Park 264
Playa de Tesoro 218
Playa del Rosario 126
Playa el Médano 71, 238, 241
Playa Independence 53, 208
Playa la Costilla 268
Playa la Perla 188
Playa las Margaritas 243
Playa las Palmas 244
Playa las Viudas 237
Playa los Cerritos 74, 243
Playa los Cocos 186
Playa los Naranjos 185
Playa Malarrimo 161, 163
Playa María 159
Playa Notrí 201

Playa Punta Arena 71, 185
Playa Requesón 71, 186, 188
Playa Santispac 71, 179, 183, 185, 188
Playhouse Cave 75, 136
Playon, Bahía el 105
Plaza las Glorias 238, 240, 241, 242
Plutarco Elías Calles 243
Point Loma Sportfishing 34, 78
Point South RV Tours, Inc. 62
police 43, 54, 62, 78, 83, 84, 86, 121, 166, 178, 245, 253
Pomo, Isla 269, 270
Poncho's RV Park 181
ponds 12, 46, 53, 116, 117, 133, 136, 137, 138, 145, 157, 163, 167, 172, 179, 200, 224, 225, 232, 233, 249, 252, 255, 259, 260, 261, 262
Pool of the Virgin 255
Popotla Trailer Park 98
porpoises 8, 9
Porter, George 282
Posada Concepción 185
Posada Concepción RV Park 186
Posada Don Diego 60, 121
Prieta, Punta 48, 58, 85, 87, 148, 165, 170
prisons 88, 135, 178, 181
propane *See* liquefied petroleum gas (LPG)
Providencia, Cañada la 119
Pueblo la Playa 231, 235
Puercos, Bahía de los 183, 184, 189
Puertecitos 58, 66, 68, 137, 162, 198, 264, 266, 267–68, 271
Puerto Alcatraz 212
Puerto Almeja, Ensenada *See* Ramada, Caleta
Puerto Balandra 53, 192
Puerto Calamajué 137, 270, 271
Puerto Chale 68, 70, 211, 212, 213
Puerto Cortés 210, 212
Puerto Cueva 95
Puerto Don Juan 55, 141, 142, 147, 273
Puerto Escondido 40, 41, 58, 78, 190, 192, 202–03, 207
Puerto Gato 197
Puerto Lopéz Mateos 10, 14, 206
Puerto Magdalena 207, 212
Puerto Nuevo 62, 98, 99
Puerto Refugio 9, 56, 78, 92, 143, 144, 270
Puerto San Carlos 10, 14, 22, 79, 207, 212
Puerto Santa Catarina 134
Puerto Santo Tomás 108–09
Puerto Viejo 158
Pulmo Reef 15, 18, 20, 22, 36, 52, 60, 68, 229, 230, 231, 237, 238, 241
Pulmo, Cabo 71, 82, 230–31
Púlpito East, Caleta 145
Púlpito West, Caleta 145
Púlpito, Bahía el 145
Púlpito, Punta 18, 56, 184
Púlpito, Punta el 145

Purgatorio, Arroyo del 175
Purísima, Arroyo de la 200

Quatro Casas *See* San Telmo, Punta
Quemado, Ensenada el 141, 142
Quemado, Punta 56

rabbits 7, 13, 74, 106, 154, 192, 220
rabies 80
Racito, Isla el 19, 141
Racito, Islote el 147
radio 42, 43–44, 54, 60, 89, 103, 123, 218, 241, 264, 273
Rafael's Sport Fishing Fleet 241
Ramada, Caleta 184
Ramona Beach Trailer Park 100
Rancho Agua Caliente 257, 260
Rancho Buena Vista 34, 229
Rancho Cerro Colorado 260
Rancho de San Baltizar 179, 181
Rancho el Porvenir 260
Rancho el Progreso 134, 162
Rancho el Rayo 253
Rancho el Salto 189
Rancho Huatamote 206
Rancho Johnson 113
Rancho la Poderosa 255
Rancho la Trinidad 180–81, 190
Rancho las Destiladeras 231
Rancho las Parras 200
Rancho Leonero 229
Rancho Ligui 203
Rancho los Dolores 197
Rancho Manzanos 114
Rancho Mother Teresa Trailer Park 258
Rancho Nejí 248
Rancho Nuevo Chapala 137
Rancho Ojai RV Park 247
Rancho Playa Monalisa 104
Rancho Renteria 189
Rancho San Andrés 148
Rancho San Dionisio 225, 232, 244
Rancho San Ignacio 249
Rancho San Ignacito 137
Rancho San José 62, 114
Rancho San José de Castro 163
Rancho San Juan de las Pulgas 112
Rancho San Juan del Aserradero 244
Rancho San Juanico 184
Rancho San Luis 253, 255
Rancho San Nicolás 183, 184, 189
Rancho San Regis 149
Rancho Santa Martha 75, 167, 171, 173
Rancho Santa Ynés 136
Rancho Sordo Mundo Trailer Park 257–58
Rancho Tres Hermanos 260
Rancho Verde 227
Rancho Viejo 116–17, 200
Rasco, Picacho 255
Rasita, Isla 141
Raza, Isla 13, 273, 275, 276
Real del Castillo 253
recompression *See* diving, recompression chambers

Recreation Industries Co. 39
Red Hill 240
reefs 8, 9, 15, 18, 19, 20, 22, 28, 30, 32, 36, 52, 60, 95, 108, 112, 120, 126, 127, 132, 141, 142, 143, 145, 146, 147, 148, 149, 154, 155, 164, 165, 166, 179, 180, 184, 190, 192, 194, 195, 197, 203, 216, 220, 221, 222, 224, 228, 229, 230, 231, 237, 269, 276
regulations *See* laws, regulations
Rehusa, Canal 208, 210, 211, 212
Remedios, Punta 143, 146, 270
rentals 20, 44, 52, 58, 72, 74, 83, 84, 103, 104, 105, 108, 123, 125, 139, 142, 156, 162, 179, 181, 183, 190, 192, 201, 216, 218, 219, 222, 228, 229, 231, 235, 237, 238, 241, 243, 263, 264, 266, 270, 278
repairs 41, 42, 44, 47, 49, 64, 65, 69, 70, 85–86, 87, 89, 93, 103, 104, 105, 109, 120, 121, 134, 136, 137, 139, 148, 149, 156, 157, 163, 165, 166, 178, 181, 192, 202, 206, 207, 213, 216, 218, 222, 229, 235, 238, 243, 255, 256, 257, 258, 260, 261, 270, 271
reptiles 7, 13, 91, 126, 142, 143, 154, 175, 194, 195, 220, 276, 281
reserves, refuges 13, 36, 95, 161, 190, 230, 231, 242
restaurants, cafés 80, 89, 90, 94, 98, 99, 100, 101, 103, 104, 105, 108, 109, 112, 113, 120, 121, 122, 123, 125, 134, 136, 139, 148, 149, 156, 157, 162, 163, 165, 166, 167, 171, 175, 178, 179, 181, 185, 186, 190, 197, 200, 202, 206, 207, 212, 213, 214, 215, 216, 218, 219, 222, 224, 227, 228, 229, 231, 235, 237, 238, 243, 244, 245, 248, 249, 255, 256, 258, 260, 261, 263, 264, 270, 271
Revillagigedo, Islas de 22, 34
rights, legal 88–89
Rincón, Bahía 230
ring-tail cats 7, 13, 173, 195, 220
Río Rita 22, 218
Risco Colorado, Punta 277, 278
rivers, streams *See also name* 4, 67, 68, 87, 93, 112, 116–17, 126, 132, 136, 144, 171, 181, 199, 200, 206, 224, 225, 231, 248, 252, 255, 257, 261, 262
Rob's Baja Tours 256
robin, San Lucas 7, 225
Robinson, Edward G. 159
Robinson, R. E. L. 259
Roca Ballena 166
Roca Ben 15, 18, 38, 123–24
Roca Blanca 273
Roca Consag 266
Roca la Foca 277
Roca Lobos 18, 179, 219
Roca Montaña 222
Roca Pináculo 18, 154, 207
Roca Raza 276
Roca Solitario 196–97, 206
Roca Timón 127

Roca Vela 143
Rocallosa, Isla el *See* Pescador, Isla el
Rocas Alijos 27, 34
Rocas Soledad 15, 18, 109
rock art 46, 51, 53, 58, 62, 74–75, 132, 136, 149, 166, 167, 171, 173, 179, 180–81, 186, 190, 194, 216, 228, 238, 255
Rockpile 95
Rocosa, Punta 145
Romero, Chico 278
roosterfish 18, 24, 28–29, 179, 180, 183, 189, 197, 202, 206, 216, 222, 228, 230, 240
Rosa de Castilla 51
Rosario, Bahía del 126, 128
Rosarito 74, 79, 82, 89, 95, 98, 99
Rosarito Sur 74, 76, 149
Rosarito, Punta 148, 149
Ruben's Trailer Park 264, 266
Russia 152, 258
RVing, RVs 21, 31, 48, 50, 52, 59–70, 74, 83, 84, 85, 86, 89, 90–91, 92, 98, 99, 114, 126, 132, 147, 148, 156, 157, 161, 163, 166, 178, 190, 202, 207, 228, 230, 235, 243, 264
  boondocking 99, 105, 112, 120, 139, 165, 174, 179, 185, 188, 189, 203, 212, 213, 218, 224, 230, 231, 243, 244, 245, 248, 268, 270
  motor homes 39, 50, 59, 80, 114, 157, 166, 170, 178, 181, 189, 203, 214, 261
  parking 60, 99, 108, 109, 112, 113, 123, 125, 134, 136, 139, 148, 157–58, 167, 171, 180, 185, 186, 188, 207, 219, 222, 237, 243, 248, 255, 256, 260, 267, 270, 271
  parks *See also* name 21, 52, 60, 61, 70, 74, 78, 80, 82, 98, 99, 100, 103, 104, 105, 109, 112, 114, 121, 122, 123, 125, 126, 136, 137, 138, 139, 157, 163, 166–67, 178, 179, 181, 183, 185, 186, 188, 190, 206, 207, 215, 216, 218, 227, 228, 229, 237, 243, 244, 245, 247, 248, 257, 258, 259, 260, 263, 264, 267, 270
  repairs *See* Wahoo RV Center, S.A. de C.V.
  trailer parts 60, 69, 86, 180, 218, 237
  trailers 21, 39, 40, 41, 59, 60, 62, 68–69, 84, 85, 86, 90, 91, 98, 99, 104, 105, 112, 114, 132, 147, 156, 178, 181, 189, 203, 206, 216, 228, 261, 268

S.S. Catalina 101
Sacramento 19, 127
Sacramento Reef 15, 18, 19, 124, 126, 127–28, 154
safety 15, 21–22, 24, 43, 44, 48–49, 56–57, 58, 70, 72, 86, 87, 93,

128, 137, 138, 154, 166, 180, 185, 194, 202, 203, 256, 273, 278
sailfish 24–27, 40, 183, 184, 207, 216, 222, 224, 228, 230, 231, 240
Salada, Laguna 4, 252, 255, 256, 259
sales 19–20, 57, 72, 77, 84, 91, 103, 104, 105, 123, 157, 178, 183, 188, 190, 201, 206, 216, 218, 229, 238, 241, 270
Salina, Punta la 147
Salinas de Gortari, Carlos 278
Salinas, Bahía 53, 192
Salinas, Punta 197
Salsipuedes, Canal de 162, 276
Salsipuedes, Cerro 53, 225, 232, 233
Salsipuedes, Isla 18, 273, 276
salt 12, 13, 152, 157, 158, 192, 195, 224
Salton Sea 7, 13
Salvatierra 18, 19, 22, 218, 219
Salvatierra, Isla 269
Salvatierra, Juan María 189, 190
San Andreas Fault 1
San Andrés, Punta 148
San Antonio 98, 116, 117, 222, 224, 227
San Antonio del Mar 113
San Antonio, Arroyo 116
San Antonio, Punta 183, 184
San Aremar, Isla 141
San Benito, Islas 4, 9, 15, 18, 19, 30, 34, 38, 154–55, 163
San Bernardo, Cañon 53, 225, 227, 232, 244
San Borja, Misíon 149
San Borja, Sierra 1
San Bruno, Boca 184
San Carlos, Bahía 127, 129, 132, 132, 148, 197
San Carlos, Punta 73, 132, 147
San Diego 5, 10, 17, 22, 25, 28, 34, 35, 38, 41, 43, 53, 55, 57, 62, 68, 78, 80, 94, 95, 98, 109, 121, 123, 124, 126, 128, 133, 134, 152, 155, 156, 165, 207, 237, 249, 260, 271
San Diego, Isla 22, 39, 124, 194, 195
San Dionisio, Cañon 225, 232
San Esteban, Isla 273, 276, 277
San Evaristo 39, 192, 213, 218
San Evaristo, Bahía 197
San Faustino 248
San Felipe 5, 14, 19, 24, 34, 38, 41, 48, 51, 54, 58, 60, 62, 68, 72, 79, 82, 85, 86, 89, 91, 95, 137, 247, 256, 259, 263–66, 267, 270, 273
San Felipe Marina Resort and RV Park 264
San Fernando, Cañon 132
San Francisco 62, 75, 166, 172, 210
San Francisco, Isla 194, 195, 196, 197, 218, 221
San Francisco, Sierra de 1, 74, 166, 167, 238

San Francisquito Resort 22, 148, 162
San Francisquito, Bahía 18, 19, 39, 51, 56, 68, 77, 79, 136, 137, 142, 146, 147–48, 162, 273
San Francisquito, Ensenada 270
San Francisquito, Punta 162
San Gabriel, Bahía 220, 230
San Gregorio, Arroyo 171
San Hipólito 165
San Hipólito, Bahía 164, 165
San Ignacio 7, 48, 51, 58, 62, 68, 74, 75, 82, 89, 156, 163, 166, 167, 170, 171, 173, 175, 200, 202, 206, 214
San Ignacio, Laguna 1, 10, 11, 12, 13, 14, 58, 60, 62, 68, 70, 161, 166, 167, 170–71
San Ignacio, Laguna de 170
San Isidoro 171, 200
San Isidro, Punta 109, 112, 195
San Jacinto, Punta 73, 120
San Jaime, Banco 27, 240
San Javier 51, 68, 190, 199, 200
San Jerónimo, Isla 9, 34, 53, 126–27, 128
San José de Comondú 51, 199, 200
San José del Cabo 5, 20, 26, 32, 51, 68, 74, 82, 83, 86, 89, 229, 231, 235–37, 240
San José Viejo 235
San José, Isla 13, 78, 146, 188, 194, 195
San José, Punta 68, 73, 109, 112
San Juan Bautista, Punta 147
San Juan de la Costa 68, 197, 213, 214
San Juan del Aserradero 225
San Juan del Dios, Arroyo 133
San Juanico 171
San Juanico, Bahía 166, 171
San Juanico, Caleta 183, 184, 189
San Juanico, Punta 73, 171
San Lázaro, Cabo 19, 207, 211
San Lázaro, Picacho 53, 225, 233
San Lorenzo Shoal Light 219
San Lorenzo, Canal de 55, 219
San Lorenzo, Isla 9, 13, 18, 30, 273, 276
San Lucas Trailer Park 178, 179
San Lucas, Caleta 18, 178–79
San Luis Gonzaga, Bahía 30, 38, 51, 137, 264, 267, 268
San Luis, Bahía 137
San Luis, Isla 268, 269, 270
San Marcial, Punta 197
San Marcos, Isla 13, 18, 179
San Martín, Isla 8, 9, 11, 15, 22, 30, 34, 38, 53, 77, 109, 113, 121, 123–25, 154
San Matías 262
San Matías, Cañada 244
San Miguel 73, 74
San Miguel de Comondú 51, 200, 206
San Miguel Surf Shop 103
San Miguel Village RV Park 100
San Miguel, Cabo 146, 147
San Pablo 247

San Pablo, Bahía 164, 165
San Pablo, Cañon 166, 171–73
San Pedro Mártir, Isla 9, 13, 29, 53, 273, 278, 280
San Pedro Mártir, Sierra 1, 6, 7, 46, 53, 54, 55, 117, 129
San Pedro, Punta 185
San Perdito RV Park 244
San Quintín 24, 32, 38, 82, 89, 121, 122, 157
San Quintín, Bahía 71, 121–23, 211
San Quintín, Cabo 123, 125
San Rafael 147
San Rafael, Arroyo 114, 116
San Rafael, Bahía 147, 162
San Rafael, Río 116, 261
San Roque 165
San Roque, Bahía 164
San Roque, Isla 19, 165
San Roque, Punta 165
San Sebastián 20, 68, 183, 184, 188–89
San Telmo 114, 119
San Telmo, Punta 73, 120, 197
San Vicente 76, 112, 113
San Ysidro 84, 94, 95
Sand Island 158, 159
sandfalls 15, 242
Sandy Point 148
Santa Ana, Punta 147
Santa Anita 235
Santa Catalan, Isla See Santa Catalina, Isla
Santa Catalina, Isla 13, 192, 194
Santa Clara, Sierra 166
Santa Cruz 229
Santa Cruz, Isla 17, 18, 194
Santa Inés, Islas 180, 183
Santa Inés, Punta 179–80
Santa Margarita, Isla 77, 207, 208, 210, 211
Santa María, Bahía 71, 123, 166, 209, 211, 212, 237, 240
Santa María, Caleta 147, 174
Santa María, Punta 147
Santa Monica, Pico 166
Santa Rita 213
Santa Rosa 235
Santa Rosa meadow 116
Santa Rosa, Punta 184
Santa Rosalía 6, 30, 38, 41, 48, 55, 62, 75, 76, 77, 78, 83, 84, 89, 142, 146, 147, 157, 162, 175–78, 189, 190, 215, 227, 263, 275
Santa Rosalía Marina 178
Santa Rosalía, Río See Mulegé, Estero
Santa Rosalillita 55, 57, 71, 126, 141, 148-49
Santa Rosalillita, Bahía 148
Santa Rosalillita, Punta 73, 132, 149
Santa Teresa, Punta 147, 184
Santiago 227, 231–32
Santo Domingo 225, 232, 244
Santo Tomás meadow 116
Santo Tomás, Bahía 107, 109
Santo Tomás, Punta 15, 109

Sargento, Punta (Sonora) 279
Sauromalus varius 276
Scammon's Lagoon 9, 10, 12, 14, 18, 36, 60, 157, 161
Scammon, Charles 9, 10
scorpions 47, 195
Scout Peak 117
Scout Shoal Light 219
Scu-Baja Dive Center 22, 218
Scuba Baja Joe 216
sea cucumbers 146, 197
sea fans 141, 194, 195, 230
sea lions 9, 31, 57, 95, 105, 125, 126, 127, 142, 144, 155, 194, 220, 238, 243, 276, 281
Sea Trek Ocean Kayaking Center 58
seals 9, 31, 57, 125, 152, 155, 212
seamanship 42–43, 146
seamounts See also name 15, 16, 18, 22, 26, 34, 123, 124, 154, 218, 221, 240, 242
Señor Diver 235
Seraffyn 195
serapes 91, 215, 238
Sergio's Sport Fishing Center 14, 103
Serra, Junípero 134, 137
services 19–20, 41, 58, 60, 80, 82, 83, 84, 85, 86, 87, 89, 94, 98, 103, 104, 105, 121, 137, 139, 157, 175, 178, 190, 207, 215, 216, 218, 237, 241, 243, 244, 247, 256, 278, 281
sharks See also whale sharks 8, 15, 16–18, 21, 22, 104, 127, 161, 165, 195, 203, 211, 221, 238, 242, 276
Shell Beach 180
shell collecting, shells 22, 75–76, 101, 106, 139, 158, 162, 164, 180, 183, 184, 188, 189, 196, 197, 201, 215, 216, 220, 224, 230, 231, 266, 270, 278, 282
Shipwrecks 231, 235
shovels 31, 61, 64, 67, 87, 159, 271
Sierra, Boca de la 225, 232
siesta 46, 50, 139, 215
Sinai RV Park 126
Siren Bay 164
6 Spot 165, 207
6 1/2 Spot 124
Slot Wash 117, 119
Smithsonian Institution 158
snakes 7, 13, 51, 107, 126, 145, 154, 175, 192, 194, 276, 282
snow 6, 46, 54, 114, 117, 263
Soc. Coop. de Producción Pesquera See Aero Cedros
Socorro, Isla 22, 241
Soldado, Punta el 141
Soledad, Arroyo de 175
Soledad, Bahía 109
Soledad, Boca la 211, 212
Solmar Fleet 240, 241
Solmar V 22, 241
Sonora 5, 38, 43, 48, 129, 133, 177, 273, 278, 279, 282
Southern California (USA) 1, 5, 6, 8, 24, 62, 71, 72, 73, 74, 80, 103, 141, 264

Southwest Onyx and Marble 134
Southwest Sea Kayaks 57, 106, 108, 126, 142, 157, 183, 278
Spanish 77, 80, 86, 87–88, 99, 149, 167, 189, 230, 238, 253, 278, 279, 280, 282
spearfishing See diving, spearfishing
Special Expeditions, Inc. 14
Spirit of Adventure Charters 14
springs See also water, potable 4, 58, 114, 116, 135, 138, 181, 186, 219, 224, 227, 255, 260
spy-hopping 11, 161, 170, 211
State Secretary of Tourism of Baja California 51, 84, 88, 91, 98, 103, 104, 121, 215, 216, 218, 247, 266
Steinbeck, John 230
Stepping-Stones Trip 38, 55, 273–81
sterndrive engines See boating, sterndrive engines
Stevenson, Robert Louis 107
stoves 42, 47, 70, 85, 112, 211, 216
sun burn 46, 70, 90, 271
supermarkets 20, 31, 89, 104, 125, 128, 129, 157, 190, 216, 228, 235, 243
Sur, Bahía del 152
Sur, Punta 222
Surf Check 74
surfing 15, 58, 59, 71, 72–74, 84, 98, 99, 100, 103, 104, 105, 107, 108, 109, 112, 113, 120, 121, 122, 123, 125, 126, 132, 148, 155–56, 164, 165, 171, 211, 213, 222, 231, 237, 238, 243, 244, 245
Surfline 74
Swiss, Switzerland 48, 238

Tabor, Cañon 203
Tajo, Cañon 48, 53, 166, 249, 255
Tanamá 256
Taraval, Sigismundo 152
Tasajera Meadow 116
Tecate 48, 58, 79, 82, 86, 95, 100, 247, 256
Tecate Resort and Country Club 256
Tecolote 218, 219
telephones 32, 60, 78, 82–83, 85, 86, 87, 89, 95, 100, 101, 103, 105, 109, 112, 113, 120, 121, 125, 139, 156, 157, 164, 165, 167, 178, 181, 185, 206, 207, 213, 215, 216, 218, 222, 224, 227, 228, 229, 231, 232, 235, 237, 243, 247, 256, 257
temperatures 1, 4, 5, 6, 8, 10, 16, 27, 29, 30, 31, 33, 34, 46, 47, 78, 101, 114, 116, 124, 132, 185, 207, 224, 230, 240, 264, 267, 273
10 Spot 164
Ten Kate, Herman 75
tents, tenting 14, 47, 59, 90, 98, 99, 104, 132, 207, 211, 262, 264
terns 13, 273, 275, 280
Terrible Three 66, 162, 268, 271
Teta de la India, Cerro 53, 254–55
The Hole 109

The Log From the Sea of Cortez 230
The Moorings 44, 218
The Net Cyberservices 266
The Rock 235, 237
The Sea of Cortez 24
The Shop 183
The Slot 142, 147
Thetis, Banco 27, 38, 207
38 Spot 164
thrasher, gray 7, 163, 276
3 Spot 207
Tiburon's Pangas Sportfishing 123
Tiburón, Isla 9, 13, 18, 57, 142, 145, 273, 275, 276, 277, 278, 279, 281, 282
tidal bores 4, 259
tide pools 107, 179, 184
tides, tide tables 4, 21, 41, 42, 56, 70, 71, 77, 78, 79, 93, 104, 105, 106, 108, 113, 123, 126, 139, 141, 142, 143, 145, 147, 149, 156, 166, 171, 179, 181, 183, 186, 203, 206, 207, 208, 210, 211, 219, 231, 259, 264, 266, 267, 268, 269, 273, 276, 278, 280, 281
Tierra Firma, Punta 184
Tijuana 5, 15, 48, 51, 62, 63, 73, 74, 78, 79, 80, 82, 83, 86, 88, 89, 94, 95, 107, 166, 247, 256
Tijuana Flats 95
Tijuana Tourism and Conventions Bureau 94
Tijuana/Mexicali Toll Road 247, 256
Timbabichi, Bahía 197
Tinaja de Yubay 53, 137–38
Tinajas, Sierra las 259
Tío Sports 237, 238
tires, tire repair 49, 50, 60, 62, 63, 64–65, 66, 69, 85, 86, 87, 98, 104, 105, 109, 112, 113, 120, 121, 125, 128, 134, 136, 137, 148, 149, 156, 157, 162, 163, 165, 166, 171, 178, 181, 206, 207, 213, 216, 218, 222, 229, 235, 255, 256, 257, 258, 260, 261, 270, 271
toads 7
Todos Santos 48, 51, 86, 243, 244–45
Todos Santos, Bahía 57, 104, 105
Todos Santos, Islas de 9, 15, 53, 55, 57, 58, 73, 98, 103, 105, 106–07, 108
toll roads 94, 95, 98, 99, 100, 103, 247, 249, 255, 256
Tony Reyes Fishing Tours 34, 218, 273
tools 44, 47, 49, 63, 65, 69, 78, 153, 178, 216, 277
Topolobampo (Sinaloa) 38, 83, 218
torote 6, 136, 142, 174
Tórtolo, Cabo 164
Tortugas, Bahía 22, 24, 32, 38, 47, 51, 68, 71, 82, 83, 89, 152, 161, 163, 164
Tortugas, Isla 147, 174–75
Tosca, Punta 70, 207, 208, 210, 211, 212

totuava 13, 35, 263

tourist cards 36, 79, 80, 84, 90, 103, 104, 157, 247, 266

tours 13, 14, 48, 61, 62, 77, 80, 104, 116, 181, 190, 194, 206, 238, 256, 276

tow, towing 39, 40, 41, 59, 60, 62, 64, 69, 84, 89, 105, 137, 149, 181, 206, 228, 266, 268

Toxostoma curvirostre insularum 276

Tracks to Adventure 62

Trailer Park la Curva 207

trailers *See* RVing, RVs, trailers

Transpeninsular Highway 14, 18, 21, 24, 36, 39, 40, 46, 47, 48, 49, 50, 51, 52, 55, 58, 59, 60, 63, 68, 74, 75, 76, 82, 86, 87, 89 *passim*

travel agents 79, 121, 206, 216, 235

travel clubs 35, 41, 44, 60, 61, 80, 84

Treasure Island 107

Treaty of Guadalupe-Hidalgo 215

tree-ring analysis 212

trees *See also species name* 6, 7, 46, 50, 51, 104, 105, 114, 116, 117, 119, 125, 132, 133, 136, 142, 147, 149, 152, 153, 163, 166, 167, 172, 173, 174, 179, 180, 181, 186, 188, 199, 200, 201, 202, 203, 215, 216, 222, 225, 231, 232, 237, 243, 244, 245, 247, 248, 249, 252, 253, 254, 255, 258, 260, 261, 263, 276, 278

Tres Pozos 259

Tres Vírgenes 129, 173–74

Trinidad, Crucero la 85, 247, 258, 260, 262

Trinidad, Punta 147

trips 10, 11, 13–14, 16, 18, 19–20, 22, 24, 27, 28, 31, 34–35, 36, 38, 44, 46, 47, 48, 50, 51–52, 53, 55, 56, 57, 58, 59, 60, 61, 62, 63, 66, 68, 72, 74, 75, 78, 80, 83, 84, 86, 87, 89, 91, 92, 103, 104, 105, 106, 108, 114, 116, 123, 124, 126, 139, 142, 143, 148, 157, 161, 162, 163, 167, 171, 186, 190, 192, 194, 196, 199, 201, 207, 211, 216, 218, 222, 225, 228, 229, 231, 232, 237, 238, 240, 244, 248, 249, 254, 264, 273, 278, 281

TRIPUI Resort RV Park 60, 202

Triunfo Gold and Silver Company 227

Tropic of Cancer 181, 225, 232, 245

Tropicana Inn 235

tropicbirds, red-billed 280

trout 114, 116, 117, 261

trucks 50, 60, 62, 63, 66, 70, 85, 86, 87, 89, 93, 95, 112, 134, 135

trucks four-wheel-drive 40, 47, 50, 52, 54, 63, 66, 68, 70, 85, 112, 128, 132, 135, 136, 138, 147, 148, 156, 161, 162, 171, 214, 227, 255, 257, 262, 267

Tule, Boca de *See* Peruchera, Punta

Tuna Canyon 32, 228

Turners, Isla 30, 198, 273, 277, 280

turtles 7, 13, 35, 91, 126, 145, 167, 214, 224, 230, 276, 278, 282

24 Spot 165

22 Spot 109

240 Spot 123

Two Parks Loop Trip 68, 112, 113, 254, 262

Ugarte, Juan de 200, 215, 276

Ulloa, Francisco de 152, 259

Underwater Diversions 238

Unhappy Coyote 75, 186

Unidad de Tratamiento Hiperbarico Fanavi 105

Union 126

United Nations 19, 91

United Parcel Service 86

United States 5, 19, 22, 24, 36, 38, 41, 43, 46, 47, 49, 50, 51, 52, 59, 60, 74, 78, 79, 80, 81, 82, 83, 84, 85, 86, 87, 88, 89, 91, 94, 104, 116, 137, 157, 163, 165, 175, 177, 179, 180, 181, 210, 216, 218, 219, 225, 230, 231, 243, 247, 249, 255, 256, 264, 273, 279

United States Coast Guard 43, 74

United States Consular Agency 243

United States Customs Service 80, 91

United States Fish and Wildlife Service 10

United States Navy Historical Center 210

University of Arizona 79

University of Arizona Dendrochronology Laboratory 212

Ursula's Sport Fishing Charters 240

Uruapan 68

Vagabundos del Mar Boat and Travel Club 35, 41, 44, 60, 61, 80, 84, 91

Vagabundos del Mar RV Park 237

Valle de Trinidad 261

Valle las Palmas 256

Valle Santo Tomás 108

Vallecitos meadow 116, 117

vans 39, 58, 59, 62, 63, 64, 65, 66, 67, 68, 70, 83, 128, 132, 161, 162, 167, 199, 211, 221, 233, 234, 238, 245, 262, 264, 268, 271, 278

Vaquitero 143, 144

Vela Windsurf Resorts 52, 72, 228

Venado Blanco, Cerro 116

Ventana Windsurf 72, 222

Ventana, Isla la 18, 141, 142

Venture Quest Kayaking 58, 142

Vestal 210

veterinarians 80, 104, 105, 112, 121, 181, 206

Victor's El Cortez RV Park 264

Victor's Sportfishing 235

Villa de Juárez 258

Villa Insurgentes 58, 87, 170, 171, 200, 206, 221

Villa Jesús María 87, 129, 156

Villa María Isabel RV & Trailer Park 181, 183

Villa Morelos 212–13

Villa Vitta Hotel Resort 138

Villa Vitta Motel 139

Villa Zaragoza 206

Villa, Pancho 177

Villarino Camp 105

Villas de Loreto 58, 190

Villavicencio, José Rosa 175

VIP (Visual Inspection Program) 20, 229

Virgin of Guadalupe 255

Vista Sea Sports 229

Vizcaíno 51, 68, 152, 163, 166

Vizcaíno Loop Trip 51, 68, 163–66

Vizcaíno, Bahía 159, 161

Vizcaíno, Sebastián 152, 215

Volcán Prieto 268

Volcán, Arroyo el 135, 270

volcanoes 38, 53, 77, 121, 123, 124, 125, 129, 139, 142, 167, 173, 174, 190, 192, 195, 268, 269

wahoo 24, 27–28, 34, 38, 86, 207, 216, 222, 224, 228, 240, 245

Wahoo RV Center, S.A. de C.V. 86, 237

Waiting Room 203

Walker, William 215

Wall Street 119

warbler, mangrove yellow 7

washboard 51, 69, 166, 170, 214, 230, 268

water, potable 13, 41, 42, 46, 47–48, 50, 51, 52, 53, 54, 55, 56, 58, 60, 61, 62, 64, 66, 70, 77, 78, 85, 89, 90, 98, 99, 100, 103, 104, 105, 109, 112, 114, 116, 119, 121, 123, 125, 126, 134, 135, 136, 137, 138, 147, 148, 149, 152, 157, 162, 163, 164, 165, 166, 167, 177, 178, 179, 180, 181, 183, 186, 190, 192, 195, 197, 199, 200, 202, 203, 206, 207, 212, 214, 215, 216, 218, 219, 220, 225, 227, 228, 229, 232, 235, 237, 241, 243, 244, 245, 247, 252, 253, 255, 256, 257, 258, 259, 260, 263, 264, 266, 267, 270, 271, 276, 279

waterfalls 117, 119, 232, 252, 255, 257, 262, 263

waverunners 219, 237, 238, 241

waves 1, 4, 21, 26, 32, 42, 44, 45, 55, 56, 58, 71, 72, 73, 74, 95, 99, 100, 105, 107, 108, 113, 120, 122, 123, 124, 125, 126, 127, 128, 132, 142, 143, 145, 146, 148, 149, 155, 156, 164, 165, 171, 180, 185, 192, 208, 210, 213, 219, 221, 222, 228, 230, 231, 235, 237, 240, 243, 244, 245, 259, 266, 267, 270, 278

weather *See also* climate; *cordonazo; coromuel* 4, 5, 6, 7, 15, 32, 38, 40, 43, 47, 55, 56, 60, 71, 73, 74, 78, 80, 86, 87, 95, 103, 104, 109, 112, 113, 119, 121, 123, 124, 128, 132, 135, 137, 139, 141, 142, 143, 144, 145, 146, 147, 148,

152, 153, 156, 158, 159, 164, 166, 171, 179, 184, 185, 192, 194, 195, 196, 197, 199, 202, 206, 207, 208, 209, 210, 211, 212, 213, 214, 215, 219, 220, 221, 224, 225, 228, 231, 237, 241, 243, 262, 266, 270, 273, 278, 280, 281

West Virginia 210

whale sharks 8, 15, 17–8, 203, 242

whale-watching, whales 8–3, 14, 17, 18, 46, 52, 55, 57, 58, 60, 62, 93, 100, 125, 138, 139, 141, 145, 156–57, 158, 161, 164, 166, 167, 170, 190, 192, 201, 206, 207, 208, 211, 212, 216, 218, 219, 235, 237, 238, 241, 242, 266, 273, 278

Wilderness Alaska/Mexico 14, 55, 211

Willard, Punta 18, 270

winds 4, 5, 6, 26, 39, 42, 44, 45, 46, 50, 51, 55, 56, 71, 73, 95, 105, 122, 123, 125, 132, 138, 141, 142, 143, 145, 146, 147, 148, 149, 152, 153, 155, 156, 161, 163, 164, 165, 180, 183, 184, 185, 186, 192, 195, 203, 207, 211, 213, 220, 222, 224, 228, 229, 230, 231, 243, 244, 259, 266, 267, 268, 276, 278, 281

wrecks, ship and aircraft *See also name* 4, 15, 18, 19, 22, 58, 70, 79, 87, 106, 108, 109, 113, 120, 123, 124–25, 126, 127, 132, 134, 141, 143, 146, 152, 154–55, 156, 157, 158–60, 163, 164, 165, 179, 180, 183, 185, 186, 188, 192, 194, 202, 203, 208–11, 212, 218, 219, 220, 224, 229, 230, 231, 242–43, 259, 278, 279

Wright Shoal 166

yachting, yachts *See* boating, yachts

Yellow Pages 60, 104

Yellowtail Alley 154

yellowtail, California 18, 24, 30, 33, 34, 37, 95, 103, 106, 109, 123, 124, 139, 141, 144, 152, 154, 156, 162, 164, 165, 166, 179, 180, 183, 189, 192, 197, 202, 203, 206, 207, 208, 216, 221, 228, 240, 245, 269, 270, 273, 276, 277, 281

yellowthroat, Belding's 7

Zacatosa, Cerro 53, 225, 232–33

zalates 149, 199, 202, 231, 276, 280

Zedillo, Ernesto 190

Zippers 235, 237